CONSPIRACIES OF CONSPIRACIES

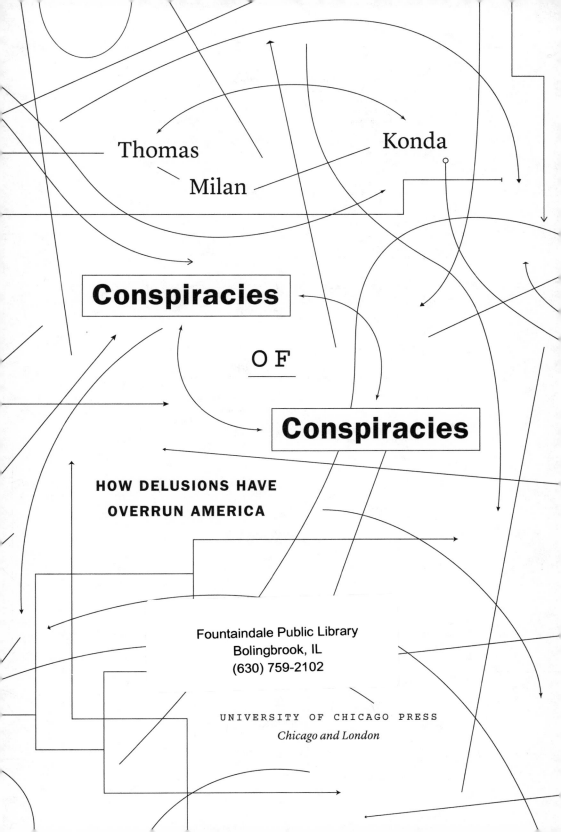

Thomas Konda
Milan

Conspiracies

O F

Conspiracies

**HOW DELUSIONS HAVE
OVERRUN AMERICA**

Fountaindale Public Library
Bolingbrook, IL
(630) 759-2102

UNIVERSITY OF CHICAGO PRESS
Chicago and London

The University of Chicago Press, Chicago 60637
The University of Chicago Press, Ltd., London
© 2019 by The University of Chicago
Published 2019
Printed in the United States of America

28 27 26 25 24 23 22 21 20 19   1 2 3 4 5

ISBN-13: 978-0-226-58576-5 (cloth)
ISBN-13: 978-0-226-58593-2 (e-book)
DOI: https://doi.org/10.7208/chicago/9780226585932.001.0001

Library of Congress Cataloging-in-Publication Data

Names: Konda, Thomas Milan, author.
Title: Conspiracies of conspiracies : how delusions have overrun America / Thomas
Milan Konda.
Description: Chicago ; London : University of Chicago Press,
  2019. | Includes
bibliographical references and index.
Identifiers: LCCN 2018034310 | ISBN 9780226585765 (pbk. : alk.
  paper) | ISBN
80226585932 (ebook)
Subjects: LCSH: Conspiracy theories. | History—Errors, inven-
  tions, etc.
Classification: LCC AZ999 .K65 2019 | DDC 001.9—dc23
LC record available at https://lccn.loc.gov/2018034310

♾ This paper meets the requirements of ANSI/NISO Z39.48-1992
(Permanence of Paper).

For June

CONTENTS

INTRODUCTION

CONSPIRACY THEORIES
AND CONSPIRACISM

> The definition of conspiracy theory poses unexpected difficulties.
>
> Brian Keeley, "Of Conspiracy Theories"

Americans see hoaxes and plots everywhere: from climate change to immunizations to almost anything having to do with Hillary Clinton. But why? Is the constant stream of conspiracy theories a side effect of social media? Are conspiracy theories a product of the increasing polarization of politics? Or have they always been around and for some reason we just notice them more now?

We can start to answer the last question: in their modern form, they have been around for at least two hundred years. The United States was less than ten years old when New England religious leaders sounded the alarm about the Illuminati's plans to destroy the republic. And this was only the beginning. In 1831, the Anti-Masonic Party held the first national political convention. Perhaps predictably, speeches there were peppered with conspiratorial rhetoric about Freemasonry. Before inventing the telegraph, Samuel Morse gained fame by warning that the Austrian emperor had orchestrated a conspiracy to undermine the world's

1

greatest Protestant republic by flooding America with Catholics. By the end of the nineteenth century, free-silver populists were portraying their economic plight as the result of a British (and often Jewish) banker conspiracy.

By the end of World War I, conspiracy theories began to have more staying power. The lasting menace of Bolshevism-socialism-Communism contributed to a certain constancy of conspiratorial thinking. At the same time, the idea of the "International Jew" (largely the creation of the fraudulent *Protocols of the Learned Elders of Zion*) gave rise to a series of antisemitic conspiracy theories that have still not run their course. America's turn toward international involvement powered conspiracy theories from isolationists and "America Firsters." The growing presence of the federal government—Wilsonian progressivism, FDR's New Deal, Lyndon Johnson's Great Society—fueled another array of conspiracy theories: federal support of civil rights was said to be part of a conspiracy against the white race; federal reorganization schemes were said to be part of the conspiracy to destroy the states. And, of course, the Kennedy and King assassinations contributed their share of conspiracy theories.

So, yes, there have been conspiracy theories all along. But there is also something new that has transformed the conspiratorial landscape: *conspiracism*—a mental framework, a belief system, a worldview that leads people to look for conspiracies, to anticipate them, to link them together into a grander overarching conspiracy.[1] Conspiracism has been building for some time, and by now it appears to have emerged as the belief system of the twenty-first century. Its adherents range from people who are beside themselves with conspiratorial rage, such as radio-show host Alex Jones, down to everyday people who are reluctant to have their children immunized because they accept vaguely conspiracist claims about vaccines. While many analysts believe that social media have accelerated conspiracism's growth, the reason for its prominence is still an open question.

This book analyzes conspiracism from three perspectives. First, research about the nature of individual people's beliefs—primarily cognitive research in psychology and epistemological research in philosophy.

The psychology deals with the question of why people believe conspiracy theories, while the philosophy deals primarily with what a conspiracy theory actually is. Second, historical research on the political, social, religious, and other developments that can create circumstances conducive to conspiratorial thinking. The history shifts the questions away from the individual to the level of society as a whole. And third, the actual writings of conspiracy theorists and their followers. These, although often disturbing, can provide visceral insight into both the thought processes of conspiracists and their perceived social circumstances. Taken together, these different approaches yield a new and, I believe deeper, analysis of conspiracism and the theories it generates than has been available before.

Problems of Definition

Conspiracists—that is to say, those whose belief system is conspiracism—have a predilection, perhaps even the need, to see conspiracies behind events, and not just major events such as the Kennedy assassination or the 9/11 attacks, when doubt and suspicion are widespread. Conspiracists consistently find conspiracies where others do not. For example, the creation of nonbinding recommendations for sustainable growth at the 1992 Rio Earth Summit was a thoroughly routine event, but many conspiracists view what they call Agenda 21 as the work of "global Communism," or part of an evil plot to "have 90% of the world's population murdered by abortion and aborting life by disease, famine, wars, wrecking of the economy, industry, technology, giving vaccines and medicines which give a slow death."[2] Even more prosaically, while the introduction of bar codes in 1974 barely qualifies as an event, religious conspiracists continue to warn that "those black lines on every product you buy!" signal a satanic conspiracy. There need not even be an event to inspire conspiracist thinking. The contrails of jet aircraft crisscrossed the skies for decades as a nonevent before conspiracists began to claim that they were really "chemtrails" secretly laced with "pathogens, chemicals, and fungi" by the government to poison or stupefy the citizenry.[3]

In 1965, historian Richard Hofstadter wrote that the "distinguishing thing about the paranoid style is not that its exponents see conspiracies here and there in history, but that they regard a 'vast' or 'gigantic' conspiracy as *the motive force* in historical events."[4] It may not be necessary to go quite this far. People can compartmentalize their thinking and hold conflicting ideas associated with different belief systems. Nevertheless, conspiracism as a belief system is generally very broad and influences its adherents' thinking across many subjects. Conspiracism is also distinctive as a belief system for two reasons. First, it is inherently negative. Conspiracists fear and oppose the conspiracies they envision, because those conspiracies are invariably aimed at destroying their way of life. Hence, the struggle against the unending stream of Illuminati, Zionists, forces of Satan (or Lucifer), mind controllers, and the global elite ensconced in its many secret societies. Second, conspiracism as a belief system lends itself to obsessiveness. Conspiracists seem much more aware of their belief system than most people are, leading them to consciously apply it to events on a daily basis.

The manifestation of conspiracism is, of course, the conspiracy theory. In principle, the idea of conspiracy theory seems straightforward, and most people think that they would recognize one without difficulty. But the term "conspiracy theory" has been so poorly defined and so loosely used as to become useless, if not actually misleading.[5] Some research has confounded conspiratorial beliefs with beliefs that are merely unconventional or about offbeat topics such as the prophecies of Nostradamus or the curse of Tutankhamen. Worse, people have been counted as adherents of conspiracy theories on the basis of their views about normal historical incidents such as John Brown's raid on Harper's Ferry or the charges that Anita Hill and "others" brought against Clarence Thomas during his Supreme Court confirmation hearings.[6] An early study of conspiracism among African Americans in the South concluded that they had "a surprisingly strong belief in most conspiracy theories involving government. Over 85% of respondents agreed or strongly agreed that African Americans are harassed by police because of their race and that the criminal justice system is not fair to Blacks."

Using such commonplace observations about racism in society as evidence for conspiracist thinking can only undermine research. More recently, a much noted 2013 survey conflated non-conspiratorial questions about politics with ones about space aliens, Bigfoot, and whether Paul McCartney died in the 1960s.[7]

In the last few years, some researchers have criticized loose or misleading definitions of conspiracy theory and made serious efforts to come up with good measures of conspiracy ideation.[8] Such academic and professional efforts have not filtered into the popular press or the internet, however, and the 2016 presidential campaign brought about a resurgence of the problem. A story about Republican complaints over the possibility of the Federal Elections Commission's opening the presidential debates to third party candidates was headlined as a "GOP conspiracy." A sermon about religious persecution given by presidential hopeful Ben Carson to a congregation of his fellow Seventh Day Adventists was depicted as his "Satanic Sabbath persecution conspiracy." AlterNet created "The Definitive Donald Trump Conspiracy Guide," a messy list of fifty-eight simple accusations (e.g., that Bill Ayers had ghostwritten Obama's memoir), speculations (Trump's 2012 musing about Obama's strategy for reelection: "Looks like he'll have to start a major war or conflict to win. Don't put it past him."), and random claims (27–35 percent of Muslims "would go to war" with the United States). That Trump believes these things may be important, but lumping them all together under a conspiracy theory heading only clouds the issue.[9]

Poor definition is only one of the factors that has made conspiracy theory a tricky concept. Equally troublesome is the existence of two conflicting camps, which see conspiracism from wholly different perspectives. One camp sees conspiracism essentially as a psychological problem afflicting certain individuals, while the other considers it to be a reasonable response to the modern world—perhaps the only response capable of setting things right. This conflict is rendered all the more intractable by the fact that the negative camp, dominated by psychologists, focuses all its attention on the individual, whereas the positive camp deals largely with the sociological and political context that gives rise to conspiracist thinking. Thus, the two groups often talk past each other.[10]

The negative camp tends to define conspiracy theory pejoratively, as the "unnecessary assumption of a conspiracy when other explanations are more plausible," or "unproven, often rather fanciful alternatives to mainstream accounts."[11] From this point of view, conspiracy theories are not real theories at all but, rather, a "subset of false beliefs" or a "pseudoscience." They are based on weak evidence and perceptual biases, stemming from conspiracists' "crippled epistemology" (i.e., they accept conspiracy theories because they seek out only information that reinforces their suspicions); they are "nihilistic" in their rejection of authority; and they succumb to "magical thinking," as opposed to rationality.[12]

If any one person inspired this negative view of conspiracy theory, it was the philosopher of science Karl Popper; certainly the supporters of conspiracy theories blame him for it.[13] Whether, as some maintain, Popper was the first to use the term "conspiracy theory" in a pejorative way, he certainly disparaged it as a "mistaken theory" that was merely the "secularization of religious superstition" in which "the Gods are abandoned. But their place is filled by powerful men or groups whose wickedness is responsible for all the evils we suffer from."[14] Popper's equating conspiracy theory with superstition was intended to undermine its advocates. The implied combination of cognitive shortcoming and emotional appeal has inspired subsequent opponents of conspiracism to liken conspiracy theories to accounts of miracles, which can be dismissed without assessing their claims in detail.[15] Many researchers agree with Popper (and with the scientific community generally) that genuine theories must be falsifiable, which conspiracy theories are not.[16] Other researchers conclude that conspiracists are much the same as religious fanatics in their delusional thinking.[17]

The positive camp argues that conspiracy theories are often true and that they are socially beneficial. Members of this camp are constantly on the lookout for pejorative labels and loaded terms applied by their opponents. Foremost among those terms is "conspiracy theory" itself, which is routinely argued to have been "implanted" in popular discourse to make serious criticism of society or government seem "paranoid, nutty, marginal, and certainly untrue." It is purposively chosen to "discredit advocates of a certain persuasion," by labeling them as an "unwanted remnant" of prescientific thinking.[18]

Supporters of conspiracism wage a constant battle against the effort to write off conspiracy theories. They frequently portray their opponents as fearing conspiracy theories to the point of panic. Ginna Husting argues that "the emotionality of U.S. conspiracy panic discourse effectively polices the boundaries of what is sayable, knowable, thinkable, and perhaps feelable." Jack Bratich also uses the term "conspiracy panic" to describe the reaction of respectable opinion to conspiratorial interpretations of events, arguing that the panics "help to define the normal modes of dissent" and to rule out anything beyond them.[19] Lance deHaven-Smith goes further, positing conspiracism as our last line of defense against SCADs—state crimes against democracy. Conspiracism provides hope by creating "a 'well-tempered' citizen in liberal politics who is vigilant but not obsessive about the state and its power."[20] Lee Basham and Matthew Dentith, in what amounts to a manifesto, argue vigorously that "the danger" lies not in conspiracy theories but in "the pathologizing response to conspiracy theories. The antidote to whatever problems conspiracy theories present is vigilance, not some faux intellectual sophistication which dismisses conspiracy theories out of hand. It's really quite simple when you think about it: conspiracy theorising is essential to the functioning of any democracy, or indeed any ethically sensitive society."[21]

Increasingly, conspiracists and their supporters pointedly avoid the term "conspiracy theorist" altogether, favoring more positive designations of "skeptic" or "critical thinker" instead. Those whose ideas flood the internet are considered "citizen journalists" whose hallmark is their "will-to-moderation."[22] Similarly, conspiracy theorizing is praised as "naïve" deconstructive history, reflecting the belief that untrained amateurs are not blinkered by conventional thinking. Rebelling against the "orthodox," they take a "radically" empirical approach to history in which "tangible facts are the focus, especially the facts that the standard stories try to overlook. There is a ruthless reduction down to what is without doubt real, namely, persons." In one example of this approach, Mark Lane—a prominent Kennedy assassination conspiracy theorist—is equated with Galileo as someone who changed humanity's thinking.[23]

Supporters of conspiracism frequently point to historical conspiracies that everyone agrees actually took place.[24] Watergate is the most popular of these, and the Iran-Contra scandal and the Kennedy assassination are fairly widely noted. But, what counts as a conspiracy is rather broad, with the concept stretched to include medieval witch panics and the Holocaust. Supporters assume that, since some conspiracies are demonstrably true, some conspiracy theories must be true as well. Thus, conspiracy theories should be seen as plausible "master narratives" that demand serious examination, especially in "the absence of a credible narrative" from the authorities. The term "narrative" skirts the issue of falsifiability. It can be argued that, as narratives, even if some conspiracy theories are "nutty" or just "silly," this is not due to their genre but "because they suffer some specific defect—for instance, that the conspiracies they postulate are impossible or far-fetched." If *any* conspiracy theories are "warranted," supporters contend, then each of them must be assessed on its merits.[25] Supporters also point to research suggesting that "ordinary people" will make conspiratorial judgments if presented with compelling information, and at least one advocate has claimed that "when conspiracy theories turn into conventional wisdom, people cease to call them conspiracy theories."[26]

Definitional Points of Agreement

All these problems—stemming both from meager definitions and from loose or loaded terms—combine to cause confusion over the exact meaning of "conspiracism." There are, however, some points of agreement that are widely accepted. Centrally, conspiracism has an overarching narrative of good versus evil: a classic Manichean dichotomy. Among religious conspiracists, this takes the form of the righteous fighting the forces of Satan and is usually cast in terms of the apocalypse and the

Antichrist.[27] At the secular level, conspiracism is frequently linked with populism, a similarly dualistic ideology that posits "two homogenous and antagonistic groups, 'the pure people' versus 'the corrupt elite.'" The elite is frequently alien, but homegrown elites can become "disloyal" and betray the people. Both populism and conspiracism are considered "thin-centered" ideologies (i.e., there is not much substance at their core), which can be easily combined without conflict.[28]

As a corollary to the dualism, the people and the elite are cast very differently in conspiracist thinking. The elite conspirators are, of course, malevolent and sinister—and may well be the very embodiment of evil. They operate behind the scenes, their "malevolent collusion" and "secret machinations" unsuspected until it is too late. Thus, they are able to corrupt not just government but any institution: from elementary schools to the Intergovernmental Panel on Climate Change.[29] The elite conspirators are also extremely single-minded and competent, to the point of being "preternaturally effective."[30] The "pure people," by contrast, are generally clueless; they are trusting to the point of gullibility and certainly no match for the conspirators. This point stands out sharply in the writings of actual conspiracists.[31]

A third point is less widely agreed on: namely, that conspiracism is not politically symmetrical but primarily associated with the political Right. It is important to note that conspiracism is not associated with traditional conservatism but with what Richard Hofstadter described as a right-wing "pseudo-conservatism," which even he found "more than ordinarily incoherent."[32] In brief, while pseudo-conservatives tend to favor small government, they do not embrace classical conservative values like moderation. Recent studies find conspiracism rife among those on the right who are particularly fearful, anxious, and frustrated, many of whom are suspicious even of "mainstream" conservatives.[33] The distinguishing psychological attributes that push them off the end of the political spectrum may be tendencies toward authoritarianism and social dominance.[34]

As a belief system, conspiracism is generic, whereas any conspiracy theory that it generates is specific. An individual with a conspiracist belief system may not be aware of that fact, but will still use a conspiracy theory as the framework for understanding the world. This framework can be thought of as hermetic—that is, seeing the hand of God at work everywhere. Whether religious or secular, hermetic narratives "present 'airtight' all-encompassing explanations of past events. They are totalizing histories," in that the "ultimate causes" of events are "secret plots by powerful forces" as opposed to "mundane human (in)activity or natural forces."[35] They differ from one another on the exact mix of conspirators (e.g., Illuminati, Jews, Bilderbergers, FEMA, Zeta Reticulans), their specific tactics (assassination, sex education, false flag operations, chemtrails, mind control), and their exact goals (eliminating freedom, destruction of Christianity, population reduction, Luciferian control, or just general world domination). How many conspiracy theories exist depends on how many of these distinctions one cares to make.

For a belief to count as a conspiracy theory, it must be more than a simple claim or accusation. There is nothing unusual or distinctive about the occurrence of a conspiracy; in politics it is no more esoteric or mysterious than bribery or nepotism. Indeed, in a legal sense, a case of bribery is a conspiracy. Some semblance of an actual theory—or at least a narrative—is required. Any theory or narrative will posit a conspiratorial elite working against the wishes and interests of the people in general, but it must also be "a counter-discourse of some sort: that is, a discourse seeking to challenge the orthodox or dominant explanation for an event." Conspiracy theories are necessarily at odds with the consensus of "epistemic authorities" (i.e., societally endorsed sources of information). Combatting the official version of events is the "central logic" of a conspiracy.[36] Thus, the idea that followers of Osama bin Laden carried out the 9/11 attack is not a conspiracy theory. The normal explanatory context of ongoing conflict between al-Qaeda and the United States is the "dominant explanation" and provides some understanding of why it happened. The counter-discourse that Bush administration neocons actually carried out or approved the attack, in contrast, can only exist by generating a conspiracy theory. By being at odds with the "epistemic authorities" the idea has to be supported by some larger narrative or theory that explains how the authorities are wrong, why what appeared to have happened is not *really* what happened, and—most importantly—why the neocons orchestrated a deadly attack on their own country. A conspiracist counter-reality must be constructed either from the ground up or as a manifestation of an ongoing conspiracy theory, such as a Zionist version of the new world order.[37]

Regarding Terminology

There are three closely related terms that we must be clear about: conspiracy, conspiracy theory, and conspiracism. There have been many workable definitions of conspiracy, all along the lines of: "A group of people acting in concert secretly in order to deceive the public about the true nature of their goal." A great many plots, coups, and even everyday crimes, few of which are momentous enough to merit a conspiracy theory to explain them, are covered by this definition. However, I use the term "conspiracy" to indicate only those conspiracies that lie at the core of a conspiracy theory. This usage implies that a "conspiracy" constitutes a threat and that it is probably an imaginary construct. The term "conspiracy theory" is little used because it is reserved for genuinely theoretical ideas. Thus, the term for an individual, "conspiracy theorist," is not applied to, say, the array of assassination buffs, birthers, truthers, and aggrieved white supremacists fighting the Racial Holy War. Rather, actual conspiracy theorists (and their corresponding conspiracy theories) probably number no more than a few dozen since the French Revolution. To capture this, a plausible definition for "conspiracy theory" needs to be rather detailed: "A narrative centered on the idea that a malevolent group of people is conspiring to bring about some state of affairs to the detriment of the people in general. Their conspiracy lies behind a variety of events with which at least some of the conspirators have no apparent connection." Because of the scope of its goal, the conspiracy involves a long-term plan.

By this conservative definition, there are perhaps a dozen major conspiracy theories, along with a few niche ones with dedicated followers.

Many of these conspiracy theories overlap; conspiracists borrow terminology, ideas, and villains from one another constantly. Nevertheless, each has a distinctive emphasis. Together, they can guide us in detailing the career of conspiracism and the work of conspiracists themselves. In a nutshell, the career of conspiracism begins with the Illuminati at the end of the eighteenth century. It proceeds in fits and starts during the nineteenth century, mostly in the United States. In the twentieth century, conspiracism gained a permanent foothold in the public consciousness first as an antisemitic conspiracy, then as a globalist-Communist–new world order conspiracy. Finally, conspiracism proliferated into an array of conspiracies, ranging from deadly serious to gratuitously silly. Today, conspiracism stands at the threshold of being a major belief system, albeit a fragmented one. Conspiracism has reached such a point of prominence today that we must ask whether it is about to destroy democracy and civil society. This is not an idle question.

1

THE INVENTION OF
CONSPIRACY THEORY

THE FRENCH REVOLUTION AND THE
BAVARIAN ILLUMINATI

The intelligent saw in the open system of the Jacobins the complete hidden system of the Illuminati.

John Robison, *Proofs of a Conspiracy* (1798)

It is not at all unusual for people to think that conspiracism and the conspiracy theories associated with it have a "deeply rooted" past. Conspiracists themselves frequently extend their conspiracies back to ancient times in order to add mystery to their narratives, suggesting constant linkages over long periods between suspicious groups and events. Nesta Webster, whose writing in the wake of the Russian Revolution set the template for modern conspiracy theory, claimed to have traced the origins of revolutionary activity to the "first century of the Christian era." In fact, Webster went back even further, to the time of Moses, in order to capture the "forces" that had been "gathering for an onslaught not only on Christianity but on all social and moral order."[1]

The mere existence of conspiracies does not, however, automatically give rise to conspiracy theories or conspiracism. Conspiracies, in the sense of the plots that pepper history, have been integral to politics from the beginning and, thus, unremarkable. Julius Caesar was, after all, the victim of a conspiracy. The historian Gordon Wood has argued that the innumerable "schemes of antiquity and the Renaissance . . . flowed from simplicity and limitedness" of a politics dominated by elites, and so the conspiracy "was taken for granted as a normal means by which rulers were deposed."[2] In such times, there was no need for theory beyond the all-encompassing one that elites are constantly conspiring against each other.

Writing in late seventeenth-century England, Daniel Defoe described an "Age of Plot and Deceit" featuring "court conspiracies, backstairs conspiracies, ministerial conspiracies, factional conspiracies, aristo-cratic conspiracies."[3] It is important to note that none of these plots or coups involves any effort to deceive the public—an essential aspect of a genuine conspiracy theory—because the public played no role in politics. In fact, from a political standpoint, "the public" did not exist; people were subjects, not citizens, and no one thought them important enough to try to deceive.[4] By the eighteenth century, a somewhat wider array of participants was making politics more complex. Conspiracy explanations became broader and more subtle: "Accounts of plots . . . were no longer descriptions of actual events but interpretations of oth-erwise puzzling concatenations of events."[5]

The increasing tensions between the British government and the col-onists of North America illustrate the point. The British perception of discontent in the colonies began to turn toward conspiracy in the 1770s, and "secret emissaries" from France were credited with fomenting dis-content. Shortly before the revolution, General Burgoyne reported that John Adams was "as great a conspirator as ever subverted a state."[6] In the American colonies, where political control was still narrowly applied, people had originally thought of "political conspiracy in terms of self-ish factions of public officials seeking personal power and wealth by manipulating the machinery of government." This view gradually was supplanted by the more conspiratorial idea of "a coterie of the King's friends . . . working secretly to deprive them of their liberties."[7]

The eighteenth-century conspiracy explanation was a rational assessment of politics, even if not always accurate. It combined a modern approach to understanding social change with a traditional determination to hold individuals accountable for their actions. Instead of offering a counter-discourse, as today's conspiracy theories do, conspiracy explanations were widely shared, thus becoming mainstream views of how politics operated.[8] This enlightened view was, however, overwhelmed by the complexity and confusion of the French Revolution, which seemed to require some theory to explain its scope and force, for "no small group of particular plotters, ... only elaborately organized secret societies like the Illuminati or the Freemasons, involving thousands of individuals linked by sinister designs, could be behind the Europe-wide upheaval."[9]

The French Revolution was the most dramatic threat to the established powers in Europe since the fall of Rome. Soon, people were imagining the vast sinister designs of unseen manipulators.

The First Conspiracy Theory: Illuminized Freemasonry

Two prominent opponents of the French Revolution took up the challenge of uncovering these sinister designs: John Robison, a Scottish chemist of considerable reputation, and the Abbé Augustin Barruel, a French cleric living in England. Robison's *Proofs of a Conspiracy against All the Religions and Governments of Europe, Carried on in the Secret Meetings of Freemasons, Illuminati, and Reading Societies* was published in 1797 and achieved immediate widespread success. At the same time, Barruel published the first part of his multivolume history of Jacobinism to roughly equal acclaim. Neither publication was an accurate or even plausible guide to the revolution, but they did mark the beginning of conspiracy theory.[10]

Robison, a traditionalist, had been fighting for some time against Enlightenment chemistry, which he found godless and mechanistic. This view put him at odds with Antoine Lavoisier, Joseph Priestly, and his own colleagues. By the time he began work on *Proofs*, moreover, Robison was a very sick man, subject to bouts of insanity and "vulnerable to melancholy, confusion, and paranoia." In *Proofs*, Robison denounced Lavoisier and Priestly as Illuminists and accused Madame Lavoisier of using her famous salons as "venues for sacrilegious rites where the hostess, dressed in the ceremonial robes of an occult priestess, ritually burned the texts of the old chemistry."[11] His defenders attributed questions about Robison's mental state to the fact that he had exposed the "dark designs" of his attackers.[12]

His idiosyncratic arguments about chemistry aside, Robison's basic contention was that Adam Weishaupt's Bavarian Illuminati, created in 1776, led the conspiracy behind the French Revolution in order to destroy all the religions and governments of Europe. The Illuminati, he maintained, had infiltrated French Freemasonry and brought the revolution about, under "the specious pretext of enlightening the world."[13] Robison himself had been a Scottish Rite Mason but had been shocked to find continental Masonic lodges to be, as he saw it, irreligious and decadent. Accordingly, in his conspiracy, Scottish Rite Masons were blameless while French Grand Orient Freemasonry bordered on the diabolical. (This distinction between blameless and corrupt Freemasonry is still observed by some conspiracists, causing confusion to this day.) Within a few years, *Proofs* began to besmirch Robison's professional reputation; even Barruel criticized his errors of fact. A fellow chemist handled the issue delicately: "The alarm excited by the French Revolution had produced in Mr. Robison a degree of credulity which was not natural to him."[14]

Augustin Barruel had been an anti-Enlightenment, anti-philosophe writer even before the revolution. Having fled France, he wrote his call to arms against the revolution in London, publishing the first two volumes of *Memoirs* in 1797. An abridged English translation appeared in 1798. Barruel's conspiracy outdid Robison's in both complexity and duration. He linked continental Freemasonry to the Knights Templar, implicitly pushing the origin of the conspiracy back at least to the Crusades. Barruel did not invent this historical linkage; as early as 1736 some Freemasons had tried to establish it. But by portraying the Knights Templar as bitterly anti-Christian, Barruel could link them—and thus Freemasonry—to

Enlightenment figures such as Voltaire and Weishaupt. All these links are uncertain at best, and Barruel appears to have confused the Illuminati with mystical groups such as Martinists and Rosicrucians on occasion.[15] The poet Shelley reviewed Barruel's tome as "half filled with the vilest and most unsupported falsehoods" but recommended it anyway.[16]

Barruel's views changed with newer editions of his work, each one "wilder and more vituperative than the last."[17] The most important change was inspired by a letter purportedly from a Captain Simonini, known as the Simonini letter, which ostensibly exposed the role of the Jews in the revolution as an "unseen and controlling presence" over the Freemasons, Knights Templar, and even the Illuminati. Despite doubts about the letter's authenticity even at the time—it seems to have been the work of the French police—editions of Barruel's work from 1806 on endorsed the idea and, indeed, seem to have created the enduring notion of the Judeo-Masonic conspiracy.[18]

What Makes All This a Conspiracy Theory?

By today's standards, neither Robison's *Proofs* nor Barruel's *Memoirs* seems powerfully conspiratorial. Each work incorporates lengthy descriptions by other writers of specific Freemasonic lodges and the careers of Jacobin leaders. The critical feature that makes their ideas conspiracy theories rather than mere explanations lies in how they piece together disparate facts and notions into a story they imbue with a deeper meaning. Each creates a dualistic narrative in which the malevolent conspirators secretly work to destroy everything that is good and pure. This amounts to an alternative historical "construct," which one scholar has likened to "a theatrical performance" embodying the fears and fantasies of its creators. Its conspiratorial dualism makes the construct an oversimplification that ignores the "complexity and dynamics of historical processes."[19] The underlying psychological mechanisms that conspiracy theorists use to piece things together in this way are today referred to as patternicity and agenticity—both normal mental processes carried to an extreme.

Contemporary researchers have placed these mental processes at the forefront of their attempts to understand conspiracist thinking. As Michael Shermer, who coined the term "patternicity" put it: "Conspiracy theories connect the dots of random events into meaningful patterns (patternicity) and then infuse those patterns with intentional agency (agenticity)."[20] Conspiracy theorists themselves are often aware of this process, which they sometimes report as an epiphany, although their sudden awareness may well be apohenia, which, "unlike an epiphany—a true intuition of the world's interconnectedness—is a false realization . . . a weakness of human cognition."[21] Contemporary conspiracy theorist James Perloff, describing his first encounter with Gary Allen's *None Dare Call It Conspiracy,* recalls: "For the first time, history began making sense: it had a pattern to it, and was not the haphazard amalgamation of events I had been taught in school." Even more dramatically, Gary Wean prefaced his revelations about the O. J. Simpson case with this explanation: "Suddenly you realize, you awaken, the picture is clear, you are not becoming mentally disordered at all. You have been merely, slowly becoming aware that all the dastardly, evil past events that have been occurring have emanated from a single source; *everything* is connected."[22]

Researchers have noted that such extreme versions of patternicity amount to "illusory pattern perceptions," typically accompanied by "hyperactive agency detection." The first step in this process depends on the certainty that there must be an agent, whose nature is informed by one's fears or obsessions. The Depression era conspiracy theorist Gerald B. Winrod explained to his readers that he simply "knew" that the "hellish" events of his day "had to have their secret octopus-roots fastened in demon-possessed brains somewhere."[23] Together, excessive pattern and agency awareness are vital conditions for conspiratorial thinking (which psychologists often call conspiracist ideation), as they allow the conspiracist to assign blame.[24] As Richard Landes writes, such thinking creates a belief system in which "all details cohere, unnoticed or unexplained facts fit into place, and patterns emerge. Everything connects, gains shape, texture, and color. To the believer, now semiotically aroused with his new hermeneutic, the troubling world makes sense, compelling sense."[25] Psychologists overwhelmingly consider conspiracist ideation as confused, and not just because of excess patternicity. The attribution of a purposive agent behind the pattern puts conspiracist ideation on a par with belief in the supernatural or in paranormal phenomena. This is, of course, the standard fixation of the schizophrenic.[26] Less dramatically, it has been called the patchwork quilt fallacy. By either name, it describes how unconnected facts and claims are linked under a conspiratorial hypothesis to "explain" them even though "there is no real need to explain the unconnected facts, so the evidence does not help to take the hypothesis seriously."[27]

The looseness of extreme patternicity makes it easy to define any person or group as the agent behind one's conspiracy. Thus, Barruel had no difficulty adding Jews to his conspiracy of Illuminists, Freemasons, Templars, and others. Over a hundred years later, Nesta Webster reinvigorated the Jewish-Freemasonic-Illuminist triad and added Bolshevism to bring the conspiracy up to date. Later, Webster managed to detect further patterns involving agents of Theosophy, birth control, the "Freud theory," the proposed universal language Esperanto, pan-Germanism, and the worship of Baphomet, the goat-headed pentangle-inscribed version of Satan.[28] During World War II, the poet Ezra Pound, in his exposé of the "usurocracy," found conspiratorial connections between the American Revolution, Regius professorships ("founded to falsify history"), Alexander Hamilton's racial background, the supposed suppression of the works of Aristotle and Demosthenes, the Rothschild family, Lincoln's assassination, and Franklin D. Roosevelt ("a kind of malignant tumour"). Similarly, Christian Identity preacher Wesley Swift forged a vision linking Jewish control of the press, the Federal Reserve System, miscegenation, the Asiatic flu ("the devil's work, too"), World War II, and Hinduism.[29]

The most critical aspect of this conspiracy-building process lies in making what Richard Hofstadter called the "curious leap" from everyday reality to the conspiracy theory, which he illustrates with Robison's *Proofs*:

For page after page he patiently records the details he has been able to accumulate about the history of the Illuminati. Then, suddenly, the French Revolution has taken place, and the Illuminati have brought it about. What is missing is not veracious information about the organization, but sensible judgment about what can cause a revolution. The plausibility the paranoid style has for those who find it plausible lies, in good measure, in this appearance of the most careful, conscientious, and seemingly coherent application to detail, the laborious accumulation of what can be taken as convincing evidence of the most fantastic conclusions, the careful preparation for the big leap from the undeniable to the unbelievable.[30]

The creation of patterns and attribution of evil forces behind them makes such a leap of faith seem natural and defensible. Nesta Webster belittled her critics for maintaining that revolutions arose out of popular discontent when she had clearly demonstrated that revolutions were the work of "a deep-laid conspiracy that uses the people to their own undoing."[31] It is primarily this leap that distinguishes everyday reality, in which "actual conspiratorial politics" may well take place, from the imaginary realm of "bona fide conspiracy theories."[32]

The leap also reveals a key distinction between social critics whose work focuses on powerful elites and conspiracy theorists—a distinction the social critics have often noted. The "construct" created by conspiracy theories is a simplification that, social critics complain, ignores the fact that power structures can be "weak, fragmented, or pluralistic."[33] Although power structure researchers and conspiracists do "share some specifics about how the social world actually works," the conspiracists "baffle us" only when they make the leap to the definitional "separation of conspiratorial groups from the rest of society, their boundless power and lack of scruples, as well as the no less boundless ignorance of ordinary people outside the conspiracy."[34]

The putative conspirators are invariably monolithic, typically omniscient, and often enough "evil incarnate"—a "perfect model of malice, a kind of amoral superman; sinister, ubiquitous, powerful, cruel."[35]

But beyond such comic book attributes, the nature of the conspirators is often left rather vague. Even when a specific organization is named, its conspiratorial activities are rarely spelled out. In a typical leap, the Christian Identity preacher Oren Potito slides right past the normally all-powerful Council on Foreign Relations (CFR) to the "even more exclusive club" within the CFR, the Business Advisory Council. But how this group of roughly 160 businessmen that meets only sporadically controls the CFR or anything else is unspecified.[36] Of course, when the conspiracy is headed by amorphous entities such as Illuminized Freemasonry or the Synagogue of Satan, specificity is impossible and probably pointless.

Vague yet menacing conspirators work well for conspiracy theorists. As Ernie Lazar has argued: "Most political conspiracy theories are primarily an intellectual device by which individuals and organizations demonize their perceived enemies whom they propose to vanquish."[37] Vagueness can also help conspiracists survive as their context shifts. For example, by abandoning their straightforward Soviet conspiracy in favor of a metaphorical "cancer of collectivism" masterminded by the Illuminati, the John Birch Society was able to survive the demise of the Soviet Union and the end of the Cold War. With the adoption of such terms as "invisible government" and "new world order," the collapse of Communism "was transformed by true believers into a mere 'phase' in the grand conspiracy of collectivization."[38]

In keeping with the patternicity used to build conspiracy theories, an array of conspirators is frequently thrown together in a shotgun blast of people and organizations, well-known and obscure ones alike. Frank Capell, best known for claiming that John and/or Robert Kennedy had Marilyn Monroe murdered, pulls together "Communists, the Fabian Society, the One-Worlders, the Pacifists, [and] the Occult Religion-Destroyers" to run a "conspiracy to bring about the 'New World Order.'" Ameen Rihani's 1920 version of the Great Conspiracy connected Ismailites, Mazdakites, and the Assassins—all "clothed, for the benefit of the Illuminati, in rags picked up at the doors of Spinoza and Plato." And the occult-UFO enthusiast Jim Keith relies on the Elizabethan-era philosopher John Dee to link Rosicrucianism and the Qabbalah with the British

Royal Society and MI5 as part of "the long-term occult agenda in geopolitics that is just now coming to poisonous fruition."[39]

The leap to some sort of evil cabal bent on world domination is not merely a feature of the conspiracy theory but also the key to so many conspiracy theories' longevity, as the continued availability of Robison's *Proofs* and Barruel's *Memoirs* attests. Once the impetus behind a conspiracy is established as a long-standing shadowy force, it becomes easy to attribute other suspicious actions to it, giving the theory permanence and expanding its scope. Once the initial leap is accepted, other claims can be accepted as well, even if they are clearly based on nothing more than a visceral emotion. For example, in a 1950s diatribe against the United Nations (UN), the roster of one-worlder conspirators was expanded to include the Mattachine Society, a pioneering gay rights group having nothing to do with the UN. There are other features common across conspiracy theories, but spotting patterns others do not see and attributing the existence of those patterns to a malevolent power are the most important. It is impossible to generate an actual conspiracy theory without them, as they constitute the mechanism that enables people to make the leap into an alternate reality.

The Illuminized Freemasonry conspiracy theory is one of the building blocks of modern conspiracism. But it also continues to exist on its own in several versions. Some are remarkably pure renditions of Robison or, more often, Barruel's basic story. William Schnoebelen's constant stream of books and DVDs reiterates the Illuminati's infiltration of Freemasonry, while Michael Howard's investigation of "secret societies—their influence and power in World History" extrapolates Barruel's approach to cover the last two hundred years. Jan van Helsing goes in the other direction, dropping back to the "Brotherhood of the Snake," which was an Illuminati precursor over three hundred thousand years ago.[40] Other variants of the conspiracy generally reflect the fears and obsessions of different conspiracists. John McManus envisions a vaguely Jewish Illuminized Freemasonry at the heart of a long-term plot to destroy the Roman Catholic Church. Jim Marrs has been quite prolific in developing his Illuminized Freemasonry new world order conspiracy. Des Griffin lays out a full Rothschilds-centered version in a mere twenty-four pages. Terry Melanson brings in the Rockefellers and the Rothschilds but still bases his new world order on Weishaupt's infiltration of Freemasonry "to establish a universal regime over the whole world."[41] The Overlords of Chaos, an extensive anti–new world order website, focuses on the threat posed by environmentalists, who, in their desire to achieve a "balance in nature," plan to carry out a "Mass Culling of the People via Planned Parenthood, toxic adulteration of water and food supplies, release of weaponised man-made viruses, man-made pandemics, mass vaccination campaigns and a planned Third World War."[42] There is at least one version of Illuminized Freemasonry that includes the Scottish Rite Masons (generally exempt from blame since Robison's time), whose headquarters is adjacent to the original church of the Jesuits in Rome—"the city that sits on the seven hills, 'the Mother of Harlots and Abominations of the Earth!'" And, of course, "Illuminized Freemasonry has controlled the worldwide Zionist movement since 1896, as evidenced by the use of the hexagram symbol."[43]

The Creation of the Modern Illuminati

The French Revolution, the contagious spread of radical ideas across Europe, and the rise of Napoleon all combined to paralyze European conservatives with fright for decades. The more repressive the regime, the more likely its leaders were to envision conspiracies.[44] At one end of this spectrum lay England, which was never consumed with conspiracy mania. Even a House of Commons investigative report undertaken during the worst days of the French Revolution expressed concern only over actual threats to the government—notably the United Irishmen. The report did not mention the Illuminati or even Freemasonry.[45] At the other end of the spectrum of fear, one Russian tsar after another was fed a steady diet of conspiratorial warnings by advisers and police officials. These warnings reflected the conspiratorial links that Augustin Barruel had come up with; Nicholas I was advised early and often that Russia was a key target of "conspirators of whatever name against

God and rulers, Masons of various degrees, Rosicrucians, Knights of the Sun, pupils of Voltaire and Rousseau, Templars, followers of Swedenborg, Saint-Martin and Weishaupt, all . . . together under the name of Jacobins." Lurid accounts of Illuminati assassinations by means ranging from slow poisoning to exploding boxes added frisson to the warnings.[46]

The fear of conspiracies manifested itself specifically as a fear of secret societies, the threat of which haunted European leaders throughout the nineteenth century. During the Napoleonic wars, from roughly 1802 to 1815, secret societies of all types were ruthlessly rooted out by the police. These years were marked by "a peculiar hostility to all forms of voluntary organization": labor unions, student societies, and, in Russia, even poetry groups.[47] After Napoleon's defeat, the restored regimes continued to clamp down on anything they saw as a secret society. Freemasonry, for example, had been tolerated, even by Russia and the Vatican, before the French Revolution. But in the wake of twenty-five years of revolution and war, leaders of the more repressive of the restored governments took advantage of the idea that a "Masonic conspiracy 'explained' the Revolution without requiring social change." The natural result of such repression was a self-fulfilling prophecy: members of any groups favoring social change or reform had to act secretly to avoid imprisonment, and so "secret societies" actually proliferated.[48]

The focus on secret societies brought European notions of conspiracy back from the extremes of Barruel's massive theory to a more realistic position. The Illuminati became less of a concern as time wore on and, despite the Simonini letter, the conspiratorial role of Jews was fading away as well.[49] Secret societies instead became focused on actual politics. Some were mystical or cultish, but, across Europe, most were related to independence movements. The Hetairia trying to free the Greeks from Ottoman rule, the Irish Republican Brotherhood, the Carbonari in Italy, and many other organizations did conspire in their fights for political self-determination. Accordingly, most of the concern over conspiracies in government and religious circles focused on realistic, if exaggerated, fears of subversion, not on giant Illuminati-based or Judeo-Masonic conspiracies.[50]

Today, however, even the most cursory search on the internet will "reveal" constant and wide-ranging activity by the Illuminati between their destruction of France in 1789 and their establishment of Bolshevism in Russia in 1918. Conspiracist websites routinely quote Prime Minister Benjamin Disraeli ("The world is governed by far different personages from what is imagined by those who are not behind the scenes") to provide support for their claims. In France, for example, the Dreyfus Affair in the 1890s is said to have been orchestrated by the Illuminati and "transformed France into the Masonic Jewish sock puppet it is today."[51] In the United States, Abraham Lincoln was killed by agents of the Rothschilds because of his opposition to the "London Banksters." John Wilkes Booth, the Rothschild-Illuminati cat's-paw, escaped, only to be gunned down fifty years later by Illuminati assassin Jesse James because Booth had decided to expose the conspiracy.[52] And in the Middle East and North Africa, an Islamist revival giving rise to Wahhabism was the result of a conspiracy by European agents of the Illuminati.[53]

All such accounts of nineteenth-century intrigue by the Illuminati are twentieth-century inventions of conspiracists to improve on a threadbare story. The Illuminati's reputation, created by Robison and Barruel, as the force that had infiltrated French Freemasonry to bring about the revolution was formidable enough to sustain the Illuminati as a symbol, but not much more. The Illuminati barely figured into the nineteenth century's own accounts of subversion or conspiracy. Thomas Frost's 1876 two-volume history of secret societies over the previous hundred years begins with a thorough, if overwrought, account of the Illuminati in pre-revolutionary France—yet after that he barely mentions the Illuminati and never claims that the group had any notable impact on subsequent secret organizations.[54] An unusually strong statement of Illuminati influence was provided by the anti-Masonic Monsignor George F. Dillon, who raged that the Illuminati's "fanatical and deep director" Adam Weishaupt's "wily confederates were ministers in every court of Europe. Then, as now, the invincible determination with which they secreted their quality from the eyes of monarchs as well as of the general public enabled them to *pose* in any character or capacity without fear of being detected as Freemasons, or at least as Illuminati." But, again, Dillon's Illuminati soon languish; none of Weishaupt's "wily confederates" are shown to have done anything.[55]

The most prominent nineteenth-century Illuminati legend, at least in the United States, centers on Albert Pike, who "continued the work of Adam Weishaupt, introducing Lucifer to the Supreme Council as the Masonic God."[56] In the world of conspiracism, Pike, a Confederate general who later became the leading Freemason in North America, has achieved a cultlike status as the embodiment of occult Freemasonry, Illuminism, Luciferianism, and even Zionism. Pike is said to have founded a particularly insidious form of Masonry called Palladism, which favored Lucifer (the god of light and goodness) over Adonay (a god of darkness and evil) and spread the influence of Illuminism far and wide. Pike's letter of "instructions" to his fellow conspirator Giuseppe Mazzini in Italy laid out the Palladian-Zionist-Illuminati plan for three "world wars" that would culminate in the destruction of Christian civilization.[57]

The only aspects of Pike's legendary influence that actually date from the nineteenth century are the Masonry and Palladism; the Illuminati and Zionism are twentieth-century additions. Moreover, Palladism was revealed as a fraud by its creator, the French hoaxer Leo Taxil, in 1897. Taxil had simply taken Pike—an important Freemason relatively unknown in France—and attributed to him an imaginary doctrine (Palladism) as part of Taxil's ongoing anticlerical hoax involving a supposed victim of satanic Freemasonry. The all-important letter to Mazzini was added to the story well after the exposure of the fraud and did not become well known until William Guy Carr featured it in his conspiracy theories in the 1950s.[58] Everything about the Pike story illustrates the capacity of conspiracists to build, maintain, and defend an alternative history that keeps the Illuminati in the picture.

Despite the efforts of twentieth-century conspiracists, the Illuminati had no history after its dissolution in the late eighteenth century. In 1880, Theodor Reuss tried to revive the Illuminati with his occultish group Ordo Templi Orientis, but without success. In the 1890s, Reuss tried again, joining forces with a freelance occultist named Leopold Engel to form an "Illuminati" Masonic Lodge, apparently to the displeasure of the Freemasons themselves, and again unsuccessfully.[59] Even so, contemporary conspiracists occasionally dredge up Reuss's Ordo Templi Orientis and link it to anything from Area 51 to Obama's birth certificate.[60] Yet in the early twentieth century, the Illuminati was so little known that even Barruel's work was called a "now obscure treatise on Jacobinism."[61] Illuminism reappeared only with the books of Nesta Webster, who transposed Robison and Barruel's idea of a string-pulling Illuminati from the French Revolution to the Russian one. It was only with Lady Queenborough's 1933 *Occult Theocrasy* that the saga of Albert Pike reemerged, and only with Carr's work in the 1950s that an explicit continuity between eighteenth-century and current Illuminism was created. The entire body of occult Illuminati historical lore, the link between Illuminism and Lucifer, and any connections between Illuminism, Communism, and Zionism have been built on this weak foundation.

2

CONSPIRACISM TAKES SHAPE
IN THE UNITED STATES

Shall our sons become the disciples of Voltaire, and the dragoons of
Marat; or our daughters the concubines of the Illuminati?

Yale University President Timothy Dwight, "The Duty of Americans, at the Present Crisis," 1798

The United States took the lead in the creation of conspiracy theories
during the nineteenth century. Up through the Civil War, hardly a year
went by that some region or segment of the population was not swept
up in conspiratorial fervor. First, New Englanders discovered the Illuminati's threat to America. Then across the northeast, Masonic lodges
became hives of conspiratorial activity. By the 1830s, cities up and
down the eastern seaboard felt the brunt of the conspiracy to flood their
streets and polling places with Catholics. And, right up to the outbreak
of the Civil War, northern abolitionists recounted the "Slave Power"
conspiracy. As the century drew to a close, agrarian populists were moving beyond resentment of East Coast bankers and constructing a primitive international conspiracy to explain their plight.

In every instance, those most obsessed with conspiracy theories saw themselves as besieged by changes in society that they did not like and that threatened their position. And in every case, they saw their position as embodying proper and enduring values. The two dominant values were piety and Americanism—the latter a notoriously slippery concept. The actual conspiracy theories do not seem impressive by twenty-first-century standards. Arguably, some do not rise to the level of conspiracy at all. Still, taken as a group, they contributed elements of conspiratorial thinking and rhetoric that have had a lasting impact.

The Illuminati Invades Virginia

The underlying political situation in the United States was quite different from Europe's. The American Revolution was barely twenty years old when Robison and Barruel published their indictments of the Illuminati and the French Revolution. The founders of the new nation had gone to great lengths to avoid monarchy or anything that smacked of hereditary power. Nor had they allowed for the possibility of an established religion. In short, the very things that Illuminati conspirators were presumably intent on destroying were missing in the United States. Robison and Barruel's fearsome scenarios thus seemed unlikely to gain any traction there.[1]

Nevertheless, Robison's *Proofs* was widely excerpted and then printed in its entirety in New York and Philadelphia in 1798 and in Boston the next year. Barruel's *Memoirs* was less widespread but still easily available in English. Moreover, Barruel clearly warned Americans that "Republics are equally menaced with Monarchies; and that the immensity of the ocean is but a feeble barrier against the universal conspiracy of the Sect!"[2] Robison's conspiratorial ideas were repeated endlessly in New England sermons and pamphlets as that region suffered a loss of power and prestige. In that context, a subversive conspiracy made sense to many distressed New Englanders. As historian Gordon Wood noted, the idea that Jefferson's "Republican Party was in league with an international Jacobinical conspiracy dominated by the Order of the Bavarian

Illuminati" seemed not too far-fetched at the time.[3] Still, the Enlightenment principles on which the Illuminati had been based did not actually threaten America's republican government or its religious practices, so European images of subversion "had to be shaped and blended to fit American considerations." Opponents of Illuminism began to stress its threat to "a way of life," marking the beginning of that metaphor, which has been the target of conspirators ever since.[4]

Most of the New England sermons, pamphlets (mostly transcripts of sermons), and newspaper articles (likewise) focused on the evils being perpetrated in Europe without explaining how or why they might cross the Atlantic. The Reverend David Osgood, in one of the earliest sermons concerning the threat (1795), stressed the "ferocious and atheistical anarchy in France" and how revolutionaries were intent on "bringing to other nations . . . their infernal principles and conduct." Osgood claimed that the "same spirit, and some of the identical agents, found their way into these states and began here their fraternizing system."[5] As Robison's and Barruel's conspiratorial interpretations proliferated, Timothy Dwight, pastor and president of Yale, cited them both heavily in laying out the threat to his listeners' sons and daughters. Fisher Ames, best known for his oration at Washington's funeral, painted a hellish picture of France "and perhaps our future state" unless Americans rose up "like a body of minute-men" to repel the forces of Jacobinism.[6]

The best known of the New Englanders was Jedidiah Morse, a pastor and geographer who in 1798 gave three widely reprinted sermons supporting Robison's *Proofs*. The following year, Morse overreached somewhat, claiming to have in his possession "an official, authenticated list . . . of the officers and members of a society of Illuminati . . . consisting of 100 members, instituted in Virginia, by the Grand Orient of France." A lack of evidence undermined his claims and even subjected him to occasional ridicule.[7] None of Morse's claims impressed Thomas Jefferson, who wrote Bishop Madison in Philadelphia: "I have lately by accident got a sight of a single volume, (the 3d.) of the Abbé Barruel's 'Antisocial Conspiracy,' which gives me the first idea I have ever had of what is meant by the Illuminatism, against which 'illuminati Morse' as he is now called, &

his ecclesiastical and monarchical associates have been making such a hue and cry. Barruel's own parts of the book are perfectly the ravings of a Bedlamite. But he quotes largely from Weishaupt whom he considers as the founder of what he calls the order."[8]

The Federalists made little headway with their thinly veiled accusations against the Jeffersonian Republicans, as people "generally began to admit the baseless nature of the alarm that Morse had sounded."[9] In 1802 when the Reverend Seth Payson published *Proofs of the Real Existence, and Dangerous Tendency, of Illuminism*, most of his effort was devoted to defending the reputations of Robison and Barruel against "shafts of ridicule and defamation" such as Jefferson's. Also in 1802, an attack on the faction of DeWitt Clinton, although couched in terms of the "Columbian Iluminati," was devoid of any conspiracism at all. Still, even as late as 1828, when the anti-Mason movement was getting underway, Henry Dana Ward, the well-known abolitionist, tried to keep the Illuminist threat alive in his *Free Masonry: Its Pretensions Exposed. . . .*[10]

The Illuminist conspiracy in the United States lasted only a few years and was limited largely to New England, where conditions were ripe. Not only was the Federalist Party losing ground to the Jeffersonians, but the more stringent and hidebound New England religions were rapidly being displaced by upstart religious groups such as the Methodists.[11] From the traditional Puritan viewpoint, America was spiraling out of control. Timothy Dwight's 1801 sermon marking the new century lamented markers of the decline—"profanation of the Sabbath, . . . drunkenness, gambling, and lewdness." The Puritan heritage had also promoted a strongly Manichean, good-versus-evil outlook, and early Puritans saw themselves as doing God's work in the wilderness— building "a city upon a hill"—that led easily into a "sense of mission that convinced Americans of their special role in history." In one of his Illuminati-inspired sermons, Harvard divinity professor David Tappan expounded on America's "all-important mission of thwarting world revolution and saving the world from atheism and moral ruin."[12]

The Illuminati conspiracy arrived ready-made from Europe, and its American propagators were not actual theorists. They found an audience among elites whose power was in decline and who were deeply concerned about the direction of the new nation. Their situation was so dire that by 1804 New England Federalists were seriously considering secession. Contemporary research has found that people who see their situation deteriorating are particularly susceptible to conspiracy theories. Feelings of increasing powerlessness, especially of a diminution of sociopolitical control, lead people to conspiratorial conclusions. Believing that one's plight is caused by a conspiracy can provide "a clear explanation for a negative outcome that otherwise seems inexplicable."[13] Such powerlessness can also lead to increased religious intensity or greater acceptance of authoritarian leaders, but when these feelings are linked with overwhelming, shocking events—such as the French Revolution and its associated terror—the odds of turning to conspiracy theory are increased.[14]

Homegrown Conspiracies: Freemasons, Catholics, the "Slave Power"

Unlike Europe, nineteenth-century America was a secular republic that did not have residual Bonapartist secret societies or insurgent nationalist groups such as the Hetairia or the Carbonari to contend with. But even in Europe, fear of conspiracy was mostly the obsession of a small number of autocrats and the "aberration of a few hundred writers," whereas conspiracy thinking sporadically cut a wide swath through the American populace.[15] There was a seemingly constant parade of imagined conspiracies in the antebellum years. But why?

Part of Americans' penchant for seeing conspiracies stems from the nature of religious belief in the United States, which is rooted both in its Puritan heritage and in a related strain of antipapism that never faded away. In addition, the rise of evangelical Protestantism, peculiar to the United States and manifested by the Second Great Awakening—is a factor in conspiracy thinking, as was America's exceptional mission to civilize the world and spread republican virtue. This mission naturally made the United States a target for conspirators, all the more so because of particularly fragile form of government, which could be easily undermined. Richard Hofstadter observed that nineteenth-century conspiracy believers always felt as if they were "fending off threats" to the nation.[16]

Several related factors have been seen as contributing to Americans' tendency to turn social problems into conspiracies. Traditionalists often felt threatened by growth, increasing prosperity, and encroaching cosmopolitanism—all exacerbated by the influx of immigrants. Nativists feared betraying—or at least failing to live up to—the spirit of the American Revolution. This fear was catalyzed by the fiftieth anniversary of the revolution in 1826, which generated an almost cultish fervor for the founding fathers, the Minutemen, even the Pilgrims. In addition, Hofstadter famously stressed a distinctively American anti-intellectualism as a factor.[17] Another possible factor, noted in passing by many, is a severely repressed sexuality, which played up threats to the purity of American womanhood. To some degree, this reflected an obsession of Robison's: that the French Revolution was a victory for libertinism, the corruption of women, and the "cultivation of sensual pleasures." However, most of the "affinity of paranoia and pornography" appears to have been homegrown.[18]

What is widely considered the first indigenous American "conspiracy theory" grew out of the anti-Mason movement.[19] In 1826 in western New York, one William Morgan, a disgruntled ex-Mason about to publish an exposé of Freemasonry, was arrested, jailed, and then abducted. Neither he nor his book was ever seen again, and he was widely assumed to have been murdered by Freemasons. This incident was seized on by people who already found Masonry suspicious and by New York opponents of President Jackson (himself a Freemason). Fostered by friendly newspaper publishers and by New York politician Thurlow Weed, the movement was quickly transformed into a political party—the Anti-Masonic Party—that became quite successful in New York, as well as in Vermont and Pennsylvania.[20]

The unanswered question in this tale is why people found Freemasonry so suspicious and threatening that an incident in a remote backwater could inspire a national movement. One reason was the relentless flogging of the incident by Weed and his allies. But, beyond that, there was a widespread perception that, in town after town, Masonic lodges had become the headquarters of a coterie of important, well-to-do citizens. It was easy to imagine all sorts of backroom deals and minor conspiracies against the general public. Freemasons began to be viewed as a local aristocracy, cosmopolitan and secular. Masonic titles and rituals were easily portrayed as antirepublican, and the lodges' acceptance of non-Christians was unpopular among the growing body of evangelical Protestants. Masonic secrecy allowed people's imaginations free rein, and the image of Freemasonry shifted from that of an elitist club to that of an organization that threatened traditional values with its "un-American activities" and its plotting against religion.[21]

While the original charge that Freemasonry amounted to a "fraternity for the privileged classes" was not conspiratorial (or even untrue), conspiratorial ideas began to percolate in "the apocalyptic and absolutist framework in which this hostility to Masonry was usually expressed." Freemasonry suddenly became "one of the greatest evils that ever existed in any age or country;" "an engine of Satan;" its members, "enemies of the human race." The fraternity of privilege had been transformed into a conspiracy of criminal antirepublicanism, as asserted at the first Anti-Masonic Convention: "The abuses of which we complain involve the highest crimes of which a man can be guilty, because they indicate the deepest malice, and the most fatal aim. They bespeak the most imminent danger, because they have proceeded from a conspiracy more numerous and better organized for mischief, than any other detailed in the records of man, and yet, though exposed, maintaining itself in all its monstrous power."[22] As this rhetoric proliferated, paranoia flourished. Anti-Masons undertook surveillance of lodge members; questions about licentiousness in the all-male lodges arose; speculation about Masonic rites and oaths became increasingly blood-soaked and occultish (temperance advocates took a dim view of drinking wine from human skulls).[23]

A noteworthy aspect of these conspiratorial accusations is the absence of any insidious manipulation behind the scenes. Even though it had been only twenty-five years since the Federalists' Illuminati frenzy, allusions to Illuminati influence were rare and generally incidental.[24] Mistrust of Freemasonry was based solely on perceived characteristics of the group itself: elitism, secrecy, and peculiar rites. Most of the specific accusations of conspiratorial behavior dealt with Masons' using their connections to shut everyday people out of lucrative business opportunities and to monopolize local political offices. Building on this was the additional accusation of Masons' covering for one another's crimes and thwarting the cause of justice. While exaggerated, and in some cases even paranoid, conspiratorial ideas about Freemasonry were grounded in reality.

So, although frequently cited as a conspiracy theory, the Freemasonry episode barely qualifies as one. As Freemasonry became less appealing under the onslaught of the anti-Masons, membership fell precipitously and many lodges closed, whereupon anti-Masonry lost its rationale and faded away. Accordingly, anti-Masonry is best thought of as a crusade with some conspiratorial thinking on its fringes.

But hard on its heels emerged the fear of a Roman Catholic conspiracy, originating in an avowedly nativist response to the influx of Catholic immigrants, especially from Ireland, which catalyzed the fear of "popery" shared by puritans and evangelical Protestants. A burgeoning array of books about innocent girls and young women being abducted and corrupted by priests and nuns helped push anti-Catholicism in a conspiratorial direction.[25] A major voice against popery was that of Samuel Morse, son of Jedidiah ("Illuminati") Morse and inventor of the telegraph. Writing as "Brutus," Morse, in his 1835 *Foreign Conspiracy against the Liberties of the United States*, set forth a full-fledged conspiracy theory complete with an organized hierarchy of manipulators behind the scenes. According to him, the pope was not at the center of the web of conspiracy, for he reported to Chancellor Metternich of the Austrian Empire, who in turn "obeys his illustrious master, the Emperor," Francis I. These three "conspirators against our liberties," Morse argued, controlled agents "now organized in every part of the country . . . from the most abject dolt that obeys the commands of his priest," and up through the Catholic hierarchy.[26]

Morse buttressed the role of Metternich by incorporating Austria's 1815 Holy Alliance with Prussia and Russia into the conspiracy. More plausibly, he stressed the role of the St. Leopold Foundation, an organization that was in fact dedicated to spreading the Catholic faith. Closer to home, Morse excoriated politicians whose "*recklessness* and *unprincipled* character" made them seek out short-term gain by giving "great advantage to these conspirators," along with those craven newspaper editors who "can easily be made into tools of a despot to subvert the liberties of their country."[27]

Morse's contemporaries made similar arguments. Lyman Beecher, a Christian millennialist, saw the influx of Catholics to America as the key part of a conspiracy by "the potentates of Europe" to undermine the world's great Protestant Republic. Representative Lewis Levin of Pennsylvania claimed that the pope had convened a secret meeting of wealthy and influential Catholics in London to "overthrow . . . Protestant rights and Protestant freedom in the United States." Catholics were not fleeing deprivation or starvation; they were actively being sent as part of the conspiracy "to overthrow our republic." Beecher, like Morse, made this argument with a seemingly endless stream of rhetorical questions: "What means the paying of the passage and emptying out upon our shores such floods of pauper emigrants—the contents of the poorhouse and the sweepings of the streets?— . . . sending annually accumulating thousands to the polls to lay their inexperienced hand upon the helm of our power? Does Metternich not imagine that there is no party spirit in our land, whose feverish urgency would facilitate their naturalization and hasten them to the ballot box?—and no demagogues, who, for a little brief authority, however gained, would sell their country to an everlasting bondage?"[28]

Most Catholics, according to such writers, simply obeyed their priests, voting en masse to "decide our elections, perplex our policy, inflame and divide the nation, break the bond of our union, and throw down our free institutions." Levin even linked this argument to the ongoing "Slave Power" conspiracy, maintaining that the Vatican's plan included adding more states where slavery would be "made eternal by modern rivets forged in the fire . . . of tyranny and . . . imbecility." But in addition to this regular army of "abject dolts," there were Catholic shock troops, the Jesuits. Members of this order, "silent, systematized, unwatched, and unresisted," were "prowling about all parts of the United States in every possible disguise, expressly to ascertain the advantageous situations and modes to disseminate Popery." One particularly insidious Jesuit practice had servants, especially maids, spying on their employers. A fictitious oath making the rounds had Jesuits swear to "place Catholic girls in Protestant families that a weekly report may be made of the inner movements of the heretics."[29]

The anti-Catholic conspiracy theory was notable for its prejudice against and scapegoating of immigrants. Contemporary psychological research links these attitudes to conspiracy mentality through right-wing authoritarianism and social dominance orientation. Right-wing authoritarians have a "markedly negative attitude" toward groups that deviate from their accepted norms. They are likely to scapegoat and actively persecute such groups as well. People with a strong social dominance orientation behave similarly, but they single out groups they perceive as having low social status. Right-wing authoritarianism and social dominance orientation are similar in their relationship to conspiracism, as both transform passive attitudes into active behaviors when serious threats are perceived.[30] Some researchers have concluded that "conspiracy mentality" should constitute a third "negative political attitude," similar to the others in terms of negativity and prejudice but distinct from them in that its practitioners single out "high power groups" as their target. However, the "high power" of such scapegoated groups may well exist only in the minds of the conspiracists.[31]

Anti-Catholicism was more than a resurgence of antipapism; it was an actual conspiracy theory, more than anti-Masonry had been. It reached beyond the obvious hierarchy of the church to a cabal of European powers under the direction of the most powerful emperor on the continent. Morse's Manichean narrative posited "a war going on between *despotism* on one side, and *liberty* on the other," a fight to the death between "bands of darkness" and the "light of a new age." Beecher relied on much the same rhetoric: the "forces of despotism" had "no hope of rest and primeval darkness, but by the extinction of our light."[32] As an actual conspiracy theory, depending on a leap of imagination for its coherence, anti-Catholicism did not fade away as the threat receded—as had happened with anti-Masonry. Protestant concern over parochial schools toward the end of the nineteenth century would not have generated conspiracy rhetoric without the conspiratorial framework laid down before the Civil War. Parochial school opponent Reverend Justin Fulton brought back the ideas of Morse and Beecher in language laden with intrigue:

> Romism is the dominant power in the Capitol of the United States. Lincoln, Grant, and Arthur withstood it, and suffered the consequences. The power is unseen. It is shadowy. It inhabits the air and infects it. Romanism is the malaria of the spiritual world. It stupefies the brain, deadens the heart, and sears the conscience as with a hot iron. . . . The surrender to Rome of the Capitol of the Great Republic means death to liberty. The people of all lands and climes are interested in the conflict. The facts given will ripen the indignation of pure-minded men and women against the Jesuitical foe, who no longer creeps under cover or hides in the shadow of some wall, but stalks boldly forth on his errand of wickedness.[33]

As typically happens with conspiracy theories, the "facts given" are often fanciful and occasionally run up against reality. Fulton claims that thousands of government clerks are "under the surveillance of Rome" but has to admit that it may not be true that "a private wire runs from the White House, in Washington, to the Cardinal's Palace, in Baltimore," ultimately falling back to a much less impressive position: "It *is* true that the Cardinal is a factor in politics." Anti-Catholic organizations spread the "fact" that a Catholic-orchestrated run on the banks caused the panic of 1893, and they circulated a fraudulent papal encyclical giving the date when Catholics should begin exterminating all heretics.[34]

The third antebellum conspiracy was supposedly perpetrated by the slaveholding class in the South to preserve and expand slavery. This was mirrored by a corresponding abolitionist conspiracy believed by Southern slave owners, especially after Great Britain abolished slavery in its territories. In addition to overestimating the influence of abolitionists, slave owners envisioned "fleets of armed steamers, loaded with black troops from the West Indies" attacking Southern ports. Robert Goldberg sees the slave owners not as conspiracy minded but merely as having "lost perspective and created a menace out of scale and more cohesive than the evidence allowed."[35] The same could be said for most of the abolitionists worrying about the Slave Power conspiracy, which David Brion Davis considers to have been at least in part a matter of strategic rhetoric—a "necessary means of arousing the fears" of those northerners not concerned with the plight of slaves. During the Civil War, this rhetoric portrayed slave owners as an "aristocracy against democracy" whose members planned to "establish a monarchy."[36]

The basic argument made by adherents of the Slave Power conspiracy was that slave-state politicians wielded disproportionate clout in Washington, DC, which was true enough. As one abolitionist calculated, slave owners, while only "one fortieth of the entire population of the South, and one hundredth the part of that of the Union, are yet the real sovereigns of the Republic." Yet most Slave Power conspiracists described normal political backroom deals and some corruption, and most historical accounts, including those accusing Southern political leaders of planning a secessionist rebellion, have depicted Slave Power activity as taking place in the open.[37]

A few conspiracists made the effort to build a more substantial theory. Episodes from American history were retrofitted to accommodate a belief that the Slave Power had long been operating behind the scenes. Making the most out of the commercial affinity between the South and Great Britain, the War of 1812 was reinterpreted with conspiratorial implications. This retrofitting was extended to the earliest years of the nation and to institutions such as the Bank of the United States, with the argument that the true purpose of the bank was to support slavery. Dramatic events such as the 1835 assassination attempt on President Andrew Jackson could be made to fit into the Slave Power conspiracy as well.[38] Even after the Civil War, a few dedicated souls tried to keep these ideas going. Building on Lincoln's assassination, John Smith Dye lamented "the assassination of three of our most illustrious Presidents, all of whom were swept aside like cobwebs when they stood in the way of the conspirator's unholy designs."[39]

Still, the Slave Power conspiracy was not as much a conspiracy theory as anti-Catholicism had been. The latter featured European potentates manipulating the Vatican, the Roman Catholic hierarchy manipulating its parishioners, and the cardinal in Baltimore manipulating the White House, all in pursuit of an existential goal: the destruction of liberty and of the Protestant republic. The Slave Power conspiracy was limited largely to senators manipulating the legislative process to maintain slavery. In fact, the Slave Power conspiracy was very much a throwback to the conspiratorial analyses of politics that had been common in the eighteenth century.

Populism's Financial Conspiracy

After the Civil War, conspiracies loomed less large on the American political scene. There was a brief resurgence of anti-Masonry around 1870, linking it with every other unsettling occurrence and trend of the day: Jesuits, the Paris Commune, spiritualists, "free love." But this hodge-podge of threats never congealed into a conspiracy. Anti-Catholicism did not entirely disappear and was reenergized by the debate over parochial schools during the Grant administration. But, with Metternich's death and the decline of the Austrian Empire, anti-Catholicism was increasingly organized around nativism rather than conspiracies against liberty.[40] Beginning in the 1870s, however, a new financial conspiracy developed into what would become the dominant political issue at the end of the century.

The conspiracy centered on a "cabal of coastal political elites [and] bankers" (At this time, "banker" was sometimes, but not always, a code word for Jews) and was driven by the demonetization of silver in the Coinage Act of 1873: "The greatest crime ever committed in the world—one that was to cause more suffering than all other crimes committed in a century."[41] Originally the silver advocates simply saw East Coast bankers as a "money trust," having so much clout in Washington that they were able to maintain the gold standard—benefiting their banks at the expense of southern and western farmers.[42] But this explanation became enveloped in an ever-expanding and increasingly distant array of conspirators.

In the 1870s, the Greenback Party convinced many people that a "bondholders' conspiracy" was selling out the interests of the United States to "foreigners" (which was understood to mean British banking interests). By the 1880s, England was sliding into the driver's seat of this conspiracy, apparently in an effort to reconquer America: "She has conspired with the Tory capitalists of our Eastern States to rob us of our possessions as surely as she conspired with Benedict Arnold to betray to her our armies in the days of the Revolution. This England has never yet given up the idea of victory over the material resources of America. . . . She reaches forth her golden arm to destroy the value of our silver, and she finds her dupes and her coconspirators amid the bankers of New York and Boston."[43] By the heyday of the Free Silver movement in the 1890s, English dominance of the conspiracy could "no longer be rationally doubted."[44] This conspiracy theory expanded by being retrofitted to explain seemingly unrelated historical events—as had been true of the most determined propagators of the Slave Power conspiracy. An 1895 Populist Party manifesto castigating the "secret cabals of the international gold ring" claimed that "as early as 1865–66 a conspiracy was entered into between the gold gamblers of Europe and America." One H. C. Baldwin pushed the conspiracy back to 1820, when Great Britain abolished slavery. Baldwin was able to see through "that philanthropic act" to the underlying "unholy conspiracy to establish a system of finance which is fast reducing the whole people to the conditions of debt slaves."[45]

The other element expanding the financial conspiracy was its internationalization. Although still headquartered in Britain, the "Money Power . . . knows no boundaries except to fix its tentacles wherever the foot of industry treads or the hand of industry toils. There it puts its blood-sucking tentacles, and is putting them the world over." Even at this early date, a key element of an international money power conspiracy was Jewish bankers in general and the Rothschilds in particular. Rothschild financial power was well known even in America, although generally without any conspiratorial dimension. Most of the language employed by the silver advocates was circumspect about Jews, who were used as a "rhetorical symbol for the ills of society and an economic system that were beyond the control of the average citizen."[46] Still, the Jews were clearly an underlying presence. In *Coin's Financial School* (the Bible of the silver movement, in which a child explains free silver to a group of thick-headed economists), William Harvey's language is very restrained. The book's illustrations, "simple and striking images," are another matter. These include Gold smiling over the corpse of Silver: "An octopus representing the Rothschilds, centered in England, and labeled 'The Great English Devil Fish,' grips the entire world in its tentacles; John Bull makes a brutal attack on the female figure of liberty, while virtuous Silver, helpless in chains, looks on; . . . [while] a monstrously rapacious usurer sits clutching his bags of gold."[47]

Equally important in creating this Anglo-Jewish conspiracy were contemporary novels. In 1894, William Harvey published *A Tale of Two Nations*, a roman à clef featuring a British financier "of Semitic origin," Baron Rothe. In this potboiler, the baron's agent in America divides his time between bribing or blackmailing politicians and seducing a virtuous American woman; ultimately the conspiracy against America is successful although the seduction is not.[48] Harvey's novel was published just after Ignatius Donnelly's luridly conspiratorial *Caesar's Column: A Story of the Twentieth Century*. Donnelly, an eccentric Minnesota politician, had earlier demonstrated cryptographically that Francis Bacon had authored Shakespeare's plays and created the modern myth of Atlantis.[49] *Caesar's Column* reflected Donnelly's political beliefs, which culminated in the view that "a vast conspiracy against mankind has been organized on two continents, and it is rapidly taking possession of the world."[50] A dystopian novel set in 1988, *Caesar's Column* depicts the war between a pampered ruling class and a vast underground proletariat—a war with a hundred million soldiers, zeppelins, and some sort of hyper-evolved zombies. All this takes place in a world that has been "Semitized" by a financial oligarchy of Jewish bankers under the leadership of "a Rothschild-like figure."[51]

Some of the populist writing foreshadowed later conspiracy theories rooted in the spread of *The Protocols of the Learned Elders of Zion*. Gordon Clark of the Bimetallic League published the openly antisemitic *Shylock: as Banker, Bondholder, Corruptionist, Conspirator* in 1894. And clearly, many of the illustrations of the day were in the same vein. A cartoon from *Judge* magazine in 1892 depicted a Jewish businessman on Broadway in New Jerusalem ("York" of "New York" crossed out) watching "our first families" (the Dutch) being driven out. The free silver organ *Sound Money* showed Uncle Sam literally being crucified by Jewish "Wall St. Pirates" with the help of their stooges in the Republican and Democratic parties.[52] Of all the nineteenth-century conspiracy theories, only the populist free silver one began building an alternate reality narrative characteristic of real conspiracism.

The Impact of Nineteenth-Century Conspiracy Theories

The United States proved to be fertile ground for conspiracy theories. First in New England and then across the entire nation, social changes occurred with dramatic speed: commercial growth, an increasingly transient population, westward expansion, and the influx of immigrants. These developments generated an uncomfortable tension between tradition and progress.[53] In this atmosphere, America's republican government and its foundation in revolution created an additional tension. As Lyman Beecher declared, America was, by "the providence of God, destined to lead the way in the moral and political emancipation of the world."[54] This made it a natural target of any antirepublican forces, and, to some degree, all the conspirators across the century—Illuminists, Freemasons, Catholic potentates, the Slave Power, English banks—were portrayed as antirepublican. Yet Americans worried about their own capacities as well, as "the fear of betraying the priceless heritage won by the Founding Fathers" worried many. David Brion Davis summed up these tensions by noting "a striking correlation between the fears of conspiracy and American aspirations to national greatness. It is almost as though the nation's grandiose mission to liberate and democratize the world could only be confirmed by proving the maliciousness and power of a clandestine enemy."[55] Add to these tensions the distinctively American puritanistic Protestantism and a strong anti-intellectual streak, and it is less surprising that America gave rise to so much homegrown conspiratorial thinking.[56]

In Europe, conspiratorial suspicions focused on three things, none of which generated any conspiracy theorizing. First, fears of revolutionary aftershocks in the wake of the French Revolution never quite dissipated. Relatedly, the various movements of national liberation, and the secret societies they encompassed, were a constant concern of the forces of reaction. And third, beginning in roughly the middle of the century, a new type of antisemitism arose that was to become viciously conspiratorial in the twentieth century. In America, by contrast, new conspiratorial ideas flourished. Each conspiracy, even if not much more than a simple explanation, contributed a lasting element to how conspiracy theories work.

The anti-Masons were the first to spot the conspiracy in plain sight: Masonic lodges on the main streets of towns across the country. The visibility of lodges added a stridency to conspiratorial rhetoric, similar to conspiracists today who rail against the "sheeple" who cannot see the obvious. The anti-Catholics made the conspiratorial leap from the Vatican to the Austrian Empire, shifting the target of the conspiracy from religion to politics and liberty. As a stylistic breakthrough, both Morse and Beecher turned the rhetorical question into the mainstay of their argument, allowing them to avoid making specific claims (such as had undone Jedidiah Morse) while still sowing fears. Abolitionists of a conspiratorial bent pioneered the historical retrofit in their effort to turn Slave Power from a political issue into an actual conspiracy theory. And the Populists, taking a leap as the anti-Catholics had done, and reinterpreting history in the fashion of the abolitionists, created a huge global, evil conspiracy when East Coast bankers would have been more plausible villains by themselves. In addition, all the conspiracies featured two elements that have become staples in conspiracy theories: dupes and sex.

Dupes—either hapless or willing accomplices—are what connect the shadowy and often distant conspirators to their victims. Willing or not, they betray their fellow Americans as well as their heritage. Generally, these are politicians and what is now called the mainstream press. For example, the suspicious disappearance of William Morgan, the Freemasons' nemesis, generated a conspiracy theory only because the Masons, "through their political and social influence, . . . induced the press to remain silent about the true facts of the case."[57] By the end of the century dupes were portrayed as knowingly doing the bidding of forces determined to destroy America.

The question of sex seems strongly linked to concerns about loss of power. From one's daughter becoming a "concubine" of the Illuminati, to the questionable practices common in the all-male Freemason lodges, to the "Awful Disclosures" of Maria Monk about her captivity in a Montreal nunnery, to the seduction of America's womanhood by foreigners working for the Rothschilds in novels, the plight of women appears with surprising frequency—almost always in a context suggesting that a better showing of manly fortitude would have saved them. For some time, it appeared that the obsession with women as sexual victims was a nineteenth-century artifact, though it rebounded with unprecedented force during the civil rights era of the 1960s, when the prospect of interracial sex unhinged some conspiracists to the point of incoherence.

And yet, at the end of the nineteenth century, even as these conspiratorial tropes were sinking in, conspiracism was losing ground. The republic no longer seemed so vulnerable. People were acclimating to progress. The Populists were defeated soundly in elections while the silver advocates found a home in the non-conspiratorial Republican Party. In addition, science—even social science—stressed complex explanations of events, undermining the conspiratorial approach. The historian Gordon Wood, writing in 1982, concluded his defense of earlier conspiracy thinking with the observation that, by this time, "attributing events to the conscious design of particular individuals became more and more simplistic. Conspiratorial interpretations of events thrived, but now they seemed increasingly primitive and quaint."[58] Nineteenth-century America had generated specific, event-driven conspiracy theories but no framework capable of sustaining a full-blown conspiracy theory.

3

PRECONDITIONS FOR MODERN CONSPIRACISM

JEWISH ASSIMILATION, PREMILLENNIALISM, AND ARYAN OCCULTISM

> Fantasies can achieve a causal status once they have been institutional-
> ized in beliefs, values, and social groups.
>
> Nicholas Goodrick-Clarke, *The Occult Roots of Nazism*

Although short-lived conspiracy theories cropped up regularly in the United States, and although monarchists in Europe were constantly on guard against secret societies, the nineteenth century was essentially devoid of conspiracism as a worldview. But in the aftermath of the Bolshevik revolution in Russia, conspiracism began to flourish. In 1919, Nesta Webster's *The French Revolution* brought the ideas of Robison and Barruel back into print, the Illuminati was rekindled as a threat to civilization, and modern conspiracism began to develop in earnest. The conspiracy theories spawned at this time were much broader than earlier ones, which had been more constrained by reality and featured secretive groups with limited, comprehensible goals. Nationalist movements were active from Ireland to Greece; Freemasons' numbers and influence had grown dramatically in the United States; political machines had tried to mold Catholic immigrants into a voting bloc; powerful slave-state politicians schemed to defeat abolitionists; and East Coast bankers defended the gold standard. But the conspiracy theories built around these groups did not last—in part because the narratives around them were grounded in reality enough to be held up against actual events and shown to be untrue or, at least, overblown.

Twentieth-century conspiracy theories, by contrast, dealt with larger, more diffuse groups, like the Illuminati, and with more comprehensive and menacing goals, typically world domination. The very breadth of the goals makes it much harder to hold these conspiracy theories up to reality, and thus they endure. Even when these conspiracy theories center on real groups, such as Communists or Jews, the groups are redefined in a way that make them less identifiable. Reds, pinks, one-worlders, fellow travelers, and liberals; International Jews, Talmudists, the Hidden Government, the Synagogue of Satan—all this terminology casts a net wide enough to capture any perceived enemy. And this does not take into account the conspiracies controlled by the Aldebarans, the Vril, the Ascended Masters, or even, still, the Illuminati.

Some of the reasons behind the changing nature of conspiracy theory are not surprising, while others are rather unexpected. But it is not possible to understand twentieth-century conspiracism without examining such earlier developments. Three of these developments stand out, the largest and most important of which has to do with the widespread assimilation of European Jews and the reaction against them. The second, more a distinctly American phenomenon, is the growth of apocalyptic and millennialist religious thinking. And the third is the occult revival, which ranged from gothic revival literature to mythic racism.

Changing Ideas about the Jews
FROM THE JEWISH ENLIGHTENMENT TO THE *PROTOCOLS*

Jews in Europe had been subject to religious prejudice for centuries. Sometimes tolerated, sometimes persecuted, their situation had changed relatively little since medieval times. Toward the end of the eighteenth century, however, some within the Jewish community began supporting the secular, liberal ideas of the Enlightenment. Over the next hundred years, during the period known as the Haskalah (or Jewish Enlightenment) Jewish assimilation progressed with varying success across Europe.[1]

Early in the nineteenth century, assimilation received some peculiar support from Christian millennialist Restorationists, for whom the arrival of the millennium depended on the restoration of the Jewish kingdom in Zion. The restoration in turn depended, as they saw it, on Jews' converting to Christianity. The London Society for Propagating Christianity among the Jews (1809) spearheaded the drive for conversion. In France, Napoleon encouraged assimilation by liberalizing laws and even convoking Jewish leaders to deal with pressing issues between Christians and Jews. This effort was successful enough to earn Napoleon a nomination as the Antichrist.[2]

Jews, by and large, were not interested in converting to Christianity, but many became secular in practice, abandoning traditional garments, speaking their national language instead of Yiddish, trading in their religious education for a secular one. By the second half of the century, many Jews—mostly in western Europe—were active in legal, scientific, and cultural professions and were beginning to make their way into politics, as barriers to their participation fell. The acculturation of Jews in western Europe was so strong that it overrode the burgeoning Zionism common among east European Jews: "In Western Europe, the Zionist movement faced strong opposition from most Jews. They had not only become acculturated but were by now patriotic citizens of their countries and in large part, became middle class. They felt threatened by Zionism because they had a lot to lose. They did not want their loyalty to their country to be questioned or to endanger their citizenship."[3]

None of these changes went unnoticed by Judeophobes. On the contrary, Jewish assimilation into modern bourgeois society provided an additional basis for anti-Jewish sentiment: on top of the traditional religious intolerance and social prejudice, a political antisemitism could now emerge. Norman Cohn, in his study of antisemitism, noted that political antisemites "see 'the Jew' not only as an uncanny, demonic being but also as . . . a symbol of all the force in the modern world which they themselves hate and fear."[4] Before the middle of the century, pamphlets condemning Jews circulated. One of the first, written under the appellation Satan, introduced the canard that the Rothschilds had built their wealth on advance information about the outcome of the battle of Waterloo. In the wake of the revolutions in 1848, a steady stream of periodicals, novels, and tracts portrayed Jews as a threat. Benjamin Disraeli's novels of political machinations by Jews were quite popular. Pamphleteers such as E. E. Eckert revived Barruel's link between Jews and Freemasons. And ultimately most influential, Hermann Goedsche's 1868 novel *Biarritz* depicted the leaders of the Israeli tribes of Israel meeting with the Antichrist in the Jewish cemetery in Prague.[5]

Goedsche's tale became a key part of what would become *The Protocols of the Learned Elders of Zion*, but others contributed to this effort as well. In the 1860s a Russian Jew who had converted to Christianity, Jacob Brafman, exposed readers to the Kahal, "a secret, uncanny sort of organization which wielded despotic power . . . , incited the Jewish masses against the State, the government, and the Christian religion, and fostered in these masses fanaticism and dangerous national separatism."[6] Around the same time in France, Gougenot des Mousseaux was creating the idea of "Kabbalistic Jews" by reimagining the Kabbalah (a loose-knit body of mysticism and metaphysical doctrine) as the work of an ongoing Jewish Satan-worshipping cult that celebrated the serpent and the phallus with a constant stream of orgies and murders. In 1873, Frederick Millingen, writing as Major Osman-Bey, laid out the whole conspiracy in *World Conquest by the Jews*, the first work of its type in English.[7] The culmination of these efforts was the infamous *Protocols*.

The primary source of the *Protocols* was the Jewish cemetery scene in Goedsche's *Biarritz*. Lifted from the novel and published as a pamphlet in 1872, this story and variants spread westward, becoming less fictional as it went. By the time it emerged in Paris in 1886, it was prefaced as "the program of Jewry, the real program of the Jews, expressed by . . . the Chief Rabbi. . . . It is a speech made in the 1880s."[8] According to most sources, the cemetery scene, other antisemitic writing, and an otherwise harmless satire by Maurice Joly were pieced together by (or at least under the direction of) Pyotr Rachkovsky, head of the Russian secret police. This farrago emerged in the early years of the twentieth century as an official-looking and detailed document revealing a multifaceted conspiracy by Jewish leaders to destroy Christian civilization and to rule the world.[9]

Different editions and versions of the *Protocols* altered its text; sometimes it was even supplemented with anti-Masonic content. The 1917 version that was distributed to Russian soldiers, titled *He Is Near, at the Door . . . Here Comes Antichrist*, made its way to the West and was translated into English by Victor Marsden.[10] The *Protocols* provided an absolute and unavoidable framework for a global Jewish conspiracy, which would have been impossible before the Jewish Enlightenment. The *Protocols* clarified the new picture of the Jews: "Pulling the strings behind the scenes, dominating the new system of modernity, the Jew becomes the cause of every catastrophe."[11]

Ironically, given Jewish acculturation and assimilation into the nations in which they lived, the image of "The International Jew" had been gaining ground and was made into a pillar of antisemitic conspiracism by the *Protocols*. Henry Ford published his famous series of anti-Semitic articles in the *Dearborn Independent* under the heading, "The International Jew: The World's Foremost Problem."[12] The 1920 British government pamphlet, *The Jewish Peril*, was among many works echoing this theme. Even increasing evidence that the *Protocols* were "forgeries" did not stop such articles. *America*, a Catholic weekly magazine, after allowing that the *Protocols* "may or may not be authentic," linked the Jew to every revolutionary movement imaginable. As Norman Cohn summed up: "The Myth of the Jewish world-conspiracy, then, has very little to do with real people and real situations and real conflicts in the modern world, and this seems natural enough when one considers how it originated."[13]

The *Protocols* "new political superstition concerning a secret Jewish government" led directly to two antisemitic conspiracy theories: the finance-based "secret government" and the anti-Christian "hidden hand" plot.[14] By envisioning Jews as a powerful cohesive international organization devoted to world domination, the *Protocols* made it impossible for anyone to be a serious antisemite without becoming a conspiracist as well. In the United States, this was clear by the 1930s as "explanations" of the *Protocols* were distributed and antisemitic right-wing isolationists moved rapidly into conspiracism.[15] Elizabeth Dilling, one of the leaders of the isolationist "mothers' movement," began her career blaming Jews for Communism and for overrunning the Holy Land. In 1934 Dilling was sketching out a Jewish-led Communist conspiracy, and by 1940 her self-published book *The Octopus* was wholly conspiratorial. Her conspiracism became all-encompassing after World War II, including the usual evils (foreign aid, income tax, water fluoridation, race mixing) as well as less typical ones—such as the use of the term "Standard Metropolitan Statistical Area," which "signaled a plot to obliterate state and national boundaries and place communities under the rule of 'commisars.'" Shortly before her death in 1966, Dilling set about trying to expose the Vietnam War as a Jewish plot, an example of the *Protocols* (specifically, number 10) at work.[16]

Other prominent isolationists followed a similar path. Lois Washburn came to identify the Jews as controlling both the Boy Scouts and all the Yellow Cabs. Lyrl Van Hyning, who had identified several presidents as secret Jews (Woodrow "Wohlson," for instance), was among the first to observe concentration camps under construction to hold those determined to resist "the Freemasonic State ruled by the statue of King Solomon" that America had become.[17] Across the board, antisemites of the 1930s had evolved into conspiracists by the 1950s, if not earlier. Gerald Winrod, a one-man defender of the Christian faith, moved rapidly from the *Protocols* in 1934 to a Soviet-Zionist-Illuminati conspiracy the next year. Gerald L. K. Smith became strongly antisemitic only in the late 1930s, but by the 1960s his overriding concern was "the conspiracy led by the Jews who plotted the destruction of Christian civilization." By the time the second generation of post-*Protocols* antisemites—Southern Methodist University English professor John O. Beaty, for example, or California state senator Jack B. Tenney—came along, their antipathy toward Jews and their conspiratorial worldview were merged from the beginning.[18]

A separate, intensely bizarre strand of antisemitism, known as British Israelism, emerged during the nineteenth century. The underlying idea seems to date from 1794, when Richard Brothers, a self-proclaimed prophet and healer, published *A Revealed Knowledge of the Prophesies and Times*. One revelation was that Brothers himself was a direct descendent of King David, giving him the right to the English throne—a self-serving consequence of the more general revelation that Anglo-Saxons were descended from one of the tribes of ancient Israel. This eccentric notion nearly faded away before John Wilson revived it by giving it "scientific" validation in his 1840 *Our Israelitish Origin*. Over the next fifty years, Wilson and others spread the word about the British Israelites. This school of thought was not originally antisemitic; on the contrary, it seems to have been inspired by the desire to join the Jews as God's chosen people. Nevertheless, by 1876 Wilson had begun to see the difference between the southern kingdom of Judah, where Jews originated, and the northern kingdom of Israel, where the newly discovered Anglo-Saxon "Jews" originated. Wilson argued that: "It is for the northern kingdom and their descendants in particular that the bulk of God's blessings were intended. They are the chosen among the chosen people, considered far more important instruments of God's purposes and destined for greater blessings than the Hebrews of the southern kingdom. The southern Jews' status has been further diminished by intermarriage with inferior peoples, the 'worst of the Gentiles.'"[19]

British Israelism spread to North America in the 1880s, where it began to take on a more antisemitic and racist cast. The writings of Charles Totten and John H. Allen contributed to this end, inspiring 1920s Klan leader Reuben Sawyer to link the southern kingdom's "counterfeit Israelites" to the Jews' hidden "government within our government." Another follower of Allen, Howard B. Rand, joined with W. J.

Cameron (who oversaw the distribution of Henry Ford's antisemitic ideas) to create the Anglo-Saxon Federation of America. The relationship between ancient Hebrews and Anglo-Saxons was obvious to Rand, since "Saxon" is clearly derived from "Isaac's Son," while "British" combines the Hebrew words "Berith" (covenant) and "Ish" (man). Britain is thus home to Isaac's sons, the men of the covenant.[20]

British Israelism was also merged with the flatly racist pre-Adamite theories of Dominick M'Causland and Alexander Winchell. The pre-Adamites, primitive races that predated the Garden of Eden, were the progenitors of every nonwhite race from Eskimos to Australian aborigines. These races were, naturally, far inferior to the Caucasians descended from Adam and Eve. This quasi-theological notion proved easy to combine with antisemitism by way of a two-seed theory. In seed one, Adam and Eve's son Abel becomes the origin of the white Europeans already established as the true Israelites. In seed two, Eve is seduced by Satan, and gives birth to Cain, the precursor of the Jews—who are by this logic the literal children of Satan. This two-seed version of British Israelism is the underlying "theology" of today's Christian Identity movement.[21]

A final element in this was contributed by obscure academic interest in the conversion to Judaism of Khazars around the ninth century. Escaping repressive regimes, many Jews had fled to Khazaria, a region largely east of the Black Sea, and some Khazarian leaders had subsequently been converted to Judaism. In the late nineteenth century, the idea of Khazarian Jews was hijacked by British Israelite antisemites claiming that Ashkenazi Jews were not even descended from the southern kingdom of Judah (and, thus, not Jewish in any sense) but were, rather, a wholly nonbiblical group of people descended from Khazars. This idea reinforced the British Israelites' increasingly antisemitic stance that only white northern Europeans could trace their lineage back to biblical times. It is not surprising that the Khazarian Jew became part of the Ku Klux Klan's ideology, along with the two-seed theory.[22] All this means the antisemitism behind so much of modern conspiracism is based on a thoroughgoing reconstruction of the Jews. What most people accept loosely as the Judeo-Christian heritage is recast as a narrowly conceived birthright of the Aryan race, while actual Jews are themselves recast as an alien force trying to destroy that heritage.

Premillennial Apocalypticism

Hard as it may be to follow the logic of British Israelism and its interactions with two-seed theology and Khazarian Jews, the various millennial sects and their interactions with apocalypticism do not offer any respite. American religion had long been distinctly apocalyptic, giving it a "chronic predilection to locate and identify external antichrists," finding them embodied in "ecclesiastical institutions, nation states, alien ideologies, and even specific individual[s]."[23] But, toward the end of the nineteenth century, religious changes were underway that would make American religion even more focused on the apocalypse and the Antichrist.

Many have attributed outbreaks of conspiracist thinking partly to religious enthusiasm. In the nineteenth century, a puritan-infused Protestantism highlighted both American exceptionalism and a Manichean dichotomy of good versus evil. In addition, outbursts of evangelism such as the Second Great Awakening have been linked to intolerance and suspicion, thus contributing to early conspiracy theories such as anti-Masonry and anti-Catholicism.[24] But to explain the rise of twentieth-century conspiracism, religion—or even Protestantism—is much too broad a concept. The specific aspects of religious belief that incline people toward conspiracy theories are millennialism and apocalypticism.[25] In particular, premillennialist beliefs (in which the second coming of Jesus Christ precedes the millennium rather than following it) led people to anticipate the rise of the Antichrist and the resulting apocalyptic battle between good and evil. And while millennialism has existed for centuries, the main premillennialist variants—Fundamentalism, dispensationalism, and Pentecostalism—were early twentieth-century creations. Thus the link between millennialism and conspiracism is relatively recent.[26]

The most important source of this religious change arrived in America from British evangelist John Nelson Darby's literalist reading of the book of Revelation. Darby taught that God's next "dispensation" (the last had been the crucifixion) would be the Rapture, "followed in quick order by Antichrist, tribulation, Armageddon, millennium, Satan's comeback and final defeat, resurrection and the last judgment." Against a late nineteenth-century context of "rampant scientism" and overly sophisticated biblical criticism, Darby believed that "an interpretation that was simple, clear, and assured would be compelling. The divine authority of Scripture required literal fulfillment of the prophecies. The end was very near; but it was not predictable. . . . Only one thing was known for certain: the Bible was never wrong. Biblical inerrancy became an article of faith . . . among American fundamentalists."[27]

Premillennialism in general, Darbyist or not, carried with it a distinct set of social ideas. Postmillennialism, which had dominated American evangelism until after the Civil War, had been associated with reform movements such as the Second Great Awakening, abolition of slavery, and temperance, as well as with anti-Masonry. Its positive outlook also made it compatible with America's mission in the world. This positivity followed from postmillennialism's core eschatological point: "The belief that Christ will return after the thousand-year reign (Rev 20:4). God's will is achieved by improving the world rather than destroying it. The churches can hasten the millennium through evangelism, prayer, and reform. Post-millennialists combine a prophetic eschatology with an essentially optimistic and progressive view of history."[28] By the end of the century postmillennialists had largely been drawn into the Social Gospel and Progressive Era reform movements, leaving traditional religion open to a more conservative direction.

Premillennialist apocalyptic eschatology led directly down this conservative path. Anticipating the rise of the Antichrist and Armageddon, premillennialists devoted their efforts solely to converting people to their brand of Christianity before this final cataclysm. Reform movements, from this perspective, were worse than useless; they gave people false hope and distracted Christians from their true task. During the

Progressive Era, religious fundamentalists in general and premillennialists in particular began to feel that they were losing ground to a Christianity "busied with such secular things as labor unions, social settlements, and even the promotion of socialism." In response, dispensationalist premillennialism was "shaped by a desire to strike back against everything modern—the higher criticism, evolutionism, the social gospel, rational criticism of any kind."[29]

The backlash of theological and social conservatism was institutionalized over the next few years. In 1909, the Scofield Reference Bible was published, containing dispensationalist, premillennialist commentary alongside the King James text. Beginning in 1910, Lyman Stewart, president of Union Oil of California, began a project that actually created the term "fundamentalist." Along with his brother Milton, Stewart oversaw the production of ninety essays into a twelve-volume work titled *The Fundamentals: A Testimony to the Truth*. Inspired by his desire to "stem the tide of liberalism," Stewart funded the world-wide distribution of these essays through the Bible Institute of Los Angeles, which he had founded in 1908.[30]

At its extreme, this newly codified fundamentalist, premillennialist dispensationalism was antisemitic as well. One of the most prominent fundamentalist preachers of the era, William Bell Riley, explicitly linked the Jews to the *Protocols* and thus to Communism. James Gray, president of the dispensationalist Moody Bible College in Chicago, found the just-published *Protocols* to be "a clinching argument for premillennialism and another sign of the possible nearness of the end of the age." Evangelist Arno Gaebelein used the *Protocols* to bolster his argument (one repeated regularly ever since) that, while many Jews were blameless, "apostate" Jews were busy spreading Bolshevism, bootlegging liquor, and undermining the morals of America.[31]

Premillennialism and conspiracism both rely on a Manichean outlook. Richard Hofstadter described the connection as "the megalomaniac view of oneself as the Elect, wholly good, abominably persecuted yet assured of ultimate triumph; the attribution of gigantic and demonic powers to the adversary." A millennialist drawn into a political battle, he concluded, "is always manning the barricades of civilization.... It is now or never in organizing resistance to the conspiracy."[32] Early in the twentieth century, events such as the Russian Revolution and British support of Zionists in Palestine were interpreted by premillennialists as fulfilling biblical prophecy. Such events, among other signs of the impending apocalypse (the Great War, the influenza pandemic, global economic collapse), readied American premillennialists for the end-of-days scenario.

A separate but overlapping religious impetus toward conspiracism has traditionally featured Satan, with or without Armageddon. As far back as the eighteenth century, people had linked Satan to political plots. Satan's role in politics waned in the nineteenth century but rebounded strongly in the more apocalyptic religious milieu of the early twentieth century. In addition, the bizarre theory combining Satan's pre-Adamite role, his fathering of Cain, and his Synagogue of Satan became an integral part of Christian Identity conspiracism.[33] While the central features of this religious movement were antisemitic and racism, its political messages embodied unusual satanic connections. Christian Identity leader William Potter Gale's call to arms demanded that "we must oppose Satan and his evil ways with every power that God has given His children. The philosophy of Communism which is Satan's form of government is being imposed on God's Is-ra-el in their land. Communism ... is atheistic and believes that the created are above the creator. Those who believe that the federal government is above the states that created it have accepted Satan's Communistic philosophy." This same logic was later used to oppose both one-world government and the admission of Alaska and Hawaii to the union.[34] Many conspiracists have placed Satan at the center of their conspiracies. Take Gerald Winrod's account of the Illuminati, for instance: "No matter where we find Illuminism or how we trace its ramifications, Satan is always the mastermind behind it." And also Gerald L. K. Smith's "blueprints of conspiracy in the great centers of Satanic power the world over," and Tal Brooke's new world order, "directly empowered by Satan himself."[35]

The Occult Revival

The romance of the occult, the major nineteenth-century reaction against the growth of scientific thinking and Enlightenment rationality, contributed more ideas to twentieth-century conspiracism than one might imagine. Literary and artistic romanticism provided the groundwork for occultism. The rediscovery of medieval glories, especially in English literature, brought back images of knighthood—and with it the legends of the Templars and Knights of Malta. The arts aside, the last half of the nineteenth century spawned an incredible array of philosophical and quasi-scientific ideas, some of which had a direct impact on conspiratorial thinking in the twentieth century: first, spiritualist-based quasi-religious organizations; second, ancient knowledge (some perhaps true but most of it imaginary); and third, certain ancient races (again, some passably real but most of them imaginary). These three products of conspiratorial thinking were not entirely separate; the ancient knowledge, imagined to be far superior to mere science, belonged to the civilizations populated by the ancient races, and this same knowledge became the core ideology of the quasi-religious organizations. Taken together, they amount to what political scientist Michael Barkun referred to as a "cultural dumping ground of the heretical, the scandalous, the unfashionable, and the dangerous."[36]

SPIRITUALIST ORGANIZATIONS

Originally, "spiritualism" was a term limited to communication with the dead, as in séances, but grew to encompass much more. One group associated with its positive aspects was the Rosicrucians, who had faded in the eighteenth century but rebounded in the mid-nineteenth century. Their leader in America, William Beverly Randolph, stressed love and healing, while his European counterpart, Eliphas Levi, stressed the occult in his Qabalistic Order of the Rose Cross headquartered in France. There were some connections between the Rosicrucians and

Freemasons, who were also enjoying a resurgence, despite being viewed with some suspicion.[37]

Far and away the person who was most important to spiritualism was Madame Helena Blavatsky, who began her career as a medium and then explored Western occultism before cofounding the Theosophical Society in 1875. Moving to India, Blavatsky and Henry Steel Olcott developed a philosophy based on Eastern traditions. An account of the history of humanity, seemingly a struggle between the Ascended Masters of the Great White Lodge and their Black Lodge enemies, was given by these masters to "select messengers" such as Blavatsky. According to theosophical doctrine, the history of humanity was divided into five periods, each with its own "root race." Beginning before history with beings from "The Imperishable Sacred Land," new races emerged every several thousand years. The Hyperboreans, whose civilization lay in extreme northern latitudes, gave way to Atlanteans and then to Lemurians, before they were succeeded by the present race (begun in America, but not American Indians).[38]

Theosophy spawned several similar spiritualist organizations; at least two or three Rosicrucian organizations had essentially theosophical beginnings. The Vril Society in Germany used theosophical ideas, although the group's main inspiration was Edward Bulwer-Lytton's 1871 novel, *The Coming Race*.[39] The most disturbing of these subsequent organizations is likely Rudolph Steiner's Anthroposophical Society, founded in 1913. Steiner's society was theosophical but with much more racism. In general, Steiner held that "'lower races' of humans are closer to animals than to 'higher races' of humans. Aboriginal peoples, according to anthroposophy, are descended from the already 'degenerate' remnants of the third root race, the Lemurians, and are devolving into apes. Steiner referred to them as 'stunted humans whose progeny, the so-called wild peoples, inhabit certain parts of the earth today."[40] Confusingly similar to the Anthroposophists were the Ariosophists, also a creation of the early twentieth century. Largely organized by one Jörg Lanz von Liebenfels, the Ariosophists grafted German *völkisch* racism onto Theosophy. Ariosophy described "a prehistoric golden age, when wise gnostic priesthoods had espoused occult-racist doctrines and ruled over a superior and racially pure society." Sadly for them, a conspiracy advocating a "spurious egalitarianism" brought about by non-Aryans destroyed this civilization. To fight back Lanz von Liebenfels organized his followers into a semisecret organization not unlike the Knights Templar.[41]

ANCIENT KNOWLEDGE AND RACES: ARYANISM

The wisdom of the ancients (no matter which ancients) invariably involves what James Webb has called "flight from reason." Much of this lore is, in one way or another, magic—ceremonial magic, astrology, psychic powers, "and a multitude of similar topics of doubtful intellectual responsibility."[42] Theosophists learned of astral projection from the Ascended Masters; Vril ideas encompassed the notion that Jesuit thinking is a remnant of Atlantis's civilization; Anthroposophists emphasized the Atlanteans' mental telepathy; and Lanz von Liebenfels's neo-Templars discovered that the Holy Grail was actually "an electrical symbol pertaining to the 'pan-psychic' powers of the pure-blooded Aryan race.[43] The role of race in this ancient knowledge is second only to occultism as a theme. Ideas of racial dominance and degeneration suffuse Theosophy and, even more so, its offshoots. Not surprisingly the emphasis on race consistently demonstrated the greatness of the Aryans.

Aryans had been invented by eighteenth-century linguists as a hypothetical people whose Indo-European language underlay more recent languages. Often referred to as Caucasians because they presumably hailed from somewhere in the Caucasus Mountains, the Aryans were increasingly romanticized as a cultured pastoral civilization. By the mid-nineteenth century, Aryans were being cast as race of such "near heroic proportions" as to make their modern-day descendants "seem degenerate in comparison." This idea was the antithesis of evolution and led naturally to concerns about further degeneration through the mongrelization that had destroyed the purity of south Europeans.[44] The concept of an Aryan race, steeped in antiquity and naturally dominant, was appealing to a great many European Theosophists, but the peculiar origins of Aryanism were often downplayed. The Vril-ya, Bulwer-Lytton's fictional ancient race who derived supernatural powers from the Black Sun in the center of the earth, were "descended from the same ancestors as the great Aryan family, from which has flowed the dominant civilization of the world."[45] Madame Blavatsky had expanded her original hierarchy of "root races" to stress the "spiritual advance" marked by the Aryans. Blavatsky's "cosmic evolution" provided a "ready-made account of Aryan superiority against the debris of lower unnatural half-breeds originating in racial defilement."[46] These actual sources of Aryanism were increasingly obscured as people would either present them vaguely as "gnostic" or emphasize their fairly respectable Hindu and Buddhist elements. But the key idea remained—not merely Aryan superiority, but something approaching a godlike superiority. Steiner's anthroposophy drew out this idea, as did the ariosophy of Lanz von Liebenfels, whose neo-Templars were to replicate the "strict eugenic practices of the Templar Knights designed to breed god-men."[47]

The flip side of Aryanism was, of course, the peril presented by other races and especially "racial mixing." Blavatsky blamed the fall of the Lemurians on racial mixing, which led to the "breeding of monsters and inferior races." This antipathy to miscegenation extended even to the mixing of blood through transfusions. Steiner, in his *Occult Significance of Blood*, claimed that, although blood from other races would not kill Aryans, it would destroy their "clairvoyant power."[48] The outlier facing Aryan racists was the Jews, who, after the Jewish Enlightenment, could not simply be dismissed (as other races were) as distant, primitive peoples.

As the "origin" of the Aryans shifted over time from the Himalayas to northern Europe, they emerged as the embodiment of "the purity of Germanic 'blood.'"[49]This new Aryanism was developed by a variety of writers and scholars, who downplayed its occultism. Ernest Renan, a French scholar who was a key figure in propagating the notion of Khazarian Jews, contrasted Aryans and "Semitic spirit." One of the strongest

Aryanists was an expatriate Englishman in Austria, Houston Stewart Chamberlain, who interpreted history as an "elemental conflict between the 'Aryan' and the Semite, between the forces of strength and weakness, of idealism and materialism, of nobility and servility."[50] The Jews were being painted as the evil counterforce to Aryan civilization, an idea that meshed extremely well with both the *Protocols* and the two-seed idea of Jews as Satanic.

The Contribution to Conspiracism

Taken together, *Protocols*-based anti-Semitism, occultism, and Aryan racism contributed heavily to some of the most horrifying aspects of the twentieth century—above all, Nazi Germany.[51] Those aspects of Nazi ideology most influenced by these forces were heavily conspiratorial and remain so. Indeed, over the last fifty years the residue of Nazism has spawned an array of bizarre theories incorporating conspiratorial ideas—for example, "Vril-Powered Nazi UFOs." Illustrating a generous array of conspiratorial beliefs, one Wilhelm Landig "revived the ariosophical mythology of Thule, the supposed polar homeland of the ancient Aryans. He coined the idea of the Black Sun, a substitute swastika and mystical source of energy capable of regenerating the Aryan race. He popularized esoteric ideas current among the pre-Nazi *völkisch* movement and the SS relating to Atlantis, the World Ice Theory, prehistoric floods and secret racial doctrines from Tibet. He also drew attention to Nazi interest in the medieval Cathars and Grail traditions as an alternative Germanic religion of dualist heresy."[52]

Beyond the Nazis, the racism and antisemitism distilled into the *Protocols* clearly influenced twentieth-century conspiracism in America. The conspiratorial content of this antisemitism is sometimes obscure but always present. From the 1920s onward, Jewish conspiracies abounded, as the following four examples show. Representative Louis McFadden of Pennsylvania relied on the *Protocols* as he regularly excoriated the Jewish financial conspiracy to destroy America from his position on the House Banking Committee. Science fiction writer Charles

Hudson, an "obsessive conspiracy theorist," published a regular bulletin that "ascribed to the Jews every calamity in American history from the assassination of Lincoln to the Johnstown flood." The Russian refugee Count Cherep-Spiridovich spent a decade developing the *Protocols* into the conspiracy of "the hidden hand" (i.e., the "Judeo-Mongol world government"). Eugene Sanctuary, of the World Alliance against Jewish Aggressiveness, described the Jews as "Conspiring Termites" who cannot be exterminated or even seen. Only "the occasional collapse of some phase of governmental activity is proof that the form of termite we describe is assiduously working at his task the objectives of which are ably portrayed for us in the Protocols."[53]

Dispensational millennialism similarly found its way into a great many twentieth-century conspiracy theories. Richard Hofstadter sketched out the influence of 1920s fundamentalism on antisemitic conspiracists such as Gerald Winrod, William Dudley Pelley, and Gerald L. K. Smith, as well as anti-Communist conspiracists who headed the various "Christian crusades" and the John Birch Society. Hofstadter's view that an "essentially theological concern . . . underlies right-wing views of the world" has been extended to show how the 1920s Klan revival was based on premillennial conspiracism. [54]

William Pelley, generally thought of as a fascist leader rather than a millennialist, revealed this influence on his thinking in his "Private Manual, Number One," a set of instructions to his fascist "Silver Shirt" followers. This call to action advised them on its opening page to "look out for the Hidden Hand and Cloven Hoof" behind any crisis, and continued with: "A Challenge to this Crisis. The Silver Shirts of the Liberators are a great Christian militia, swinging into disciplined ranks to challenge and annihilate the alien debaucheries of a Distressed Hour and in obedience to Divine Prophesy bring into practical action an Age of New Chivalry."[55] Similarly, Elizabeth Dilling, known primarily as a virulent anti-Communist, followed her exposés *The Red Network* and *The Roosevelt Red Record* with a vigorous attack on "Modernist 'Christians,'" postmillennialist liberals who "persist in preaching that Lenin-inspired 'peace' movements and collectivized state power can bring humanity in its present sinful state into a millennial kingdom without Christ. . . . In their desire to find their life without disagreeable sacrifice, they fulfill part of the scripture verse: 'He that findeth his life shall lose it, and he that loseth his life for my sake shall find it.' (Matt. 10:39)"[56] Methodist minister Arno Gaebelein, a prominent premillennialist, wrote a much more sustained attack on "the road of modernism." In his *The Conflict of the Ages*, the Manichean struggle between the forces of light and darkness was replicated as the Communist conspiracy against traditional Christianity. Modernist, progressive Christians would find that this road would "lead on, on, on to atheism, to world revolution, national disaster and finally to the judgment of an Almighty God." Gerald Winrod, a dispensationalist evangelist from Kansas, interspersed his religious works (e.g., *Science, Christ, and the Bible*) with intensely antisemitic conspiracy theories such as *The Truth about the Protocols* and *Adam Weishaupt, a Human Devil*.[57]

As early as the 1930s, many supporters of fascism in general and the Nazis in particular were steeped in the occult. In England, Edith Starr Miller's conspiracy opus, *Occult Theocrasy*, relied heavily on Masonic works, on theosophical sources, and even on the occult hoaxes of Léo Taxil. Also in England, Christina Stoddard built on the foundation of Illuminized Freemasonry a superstructure of Gnostics and Cabalists to develop her lurid conspiracy of the "ancient serpent." Stoddard's conspirators aimed "to awaken this serpent, the sex-force or 'God within' man, raising it by processes and Yogic methods" to unleash the "Universal Creative Principle." In a convoluted fashion, this allowed the conspirators to dominate "the masses" and lead them to internationalism and "universalism."[58] In America, the most notable of occultist conspiracy theorist was the aforementioned William Pelley, founder of the crypto-Nazi Silver Shirts, whose work was infused with an extraterrestrial dimension. Pelley was not alone in fusing the occult and the political. Eugene Sanctuary's *Are These Things So?*, which rehashes Robison's and Barruel's conspiracies, includes an appendix explaining "some claims of the occult forces" used by conspirators—specifically thought transference and astral projection. Although Sanctuary maintains that these abilities are "merely intangible forces of nature which science has not, as yet, definitely recognized," he tries to buttress this claim with lengthy quotations from *The Secret of the Zodiac* and an article about Freemasonry from the *Rosicrucian Magazine*. And West Coast magazine publisher William Kullgren embedded most of his conspiratorial ideas in his astrological pronostications.[59]

Without these disparate nineteenth-century developments, the modern conspiracism of the twentieth century would not be the same and might not have come into being at all. In this regard, the antisemitism of the *Protocols* stands out as obvious, while Aryanism and the occult are more muted in their effects. But Aryanism underlies a great deal of right-wing militia conspiracism, and occult thinking has expanded greatly, inspiring some of the more peculiar conspiracy thinking of the last fifty years. Of the three influences, antisemitism flourished earliest, as the mainstay of the conspiracism opposing the New Deal. After World War II, the flagrant antisemitism of the 1930s subsided, kept alive only by a fairly small band of unrepentant Nazis. Taking its place, especially as the civil rights movement emerged, an Aryan-based racism revived, including new developments in British Israelism conspiracy theories. Then, accompanying the rise of "new age" thinking in the 1960s, occultism became increasingly an integral part of conspiracy theories. This is clearest in UFO conspiracies but is also present in most contemporary religion-based conspiracy theories as well.

4

THE INTERNATIONAL JEWISH CONSPIRACY AND THE SECRET GOVERNMENT

Your literature does not have to state the word: Jew. All you have to do to place the blame where people can understand it is to accuse the international bankers.

George Deatherage, American Nationalist Confederation[1]

The idea of a "secret government" is the core of the most widespread and durable conspiracy theory of the twentieth century: the Jewish conspiracy for world domination. The basic idea grew out of a Jewish banking conspiracy already established by the time of the Populists' conspiracism of the 1890s—but strengthened and broadened by the *Protocols* and fleshed out with Aryan-racist and occult concepts. The catalyzing event that turned many people's attention to the "Jewish peril" was the Russian Revolution. For the most prominent conspiracist of that time, the Englishwoman Nesta Webster, Bolshevism amounted to a rebirth of the Jacobinism of the French Revolution. Accordingly, her work revived the ideas of Robison and Barruel and rescued the Illuminati from decades of obscurity. By giving the Jews a prominent role, Webster shaped the thinking of a generation of conspiracists. The heyday of the so-called secret government occurred during the 1920s and 1930s, but it continues today as, among other variants, the Zionist Occupation Government conspiracy theory.

The International Jew

In several books, beginning in 1919 with *The French Revolution: A Study in Democracy*, Nesta Webster developed her belief in a long-standing "co-ordinated and continuous conspiracy of Jews to destroy Christianity and dominate the world." Her early emphasis on the Illuminati and continental Freemasonry as agents of revolution slowly gave way to the idea of "the Jewish peril," which she envisioned as a Cabala-based conspiracy whose "forces" had been "gathering strength for an onslaught not only on Christianity, but on all moral and social order" since "the first century of the Christian era."[2] Webster's Cabalists used a succession of secret societies to obscure their role. By her own day, Webster claimed, the influence of Jews in what she deemed "the five great powers at work in the world," Freemasonry, Theosophy, Pan-Germanism, international finance, and revolution, could no longer be considered "a matter of surmise but of fact."[3] Although others concerned about "the Jewish peril" usually ignored the first three of these "great powers," the last two began to coalesce into a widely accepted vision of conspiracy.

Many respectable British commentators had already accepted the Jewish peril in light of the Russian Revolution. Winston Churchill, a member of the Lloyd-George government, questioned the loyalties of "international" Jews. The British government issued a booklet titled *The Jewish Peril* in 1920. At the same time, Howell Arthur Gwynne, editor of the *Morning Post*, collected into a book his writings on the Jewish peril. As judiciously as he could so as to skirt the obvious charge of antisemitism, Gwynne laid out his premise "that there has been for centuries a hidden conspiracy, chiefly Jewish, whose objects have been and are to produce revolution, communism and anarchy, by means of which they hope to arrive at the hegemony of the world by establishing some sort of despotic rule. . . . The Jewish Bolsheviks are to-day carrying out almost to the letter the programme outlined in the Protocols."[4]

The threat allegedly posed by Jewish Bolsheviks was not long in reaching the United States. Most famously, Henry Ford serialized and commented on the *Protocols* in his newspaper, *The Dearborn Independent*, and collected the series into a book, *The International Jew: The World's Foremost Problem.*[5] At the same time however, the authenticity of the *Protocols* had come under serious attack in at least three countries. One writer noted somewhat mockingly that "the names of the 'Elders of Zion' are not given. The dates of their 'Protocols' are not given. The names of the assistants or followers to whom the 'Protocols' were addressed are not given. The names of the Jews who are to execute, or who have already executed, the plottings detailed in the 'Protocols' are not (with the exception of Karl Marx) anywhere given. But the plot to wreck and conquer the world is given in full."[6] A common reaction to the exposure of the *Protocols* as fraudulent was to concede the possibility and move on, as Gwynne had done. The *Christian Science Monitor* editorialized that, "for the present, it is sufficient to draw attention to the fact that these ideals keep reappearing with a curious and significant regularity, at moments of great political commotion, and exercising an extraordinary and appalling effect upon world politics." Without actually using the word "conspiracy," the *Monitor* did link the *Protocols* to "the naked theory of Adam Weishaupt." A Catholic weekly similarly offered its view that the *Protocols* "may or may not be authentic" before claiming that Jews had dominated the Bolshevik revolution (as they did all revolutions) as well as the Communist government of Russia.[7]

Fear of the Jewish peril in the United States increased during the first "Red Scare." In 1919, the Overman Committee of the House of Representatives, the first of many congressional committees to investigate the threat of Communism in America, heard testimony about the Bolsheviks in Saint Petersburg. Not only were 372 of the 386 Bolsheviks in Saint Petersburg Jews, but over two-thirds of these were from the lower east side of Manhattan. Numbers such as these provided "evidence" for antisemitic conspiracists for decades. Howell Gwynne had estimated 95 percent of the revolutionary leadership in Russia was Jewish. Victor Marsden (translator of the *Protocols*) came up with 545 Bolshevik officials, of whom 447 were Jews. After Stalin rose to leadership, lists such as these were expanded to include those who, like Stalin, were "married to Jewesses."[8]

Fear of Communism in the 1920s was focused sharply on aliens since "Bolshevism is not indigenous to American soil. It is a disease that . . . comes from overseas, and with which no native-born American would be likely to be afflicted unless there were something about him congenitally abnormal."[9] Various "patriotic" organizations and individuals reported on threats across the board. Ralph Easley, who promoted the idea of "fantastic conspiracies" from abroad, exposed Bolshevism in churches, the press, unions, and schools and colleges, and led the effort to scrutinize textbooks for suspicious content. The Daughters of the American Revolution, declaring that "Communism, Bolshevism, Socialism, Liberalism, and Ultra-Pacifism tend to the same ends," came up with a blacklist of "the Common Enemy"—over two hundred people barred from speaking under their aegis. Bolshevism was also becoming embedded in "cultural conflicts that had previously been viewed as homegrown battles between traditional religion and secularization" such as evolution. By 1924, William Jennings Bryan was blaming the "scientific soviet" as the force behind Darwinism being taught in schools.[10]

Throughout this period, and even earlier, Jews were portrayed as alien to the United States in much of the academic and quasi-academic literature about race; in 1908 Alfred Schultz had singled out Jews as one of the "alien stocks" that threatened "Aryan purity."[11] Immigration opponent Prescott F. Hall, railing in 1921 against the westward movement of the "brown and yellow races of Asia, described the threat of Bolshevism as "essentially . . . a movement of oriental Tartar tribes led by Asiatic Semites against Nordic bourgeoisie." By 1921, the idea that East European Jews were actually descended from the Khazars was making its way into the mainstream via H. G. Wells's popular *The*

Outline of History. Pulitzer Prize–winning historian Burton Hendrick brought this seemingly exotic idea home in his book *The Jews in America*:

> The blood of this Turkish or Mongol people flows extensively in the veins of the Eastern Jew of to-day. A further large Slavic mixture makes the Eastern Jew racially alien to Jews from other parts of Europe. Thus the masses that comprise one fourth the present population of New York City trace their beginnings, in considerable degree, to certain tribes that roamed the steppes of Russia in the Middle Ages and happened to accept the religion of Judah as their own. . . . As candidates for assimilation, these Jews, as they land at Ellis Island, are about as promising as a similarly inflowing stream of Hindus or Syrian Druses.[12]

The idea of Jews as truly alien—not even "true Jews, but only Judaized Mongols," as Klan leader Hiram Wesley Evans referred to them—fit nicely into a conspiratorial framework. Alien Jews were even joined with the Catholics in a conspiracy of "Romanism, alienism, Bolshevism, internationalism, political debauchery and lawlessness." An expatriate Russian known as Major-General, Count Cherep-Spiridovich, routinely referred to the "Judeo-Mongol World Government" which he said sought "nothing more or less than the deliberate murder of the intelligent Aryan classes in order to substitute the Asiatics."[13]

Taken all together, these components—the purely racist antisemitism, the conspiracism of the *Protocols*, and the alien threat—brought the Jewish conspiracy into being. So recognizable were they, in fact, that all three were combined in Marcus Eli Ravage's 1928 satire, "A Real Case against the Jews" (subtitled, "One of Them Points Out the Full Depth of Their Guilt"). Tossing aside war and revolution, Ravage confesses the Jews' deepest conspiracy: imposing Christianity on the Aryans, a previously "innocent, care-free pagan race":

> Our ancient little country is your Holy Land. Our national literature is your Holy Bible. . . . A Jewish maiden is your ideal of motherhood and womanhood. A Jewish rebel-prophet is the central figure in your

religious worship. . . . In Dayton, Tennessee, a Bible-bred community forbids the teaching of your science because it conflicts with our ancient Jewish account of the origin of life. . . .

Is it any wonder you resent us? . . . We have imposed upon you an alien book and an alien faith which you cannot swallow or digest, which is at cross-purposes with your native spirit.[14]

By the end of the 1920s, conspiracists saw an international Jewish conspiracy clearly in place, although its proponents were less numerous than they had been during the height of the Red Scare. The onset of the depression reversed this decline, however, and by 1933 antisemites had a new common enemy: Franklin D. Roosevelt.

International Jewish Finance

By the time Roosevelt was elected president, "Bolshevism" was fourteen years old and thus less threatening than it had been during the Red Scare. Moreover, the *Protocols* had been shown, to most people's satisfaction, to be fraudulent, and the notion that most Jews were actually Khazars was fading away with the Ku Klux Klan. With the onset of the Great Depression, negative attention to Jews became increasingly focused on their financial activity rather than their Bolshevik plotting. The old populist conception of British bankers as the enemy was making a comeback, as were the Rothschilds, but with a stronger focus on that family's American agents. Jacob Schiff was the favorite candidate of many conspiracists. Gerald Winrod saw Schiff as the agent of not only the Rothschilds but revolutionary Jewry as well: "Schiff . . . was born in one of the Rothschild houses in Frankfort, Germany and after arriving in America married the daughter of Loeb, thus becoming part of the banking family Kuhn, Loeb and Company, the concern which is credited with having financed Lenin and Trotsky in overthrowing the Russian Empire."[15] Other presumed agents included Paul Warburg and August Belmont. But ultimately it did not matter. As Henry Ford's *Dearborn Independent* put it, "Rothschild power . . . has been so broadened by the entry of other banking families into governmental finance, that it now must be known not by the name of one family of Jews, but by the name of the race. Thus it is spoken of as International Jewish Finance."[16]

Some of the rhetoric describing the Jewish financial conspiracy was taken wholesale from the populists' fixation on gold, as filtered through the *Protocols*. Winrod quoted the third Protocol as particularly "prophetic": "We shall create by all the secret subterranean methods open to us and with the aid of gold, which is all in our hands, a universal crisis." Father Charles Coughlin, in one of his early radio addresses, castigated any government that let International Jewish Finance "dictate that gold alone shall be its basic money." The Jews' "shuttling of gold and credits," Coughlin followed up, would make "scepters fall; crowns roll in the dust." A pamphlet by the avowedly fascist American Guards claimed, "It is known that the Jews control the finances of the world through their gold fetish." How financial control through gold actually worked was handled with generic rhetoric such as Robert Edward Edmondson's: "The power of gold enables Jews to crowd Gentiles out of and monopolize the avenues of opportunity." Count Cherep-Spiridovich noted how easy it was for the Rothschilds to subvert politicians, professors, and preachers "contemplating the mountains of gold on which the Rothschilds are seated."[17]

One specific claim was widely made: Jewish financiers had conspired to overthrow the Russian government and install Bolshevism. A supposedly suppressed yet frequently cited British white paper had made this accusation in 1919:

Section 1—In February, 1916, it was first discovered that a revolution was being fomented in Russia. It was found out that the following persons as well as the banking-house mentioned were engaged in this work of destruction: Jacob Schiff (Jew); Guggenheim (Jew); Max Breitung (Jew); Kuhn, Loeb & Co. (Jewish Banking-house), of which the following are directors: Jacob Schiff, Felix Warburg, Otto Kahn, Mortimer Schiff, S. H. Hanauer (all Jews).

There can be no doubt that the Russian revolution, which broke out a year after the information above had been received, was launched and fomented by distinctly Jewish influences.[18]

Schiff and Kuhn, Loeb & Company became the linchpins of this conspiracy. They backed "the syphilitic Jew Lenin" and the rest of "Trotsky and Co." For years, claimed Gerald Winrod in 1935, "the connection between Bolshevism and international Jewish financiers was kept out of sight," but now no informed person "doubts that Bolshevism is controlled and directed by a mysterious hierarchy of Jewish financial wizards."[19] Schiff and his associates became such touchstones of antisemitic conspiracism that Antony Sutton, whose more recent exposés of Wall Street financial influence have been widely cited by conspiracists, felt compelled to set the record straight:

> Investment banker Jacob Schiff . . . was in fact *against* support of the Bolshevik regime. . . . The persistence with which the Jewish-conspiracy myth has been pushed suggests that it may well be a deliberate device to divert attention from the real issues and the real causes. . . . New York bankers who were also Jewish had relatively minor roles in supporting the Bolsheviks, while the New York bankers who were also Gentiles (Morgan, Rockefeller, Thompson) had major roles.[20]

Conspiracists also maintained that the Jews had conspired to destroy the American financial system, a process culminating in the establishment of the Federal Reserve System. The leading voice against the Fed was Representative Louis McFadden's. The Pennsylvania Republican ultimately destroyed his political career with a series of increasingly antisemitic tirades against the Fed, beginning with a 1932 attack on "the evil practices of the Federal Reserve Board and the Federal Reserve banks and the interests which control them." These "interests" came into sharper focus the next year, as McFadden expanded on his theory: "In the United States today, the Gentiles have slips of paper while the Jews have the gold and lawful money." Quoting Protocol twelve on "modern power-gold," McFadden laid the groundwork for an argument that still has adherents today—that Jewish financiers created a system to foist worthless paper money backed by nothing on Americans, leading the nation to fall into their debt. McFadden challenged the House Democrats to fight the alien forces trying to destroy the economy: "Do not force Americans to pay tribute to foreign ruler and potentates. Take back this country or perish in the attempt. Let this be our country again. Let us rebuild it for our own. . . . Remember, Mr. Chairman, that the ship of state has women and children aboard. Do not, therefore, guide it into uncharted waters. Do not allow the great Democratic Party to steer it onto the rocks . . . so that the international salvage crews may set to work on the wreck of it."[21] Variations on McFadden's charges have appeared routinely over the years. Pedro del Valle interrupted a diatribe against Lyndon Johnson's civil rights agenda to hail McFadden and berate the "moral cowards" in the House of Representatives who failed to support him. A 1970 tribute to McFadden came remarkably close to portraying the Great Depression as a sort of "false flag" operation by the Fed, which somehow managed to hide the nation's wealth to make it appear that the economy had collapsed. Today, McFadden is something of an icon on anti-Fed conspiracy websites, where the antisemitism is cleansed away and he is portrayed as a populist martyr—silenced for speaking out against powerful financial forces.[22]

McFadden's was not the only voice. New Zealander A. N. Field had independently stressed the "strange story of the Federal Reserve board" and the *Protocols* in his 1932 explanation of "the Slump." Gerald Winrod stressed the sixth Protocol in order to indict the Jews for the "wild business orgy of insane spending . . . deliberately planned by the Elders." William Pelley alluded to the same thing as following from the "Satanic plans of the Red Jews." George E. Sullivan painted the Jewish forces "bent on world conquest" not merely as "financially powerful" but as "occult" as well. In "The Subjugation of America," part 2 of Texas judge George Armstrong's book on the Rothschilds, the *Protocols* actually take second place to a nineteen-point plan for world takeover masquerading as an 1869 funeral oration by a Rabbi Reichorn. Less convincing even than the *Protocols*, the oration's point number nine was most germane: "Let us try to replace the circulation of gold with paper money; our chests will absorb the gold, and we shall regulate the value of the paper which will make us masters of all the positions." Investment adviser and economist Robert Edward Edmondson issued numerous leaflets warning of a Jewish takeover of the economy as part of "The Edmondson Jew-Exposure Publicity Campaign." In his typically florid style, Edmondson described how the "tribe" of "foreign-born Jews" would "'settle upon the glands' of our American System . . .—parasitically eating out the substance we have created with the vampirish voracity of a plague of locusts."[23]

The Secret Government behind the New Deal

The election of Franklin D. Roosevelt in 1932 generated a frenzy of activity on the Right, among which was a "small proportion" of antisemites. An Anti-Defamation League study concluded that from 1933 to 1939 "some hundred organizations, large and small, drew together the Jew haters into a potentially dangerous force." The people involved in these groups were, the study found, "markedly diverse"; a remarkable description of them was provided in retrospect by Carey McWilliams: "A most heterogeneous lot: monetary reform addicts; Pope-baiters; mystics of the Pelley variety; pension plan schemers; professional God-killers; Bible-Belt fundamentalists; West Coast sun worshippers and vegetarians; warped zealots of the John Rankin breed; Negro-haters and whatnot. . . . To the extent that they have been able to work together at all, it has been by reason of their hatred of progressive political action, their strong antipathy to the trade union movement, and their uniform and consistent anti-Semitism."[24] During the 1920s, antisemites had been able to focus their rhetoric on "International Jewish Finance," but in the political realm no such focus existed. But as Roosevelt's "Red Record" began to reveal itself, the term "the Jew Deal" came into being.[25]

For the conspiracy-minded antisemite, the problem with the New Deal did not lie in its actions or accomplishments. These were little touched on and, even then, often symbolically—the Blue Eagle logo of the National Recovery Administration struck Gerald Winrod for its resemblance to the Beast of Revelation, whereas it struck Pelley's Silver Shirts as having a "Red Communist derivation." Rather, the conspiratorial focus on the Jews in the New Deal encompassed both specific individuals as well as their overall numbers. Three individuals vied for the top spot. Bernard Baruch, a Wall Street banker and onetime adviser to Woodrow Wilson, was often referred to as "the unofficial president." Supreme Court justice Louis Brandeis, whose famous dissenting opinions constituted FDR's "underlying philosophy," was dubbed "the father of the New Deal." The third contender, Felix Frankfurter, was until 1939 only an adviser to FDR. However, as a law professor at Harvard, Frankfurter contributed any number of "protégés" to the ranks of the New Deal. One conspiracist effort combined anti-Communism and anti-intellectualism to come up with the menace of the "Scarlet Fever Boys, a swarm of Felix Frankfurter disciples, all under the domination of young, free-thinking collegians of no practical experience, whose theories have only been partially tried in Russia." Frankfurter was still being singled out as late as 1970 by the Ku Klux Klan because his ideas supported school desegregation.[26] That Frankfurter was born in Austria was a fact frequently highlighted by anti-Semites—though Baruch's South Carolina origins and Brandeis's birth in Louisville, Kentucky, were never mentioned.[27]

Beyond these three, lists of Jews making up the secret government varied. William Pelley included Treasury Secretary Henry Morgenthau Jr. (another very popular choice), then moved on to thirty-one lesser threats, ranging from Judge Rosenman ("Roosevelt's Right Arm") to Henrietta S. Klotz, a Morgenthau assistant. He also sold a booklet of "nearly 300 Jews who have gained to [sic] the most vital positions in our Federal Government."[28] Carl Mote added legal advisers Ben Cohen and Jerome Frank, along with Tennessee Valley Authority administrator David Lilienthal and an array of "economists," using quotation marks perhaps as a nod to the *Protocols*: "We shall surround our government with a whole world of Economists."[29] With the dearth of actual Jews in important positions, non-Jews were frequently included in such lists.

Pelley's followers included Secretary of Labor Frances Perkins, who Pelley claimed was not in fact a Bostonian but a "Polish-born Jewess." A West Coast Silver Shirt reportedly offered $1,000 to "the person who will bring me her American birth certificate." Eugene Sanctuary's list of five Jews gives way to people who, "if not Jews, were closely connected with Jews." These connections could be fairly tenuous. One could be "connected with" the League for Industrial Democracy, which "runs parallel to the Ethical Culture Society, founded by the Jew Felix Adler." The shortage of Jews was also behind Edmondson's designation of New Dealers General Hugh Johnson and Tommy "The Cork" Corcoran as "protégés" of Jews.[30]

The Jews in the New Deal were only the visible part of their otherwise "invisible empire," as Gerald Winrod called it. Winrod's assessment of the threat followed naturally from his apocalyptic worldview, but he found it difficult to describe: "It is possible that this invisible empire has existed as a self-propagating body ever since the Jewish leaders contacted the Chaldeans while in Babylonia. . . . The entire cabal is so large and far-reaching, its motives so hellish, its plan of attack so contrary to Christian thinking, that it simply staggers the mind. . . . This anti-Christ force has apparently manifested itself from its underground sources in different ways at different periods of history, but never with the boldness and permanency that it has since it came to the surface eighteen years ago."[31] The idea that Jews were inherently alien made a strong comeback in this atmosphere. Carl Mote expressed his concern but no surprise over "alien and Jewish Communists" in the New Deal, since, "instinctively, the Jews are very much at home in the New Deal and fit snugly into its pattern for the simple reason that the warp and woof of the pattern are *change, confusion, disturbance,* even *revolution,* to which the Jew is accustomed." Eugene Sanctuary painted New Deal Jews as agents of "the secret councils of the central Jewish Kahal." Americans had a difficult time grasping Jewish motives, according to William Pelley, since "the Jew is not a white man, but an oriental." Even more bluntly, Kansas publisher E. J. Garner used his newspaper *Publicity* to rail against "the Mongolian Jew Controlled Roosevelt Dictatorship."[32]

Roosevelt's role in all this was a matter of dispute among conspiracists. One view was that FDR was merely, in Gerald L. K. Smith's words, a "grinning manikin [*sic*] that was some day to serve as the ruling figurehead over a once free people." As "the pampered son of a rich family in New York, who had never done a day's work in his life," William Pelley's FDR was the perfect stooge for "the world-wide coalition of great banking Jews who really constituted a Hidden Empire." Why would Roosevelt agree to such a role? Elizabeth Dilling answered: "Roosevelt is merely an ambitious rich man's son, eager for honors and dictatorial power and flattered with the idea that his 'reign' is a beneficent one, and that he has been promised enjoyment of the Presidential plum and still more power if he continues to 'behave.' If he but takes the time to smile for publicity cameras, and to deliver some prepared radio speeches in a warm fireside manner, the Red ruling clique running him and the government with his full approval and cooperation are well satisfied."[33] Smith, despite his portrayal of Roosevelt as a figurehead, was one of many conspiracists holding the view that FDR was actually a Jew himself. Winrod agreed, while Pelley held that FDR was three-fourths Jewish.[34] According to the World-Service, the press agency of Nazi Germany (created "to enlighten ill-informed Gentiles"), Robert Edward Edmondson created the Roosevelt "family tree" on which Smith and Winrod relied. Roosevelt himself told reporters: "My forefathers came to America from Holland about 300 years ago. Whether these ancestors of mine were Jews, Catholics, or Protestants—this question does not disturb me." The World-Service found this answer "evasive."[35]

The idea that Roosevelt was Jewish was more than an ad hominem attack; it proved, "from the viewpoint of eugenics, his natural bent toward radicalism." It made him an integral part of the conspiracy:

Roosevelt inevitably draws upon his Semitic ancestry. It is, therefore, as natural for him to be a radical, as it is for others to be true Americans. This is why he can boast of flaunting conventionalities, and publicly gloat over destroying those traditions which are fundamental to our national character. HE IS NOT ONE OF US! This may also explain why he attaches so little importance to his word of honor, and has no hesitation in breaking his promises. It is to be doubted if he, himself, understands the inner forces that surge through his being, driving him further and further toward the Left. It's in his blood.[36]

For those who took this view, blood was not a metaphor. William Pelley, claiming everyone knew "the bloods of the three great racial divisions of the world; white, yellow, and black, all test differently under chemical analysis," added that "it is not generally known that the Jew's blood tests yellow." Eugene Sanctuary, however, went with cultural determinism over biological determinism, taking the view that "Rabbinical Judaism with its unyielding laws and fettering customs 'cuts off the Jews from the great family of mankind.'" And Edward Edmondson singled out centuries of "nomadic desert life" for making Jewish tribes "Communistic in structure" and thus "non-assimilable." Either way—by blood or custom—Jews were inexorably alien; FDR and his New Deal were inexorably alien; and there was only one possible cure. Pelley instructed his followers to "be prepared to strike directly at the heart of the whole racial conspiracy." Sanctuary looked to the new fascist regimes in Germany and Hungary, where the people "had the courage of their convictions and dared to meet this slimy thing, although in human form, and thrust it from their midst."[37]

Antisemitic conspiracists expended considerable effort moving the Jewish conspiracy from the financial realm into government. They created a government run by Jews, perhaps even headed by a Jew, an alien presence controlling America. Gentiles were summarily "ruined," "turned into the streets," "foreclosed upon," their prospects "gutted."[38] Such rhetoric was commonplace; more precise outcomes, however, were in short supply. Even Representative McFadden's diatribes against the Federal Reserve dealt more with its existence than its actions.

Gerald Winrod was among a handful of fundamentalists who occasionally focused on actions, linking the repeal of prohibition, for example, to a larger anti-Christian conspiracy. James B. True found Roosevelt's foreign policy to be "identical with the policy of International Jewry."

And a fair number of conspiracists brought up the Recognition of the Soviet Union. Elizabeth Dilling was one of very few detail-oriented conspiracists. Just as her *Red Network* had named every leftist and liberal she could think of, her follow-up book, *The Roosevelt Red Record*, listed every administration action she found objectionable. On just one page, Dilling castigates the Emergency Leasing Corporation, the Agricultural Adjustment Act ("The thoroughness and audacity of dictatorial provisions along these lines make one gasp."), and the Works Progress Administration.[39]

Still, most antisemitic conspiracists stuck to the big picture. In his 1939 testimony before the Dies Committee—officially excluded from the committee report as embarrassing—George Van Horn Moseley challenged the committee to expand its horizons to include "organized Jewry": "It is not generally realized how complete is the *Jewish State* as it is organized and operating *within* the United States—a nation complete within a nation. Your inquiry should include an investigation of the controlling organizations of that state. . . . I have had the temerity to challenge that great octopus and expose it in an effort to protect our Republic. I wish to see control revert to an honest government and to millions of truly loyal Christian American people."[40]

The Secret Government at War

As war in Europe threatened and finally broke out, the international Jewish conspiracy was adapted to include it. Early on, isolationist sentiment was common, but little of it could be considered antisemitic or conspiratorial. By the end of the 1930s, this opposition had been organized into a great many groups, the most famous and largest of which was the America First Committee. The career of the committee illustrates how rapidly opposition to the war was steamrolled by conspiracists and the German-American Bund. An investigation by the American Legion in California found America First chapters overtaken by antisemites and Nazi followers from the American Guards, the National Copperheads, and members of William Pelley's Silver Shirts, among others.

Bundists also worked their way into "Nativist hate-groups" such as the Ku Klux Klan.[41]

Efforts to resist the antisemitic onslaught were not successful. At a Carnegie Hall meeting of Women United, Mrs. Theodore Roosevelt Jr. told the crowd that "growing anti-Semitism in this country is the kind of thing that will destroy our republic, and should not be allowed to go on. Tolerance is as important to our national defense as armament. It is the cornerstone of the nation." The reaction to this admonition was reported by Charles Hudson, the publisher of *America in Danger!*: "Evidence of Americans' feelings and understanding of war and warmakers, seen in hearty applause to speeches made by Senators Robt. Reynolds and Bennett Champ Clark at Carnegie Hall 4-14-41, when the 2,300 peace-lovers there became cold when the honorary chmn, Mrs. Theodore Roosevelt, Jr., plead [sic] for 'tolerance.' . . . She left in the middle of the meeting. . . . Looks like Mrs. 'Teddy, Jr.' had been planted—possibly to test the reaction among Christian Americans in New York City to that 'tolerance' plea." More dispassionate reporting noted that her statement was received with "undisguised hostility" by the crowd, members of which called it "tolerance drivel" and "downright un-American."[42] Around this time, the National Legion of Mothers of America, a prominent mothers' movement voice of isolationism, was fractured by radio priest Charles Coughlin's encroachment. The leader of the National Legion of Mothers of America, novelist Kathleen Norris, fought his endorsement, along with the subsequent ones of William Pelley and Gerald L. K. Smith. Nevertheless, extremists began to take over local chapters. A Philadelphia extremist "said Hitler was no danger to America, but she wished he would come over and clean up the 'damn Jews.'" In the wake of this hostile takeover, chapters seceded and a markedly more violent group splintered off, the Molly Pitcher Rifle Legion, whose flyers urged women to "Buy Christian, Vote Christian, Employ Christian."[43]

Despite the high visibility of respectable individuals, such as American icon and tragic hero Charles Lindbergh Jr., the most active members of groups fighting American involvement in the war were well-established conspiracists such as Pelley, Sanctuary, Dilling, and Coughlin. They were joined by less familiar but equally antisemitic conspiracists. Francis Moran, of the Christian Front, attacked "war-mongering, chiseling Jews." George Deatherage, promoter of the umbrella organization the American Nationalist Confederation, found the coalescence of American fascist groups "gratifying." Catherine Baldwin founded the Defenders of the Constitution, in part because "the big public outfits are all run by Jewish stooges," who "operated their outfits as traps to get good people in, who will all be prosecuted at a later date."[44]

Blaming the Jews for working against the "good people" was common in these circles; a West Coast Christian patriot publication headlined one story: "Jewry Declares War—Christian Patriots Are Ready." Elizabeth Dilling was one of many who blamed B'nai B'rith for "breeding, instead of lessening, anti-Semitism." George Deatherage tried to defend the swastika from Jewish propagandists in America ("where they control the press") who were doing their best "to cast odium on the emblem." In his Dies Committee testimony, George Van Horn Moseley took umbrage at having been called a Fascist for his remarks about Jews, claiming that, "as far as I know, I have never seen a Fascist. I belong to no organization. The Jews have forced me to discuss the problem of the Jew in self-defense. They are doing everything in their power to intimidate me and to force me into the camp of their enemies." Also blaming the victim, Edwin Westphal simply disclaimed credit for starting his own organization. "We Christians didn't start the Christian Mobilizers," Westphal told supporters. "The Jews started it for us. If it weren't for their intolerance, there wouldn't be any of these organizations."[45]

Pamphlets and speakers representing these organizations made two layers of claims: the general contention that Jews caused wars on purpose for their own benefit and the specific claim that they were behind the war against Germany. Back in 1921, Henry Ford's *Dearborn Independent* had gone with the general claim, writing that the Rothschild fortune was "founded in war. The first twenty million dollars the Rothschilds ever had to speculate with was money paid for Hessian troops to fight against the American colonies." George Armstrong supported his view of Jewish warmongering by pointing to the *Protocols*. C. Leon de Aryan suggested a continuum back to Old Testament days with his remarkable observation that Winston Churchill's *V* for "victory" salute was a secret Jewish sign for "violence, vengeance, and sabotage" "dating back to 'the Feast of Belshazzar.'"[46]

More commonly, Jewish conspirators were blamed for bringing about the current war. Eugene Sanctuary issued a series of pamphlets explaining the Jews' role in "This War, the Second Major Crime in History, the First Being the Crucifixion of Jesus Christ." The conspirators' exact reasons varied but were always nefarious. In George Deatherage's view, the war was actually a struggle between the Rothschild and Warburg financial interests.[47] To Howland Spencer, the "zealots who seek world domination" needed first to force the United States into the League of Nations by way of a neutrality bill. Spencer placed long-time presidential adviser Bernard Baruch at the apex of this conspiracy:

> To win world domination by 1941—the year of triumph announced by the Communist, Einstein—the next few months are vital to the conspirators. This was admitted by one of them—the man Tugwell—in his Los Angeles speech. Another world war must be brought about and the United States involved in such a war through the *lunacy* of a dictatorship or the dictatorship of a lunatic. Such plot and such madness is the original neutrality bill, involving sanctions. . . .
>
> We have Baruch's own boast of his part when in the Waldorf-Astoria hotel he met Captain Jefferson Davis Cohen, then a recent guest of the President at Hyde Park. 'What have you been doing?' asked Cohen. '*I have been writing the Neutrality bill*,' replied Baruch.[48]

In a warning addressed to "Gentile Freemasons," Ernst Goerner portrayed the crisis in Czechoslovakia as "just another conspiracy to start the conflagration." He continued: "The people of Europe do not want to fight each other. They have no grievances. But it is the Jew-controlled governments of the so-called Democracies who try to make their people fight just to satisfy Jewish hatred." On the same basis, the Anti-Communist Federation of America mockingly advocated funding a "Jewish Expeditionary Force" composed of Jewish New Dealers (along with celebrities such as Edward G. Robinson and the Marx Brothers). "Fellow Americans!" the federation said in conclusion. "Give the Jews a chance . . . If THEY want WAR against Germany, let THEM fight it, while we attend to our people our problems and our nation." At what has to be the extreme position, one Rosa Farber of the Detroit-based Mothers of the U.S.A., maintained that the Jews—through a world Jewish council, or Sanhedrin—had installed Hitler in Germany to make their plans for Communism seem more appealing. American entry into the war did not eliminate such rhetoric; according to Agnes Waters, the attack on Pearl Harbor was "an inside as well as an outside job . . . part of an international plot to get us into the holocaust of world revolution."[49]

The loudest voice urging the United States to join the war came from Britain, and so the British were increasingly linked to "International Jewry" as a "powerful and rich sugar daddy to foot the bills and do their fighting."[50] Catherine Curtis, head of the National Legion of Mothers of America, railed against "the British and the Jews" as part of "a worldwide conspiracy that included communists and international bankers." The purpose of Goerner's warning to Gentile Freemasons was to erase the distinction (in place since the days of John Robison's *Proofs* and maintained by Nesta Webster) between continental and British (Scottish Rite) Freemasonry and to argue that the latter was also subservient to the Jews. The Molly Pitchers told women in America to "Boycott all Sponsors on the English Jew Controlled Radio." George Moseley argued that England, not Germany, was "the real threat to America" and that we should ally with Japan. The president of Defenders of the Constitution of U.S.A., Catherine Baldwin, put out numerous pamphlets and charts to show the "alleged effects of British domination in the United States." And Representative Jacob Thorkelson of Montana interrupted his nine-part attack on Great Britain to insert an attack on the Jews published by London's Imperial Fascist League. A several page list titled "Hereditary Titleholders of Jewish Blood" pertaining to nobles in Great Britain followed, since "it has long been one of the Jewish methods in the attainment of world domination to penetrate into privileged circles where political power is greatest." At a "patriotic" forum, one such penetration was credited to British foreign minister Anthony Eden's wife. "She is JEWISH," was the charge. "Her name is Litvinov, alias Finkelstein!"[51]

As America seemed increasingly likely to join the war effort, the tone of the antisemitic attacks became even sharper. Judge George Armstrong explained how the Jewish "undeclared war against Germany" was just part of their plan for world conquest as revealed in the *Protocols* ("authentic") and funded by the Rothschild "Dynasty." Representative Thorkelson, newly defeated in Montana's Republican primary, gave a radio address blaming shifting public opinion on the international bankers' control of gold, which in turn "controls the press, radio, news services, and cinema; the four mediums which these men use to soften public opposition to war." William Kullgren, an occultist antisemite from Atascadero, California, predicted in January 1942 that FDR would cancel the elections that year. Roosevelt would get away with this move because Americans had become "a race of synthetic Jews" living under "the law of the Talmud."[52]

The secret government had always been rather strictly defined by the concept of international Jewish finance. By controlling banking systems, Jews were presumably able to foist worthless "fiat money" onto Gentiles while amassing "real" wealth for themselves. They financed wars and revolutions and infiltrated government to institute policies—such as the Federal Reserve System and the abandonment of the gold standard—to manipulate debt and finance to their advantage. This conspiracy was carried into the New Deal but, by the mid-1930s, was giving way to a broader Jewish conspiracy that could be traced back to biblical times and sought to destroy gentile civilization itself. This broader conspiracy was often called "the hidden hand."

The narrower finance-based secret government conspiracy theory did not altogether disappear. Long after World War II, Don Bell, a new world order conspiracist, used it—and included a list of important Jews in government—to answer his rhetorical question, "Who are our rulers?" A pamphlet distributed by right-wing publisher Conde McGinley used the secret government to describe how the Jews secretly ruled the Soviet Union. A Jewish network of "secret boards," often headquartered in local synagogues, controlled the population through a campaign of fear.[53] The secret government remained a fixture in the rhetoric of the extreme Right fringe (including neo-Nazis) of the American political landscape. Secret Government conspiracism became the favored position of violently right-wing anti-Christian conspiracists—beginning with the iconic "theoretician" Francis Parker Yockey and including William Pierce, whose 1978 novel *The Turner Diaries* is nearly a sacred text. It was even applied to explain the trial of O. J. Simpson as part of the Jewish conspiracy to create race wars (their earlier effort—the prosecution of Charles Manson—having failed in this regard).[54] Other notable late twentieth-century secret government conspiracists include University of Illinois classics professor Dr. Revilo P. Oliver and Eustace Mullins. Today, in its purest form, the secret government conspiracy survives most clearly in the wealth of books and websites devoted to what G. Edward Griffin terms "the creature from Jekyll Island," the Federal Reserve System.[55]

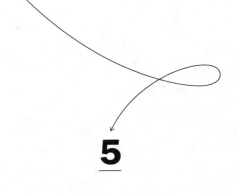

5

THE EMERGENCE OF
THE HIDDEN HAND

The present world-wide economic collapse, the breaking down of moral standards, . . . the general disregard for God, the birth and development of Communism, and the atheizing of the masses of people, may all be explained by the hypothetical proposition that behind the scenes there is A HIDDEN HAND; a small group of super-intelligent personalities who control the gold of the world and pull wires for the deliberate purpose of tearing down the Gentile peoples.

Gerald Burton Winrod, *The Hidden Hand*

Given the tumult of the 1930s—a worldwide economic depression, the rise of fascism, and the dramatic political shift into the New Deal—extremist reactions were to be expected. In the United States, adherents of Stalinist Russia and of Nazi Germany probably had a greater political voice than their numbers justified but were nevertheless remarkably numerous. Mainstream political ideology was also sharply antagonistic, with FDR's followers seeing him as a savior while his opponents saw him leading the nation to ruin. In the background of this political strife, the antisemitism that had become more common in the wake of the

Bolshevik revolution and the spread of the *Protocols* intensified along with fascist propaganda.

Even so, there was no need for oppositional views to be couched in the rhetoric of conspiracism, and, in fact, most anti–New Dealers were neither conspiratorial nor antisemitic. The business community, especially through its organizational fronts, such as the National Association of Manufacturers and the American Liberty League, relentlessly castigated Roosevelt, his policies, and the New Deal in general without mentioning Jews or laying out a conspiracy theory. In addition, many independent voices attacked the New Deal as a revolution, not a conspiracy. For example, Garet Garrett, a journalist who despised the New Deal to the point where he "retired to a cave on a river bank at Tuckahoe, New Jersey," took the view that most political observers misunderstood the New Deal by trying to fit it into normal American politics: "No matter how carefully a revolution may have been planned there is bound to be a crucial time. That comes when the actual seizure of power is taking place. In this case certain steps were necessary . . . to keep people excited about one thing at a time, and divided, while steadily through all the uproar of outrage and confusion a certain end, held constantly in view, was pursued by main intention. The end constantly held in view was power."[1] For almost fifty pages, Garrett kept up a barrage against the administration, its "captive" Congress and "domesticated" supporters, without falling into conspiracism or singling out Jews.

It might seem predictable for the fascist voices—especially those linked through the German-American Bund to Nazi Germany—to use conspiracism. However, despite the occultish dimension to Nazism, their racism was built on the nineteenth-century emergence of Aryanism. The supremacy of the Aryan "race" and the corollary necessity of maintaining its purity, combined with resentment of Jewish assimilation, was sufficient to scapegoat Jews and link them to revolution without recourse to conspiracism. In the United States, evidence of this lies among the defendants in the massive sedition trial that took place during World War II. Those defendants connected to the German propaganda effort (e.g., Frank Ferentz, Peter Stahrenberg, George Viereck) were violently antisemitic, but not conspiratorial. Defendants without those kinds of connections, such as William Dudley Pelley, Elizabeth Dilling, or Gerald Winrod, were intensely conspiratorial.[2]

The Core Conspiracy of the Hidden Hand

The term "hidden hand" has never been unique to antisemitic conspiracy theories; it was the title of an innocuous nineteenth-century novel and had long been used to indicate surreptitious behavior. An early use of the "hidden hand" as a conspiratorial term for Jews occurred in 1921 when The Britons, a right-wing nativist group in England, changed the name of its signature publication from *Jewry Über Alles* to *The Hidden Hand*. Cherep-Spiridovich used it as a synonym for the secret government in 1926. Since then, it has usually been aimed at Jews, although recently its nineteenth-century application to Freemasons has returned, as some internet conspiracists have interpreted the old-fashioned practice of men placing their hand inside their coat for formal portraits as a literal sign of the hidden hand of Freemasonry. The actual hidden hand indicates one's "hidden power," which "revolves around the power of the occult."[3]

In light of the already well-established secret government conspiracy theory, it is worth clarifying how the hidden hand differed from financial control by international bankers and the idea that Roosevelt was dragging the nation into socialism. First, the conspirators were all the Jews— not merely bankers and government officials, but the entire "race." Jewish "domination" of science, literature, and especially popular culture are at least as important as finance and politics to the hidden hand. Building on this, the second distinct aspect of the hidden hand is that, despite their connection to Communism, the Jews' goal is not political or even to be found on the Left-to-Right political spectrum. Their goal is world domination, as referenced vaguely throughout the *Protocols*. As far back as 1920, Howell Arthur Gwynne, reflecting the casual widespread antisemitism in England, made the point that, through Communism, Jews "hope to arrive at the hegemony of the world by establishing some sort of despotic rule."[4] Such generic "some sort of" explanations were common among hidden hand conspiracists throughout the 1930s.

Third, the distinction between simply scapegoating Jews and painting them as the force behind a relentless conspiracy for global hegemony is evidenced by hidden hand conspiracists' attention to ancient Jewish lore. The "mystical cabalah" and the Talmud were used to explain why Jews needed to go beyond Communism to find a more agreeable "sort of despotic rule." Despite its title, the first topic discussed in Gerald Winrod's *The Truth about the Protocols* is the Talmud's relationship to "the secret operations of the ancient Jewish Kahal." William Pelley introduces his argument with a cartoon of a Jew reading a *Protocols* recipe book while he whips up a big pot of "World Revolution." The *Protocols*, according to Pelley, reveal the Jews' "most secret . . . and secular aspirations": "Indeed, if one compares the Protocols with the traditional works such as the 'Zohar,' the 'Schulchan Arukh,' and the 'Talmud,' one is easily convinced that they all set forth the same doctrine and the same sentiments. Thus the Protocols are but an aspect of Jewish thought— its modern aspect. . . . They may also be regarded as a crystallization, necessitated by the conditions of the time, of the fundamental ideas codified in the Talmud by the Rabbis of the past."[5] The idea that global domination reflected "a very real and essential part of their traditions" had been broached by Nesta Webster in *Secret Societies* and implicitly or explicitly underlay all versions of the Jewish conspiracy. Despite the pretense of expertise, such as Pelley's exegesis, few conspiracists studied the actual substance of the ancient documents, which were merely symbolic referents, and even those who did relied heavily on suspect translations.[6]

The fourth and last distinction—a corollary to the religious nature of the conspiracy—is that the victims of the conspiracy must be the Gentiles. Ignoring other continents and their various religions, conspiracy theorists invariably divided the world between Jews and Gentiles. A 1936 pamphlet by the Twentieth Century Crusaders presents "the case of Judaism vs. Christianity with evidence from the Jewish Rabbi Scriptures" (i.e., the Talmud). And Eugene Sanctuary's 1939 edition of *The Talmud Unmasked*, an 1892 Russian attack on Jews, includes an entire chapter explaining how "Christians are to be exterminated"("indirectly" by conspiracy or, if that fails, "directly" by killing them).[7] The hidden hand conspiracy portrayed Jews as having "powerful Jewish intellects," which they put to cunning and ruthless use. By contrast, the Gentile, trusting and gullible, was "asleep in his own tractability." Gentiles never suspected they were "merely the puppets and monkeys" of the Jews, who "possess rare ability for stirring up strife among the Gentiles.... They are experts in arousing human passions by producing mob psychology. They are able to stampede crowds into croaking special phrases like frogs."[8]

These four features constitute an outline of the conspiracy constructed by a relatively small number of individuals. The conspiracists attempt to explain America's shift to the left, embodied in the New Deal, as the current manifestation of a centuries-old Jewish plot to dominate the world and destroy Christianity. Whatever shape the Jewish hegemony takes, it will represent an alien force and an alien way of life. This is, by any measure, a true conspiracy theory. It contains what Richard Hofstadter called "the big leap from the undeniable to the unbelievable."[9] It leaps from an economic collapse and a nation's political scramble to a Jewish conspiracy, backtracking into the Talmud and other religious esoterica, then using those sources to justify belief in the *Protocols* —which, of course, prove Jewish guilt.

The Conspiracy Expands

A key tenet of our understanding of conspiracy theories today is that they inexorably expand in order to explain how the conspirators fend off exposure. Questions about how a conspiracy is able to operate secretly, about why the general public is so oblivious to it, are invariably answered with explanations centering on the conspiracy's control of channels of information. Thus, the press, schools, churches, and popular entertainments are folded into the original conspiracy, and its size increases accordingly. This process is also the primary element in the self-sealing nature of conspiracism; it underlies the "that's what they want you to think" argument conspiracists so often fall back on. Researchers contend that conspiracism as a belief system is unique in having this "self-sealing" (or "self-validating" or "self-insulating") quality.[10] This gives every conspiracy theory the distinctive common feature that any evidence against it can be explained a part of the conspiracy—an effort by the conspirators to discredit those who are trying to expose the conspiracy. Thus, conspiracy theories have "built-in protection against empirical failure and hostile criticism from outsiders. . . . Their epistemic structure guarantees that believers will always have some way of explaining away difficulties."[11] This is what makes conspiracy theories unfalsifiable; they are "the only theories for which evidence *against* them is actually construed as evidence *in favor* of them."[12]

While this "epistemic defense mechanism" does make conspiracy theories self-insulating against disconfirmation, it also causes them constantly to expand. A kind of cascade logic causes conspiracy theories to grow when, in the words of Ted Goertzel, "defenders of one conspiracy theory find it necessary to implicate more and more people whose failure to discover or reveal the conspiracy can be explained only by their alleged complicity." Expanding circles of complicity invariably encompass communication media, especially those in the "mainstream," and are clearly a part of the cover-up process of conspiracy building. Researchers focusing on cover-up conspiracies have compared them to "viruses" that expand by mutation: "As one version approaches extinction, a new, slightly different version gains strength."[13] The expansion of the conspiracy is not just a matter of the number of conspirators. The conspirators' power expands "to explain how they were able to intimidate so many people and cover their tracks so well." In addition, the range of topics inevitably expands along with the structure of the conspiracy.[14]

This process was clearly at work among the hidden hand conspiracists. Its inspiration was laid out, with some unintentional irony, by Gerald Winrod in his claim that an "elaborate and almost fantastic system for dominating the newspapers of the world is presented in the Protocols." The press, under this system, refused to expose the conspiracy and even lied on its behalf. The public was constantly fooled by "America's kept press, tinctured with its 'progressive' doctrines of 'liberalism.'" "Can you," asked Ernst Goerner after having explained the truth to his Masonic Brothers, "finally recognize that the Germans are not the brutal conquerors as pictured by the Jew-controlled press?" Equally important, the press "smeared" all those who tried to expose the conspiracy. The New Deal smear gang (or, more militarily, the smear brigade) was always prepared to do the bidding of the hidden hand. On the eve of World War II, Joseph Kamp portrayed the press as part of a fifth-column attack on the House Committee on Un-American Activities: "Throughout the entire life of the committee, Chairman Dies and his colleagues have faced contempt, derision, denunciation and wrath from prejudiced individuals, liberal-to-Red organizations, and a considerable portion of the press. They have been subjected to every manner of intimidation and scurrilous disparagement. They have been maliciously castigated and deliberately lied about by unscrupulous public figures."[15]

Control of the press, like everything about the conspiracy, operated behind the scenes. Sometimes this point was made subtly, as when Father Coughlin's *Social Justice* periodical selected the heads of the three radio networks to share its "Man of the Week" award. This was the "triumvirate, whose guiding hand—sometimes hidden but always present" informed ("or subversively influenced") the public. Usually, however, claims of Jewish control were blunter: "In the United States the 'great power of the press' is very extensively controlled by advertisers, money-lenders and writers who are Jewish or under such influence. The ... free exchange of vital politico-economic information is therefore treasonably suppressed."[16]

Deeper control over information was achieved by suppressing information before it ever reached the press. Books might just disappear. Father Coughlin's open letter of encouragement to Charles Lindbergh Jr. brought up how Lindbergh's father, a prominent isolationist in his day, "was almost censored out of existence when his books were pulled from the library shelves." George Armstrong complained that all the histories of the Rothschilds he could find were "either Jewish or strongly pro-

Jewish." And surprisingly, given how often Webster's works were cited, Eugene Sanctuary claimed that "the writings of Nesta H. Webster have been suppressed in this country and England."[17]

In addition to the press, the entertainment media conveyed information that could be controlled by the conspiracy, either to mislead the public or, worse, to corrupt morality. William Dudley Pelley had attacked Jewish propaganda through movies as early as 1934, when he explained that *The House of Rothschild* was part of the Jews' plan "to dominate the nation in the age-old manner prescribed in the Talmud."[18] Pelley later laid out how this plot worked: "The average person goes into a theatre or a movie temple to relax, to be entertained. His defenses are down, and the subversionists know it. *Subtilely [sic] into his mind can be inculcated ideas that are scarcely ever recognized for the vicious things they are. He receives them subconsciously*, intent on the dramatic story being played before his eyes. Hours, days, months later, he finds his psychology trending into avenues that are but the regurgitation of what he has been incessantly fed in his hours of recreation."[19] Robert Edward Edmondson covers the same ground and builds on Father Coughlin's concern over a radio broadcasting monopoly, arguing that the "screen and radio are powerful moulders of public opinion" on his way to excoriating "the **economic masters**" of those industries—Laemmle, Zukor, Goldwyn, Fox—"**all Jews**." Edmondson provides a more detailed rundown of the Jewish movie monopoly in a 1938 bulletin, which explains that as "earnest and fair-minded American patriots, **deeply concerned** over the jazzy, communistic eye-and-ear 'education' American Youth is receiving via the 'movies,' we are repeatedly asked this vital question, strange as it may seem: 'IS the motion picture industry really Jewish-controlled?'"[20] Edmondson's answer is an unequivocal yes.

This view of the movies made it natural to connect them with a variety of other vices, all designed to destroy morality. Early on, Nesta Webster had linked movies with "minor subversive movements": drugs, degenerate art, and psychoanalysis. Gerald Winrod paired the "constant carnival of immorality" of the movies with the "vile literature . . . released every week on the news-stands of America." A handbill circulated on the West

Coast, calling for a movie boycott, featured a drawing of a man (identi-fied by a Star of David) and a seemingly naked woman above the head-line: "Hollywood is the Sodom and Gomorrah where INTERNATIONAL JEWRY controls VICE—DOPE—GAMBLING."[21]

The conspiracy did not appear to dominate other American insti-tutions to the degree that it dominated mass communications media. Nevertheless, vigilance was necessary, particularly to protect children, and so the conspiracists expanded their areas of concern to include the infiltration of churches and schools. Actual churches drew little atten-tion from conspiracists, aside from the obviously suspicious Riverside Church in New York City. This interdenominational cathedral estab-lished in 1930 with Rockefeller money was a bastion of social gospel, which, as a result of "introducing modern scientific methods and mass social reforms," conspiracists saw as a threat to Christianity. When Eugene Sanctuary included among his "foes of Jewish aggressiveness" the "Theological Seminaries not Teaching 'Another Gospel,'" his read-ers understood what that other gospel was.[22]

Conspiratorial infiltration of religion encompassed many church-based organizations. One of the stated objectives of American Women against Communism was "to oppose all subversive activities in Churches, Church Organizations, the Y.M.C.A. and Y.W.C.A." They were particu-larly concerned by the Methodist Federation for Social Service (or "Red" Service, as Elizabeth Dilling put it). Its leaders were those "Christian Dupes" Dilling claimed the communists rejoiced over—namely, the Christian Gentiles that the B'nai B'rith preferred as "fronts . . . for any kind of statement likely to be swallowed by the uninformed Gentile pub-lic."[23] The mainstay for conspiracists, however, was the Federal Council of Churches of Christ in America. Eugene Sanctuary saw in the council evidence of "the penetration of Fabianism in the church of America," while William Pelley charged that it had been formed "to promote rad-ical thought in our Protestant Christian churches." The council might turn up anywhere. Representative Jacob Thorkelson of Montana con-cluded his nine-part diatribe against the conspiracy by the British and the Jews with this parting shot: "In concluding this speech, may I say that the Federal Council of Churches is a subversive organization, the members of which are clothed in garments of pink, red, and scarlet, all the colors of radicalism and communism. It is now well to take heed, for this movement is carrying this Nation into trials, tribulations, and war."[24]

Whereas the corruption of churches was couched in political terms, the corruption of schools was portrayed as a Jewish plot to undermine Gentile morality. As usual, the conspiracy is admitted in the *Protocols*—in this case, number 16: "We must introduce into their education all those principles which have so brilliantly broken up their order." Public schools had been "the bulwark of our national existence," but now the "dangerous termite" of conspiracy had gotten a "strangle-hold on the educational system of this country."[25] Elizabeth Dilling cited an inflammatory report on Soviet schools to show "that the most terrible kinds of vice are encouraged among the young school children in order to break down their family influence." Father Coughlin lamented that "we have seen Christ scourged from our schools." As another "corroding influence," Robert Edward Edmondson cited an editorial in a Jewish newspaper, stating that "the public schools must be kept clear of Christmas carols and other Christmas influences." Colleges, of course, were beyond the pale, effectively "kidnapping" America's youth to poison "their minds and morals."[26] Jewish corruption of the schools faded as an issue until the Supreme Court's *Brown v. Board* ruling of 1954, whereupon racist antisemites revived it. In his call to "abolish the public schools! Now!" John Kasper tied together all the aspects of the "*menace to American liberty*" represented by the Jews: the Communist Party, the National Association for the Advancement of Colored People (NAACP), the Federal Reserve System, and the World Bank.[27]

In many areas, where the conspiracy expanded beyond the government and its minions in the press, there was a menacing undercurrent of lurid immorality and unbridled sexuality. Nesta Webster had made this point in *Secret Societies*: "Monsieur de Lannoy, a member of an antimasonic association in France, at a conference on 'the influence of judeo-masonic sects in the theatre, in literature, in fashions,' showed how 'orders of things which appear to have no connexion with each other are skilfully [*sic*] bound up together and directed by a single methodical movement towards a common end. This common end is the paganization of the universe, the destruction of all Christianity, the return to the loosest morals of antiquity.' The same glorification of vice has found exponents amongst the modern Illuminati in this country."[28] Gerald Winrod echoed Webster's concern about the glorification of vice, with the standard allusion to the *Protocols*: "Realizing that no nation can survive a moral collapse, it is explained that the Elders have been determined to promote immorality among the Gentile masses." The temptations "flaunted" before the Gentiles included "sexual vice," along with alcohol, pornography, and "polluted amusements." Quoting an unnamed preacher's bafflement at this "avalanche" of immorality, Winrod explained that "had this noted preacher been familiar with The Protocols he would have had an idea as to the possible cause of the calamity." Even Winrod failed to mention what Protocol one referred to as "our special agents" of immorality: the "tutors, lackeys, governesses in the houses of the wealthy."[29]

Elizabeth Dilling reached back to *The Communist Manifesto* for inspiration, citing its disparagement of "Bourgeois marriage" and promotion of what she called "an openly legalized community of women." After a tangential point about the evils of abortion and child care, Dilling quotes "socialist authority" August Bebel: "In the new society women will be entirely independent both socially and economically. . . . In the choice of love she is as free and unhampered as a man." This new society would mark the end of marriage and the family, evidence of which could be found in the "Red women who do not bear their husband's name." Immorality and vice were widely noted in a variety of settings. Arguing against the immigration of Jewish refugees, Agnes Waters exclaimed: "There are 200,000 Communist Jews at the Mexican border waiting to get into this country. If they are admitted they will rape every woman and child that is left unprotected." Gerald L. K. Smith concerned himself with "rampant" homosexuality in the State Department, "symptomatic of the terrible decay and degeneration in the City of Washington." Unable to stop himself, Smith concluded with the observation that these "were men who enjoyed the favor of both Franklin and Eleanor.

In fact, the escapades of Eleanor and the conduct of her many youthful boyfriends in New York have never been fully discussed anywhere in print. . . . What a filthy lot of traitors, Communists, wasters, perverts! Shall these people rule America? God forbid!"[30]

The Conspiracist Pyramid: Theorists and Their Followers

One can think of conspiracists as forming a hierarchy, topped by a small number of true theorists with a much larger array of conspiracy propagators who spread these theories and keep them up to date. The more passive lower levels of the hierarchy are composed of serious followers and then casual adherents. Serious followers maintain an active interest in their chosen conspiracy theory and are usually rather knowledgeable about its nuances. Casual adherents, in contrast, are less involved and may be unaware that views they hold follow from a conspiracy theory at all. There is, of course, no line of strict separation between these groups, and individuals may be difficult to categorize, but the hierarchy is useful as there is no reason to think that conspiracists across it share the same mix of psychological attributes. This is one reason why studies of psychological correlates of conspiracist ideation—mistrust, anomie, paranoia, narcissism, authoritarianism, schizotypy, and simply bad thinking—have proven hard to replicate.

THE BOTTOM OF THE PYRAMID: THE PSYCHOLOGY OF FOLLOWERS

During the 1930s, active followers of the hidden hand conspiracy were fairly numerous, but there is little information available about them. The number of casual adherents is impossible even to estimate. Only in recent years have there been studies of people who seriously believe, but do not spread, specific conspiracy theories. The findings of these studies are somewhat impressionistic, but overall, serious believers exhibit considerable paranoia, are extremely intransigent about their beliefs, incline toward political extremism, and are given to racial and ethnic prejudice. Paranoia was famously the distinguishing characteristic used by Richard Hofstadter, and even critics who think he "pathologized conspiracy thinking" still find evidence of paranoia in conspiracists.[31] A willful imperviousness to evidence is widely noted in academic studies of conspiracy believers, reflecting a severe mistrust of accepted authorities. Many critical assessments of intransigence link it, explicitly or implicitly, to "low complexity cognitive styles" that make people want simple, unambiguous answers to problems.[32]

Not surprisingly, serious followers tend toward extremist views—occasionally a leftist extremism, sometimes a libertarianism that is hard to place on the normal Left-to-Right spectrum, but most frequently a right-wing extremism that incorporates racism, antisemitism, or other manifestations of bigotry. As a large, international assessment of counterterrorism noted, "Conspiracy theories are widely prevalent across this extremist spectrum, despite the vast differences in the extremist ideologies themselves."[33] Until recently, serious believers had little opportunity to make their views known, but enough examples have survived to add weight to the academic findings. Here, for example, is a 1946 reader's letter to *Women's Voice*, a publication devoted to fighting the hidden hand:

> This is to inform you that the Pearl Harbor Investigating Board is investigating their own crime, committed by the Free-Masonic Jew Deal. It is a waste of time and money[.] Baruch tells them what to do. They do it or die.
>
> Judah P. Benjamin put the north and south to war in the same manner. A Jew and a Mason, Jef Davis, gave the Masonic distress signal and saved his life.

The magazine's publisher and editor, Lyrl Van Hyning, found this letter worth printing.[34]

Casual adherents are an even more difficult group to assess. Many are not believers at all but just willing to entertain the idea of a conspiracy. Recent research suggests that many people who resist having their children vaccinated are unfamiliar with the claims of conspiracy propagators about mercury, autism, or medical cover-ups. They have just heard about the "controversy" and express vague notions about the possibility that "too many immunizations . . . could 'overload' a child's immune system."[35] The same sort of unwitting acceptance of conspiratorial ideas has been noted in people's views on globalization. In a variety of areas, psychological studies have found that people "significantly underestimated how much the conspiracy theories influenced their own attitudes" and had a "hidden impact" on their thinking.[36]

People do not always think through the implications of casual beliefs. For the vaccine and autism story to be true would necessitate a huge and sociopathic medical conspiracy that few people would accept. Conspiracists play into this thoughtlessness by avoiding conspiracist rhetoric while presenting their ideas as simple facts.[37] An analysis of 9/11 "truthers" in the United Kingdom found serious believers but also "a much larger, more diffuse group, which we term the illiterari." For these people, "membership in 9/11 Truth is as much social and recreational as an exercise in critical inquiry. . . . The illiterari have not actually looked at much of the material." Even though their attachment is casual, these people do accept that there was a conspiracy. It is a belief "to which they have committed socially and around which they have formed an identity." This emotional attachment makes conspiracy theories very hard to overcome. As pseudoscience opponent Ben Goldacre has pointed out, "You cannot reason people out of positions they did not reason themselves into."[38] Any conclusions about the psychological characteristics of casual adherents are problematic, but they seem better adjusted than other conspiracists. They are presumably mistrustful enough of the authorities to entertain conspiracy theories, but they do not seem paranoid or hostile. Nor is there any reason to consider them delusional. The worst that can be said about them—as is implicit in the term "illiterari"—is that they do not think much about what they believe.

THE APEX OF THE PYRAMID: THE PSYCHOLOGY OF THEORISTS

True conspiracy theorists—those who construct the alternative narratives that eventually filter down to their followers—have quite a different psychological profile. The emergence of the hidden hand conspiracy owes a great deal to a loose cadre of conspiracy theorists, whose work can be assessed in terms of psychological characteristics ranging from the patternicity inherent in conspiracist thinking, through the array of "negative political attitudes" (e.g., mistrust, alienation, hostility), to actual personality disorders and delusional thought patterns. Determining who is a true theorist and who falls short of being one is not an exact science, but three hidden hand theorists stand out: Nesta Webster, William Dudley Pelley, and Gerald Winrod. Webster's main conspiratorial works were published in the early 1920s and were widely cited as late as World War II. Pelley and Winrod were quite prolific throughout the period. Each of the three worked at an abstract level to give meaning to the events of their times by exploring patterns no one else seemed to notice—patterns that could be explained only by a conspiracy.

Webster was unparalleled at this. In *Secret Societies*, she ran through analogies, resemblances, modes of recognition, and spiritual descent to make connections such as those among "the Dar ul Hikmat or Grand Lodge of Cairo," Weishaupt's Illuminati, the Syrian Druses ("their organization presents analogies with that which we now know as 'masonic'"), the "Hashishiyin or *Assassins*," their "spiritual descendants, the Jacobins of 1793," and the sect of Hasan Saba ("the supreme model on which all systems of organized murder working through fanaticism such as the Carbonari and the Irish Republican Brotherhood, were based").[39] Webster managed to cast all these groups and many others, modern and ancient, as subsidiary to the Jews in her version of a hidden hand conspiracy. A contemporary review summed up Webster's method as a "farrago of undigested nonsense combined with occasional glimpses of common sense."[40]

Gerald B. Winrod "Americanized" Webster's work by coming at the conspiracy from a biblical perspective. The threat posed by secret societies was of negligible interest to Americans, but Winrod's version downplayed these societies along with their occult precursors. The few he felt compelled to leave in simply buttressed the role of the Illuminati. Relying on his extreme version of premillennial apocalyptic Christianity, Winrod created a conspiracy that Americans—especially fundamentalist Christians—felt at home with. Nowhere are Winrod's ideas better encapsulated than in *Adam Weishaupt—a Human Devil*, where the believer protected by "Bible truth" discovers,

> in this weird system of occultism[,] a demonic principle capable of warping and twisting the minds of those who allow themselves to come under its influence. . . . Illuminism is rooted in black magic. It produced a mighty wave of occultism in the eighteenth century which even swept governments from their foundations. And the end is not yet! . . . These same hidden forces, often using influential leaders as their pawns, are still actively engaged in pushing their program of world chaos with the final objective in view of pulling down the temple of civilization and blotting Christianity from the face of the earth.

Winrod exchanged Webster's patterns linking secret societies for patterns of biblical verse linking Satan to the Illuminati. This interpretation might seem to leave little or no room for the Jews, and yet: "The real conspirators behind the Illuminati were Jews. The whole scheme was a Jewish plot to the core."[41]

The contributions of William Dudley Pelley to the conspiracy of the hidden hand are much harder to pin down. Where Webster and Winrod were thorough and organized, Pelley was haphazard—a "fusion of right-wing political organization with anti-Semitism, paramilitarism, and millennialism." Pelley's millennialism was intensely apocalyptic but idiosyncratic. Even while leading his Silver Shirts, Pelley continued to publish *Reality*, a magazine devoted to the idea that "consciousness has many octaves and all together produce reality."[42] Nevertheless, while Webster's conspiratorial vision began with the Illuminati and Winrod's with Satan, Pelley was inspired primarily by antisemitism. Not traditionally religious, and seemingly little interested in Adam Weishaupt, Pelley constructed his own vision of the apocalyptic clash between American Christians and alien Jews. Convinced that Jews secretly amounted to a full 20 percent of the American population, Pelley portrayed them all as under the control of their rabbis, who "as a religious oligarchy are all for communism because . . . it exterminates by mass murder or starvation all those who are believers in the Christian religion." This was a more streamlined version of the conspiracy, but, equally important a more immediate one. Pelley's apocalypse was already underway and needed to be fought.[43] Sadly, Pelley found the Gentiles ill-prepared for the fight: "gullible," "dumb workingmen," "unenlightened" souls who "never suspect" that they are the victims of a conspiracy. Pelley despaired of getting across the truth about the "Machiavellian Conspiracy . . . to Gentile America— asleep in its own tractability."[44] His instructions to the Silver Shirts, his personal militia, tried to prepare his followers for "the Great Armageddon designated in Divine Prophesy." The fight would not be easy:

> In the archives and minds of the leaders of **The Silver-Shirts** is irrefutable information that if improperly or prematurely released would bring the swift murdering of its custodians. . . . The men at the head of **The Silver Shirts** are taking their lives in their hands to arouse and organize the Christ Forces of this nation. . . .
>
> **This is no Children's Crusade** that is now swinging into reality. It is the open challenge of an organization of New Vigilantes that purpose [sic] to accomplish works under leaders who have proven that they cannot be bought or debauched, and who are fully acquainted with the character and identity of the enemy whom they accost not only in the underworld but in the world of respectability and abstruse finance.[45]

Despite their differences, each of the three versions of the conspiracy posited a Manichean struggle between the forces of evil and the good Gentile population. The common factor in the evil forces was, of course, the Jews, whether alone (Pelley), in league with Satan (Winrod), or behind the Illuminati (Webster). These were not mutually exclusive versions, but each emphasis generated its own cadre of followers.

As they made sense out of the patterns they recognized, the hidden hand theorists described a reality in which the good Gentile people were rapidly losing control of the society—even the civilization—they had built to an insidious alien force. None of the three, however, dwelled on this catastrophe. Rather, by couching it in apocalyptic terms, they heralded an opportunity to rise up and destroy the evil force. This "little island of ours," Webster wrote of England, may "finally stem the tide of World Revolution and save not only herself, but Christian Civilization."[46] This peculiarly positive outlook meant their writing was relatively free from the negative political attitudes that pepper the writing of most conspiracy propagators. For paranoia, only Pelley's writings stand out. Webster borders on paranoia in her lengthy responses to criticism, but her associate Leslie Fry, in private communications with Nazi agents, described her as insufficiently paranoid to trust.[47] And Winrod evidenced no paranoia to speak of.

Pelley's paranoia may well have stemmed from his delusional beliefs. He frequently claimed to "just know" things: in Russia in 1918 ("Privately I knew that the whole dastardly mess was a Yiddish scheme to subdue the world's Gentiles") or in America ("I had means of knowing in advance that the whole New Deal nonsense was Yiddish in origin"). Such remarks might be written off as hollow rhetoric but for claims of information "received 'clairaudiently,' via the Psychic Radio, from Great Souls who graduated out of this three-dimensional world into other areas of Time and Space."[48] It may well be that Pelley suffered from schizophrenia to the point of hearing voices, but regardless, his paranoia bordered on a persecution fixation. In his instructions for the Silver Shirts, he warns of bribery, public slander, and whispering campaigns on his way to this crescendo: "If a real leader contrive to survive such attacks, lethal expedients are next in order: motor cars in which they are being transported are forced at high speed off the public highways, 'accidental' gunfights of gangsters break out where they are exposed to the fusillade of bullets, they are invited to banquets where slow-working poisons are introduced into their foods, or they are 'snatched' by insolent extortionists and 'taken for a ride.'" Pelley's writing includes such scenarios regularly, in enough detail that they sound as though he is relating events he experienced. But then Pelley had worked in Hollywood as a scenario writer. Pelley also harbored occult delusions, unaccompanied by paranoia. Many of these are essentially random, such as "The mystical number '17' which has symbolized all major operations in Chief Pelley's career to date."[49]

Delusional thinking without accompanying paranoia runs through Webster's work, starting with her revelatory insights into eighteenth-century France, which led her to believe that earlier accounts of the French Revolution misunderstood it. Webster credited her revelations to reincarnation but left open the possibility of extrasensory perception or "spirit presences." By the time Webster published her third opus, *Secret Societies*, her observations frequently reflect her peculiar beliefs— "The part," she writes without any further clarification, "played by magicians during the period preceding the French Revolution is of course a matter of common knowledge."[50] This sort of claim was fairly routine for her. Pelley, too, peppered his writing with mundane weirdness. Pelley obsessively applied his antisemitism to any event, using the type of backwards syllogism common among conspiracists. When the government undertook a campaign to reduce the incidence of venereal disease in 1938, Pelley was struck by the fact that the wire service stories were "almost identical in their phraseology." Putting this together with the fact that "the Jew, Morris Fishbein" was the head of the American Medical Association, Pelley saw a "concerted, consistent and continuous propaganda barrage" being orchestrated by the Jews. He concluded that, "obviously, the ultimate objective is to have laws passed in all states compelling everyone to take the syphilis tests. Judging from other Jewish New Deal governmental agencies set up, we know the various administrative boards would be packed with Jews, all of which leads to the logical conclusion that this entire scheme is one leading up to wholesale innoculation [*sic*] of Gentiles with vaccine syphilitic germs."[51]

Winrod presents a challenge in that anyone whose primary reference is the book of Revelation can easily appear delusional. He exaggerated this appearance by interpreting scripture as prophetic of automobiles (with headlights), radio, and Great Britain. Winrod also seemed to go beyond the rational when he brought the Antichrist up to date as a veritable Judas-

Nero-Napoleon-Mussolini-Nietzsche, all rolled into one superpersonality: "This man is in the flesh at the present time. In the not distant future he will be unveiled as the world's most powerful potentate, a high-brow, a scholastic, a wizard in finance, a superman. . . . For over twenty years I have been familiar with the facts relating to the coming of a world dictator, and have proclaimed them constantly but only in recent years have I learned of a HIDDEN HAND consciously preparing the way for his coming."[52] Although most of the space in Winrod's publications is devoted to lengthy quotations from other sources, his connecting prose is uniformly similar in tone to this excerpt.

Given their high level of delusional belief, Winrod, Pelley, and Webster, not surprisingly, demonstrate innumerable instances of bad thinking. Weird claims are passed along without attribution. From Winrod, we learn that "Einstein, the Jew who was expelled from Germany, is a high up Rosicrucian and has been able to communicate with the 'Invisible Master' by means of spiritualism, from which source he is said to have come into possession of his theory of relativity." Other claims arise spontaneously, probably out of the simple desire to believe them; Pelley declares flatly that "love of humanity is an Aryan affection, foreign to most other races." And some are a combination of both; Nesta Webster excelled at embedding odd claims in her chain-link verbiage:

> The Stella Matutina may be only an obscure fraternity, even the Theosophical Society . . . may not be of the greatest importance in itself, but will anyone . . . seriously maintain that the Grand Orient is a small or unimportant organization? . . . These amazing cults, these strange perverted rites which we associate with the dark ages, are going on around us to-day. Illuminism, Cabalism, and even Satanism are still realities. . . . In 1908 Monsieur Copin Albancelli stated that circumstances had afforded the proof that—"certain masonic societies exist which are Satanic."[53]

With regard to the rest of the psychological characteristics, the only one that stands out is the personality disorder of narcissism. The casual ease with which Nesta Webster dismisses other authors' work ("French writers of the past had distorted facts to suit their own political views") shows it, as does her intense reaction to any criticism. Gerald Winrod's blurb for his *Three Modern Evils* ("This fearless book, bound in beautiful art covers, deals with Modernism in the Church, Atheism in the schools, and Communism in the world. It takes courage to write a book like this") exemplifies Winrod's sense of himself.[54] Neither, however, comes close to William Pelley in terms of narcissism, which trait also appears to underlie a severe authoritarian streak (as perhaps befits a man who created an avowedly fascist paramilitary organization). Pelley's "private manual" to his troops explains precisely what is expected of them, their code of morality, and their dress code. He also describes the leader of the Silver Shirts: "At their head is their supreme ranking officer known as THE CHIEF, holding his position until the purposes of the Silver Shirts are declared accomplished, because of his projection of the organization, his intimacy with the national and international political and economic situation, and his knowledge of the ramifications of the public enemies. His office is not elective excepting in the case of his death." It was, of course, understood that "the chief" would always be Pelley himself, a point underscored in *The Reds Are upon Us*, written by Pelley but officially credited to "The First Council." Also an introduction aimed at incoming recruits, the book is written with constant references to Chief Pelley, the ideas he "has set forth for us," and threats about which he "solemnly advises us."[55]

These were not the only original voices of hidden hand conspiracism. One could include William Kullgren, publisher of the magazine the *Beacon Light* of Atascadero, California. Kullgren regularly railed against the "Talmudic, Babylonian System" that ruled the United States in standard hidden hand fashion. But his views also reflected Theosophy (Hitler as "the reincarnation of one of the lords of the dark race of Lemuria") as filtered through the Aryan Astrological Occult Church of Christ. Occasional references to Marx and Weishaupt peppered Kullgren's essays, but even his most political observations were couched in the framework of astrological predictions. Kullgren also espoused a variety of medical oddities ranging from craniopathy to chiropractic and sold equipment to make raw vegetable juice. As the war loomed, his magazine increasingly promoted survivalism in remote areas.[56] Eugene Sanctuary, head of the World Alliance against Jewish Aggressiveness, offered some original ideas. He was perhaps the first to bring into the conspiracy the Fabian Society, "a rebellious intelligentsia whose accomplishments seem the realization of Weishaupt's dream of Masonic Illuminism (Haskalah)." The Fabians and their progressive allies in America were able to "gain dominance over certain individuals and use them in accomplishing their nefarious schemes" by means of "Thought transference" and "projection of the astral," occult abilities learned from "metaphysical societies" and the Rosicrucians.[57] Most of the prominent voices behind the hidden hand conspiracy, from the early 1930s to its eventual decline after World War II, did not, however, produce any notable theory. They reiterated the ideas of the few theorists and applied these ideas to new issues and social developments.

6

THE RISE AND FALL
OF THE HIDDEN HAND

Will others just miss death by being driven off the road, as Henry Ford
was, before being made to recant critical truths about subversive Jewry?
Or Else?

Elizabeth Dilling, *The Octopus*

The handful of theorists who managed to expand the original Jewish
secret government into a hidden hand conspiracy determined to wipe
out Gentile civilization were soon joined by a remarkable number of
active propagators of the conspiracy. In part this was due to the influence of Nazi Germany, which as early as 1933 was cultivating antisemites in America as propagandists, especially among isolationists. By
the very late 1930s the idea of a Jewish conspiracy had attracted a considerable number of adherents, but many of these fell away as the war
intensified, and when America entered the war, their numbers were
seriously depleted. Those who remained devoted to the global Jewish
conspiracy were among the most intense and vicious conspiracists of
any time, and a remarkable number of them continued to propagate an
openly pro-Nazi version of the hidden hand conspiracy during and even

after the war. Although their influence lingered for years, their central Jew-versus-Gentile narrative faded and subsequent conspiracists were markedly less religious.

Propagators of the Hidden Hand: The Psychology
of Hard-Core Conspiracism

No doubt other individuals contributed original ideas to the hidden hand conspiracy besides Webster, Winrod, and Pelley, but these theorists account for the lion's share. Most of those who actually spread the conspiracy just shaped the basic idea according to their predispositions and fitted the events of the day into the already established conspiratorial framework. Some of these people were household names in their day and are still fairly well known. Father Coughlin's radio audience ran into the millions. Gerald L. K. Smith was renowned as an orator who could fill stadiums with his followers. Elizabeth Dilling, in addition to writing books about the New Deal, was also a popular speechmaker, who occasionally "faked a Yiddish accent her audiences found hilarious." Dilling fell into obscurity until self-appointed pundit Glenn Beck began touting her books.[1]

There were many other national figures: Robert Edward Edmondson produced over four hundred *American Vigilante Bulletins*, most having to do with the conspiracy; Lyrl Van Hyning, founder of We the Mothers Mobilize for America, promoted the conspiracy through her magazine *Women's Voice*; Eugene Sanctuary of the World Alliance against Jewish Aggressiveness stuck to a combination of Webster's and Winrod's work, centering on the Talmud. And regional voices were well represented by periodicals. The West Coast had several, led by C. Leon de Aryan's the *Broom* (San Diego) and William Kullgren's *America Speaks* (Atascadero). Other widely distributed periodicals included Harvey Springer's Colorado-based *Western Voice*, Court Asher's the *X-Ray* (Muncie, Indiana), E. J. Garner's *Publicity* (Wichita, Kansas), the Crusading Mothers of Philadelphia's *Cradle of Liberty*, and North Carolina senator Robert Rice Reynolds's the *Vindicator*.

With a decent number of prolific conspiracy propagators to examine, their psychological makeup is easier to assess. While the full-fledged delusional thinking that marked the theorists is rare among the propagators (Eugene Sanctuary's ideas about conspirators' using their psychic powers to organize is the stand-out exception to the rule), something between delusional and just bad thinking is common.[2] As one example, seriously bad (and self-serving) thinking abounds on the question of antisemitism itself. The claim that one is, despite the evidence, not an antisemite was well established by Nesta Webster and was used far and wide. A striking example is Robert Edward Edmondson's claim that his "Jew-Exposure Publicity Campaign" was not antisemitic. George Armstrong, in his book about the Rothschild "empire" and its planned "subjugation" of the United States, is at pains to point out that "this book is not written in a spirit of anti-Semitism, for I have Jewish friends that I do not wish to injure." Equally reassuring are Father Coughlin's words appended to a lengthy diatribe against the Jews: "Believe me, my friends, it is in all charity that I speak these words." Eugene Sanctuary offers a more formal disclaimer in *Are These Things So?* where he writes: "Except for a few, neither the author nor anyone he quotes have any personal animosity towards any particular race other than that which is developed by the evidence." Often the authors seem personally affronted by the idea that others might see them as bigots.[3]

The bad thinking really kicks in as denials of antisemitism are couched in defensive terms. Representative Louis McFadden, citing the *Protocols*, blamed the Jews for antisemitism before explaining that he personally was not antisemitic and that "some of my best friends are Jews." A reporter for the Jewish Telegraphic Agency had heard this before: "In precisely the same terminology the most bitter anti-Semite in the entire realm of Hitlerdom, Julius Streicher, told me that at core he was a friend of Jews." Robert Edward Edmondson devoted an eleven-page pamphlet to blaming the Jews for their own persecution. He articulated the thinking implicitly underlying the blame-the-victim argument: "Where there is an effect there must be a cause. There must be an **offensive** Jewism before there can be a **defensive reaction of anti-**

Jewism." Thus, by declaring antisemitism to be "an effect," Edmondson has no trouble coming up with a "cause" that fits his preconceptions. This self-serving notion became so commonplace, conspiracists made it casually to set up further arguments. Coughlin used it to explain an "incident" against one of the newsboys selling his *Social Justice*: "Ever since the days of the Jewish captivity into Egypt and Babylon, . . . the Jewish people have been incited to actions from which they become victims of persecution, actions provoked by the lying of false leaders."[4]

The fact that Jewish organizations fought antisemitism was folded into the conspiracy, which naturally increased the conspiracists' delusion of being victimized themselves, particularly by the B'nai B'rith and its Anti-Defamation League. These organizations were the cornerstone of George Van Horn Moseley's "*Jewish State . . .* operating *within* the United States," in charge of "the espionage work of the Jews." Elizabeth Dilling not only made B'nai B'rith itself the title creature in *The Octopus*, she also likened it explicitly to the Soviet secret police: "The most colossally-financed, 'O.G.P.U. [secret police of the Soviet Union],' coercive spy and propaganda machine in the United States is the pro-Red, anti-Christian B'nai B'rith Anti-Defamation League. . . . Its aim, in which it largely succeeds, is national control, through coercion or inducements of speakers, books, articles, sermons, radio preachers, renting of halls for public meetings—in brief, of American freedom of speech, press, and assembly. It stops at nothing in its efforts to publicly discredit any individual who dares oppose or expose any subversive activity that is Jewish, or who mentions anything unflattering to Jewry."[5] Very likely every hidden hand conspiracist of the day felt persecuted by the Anti-Defamation League (ADL), although there is no evidence that any of them ever suffered much at that organization's hands.

The underlying issue was not the ADL but a high level of paranoia—perhaps not quite matching William Dudley Pelley's, but still serious. Fears of persecution knew no bounds. Remarks such as George Armstrong's in *Rothschild Money Trust* were standard fare: "In writing and publishing this book I am inspired by no other motive than to render a service to my country. I realize that I am taking some risk in doing so—at least that of persecution." More pointedly, William Pelley, in his introduction to Ernest Elmhurst's *World Hoax* accused "some Jews of Manhattan" of financing a campaign to "put me behind bars to silence my writings on this most perilous of all menaces which the United States confronts." Elizabeth Dilling took some pride in her brave declaration that World War II was "a Jewish war" since, "I don't doubt that I will be sent to a concentration camp but I will not be silenced." C. Leon de Aryan of San Diego was subject to threats over the telephone from Communists—he could tell they were Communists, de Aryan told an investigating committee, by the "guttural sound" of their voices. And Gerald L. K. Smith interrupted a string of accusations against FDR to make a personal observation: "The top of the list of men Roosevelt wanted to imprison was Gerald L.K. Smith. . . . He had enough power and enough evil intent to do it. But I say without embarrassment or blush that God just wouldn't let him do it. There is no other way I have of explaining how I escaped either being shot or imprisoned, or both, by this evil man whom I have never ceased to expose."[6] Beyond paranoia, such fears appear to be steeped in narcissism, especially the belief that you are so much on the minds of the conspirators that they will stop at nothing to keep your vitally important revelations from the public. Perceived persecution could even increase narcissism. One assessment of Elizabeth Dilling as a prominent representative of the mothers' movement, concluded: "Evincing the desire for martyrdom that characterized several of the mothers' leaders, Dilling relished the persecution she received, taking it as a sign that she was accomplishing something."[7]

Vindication through persecution seems evident in the more severe paranoid fantasies that pop up in the writings and speech of the conspiracists as they took the idea of their enemies' stopping at nothing to its logical conclusion. Howland Spencer, in an Ulster County, New York, newspaper editorial, told readers of "*dark forces* arrayed against us" in the form of the administration's neutrality bill. This bill had been the subject of a "warning" by journalist Frank Simonds, but "before the ink was dry upon his warning, *Frank Simonds was dead*. His death was sudden—and one wonders again at the curse, 'Oppose Roosevelt, anddie.' . . . With Frank Simonds' keen and experienced brain suddenly stopped, the conspirators' 'administration neutrality bill' was pushed before the Senate Foreign Relations Committee. *Who wrote this bill? Who but Bernard Baruch himself.*"[8] When Senator Dwight Morrow of New Jersey, a well-regarded politician and former ambassador, died in his sleep in 1931, William Pelley sent out a confidential official "despatch [*sic*]" reading: "In America there are hundreds of men who see nothing extraordinary that Senator Morrow 'happened' to be stricken fatally the day after his attendance at a Jewish banquet."[9]

In the same spirit, General George Van Horn Moseley, in his testimony before the Dies Committee, read from "one of those highly confidential reports" he claimed to receive. Although not quite clear, the report seems to describe a plot headed by investment banker Lewis Strauss against Moseley and his ally General Malin Craig:

> This, Gentlemen, is the Meranus Plan. It might interest you to know that we have tried to find Moseley's price. We even tried to arrange a meeting in Sir Bill's office, but were unsuccessful. Other means will be used to render him harmless, as we cannot tolerate his actions. He is becoming a menace to us. . . .
>
> . . . Our enemy, Gen. Craig, will soon retire. If after he does he should suddenly, due to acquiring heart trouble, or because of acute indigestion of some sort, change his address to—Arlington! We would be well rid of him. We cannot afford any more Moseleys!"

Moseley's testimony was interrupted by his associate Charles B. Hudson, who knocked Moseley's water glass over and shouted, "This water might have been poisoned by the Hidden Hand!" This may have been a theatrical gesture, but years later, Hudson claimed that "FDR retired Craig and told him to keep his mouth shut. Craig did not live long, and Moseley was poisoned at a New York City banquet, and only rushing to his hotel and using a stomach pump which he carried due to threats he had received, saved his life."[10] If we believe Hudson's anecdote, General Moseley actually traveled with a stomach pump. On another occasion, Agnes Waters, on being ejected for disrupting a House committee hearing, complained, "I had heart attacks after. I feel sure this was a deliberately planned attempt to murder me." And in one of the more remarkable instances of this kind, Robert Edward Edmondson, writing in his capacity as an investment economist to Chief Justice Charles Evans Hughes about monetary cases before the Supreme Court, felt compelled to add: "It is a singular and sinister fact that those who, like the late Speaker Rainey, have been active in a monetary or anti- otherwise, have in a number of cases either died suddenly or have become seriously ill without apparent reason."[11]

A side effect of narcissism may reveal itself among negative attitudes such as mistrust and alienation. Given the nature of the conspiracy being promulgated, it is not at all surprising that none of the conspiracists shows any trust in the government. It is similarly not hard to believe that, to the degree that they imagine the press, religious groups, and schools being infiltrated, they show considerable suspicion of these institutions as well. Fairly regularly, however, conspiracists evidenced mistrust of, alienation from, and even contempt for the public at large— the very people they were trying to reach. The frustration of trying to motivate a comatose populace marks the starting point of alienation. Elizabeth Dilling, for example, in *The Red Network*, divides the American public into two groups, the "professional patriots," originally a term of disparagement that Dilling embraced, and the rest. She then singles out for thanks "those 'patrioteers' who have aided and encouraged the author in her effort to bring the sound but still sleeping portion of the American public the truth about the Communist-Socialist world conspiracy."[12]

Gerald Winrod was more pessimistic about the efficacy of bringing the truth to a sleeping public. "Not until the storm breaks," he wrote in 1935, "do the sleeping masses awake, yawn, stir themselves and look at the wreckage and carnage, after it is too late to help matters." In his only book, *The New Deal Goose Step*, Carl Mote found a similar problem with the masses, compounded by the fact that they were allowed to vote. While other writers were of the opinion that a "revolutionary dictatorship" could be forestalled by keeping FDR from a third term, he thinks this unlikely: "The masses who have already enjoyed the bounties of the state for five years are badly spoiled and will use their political power, which universal suffrage and our party system invite, to prevent any major abatement of the bounties. No way of escape from steadily increasing bounties has been divulged and we only save ourselves now from the misery of contemplating our *ultimate* disaster— and the abyss—by practicing the ways of an ostrich in a sandstorm."[13] Not realizing their true interests, the masses amount to no more than "Gentile dupes." As William Dudley Pelley argued, Jewish labor leaders "can get the dumb workingman to do the battling" so the Jews can take over. If the "violence-gesture," as Pelley called it, is unsuccessful, "the poor gullible workingman can be left to 'take the rap' while the Jew gets off scot-free." Trying to explain the situation to such people is fruitless, as Ernest Elmhurst relates in *World Hoax*: "Determined to put a halt to your 'Nazi Jew-baiting,' Mr. Average Citizen stalks off and will have no more to do with you. His colossal ignorance about what is going on is not only tragic. It is heartbreakingly pathetic." Court Asher's weekly newspaper the *X-Ray* summed up the plight of the people in a headline: "We Are Herded as Sheep." Even after Roosevelt's death and the end of the war, Gerald L. K. Smith was still bitter about "the great stupid mass of uninformed illiterates who were taught by *Government-bought* and *treasury-paid-for* propaganda to worship the late FDR."[14]

All in all, a profile of these early conspiracy propagators emerges out of their writings and speeches, even though they vary considerably in their characteristics. Some, notably Joseph Kamp and Allan Zoll, were widely accused of promoting the conspiracy to antisemites as a moneymaking operation.[15] Others, especially later in the thirties, were pragmatic mouthpieces for the Nazis and did not deviate from a simple script blaming the Jews for everything. But many were possessed of the same fervor that motivated the theorists. It is often easiest to identify such driven souls by their continuing activism even well after World War II had so badly harmed their cause. Winrod, Dilling, Smith, Armstrong, and others became, if anything, even more extreme and vituperative.

The exception was William Pelley, who had been imprisoned for treason and insurrection in 1942. Pelley abandoned political activism as a condition of parole in 1950 and turned his attention back to the occult.[16]

Even with individual variations, however, some characteristics are uniform. The propagators share the delusions of the theorists and, sometimes, add to them. Dilling was so fixated on Sigmund Freud as a hidden hand influence that she inspected library copies of his books to determine how "well-thumbed" they were. Alexander Cloyd Gill's obsession with youth organizations earned him a position as Joseph Kamp's research director. E. J. Garner regularly devoted space in *Publicity* to tout his friend John R. Brinkley—who posed as a physician specializing in "male rejuvenation therapy," in which goat glands were randomly embedded into men's bodies.[17]

The propagators also come across as alienated, hostile, and intensely mistrustful. The level of invective across their articles and books is astonishing. Most of this is aimed at the Jews and at their party (the JEW-O-CRATS) and its ideology (JEWocracy). But much of it is leveled at the dupes, especially highly regarded intellectuals. Eugene Sanctuary devotes five pages and all of Protocol two to the threat posed by "the politico-scientific professor" Albert Einstein, whose popularity can be attributed to "the power of the Hidden Hand." Elizabeth Dilling's *Red Network* covers the same ground while also arguing that Einstein's theory of relativity is fallacious and that other scientists "evidently figure that the best thing to do is keep quiet and leave him undisturbed on his self-erected scientific throne."[18]

Paranoia stands out clearly in the work of conspiracy propagators. The almost constant undertone of persecution and victimhood stemming from the narcissism so many conspiracists convey, combined with the reactions most people have to it, reveal visceral fears. Intimidation, imprisonment, physical attack, and murder plots frequent the world in which conspiracists live. It is in keeping with a narcissistic personality that persecution contains an element of schadenfreude or even martyrdom. In a not unfriendly assessment of Elizabeth Dilling, one writer quoted Dilling herself as ready to "serve the cause of Christianity and Americanism in whatever way is best, dead or alive, in jail or out, smeared or vindicated." Dilling reportedly took delight in being "a martyr willing to sacrifice herself for a higher purpose."[19]

The negative psychology affected conspiracy propagators' political beliefs. At the beginning of the 1930s it was still possible to detect an element of old-style populist economics among the conspiracists. Early in his career, William Dudley Pelley organized a Foundation for Christian Economics, a compound of mysticism and neo-populism. Gerald L. K. Smith, before turning to the Right, had been closely associated with Huey Long's Share the Wealth crusade. And, as late as 1938, Father Coughlin's *Social Justice* was still touting populist movements such as the Ham and Eggs pension plan.[20] By the end of the decade, however, the residue of populism was gone, swamped by antisemitism, isolationism, and fascism.

This shift, by a group that was reactionary and nativist to begin with, seems to place the hidden hand conspirators solidly on the conservative end of the political spectrum. But the reality may not be that straightforward. In the breakthrough study of the authoritarian personality, Theodore Adorno and his colleagues came up with the term "pseudo-conservative" to describe a person whose thinking is conventional yet chaotic, who yields easily to authority while trying to dominate his perceived inferiors. Applying this idea to the conspiracists of his day, Richard Hofstadter characterized them as a group who, "in the name of upholding traditional American values and institutions and defending them against more or less fictitious dangers, consciously or unconsciously aims at their abolition."[21] Such people, Hofstadter noted, have little to do with traditional conservatism. They are clearly anchored on the Right end of the political spectrum but seem in some important way to have drifted off the spectrum entirely.

The Slow Decline of the Hidden Hand

The onset of World War II began the inexorable contraction of hidden hand conspiracism. Hard-core fascists did keep up the rhetoric, Major

General George Moseley telling a Philadelphia "National Defense Meeting" in early 1939 how the "war now proposed is for the purpose of establishing Jewish hegemony throughout the world." William Dudley Pelley took the position that the United States should not fight on behalf of "Mongolic Judaists."[22] In 1939, Martin Dies, head of the House Committee on Un-American Activities, had publicly demanded that the attorney general prosecute bundists, causing George Deatherage to claim that Dies had "sold out to the Jewish bankers." In late 1939, a last-ditch effort to keep America out of the war emerged with the politically broad America First organization. But even this group's most prominent spokesman, Charles Lindbergh Jr., eventually began to sound like an antisemitic conspiracist.[23]

Among the more strident conspiracists, rhetoric became more pointed. Lists of Jews began to focus on everyday people who had somehow wormed their way into the government. Fueled by the Dies Committee, Joseph Kamp exposed these members of "America's fifth column"—a term from the Spanish Civil War that described organized spies and saboteurs. Kamp's first list, headed oddly by secretary of the Virgin Islands Robert Morss Lovett, included almost no policy makers but a great many low-level employees with obviously Jewish names: Social Security Board stenographer Frieda Cohen, for example, or DC Juvenile Court probation officer Max Kopelman. Kamp never accused these people of anything; he merely used their names as window dressing for his general charges of Communist infiltration of government. The 579 Red fifth columnists listed by Kamp in 1940 swelled to over four thousand "Communists, Communist sympathizers, and fellow travelers" by 1942.[24]

Anti-Jewish rhetoric became more threatening as the war progressed, some of it clearly a reaction to Jewish war refugees. C. Leon de Aryan attacked Jewish refugees who were "scuttling like cockroaches out of Europe. Their international bankers and wholesale murderers and betrayers of France are safely ensconded [sic] in New York and Canada." A group of disgruntled movie industry workers claimed that Jewish refugees were taking all the jobs in Hollywood, blaming this outrage on the "vengeance" of the "Anti-American, shameless Jew producers." William Dudley Pelley predicted that "a coast-to-coast pogrom is inevitably ahead for the Jews of America as more millions of them crowd in with immigration barriers lifted." Joseph "McNazi" McWilliams's address on immigration policy to the Crusaders for Americanism was titled "A Jew-free America." And the Molly Pitchers helped spread a conspiratorial rumor that Secretary of State Cordell Hull planned to ship two million American farmers to Brazil and to give their farms to Jewish immigrants. The group's pamphlet concluded: "Americans have nothing in common with the greedy Jew Bolshevik parasite who would lash us into serfdom and crush us with his might."[25]

Wartime shortages were interpreted as part of the conspiracy against America at different levels of stridency. The relatively restrained *Chicago Tribune* told readers, "Americans are deprived of food in order that the international banker, Lehman, and Stettinius, the son of a Morgan partner, may be established in world trade." Agnes Waters simply wrote off sugar rationing as "Barney Baruch's Jew plot left over from the first World War to communize America."[26] Joseph Kamp's Constitutional Educational League put out a booklet devoted to "the truth about rationing." In keeping with Kamp's predilection for naming names, the author of the booklet, Carter O'Connor, offered up several hapless bureaucrats before settling on the "all-seeing, all-knowing deity" Harold Loeb—senior business specialist with the office of Price Administration ("at $4,600 a year"). Carter did not accuse Loeb of any misdeeds but did spend some time characterizing the man: "Aloof and withdrawn, he broods in the deeper shadows of the Washington jungle.... 'Obstructionist' explorers of the dark swamps of the capital have come across his Signs, read his Portents, or listened to his intonation of the canon of the Future—a future in which all personal liberty, all industrial progress, all institutions of a decent civilization are to be sacrificed to 'world freedom.' ... Loeb is all things to all isms. He is the Infinite Spirit, the Giver of Life, the Oracle of the New World Order."[27]

As England implored the United States to join the war, that nation was folded into the hidden hand. The *Gaelic American*, playing into Irish antipathy for the United Kingdom, blamed British "planners for dictatorship" for food shortages. The supposed "make America hungry" plot by Britain's Israel Jew Moses Sieff was intended to create "chaos to put over totalitarian scheme here." The works of British fascists were used to explain things to Americans. Eugene Sanctuary distributed copies of a "British document" about the takeover by the "alien menace" in that country. Robert Edward Edmondson devoted one of his Jew-Exposure Publicity Campaign leaflets to a letter from Arnold Leese, a British fascist who claimed to be "still at large" and on the run from "Churchill's Jewish OGPU." Leese's message was that the cooperation between Britain and France against Germany was part of a conspiracy "in the Rothschild interest."[28]

The rhetoric became even less restrained as antisemitic conspiracists found themselves under attack from anti-Nazis and even the government. William Pelley's *Liberation* newspaper featured headlines such as "Will It Take a Civil War to End Jew Control?" Pelley also began to argue for the "forcible removal of the Jews from office." General Moseley (who reported that he had been "flayed" by the secretary of war on a trumped up charge of "flagrant disloyalty") looked forward to a patriotic uprising, "which will make the massacres now recorded in history look like peaceful church parades." Even more directly, Agnes Waters favored removing Roosevelt and his cronies from office by shooting them, as this was "easier than to fool with the elections and a lot more certain." Roosevelt's allies in Congress would not be spared Waters's firing squad; she singled out "that Senator Pepper" because he "hangs around with Moscow Jews and Negroes. Also, he is part Indian, I hear. We want real Americans." Joe McWilliams shared his dreams of sweeping the New York streets with machine gun fire as part of his plan "to make this country the paradise that Hitler has made Germany."[29]

Finally the government clamped down on the bundists and their allies in what became known as the Great Sedition Trial. A fiasco from beginning to end, with three rounds of indictments in 1942, 1943, and 1944, the trial was essentially abandoned shortly before the war ended. Some of the defendants used their indictments as fundraising opportunities. The Protestant War Veterans protested the "UnAmerican Persecution of Christian Patriots" in their fundraising letter. Elizabeth Dilling bragged about having been indicted in all three rounds, telling her followers in "a special appeal" for money about her "third annual Jewish B'nai B'rith-inspired New Deal indictment."[30] The trial marked the end of the bund, and some conspiracists abandoned the public arena, but others continued unfazed by prosecution or social obloquy. Henry H. Klein put out a pamphlet version of his own testimony on behalf of Pelley under the title *Republic on Trial: Washington Bar, a Bar to Justice.* Agnes Waters, predicting that she would be elected president in 1944, gloated "then I will take every Jew to the cleaners if I allow him to live at all."[31]

Even as the end of the war was in sight and the postwar world became the topic of the day, this rhetoric did not let up. Pleading "don't stab our boys in the back," the American Mothers of Detroit saw America falling prey to the conspiracy orchestrated by the Cecil Rhodes fund to return the United States to British rule. More typically, the Protestant War Veterans of the United States saw a Jewish conspiracy and, mocking the great sedition trial, offered its own "indictment containing 23 counts wherein the Jew-Communists in furtherance of world domination have conspired to wreck the American Republic and enslave its people under a Jewish-Communist-Dictatorship." Whether the "Jew-Communists" were actually guilty of this conspiracy—"YOU THE JURY MUST DECIDE!"—hidden hand conspirators were already moving on to the Jews' plans to control events after the war. Homer Maertz "unmasked" the Jewish conspiracy behind the efforts in San Francisco to establish an international organization.[32] And once again Agnes Waters staked out the most repellant position by writing to bereaved parents of soldiers killed in the war: "How long, how long are we going to permit our men to be slain to save the Jewish empires all over the world? Did you know that certain Jews by the hundreds are being trained to follow the armies and to be the ARMY OF OCCUPATION with all the prostrated nations under their control? These men will be the rulers of the Army of Industrial Occupation. Is that what your boy was fighting for?"[33]

While the careers of most of the conspiracists who were active in the 1930s came to an end during World War II, there were those who persisted. Lyrl Clark Van Hyning was one of these; she continued to publish

Women's Voice into the 1960s, exposing the presence of the hidden hand in article after article, since "the one battle in which every American should enlist is cleaning the orientals out of our Government." Van Hyning also discovered the related conspiracy of Freemasonry's "Luciferian Doctrine" but returned to the Jews as the main problem: Americans had to "throw out the International bankers by a return to our own money—no more interest to private-Federal Banks—no more fighting their wars!" Her version of the new world order was the "Jewish World State" with its motto: Ordo ab Chao (Jewish order out of chaos). Able to detect the hidden pattern in any array of events, Van Hyning found it suspicious that four of "the world's most powerful and influential Jews" had each resigned from some position within a fairly short period of time. "Your editor," Van Hyning wrote, "will be interested to learn what is behind these withdrawals."[34]

Others who stayed the course included Gerald Winrod. As early as 1946, Winrod published an attack on Communism that essentially rehashed his hidden hand argument from 1933. Still fixated on Weishaupt, Winrod also maintained that the Illuminati's conspiracy "has continued as a tangible organization, down to the present hour. It is operating secretly in the United States, and must be mercilessly exposed." Gerald L. K. Smith continued berating FDR, notwithstanding the president's death. Using the conspiracist's standard rhetorical device of attributing his ideas to unnamed others, Smith pondered the "super mystery" of Roosevelt's death: "Those who hold to the murder theory insist that Roosevelt was the tool of a terrible international cabal. They felt he had fulfilled his purpose. They knew he was in bad health and they feared that he might make some horrible blunder growing out of delirium or senility that might expose their hand and spoil years of successful and satanic plotting."[35] Around the same time, anonymous campaigns based on the hidden hand sprang up. There had been some of this during the war, when bogus leaflets and flyers appeared in one city or another. In 1941, a leaflet titled "Special Notice to All Jews" declared Jews exempt from military service "in accordance with the highest interpretation of Judaism." During the 1943 mayor's race in Philadelphia, a "Vote Jewish" flyer from the nonexistent B'nai B'rith Non-Sectarian Voters' League declared: "Gentiles have proven themselves too stupid. This is our golden opportunity!" A postwar campaign along these same lines featured letters mass mailed to newspapers around the country. One letter, supposedly from the World League of Liberal Jews, Western Branch, Los Angeles, California, began: "In the near future, when the Jewish people take over the rule of the United States."[36]

By the 1950s, the hidden hand conspiracy was showing signs of deterioration. Leon de Aryan expanded his roster of "secret Jewish conspirators" to include Charles de Gaulle, Winston Churchill, and Pope Pius XII. Robert Edward Edmondson reorganized dozens of his leaflets into a defense of his 1938 trial for libel and the Great Sedition Trial. Designated as an "official" document—"a Constitutional 'Petition to Congress'"— Edmondson claimed that "its legality cannot be successfully challenged."[37] General Moseley remained active, castigating the chancellor of the University of Georgia for supporting the National Conference of Christians and Jews when he should have been trying to get the Jews to "abandon their un-American world-wide plans." Robert Williams exposed President Truman's health care proposal as the work of "Red Jews" and "wholly alien to the Anglo-Saxon-Nordic individual whose race grew to greatness . . . because it produced a high percentage of persons who relied on themselves and would have no master." And the National Blue Star Mothers attacked the fundraising entity Community Chest as a Zionist organization devoted to destroying Christianity in America.[38]

Many people continued to expose "the Boss," the "Machiavellian" Marxist immigrant who "rules the Supreme Court with an iron hand": Felix Frankfurter. Through ten editions spanning seven years, Robert H. Williams's *Know Your Enemy* depicted on its cover photographs of "Stalin and the 'Secret Government of the United States'": Senator Lehman of New York, Felix Frankfurter, and Henry Morgenthau Jr. (even though Morgenthau had retired as secretary of the treasury in 1945). Even at the very end of the Eisenhower administration, one could find lists of the "Asiatic Marxist Jews"—ranging from the venerable Bernard Baruch to Albert Einstein—behind the "Coming Red Dictatorship." Remarkably, this practice lasted into the 1960s, with John Kennedy's administration reviving it among diehard opponents of civil rights. The National States' Rights Party's "latest up to date count" found twenty-six Jews in important positions in the Kennedy White House, "a completely Jew dominated conspiracy running the U.S.A."[39]

This standard version of the conspiracy declined slowly, becoming the antisemitic version of Cold War anti-Communism. It is easy to see the decline in Benjamin Harrison Freedman's 1961 speech before "a patriotic audience." After detailing how Louis Brandeis tricked President Wilson into joining World War I and spelling out how the Jews declared a "Holy War" on Germany in the 1930s, Freedman takes a couple of potshots at the Federal Reserve and the income-tax amendment of 1912. He finishes with an extended exposition on the Khazar theory of the Jews, concluding, "There isn't one Jew who's a Semite. They're all Turkothean Mongoloids." All in all, Freedman's badly dated talk covered events ranging from twenty-five to some eight hundred years back.[40] Revilo P. Oliver was still using the standard conspiracy when he wrote his infamous essay explaining the Kennedy assassination as the work of the Communists, who were dissatisfied with the speed with which Kennedy was delivering the nation into their hands. In follow-up speeches, Oliver, after disparaging the cult of "Massah Jack," returned to the core idea of FDR as Frankfurter's stooge.[41] The hidden hand was becoming stodgy and dated, and even though new versions were published occasionally, by the 1960s the overt antisemitism of the conspiracy put it well outside respectability, even for most of the right wing.[42]

Hidden hand ideas did not disappear but largely became bound up with one-worlder conspiracism. Newer versions come out from time to time: A. Ralph Epperson's *The Unseen Hand* updated the conspiracy to 1985. William T. Still's *New World Order: The Ancient Plan of Secret Societies* basically reiterates Nesta Webster's early work. Robert Henry Goldsborough warned that Soviet premier Gorbachev's perestroika reforms are part of the conspiracy. And Alex Christopher's *Pandora's Box: The Ultimate 'Unseen Hand' behind the New World Order* is a twenty-first-century version of the standard hidden hand conspiracy disguised as "a one-of-a-kind novel."[43]

7

FROM NEO-NAZI TO WHITE SUPREMACIST CONSPIRACISM

> Bitter conflict between the Christian creed and loyalty to the White
> Race convinced me more than anything that Christianity had to go, and
> that the White Race needed to replace it with a sane, basic religion of
> its own.
>
> Ben Klassen, *Dedicated to Posterity*

American politics just after World War II is remembered primarily for its anti-Communism. The Cold War, the Iron Curtain, and Russian spies all contributed to a fearful Red Scare and to the rise of McCarthyism. The years from 1945 to 1960 saw a diminution in accusations against Jews, despite occasional headlines like "Yiddish Marxists Plot USA Defeat." A 1960 University of Illinois study estimated a thousand groups distributing "great quantities of right-wing literature."[1] But how much of this right-wing output was conspiracist in nature? Just as it had been possible to oppose Roosevelt and the New Deal without being a conspiracist, it was quite possible to be a vehement anti-Communist without recourse to conspiracism.

Most of the literature examined in the Illinois study contained at least some conspiracist sentiment, enough to lead the authors to note the long tradition on the right of belief in "an international conspiracy, . . . possibly centuries old, which is destined to destroy our civilization." They saw this conspiracism along a continuum, ranging from the American Legion's unsurprising determination to "protect our country from penetration by those who would subvert it," all the way to Admiral John Crommelin's manifesto announcing his candidacy for governor of Alabama: "Whereas: The ultimate objectives of the Communist-Jewish conspirators is [sic] to use their world-wide control of money to destroy Christianity and set up a World Government in the framework of the United Nations, and erase all national boundaries and eliminate all racial distinction except the so-called Jewish race, which will then become the masters—with their headquarters in the State of Israel and in the UN in New York, and from these two communication centers rule a slave-like world population of copper-colored human mongrels. . . ."[2] However, a similar study that focused on right-wing military officers posited two distinct types of anti-Communism: one based on a rational assessment of the threat, and a second group with views "growing out of a mood of frustration . . . a form of political paranoia" in which the problem "is defined as one of evil conspiracies." This second group was what Richard Hofstadter had in mind with his concept of "pseudo-conservatives."[3]

The connection between anti-Communism and conspiracism cannot be specified exactly. There is no point at which exaggerated fear of Soviet subversion became unambiguously conspiratorial, and examples such as Cardinal Spellman's essay "Communism Is Un-American" are hard to classify as one or the other, but in practice the onset of conspiracism was generally clear. Those not conspiracy-minded might well warn of subversives worming their way into important political positions, but conspiracists would see a Communist-controlled government and would imagine the peril to all other social institutions. Nowhere is this clearer than in the publications of the John Birch Society, begun in 1958 by Robert Welch. At the society's organizational meeting, Welch laid out his beliefs: "Communists are much further advanced and much more deeply entrenched than is realized by even the most serious students of the danger among the anti-Communists. . . . I personally have been studying the problem increasingly for about nine years, and practically full time for the past three years. . . . Yet every day I run into some whole new area, where the Communists have been penetrating and working quietly for years, until they are now in virtual control of everything that is done in that slice or corner of our national life."[4] Beyond its near total domination of the federal government, Communism's "virtual control" of American life was said to be staggering. Norman Dodd, former director of research for the Reece Committee, which had investigated tax-exempt foundations, exposed the "effective contribution to Communism" made by the Ford Foundation and the Carnegie Endowment, among others. The media, notably the "controlled New York papers and radio," were also vital parts of the Communist conspiracy. Other notorious hotbeds of Communism included labor unions, the ACLU, and the motion picture business.[5]

But in keeping with the tendency of conspiracism to expand, many unlikely institutions were also exposed as communistic. As in the 1930s, religious institutions were subjected to conspiracist attention. Harvey Springer railed against the "rape of fundamentalism by the Federal Council of (Anti) Christ." A self-appointed watchdog committee found a "pink fringe" on the Methodist Church. H. L. Birum, among others, claimed the National Council of Churches was saturating its Revised Standard Version of the Bible with Communist propaganda as part of its "militant program of SPIRITUAL BOLSHEVISM."[6] On the secular side, a "giant cell of political radicalism" (actually comprising organizations as dull as the National Municipal League, which united various city reform groups throughout the country) was pursuing a plan to "plunge Americans into the bondage of political and economic slavery." The American Legion reported that even "veteran anti-communists" were "frankly baffled" by the success of *Consumer Reports*, since the magazine was put out by a well-known "Communist Party front." And there were exposés of organizations ranging from the YWCA to the Community Chest.[7]

While most anti-Communists looked to the Kremlin as the source of the subversion, conspiracists were more likely to summon up Karl

Marx himself, who was portrayed often as a puppet of the Illuminati. Some bypassed Marx in favor of Clinton Roosevelt, whose 1841 essay on the science of government was billed as "the plagiarized communist teachings of Adam Weishaupt, a renegade Jesuit, and the substance of the Communist Manifesto."[8] Equally important to conspiracists were the early twentieth-century progressives, especially those with internationalist leanings, and Fabian socialists. Depictions of these individuals blurred the lines between liberalism, socialism, and Communism, making it easier to throw them all into a single conspiracy. They also served to link leftist ideas with a suspicious cosmopolitanism. And last, as the embodiment of the new, highly educated class of political and social leaders, they were used to besmirch intellectuals, academics, experts, and other elites.[9]

Anti-Communist conspiracism proper did not outlast the Cold War, but it contributed to other conspiratorial themes that did. In combination with the residue of the hidden hand, anti-Communist conspiracism played a role in the development new world order conspiracism. But it also provided some grist for the mill of neo-Nazi conspiracism.

Residual Nazi Conspiracism

The career of the clique of conspiracists dedicated to Nazism is both clearly defined and distinct from all other strands of conspiracism, though it shares wellsprings with other racist conspiracies. A 1937 American Guard leaflet appealed both to whites ("Let us again adhere to the ideals of the White race.") and to "Gentiles!" who might not realize that Jews "actually amount to an economic dictatorship." During the war, pro-Nazi conspiracists held fast to the view that Germany was the victim of a Jewish plot to trick Britain and America into waging war against it, destroying not just Germany but ultimately the United States as well. Charles Hudson, one of the more hyperbolic conspiracists, explained that, by volunteering as air wardens, Jews "have access and full opportunity to get an absolute check (on personal firearms, etc.), block by block, of all citizens and non-citizens. Think it thru!"[10]

Immediately after the war, one event and one nonevent bonded this group in defense of Germany. The nonevent was Treasury Secretary Morgenthau's plan to destroy German industrial capacity altogether in order to prevent it from waging war again. While this plan was quite punitive, it was rejected by Roosevelt and never went into effect; still, conspiracists wrote about "Morgenthauists" as though they existed. The actual event was the Nuremberg Trials of 1945-46, disparaged as a kangaroo court for putting on trial "Germans who were doing nothing else but allowing **their** rulers to do as they did."[11]

Conspiracists saw the postwar plight of Germany as a product of the Jews' ongoing war on civilization. Conde McGinley's newspaper *Think Weekly* featured articles such as "Slave-Laboring German Prisoners-of-War" and "Ravishing the Conquered Women of Europe." The writings of eccentric Swedish Nazi Einar Åberg—much of which declared the allies and their Jewish masters to be the true "war criminals"—were distributed in the United States. So were the ideas of Ludwig Fritsch, who saw the Germans as America's "greatest benefactors." Only "Roosevelt's advisors," Fritsch claimed, hated the Nazis: "Only thus is understandable Roosevelt's demand of 'unconditional surrender' and the most inhuman 'Morgenthau Plan,' starving to death a great nation, because in the heads and hearts of our leading men all vestige of Christianity disappeared and Judaism and Paganism prevailed."[12] Francis Parker Yockey, whose vision was more encompassing than most, decried the "post-war annihilation program" for European civilization generally.[13] Not surprisingly, the victimization of the Germans was traced back to the *Protocols*, "a blueprint which forecasts the drama of destruction of all our moral and spiritual values . . . reaching its climax in the tragedy of Nuremberg." Kenneth Goff pushed back the origin of the "conspiracy to destroy Germany" even farther, to 1776, the year Adam Weishaupt founded the Bavarian Illuminati. Contemporary connections were made as well. Lyrl Van Hyning's *Women's Voice* portrayed an industrial explosion near Houston in April, 1947 as cosmic payback for the "Roosevelt-Morgentheau-Frankfurter plan." As late as 1960, Aryan diehards were still claiming that "'liberals' plot the end of a Teutonic nation."[14]

As Germany rebuilt and its "plight" diminished, leaders of the pro-Nazi conspiracy turned their attention to the United States. In establishing the National Renaissance Party, James H. Madole outlined his plan to create a new America, "subordinating the interests of the individual citizen to the interests of the national community as a whole. Whereas our doctrine of Racial Nationalism welds the nation into a united and compatible Iron Front based on the ancient ties of blood and race, the poisonous Jewish doctrines of Democracy, Liberalism and Communism seek to foment class warfare, disunity and revolution within the borders of all national states." Liberal democracy, Madole had written, was based on "mythical claims" of "Jewish intellectuals" such as Adam "Weisshaupt" and Karl Marx. Its founding doctrine of equality was merely a ruse perpetrated by Jews to pollute the Aryans' "pure blood and creative ingenuity by mixing sexually with Zulu Hottentots and Asiatic ancestor worshippers."[15]

Many pro-Nazi conspiracists published in Conde McGinley's *Think Weekly* (later, *Common Sense*), including many hidden hand conspiracists. Eugene Sanctuary, George Van Horn Moseley (and his sidekick Charles B. Hudson), and Elizabeth Dilling were all contributors. Virtually every article expounded on the Jewish conspiracy. One front-page plea, signed by McGinley, Dilling, and Lyrl Clark Van Hyning, urged readers to flood Congress with letters and telegrams that would combat the undying influence of Bernard Baruch: "Before every fresh holocaust BARNEY comes before Congress for legislation in preparation for harnessing and slaughtering 'the people who are like an ass-slaves [*sic*] who are considered the property of their master'—the Talmudists."[16]

As blatant neo-Nazis, these conspiracists were never in the mainstream even of the conspiratorial right wing. Remarkably, they managed to move still further afield by embracing the Soviet Union in the wake of Stalin's antisemitic purges and the highly publicized Prague trials, which targeted accused Trotskyists. Seemingly attracted to the sheer authoritarian antisemitism of these events, pro-Nazi conspiracists interpreted them as setbacks to "the death plans being hatched for European culture in Washington by American Jewry." The subsequent execution of Lavrenty Beria (head of the Soviet secret police), whom conspiracists said had been "designated by the Baruchs [?] to fill Trotsky's place in the near future," was an additional blow to the establishment of "the Jewish Imperium."[17] Consistent with their newfound appreciation for Stalin, and like Madole, these conspiracists openly called democracy a fraud, perpetrated by the Jews: "a small, fanatical nationalist minority which has subjugated the world."[18] In 1953, Madole's solution to "poisonous" democracy was the abolition of parliamentary government. He fleshed out this view in 1956: "Hitler, Franco, Mussolini and Peron knew that democracy was invariably an instrument in the hand of the International Jew. They knew that 'freedom and democracy' meant only freedom for the Jew to exploit and terrorize his host people hence their first move was to abolish the traditional 'democratic parties and institutions' which had become political brothels for the most shameful prostitution of the peoples interests."[19] To the neo-Nazis, democracy was not merely a fraud, it was the equivalent of a social disease.

Francis Parker Yockey and James H. Madole: Neo-Nazi Conspiracism

The transformation of postwar Nazism from Hitler-loving groups that "essentially imitated the past with uniformed cadres, swastika flags, and marches" into something focused more on the future can be attributed to a pair of actual conspiracy theorists.[20] Francis Parker Yockey, still a cult figure today, had been associated with William Dudley Pelley's Silver Shirts before the war. His intellectual inspiration, however, was Oswald Spengler's 1918 work *The Decline of the West*, a book as pessimistic as its title suggests. Spengler's treatment of the Jews was no worse than his treatment of most people and his ideas were scorned by the Nazis prior to his death in 1936—which is to say that *Decline of the West* was not a Nazi (or even fascist) manifesto. Francis Yockey's 1948 opus *Imperium* altered Spengler's ideas, linking them to Nazidom by reinterpreting the conflict Spengler has limned between the West's "Faustian" soul and the Middle East's "Babylonian-Semitic" soul. To Spengler, "Jewry represented a fateful form of 'cultural distortion'" that undercut the West's imperial destiny. For Yockey, "Jews vengefully exploited the new cultural forms of money thinking, rationalism, materialism, capitalism and democracy to destroy the traditions of the West and the authority of its old elites."[21]

Yockey saw Europe undergoing a non-Christian, slow-motion apocalypse. His ideas about the United States, however, were clearly affected by the secret government conspiracism of his youth. *Imperium* depicts a Jewish "invasion" beginning in the 1880s that replaced America's "organic individualism" with Jewish "Rationalism." The only part of the country to understand and fight the invasion was the South, which was protected by an "aristocratic traditional life-feeling." Yet when the South fought back through the Klan "as an expression of the reaction of the American organism to the presence of foreign matter," it was branded "'Un-American' by the propaganda organs of America." *Imperium* wraps up with standard secret government arguments about the Federal Reserve and the Jews' "seizure of power" with the New Deal "so that thenceforward elections were mere pageantry."[22] Yockey's combination of secret government conspiracy and distorted Spenglerism provided an avowedly non-Christian platform for gloom-and-doom racists and antisemites such as Revilo P. Oliver and William Luther Pierce.

James H. Madole does not have the intellectual reputation of Spengler or even Yockey. He did, however, become known as the "father of postwar occult-fascism." He resurrected Helena Blavatsky's nineteenth-century theosophical ideas, to which he contributed his own interpretations of ancient Vedic Hinduism. Blavatsky's theory of five planetary eras, each dominated by a "race," was vaguely compatible with Spengler's succession of "organic" civilizations. Madole believed that Aryans had once been—and should again be—worshipped as "White Gods" by the other races. He saw the Hindu caste system as the ideal vehicle to re-create an elite white government such as the one that had made Atlantis's civilization great.[23] In this way, Theosophy infused racism into Spengler's portrait of the West's decline, while its stern and hierarchical doctrine buttressed Madole's Aryan aversion to Christianity as too soft and egalitarian. Occult fascism was further distinguished by its opposition to capitalism, which followed from a more fundamental opposition to the Enlightenment and even the Industrial Revolution.[24] Stalinism, however, was acceptable, as it was now fighting against Jewish democracy.

Yockey and Madole's racist and mystical appropriation of Spengler's explanation of history amounted to a nostalgic attempt to bring back the preindustrial, racially homogenous culture of Europe, governed not by monarchs or elected officials but by an Aryan elite.[25] Standing in the way of this vision were the modern inventions, democracy and capitalism—and behind these, of course, the Jews. Madole's *National Renaissance Bulletin* asked, "America, Which Way?" over drawings indicating the choice: the "proud and free" Aryan family standing on a hill or the "Decadent Jewish-Liberal Democracy" embodied by the skid row prostitute smoking in front of a sign reading "BUY ISRAEL BONDS."[26]

The impact of occult fascism on conspiratorial thinking was narrow but important, particularly in how it emphasized authoritarian toughness, as in one of Madole's pamphlets: "Only the superbly efficient totalitarian economic systems of Fascists, National Socialist, and Communist regimes are adaptable to the strain of TOTAL WAR as practiced in the 20th century. . . . The spirit of democracy is a glorification of weakness and cowardly conduct. It glorifies the coward instead of the fighter, it raises feeble weaklings to leadership rather than a trained, iron-hard, and youthful elite."[27] In a tribute to Yockey's *Imperium*, Revilo Oliver not only warned against soft-hearted "'liberal intellectuals' or other children" reading it but also hoped that it would not "fall into the hands of tenderhearted Conservatives who want to Love Everybody." Disparaging "those dear ladies," Oliver allowed that they may have "noble souls, but they are much too good for this world." Thanks to Yockey and Madole's blurring of Spengler's ideas, Oliver attributed to Spengler a "masterful discussion" of the need to rid society of the Jewish money power. The problem, as Oliver saw it, was that "our fat, complacent Goy citizenry want to keep the nineteenth century going forever; but the twentieth century will make mincemeat of those who want to live in the past. This is the century of steel rather than gold; the century of war rather than peace; violence rather than order; of young men rather than old men. In short, this is the NAZI CENTURY."[28]

This farrago of ideas points toward another extremely influential Yockey-Madole contribution to conspiracism: what Michael Barkun has termed an "improvisational" approach to conspiracy building. Abandoning even minimal conventional limitations, the improvisational style "is characterized by a relentless and seemingly indiscriminate borrowing." Spengler's understanding of "the growth and decay of civilizations according to organic principles," Yockey's virulent antisemitism, anti-Americanism, and Silver Shirt militarism, and Madole's Vedic-pagan, Theosophist-inspired vision of an authoritarian utopia constituted an unprecedented mixture of previously unrelated ideas. This practice was picked up on by conspiracists of all stripes over the next several years and today poses considerable difficulty in making sense of many conspiracy theories.[29]

Most of those drawn to the Yockey-Madole ideology were racists and antisemites first and conspiracists only second. Yockey was a loner, but Madole was deeply involved in a network of Nazis and, later, other racist groups—Karl Allen Jr.'s White Party of America, Robert DePugh's Minutemen, George Leggett's United Nordic Federation, and others. Their conspiracism grew primarily out of a feeling that the white race had been betrayed, and they reveled in the widespread offense this view could cause. In an advertisement for its edition of *Imperium*, the National Youth Alliance bragged that the book offended black Muslims, the mainstream press, and the John Birch Society—that is, pretty much the entire political spectrum. From the beginning, Yockeyites had disparaged both "ignorant liberals" and conservatives—whether "Establishment" or "anarchistic Libertarian."[30]

Yockey's ideas had a strong impact on Willis Carto, a major right-wing force for years and the leading organizer of Holocaust denial in America. Founder of the Liberty Lobby, associated with at least half a dozen neo-fascist organizations, and publisher of periodicals ranging from the *Washington Observer* to *American Zionist Watch*, Carto worked with (and often fell out with) right-wing conspiracists from William

Pierce to Ron Paul. Every issue, for Carto, came down to "the political Zionist planners for absolute rule via One World government."[31] The influence of Yockey's preindustrial pastoral Nordic ideal shows through in an appeal to college students to join Carto's openly fascist National Youth Alliance:

> We want to achieve an organic society which will not only protect and perpetuate the great traditional values of Western civilization but will purify the Western world of the degeneracy of communism and liberalism....
>
> ... The media-peddled philosophy-religion of the present System is alien to our people and must be utterly rooted out and eliminated, along with its bearers. We want to safeguard our racial identity by putting an end to the present insanity of forced racial integration....
>
> We want to foster among our people, through the recapture of our information media and our educational system, a new spiritual outlook: the outlook of free men living and working in harmony with nature.

The alliance's first step toward achieving these goals, ahead of even opposing moral degeneracy and "race-defiling efforts of the System," was "Opposition to Zionism."[32]

But while occult fascism and its offspring seeped into and reshaped the conspiracist ecosystem, neo-Nazism itself had become a niche conspiracy by the 1970s, which was kept going by determined advocates such as William Pierce. Pierce recorded weekly messages about "black terror and Jewish degeneracy and liberal treason" for the answering machine at the headquarters of the National Socialist White People's Party.[33] Its incompatibility with Christianity dampened most conspiracists' reaction to it, as did its relative inattention to Communism or the new world order.

The 1973 Arab-Israeli War spurred a short-lived burst of activity among neo-Nazis. William Pierce renamed the National Youth Alliance as the National Alliance, which he imagined as a "superstructure" for an "array of specialized, coordinate [*sic*] groups." In 1974 another organization, the American Nationalists, tried to establish themselves as a clearing house for neo-Nazi groups with a peculiar appeal to diversity. Their manifesto noted that one of "the basic problems of such groups is their lack of prospective [*sic*] as to what their job is. They think they can beat the world with just one organization tailored to one type of person." Since it required "many kinds of people to build a movement of historical significance," the American Nationalists' envisioned themselves working alongside "the thousands of black and Mexican nationalists" who were eager to leave "this white man's land" and with whom they could "UNITE AGAINST THE ANTI-CHRIST!"[34] This combination of odd ideas failed to catch on.

The Neo-Nazi Legacy

Yet Aryan white supremacy turned out to have considerable staying power, if only for its propagation of the idea that Jews were conspiring to destroy the white race. For example, Ben Klassen and his followers in the Church of the Creator, which Klassen established in 1973, devoted their attention to the conspiracy by the Jewish Occupation Government to destroy the white race just as the Jews had "destroyed our White Racial ancestors" beginning with the "White Egyptians." Klassen was committed to the Racial Holy War (RaHoWa) that would "throw off the yoke of Jewish tyranny and control" and "make it impossible for the Jews and the other mud races to ever again threaten the existence and well-being of the white race."[35]

Also in the mid-1970s, Wilmot Robertson's monthly magazine *Instauration* took up the cause of the oppressed white majority from a self-consciously highbrow perspective. Mixing articles about racial genetics and holocaust denial with equally racist reviews of art and theater, *Instauration* marked the beginning of intellectual white supremacism. Even an article about voting was prefaced with William Butler Yeats's negative assessment of democracy before making its claim that the white majority's votes "have almost no impact because we have no one to represent us." Willis Carto's Noontide Press distributed RaHoWa material supporting a "resistance movement" to fight a government based on "conspiratorial tyranny." One of his more popular publications was an amateurish but thorough guerilla war "plan for the restoration of freedom when our country has been taken over by its enemies."[36]

But the Yockeyite tradition also had adherents determined to maintain its distinctive antimodern, Aryan supremacist paganism and its concomitant disgust with Christian "weakness." Like Klassen, William Pierce established his own non-Christian belief system, manifested in his newly established West Virginia compound, the Cosmotheist Community. The influential independent conspiracist William Gayley Simpson credited Nietzsche as an antimodern inspiration, but in his treatment titled "The Fateful Crisis Confronting Western Man," Yockey's influence is unmistakable. Revilo P. Oliver, the intensely racist University of Illinois classics professor, in Yockeyite fashion tried to rescue from obscurity the antifeminist biological determinist Anthony Ludovici, who believed that Spengler's seemingly inexorable Western decline could be reversed through "practical eugenics." Michael O'Meara portrayed Yockey as a *Vabanquespieler* (player of a dangerous game) fighting "the Jewish-dominated, liberal-capitalist, anti-European Mammon system" of America.[37] The Creativity Movement (the name Klassen's Church of the Creator adopted after a copyright infringement lawsuit) played up Yockeyite opposition to Christianity, whose emphasis on forgiveness and compassion makes the white race weak. Klassen himself disparaged Richard Butler's Aryan Nations as "schizophrenic" for "preaching that we, the White Race, are the real Israelites, and Christ was our savior" and mocked the efforts of Christian militias such as The Order (a.k.a. the Silent Brotherhood). The latter violently antisemitic, antigovernment organization, Klassen maintained, should have been able to kill hundreds of Jews with the effort they put into murdering Denver radio personality Alan Berg.[38] Today, the Creativity Movement publishes the magazine *Imperium*—yet another tribute to Yockey—which is filled with conspiratorial ideas. The negative associations many people have regarding White Racial Loyalists, for example, "have been implanted by the controlled mediums." Dylann Roof's attack on a South Carolina black church congregation is a false flag operation ("The whole thing stinks to high heaven of a conspiracy theory!!!"). And the Jewish Rothschilds ("the largest slaveowner in the South") had Lincoln assassinated.[39]

Neo-Nazi conspiracism and Yockey's iconic status have both resurged with the rise of the alt-right white supremacists. Alt-Right theorist Kevin MacDonald, who began his career as a bio-behavioral psychologist searching for a genetic justification for antisemitism, draws on conspiracies back to the hidden hand. Between 1994 and 1998 MacDonald published three books that blamed the Jews "for introducing evil social vices and other perversions into Nordic society" and portrayed them as "degenerates preying on unsuspecting, wholesome Aryans." Aside from replacing "Gentiles" with "Aryans," MacDonald's ideas are exactly the same as the hidden hand conspiracy theory. MacDonald's concerns stretch back to the 1920s—he complained that anthropologist Franz Boas had inspired an "onslaught against the idea of race and against Western culture [that] gradually had become ensconced in the universities"—and continue on up to current events: he considered Norwegian mass murderer Anders Behring Breivik "a serious political thinker with a great many insights and some good practical ideas on strategy."[40]

Yet the major split within the alt-right concerns antisemitism. To some degree the Aryan renaissance tradition has been offset by intellectuals such as Paul Gottfried, who has argued for a fashionable "Eurofascism" (such as in Mussolini's Italy and Franco's Spain) distinct from Nazi Germany and associated with alt-right favorites such as Julius Evola and Anthony Ludovici.[41] This perspective allows people to embrace elements of fascism while likening Barack Obama to Adolf Hitler. But there is at least one alt-right faction that is viscerally antisemitic: the 1488ers (fourteen for the number of words in white supremacist David Lane's mawkish homily "We must secure the existence of our people and a future for white children" and eighty-eight for the eighth letter of the alphabet—*H*—doubled to convey "Heil Hitler").[42]

But generally, the alt-right "mainstream" has been limited to rarefied intellectual antisemitism and calculated ambiguity. Jared Taylor, writing in the magazine *American Renaissance*, describes the "debate in our ranks on . . . the role Jews may or may not have played in creating the crisis we face. Some people in the AR [alt-right] community believe Jewish influence was decisive in destroying the traditional American consensus on race. Others disagree." Richard Spencer, an acknowledged alt-right leader, has soft-pedaled the "rabid" antisemitism of Andrew Anglin, telling an interviewer, "Andrew and I have different styles; we have different approaches."[43] Taylor's American Renaissance conferences have exposed the rift between "those who see Blacks, Hispanics and Muslims as the primary enemy and those who say 'the Jews' are behind every evil." Avowed Nazis such as David Duke have generally stayed with Taylor's organization, while white supremacist Jews have drifted to Michael Hart's Preserving Western Civilization, a "white nationalist venue more friendly to Jewish participation."[44]

Most alt-righters have never been strongly conspiratorial, beyond taking for granted that the government (along with its allies who control the universities and most of the media) has been purposefully undermining the white race. William H. Regnery II, longtime anti-Communist and cousin of Alfred Regnery, the right-wing publisher, became a convert to the conspiracy against the white race in 1993. Since then, his financial backing has provided a great deal of the organizational infrastructure of the alt-right. Samuel Francis, who was fired from the *Washington Times* for his war-against-the-white-race activities, took an implicitly conspiratorial approach in the statement of principles he wrote for the Council of Conservative Citizens in 2005, opposing: "All efforts to mix the races of mankind, to promote non-white races over the European-American people through so-called 'affirmative action' and similar measures, to destroy or denigrate the European-American heritage, including the heritage of the Southern people, and to force the integration of the races."[45] The alt-right has contributed to the growing conspiracist worldview by discussing race, immigration, and terrorism with constant but inferential references to the same white victimization conspiracism that has been a hallmark of the Right for decades. The alt-right also took the lead in framing "political correctness," a constant thorn in the side of white supremacists, as a conspiracy. Andrew Breitbart promoted the idea that "cultural Marxism is political correctness, it's multiculturalism, and it's a war on Judeo-Christianity."[46]

Recently, the alt-right has expanded into the online world of "Fake news, . . . hoaxes, fraudulent click-bait articles, and outright conspiracy mongering."[47] The alt-right has brought what had originally been a marginal neo-Nazi conspiracy theory to the strongest position it has ever held. When the violently racist Richard Spencer was punched in the head by a protestor while giving a television interview, the anonymous presence behind the Francis Parker Yockey website took it as a declaration of war: "We have officially entered a new and improved chapter in this race war and it has officially came [sic] at the hand of the great Richard Spencer. Unintentionally that is. I am calling this the Richard Spencer Race War Has Begun and if you copy my shit I will kick your ass for acting like a NIGGER! I can do it too."[48] This sort of gratuitously offensive, yet anonymous, tough-guy stance has become the hallmark of alt-right blogging.

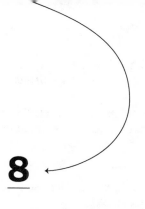

8

THE EMERGENCE OF THE
NEW WORLD ORDER

> There is a strong movement . . . to set up a World Dictatorship (known
> by various names, such as "World Government," "World State,"
> "World Federation," "Federal Union for Peace," "World Democracy,"
> "Free World," "League of Nations") with a WORLD POLICE FORCE to
> "enforce peace"?
>
> Defenders of George Washington's Principles[1]

The main concern of postwar conspiracism was not so much Jews as the
menace of internationalism. The hidden hand conspiracy had focused
on the destruction of United States, an emphasis unchanged since Jedidiah Morse's attacks on the Illuminati in the late 1700s. But now, the
emphasis shifted to the threat of international organizations and eventually a world government. The theme of postwar conspiracism became
threats to "our" sovereignty, originally the sovereignty of the nation but
shifting to the state and local level as the federal government was seen
as yielding more and more ground to the internationalists. Conspiracists
began to turn their attention to "our" local sovereignty, which they saw
as under attack by the federal government itself.

The United Nations

Not surprisingly, conspiracists devoted considerable attention to the UN. A typical early instance came in Catherine Baldwin's testimony warning the Senate: "If you sign this charter, you are signing away the sovereign rights of the people of this country, which you are not authorized to do." Baldwin detailed some of the conspiratorial ideas being attached to the UN:

> This is, to my mind, a very direct attempt to sabotage the Constitution of the United States, to take way our sovereign rights.
>
> It is not a new plan. It is one that has been going on for many, many years. Immediately after the last war the procession started. The highly financed propaganda permeated our schools, our colleges, our churches, in fact, every phase of our American life. Attempts have been made to destroy the Star-Spangled Banner—they are still going on. Our histories were rewritten so that you would not recognize American history.[2]

The United Nations did, of course, come into being, and was incorporated into the conspiracy from then on. George Armstrong, in his petition to Congress to impeach President Truman, "et al.," laid out an array of "traitors and Zionists" to be expelled from America, submitting that they were trying "to destroy our system of government and create a Zionist super state; [and] that in pursuance of said purpose they fraudulently established the United Nations and created the Atlantic Pact, and caused our government to intervene in the Korean war."[3]

As the "Jew-infested" UN was "primarily a vehicle for advancing the interests of world government under the banner of the Soviet Union," it followed naturally that the UN was anti-Christian, since the "deliberate suppression of Christianity" was necessary to establish "the tyranny and despotism of a Talmudic ONE WORLD GOVERNMENT." Americans needed to be "fully informed on the many aspects of the Judeo-CommUNists." Long time antisemite Robert Edward Edmondson singled out New York City as the "internal enemy of U.S." and indeed, "no longer an AMERICAN city, but the greatest cosmopolitan *Internationalist* center in the world since UN headquarters were located there. A recent issue of the weekly 'Human Events' of Washington, D. C., referred 'with alarm' to the alien 'problem of New York,' . . . intimating that it should be remedially acted upon through patriotic organizations before New York Socialists, Communists and Internationalists destroy The Republic 'FROM WITHIN.'" In their pledge of "everlasting defiance to the blue traitor flag of the United Nations," Vermont's Green Mountain Riflemen repeated a popular belief that the UN, as "the embodiment of modern Pharisaism and hypocrisy wishes the world to forget JESUS and forbids CROSSES on American graves wherever it can."[4]

But, reflecting the fact that antisemitism was increasingly unacceptable, most anti–world government conspiracists managed to attack the UN without it. California state senator Jack Tenney, a man consumed by the threat of Zionism, could excoriate the major parties' complacency over "the subjugation of our flag, our finances and our freedom to the sovereignty of the socialist-minded United Nations Organization and its sundry agencies" without mentioning Jews. Even Frank Britton's viciously antisemitic newspaper argued, without any reference to Jews, that once a permanent UN military capacity was established "the path toward slavery and national destruction can be charted with almost exact precision." One direction that path might take was described by Billy James Hargis: "Special U.N. froces [*sic*] have already made practice seizures of several American cities under the UN flag. What are they practicing for?"[5]

The United Nations spawned innumerable subsidiary threats to both American sovereignty and security. The prospect of American troops subject to UN control has been used to frighten people ever since. (In the 1990s, Phyllis Schlafly held that American troops would be controlled by foreigners under "a secret order!" that had been signed by President Clinton.)[6] The UN's World Court could well "invade the field of our domestic laws, already confused and muddled with international law, . . . as interpreted by Chief Justice Warren's Supreme Court, and the treason cult in our State Department." Similarly, the World Bank (created by the "International Bankers" in 1944) wielded power that "supersedes our sovereignty" and "effectually destroys our republican form of government." While not strictly speaking part of the UN, the World Bank used the UN to enforce its demands, which would put America at the mercy of a "seething vortex of International Financial Dictators." But the primary problem from the beginning had been the "flood ... of subversive organizations, many of which became 'Specialized Agencies' of the United Nations." Of these various subversive organizations, the one that conspiracists singled out as the most menacing was the United Nations Educational, Scientific, and Cultural Organization (UNESCO), whose mission they saw as: "Reduce Mankind to Uniformity."[7]

The United Nations Educational, Scientific, and Cultural Organization was a prominent cog in the conspiracy against America in several ways. Foremost among these was its "scheme to pervert public education," as a report by the American Flag Committee of Philadelphia spelled out. Under UNESCO's orders, teachers were to suppress American history and "truth" in general, teaching "disloyalty" instead. Besides "corrupting the morals of your children," they would discard "logical teaching methods" in the service of promoting a one-world government. Both the committee and Representative John T. Wood, who had the committee's report inserted into the *Congressional Record*, were particularly concerned about the teaching methods to be used by "UNESCO-indoctrinated teachers, who advocated that," "before the youngsters are given any kind of formal study of their own country, every opportunity should be taken to enlarge the child's imagination and encourage him in an interest in all that is remote and strange. . . . The purpose of this is not simply to teach our kindergarten and elementary pupils about alien peoples, but to cause them to identify themselves in their imagination with people different from themselves."[8] This reaction to UNESCO's educational component was repeated constantly. More than ten years after Wood's report, another representative, James B. Utt, placed into the record yet another exposé of how American schoolchildren were being "indoctrinated with world government ideals." By this time, school administrators had apparently become cagey, and the only way to find out if students were being indoctrinated was to ask them if they were being taught such lessons as "collectivism is inevitable" or "private property has no place in the new order."[9]

On UNESCO's cultural dimension, artwork was both disparaged and interpreted as contributing to aesthetic and moral decay. Robert Williams interrupted his 1950 exposé of the Zionists' "Ultimate World Order" for a photo of the "UNESCO Brown Man," a statue he attributes to Bernard Rosenthal. A nondescript futuristic humanoid, looking very much like a relaxed Academy Award statuette, the statue is intentionally generic so it can represent people of any race or nationality. Williams interprets this ideal as "the blending of all races of mankind into one composite, raceless, nationless, homeless, characterless, faceless brown slob—utterly lost from all heritage and completely subject to the will of the Zionist master race." Somewhat less dramatically, Dan Smoot criticizes a mural by Picasso ("the foremost communist 'artist' in the western world") for UNESCO headquarters as accurately symbolizing the agency: "degenerate ugliness parading as beauty; confusing nonsense posing as something meaningful."[10]

For the most part, UNESCO, like the UN itself, was presented as a more generalized threat. Billy James Hargis, in one of his Christian Crusade pamphlets, presents UNESCO as part of a conspiracy to undermine religion by means of "the Darwin Theory" and theological "Modernism." Another pamphlet was somewhat more scathing:

> Congressman Lawrence H. Smith, of Wisconsin, described the U.N. system and UNESCO which promotes it, as "a permanent international snake pit where Godless Communism is given a daily forum for hate, recrimination, psychological warfare against freedom and unrelenting moral aggression against peace."
>
> European writers call UNESCO the "crackpot carnival." But the best definition of all comes from a California member of the American Legion. He said, "UNESCO is the United Nations Espionage, Sabotage and Corruptive Organization."[11]

The underlying threat perceived by many conspiracists was some sort of network of internationalists relentlessly pushing America toward immersion in a world government, a threat that went back at least to the League of Nations. Despite the best efforts of antisemites, it was hard to place the Jews at the center of such a network—but the question of who else would want to destroy American sovereignty loomed large. The answer that emerged defined a class of well-to-do, highly interconnected, intellectual members of the American "Eastern Establishment" and their British coconspirators.

A major step in defining the American side of this conspiracy was Emanuel M. Josephson's 1952 attack on the Rockefeller empire, *Rockefeller "Internationalist": The Man Who Misrules the World*. The Rockefeller family had inspired attacks for decades, because of their business practices and labor tactics, but Josephson was the first to present a sustained attack on the Rockefellers' internationalist efforts. Josephson's argument is encapsulated in the caption accompanying a photograph of a Manhattan street scene that opens his book. Three buildings, designated A, B, and C, constitute the "Physical Symbol of the Rockefeller-Soviet Axis": "At West Corner of Park Avenue and West 68th Street there stand three buildings side by side that are the emblem of the Rockefeller-Soviet Axis. 'A' is the Home of Rockefeller's Council on Foreign Relations, the Foreign Office of the Rockefeller Empire. 'B,' on the opposite corner is the home of the Soviet Russian Delegation to the UN. 'C' houses Rockefeller's Institute of Public Administration, controlling city and state governments."[12] Josephson's animus toward the Rockefellers may well have stemmed from his anger over milk. Previously a writer of medical exposés, Josephson blamed the Rockefellers for corrupting the nation's public health system to force acceptance of the "adulterated . . . synthetic concoction . . . 'homogenized' milk." Accordingly, Josephson's rationale for why the Rockefellers might abandon American capitalism and become internationalist sellouts was somewhat metaphorical: "John D. Jr. about-faced. He awoke to the value of regimentation of the 'peasants' under amenable leaders, the value of 'homogenizing' mankind, about which he now appears as enthusiastic as homogenizing milk. Indeed the 'homogenizing' of the heterogeneous mass of mankind in Asia . . . may be one of the purposes of the Rockefeller Empire in turning over Asia to the Communists."[13] Even with this lactic limitation, Josephson's linkage of the Rockefellers with the Council on Foreign Relations, among a variety of other internationalist organizations, established an essential part of the new conspiracism around world government.

The Conspiracy of Cecil Rhodes

A more thorough articulation of the internationalist conspiracy theory incorporating British coconspirators was introduced to American readers in Catherine Palfrey Baldwin's 1954 book *And Men Wept*. The ideas behind such a conspiracy had, however, been percolating for some time. In the early 1930s, Representative Louis McFadden had proposed barring from the presidency any American who had ever "expatriated himself" on the grounds that "such a man is likely to think of himself as a cosmopolitan." Baldwin herself had been a violent enemy of British Israelism, involving her in numerous feuds with other rightists who were unaware of that peculiar sect. Her interpretation of British Israelism as part of a plot against America led her to create the Defenders of the Constitution of the United States of America to fight against its internationalist agenda.[14] In her 1940 pamphlet *Undermining America*, Baldwin set out an early version of her theory, the foundation stone of which was British imperialist Cecil Rhodes's dying wish "that a secret society should be endowed" to extend British rule worldwide, including "the ultimate recovery of the United States of America as an integral part of the British Empire."

Baldwin had no trouble linking this pipedream to Andrew Carnegie's well-known desire to create a British-American free trade union.[15] Although Cecil Rhodes's role in the conspiracy was not great, he helped provide a focus. The program of his that established Rhodes Scholars was tailor-made for conspiracists looking to link progressive American internationalists and English socialists. Initially, Baldwin omitted the

Jews from her conspiracy. After the war, however, her new organization, Women for the United States of America, worked with antisemites such as Father Coughlin and Elizabeth Dilling before abandoning antisemitism. Others never made this transition. Wesley Swift, after linking Rhodes to the Illuminati (a creation of Mayer Amschel Rothschild, head of the Rothschild family), concluded that a Rhodes Scholar was simply "a conceited instrument of International World Jewry."[16]

Baldwin's *Undermining America* pamphlet attacked the philanthropic foundations established by Carnegie, Rockefeller, Duke, Russell Sage, and Edward Filene, all of whom she considered internationalists. With a nod to Elizabeth Dilling's *Red Network*, Baldwin listed the members of these foundations "from which funds go subsidies [*sic*] to subversive, communistic, socialistic and all peace movements" such as the International Labor Organization, the Foreign Policy Association, and the League of Women Voters. Baldwin also offered a set of ten charts titled "Undermining America for World Government, World Police, World Currency, and World Religion."[17]

The election of a Labour government in England in 1945 turned more people's attention to the threat posed by British Fabian socialism, defined by Tennessee representative B. Carroll Reece as "a technique of nonviolent revolution by the consent of a duped, propagandized population."[18] In a speech before the National Society of New England Women, Augustus Rudd encouraged his audience to find the pattern and reflect on who must be behind it:

> You should follow closely the program of the Socialist labor government in England . . . the child of the Fabian Society pioneered by Sidney and Beatrice Webb in London in 1884. As you see one industry after another being nationalized . . . you can see liberty rapidly disappearing and the hollow mockery of Britain's proud boast of centuries that every man's home is his castle.
>
> And when you read that the nationalization of the medical profession, with all the evil consequences, is being ruthlessly pushed . . . you

should shudder at the bills now pending in our Congress for socialized medicine, for it is the same plan.

Yes, you are now being afforded a dress rehearsal of what these professors have planned for our country and are successfully carrying out.[19]

The "professors" Rudd referred to were the key carriers of British Fabian socialism. While colleges up and down the East Coast were involved, Columbia University was particularly "well-known as a hotbed of British Fabianism, that peculiar type of 'creeping' socialism which sired the present 'Labour Government' which has reduced England to a fourth-rate power."[20]

In a series of articles in the *Chicago Tribune*, columnist William Fulton linked America's situation to Cecil Rhodes's living legacy, the Rhodes Scholars, who, "returning from schooling and indoctrination at Oxford University, England, are the principal hawkers of globalist propaganda in the United States." Almost half of the Rhodes Scholars enumerated by Fulton were teachers, professors, or presidents of schools, far and away the largest occupational group. These people were infiltrating the American government "in increasing numbers . . . particularly in the vital foreign policy-making state department." Detailed lists of Rhodes Scholars showed them to be prominent in the UN and many internationalist organizations—United World Federalists, the Institute for Pacific Relations, the Foundation for World Government, the Atlantic Union Committee, the Council on Foreign Relations (CFR), and many more.[21] In 1953, Congress joined in, establishing a special House committee (the Reece Committee) to investigate tax-exempt foundations in order to determine whether their activities were "un-American . . . subversive . . . political" and whether they had "resorted to propaganda." Originally focused on the Carnegie and Rockefeller Foundations, the committee expanded its scope to include academic organizations such as the American Historical Association, the Social Science Research Council, and the American Council of Learned Societies. Representative Reece himself viewed "the left-wing intellectuals, whose prestige and influence seemed to be the product of the tax-exempt foundation grants" as the "nerve center of subversion in America."[22]

Building on these sentiments, Catherine P. Baldwin constructed her conspiracy in *And Men Wept* on the contemporary feeling that internationalist, pro-UN fervor was, somehow, part of a more general plot among the intelligentsia to victimize America. Baldwin not only identified the perpetrators but also explained how they came to betray their own countrymen. With Cecil Rhodes's last will playing the role of a cryptic *Protocols*, laying out the plan for all to see, Baldwin quoted Carnegie as saying about world government: "Do it by peaceful means if possible, if not, then by war, not by one big move but little steps, one by one."[23] Baldwin described a network of people—Columbia University president and director of the Carnegie Endowment Nicholas Murray Butler, Carnegie himself, Woodrow Wilson and his conduit to the Fabians, Colonel Edward House—and organizations—the Anglo-American Society, the Pilgrim Society, the Atlantic Union—all determined to bring America under the control of Great Britain. Linkages among these organizations and between them and the federal government were easy to find; any number of people were involved with more than one. Baldwin singled out one Carter Goodrich, for example, who once headed the International Labor Organization, freely admitted that it had been established under the aegis of the League of Nations ("the stepping stone to World Government"), and currently taught under Nicholas Murray Butler's reign at Columbia.[24]

The entity composed of the Rhodes Scholar, the Carnegie Endowment, the Fabian Society, and Columbia University was fleshed out and reshaped by other conspiracists, some more exercised by Rockefeller, others by an Ivy League "old boy" network. Baldwin's bitter antipathy toward the British Israel believers, in contrast, faded away. This idiosyncratic aspect of her conspiratorial vision had been a regular source of her more peculiar claims. Where other conspiracists saw a Jewish or Illuminati plot in the presence, on the dollar bill, of the reverse of the great seal (the pyramid with the eye atop it), Baldwin asked: "Why was it placed only on the ONE dollar bill? Could it have been to signify that we were to have a ONENESS with Britain?"[25]

The central idea behind this conspiracy theory—that a network of Progressive Era organizations, founded with money from monopoly capitalists, filled with liberal and socialist academics, and having tremendous influence over government from the Wilson presidency onward—caught on with conspiracists of all stripes. Some, such as Rose Martin, stressed the role of the Fabian Society, whose identity in the United States is "carefully concealed and where its practitioners are usually known as liberals rather than socialists." The foundations and associations through which the Fabians work to destroy the "free world" are simply "a beguiling false front of benevolence and learning." R. J. Rushdoony and his followers, such as dominion theologian Gary North, painted liberals and socialists as "a band of bloodless revolutionaries" whose "manifesto" was a 1912 novel by Wilson adviser Colonel House. The eponymous hero of *Philip Dru, Administrator* "takes over the government and imposes a new order on society."[26] The American Legion saw internationalists as "descendants of 18th Century Illuminists." Kenneth Goff detected the Illuminati behind the internationalists' efforts to build a "world order of Anti-Christ power." And conspiracist William Guy Carr placed the Illuminati behind everything, with Rockefeller seizing control from the Rothschilds.[27] Don Bell tried to bring the Rothschilds back into the picture, claiming that the "coterie of powerful international bankers" had financed Wilson's election and so had him "under its thumb." These bankers assured their "organizational control of government through the Council on Foreign Relations." Myron Fagan, whose earlier career of naming "Reds" in Hollywood had run its course by the 1960s, threw everything together in a series of pamphlets: the British (*"You know what a Rhodes scholarship means!"*), the Rothschilds, the Illuminati (*"CFR in our day"*), and "students who had been specially educated and trained, . . . to be used as Agents and placed behind the scenes of ALL governments as 'Experts' and 'Specialists,' so they could advise the top executives to adopt policies which would, in the long run, serve the secret plans of the 'One-Worlders' and bring about the ultimate destruction of the governments and religion they were elected or appointed to serve."[28] Academic organizations in particular, such as the Rand School for Social Sciences, the Intercollegiate Socialist Society, and the American Association of University Professors, combined to point the way to UNESCO and its campaign of indoctrination for "Peace" and "the great world brotherhood now about to dawn."[29]

The network began to be referred to as an "invisible government," one "that controls both parties; that . . . forced 'One-World Willkie' to help elect Roosevelt in 1940. Something that positively and actually exists here in the United States today: an International Conspiracy."[30] In his *Blue Book of the John Birch Society*, Robert Welch dates the beginning of America's downfall to the Wilson administration. Manipulated by "the collectivists of Europe," Wilson "put his healthy young country in the same house, and for a while in the same bed, with this parent who was already yielding to the collectivist cancer." Dan Smoot, in his first foray into the origins of the invisible government, argued for the importance of the failure of the League of Nations. Smoot wrote about how "eager young intellectuals around Wilson, under the clear eyes of crafty Colonel House, drew up their charter for world government (League of Nations Covenant) and prepared for the brave new socialist one-world to follow World War I. But things went sour. . . . Bitter with disappointment . . . , House called together . . . his most dedicated young intellectuals . . . and arranged a dinner meeting with them and with a group of like-minded Englishmen." Thus was created the Council on Foreign Relations, cornerstone of Smoot's invisible government and "dedicated to the ideal of pushing America into a one-world socialist system." Others took a slightly different approach, defining the invisible government as an "arm of the international bankers and their pet project the United Nations." Occasionally, the Illuminati would still turn up behind the secret government.[31] In 1962, Smoot published his still popular book *The Invisible Government*, but within two years the term was appropriated by David Wise and Thomas B. Ross to describe the Central Intelligence Agency (CIA) as the "heart" of a new and different system that had "grown so big in men, money, and power that it has become an invisible government threatening the very freedoms it was designed to defend."[32] Since that time, the term "invisible government" has been associated with the intelligence community and deep state conspiracism.

The term that would emerge to replace both "one-worlder" and "invisible government" was "new world order." Although it meant nothing specific, it had popped up occasionally after H. G. Wells used it in 1940 to describe his vision of global cooperation that could follow the defeat of Hitler. By 1941, conspiracists had begun to appropriate it as a fear-inspiring umbrella term for the ultimate goal of the internationalists. And by the 1960s, "new world order" was a sufficiently recognized term that it could be used in a political cartoon to label the menacing figure using his "UN" broom to sweep away "freedom and independence," "different races," and "different gov'ts."[33]

The New World Order

Even before the term "new world order" took on particular prominence, conspiracists focused on the network behind the "new international order." Immediately after the war, considerable conspiratorial attention had been focused on the United World Federalists, an antiwar organization originally dedicated to world government. This group was so badly Red-baited, mostly by Joseph Kamp, that its agenda deteriorated to simple support of the United Nations.[34]

Some conspiracists continued to flog the United World Federalists, but more turned to the Council on Foreign Relations because of its numerous "fronts," ranging from Harvard's Center for International Affairs to the Roper Poll, and control over both political parties. The "brainwashing" department of the CFR was particularly important in that it explained the presence of so many respectable business and military leaders in the organization. Besides the "thought control" it exercised through the captive news media, the CFR swayed key individuals through its "carefully planned six-week seminars . . . by so-called experts" at the lavish Arden Estate owned by Nicholas Murray Butler's Columbia University. Aside from the brainwashing, most of the articles about the CFR were fairly sedate. Oren Potito, whose religious conspiracism could be extreme, limited himself to the "even more exclusive club" within the CFR: the Business Advisory Council. Don Bell, who twelve years earlier had cast the Rothschilds as the force behind the CFR, abandoned that effort in favor of the CFR's push toward world government by means of Fabianist planning and budgeting reforms.[35]

The purported British role in the new world order was strengthened following the publication of Carroll Quigley's *Tragedy and Hope* in 1966. Quigley's opus included a section on the organization called the Round Table that was inspired by Cecil Rhodes and that struggled in the early twentieth century to maintain British imperial power. Quigley, although agreeing with their general goals, found the group's activities secretive to the point of being seriously undemocratic.[36] The book was the subject of a 130-page "review" by anti-Communist entrepreneur W. Cleon Skousen, which he published as *The Naked Capitalist*. Skousen recast Quigley's Round Table section in conspiracist terms, essentially rewriting the book so badly that Quigley threatened to sue.[37] Immediately afterward John Birch Society stalwart Gary Allen also cannibalized *Tragedy and Hope*, explicitly painting Quigley as supporting a "trilateralist" conspiracy. Allen had become fixated on the Trilateral Commission as the core of the new world order from the moment (as he saw it) that David Rockefeller had ordered its creation. Allen's *None Dare Call It Conspiracy* had considerable influence, in part because the John Birch Society distributed millions of copies of it prior to the 1972 elections.[38]

Skousen's and Allen's reworking of Quigley has had a lasting impact on the internationalist conspiracy. Long-time television conspiracist Glenn Beck revived Skousen's work, and Beck's "signature, and much-ridiculed, chalkboard lectures have been based on the ideas expressed in Skousen's books."[39] Currently, conspiracy theorist and medical quack G. Edward Griffin continues to treat Quigley as a fellow conspiracist. By appropriating a work such as Quigley's, conspiracy theorists are able to give their own work a patina of academic credibility. This works well if the author has died; Spengler was unable to complain about Yockey's interpretation of his thesis, much less Robert Welch's treatment of it.

In internationalist conspiracism, misrepresentation of respectable research also serves to blur the line between serious analysis of power elites and conspiracism. Quigley complained vigorously about this, calling conspiratorial interpretations of his work "garbage." Nevertheless, in his Fabian socialist new world order conspiracy, G. Edward Griffin leans heavily on Quigley, quoting him at length on Cecil Rhodes's well-known "secret society" the Round Table.[40]

Internationalist conspiracism appealed as well to the anti-Communist right as anti-Communism became passé. Mary Davison's book *Profound Revolution* did not originate in Marxism but with the direct election of senators. Repealing the seventeenth amendment was necessary so that "the STATES and NOT the United Nations or the Council on Foreign Relations" would once again "control" the Senate. Also moving away from simple anti-Communism, the Patriotic Party warned of the UN's plan to create "a 'World Tribunal' which will seize all possessions, and all savings and bank deposits" and then issue every person "a number."[41] Edward J. Hatfield Jr., head of Citizens for American Survival, took the opportunity of J. Edgar Hoover's death in 1972 to lay out a new revolutionary scenario, in which it is "almost inconceivable that President Nixon, outright tool of the Rockefellers and the Council on Foreign Relations, will replace Mr. Hoover with someone *not* of, or controlled by, that ruling power behind the government.... Therein lies the threat of the CFR and its financial revolutionary Left to capture the FBI [Federal Bureau of Investigation] files and perhaps meld them with those of the Anti-Defamation League. Therefore, their use for the persecution of patriots who object to treasonous federal government can be expected."[42] Even Robert Welch, and his John Birch Society, shifted their emphasis away from Communism and toward the "eternal war between good and evil" as embodied in the struggle against the Illuminati. By the 1970s, the society was using its *Family Heritage Series* of publications to ask: "Do you see similarities between the ideas of the Communists, the Anarchists, and the *Illuminati?* (encourage family discussion)."[43]

Over the years, this internationalist conspiracy splintered into countless subtle variants, each continuing to inspire followers. In the National

States' Rights Party version, the influence of globalist institutions was channeled through Henry Kissinger—"the '*Secret President*' of America." In 1992, Gary Kah laid out his "stepping stones" to world government, starting with the Council on Foreign Relations and its progeny the UN, the Bilderbergers, and the Trilateral Commission. D. L. Cuddy's chronology of the new world order begins with Colonel House, the Fabians, and the CFR and ends with the observation that the term "new world order" has become a political liability; the new ideal is "global governance." In order to fold the "German-Jewish bankers on Wall Street" into the conspiracy, Eric Samuelson pushed the origin of globalism back to 1837. Recently, John Coleman uncovered the centerpiece of the internationalist conspiracy, the Tavistock Institute for Human Relations—"shaping the moral, spiritual, cultural, political and economic decline of the United States of America" since 1913.[44]

The main difference between the internationalist conspiracy theory, as it has developed since the 1950s, and the secret government–hidden hand conspiracies of the 1930s is not the latter's dependence on international Jewry. That is an important difference but not vital; conspiracists can still place Jews at the center of the new world order. Rather, the key difference lies in what is meant by government. In the hidden hand the government was, in fact, our American institutions of government (Congress, the presidency and the executive branch in general, the courts), along with the military, political parties, state and local governments, and perhaps a few well-known interest groups. The conspiracy held that most, if not all, of these actual institutions had been infiltrated and subverted by agents of the conspiracy. In this sense, there is no fundamental difference between the nineteenth-century conspiracy theories such as anti-Catholicism or the Slave Power, the secret government of Zionists behind the New Deal, and the McCarthyite charges of Communist infiltration of the State Department.

In the internationalist conspiracy, by way of contrast, the "government" is a mental construct, an abstraction created by the conspiracist— the "order" in the new world order. It is never merely the United Nations; that organization is just a front, like the North Atlantic Treaty Organization or the Soviet Union. The "government" is composed of whatever organizations and people the conspiracist chooses. Its members may be referred to as neutralizers, masterminds, usurpers, or mattoids. They may be identified as the "wire-pullers" who use President Eisenhower as their "front man." They may be called the invisible government or just the eastern establishment.[45] The center of the conspiratorial web may be the Council on Foreign Relations, or the Rockefeller Foundation, or even the United World Federalists. There may not even be center of the web. The conspiracy may be an outgrowth of Clinton Roosevelt's 1841 booklet *The Science of Government Founded on Natural Law*, or of the founding of the Fabian Society in 1884, or even of Colonel House's *Philip Dru, Administrator*. However the pieces are put together, they constitute a network with powers greater than those of the United States or any nation. The people who run this network are largely unknown to the public; they work behind the scenes and their decisions are not public. This is not a captive or subverted government; it is a truly secret government. It is to this approach to conspiracism that we owe the well-known conspiracy chart connecting disparate components of the plot with arrows going every which way. It is also the reason why this chart can be filled with whatever international organizations come along: from the World Health Organization to the Bilderbergers.

Internationalist conspiracism marked a watershed in how conspiracies were made. It was completely improvisational, and thus anyone could alter it, bring in new components, or discard them. Accordingly, internationalist conspiracism was not as coherent as its predecessors had been. At the individual conspiracist level, it reverts back to the Nesta Webster practice of simply mentioning several organizations in rapid succession to suggest that they are linked. As a school of thought, it may include anything from Jesuits to adulterated food. This can be illustrated with an extreme (but far from the most extreme) example: Brian Desborough's reaction to *The Century for Young People*, a book by Peter Jennings of ABC News. The book "imparts the same misleading political spin on historical events as we have come to expect from our Illuminati overlords," and so Desborough tries to set the record straight.

Desborough explains world politics by rapidly linking the Royal Institute for International Affairs, the "Rockefeller-funded" Institute for Pacific Relations, the City of London, Wall Street, the North Atlantic Treaty Organization, the Tavistock Institute, the Children of God church, the Stanford Research Institute, and the Office of Naval Research. These entities combined in unspecified ways to attack Pearl Harbor (planned "not in Japan as is popularly believed"); to bring Nazi Joseph Mengele to America "to implant technologically-advanced mind-control techniques upon many hapless Americans"; to perpetrate the "ritual murder" of River Phoenix; to lure America's youth into the New Age movement; and to thwart John F. Kennedy's space program. Finally, this conspiracy has devoted itself to the deindustrialization and consequent ruin of the Western world. This "government" controls "vast environmental agencies staffed with bureaucratic parasites" who have no interest in curbing pollution with "proven over-unity (free-energy) devices" and "the application of Schauberger vortexian technology." According to Desborough, the Tavistock Institute admitted all this in a 1974 report revealing that environmentalist, New Age, and religious organizations are, in actuality, all "part of a unified, planned social engineering conspiracy . . . as a precursor to the establishment of a global totalitarian government."[46]

9

THE CONSPIRACY OF PERSONAL DESTRUCTION

> Remember that the tentacles of the conspiracy reach into your home town, where its puppets are promoting fluoridation, "mental health," and innumerable other plans to accustom us gradually to increasing slavery and intimidation.
>
> Revilo P. Oliver, *All America Must Know THE TERROR That Is upon Us*

Intellectuals

The plot to create a new world order was too distant from many people's lives for them to become alarmed; even warnings about the conspiracy to "enslave Congress and You (documented)" could fall on deaf ears.[1] One way to shake up the public was to personalize the conspiracy, as had been done by listing members of the hidden hand who controlled the New Deal. Disparagement of FDR's "brain trust" had led quickly to a wider attack on intellectuals, even those not involved in politics. For example, Max Lerner, "who took over the department of political science at Williams College for Moscow in the fall of 1938," was accused of "intellectual arrogance" for his pro-New Deal writings, which were described as a "potpourri of Polish Judaism and Yale Dialectics."[2] By the

1950s, Senator Joseph McCarthy's crusade against the Communist conspiracy routinely attacked intellectuals. McCarthy's disparagement of intellectuals "seemed to give a special rejoicing to his followers" and his "sorties against intellectuals and universities were emulated throughout the country by a host of less exalted inquisitors."[3] Mistrust of intellectuals became a standard trope of conspiracist rhetoric. Clarence Manion, although dean of the Notre Dame Law School himself, blamed "scholars," a word he put in quotation marks, for creeping socialism. Dan Smoot was one of several commentators who blamed academic meddling for the Supreme Court's 1954 *Brown v. Board of Education* school desegregation ruling—particularly by Gunnar Myrdal, "a Swedish socialist with a Communist front record who, in a book called *An American Dilemma*, had proclaimed his utter contempt for the constitution of the United States." Robert Welch, after pointing out Myrdal's connection to the always suspect Carnegie Endowment, lists several other intellectuals—from W. E. B. DuBois to Franz Boas—who contributed to Myrdal's findings.[4]

This barrage of invective against academics expanded into a wider mistrust of expertise, policy makers, literary icons, even scientists. Joseph Kamp, in a pamphlet attacking "the crusade for world government," characterized its proponents as "'intellectuals' without intelligence." Professors were commonly disparaged as Ivy League "Reducators" and "pseudo-intellectuals." They were the "so-called scholars" behind the suspiciously liberal New Standard Revised Bible; they were "Negro intellectuals . . . carried away" by the civil rights movement. Westbrook Pegler, while admitting that Theodore Roosevelt had gone to Harvard, took comfort in the fact that he had been "only a matriculant, never a scholar."[5] There was often a great deal of defensiveness in such harangues. Inspired by congressional hearings into Alger Hiss's Communist background, the American Legion used its Thanksgiving message to tell its members to give thanks that

> your organization's position on the twin evils of Communism and Socialism since its very founding 33 years ago, has never shifted or

deviated 1/10,000th of an inch. This despite Niagaras of ridicule, abuse, pressure, and, at times, virtual isolation. . . . Unlike some intellectuals and others, it was never flim-flammed by Soviet confidence men and grifters.

WHO IS THE FOOL TODAY? The "simple-minded" Legionnaire who "never grew up" and still believes in the homely virtues of patriotism and sound Americanism, the butt of every smart alec playwright, writer, commentator, and pseudo-intellectual; or the smart alecs, many of whom now stand exposed as Soviet spies, commies, commie fronters, or saps and easy marks for every Stalinist con game pulled off in this country? . . .

WHO PLAYED THE FOOL, THE LEGION OR THOSE BLATHERSKITE "INTELLECTUALS"?[6]

Conspiracists often felt persecuted, first by the Anti-Defamation League in the 1930s, and then by anti-Nazi writers. As the New Deal gave way to internationalism, a feeling of persecution at the hands of a much wider array of intellectuals and their organizations began to grow. When Gerald Winrod blasted America's "Gestapo" for persecuting radio preachers in 1949, he was referring to more than the Anti-Defamation League; his primary enemy was now the Federal Council of Churches, the main ecumenical organization in the country. This church group, working in league with organized labor and the NAACP, could bring tremendous pressure to bear against right-wing radio preachers, Winrod complained, since they knew the liberal Supreme Court would support them. Under these conditions, even Jesus would be "immediately banned from the radio as an 'anti-Semite.'"[7] Upton Close, whose radio commentaries were not aired on WOR in New York, maintained he was being censored at the behest of "officials at Macy's" who found his program "un-Soviet." Persecution by law enforcement agencies, Close also complained, was orchestrated by the Anti-Defamation League, "a mysterious network organization with vast funds and agents available to follow cases anywhere"—like "private secret police."[8] The arrest and subsequent trial of the suspects of the 1958 Atlanta synagogue bombing was deemed persecution by those who believed the bombing to be a false flag operation undertaken by "Jewish organizations." The membership gained and money raised as a result of "this successful 'coup!'" would help the ADL in its campaign to destroy America's "White Christian Founding Race."[9]

Myron Fagan, whose career began by exposing Reds in Hollywood and finished with diatribes against the Illuminati, faced constant persecution at the hands of one-worlders. His enemies were a "SECRET POLICE" as bad as the Soviet Union's: the United World Federalists, the *Christian Science Monitor* (under the editorship of Erwin Canham, "Rhodes Scholar, a zealous 'one-worlder' and frantic supporter of the 'United World Federalists'") and CBS News's Chet Huntley, "a *wild-eyed* 'Liberal' Radio news commentator." Fagan's sense of persecution only intensified when he tried to sue his persecutors. His lawyer "betrayed" him and the California Bar Association refused to consider his subsequent complaint. Similarly, Robert H. Williams took such umbrage over questions about his background in U.S. Army Intelligence by the ADL and "Communist publications" that he included photostats of his performance evaluations in one book. Even with these, "the author expects renewed attacks by the alien cults to keep people from heeding his warning."[10]

Responding to the persecution he suffered at the hands of radio personality and press columnist Walter Winchell, Joseph Kamp told his readers that Winchell "had been bribed or cajoled by an International Cabal into service as a frightening Twentieth Century Golem made of newsprint pulp." Many others suffered similar persecution. After Eustace Mullins founded the Aryan League of America, the American Petroleum Industries broke off their contract with him, who had been their "propagandist." In New York, "Jewish Civil Officials" used legal methods to deny meeting venues to James Madole's National Renaissance Party, and in Chicago, heavy-handed FBI surveillance of Mullins, according to him, amounted to "siege conditions."[11]

By the 1960s, this level of persecution was taken for granted and featured strongly in communications with members of conspiracist groups. In his year-end report for 1961 (attached to a fundraising letter), Myron Fagan enumerated some of his persecutors, Chet Huntley having been joined by unnamed "Hollywood producers," "TV sponsors," and even the California American Legion. Fagan maintained that, although his persecution might seem trivial, "it is NOT trivial. Control of Hollywood, Radio and TV, *especially TV*, is even more vital to the Masterminds of the Great Conspiracy than the *already controlled* Press." Faced with similar persecution, Fred Schwarz attached a form letter to the program for his 1961 anti-Communist "school" for attendees to copy and send to *Life* magazine, which had disparaged some of the school's faculty as "crackpots": "Please make a copy of this letter, or one in your own words, and send it to the editors of Life Magazine. Let them know by action and swamping them with paper and ink that we true Americans and freedom loving people do not like subversive and Communist sympathizing editors or writers on there [*sic*] staff." Karl Prussion, conversely, expressed pride over being attacked by "collaborators and appeasers of communists" such as the California Board of Education. Robert Welch seemed fatalistic in the foreword to the 1961 edition of the John Birch Society's *Blue Book*, mentioning in passing: "Naturally, we have faced extensive and malicious attacks from the open and disguised left." Later, describing the 1960s as "the era of 'be kind to communists and their friends,'" Welch scoffed that "the whole left-liberal cabal of the religious, educational, entertainment, labor and communications world has tried to erect a 'Nazi or Fascist threat' out of the John Birch Society."[12]

In the eyes of those trying to stop the march toward world government and the implicit end of sovereignty at any level, most of the persecution originated with the media, increasingly part of the conspiracy. The media's role had become obvious with the attacks on Senator Joseph McCarthy by the Communists "and their dupes and stooges whose influence extends into the newspapers, magazines, radio and television."[13] The drumbeat against what has come to be called the mainstream media stressed the need to "attack directly the lies, distortions and propaganda of the Establishment's communications media . . . and entertainment industries." The "good people," as Gerald L. K. Smith pandered to them in a fundraising letter, "are in the majority, but they have been chloroformed, mesmerized, hypnotized and blinded by a news media that does not tell them the truth." The idea of the media extended well beyond just the news. The "printed and electronic press" worked with "the pedagogy, the pulpit and the political sectors of society" in order to "orchestrate in concert, distortions, deceptions, deletions and demi-truths because truth is anathema to their grand design." A few voices took this issue beyond the rhetoric of alliteration: "Mr. John Doe, Citizen, U.S.A., has been treated to the full effect of MASS CONDITIONING via the CONTROLLED COMMUNICATIONS MEDIA. The caldron of witches brew of news and views has been allowed to roll & tumble until the ordinary citizen, sitting in front of his 'boob-tube' has been bombarded into a state of conditioned confusion. He is now willing to grasp at any straw and believe anything as long as 'THEY' do something to end this mess. But THEY are not through with him!"[14] This insistence that the media are not merely biased but an active participant in a conspiracy against the truth was a key part of the expansion of the hidden hand conspiracy twenty years earlier and has continued as an article of faith among conspiracists ever since. The news media have been the object of explicit attacks from such luminaries as Eustace Mullins and Michael Collins Piper, and their malfeasance has most recently been enshrined in the presidential "FAKE NEWS TROPHY!"[15]

The Threat of Mental Health

The most viscerally frightening arena in which intellectuals and experts threatened people was mental health. The problem burst into the public's awareness in 1955 with the publication of *The Brainwashing Manual* by Kenneth Goff.[16] Purportedly a "synthesis" of a Russian text on "psychopolitics," introduced with a lecture to American students at Lenin University by Lavrenty Beria, head of the Soviet secret police, the book was entirely fraudulent.[17] Regardless, Goff maintained that psychopolitics, practiced under the harmless-sounding cover of "mental healing," provided the rationale for the plan "to subject to torture and imprisonment those who preach the gospel of our Lord and Savior Jesus Christ, and who oppose the menace of Communism." Others echoed Goff's fears. Fred Schwarz, head of the Christian Anti-Communist Crusade, described how "the mind smashes into fragments" that can later be reassembled "for whatever Communist purpose is designated." And in a wide-ranging anti-intellectual "challenge to the devotees of Freud, Pasteur, Darwin and Marx," Herb Blackschleger warned of "an entire nation brainwashed for decades by mind-control experts."[18]

This fear was applied immediately by conspiracists alarmed over the Alaska Mental Health Act, which would bring mental health services to what was then a territory. The costs of the services would be defrayed by giving the territorial government millions acres of federal land to develop (or even just sell). Conspiracists, however, saw the land as "Siberia, U.S.A." "Is it the purpose of H.R. 6376 to establish a concentration camp for political prisoners under the guise of treatment of mental cases? The answer, based on a study of the bill, indicates that it is entirely within the realm of possibility that we may be establishing in Alaska our own version of the Siberian slave camps run by the Russian government."[19] The bill, "the most sinister, deceptive, subversive law ever, concocted, passed both Houses by 100% voice vote, like a cat in the stillness of the night." For years afterward, however, opponents in the House continued to warn that mental health was being used "to railroad more and more people into mental institutions."[20]

Despite its presumed origin with Beria, the psychopolitics literature did not feature Soviets very prominently.[21] The primary concern was the psychological establishment itself as an arm of the new world order. Sometimes the menace of mental health seemed to spring up spontaneously, as in this 1957 "news" story: "In 1948 the mental health concept was originated for political use. At a World Citizenship Conference in London, it was agreed that any person who objected to one worldism should be stigmatized as mentally suspect." The specter of forced mental orthodoxy was embodied by Dr. G. Brock Chisholm, of the World Federal Mental Health Association, who openly favored "eliminating such boundaries to brotherhood as color, creed, and geography"; this view amounted to "psychopolitics in the raw."[22] Aside from Chisholm's organization, mental health was being forced on the American public by the World Health Organization, UNESCO, the National Association for Mental Health, and the recently established Department of Health, Education, and Welfare. In the face of all this, conspiracists decided that "we must draw the terrifying but logical conclusion that the conspiracy now has control of so large a number of psychiatrists and similar 'experts' that . . . the plan can be put into operation without effective opposition."

The idea that the mental health profession itself was part of the conspiracy to establish a global dictatorship grew rapidly, becoming a standard element of conspiracist thinking in only a few years. Eugene Pomeroy, listing the main threats to America in 1958, included the "subversive" psychiatrists who "developed the 'Mental Health' program that enables American patriots to be easily and illegally confined in mental institutions," adding: "From these institutions there is no escape." Revilo Oliver focused his attention on the Jews' conspiracy to dominate America by "controlling the minds of the politically dominant majority of its population" under the guise of "mental health." Americans, Oliver complained, were all too willing to "acquiesce in legislation to authorize the 'legal' kidnapping of troublesome Americans and their incarceration in prisons (to be called 'hospitals') in which 'trained psychiatrists' of alien origin and their brutish assistants can induce insanity, imbecility, or, if necessary, death by means of scientific tortures, . . . or mind-destroying drugs, such as the now famous L.S.D., which was only later produced by the Weizmann Laboratories in Israel and shipped to the United States for surreptitious sale to adolescents and children whose minds had been given a preliminary conditioning in the public schools."[23] An important advantage conspiracists imagined for the authorities' declaring patriots to be "mentally ill" was that such an assertion allowed for "No martyrs!" since opponents of "one-world government are disposed of as members of the 'anti-social, crack-pot fringe.'" However, whenever a case arose, as in the 1962 pretrial commitment of

General Edwin Walker for his actions during the anti-integration riots at the University of Mississippi, martyrdom was immediate.[24]

The concept of mass brainwashing arose during this period most strikingly in the opposition to water fluoridation. While much of this opposition was based on medical criteria (whether sensible or "crack-pot fringe"), a surprising amount of it represented conspiratorial thinking. A relatively mild version hypothesized an economic conspiracy based on the power of the aluminum industry. Antisemitic conspiracists saw a Zionist plot, of course, similar to the one behind the Salk vaccine for polio. Charles B. Hudson was the first to see the true magnitude of brainwashing involved, in that "fluorination" affected "brain cells that are the source of resistance to slavery and a desire for freedom." Fluorinated water, Hudson opined, was probably responsible for Britain's electing a Labour government. He went on to claim that "the ancient civilizations were destroyed by such poisons fed the bodies and brains of the people by the ruling caste who desired to perpetuate their dictatorships by wiping out resistance in the people. It seems that the White Race bodies and brains react more disastrously to such poisons."[25] Everyone knew the power of fluorination. Kenneth Goff had, as a young Communist, conspired with his fellow cell members to poison water supplies with fluorine to "bring about a spirit of lethargy in the nation." Fluoridated water was also reportedly used by the Russian secret police "to make their prisoners stupid so they can be more easily brainwashed."[26]

The fear of fluoride poisoning was frequently connected with both polio vaccine conspiracies and the mental health threat. One flyer, with a weirdly frightening drawing of a little girl cringing before a grinning skeleton wielding a pawn shop sign, asked:

Are you willing to PUT IN PAWN to the UNHOLY THREE all of the material, mental and spiritual resources of this GREAT REPUBLIC? . . .

1. Water containing Fluorine (rat poison—no antidote) is already the only water in many of our army camps, making it very easy for saboteurs to wipe out an entire camp personel [sic]. . . .

2. Polio serum, it is reported, has already killed and maimed children. . . . This vaccine drive is the entering wedge for nationwide socialized medicine. . . . In enemy hands it can destroy a whole generation.
3. Mental Hygiene is a subtle and diabolical plan of the enemy to transform a free and intelligent people into a cringing hoard of zombies. . . .

FIGHT COMMUNISTIC WORLD GOVERNMENT It is later than you think![27]

The flyer further declared the U.S. Public Health Service to be "heavily infiltrated by Russian-born doctors, according to Congressman Clare Hoffman." This idea caught on with antifluoridation groups around the country, like the one in La Crosse, Wisconsin, that said: "Considering the recently-exposed infiltration of the many departments of our federal government by Communists, it is not unreasonable to suppose that the fluoridation-program could be subversive, since the U.S. Public Health Service has mothered the fluoridation program in the U.S." Unreasonable or not, such fears were widespread. A study of the local referendum that stopped fluoridation in Northampton, Massachusetts, concluded that the defeat "resulted largely from growing anti-intellectualism and the 'current suspicion of scientists, a fear of conspiracy, the tendency to see the world as menacing.'"[28] Suspicion of government agencies spread rapidly on the conspiratorial Right. Alarmed by data collection by the Department of Health, Education, and Welfare, Jo Hindman expanded on the "years of surreptitious planning and experimental action on the part of social engineers embedded in our various school systems, professions and agencies." These experts were secretly "dedicated to reshaping American society into an alien, unconstitutional, and collectivist State mould." Buttressing Hindman's claim, Revilo Oliver told a meeting of the Illinois Daughters of the American Revolution that the Department of Health, Education, and Welfare employed a full third of "the top echelon of international conspirators in this country."[29]

The "Menticide" of Our Children

Of particular concern was the victimization of children and youth. W. Cleon Skousen lectured parents on "the so-called 'Mental Health,' program and the dangers of coercive control psychiatry."[30] More impressionable than adults, children did not need to be institutionalized to be brainwashed; schools could be used for that purpose. Moreover, mental health professionals seemed to be singling children out for treatment. In 1959, a Houston youth study evoked several "bogeymen" of the Right—"the outside agitator, the academic expert, and the philanthropic foundation"—and generated a massive backlash. A local newsletter placed the blame on "the foggy advocates of federal control, the socialists, the do-gooders, and especially the Hogg Foundation for Mental Health—that perversion of a great Texas family tradition through the ill-advised, tax-exempt use of its fortune. This meddlesome, misguided outfit, long aggressive in sinister mental health intrusions into private affairs, is pushing seminars at chosen colleges throughout the state . . . with six-week courses for pseudo-psychiatrists, hand-picked in accord with U.S. Office of Education 'criteria,' and financed individually by federal grants." Local opposition to the survey was so intense that the results were publicly and ceremoniously burned.[31] Nationwide opposition was led by the Minute Women, a group devoted to ferreting out subversive influences in public schools. In a magazine article, Minute Woman Gene Birkeland, California "chairman" of the group, delved into the problem with an anecdote about a child sociopath, asking, "Why was there no saving voice of conscience in this child-strangler?" and answering by pointing to the "'revolutionary' doctrine" of G. Brock Chisholm and the half dozen organizations that embody his views. Chisholm's actual "doctrine" was that sex education should be taught in schools, which was not merely deemed immoral but which also underlay "the Soviet use of unrestrained sexual license as a key weapon in subjugating the youth of captive nations."[32]

The menace of psychology rejuvenated what had become a relatively moribund area of conspiratorial interest: the public schools. Fear of Communist subversion had faded along with the Red Scare, progressive education based on the ideas of John Dewey was perhaps too arcane a threat to capture the public's imagination, and the Daughters of the American Revolution had been reduced to declaring textbooks of being "guilty of special pleading from the liberals and internationalists." In the absence of any other serious threats, mind control fears loomed large.[33] The increasing use of psychology in schools led to a wave of books and articles, starting with E. Merrill Root's *Brainwashing in the High Schools* and Matt Cvetic's articles about "thought control" in the magazine the *American Mercury*. Dan Smoot revived anti-UNESCO rhetoric by portraying a ten-year-old series of its booklets on education as mind control, expounding the "urgent duty to develop informed and competent world citizens." Smoot found certain UNESCO statements to be un-American, such as, for instance: "As long as the child breathes the poisoned air of nationalism, education in world-mindedness can only achieve precarious results."[34]

"What is in your child's textbook?" is a question that was applied to much of the curriculum, where even game preserves and fish hatcheries were among the "government tentacles" intruding into "every walk of life." And, of course, the science that "teaches as fact the theory (man's guess) that man 'evolved' from lower animal [*sic*], contrary to Bible teaching" was indoctrination at its worst.[35] Thus, it was not only the campaign of desegregation that led some to advocate the abandonment of public education but what the students were forced to learn as well. Private schools without federal interference would ensure that "every parent and every child can keep a close watch on the 'materials' of education" to protect students from "any left-wing National Education Association . . . trying to brainwash American children to accept a *one world, one race, one color* super-state set up with Jew control at the top."[36]

The threat posed by psychology went well beyond the textbooks and curriculum, sometimes to areas too delicate to mention. Gene Birkeland had some difficulty finding "printable quotes" in an instructor's guide on sex education, which she viewed as Pavlovian "mind-conditioning." Even Dan Smoot, no-nonsense ex-FBI agent, found a UNESCO paper "too obscene to read publicly," hinting at surveys in which children were asked about their parents' sex lives.[37] Sex education in schools was, to some of its opponents, part of a larger conspiracy against morality. An article lionizing the opponents of "blatant" sex education in Anaheim, California, schools described the forces mobilized against them under the heading, "Leftists Defend Programs":

> The behaviorists, entrenched in major universities all over the country, were in a perfect position to bring up their big guns. And so they did. Clergymen of the liberal persuasion rushed to the defense of SIECUS [the Sexuality Information and Education Council of the United States], while doctors and educators vied with one another to secure favorable comment about the sex programs from the mass media.
>
> *Psychology Today*, with expensive packaging and seemingly limitless funding from mysterious sources, ran a series of articles ridiculing all those gallant little people who had fought so hard for their children.
>
> *Playboy Magazine* ran laudatory reviews of books written by the sexologists and carried a lengthy interview with Dr. Mary Calderone, during which she was given ample space to attack her critics.

When the issue began to wane, generating less press coverage, this was interpreted as the Sexuality Information and Education Council of the United States going "underground."[38]

Even more menacing than sex education was "its twin": sensitivity training. Ezra Taft Benson, apostle of the Mormon Church and former secretary of agriculture, lumped sensitivity training in with the other "atrocious, destructive evils" perpetrated by the "Communist conspiracy, fellow-travelers, and dupes." The evils could be found "in our music, in our art, in sex perversion and so-called sex education in the schools, in destructive sensitivity training—a powerful form of Pavlovian brainwashing." Others who found sensitivity training conspiratorial included Gary Allen, Don Bell, and the Ku Klux Klan, which declared it to be "mental suicide!"[39] The deepest conspiracy was unraveled by Ed Dieckmann Jr., San Diego policeman and pulp fiction author. Dieckmann's conspiracy involved all the expected participants: psychologists (Carl Rogers) and psychiatrists (G. Brock Chisholm), the "leftist" American Psychological Association, the Sexuality Information and Education Council of the United States, the National Training Labs, the Department of Health, Education, and Welfare, and at least a dozen other organizations. Dieckmann declared that sensitivity training "is the most poisonous legacy the *Illuminati* left us," and so we should not be surprised to learn that

> the "sex ed" of the kind now being pushed *is* sensitivity training and that's what is wrong with it! All the ingredients are there: self-confession, the lack of right and wrong, group consensus, the "New Morality," and the only loyalty that toward One-World, as condensed in the *World Citizenship Credo* of the United Nations: "World Citizenship and Mental Health."
>
> Get it? If you are so blind as to not perceive the blessings of One-World, you are less than healthy and ready for shock treatments.[40]

The 1960s saw a variety of "sensitivity trainings": Gestalt therapy, human relations workshops, Esalen, psychodrama. To conspiracists, the point of them all was the same: people would lose their individuality and "become homogenized into a group . . . subject to the will of a leader." In this context, self-criticism forms the basis of "voluntary" confessions of the type used by tyrants who want people's minds "influenced, tamed and broken down into servility." This Pavlovian "brainwashing" technique is, according to the conspiracists, a variety of "menticide." It can even be "used through the mass communications media . . . to turn the U.S. into a nation of mental robots." Even the most harmless versions, such as that practiced under the aegis of the National Council of Churches, could generate an editorial charging that "sponsors and participants could have called it appropriately a workshop on How to Recruit and Brainwash Teenage Children."[41]

All these elements were seen as part of one conspiracy to destroy the will to resist subjugation. It was orchestrated either by Communists or by one-worlders and was particularly responsible for what had gone wrong with America's young people. It was centered in psychology, but the conspirators also pointed to "their scientists, educators, and entertainers. . . . rendering a generation of American youth useless through nerve jamming, mental deterioration, and retardation." This, too, was menticide: "a literal suicide of the mind."[42] Sex education and sensitivity training were only one part of the plan. There were drugs ("it is generally accepted that Communism is behind the narcotics drive"); movies ("naked women, blasphemous portrayals of the Lord Jesus, and certain avowals that automation will deprive these youth of their future"), folk songs (with "subtle, Marxist content"), and, of course, rock and roll. Representative James Utt of Orange County, California, explained: "The Beatles, and their mimicking rock-and-rollers, use the Pavlovian technique to produce artificial neuroses in our young people. Extensive experiments in hypnotism and rhythm have shown how rock-and-roll music leads to a destruction of the normal inhibitory mechanism of the cerebral cortex and permits easy acceptance of immorality and disregard to all moral norms." Hardly surprising, then, that "the Beatles ability to make teenagers take off their clothes and riot is laboratory tested and approved."[43]

The public school as purveyor of psychopolitics persists in mind-control conspiracy theory. In 1976 Jo-Ann Abrigg's account of "psycho-social education" explicitly connected humanism and Pavlovian behaviorism, a combination that turned classrooms into "mental health clinics" devoted to "behavior modification." Ten years later, New Age philosophy opponent Constance Cumbey reiterated the menace of humanistic principles in schools, calling these "the exact same beliefs with which our children are brainwashed in public schools beginning in kindergarten. . . . No conspiracy?" And long-time public school opponent and Reagan administration education adviser Charlotte Iserbyt agreed. The "brainwashing for the acceptance of the 'system's' control," she wrote, "would take place in the school—through indoctrination and the use of behavior modification." Iserbyt singled out for particular opprobrium "critical thinking" as "nothing but pure unadulterated destruction of absolute values of right and wrong."[44]

Mind-Control Conspiracism

Mind control was a growing area of conspiracism outside education as well, particularly as an outgrowth of concern over the military and intelligence agencies' forays into psychological operations. In the 1980s, allusions to the military's "mind war" program of psychological operations began to proliferate, "with its 'sinister' title quickly winning it the most lurid conspiracy theory reputation." The psychological operations program was becoming a conspiratorial "blueprint . . . for world domination."[45] Early on, in what he called "an exercise in citizens' intelligence," Walter Bowart had laid out the connections between the CIA's MK-Ultra, or mind control, program and the "lone nuts" behind various assassinations. In his foreword to Bowart's book, Richard Condon (author of *The Manchurian Candidate*, the bestselling thriller about a mind-controlled assassin) summarized the case against educators, the military, the medical profession, lawyers, and "our esteemed statesmen": "Each one of those groups is involved in this dismembering of the mind. Taxes and the collective conscience make the urination of the secret police upon the human mind possible. 'Brainwashing' per se is no news to any of us. Controlled assassins are not known to us only through fiction. Advertising assaults on behalf of poisonous materials to induce us successfully to buy and consume are early bastions of mind control."[46] While Bowart and Condon were attacking the mind-controlling police state more or less from the Left, it was more regularly being attacked by the well-established right-wing new world order conspiracists. Antigovernment stalwart William Pabst once filed a class action lawsuit on behalf of the American people against "various personages that had a key part in a conspiratorial program to do away with the United States as we know it." Pabst's lengthy argument swept up UNESCO, the Alaska Mental Health Bill from twenty years earlier, and the abolition of state governments by executive order under the Law Enforcement Assistance Administration's objective of "Controlling the Masses." Pabst described the federal prison camps being built to house patriots in ways that became the template for Federal Emergency Management Agency camps. There, government "psycho-surgery" would make you "as cooperative as an adding machine," and drugs, such as "something called anectine (phonetic spelling)" could be used to torture you. To ensure that people go willingly to the camps "in a tranquil state of mind," incapacitating nerve gas could be released from aircraft as an aerosol.[47]

By the 1990s, the prospect of mind-controlled slaves had become a well-established element of conspiracism. Jack Mohr's "Talmudic/ Communist" assessment of "psychopoliticians" led him to see their work as part of a much larger conspiracy. For example, in 1996, Alaska Representative Don Young's emergency American Land Sovereignty Protection Act, intended to protect the United States from the establishment of any World Heritage Sites, failed to pass the House. Mohr's take on this was that representatives had "voted in favor of the New World Order over the rights of their constituents," and he wondered whether "psychopoliticians have had a part in this?"[48] Mohr's psychopoliticians were hard to identify, though Eustace Mullins predictably identified them as Freudians working for the Zionist-controlled CIA. The high visibility of Kurt Lewin, a behavioral scientist from Germany, was used to establish psychopoliticians as ex-Nazis brought to the United States by the CIA during the Cold War. Aside from the CIA and behavioral science organizations such as Lewin's Tavistock Institute, the military was the only institution widely credited with having a mind-control agenda, although Martin Cannon, in his book *The Controllers*, included the National Aeronautics and Space Administration (NASA) and the Atomic Energy Commission to buttress his argument that "the 'UFO abduction' phenomenon MIGHT be a continuation of clandestine mind control operations."[49]

Mind control is applicable to any purpose, and, thus, it turns up in many conspiracies. Cannon's hypothesized UFO abductions were critical to the government's MK-Ultra mind-control experiments, in that they solved "'the disposal problem,' i.e., the question of 'What do we do with the victims?'" More typically, mind-control victims are turned into assassins and superhuman agents who do the bidding of intelligence or military organizations. Often, the victims are serving deeper, occult forces, but sometimes they are merely victims of "research" such as that conducted by the CIA into cannibalism and "blood rituals." Regardless, the danger is severe. Cisco Wheeler and Fritz Springmeier preface their book on Illuminati mind control with a "WARNING . . . If there is any chance you the reader have had mind control done to you, you must consider the following book to be DANGEROUS. . . . The complications that could result for those under mind control learning the truth—could be fatal."[50]

Mind-control conspiracy theory has also come to play a significant role for those who believe in child ritual abuse and Satanic and cult-related abuse. When the premise behind repressed and recovered memories was shown to be fraudulent by researchers associated with the False Memory Syndrome Foundation, believers called the researchers mind-control agents who had helped perpetrate the abuse in the first place and were now trying to cover it up.[51] Walter Bowart explained this in remarks to the Society for the Investigation, Treatment and Prevention of Ritual and Cult Abuse. According to a reporter: "Bowart claimed that the False Memory Spindrome [sic] Foundation . . . is a Central Intelligence Agency action. It is an action aimed at the psychological and psychiatric mental health community to discredit you, to keep you in fear and terror. Bowart stated that everyone connected with the False Memory Syndrome Foundation (FMSF) will be shown to be 'spooks or dupes.' According to Bowart, the CIA is currently conducting a campaign of mind control against the American public and wants to discredit victims of these experiments so that their stories will be seen as false memories."[52] Beyond all this, the idea of a mind-controlled slave naturally led to visions of perverse sex. Thus, the military used mind control to create "a coterie of hypno-programmed soldiers" and to brainwash women to "reward" them with "unlimited sexual access." One Brice Taylor wrote an account of her brainwashing subtitled "The Memoirs of Bob Hope's and Henry Kissinger's Mind-Controlled Slave. Used as a Presidential Sex Toy and Personal 'Mind File' Computer." Similarly, CIA-created slave Cathy O'Brien was placed in "forced prostitution (white slavery) with those in the upper echelons of world politics," and orphans from Boys Town were programmed and forced into prostitution "with several of the nation's political and economic power brokers."[53] And, as Jack Mohr made clear, you are merely naive if you thought Christian faith would protect you from such a fate: "'Just as a dog can be trained, so a man or woman can be trained . . . Sexual lust, masochism, . . . and other desirable perversions (such as Sodomy), can be induced by pain-drug hypnosis, to the benefit of the psychopolitical operator.' Don't be so naive as to believe that you will be able to withstand the use of pain-drug hypnosis."[54]

Aside from the creation of sex slaves, mind-control conspiracism is generally subsidiary to some other conspiracy theory. Presumably, conspirators are trying to brainwash the public to go along with some malevolent plan. But over the years a mind-control conspiracy theory with its own raison d'être began to take shape, at least to the degree that conspiracists became increasingly fixated on the techniques of mind control while paying less attention to its purpose.

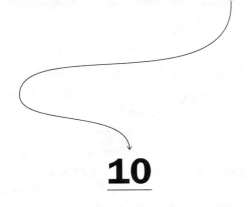

10

THE PLANNERS TAKE OVER

> When the planners began restructuring the United States, one of their
> first ideas was to get rid of the States and State governments.
>
> Don Bell, "Toward Ecumenopolis, the World-City

As the new world order conspiracy developed, its increasingly ad hoc and improvisational character emerged—and as a result it became increasingly complex and variegated. Different conspiracists pieced together the components they saw as central to their version of the world government and began to create alternate histories to back up their alternate versions of the present. American history could, thus, be full of surprises. Former secretary of agriculture Ezra Taft Benson told readers of America's "abandonment of the inspired Monroe Doctrine." People may well have been surprised to find that at least three amendments (the fourteenth, sixteenth, and seventeenth—and possibly the fifteenth) had been illegally attached to the Constitution. And while they may not have been shocked to learn that the "headquarters of the international Communist conspiracy were openly and officially transferred to New York City" in 1872, or even that the Federal Reserve System was designed to steal their money, they were probably stunned to discover that Marilyn Monroe had been murdered by the Communists because she had become a "liability."[1]

Conspiracy theorizing also became increasingly entrepreneurial. Full-page ads listing dozens of books one should buy appeared in periodicals such as *Women's Voice, American Opinion*, and the *Bulletin of the Committee to Restore the Constitution*. The 1967 catalog of publications for Edgar Bundy's Church League of America listed 154 reports, pamphlets, and booklets and ten years' worth of back issues of the league's monthly magazine, plus dozens of books, tape recordings, and films. Topics ranged from "Commander" Karl Baarslag's *Manual for Survival* ("suitable for high school") to *Necessity for Creationism* ("scholarly exposé of the evolution hypothesis as a fraud"). The Key Records catalog ("record albums dedicated to saving the United States") featured a similar array of topics.[2] Speakers' bureaus dealing with conspiratorial topics also sprang up. Open Forum, headquartered in Amarillo, Texas, was a formidable one. In addition to several straightforward John Birch Society anti-Communists, Open Forum featured well-known conspiracists such as David Noebel (*Communism, Hypnotism, and the Beatles*), Rose Martin (*Fabian Freeway*), and Gary Allen (*None Dare Call It Conspiracy*), along with stars of the future such as Jack Mohr (*The Psychopolitical Indoctrination of America!*) and G. Edward Griffin (*The Creature from Jekyll Island*).[3]

The mainstay of entrepreneurial conspiracism was the event—the rally, the forum, the "school." Fred C. Schwarz, head of the Christian Anti-Communist Crusade, excelled in this area. Primarily an anti-Communist, Schwarz peppered the "faculty" of his many "schools" and "seminars" with minor conspiracists. Schwarz also worked closely with W. W. Lynch, president of Texas Power and Light, to put on the Dallas Freedom Forums in the early 1960s. Along with Schwarz's regular faculty, these forums featured W. Cleon Skousen and Ronald Reagan. Also in Dallas, local John Birch Society members began a National Indignation Convention, a series of rallies featuring conspiracists such as Dan Smoot and Tom Anderson. A strong military presence was evident in the 1961 West Coast "school of anti-communism": "Project Alert!" The topic for this group's first session was the loaded question, "Is the news media suppressing the facts through communist infiltration?"[4]

Billy James Hargis, head of the Christian Crusade, held his first annual National Anti-Communist Leadership School in Tulsa, his base of operations, in 1962. Generally regarded as an anti-Communist, Hargis often used the language of premillennialism to convey a genuinely satanic conspiracy. Hargis put together a much more conspiratorial event than Schwarz's, with speakers R. Carter Pittman (civil rights), Edward Hunter (brainwashing), Myers Lowman (church subversion), and Revilo Oliver (American society).[5] The Congress of Freedom, which had begun small in Omaha in 1953, had morphed by 1960 into a vehicle for vaguely conspiracist tax resisters and a more seriously conspiratorial group called the Independent Farmers whose members had personally "tasted the bitter pills of Government and Bureaucratic persecution and vindictiveness."[6] And Kenneth Goff's Soldiers of the Cross Training Institute and Bible School in the Colorado Rockies offered courses with names like The United Nations and the World Revolutionary Movement, along with exposés of psychopolitics and evolution. The institute became increasingly radical, adding to its curriculum such courses as Survival and Christian Resistance by 1969. Goff also ran a publishing operation, the output of which included Dallas Roquemore's survivalist epic, *Get Ye Up into the High Mountains.*[7]

Government Control

A dominant theme among conspiracist speakers was the ever-increasing mistrust of the federal government. More than lingering opposition to the New Deal or Truman's Fair Deal, this mistrust grew out of fear of internationalism, which political leaders in both parties were embracing, as well as federal revenue sharing with state and local governments. Conspiracists saw these developments as evidence of federal encroachment on local sovereignty and as a conduit for the demands of the UN. The UN's efforts to combat genocide, for instance, were seen as part of a larger initiative, under which causing anyone "mental harm" would be a crime under the "Nero-like powers of the Genocide Convention." Thus, by calling a black person a "nigger" ("even jokingly"), you could be "hauled off to court in Tel Aviv or Afghanistan, as decided by the UN, and if found guilty, shipped off to hard labor in a Siberian Slave Labor Camp."[8] This combination of racism and fear of the UN was not at all unusual. Chicago's White Circle League merged the two regularly in leaflets warning of the threat posed by blacks and Jews: "White Americans—wake up—save your own beloved land—the federals will take it—as soon as they can. Get every Southern Rebel who can man a gun—we will need to arm our women. . . . Our government has betrayed us—to United Nations band. [?] Better to fight on American soil—and be a 'free man.'"[9]

Many conspiracists took Britain as a model of what Americans could expect if they were not vigilant. Clarence Manion, dean of the Notre Dame Law School, called the Labour program a type of "State Absolutism," which must be fought here, because "unless you counterattack swiftly and sharply you are likely to be denatured." Manion was one of many who argued that the federal government's grants-in-aid to local governments would allow it to "buy its way into complete centralized control" of all local functions.[10] The same note was sounded by Ben Moreell, a Navy engineer turned steel company executive. Moreell's 1952 speech to the American Petroleum Institute was entitled "To Communism . . . via Majority Vote" to underscore the method by which Communism had taken over England. Moreell designated the threat faced by America as "planning," a practice of "social engineers," and "dedicated to the thesis that, by using the force of government, mankind in the mass can be changed and molded to conform to a master plan." Famous social engineers included Robespierre and Hitler, but explicitly not Jesus. Spurred on by the UN, social engineers were dragging Americans inexorably to the "bondage of the welfare state," which Moreell saw as equal to the "bondage of slavery."[11]

Opposition to what was usually referred to simply as planning was not at all unusual among conservatives from the 1950s onward. In his

1954 report to the Reece Committee, Norman Dodd expressed concern about the academic research organizations that received funds from philanthropic foundations: "It is difficult to avoid the feeling that their common interest has led them to cooperate closely . . . in the planning and control of certain aspects of American life through a control of the federal government and education." Dodd imagined that people in these organizations called themselves social engineers, suggesting that "freedom . . . has already been abandoned." As it happened, many of the social engineers were headquartered in one building at the University of Chicago—depending on the year, anywhere from seventeen to twenty-two organizations, such as the National Association of Budget Officers and the Council of State Governments. This building came to be known by its street number, 1313, which became a shorthand term among conspiracists.[12]

While others may also have objected to specific policies emerging from 1313, conspiracists articulated the true threat: world government "to be operated by appointed social science 'experts.'" Prolific 1313 opponent Jo Hindman imagined "swift moving teams of social engineers, self-described 'experts'" as the "1313 carriers" of what she called "political leukemia."[13] Some saw deeper conspiracies than others. William Guy Carr identified 1313 as an "Illuminist training centre" funded by the same foundations that provided the money for the Council on Foreign Relations. According to Carr, "The Illuminists . . . call themselves 'The Public Administration Services.' They pretend to improve Civic Governments and Social Services. In reality they train selected agentur to occupy key positions in all levels of civic government." Jo Hindman, more typically, saw the UN Charter behind the scenes, while Kent and Phoebe Courtney, Louisiana-based opponents of the federal government, stopped at the Council on Foreign Relations.[14]

Regardless of the ultimate source, the threat was essentially the same: the certain elimination of lower levels of government and, probably, the absorption of America into a world government—as there are only "four steps between city-county merging and U.S.-Foreign Government merging." The "Metrocrat" ("the individual who promotes 1313's destructive and tyrannical government") "ATTACKS American constitutional government by whacking off your limited controls from your government. '1313' then substitutes unlimited Metro in the place of the governing power formerly derived from you." As is always the case in a well-run conspiracy, the truth is censored. Metrocrat employees and "volunteers" in local government, "pro-metro" Chambers of Commerce, and civic organizations such as the League of Women Voters tout the benefits of 1313's plans, and the "Brainwashing Department of the CFR" does the rest. On those occasions when the Council on Foreign Relations' broadcasters, newspapers, and magazines "fail to drum up enough public support for CFR-recommended legislation, CFR member Elmo Roper can always be counted on to take a poll and come up with his findings that the American people 'support' the proposed legislation."[15]

Federal encroachment on local government was mostly seen as a gradual and rather programmatic undertaking. Frequently tied to federal revenue sharing, the result would be "far more centralization of power in Washington, and the practical elimination of our state lines." The National Economic Council estimated rather loosely that, for every billion dollars in federal funding, "a large number of Americans will be just so much more thoroughly regimented and brought under the control of the power-hungry Federal Administration."[16] But a more drastic federal effort to destroy the states was also underway: specifically, civil rights legislation. The proposed civil rights bill of 1963 meant "the end of the Republic, the destruction of constitutional sovereignty of the states which formed it, and direct and arbitrary federal control of every individual.... The authority of state government will be rubbed out." In a document titled "Open Letter to the Governors and Representatives of the Sovereign States," Conde McGinley urged officials to mobilize state militias. It was not the time, the letter warned, "to permit further intrusion into the States from corrupt and irresponsible—if not actually disloyal—bureaucracy."[17]

The Civil Rights Conspiracy

Federal support for civil rights in the 1960s generated a great deal of mistrust of the government in the South and among racists everywhere. As with anti-Communists, one could be a thoroughgoing racist without a conspiratorial perspective. However, once the specter of a conspiracy began to arise, few vocal opponents of civil rights ignored it. The basic conspiracy grew out of the belief common among Southern racists that blacks did not want any change in their situation and, even if they did, were incapable of bringing it about. Working backwards, as conspiracists do, the question then became: what forces are really behind the civil rights movement? Not surprisingly, the force turned out to be Communists, with Jews lurking in the background.[18]

As far back as the 1940s, opponents of racial integration cited the *Protocols* of the Learned Elders of Zion to explain the forces behind nascent civil rights efforts. Marilyn Allen's *Protocols*-based diatribe *My Country Right or Wrong My Country* led directly to her lengthy career against "Mongrelization." And the up-and-coming Klan leader J. B. Stoner advertised copies of the *Protocols* at $2.00 each next to articles advocating killing both Jews and blacks.[19] By the mid-1950s, Conde McGinley's newspaper *Common Sense* was explaining how the NAACP was controlled by Zionists and warning of social upheaval: "Jewish Marxists Threaten Negro Revolt in America! Communists Plan Black Republic in South." James H. Madole disparaged New York Jews as "professional tolerance merchants" who were actually "fomenting" a Civil War in the South. A flyer by the Christian Patriots Crusade depicted a lynching, which it described as "old-fashioned American justice" for the "JEWISH" crime of "race-mixing."[20]

The threat posed by racial desegregation evolved quickly into a conspiracy against the white race. The Anti-Defamation League, the NAACP, and other organizations were depicted as having "banded together in a vast conspiracy to destroy our heritage," causing white America to fall like "every other nation in history that allowed its blood to be mixed with that of the colored races." The media were naturally in on the conspiracy, and even the "clerical authorities" of the Catholic Church could be found working with the Jews' "vicious leftist pressure groups." More specific accusations were also common. The murder of fourteen-year-old Emmett Till in Mississippi in 1955 was purportedly revealed to have been "a hoax created by the Jewish inspired NAACP to implement racial hatred." This hoax was enabled by Jews' total control of all media.[21] J. B. Stoner's National States' Rights Party hammered away at the civil rights organizations they saw as controlled by Jews: "Our answer to the Jewish race mixers is: 'We united Whitemen will crush down into hell your satanic plot to destroy our people.'" States' Rights Party leader and Christian Identity pastor Oren Potito also refused to give in to the "International Jewish Dictators": "The Kingdoms of this world belong to you and I, of the White Christian Anglo-Saxon race. This is our Father's world and it is our inheritance, not to enslave, but to free, not to abuse, but to rule with Righteousness, and as White Christian Anglo-Saxons, rule it we shall."[22]

Stoner's rhetoric was no match for that of Chicago-based racist Joseph Beauharnais, leader of the White Circle League of America. Beauharnais's white supremacist tirade after the assassination of Martin Luther King Jr. wandered off track when he broadened it to include those who "hold every citizen and TAX SLAVE in financial and political bondage while the SHELL GAMES of regimentation and exploitation and TAX GOUGING GOES endlessly on and AMERICA sinks deeper into the PIT of the Rothschild International Financial WORLD Oligarchy."[23] More sedately, Wilmot Robertson's 1972 manifesto, *The Dispossessed Majority*, outlined in detail the conspiracy against "the truly disadvantaged"— that is, whites—who "are hated for their virtues, not their vices, . . . discomfited and threatened." Robertson clarified his definition of this dispossessed "majority," in his ill-tempered follow-up book, *Ventilations*. The battle was not between black and white, but pitted the majority— Americans of north European extraction—against "an agglomeration of minorities consisting of Jews, dark-skinned Mediterranean Whites, Chicanos, Indians, Puerto Ricans, and Negroes."[24]

The viscerally threatening prospect behind civil rights legislation and the "negro revolt" was interracial sex. Concern over so-called mongrelization was widespread and frequently presented as a key part of a conspiracy. Evil forces were hard at work, as Robert Williams demonstrated in his assessment of the problem: "We see beautiful blonde girls marrying Negroes, while we accept without protest the recent arbitrary change (by an alien-dominated New Deal bureau) of census rules so as to classify the brown and yellow Semitic and Mongoloid Jews, and the brown Mexican-Indians of our border states, as Whites. And UNESCO, a Jewish invention, recently endorsed a statement by eight so-called scientists in Paris that 'no biological harm comes from mixed marriages.'"[25] The "forces of organized INTERACIALISM" were working overtime to "destroy WHITE RACIAL IDENTITY." Yet the *Revere*, an anti–civil rights newsletter published in the Chicago suburbs, was happy to report in a 1956 article titled "Race-Mixing Scorecard" that the "mongrelizers have made very little headway." By the 1960s, the situation had become more severe. On the West Coast, Richard Butler's Christian Defense League accepted only white members in order to fight the "diabolical . . . program to wipe out the white race by mongrelization . . . in direct opposition to God's laws and instructions to His People." Race mixing was seen everywhere. After the Selma-to-Montgomery march, Alabama Representative William Dickinson was quoted as saying, "Drunkenness and sex orgies was [*sic*] the order of the day in Selma, on the road to Montgomery, and in Montgomery."[26]

For those not obsessed with interracial sex, discussion of the civil rights conspiracy took place on a slightly higher plane. Archibald B. Roosevelt's preface to a report by the Alliance cited Arnold Toynbee and Herodotus as advocates of strict racial separation before explaining that the report would reveal that "communist psychological warfare" seeks "to confuse their dupes with semantics, pseudoscience, and misrepresentation," with the pseudosciences encompassing such fields as anthropology ("there is no difference due to race") and sociology ("all differentiation of race and racial characteristics is bad").[27]

The Communist conspiracy behind the civil rights movement was different from the anti-Communism imbedded in one-worlder conspiracy theory, which might involve Fabians or the Rockefeller Foundation.

The civil rights conspiracy, while organized by Jews and buttressed by Left-leaning politicians and academics, was directed from the Kremlin. Soviet agents had "colonized in the South," and were working "with sadistic joy as their plot materializes."[28] The standard photograph of Martin Luther King Jr. at the "communist training school" in Tennessee might accompany accusations (typically described as "citations") that King belonged to sixty Communist front organizations. Smaller numbers could be affixed to Bayard Rustin, A. Philip Randolph, Roy Wilkins, Ralph Bunche, and Thurgood Marshall.[29] Only rarely did a conspiracist break away from the Communist party narrative, as *Common Sense* did with a story about a government report recommending greater "equality of treatment" across races in the armed services. The magazine declared the report to be the work of the NAACP but also linked it to the traitors who had whitewashed FDR's role in the attack on Pearl Harbor, to Alger Hiss and his single-handed creation of the UN, and to at least one Rhodes Scholar.[30]

Over time, this sort of creativity diminished, and interpretations of events became relentlessly predictable. The Selma march originated in the Communist Party's "Lincoln Project" of 1956. Race riots were orchestrated by President Johnson for the Kremlin as part of the "plan for world government." The 1965 Watts riot was "born in Moscow more than three decades and was actually planned in the Los Angeles area for many years by the vicious and insideous [*sic*] communist organization." Racial incidents in Detroit were "part of a deliberate program to drive America to communist dictatorship." And Chicago was chosen by the Communist Party and its front groups ("SCLC, SNCC, CORE, CCCO, NAACP & MFDP [to name just a few]") in order to "provoke violence, hatred, & civil war between negroes & whites."[31] In all this, the federal government was clearly the enemy, as an account of a raid in New Orleans on the Southern Conference Educational Fund headquarters demonstrated. Working with the Louisiana Joint Legislative Committee on Un-American Activities, but "refusing to confide their plans" to the FBI for fear of "leaks," the New Orleans police claimed to link the Southern Conference Educational Fund both to Communists and to

Eleanor Roosevelt. Even King's assassination was interpreted as part of the civil rights conspiracy, in which King's "Controllers"—"a small band of rich, educated and not at all oppressed conspirators secretly running the communization of America"—have him killed to ensure the passage of civil rights legislation.[32]

Conspiracists applied the same explanatory template to the anti-Vietnam War movement as they had to civil rights. Some remembered that progressive education was "sabotaging the minds and moral instincts of the children" and saw its effects in the counterculture. Others saw the Communists' handiwork in the sudden popularity of Gandhi's "heathen religion." But, again, the prevailing explanation was Communism, backed by the federal government (after all, it was Secretary of Defense Robert McNamara who allowed "peaceniks" to "swarm over" the Pentagon).[33] Robert Shelton, head of the United Klans of America, was one of many who was not fooled. "Regardless of what subterfuge they might use," he editorialized, the Communist conspiracy was behind the peace movement. Similarly, conspiracists were able to see through the many peace groups: "This labyrinth of individual groups and organizations, often supported by persons highly placed in politics, the entertainment world and industry, and 'coincidentally' dovetailing with basic philosophies and goals of other groups in divergent fields, projects an image of a movement, or even a conspiracy."[34]

The End of Sovereignty

Civil rights and the peace movement generated a great deal of conspiratorial writing but few new ideas. Among antisemites, Jews figured in prominently, and occasionally one-worlders might appear. What was notable about the main threats of the 1960s is that they turned out to be the last major use of old-fashioned Communist Party conspiracism. By the end of the decade, the civil rights and peace movements were surpassed by "emergency preparedness"—the bland-sounding pretext for the complete government takeover that had become the conspiracists' main concern. President Nixon galvanized conspiracists with his 1969 executive order delineating ten administrative regions to be used in a state of national emergency, as explained by Don Bell: "The creation of these 'Ten Provinces' has received little or no publicity; nor is it generally known that if and when the President . . . finds it expedient or necessary, he can invoke Executive Order 11490, convert this Republic into a Bureaucratic Dictatorship governed absolutely from Washington, D.C. through these Ten Regions and their Ten Capitol [sic] Cities, bypassing and ignoring all State, County, City and Local governments!"[35] Just over two years later, Nixon confirmed the conspiracists' worst fears with another executive order allowing the ten regions to be used to establish "closer working relationships between major Federal grant-making agencies and State and Local government and improved coordination of the categorical grant system." Representative John Rarick of Louisiana, a long-standing hidden hand conspiracist, saw this as a method of getting around the "problem" that "the States are managed by elected officials." Soon, the authority of state officeholders could be replaced by "Under Secretaries for regional councils."[36]

The specter of the destruction of state sovereignty—or in extreme versions, the abolition of the states entirely—became a key element in conspiratorial thinking. Citizens for American Survival warned that "all levels of government are in the process of being reduced to a conglomerate of sovietized regions."[37] Congressman Larry McDonald "revealed to Congress" that the government, which was secretly supporting domestic terrorist groups, would "activate" these groups and then use executive order 11490 to meet the "threat." William Pabst sketched a scenario of what might follow such an order:

The next day you and your family would be standing in front of your local post office with your neighbors, the front doors bursting with block-long lines of people waiting to be registered. After waiting in line with your family for hours, you finally get channeled through the doors. Once inside you hear the postal clerk with his sidearm on telling a frightened registrant, "Look, there's nothing I can do. The truck behind the building will take you to a work camp where you have been assigned. Your wife has been assigned to a factory and there's nothing I can do." Then your son or daughter looks up at you with a quivering voice and asks, "Dad, why are we here?"[38]

Concern over regionalism was remarkably widespread. Citizens for Constitutional Government lobbied against updating the Montana Constitution for fear of establishing "REGIONAL GOVERNMENT" as a step toward world government. "This is a planned dictatorship they are talking about creating. Although this is not the sole reason for revising our State Constitution, it is the reason why these proponents of Oneworldism are so actively interested."[39] Long-time anti-CFR activist Phoebe Courtney devoted her fifth book to regional government, including a look back at 1313 as regional government's original "Trojan Horse." Don Bell devoted his weekly commentaries to a twenty-one-part exposé titled "The Contrived Evolution of Regional Government," complete with maps of the ten regions and of the emerging fifteen "super-regions of the United States" based on Standard Metropolitan Statistical Areas.[40] The use of regions by the Environmental Protection Agency (EPA) and, even more menacingly, by the Federal Emergency Management Agency (FEMA) has kept conspiratorial attention focused on regions to a remarkable degree.[41] One Nate Brown, writing in the *Christian Journal*, warns Americans that the "infamous" North American Union's "plan to do away with the 50 states and create FEMA regions is happening right now." Deanna Spingola, however, under the heading "The United States Was Officially Abolished in 1972!" provides maps to show that FEMA regions have long existed, that they are the same as Nixon's regions, the EPA's regions, and possibly North American Free Trade Agreement trade corridors.[42]

By the 1960s, the federal government's threat to gun ownership had become an equally conspiratorial issue. The people needed to stand up to government, but "plans to confiscate all private firearms by the end of 1965" were in the works even before the Kennedy assassination brought gun control to the forefront. Wesley Swift castigated "the brain washed clergy" for their support of gun control. Attributing an actual plan to the clergy, Swift claimed "that they intend to start after the election on five States and then spread it through the Country, but Law Enforcement officers don't know that in this plan, it also called for the disarmament of Law Enforcement officers and the establishment now of a military police by selected man power taken out of the armed services and put under United Nation's control."[43] Conspiracists fighting proposed legislation in 1965 explained how the Soviet Jews had used gun control to keep "170 million Russian Gentiles in total submission." Pamphlets and newsletters galore warned: "Don't let them take your guns away!" To do so would "surrender your last bastion of defense against total dictatorship and enslavement!" Gun control opponents appear to have been the first to routinely use a wholly unspecified "they" to represent the conspirators: "In the final analysis . . . if political and constitutional methodology has failed to protect your life and liberty and 'they' have come to take your firearms. . . . Then give it all to them. . . . BULLET BY BULLET!!!!!!!!!!!!!"[44]

Many other issues raised right-wing conspiratorial alarms, reflecting growing mistrust of government and authority in general. The government's abandonment of silver coins in 1965 was interpreted as part of its plot to debase our currency. The UN's plan to have soccer take over our school sports ("as a way of de-emphasizing nationalism") would be implemented with even girls encouraged to play ("rather than to look forward to being a mother"). International conspirators were also pushing for homosexuals to be counted "as a 'minority group.'" They could be stopped but only if current laws were enforced so that "the control of our Federal government and deep penetration of many state governments by the combined Homosexual International and the International Communist Conspiracy could be completely broken."[45]

A Note on "They"

The disembodied "they" has long been a popular identifying trait of conspiracism. It is difficult to determine exactly when "they" shifted from a reputable pronoun to a vague substitute for identifiable people.

It may well have accompanied the 1950s emergence of the term "invisible government" as a similarly nebulous concept. Conspiracist rhetoric in the 1920s and 1930s had singled out specific Jews all too readily: from Jacob Schiff to Felix Frankfurter and Albert Einstein. Elizabeth Dilling made her reputation by compiling lists of people she considered suspicious. Well into the 1950s, conspiracists made clear just who was manipulating events behind the scenes. For Gerald L. K. Smith, it was Eleanor Roosevelt; for Joseph Kamp, it was labor leader Walter Reuther; for Myron Fagan, it was newsman Chet Huntley.[46] But by the time of the campaign against Martin Luther King Jr., specificity was dying out. Falling back on "they" as the enemy of "we" was already a common anti-Communist rhetorical tactic that blurred the lines between liberals, socialists, and Communists.[47] The implications behind "fellow traveler," "Comsymp" (short for "Communist sympathizer"), and "pink" included many more people than could possibly be actual Communists. Similarly, the condemnation of unspecified "dupes" and "stooges" had a fairly long rhetorical history. Newly coined terms such as "globalist" and "one-worlder" were even less precise and were applied to people ranging from "sexologist" Dr. Mary Calderone to President Eisenhower.

Many terms were used pejoratively rather than with any pretense of description: "pseudo-intellectual," "social engineer," "expert," "planner." Conspiracist writers typically placed these terms in quotation marks to indicate that they considered the designations fraudulent as well: William Guy Carr's "'Specialists,' 'Experts,' and 'Advisors,'" Jo-Ann Abrigg's "so-called 'Educational Experts,'" Ed Dieckmann's "class of . . . 'social facilitators' who plan to 'correct' your thinking." This vagueness blurs the lines between people and their activities. People are anonymously caricatured as the ones who make up "do-gooder groups" and disparaged as those who "pose, hypocritically, as generous philanthropists, presidential advisers, social uplifters, civil righters, and vocal champions of the downtrodden masses!" This rhetorical trick also obscures the difference between people and the occupations or organizations with which they were affiliated. Public administrators and their organizations could all be covered with the blanket term "1313." Unspecified practitioners of "Third Force Psychology" were the ones trying to force "the religion of Humanism" into everyone's brains.[48]

The same rhetorical evasiveness was used to sanitize the antisemitism behind so much conspiratorial thinking. Even Benjamin Freedman, an open antisemite, used "they" constantly to avoid having to specify his targets. For example, Freedman's account of how Woodrow Wilson was elected president includes these key statements in a single paragraph, all implicit references to the Jews:

They set up the Democratic National Headquarters.

They looked around for a man to put up as president.

They got Woodrow Wilson.

They trotted Theodore Roosevelt out of political "moth-balls."

They got plenty of money from England.

They formed the Bull Moose Party.

And, thus, "they split the Republican vote between Roosevelt and Taft, and Mr. Wilson walked in with a minority of the popular vote."[49] Others took greater pains to disguise the antisemitic basis of their ideas; eventually even the old standby, "international bankers," had become too obvious. June Grem updated that term to "international manipulators." Mary M. Davison fell back on "New York Establishment." The inclusion of "presidential advisers" in the quotation about things people "pose" as in the preceding paragraph, by the way, is a guarded allusion to Bernard Baruch, formerly of the "hidden hand."[50]

It is easy to overlook meaningless designations in conspiracist writing. Gerald L. K. Smith has used "the political sectors of society"; David Noebel has referred to the conspirators as having "their scientists, educators, and entertainers"; and Klan leader Robert Shelton brought up "other groups in divergent fields." None of these statements led to any further indication of what these sectors might be, which scientists, educators, and entertainers, or what other groups in which "divergent" fields. All these rhetorical sleights lead in the direction of the disembodied "they" and serve four related purposes. First, the vagueness allows the conspiracist writer to avoid specifics: who is actually behind some conspiratorial action? A cynical conspiracist can use this to try to fool readers, but many surely fool themselves the same way. Second, the lack of specificity allows the reader to insert whatever referent makes sense. When warned, "Don't let them take your guns away!" a relatively moderate reader might think of actual gun control advocates. Conspiracists, however, might think of those shadowy planners waiting to activate executive order 11490 to send you to the work camp. Third, the use of "they" invites readers to imagine a great many powerful conspirators. The Sexuality Information and Education Council of the United States may not be a formidable opponent, but the "they" behind "Pavlovian mind conditioning" certainly is. Fourth, and probably most important, the use of "they" makes it possible for conspiracists to ensnare any new development or event in the conspiracy. To the degree that one presents a group of real conspirators, it is necessary to explain why they would suddenly decide to, for instance, poison everyone with chemtrails. "They" eliminates this need.

11

PAN-IDEOLOGICAL
CONSPIRACY THEORIES

DENIALISM AND COVER-UP

From amongst the chaos . . . emerges one obvious question: "Is the left
wing or the right wing correct?" The answer is: Neither. These concepts
are wrong. They were implanted in the mind of man through heavy,
media conditioning.

Stan Deyo, *The Cosmic Conspiracy*

The period spanning roughly from the Kennedy assassination to the
election of Ronald Reagan marked more than just a turning point in conspiracy theorizing. Aside from the massive level of interest in assassination conspiracies, conspiracism in general seemed to be on the decline.
Beneath the surface, however, conspiracy theories were mushrooming,
incorporating new topics, a much wider segment of the public, and even
distinctively new approaches. The underlying phenomenon behind this
expansion was the unprecedented decline in trust in government as
well as other authoritative institutions, such as organized religion, the
business community, and eventually even science, the military, and the
media. With regard to the government in particular, declining trust was

transformed into active mistrust, an outlook extremely compatible with conspiratorial thinking.

The End of Trust

Many attribute the growth of mistrust in this era to high-profile events: the assassinations of John and Robert Kennedy, the King assassination, the war in Vietnam, and the Watergate hearings. There were, however, many more events contributing to mistrust, and even alienation, among different segments of the public. Some of these events seem mild today, and it is hard to recapture the impact they had. For example, environmental activism and reporting in the 1960s shook the confidence of many moderate Americans by exposing hazardous business practices and lax regulations. And during the 1970s, a relentless series of revelations of governmental wrongdoing created a climate in which conspiracism was able to flourish. In 1971, anti-war activists exposed COINTELPRO, the FBI's counterintelligence program operation against civil rights and black power activists. The *Washington Star* broke the story of the Tuskegee syphilis experiments in 1972. In 1974, investigative reporter Seymour Hersh published stories of CIA spying on Americans. Interest in JFK's assassination rebounded strongly in 1975 when the Zapruder film was shown on network television.

These and other conspiracy-friendly subjects received even more media and public attention due to a remarkable series of government investigations and hearings. Senator Edward Kennedy held hearings on the Tuskegee experiment. More prominently, the Church Committee held hearings on the FBI's counterintelligence program and various CIA practices. These hearings revealed FBI efforts to undermine civil rights organizations (including Native American and Hispanic groups) as well as the anti-war movement. More alarming to most people, they also revealed the CIA's practice of assassinating foreign leaders, including embarrassing accounts of the CIA's efforts to assassinate Fidel Castro, which also exposed the collaborative relationship between the CIA and organized crime. At the same time, Vice President Nelson Rockefeller oversaw the Commission on CIA Activities in the United States, devoted in part to uncovering the CIA's MK-Ultra (mind control) experiments. During Representative Otis Pike's tenure as chairman of the House Permanent Select Committee on Intelligence, hearings on the activities of the FBI, the CIA, and the Defense Intelligence Agency proved so incendiary that the committee's report was not even published by the Government Printing Office. Deteriorating public confidence in the Warren Commission's investigation of the Kennedy assassination led to the 1976 House Select Committee on Assassinations, the ambivalent conclusions of which fueled conspiratorial thinking about both the Kennedy and King assassinations. Also in 1976, Representative Sonny Montgomery's Select Committee on Missing Persons in Southeast Asia issued its unambivalent finding on POWs that "no Americans are still being held alive in Indochina, or elsewhere, as result of the war in Indochina."[1] However, mistrust of government had reached a point where many refused to believe this.

A conspiratorial meme took hold in popular culture alongside the news coverage and investigations, with any number of conspiratorial movies in the mid-seventies. In 1972, George C. Scott starred in *Rage* as a Utah sheep rancher faced with the cover-up of a military nerve gas leak that killed all his sheep and his son as well. *The Conversation*, from 1973, highlighted creeping surveillance technology. *The Parallax View* (tagline: "There is no conspiracy. Just twelve people dead.") and *Three Days of the Condor* (1974 and 1975, respectively) featured conspiracies by a multinational corporation and the CIA respectively. In 1976, *All the President's Men* compressed the Watergate scandal into two hours. A NASA mission was shown to be a hoax in the 1977 film *Capricorn One*. Chuck Norris faced down a military establishment determined to deny the existence of POWs in 1978's *Good Guys Wear Black*. And, wrapping up the decade, *Winter Kills*, a black comedy about the Kennedy assassination.[2]

The new conspiracy theories that grew out of this milieu of journalistic exposés, congressional investigations, and popular culture are typified by the moon-landing hoax conspiracy. This constituted a new approach to conspiracism; its proponents built it out of nothing, and it appealed to a wider array of people by avoiding the overtly political or ideological. In the years after the moon landing, public opinion surveys consistently showed that a noticeable minority of people doubted that it had in fact taken place. Seizing the opportunity, a public relations practitioner and writer of books such as *How to Eat Well on Less Than a Dollar a Day*, Bill Kaysing, coauthored a short book depicting an elaborate hoax. *We Never Went to the Moon: America's Thirty Billion Dollar Swindle* took advantage of the fact that, as Kaysing explained, "government deception, supported by a pervasive system of official secrecy and an enormous public relations machine, has reaped a harvest of massive public distrust."[3]

One problem facing Kaysing was logistics: how could NASA, or anyone, fake a moon landing? The other problem was motivation: why should they? Kaysing offered some desultory arguments about intimidation of astronauts and control of the media, but he was more interested in asking questions along the lines of "Why were all transmissions to be public via TV and radio, media of communications easily faked?" and "Why did so many astronauts end up as executives of large corporations?" Kaysing then offered up considerable technical detail, daunting, but relatively pointless: the composition of "hypergolic propellants" and a cutaway illustration of the Lunar Excursion Module to show how many parts it had that might misfunction. Third, he relied very heavily on visuals, printing grainy images of the moon, with captions such as "NO evidence of the surface being disturbed beneath the engine nozzle," "Again, no stars!" and "No dust on face shield." Less compelling were pictures of a patch of Nevada desert having a "striking similarity" to the moon and of the buffet at the Sands Hotel and Casino, where the astronauts presumably ate while the hoax was going on.[4] This scattershot approach, heavy with visuals but light on argumentation—"just asking questions"—has become a standard method of creating and defending conspiracy theories. It replaced the ideology in earlier conspiracy theories, which had given people a framework for accepting them. Disaggregated information, provided to the point of overload, with strong visuals and loaded questions turned out to be a powerful tactic for drawing people in (not to mention selling books).

The moon-landing conspiracy also illustrates the staying power of conspiracies in today's media environment. Flimsy and inconsequential as it was, Kaysing's conspiracy received a boost from the 1977 movie *Capricorn One*, a thriller depicting a Mars mission hoax. Five years later, one William Brian II went in a different direction, arguing that NASA was covering up data that proved the earth to be hollow and hypothesizing alien interference with the moon shot. This idea did not catch on but did help keep the conspiracy going. Ralph René's 1992 *NASA Mooned America!* returned to the original hoax idea, but since it was embedded in extraneous material such as a new value for the math constant pi and denial of the existence of gravity, René's work fared no better.[5] Even Bart Sibrel's "documentary" film *Astronauts Gone Wild* was marginal, although Sibrel gained some notoriety by provoking astronaut Buzz Aldrin into punching him. At the same time, Fox television, avoiding gratuitous weirdness, promoted the original hoax in a much more sophisticated way. Expanding the number of bogus missions from one to six, and hinting at a number of suspicious astronaut deaths, Fox's "news special" "let the viewer decide" whether the hoax-touting "experts" (such as Sibrel) were convincing.[6] Today, a quick Google search will bring anyone to what is essentially an expanded version of Kaysing's original book: a seemingly endless parade of photographs with loaded-question captions. Repeated efforts by NASA to explain such "evidence" have been declared to be just part of the conspiracy.

The moon-landing conspiracy is one of several conspiracy theories that can appeal to people across the political spectrum. Similarly, UFO conspiracy theories are largely pan-ideological in all their variants, including abductions, secret underground bases, and alien technologies.[7] Probably the most prominent area of pan-ideological conspiracism today deals with health and medical issues: pandemics, alternative medicine, genetically modified food, AIDS, and, of course, vaccines.[8] In a slightly different fashion, MK-Ultra-based mind-control conspiracies invariably have a political dimension, whether a left-wing conspiracy about corporate-fascism or a right-wing one about global government's plans for its critics. Even 9/11 conspiracy theories, initially dominated by leftist attacks on the Bush administration, have become more politically balanced as leftist interest has faded and rightist interpretations have emerged. And sometimes nonideological conspiracy theories have been moved by a particularly strong faction into one or another ideological camp. This is essentially what happened to the conspiracy theory that the government was covering up the existence of POWs in Indochina, which shifted violently to the Right in the 1980s.[9]

Many conspiracy theories with ambiguous politics fall into one of two general categories: denialism and conspiracy by cover-up. Both grow primarily out of mistrust of authorities and may well be most pronounced among "cynical individuals who support democratic principles." These are people who wish they were able to trust their own government. Psychologists maintain that denialists' belief in conspiracy theories "allows them to exert some control over their lives." To denialists, the "official story" comes to be thought of as a conspiratorial construct in its own right, making *any* alternative attractive by comparison.[10] The construction of a conspiracy by cover-up begins similarly but moves on to at least one widely believed conspiracy theory. The template for this method of conspiracy building is the UFO movement.

Denialism

"Denialism" is a relatively recently coined term used to differentiate between professing a conspiracy theory and merely refusing to accept a well-established official explanation. Although the term arose in the context of climate change and vaccines, denialism is of course much older. Looking back only to the beginning of the twentieth century, denial of scientific advances in any number of areas was fairly common. Flat Earth advocates published their explanatory maps, creationists resisted the onslaught of evolutionary theory, quacks stood up to the authority of the medical establishment. We can see denialism in Kennedy assassination conspiracism as well, in that, of the millions of people who disbelieve the explanation that Lee Harvey Oswald was a lone shooter, only a small percentage believe any particular other narrative. More troublingly, today there are people who consider themselves "sovereign citizens," a status rooted in their denial of the "corporate existence" of the government.[11]

Contemporary denialism, however, is more than just a refusal to believe; it is an active process—what Robert Proctor calls "agnotology" or "the cultural production of ignorance." While the earliest example of this could well be Bill Kaysing's moon-landing denialism, Proctor suggests that the "evil genius" behind it may have come from the tobacco industry: "The idea was that people would continue to smoke so long as they could be reassured that 'no one really knows' the true cause of cancer. The strategy was to question all assertions to the contrary, all efforts to 'close' the controversy, as if closure itself was a mark of dogma, the enemy of inquiry. The point was to keep the question of health harms open, for decades if possible."[12] This strategy links denialism to pseudoscience in two complementary ways. First, pseudoscientific claims are used to bolster denialist views, and second, the very concept of science is attacked and discredited. The pseudoscientific claims are sometimes the work of scientific "gadflies," or they may come out of well-heeled corporate labs. Or they may simply be made up. One study of anti-vaccination websites found that over two-thirds claimed "scientific" backing for bogus claims such as vaccines' causing "brain damage." Similarly, AIDS denialist Matt Irwin has claimed that an HIV-positive diagnosis causes stress, which suppresses the immune system, thus generating "immune system disregulation that may later be called 'AIDS.'"[13]

Denialism, pseudoscience, and conspiracism are closely related. Some beliefs begin as denialism but slowly become conspiratorial to answer critics who wonder why everyone else believes what they deny. Anticipating this, deniers frequently describe the cover-up and censorship they face. This was the case for Bill Kaysing's moon-landing exposé; HIV and polio denialists have followed the same practice; and (replacing scientists with historians) Holocaust deniers have done the same for years.[14] More frequently, denialism and the accompanying conspiracy emerge together. Vaccine-induced autism believers saw early on "massive academic fraud and conspiracy to discredit Dr. Andrew Wakefield" by authorities who spread "provably false lies about his research." (Wakefield's discredited research began the measles, mumps, and rubella vaccine scare.) Much the same is true of food-related conspiracies, such as those surrounding pasteurized milk and genetically modified organisms. A third situation arises when denialism is purposefully used in support of a conspiracy theory. This, of course, was the tactic pioneered by the tobacco companies but applied to climate change.[15]

Discrediting science outright, rather than co-opting it, is today's prominent strategy. By subtly discrediting "scientism," which suggests a gullible willingness to believe whatever orthodox science claims, conspiracists can use "alternative" scientific findings while at the same time disparaging the scientific establishment. This is where denialism most strongly intersects with conspiracism. The "conspiratorial element of denial," as Stephan Lewandowsky puts it, "explains why contrarians often perceive themselves as heroic dissenters who—in their imagination—are following Galileo's footsteps by opposing a mainstream scientific 'elite' that imposes its views . . . for political reasons."[16] For example, conspiracist Russell Blaylock, a neuroscientist, took exception to an article by the psychologist Sander van der Linden that had noted the troublesome societal implications of climate change denial. Blaylock complained: "This statement makes the declaration that the debate over climate change is finished and settled and no more discussions are needed. Despite the fact that the proposed solutions to climate change demand a virtual destruction of the free market and the private ownership of private property, this writer and the climate change scientists in general insist that we charge ahead."[17]

The mistrust that much of the public came to direct at government spilled over to science, especially in areas where the two were intertwined, such as public health. Sometimes the spillover happens naturally. A public health nurse trying to stem the Ebola outbreak in Liberia in 2014 was driven out of a village by residents who believed Ebola was part of an international conspiracy. "They thought nurses had been given poison by the president to inject into people," the nurse reported, "so they'd die and the UN would send money." More often, denialists help the mistrust spill over by stressing the politics of science. Denialists of HIV promote conspiracies involving Big Pharma, the government (including all its public health bodies), international organizations and foundations, scientists, and AIDS activists, all working to "kill healthy people with toxic drugs for a profit."[18]

Carl Sagan observed that pseudoscience set forth ideas "often framed precisely so that they are invulnerable to any experiment that offers a prospect of disproof." Then, scientists' refusal to accept pseudoscience becomes evidence of "conspiracies to suppress it." Science denialism works the same way.[19] Accordingly, the denial of science comes up in a variety of conspiratorial settings. A "creation scientist" explains that everyone was satisfied with Bishop Ussher's date for the creation of the earth (22 October 4004 BC) until "the rise of the scientific *intelligencia* [*sic*], and the woeful apostasy of modern times" created the "ridiculous THEORIES of the origin of the universe . . . used by Satan as a Trojan Horse for many other sins." No less peculiar are those who deny fiction. A lengthy reply to an article about the Lucifer Project, a conspiracy theory in Arthur C. Clarke's novel *2001: A Space Odyssey*, denied that the Lucifer Project was fictional at all, "given all the incredible **suppressed findings of the Apollo program**, as well as the **large-scale alien presence in the solar system** (as evidenced by the mind-blowing exposé of **Bob Dean** and others at the **'09 European Exopolitics Summit in Sitges, Barcelona**, which I attended), I venture that about nothing is impossible. . . . **Stanley Kubrick** codified the very impressive, silenced knowledge in **2001**, and the sequel **2010** is a worthy successor" (emphasis in the original).[20]

As a mainstay of the charge of "scientism," conspiracists frequently target the political and economic forces that they say manipulate science behind the scenes. The most prominent area where this occurs continues to be climate change. Sincere environmentalists, conspiracists contend, "have become dwarfed by those with ulterior motives," for whom environmentalism "has become a religion that worships at the altar of global socialism." College students are "brainwashed with a green agenda, a 'climate change' hoax that **no one** is backing up with science." Senator James Inhofe, chair of the Environment and Public Works Committee, claims that young schoolchildren are so inundated with the "green agenda" that "you have to un-brainwash them."[21]

Cover-up Conspiracism

Many people come to hold beliefs that are offbeat or at least out of the mainstream. Ideas about occult phenomena, unknown creatures, miracle cures, prophecies, and any number of other topics are common but not inherently conspiratorial. Psychologists, however, have linked such beliefs with a tendency to conspiracism. A series of studies has found that poor reality testing is a characteristic of people who believe in the paranormal and among conspiracists. Not surprisingly, acceptance of pseudoscience and of superstition was found to correlate with conspiratorial thinking as well. Perhaps more surprisingly, anthropomorphism correlates with conspiracism. Apparently, anthropomorphism links back to hyper agenticity by searching for an "intelligence" of some kind behind the scenes of disturbing events. This is essentially what Karl Popper had in mind by writing off conspiracy theories as the "secularization of religious superstition."[22] These correlates may lead people to embrace conspiracism if their beliefs are refuted by the authorities and belittled by intellectuals or the media. Rather than undermining the beliefs, refutation is taken as an indication that the authorities have a reason to hide the truth—a cover-up of whatever conspiracy is afoot.[23]

The template for conspiracy theory through cover-up emerged from the UFO phenomenon of the 1950s. At the beginning of that decade, most Americans had heard the term "flying saucer" but few believed in them. J. Allen Hynek, a government consultant on UFOs, recalled, "I would have taken bets that by 1952, at the very latest, the whole mess would have been forgotten."[24] As early as 1947, the military had programs devoted to UFOs. Project Sign, Project Grudge, and finally the better-known Project Blue Book collected and analyzed information about UFO sightings for over twenty years. Over the same time, amateur

UFO "investigators" were organizing into groups such as the Aerial Phenomena Research Organization (1952) and the National Investigation Committee on Aerial Phenomena (1956). Throughout this time, military authorities issued occasional reports designed to downplay UFO sightings. These reports were riddled with misinformation, since some of the "UFO" sightings were actually observations of secret, experimental aircraft. Moreover, the CIA muddied the water with misleading information to try to confuse the Russians.[25] The government's explanations of UFO sightings (e.g., clouds, planets, swamp gas, ball lightning) were rejected and even ridiculed. The first thorough assessment of Project Blue Book described the cover-up: "While the United States Air Force was offering the public pat denials that UFOs were 'serious business,' it was conducting intensive, highly secret inquiry into all UFO reports. These inquiries were being carried out by responsible Air Force personnel and respected civilian scientists. When their conclusions did not support the official position, the findings were suppressed."[26]

Looking back at this period, UFO conspiracist John Keel noted that "the whole subject had, in fact, been totally misrepresented by both the untrained and uninformed UFO advocates and the various governmental agencies that had been sucked unwillingly into the fray." Most ufologists were not as forgiving of the authorities and placed the blame for misrepresentation squarely on those "governmental agencies." Charges of cover-up increased and were joined by countercharges of fraud when, in the late 1960s, alien encounters emerged as the natural extension of UFO sightings. The first alien abduction story, recounted in 1966, established the pattern and created the now universal image of the Zeta Reticulan (more commonly known as the "Grey") alien: small and naked with a large head and huge eyes.[27]

The cover-up conspiracy-building process amounts to a backward, tautological syllogism. Beginning with the belief that UFOs are truly extraterrestrial, the authorities' rejection of that belief automatically constitutes a cover-up of the truth. As part of this cover-up, the authorities must offer some non-truth (the "official position") in place of the truth. This merely strengthens the conspiracist's belief in the first "real truth" (UFOs are extraterrestrial) and adds to it a second, conspiratorial real truth (the government knows the first real truth and is lying about it). This is the case whether one believes that the aliens piloting the UFOs are peace loving or warlike, benevolent or given to cattle mutilation, greys or angels—and thus conspiracies tend to multiply. By the late 1960s, one conspiracy was based on evidence of visits by aliens that the Air Force was suppressing, while another held that this "evidence" was part of a CIA plot to fool the Air Force.[28] Speculation proliferated. Was the cover-up "forced upon" the government by the aliens? Were UFO research organizations being "infiltrated and controlled" by the "secret government?" Perhaps everything about UFOs was a hoax, intended to distract the public from the true conspiracy being perpetrated by the occult forces of the Illuminati.[29]

The shift from simple cover-up to more complex UFO conspiracies was helped along by the passage of the Freedom of Information Act of 1975. Ufologists became prominent users of the act, which afforded the right to request for information, suddenly making hundreds of pages of documents available. Brad Steiger's 1976 bestseller *Project Blue Book* is essentially just four hundred pages of documents—some rewritten, but others merely photocopied. Steiger does not even credit himself as being the author of his book, only the editor. Steiger's work still depicts a basic cover-up conspiracy, but more serious conspiracies started to take hold. Stanton Friedman began building his conspiracy of the government working with aliens in 1978, an idea vaguely supported by the first book on the 1947 Roswell "flying saucer crash." In this context, more important than the details of Roswell was the uncovering of the government's "secret MJ-12 team," also known as Majestic 12 or MAJIC 12, or in one case MAJESTYTWELVE.[30]

By every account, MJ-12 is "a supersecret group of extremely important people" who may or may not exist, who know everything there is to know about the aliens. To some, they are behind the plan for a "world totalitarian socialist government . . . to be ruled by a behind-the-scenes *council of wise men*. A so-called *benevolent dictator*, will be presented as the *Messiah*."[31] Documents from MJ-12 became central to UFO conspir-

acies. Some saw the documents as real and as part of a CIA disinformation campaign, while others said that those who tried to cast doubt on the
documents were part of a CIA disinformation campaign. Jim Keith saw
both of those claims as part of the same CIA disinformation campaign,
designed to make us think that UFOs are "extraterrestrial phenomena." Everything about UFOs, aliens, and especially alien abductions
is, according to Keith, manufactured by the CIA to distract the public
from the agency's mind-control experiments performed at the behest of
the Illuminati. Psychopolitics conspiracist Martin Cannon has incorporated this view into his work, not, he stresses "as firmly-established historical fact, but as a working hypothesis and grounds for investigation."
Cannon cautions against being narrow-minded and wants "researchers"
to "exhaust ALL terrestrial explanations before looking heavenward."[32]

The controversy over CIA infiltration and disinformation has fractured the ufology community for years but is largely contained within
it. Many of the specific issues that first arose with MJ-12, however, have
been integrated into larger conspiracies, such as Keith's. Foremost
among these conspiracists was Milton William Cooper, whose 1991
Behold a Pale Horse connected every conspiratorial element of the day to
UFOs and aliens. By the mid-nineties, Cooper came to agree with Keith
about UFOs as disinformation. "For many years," he wrote in 1997, "I
sincerely believed that an extraterrestrial threat existed and that it was
the most important driving force behind world events. I was wrong
and for that I most deeply and humbly apologize." Like Keith, Cooper
came to believe in the Illuminati-led conspiracy, although he continued
to toy with the idea that the original Illuminati had been aliens who
established various cults across the ancient Middle East.[33] But in Oscar
Magocsi's version of this conspiracy the Illuminati-aliens have a secret
base of operations on the dark side of the moon. The "dark forces" from
the region of Ursa Major are not powerful enough to conquer earth militarily and, so, they use their moon base for "subversion . . . by proxy,
through the MIBs [i.e., men in black], the Illuminati, and other subordi-
nates." The base was discovered by NASA's secret "Apollo 20" mission,
the existence of which NASA denies.[34]

The most common large conspiracy centered on UFOs takes the view that aliens are real and that they have provided almost all of humanity's technological breakthroughs. In this conspiracy theory, the government has not merely covered up the existence of aliens but has actively worked with them—even meeting face to face with their leaders and entering into "treaties" with them.[35] The fundamental work here is Philip Corso's *The Day after Roswell*, While Corso was not the first to argue for a human/alien cooperative arrangement, the fact that he claimed to have been a party to it made the argument his own. Many other conspiracists articulate versions of this idea. Tim Swartz connected it to the idea popularized in the 1960s by Erich von Däniken that mankind's earliest gods were spacemen whose technology created ancient civilizations. The Anunnaki, Swartz's designated spacemen from the planet Nibiru, may have literally created humanity: "The Anunnaki came to earth from Nibiru to mine for gold. The Anunnaki soon grew tired of the backbreaking labor. Ninharsag—the goddess in charge of medicine—combined the genes of the Anunnaki with a primitive ape-man . . . to relieve the Anunnaki of their labor. . . . Unlike its hairy ape-man ancestor, the hybrid had—according to the Atra Hasis text—'*the skin as the skin of a god*.' Man was created in the image of gods."[36] Some conspiracists were suspicious of Corso and his claims. Martin Davis concluded that Corso was a "provocateur whose 'work' is meant to disrupt serious inquiry into UFOs, . . . since the most likely impact of his outrageous claims will be reinforcement of the notion that ufology is strictly the province of lunatics and fools." Corso's campaign was painted as part of a right-wing conspiracy organized through the Shickshinny Knights of Malta.[37]

The technological breakthrough angle also managed to connect aliens with Nikola Tesla, a truly iconic figure in the tech conspiracy world. There are conspiracy theories about Tesla that are not connected with UFOs. Some describe him as a pawn in the battle between electricity entrepreneurs Edison and Westinghouse. Others suggest that he was able to tap into supernatural forces. Tesla technology has also been used to explain what really happened to the World Trade Center towers.[38] But the most conspiratorial approaches to Tesla's work involve extraterrestrial intelligence. The foremost voice here is William Lyne's, whose *Pentagon Aliens* is typical in approaching its Tesla conspiracy from a libertarian perspective. The Pentagon in this conspiracy is merely the "enforcer" whose job is to contain the "one technology which more certainly than any other, has the capacity to drastically alter the Vested interests which sustain the elite . . . and even threatens to destroy it: electro-propulsive 'flying saucer' technology." Lyne outlines several Tesla breakthroughs beyond flying saucer technology before moving on to his own Tesla-inspired inventions (sadly, all stolen, since "mentally retarded secretaries" employed by the patent office failed to notice "under-the-table dealings between the examiners and the large interests" the patent office actually serves).[39]

The narratives of UFO conspiracists go off in many other directions. The ultimate conspirators in Lyne's rendition are a combination of the Illuminati, the Jesuits, and the Khazarian Jews. Norma Cox's conspiracy is headed by Lucifer, working with or through the Illuminati. Stan Deyo's mystical conspiracy is composed of equal parts Illuminati, Freemasonry, and the Jesuits. Brian Desborough's Illuminati hail from Atlantis but now appear to be headquartered in the Far East. He points out, for example, that Japan and Russia shared Tesla technology-based weapons capable of "not only creating earthquakes at a distance, but also flash-freezing a city's inhabitants."[40] The major contender facing the Illuminati for control over Tesla's technology were the Nazis. In this conspiracy theory, Tesla's electrogravitic technology (essentially antigravity) allowed the Nazis to colonize the moon and perhaps Mars by 1942. After Hitler's bodyguard Otto Skorzeny assassinated Tesla in 1943, the Nazis had complete control over Tesla's ideas. From there, postwar Nazis either bargained with the United States to exchange technology for a safe haven (leading back to Davis's conspiracy about the right-wing Shickshinny Knights of Malta), or they used their electrogravitic craft to establish a base in the interior of the earth accessible by way of Antarctica (leading back to an earth-bound explanation for UFO sightings).[41]

Both denialism and cover-up conspiracies are defined by their opposition to what is generally believed and to the authorities who propagate those beliefs. This provides a key to understanding why some offbeat beliefs evolve into conspiracy theories: how strongly the "epistemic authorities" try to discredit the beliefs to maintain the official orthodoxy. Thus, belief in cryptids (hypothetical animals such as Bigfoot or the Loch Ness monster) has not generated much scientific or governmental attention, and so there are no notable conspiracy theories about cryptids. A recent scholarly history of cryptids does not mention conspiracy in its index.[42]

Any official pronouncements or reports provide a target for conspiracists, and the information contained in them can generate additional questions, expanding the conspiracy. The investigations by the military and intelligence agencies turned flying saucers into fodder for an array of competing conspiracies. Reassurances from the U.S. Public Health Service helped shift opposition to water fluoridation from a crackpot health notion into a "Red conspiracy" and a plot to "weaken the Aryan race."[43] Kennedy assassination conspiracy theories were kick-started by the (admittedly inadequate) Warren Report. Congressional investigations revealing the absence of any POW/MIAs served mainly to entrench conspiracist beliefs to the contrary. Official statements by psychological organizations against the "recovered memory" craze were cast as part of a CIA disinformation campaign on behalf of the Illuminati. And NASA's efforts to prove that it truly had sent men to the moon have done nothing to thwart even the most bizarre conspiracy theories.[44]

Negative attention by the authorities is so vital to the success of a conspiracy theory that conspiracy advocates will pretend to have found it. Stan Gordon simply claims, without any specific accusations, that the government is trying to suppress the fact that Bigfoot is actually a space alien.[45] Even absolute inattention can be turned around, as by Marshall Masters, proponent of the Planet-X-as-manifestation-of-the-Mayan-prophesy-of-the-end-of-the-world-in-2012 scenario. According to Masters, the fact that mainstream media and NASA have "avoided acknowledging" Planet X should be worrying. A comment on Masters's website asks: "Why are they scared to give us the truth?!" Masters asks back rhetorically: "Why is the government quiet? Look up cognitive dissonance and put yourself in their shoes. People are denying and deflecting this threat with angry statements and acts. If they go public now, they'll get swamped by it. That is why they're waiting for something I call the britches event. When the weight of poop in the britches reaches critical mass, it pulls the ears open and shuts the mouth. Who are the stupids here?"[46] Hard to say. Nevertheless, since they had no actual official attention with which to work, neither Masters nor Gordon was successful in that neither the Bigfoot-as-alien nor the Planet X conspiracy seems to have attracted many adherents.

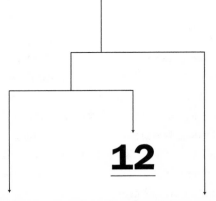

12

CONSPIRACISM PROLIFERATES

SOME ANOMALIES

Every time Spock gave the "Shin" Vulcan greeting hand sign, he was invoking Cabalistic magic.

Texe Marrs, "The Occult Magic of the Jewish Cabala"

This hologram was developed, designed and is being 'run' by both on world (Black Occult Magicians) and off world Reptilian and Human Hybrids.

Bradley Loves, "2012: What's the 'Real' Truth?"

Wait!—I haven't told you how they plan to dispose of the bodies.

Anonymous, "Blacks to Be Exterminated, Auschwitz-Style"

The breakdown of trust in and respect for institutions that began in the 1960s gave free rein to people with any number of conspiratorial notions. Moon-landing denialism and the various offshoots of UFO conspiracism have a great many followers—especially if one counts the casual adherents—but there are other conspiracy theories that, for one reason or another, are not so well known. These range from Lyndon LaRouche's intensely serious conspiracy theory, which very few people seem to understand, to purely symbolic conspiracism that sends some people into a frenzy whenever a celebrity makes a finger triangle, invoking the Illuminati. These minor conspiracies can be attached to others—as the Tesla conspiracy often gets attached to UFOs. But others are relatively freestanding, such as the conspiracy of some conservative Catholics that French Grand Orient Freemasonry is still trying to destroy the true church. Some are truly one-man operations, such as Steve Lightfoot's baffling conspiracy of how Ronald Reagan and Stephen King schemed to assassinate John Lennon.[1] The anomalous conspiracies in this chapter are more influential than these examples and illustrate something of the range of contemporary conspiracism.

Five Anomalies

THE NEW AGE CONSPIRACY

In 1928, H. G. Wells published *The Open Conspiracy: Blue Prints for a World Revolution*, classified as a novel but more his vision of a utopian future. In it, Wells promoted science, rationality, and international cooperation as forces that could lead to a "world commonweal." Wells did not posit a traditional conspiracy; he wanted progressive thinkers openly to work together to try to make the vision a reality. Nevertheless, one-worlder conspiracy theorists, fighting the international cooperation represented by the United Nations in the 1950s, seized on Wells's use of "conspiracy" (and "revolution") in the title. For them, *The Open Conspiracy* amounted to a semi-accidental exposure of the genuine hidden conspiracy to destroy American sovereignty.

In the 1980s, much the same thing happened in the wake of Marilyn Ferguson's *The Aquarian Conspiracy*. This book was the first widely read exposition on the New Age movement, loosely derived from the 1960s popular culture meme, the Age of Aquarius. Before naming the movement, Ferguson had cast it as a fundamental transformation of people's thinking that could lead to social transformation through a new politics of consciousness.[2] Ferguson hypothesized a synthesis of the "counter-culture," the "youthful opposition" to America's "technocratic society," and the mysticism largely associated with an influx of Eastern religions. The resulting synthesis would be "pragmatic and transcendental, . . . integrating magic and science, art and technology." Like Wells, she saw the process as open but chose to call it a conspiracy after Jesuit philosopher Pierre Teilhard de Chardin's phrase: "a conspiracy of love."[3]

New Age thinking comprised what Michael Barkun referred to as "odd conceptual structures" that were likely to encompass elements from "seemingly unrelated domains, such as conspiracy theories and fringe science" along with "occultism, science, and radical politics."[4] Mystical New Age ideas and conspiracy theories could be "cross-fertilized" since they "shared conceptions of the degeneracy of the modern era and a common distrust of mainstream narratives." It has also proven easy to link New Age thinking with UFO beliefs (whether conspiratorial or not). One distinctive, but far from unique cross-fertilization claims that the New Age movement "was initiated and inspired [?] by extra-terrestrial and etheric powers," which may include the theosophical "Great White Brotherhood and associates." The New Age movement, according to this view, is the only thing that can fend off "global extinction and eternal darkness."[5]

The first person to denounce New Age thinking as a conspiratorial threat was Constance Cumbey, who declared: "It is the contention of this writer that for the first time in history there is a viable movement—the New Age Movement—that truly meets all the scriptural requirements for the antichrist and the political movement that will bring him on the world scene. It is further the position of the writer that this most likely is the great apostasy or 'falling away' spoken of by the Apostle Paul and that the antichrist's appearance could be a very real event in our immediate future."[6] The main thrust of Cumbey's attack was that New Age thinking was just a new guise for the greatest threat facing Christianity: humanism, as embodied in the American Humanist Association's "Humanist Manifesto" of 1973. Cumbey claims that, although the manifesto's signatories denied involvement in any "plot to take control of the world, she finds "ample evidence for that indeed": "The

Humanist Manifesto affirms: that the universe created itself; that promises of salvation are harmful; that ethics are situational; that individuals should have the right to abortion and should have total sexual freedom; and that socialism should be in control worldwide. These are the exact beliefs with which our children are brainwashed in public schools beginning in kindergarten. They are predominant today in universities and in government. And these very same beliefs are being promoted cleverly and persistently by the national news media."[7] This view of New Age thinking became an issue in textbook censorship, as people came to believe "that 'alien' religions have invaded the schoolhouse." Indeed, many people thought that, "since the Supreme Court 'threw prayer out of' public schools, students are being indoctrinated in the religions of secular humanism, New Age, and globalism."[8]

In the wake of Cumbey's book, dominion theologian Gary North republished *None Dare Call It Witchcraft* under the title *Unholy Spirits: Occultism and New Age Humanism*. His argument was relatively straightforward: "Occultism appears at the end of a civilization," in this case, the end of Enlightenment humanism, which was giving way to "New Age Humanism," with occultism as a sort of bridge. In practice this meant that the "political ideals of the New Left" were taking over as "radical extensions of the main political goals of the Old Left." North preferred that the rationalism of the Enlightenment—which had been favored by Fabians and one-worlders—die off and that a "self-conscious Christian civilization" replace it. Religious conspiracist Texe Marrs joined in, putting out booklets exposing the "13-point hidden plan of Satan to bring to pass a One World Government and a One World Religion headed by a New Age Messiah or Christ."[9]

There was nonbiblical opposition to the imagined New Age conspiracy as well. In 1992, Lyndon LaRouche addressed Ferguson's Aquarian conspiracy directly:

> The counterculture is a conspiracy—but not in the half-conscious way Ferguson claims—as she well knows. . . . The counterculture is a conspiracy at the top, created as a method of social control, used to drain

the United States of its commitment to scientific and technical prog-
ress. That conspiracy goes back to the 1930s, when the British sent
Aldous Huxley to the United States as a case officer for an operation to
prepare the United States for the mass dissemination of drugs. . . . With
The Aquarian Conspiracy the British Opium War against the United
States has come out into the open.[10]

Around the same time, a radio broadcast by Québec journalist Serge
Monast began to make the rounds. Like Cumbey, Monast provided
a theosophical context for the New Age movement but also linked it
explicitly to the Broadway musical *Hair* (singing a bit of the song "Aquarius" over the air). Monast's conspiracy centered on Project Blue Beam,
"a gigantic space show with three-dimensional optical holograms and
sounds." Different parts of the world would receive "different images
according to predominating regional/national religious faith," but everyone would accept the "new god's image." The larger goal was, naturally,
the establishment of a new world order: "So, the goals of the New Age
movement under which the United Nations operates right now, are the
implementation of a . . . World Government under the United Nations. . . .
A World Religion where all church doctrines will be destroyed at the
roots to be replaced by the new religion of the Age of Aquarius . . . the
world concentration camp headquarters at the United Nations for those
who will not accept the new system."[11] Yet another voice against the New
Age movement was raised by radio host and retired orthopedic surgeon
Dr. Stanley Montieth, who saw its goal as Draconian population reduction. As Montieth expanded his ideas into a full-fledged "world government" conspiracy theory, the New Age segment continued to have sway
over the "destructive one-fourth" of the globe's population that needed
to be "eliminated from the social body." This, too, was a "brainwashing"
issue in the schools. A minister, learning that the theme song "Suicide
Is Painless" from the television show *M*A*S*H* had been mentioned in
school, charged that the school was in league with "environmentalists to reduce the population so that there will be enough clean air and
water."[12]

Montieth's interpretations of the New Age conspiracy, like many who opposed it, reflect a biblical traditionalism. Dennis L. Cuddy, primarily a mind-control conspiracist, peppers his analysis of the new world order with the contributions of New Agers. The new world order "is not Judeo-Christian," Cuddy contends. Rather, "it is a New Age occultic spirituality using pagan deities. That is why in America, the Ten Commandments are eliminated from public property, but courts are allowing there the pagan goddess Themis." This odd claim—using the "blind justice" statue Iustitia from ancient Rome and the equivalent of Themis, ancient Greek goddess of justice—allows Cuddy to invoke the Greek goddess Gaia, who is Themis's mother, which leads him to the New Age idea of Earth as Gaia and from there to the menace of sustainable development.[13] Tal Brooke's massive one-world conspiracy similarly sees New Age ideas as the vanguard of the new world order. Brooke also agrees with Cuddy about the threat of sustainability. Speaking of the UN's report from the 1992 Rio Environmental Conference, he explains: "You have just read part of the Marxist platform. If that means nothing to you, you are already sheep to the slaughter. . . . Mandating 'sustainable development'—could mean a scene right out of *1984*. America's good life is nothing less than 'unsustainable patterns of production and consumption.' China allows only 1 child per couple. That could become the way for America, as it shifts into a third world protectorate."[14] And even as traditional an antisemitic conspiracist as Texe Marrs manages to find space next to the Cabala for "the hottest spiritual trend" of the day. The "newfound popularity of this end-time sorcery is not by accident," explains Marrs. "Its emergence is a carefully planned Illuminati event."[15]

DAVID ICKE'S REPTILIANS

David Icke is one of the best-known conspiracy theorists in the world, his alien reptile-human hybrid shapeshifters standing out against a background of amorphous Illuminists, Talmudists, and Luciferians. But his work is not widely cited or integrated into others' conspiracies, since the only new idea Icke contributed to conspiracism was the addition of reptilians to a standard Rothschilds/Rockefellers/Council on Foreign Relations–style conspiracy. The reptilians, according to Icke, are an "extraterrestrial race the Sumerians called the Anunnaki" who originated on a distant planet and now "are one of the many **inner-Earth races** which live underground in enormous catacombs. . . . My own research suggests that it is from another dimension, the lower fourth dimension, that the reptilian control and manipulation is primarily orchestrated. . . . At the moment you are tuned to the three dimensional world. . . . It is from one of these other stations or dimensions, that the Serpent Race, the Anunnaki, is controlling the world by 'possessing' certain bloodlines."[16]

Besides building on the idea of ancient spacemen as Sumerian gods, Icke's conspiracy ties in with those who imagine Illuminati control as taking place through "bloodlines." These vary, but there are generally thirteen bloodlines, one of which is invariably linked to Britain's royal family. Indeed, Brian Desborough contends that, as the Tudors were originally not among the bloodlines, Elizabeth I seduced Edward de Vere and had his illegitimate child "to bring the reptilian blood into the Tudor bloodline."[17] Icke expanded on the bloodlines in his 2001 *Children of the Matrix*, but seemingly abandoned the Sumerians in favor of a more convoluted origin story involving the lost continents of Atlantis, Lemuria, and Mu. Icke's reptilians also became more complex, with a hierarchy of types corresponding to pseudo-racial features. (This led to Icke's being accused of coded antisemitism, but, given the obliqueness of Icke's narrative, the accusation foundered.) Later, in response to the 9/11 attack, Icke produced an Illuminati bloodlines version of the conspiracy, which largely abandoned reptilians, matrices, and other dimensions.[18]

Books about mysterious and suspicious symbolism have been popular for a great many years—and TV shows such as *Forbidden History*, which pursue the "true" story behind them, always find an audience. But these books and shows are often not conspiratorial at all, and even when they are, they just speculate on the "cover-up" by respectable scientists and historians who refuse to seriously examine the mysteries. Conspiracism in this area centered originally on Freemasonry, a practice rich in arcane symbols that could easily be billed as occult or even Illuministic. In the United States, these connections receive particular attention, as Freemasonry was common among the nation's founders.[19] At the edge of this attention to the role of secret societies in the founding of the United States, though, conspiracies have been accreting rapidly. The ad copy for the DVD *The Secret Mysteries of America's Beginnings* (vol. 1— *The New Atlantis*) draws in viewers by asking "Why is Washington D.C. build [*sic*] on the 77th Meridian?" and "Are the Revolutionary War cities really built in perfect alignment with Stonehenge?" The video makers "follow the journey of secret societies from England to the New World and learn of their ancient hope: to rebuild the lost empire of Atlantis."[20] While there is nothing inherently conspiracist about Atlantis, its emergence so soon after Freemasonry had "assumed the leadership of the New World Order, in 1782" was no coincidence. The capital of this "kingdom of the Antichrist" was Washington, DC, as revealed by its symbolism: "In 1791, Pierre Charles L'Enfant (the designer, who was a Freemason), laid out Governmental Center of Washington, D.C., he planned more than just streets, roads, and buildings. He hid certain occultic magical symbols in the layout of U.S. Governmental Center. When these symbols are united they become one large Luciferic, or occultic, symbol." The role of Atlantis fades in the mix of Freemasonry, Luciferianism, and, of course, the "Masters of the Illuminati." Some of these groups' symbolism is now familiar: the eye on the pyramid and the upside down five-pointed star (the "Goathead Pentagram") one can draw over the Washington street map. Other symbolism referred to by organizations like Freemasonry Watch—the number sixteen, representing "felicity" to the occultist—is still obscure.[21]

An important feature of this sort of symbolic conspiracism is its astonishing flimsiness. Even if sixteen is a particularly meaningful number, the facts that Sixteenth Street "emanates" north from Scott Circle and that Scott Circle "is itself the precise middle of the Goathead Pentagram" (it is not, even in the accompanying illustration) are of no importance. Nor is there anything actually "encoded" about the fact that P Street is named for the sixteenth letter of the English alphabet. The many coincidences on which symbolic conspiracists rely do not even coincide. Is it a coincidence that the old Masonic headquarters in Washington is exactly thirteen city blocks north of the White House ("Of course, the number 13 represents rebellion against God's authority, and is generally thought of as Satan's number")? Only if one begins the count at "the first city block north of Lafayette Square," a considerable distance from the White House. For that matter, the fact that the White House "forms the fifth and bottom point of the Goathead" is true only if one extrapolates the actual streets involved in the pentagram an additional four blocks beyond their southernmost point.[22] Equally unconvincing is an illustration now found in Arno Gaebelein's *The Conflict of the Ages* that depicts the "insignia of the Order of the Illuminati which is the reverse of the U.S. Seal and appears on U.S. $1.00 bills." The accompanying explanation translates *Novus Ordo Seclorum*, which also appears on the back of dollar bills, as the "New Deal."[23]

People have long used bits of arcane symbolism to buttress their conspiracy theories. A writer calling himself "Pfefferkorn" related all the symbolic points of interest on the one-dollar bill ("Above the Eagle are 13 stars . . . so placed that their contour forms the Star of David") to support the hidden hand conspiracy: "Our one dollar bill with all these curious symbols—hardly American—appeared exactly ten years ago and is for the first time in history of the U.S.A. signed by a Jew, Henry Morgenthau."[24] This sort of symbolic analysis may be the fastest growing conspiratorial activity today. Its dependence on visuals makes it perfect for online presentation. Symbolic conspiracism, like mind-control conspiracism, can serve the interests of almost any other conspiracy theory, whether Illuminati, Satanic, or Zionist. A video by Doc Marquis explains how our unwitting celebration of occult holidays like Litha (June 21, which, he claims, we celebrate as Independence Day, even though Litha occurs nearly two weeks before July Fourth) and Imbolg (February 1, which we "celebrate" as Groundhog Day on the second) plays into the hands of Satanic Illuminized Freemasonry. A wholly bizarre interpretation of the site where the Kennedy assassination took place includes the symbolism of the nearby rail yard: "Because Masonry is obsessed with earth-as-gameboard (tessellation) and the ancillary alignment necessary to facilitate the 'game' it is inordinately concerned with railroads." At the same time, a detailed numerological analysis of Dealey Plaza revealed the Freemasons' hand in the assassination because of the prevalence of "three (3 and 33)."[25]

But why would conspiratorial elites risk revealing their presence with such symbolism? If "enemies within our own government" were indeed responsible for the 9/11 attacks, leaving "occult symbolism" behind as a clue to their identity seems self-defeating.[26] One answer is that the conspirators communicate with one another with these symbols. Illuminati symbolism "serves as a 'secret' means of communication between the ruling bloodlines that the uninitiated cannot comprehend or even see." Aside from the District of Columbia street layout, examples include Saint Peter's Square in the Vatican City, the logo for the European Organization for Nuclear Research (known as CERN), the fanlight over the door of Number 10 Downing Street, and the Statue of Liberty.[27] Marginally more convincing is the idea of mind control or at least some sort of "conditioning" of the public. For example, the popularity of zombies in popular culture has been attributed to the elite's "subtly getting us ready for a planned population-culling epidemic." Symbols help build popular "frames of reference" that benefit the conspirators, but as there seems to be "no end to the fragments of information relating to the conspiracy," their meaning is elusive. It has been argued that symbols might be a "hypnotic trigger" in the *Manchurian Candidate* sense, a "territorial marking" used to display elite control, or just a way to "taunt" the public.[28]

Symbolic analysis has led to a conspiracy theory based on *The Matrix* series of movies. David Icke has become a major force in this conspiracy, linking his reptilians to it:

The *Reptilians did 'exist,'* said the **voice**, but they were holographic thought-projections of the Matrix, very much like the agents, or 'sentient programs,' that manipulate things in the Matrix movies.

They could either operate as a reptilian projection or hide behind an apparently "human" form. . . . Either way *The Reptilians* and other projected agents of the Matrix were not 'real' in consciousness terms. . . .

They are observed into illusory reality by the human mind. . . . It is so simple.[29]

In this "artificially created 'construct,' our 3-D 'reality' is actually quite similar to the Matrix as was seen and described in the TV movie" and succeeds in fooling us because its extraterrestrial creators are "Masters of both DECEPTION and MIND CONTROL. Thus, they are able to entertain themselves by taunting us with symbolism that we do not appreciate, for example, the cube."[30]

LYNDON LAROUCHE

A long-time conspiracist who seems to relish his standing as an outsider, Lyndon LaRouche abandoned left-wing politics for conspiracism around 1970. LaRouche developed a network of followers that has been almost cultlike in its single-minded devotion to his ideas. Chip Berlet, a prominent investigator of right-wing conspiracists, sees LaRouche's ideas as primarily antisemitic, but (as with Icke) this is hard to be sure of. Even in an essay attacking B'nai B'rith and its Anti-Defamation League, LaRouche's weekly newsmagazine *Executive Intelligence Review* portrays the organizations as only tangentially Jewish and ties them instead to "one of the ugliest chapters in the British-led Confederate secessionist insurrection," the Ku Klux Klan.[31] There may well be a strain of antisemitism in the work of LaRouche and some of his acolytes, but LaRouche's primary concern has always been the battle between the followers of Plato and those of Aristotle, as he explained: "One elite, the humanists, the Platonic or Neoplatonic faction, is dedicated to steering the course of history away from rule through mythologies. The other, the Aristotelians and their heirs, is committed to strengthening the rule by mythology, for the purpose of establishing a permanent 'feudal-like' Utopia of obedient simple-minded folk ruled by a tenured neo-Aristotelian oligarchy."[32] LaRouche's determination to link every event in conspiracy history to this philosophical battle (in which he sides with Platonic humanism) is the main reason why his ideas have proved too difficult for most people. But, his ideas eventually focus on Great Britain and the Royal Family, LaRouche's nemesis. He is best known for his accusations that the queen is behind the world drug trade, although recently he has focused on a British-Saudi collaboration that also involves the FBI.[33]

LaRouche does have a small group of devotees, who publish largely through LaRouche-sponsored organizations such as the Schiller Institute and periodicals such as the *Campaigner*. Some of the conspiracism put out by the "LaRouchites" is topical—Webster Tarpley has published books on the Y2K scare, on 9/11, and the Skull and Bones Club in addition to sensationalist biographies of George H. W. Bush, Barack Obama (two of them), and "Bishop" Mitt Romney, a reference to his role in the Mormon Church.[34] But, for the most part, LaRouchites isolate themselves by producing lengthy Platonic versus Aristotelian analyses of the Jacksonian populist effort (Aristotelian) to eliminate the Bank of the United States, the superiority of Alexander Hamilton (Platonic) over Thomas Jefferson (Aristotelian), and how the work of Francis Bacon (Aristotelian) set the stage for the Illuminati.[35] Very few people either understand these arguments or care to.

BLACK GENOCIDE

In 1967, John A. Williams published his fourth novel, based loosely on the career of novelist Richard Wright.[36] As part of his promotional efforts, Williams planted excerpts of the book—specifically the King Alfred Plan—in New York City subway stations. At a time of urban riots and white reaction, when the Black Panther Party was targeted by police and the FBI's counterintelligence program COINTELPRO was leaking out, the King Alfred Plan, describing the government's plan for black genocide, could seem plausible. The revelations about the Tuskegee Syphilis Experiment served only to strengthen this plausibility, and in the 1970s, the King Alfred Plan began to lose its fictional basis. Jim Jones, before moving to Guyana and establishing Jonestown, referred to it in his sermons: "There's a plan already laid aside to put you in gas chambers. It's called the King Alfred Plan." Another book argued that the energy crisis was purposively created as part of the plan. There was apparently a *King Alfred Research Newsletter* published quarterly in Jacksonville, Florida.[37]

By the 1980s, the plan was being incorporated into rap music and talked about on Black Liberation Radio, where "knowledge warriors reconstruct mainstream or suppressed knowledge into 'blackstream knowledge.'" In this context, the King Alfred Plan was a manifestation of the "paranoia that mines white information systems for clues as to how white America is preparing genocidal attack on the black population." One clue that was mined from the Iran-Contra hearings concerned a martial law contingency plan named Readiness Exercise 1984, or Rex 84, for short. Noting that *rex* was Latin for "king," some conspiratorial minded observers linked Rex 84 to King Alfred as well as a nonexistent 1970 plan to round up and imprison twenty-one million black citizens.[38] The King Alfred Plan was turning into a black version of the standard new world order conspiracy—complete with concentration camps, executive orders, and the establishment of regions. But, since this version specified black genocide as the goal, it was much more focused. It should not be surprising, then, how belief in the plan affected the black reaction to the AIDS epidemic. Early on, perhaps a third of black adults surveyed agreed that AIDS could have been engineered by the government and "white scientists" to wipe out the black race. Similar, although less extreme, suspicions have been noted regarding birth control as black genocide. More recent figures are no less troubling.[39]

Now, over fifty years after Williams's novel was published, the King Alfred Plan has become completely untethered from its origin and is simply a part of black genocide conspiracy theories. A recent internet posting described the plan as a National Security Council initiative from the early 1960s that could be traced back to the late 1940s (and even tenuously to the Japanese internment camps during World War II). The plan now encompassed a plot to wipe out sub-Saharan Africans with a combination of pollution, desertification, and weather manipulation. Another version of the plot against Africa claims that it is part of the Rockefellers' plan to seize that continent's diamonds.[40] That same posting also included the Rothschilds, along with Cecil Rhodes, the Council on Foreign Relations, and the secret MJ-12 group behind Roswell. Even Nuwaubian ideas—originally limited to the claim that ancient Egypt was a black African civilization and that white academics conspired to cover up that fact—have come to encompass a genocidal threat from the Illuminati and the Bilderbergers.[41] Perhaps the black genocide conspiracy's days as an anomaly are numbered as black conspiracism is coming to resemble its white counterpart.

On the Question of Left-Wing Conspiracism

Pan-ideological conspiracism implies that people on the Left as well as the Right may adopt a conspiracy theory. And, while the conspiracism of the twentieth century was dominated by right-wingers, nineteenth-century conspiracy theories were not. The question today is whether there are substantial left-wing conspiracy theories growing out of a leftist conspiracism. It is not unusual for people to assume political symmetry, despite the evidence. American studies professor Alasdair Spark, for instance, sees the new world order as "an equal opportunity conspiracy theory" with left- and right-wing versions. The equivalence is seriously undermined, however, by Spark's evidence. From the right-wing Police against the New World Order:

> Behind the scenes is a plan for an oligarchy of the world's richest families to place 1/2 the masses of the earth in servitude under their complete control, administered from behind the false front of the United Nations. . . .
>
> The plan calls for the elimination of the other 2.5 billion people through war, disease, abortion, and famine by the year 2000.

And on the Left, Noam Chomsky's not particularly conspiratorial left-wing interpretation of American intervention in the war in the Balkans: "The aim of these assaults is to establish the role of the major imperialist powers—above all the United States—as the unchallengeable arbiters of public affairs. The New World Order is precisely this: an international regime of unrelenting pressure and intimidation by the most powerful capitalist regime against the weakest."[42] More bluntly, journalist Jonathan Kay tries to demonstrate Left-Right symmetry by comparing *Mein Kampf,* and Hitler's "delusional fears that Jews were conspiring to destroy not only the Aryan nation, but all of humanity," with Marx's *Das Kapital.* Kay claims flatly that: "Notwithstanding the numbing jargon about Hegelian dialectics and such, the real lure of Marxism . . . is its fundamentally conspiracist vision of society."[43]

If one accepts Marxism as inherently conspiracist, then left-wing conspiracism exists, *quod erat demonstrandum.* The best-known proponent of a conspiracist Left is Daniel Pipes, who divides conspiracies into only two categories: antisemitic and secret society—with Marxism as a secret society. The reductionist simplicity of this scheme has led to the criticism that Pipes, a strong anti-Communist, "appears to be wilfully blind to the ideological implications of conspiracism." The larger question is not whether Marxism is conspiracist—few see it that way—but at what point does analysis of the power of elites in society become twisted into "conspiracy fantasy"?[44] William Domhoff, whose career has been devoted to analyzing power politics and economics from a leftist perspective, has laid out five reasons why, in his words: "There are no conspiracies." In drawing the distinction between his work (which conspiracists have appropriated) and actual conspiracism, Domhoff concludes that "careful studies show that all these actions were authorized by top government officials, which is the critical point here. There was no 'secret team' or 'shadow government' committing illegal acts or ordering government officials to deceive the public and disrupt social movements. Such a distinction is crucial in differentiating all sociological theories of power from a conspiratorial one."[45]

The closest thing to a leftist conspiracist framework is what former Berkeley English professor Peter Dale Scott has termed "deep politics," which owes its origin to the Kennedy assassination. Like all the power elite researchers, Scott tries to keep his distance from "traditional *conspiracy theory.*" Nevertheless, he finds the line between "*deep political analysis*" and conspiracism is "not always easy to draw."[46] Indeed it is not. If it is not a conspiracy theory, deep politics must be a particularly large conspiratorial explanation. It borders on creating an "alternative historical construct," but its narrative does not take Richard Hofstadter's "curious leap" to people not plausibly connected with the events in question. All in all, Scott's book appears to stop short of conspiracism, as does the 1988 memoir of the Kennedy assassination by former New Orleans district attorney Jim Garrison. In contrast, tech entrepreneur Mark Gorton's manuscript "50 Years of the Deep State," which concludes that the Bush family is a cabal, seems to be over the line. Some who could be called deep politics conspiracists, such as Kennedy assassination researchers Mae Brussell and Mary Ferrell, have written only sparingly, devoting most of their energy to amassing and collating information used by others.[47]

Interestingly, much deep politics conspiracism exists in the realm of the arts, rather than research per se. Oliver Stone certainly sees himself in this light; his film *JFK* relied heavily on Garrison's memoir. Norman Mailer viewed his novel of the Kennedy assassination as lying between fiction and nonfiction.[48] Don DeLillo's *Libra* and James Ellroy's *American Tabloid* also generate complex deep politics interpretations of the Kennedy assassination. Not as dependent on the Kennedy assassination, artist Mark Lombardi's line drawings depicting over fifty years of deep politics connections arguably constitute the most thorough deep politics work ever undertaken. Besides the success of the drawings in the art world, they have commanded the attention of both researchers and the authorities since Lombardi's suspicious "suicide" in 2000.[49]

Consistent with Michael Barkun's observation about the increasingly improvisational nature of conspiracies, the idea that a branch of conspiracism has grown out of a mistrust of government that is not defined by the standard left- and right-wing division has also taken root. "Fusion paranoia," a term coined by journalist Michael Kelley in 1995, was first used to capture an array of authors, publishers, periodicals, and online entities that combine muckraking, historical revisionism, deep politics conspiracism, and sometimes occultish and New Age ideas but are not racist or antisemitic. There are many outlets, but some are sincere, some are hoaxes, and some are, as they say, just for lulz.[50] Fusion paranoia was taken up early on the Left in articles that noted similarities between 1960s antiwar activists and later antigovernment patriots. The common "paranoia" of these groups provided a rationale for their "fusion."[51] Fusion paranoia has also been put to use by the Right. By including such nonconspiratorial beliefs as UFOs and Atlantis, Daniel Pipes was able to continue to disparage the Left as inherently conspiratorial. More recently, fusion paranoia has been used to connect all opponents of Israeli policies under the heading of antisemitic conspiracists.[52]

One area where "fused" paranoid conspiracism has long existed is health and medical concerns. In 1981, *Revelations Awareness*—subtitled the *New Age Cosmic Newsletter*—in updating the fluoride controversy to include toothpaste, lifted its arguments largely from William Guy Carr, apparently unaware of his right-wing Illuminati conspiracism. Thus, the newsletter's take on fluoridation was that its true purpose was "stupification and population control."[53] Similar notions among AIDS denialists led the medical establishment to confront the paranoia that was keeping some people from seeking treatment. Some new age alternative medicine conspiracists began to push back against the use of the term "paranoid." Dr. Alan Cantwell, a powerful voice of the "AIDS as man-made epidemic" conspiracy, complained that paranoia had become one of the key "media buzzwords" used to "silence the politically incorrect."[54]

Although deep politics is generally distinct from conspiracy theories, there is a bedrock level of conspiracist thinking on the Left. After the 9/11 attacks, rightists tried to use this to lure leftist "truthers" to right-wing conspiracies, often relying on their common rejection of anti-truther leftists such as Noam Chomsky or Howard Zinn. They met with only marginal success, in large part because the right-wing conspiracies are so often antisemitic.[55] Still, bedrock leftist conspiracism turns up from time to time as conspiracy theories centered on specific events, such as the October surprise during the 1980 election or the airplane crash that took the life of Senator Paul Wellstone. But, on the Left, these conspiracies tend to get resolved and adherents abandon them, a rare occurrence on the Right.[56] Moreover, studies, both in the United States and Europe show markedly less conspiracism among supporters of Left parties than Right parties.[57] All in all, Left conspiracism is at best a pale shadow of its right-wing counterpart. It takes up only a small part of the conspiracist stage, it has never cumulated into a sprawling theory, and it is much more in touch with reality.

13

CHRISTIAN IDENTITY AND
THE WHITE RACE

So the battle rages and many Christians do not even know there is a
war going on. . . . Certainly very few realize that it is a war between the
forces of Talmudic evil and that representing Jesus Christ.

Gordon "Jack" Mohr, *Know Your Enemies!*

The most unexpected concept in contemporary American conspiracism
is Christian Identity, which is both a theological concept and a movement based on it. As a movement, Christian Identity has generated several specific organizations and inspired other movements. As a theological concept, it has been incorporated into the framework of right-wing
conspiracism and is considered a "'motor' for militant white supremacy."[1] Christian Identity has its roots in the British Israelism movement
(also known as Anglo-Israelism), with which it is sometimes confused.[2]

British Israelism

As a coherent theological and political creed, Christian Identity dates from
around 1950, a few years after its main precursor—British Israelism—

was merged with explicitly racist and apocalyptic doctrines. British Israelism was invented in England by a loose band of religious enthusiasts who convinced themselves that the British descended from the North Kingdom of Israel and were thus the true Israelites. Over the years, they developed an idiosyncratic reading of scripture to support this belief. Toward the end of the nineteenth century, a few North American anglophiles adopted British Israelism and expanded it by replacing the biblical heritage of the royal family with a more generic Anglo-Saxon one.[3] It bears noting that little, if any, of this work denied that Jews were also Israelites.

In the 1920s, British Israelism in the United States began to merge with other ideas. Howard B. Rand, a businessman and founder of the Anglo-Saxon Federation of America, began working with W. J. Cameron, editor of Henry Ford's *Dearborn Independent*, America's foremost disseminator of the *Protocols of the Learned Elders of Zion*. While Rand toured the country giving lectures, Cameron published British Israelism pieces. Their version of British Israelism expanded the "pure" descendants of the Israelites from just the English to all the "Anglo-Saxon-Celtic and kindred peoples." On the other side of this equation, actual contemporary Jews, the "remnant who returned to Palestine," were said to have lost, through racial miscegenation, their own "purity" and the right to be called Israelites.[4] Rand also revived a nineteenth-century obscurity, seedline theology, according to which Eve's children generated two lineages: one from a "good" seed and one from an "evil" seed. Anti-Catholics traced the evil seed though Nimrod (an ambivalent Old Testament figure) and on to the Vatican. Rand and Cameron, however, used seedline theology to "literally demonize" the Jews "as serpentine connivers and a pseudo-human pestilence that had lied and tricked the White race into economic and political servitude, and spiritual and racial alienation. Their racist and anti-Semitic variant told White Gentiles: You are the lost children of Israel. Throw off the yoke of false, Judaized 'Christianity' and reclaim your birthright as the Chosen People of God, and as the masters of the planet."[5]

By 1923, Cameron was printing articles in the *Dearborn Independent* that brought the "Khazars" into British Israelism to reinforce the idea that contemporary Jews had no claim to ancient Israel. There had been medieval Khazars who converted to Judaism, but the British identity framework promulgated the notion that Khazars accounted for nearly all contemporary Jews, an idea particularly appealing to the Ku Klux Klan. In his booklet *The Jewish Question*, Klan leader Reuben Sawyer attacked the Khazarian "Ashkenazim Jew," who "has been a constant menace to every country into which he has thrust his unwelcome presence."[6] In short order, Sawyer—and the Klan—was promoting a British Israelism version of the hidden hand conspiracy. As British Israelism in the United States became subsidiary to Howard Rand's Anglo-Saxon Federation of America, it maintained a conspiracy of "Pseudo-Jewry" (i.e., actual Jews), a "Synagogue of Satan" version of the hidden hand. After World War II, Rand used this conspiracy to argue that the Jews had no right to Palestine since "it belonged to the Israelites."[7] The actual British version of British Israelism, embodied in London's British-Israel Foundation, did not take this turn and faded into obscurity.

Wesley Swift's Christian Identity

The Reverend Wesley Albert Swift is likely the most overlooked conspiracy theorist in American history. The political-theological ideas he welded together underlie some major right-wing conspiracy theories today, even if many of these theories' adherents have never heard of him. Although Swift was a religious figure, his worldview was primarily racist and antisemitic. He had been a member of the Ku Klux Klan and later toured with Gerald L. K. Smith giving sermons across California. (Smith himself was a notorious antisemite who used British Israelism ideas.) Swift had studied at the Kingdom Bible College, where he first encountered British Israelism as filtered through Philip E. J. Monson, West Coast head of the Anglo-Saxon Federation. It was from Monson's work that the core idea behind Christian Identity, two-seed theology, emerged. Monson's more traditional anti-Catholic version of seedline theology was aimed at the "Prime Minister of the Devil," that is, the pope.[8] Swift adapted it to attack the Jews.

Swift developed his ideas cumulatively through his sermons, but his basic idea was that Eve was seduced by Satan and gave birth to Cain, whose "seedline" resulted in today's Jews, who are thus literally, not just rhetorically, Satanic. The second seedline, originating with the off-spring of Adam and Eve, resulted in God's chosen people, who, by virtue of applied British Israelism, are today's white Nordic races. In lengthy theological, quasi-historical tracts, Swift and his followers described the Manichean struggle between these two seedlines across the centuries. This war, of course, was still underway, as Swift explained in his typical roundabout fashion:

> Your battle has constantly been with Satan's sons who are here to charge and to fight against the Sons of God. . . .
>
> We have troubles with this seed. They worship devils and many gods. And they wage war against you. But then the MOST HIGH said— "this evil power which seeks to do all these things, we know who they are.["] . . . They carry the mark of the serpent, the sting of the Asp, and the venom of the viper.—So we recognize them.[9]

Swift supplemented the two-seed concept with a reinterpretation of the Creation story that also traced the Jews' lineage back to the pre-Adamic races that "succumbed to the Luciferian fallen archangel's dominion." This idea also casts the Jews as Satanic, but it has not had anything like the influence of the two-seed concept. Swift did, however, use the pre-Adamites in a way that has proven very successful. Picking up the ideas from the book *Adamites and Preadamites; or, A Popular Discussion*, written by one Alexander Winchell, Swift declared the pre-Adamites to be a primitive subhuman race from which the nonwhite races of today descend. In fairly short order, "nonwhite" was replaced in seedliner rhetoric by "Negro," and often the pre-Adamites were called simply "mud people." In case whites were worried that this somehow gave blacks an earlier origin than whites, Swift reassured them: "One of the strangest things we have about your race is it was the oldest and the best. For the children of Spirit existed before the world was framed.

And you were standing by the Father's side when out of the cosmic spiral nebula of creative processes this earth and this solar system came into being. . . . The spirit of everyone [*sic*] of you in here by the antiquity of age, is older than even the oldest race that ever existed in this earth."[10]

This division of people into three basic groups—good white Christians, evil Jews, and simple other races—is fundamental to Christian Identity thinking today. The fact that these ideas are not merely supported by scripture but actually originate there makes them, for many people, perfectly acceptable. One Identity follower told two theological researchers, "Identity is not racist. Jews and blacks are what they are. God chose to . . . make blacks with the animals, we didn't. I have to believe God, and he spelled it out clear in the Bible. I'd give the shirt off my back to a black man if he came to my door. But I can't make him the same as me." What should be obvious racism and antisemitism is no longer seen as such once it is "cast in Biblical mode."[11]

Swift also absorbed a considerable amount of Pentecostalism, which itself contained a dose of British Israelism. Swift worked with Aimee Semple McPherson, the foremost Pentecostalist evangelist of her day, and adopted some of Pentecostalism's apocalyptic ideas. Under Pentecostalism's "Armageddon paradigm," the typical believer "is convinced that Armageddon is imminent, maintains intense suspiciousness toward all those deemed different, and holds to a belief that a Chosen People have a God-given role to play in salvaging the world."[12] Further still, Swift accumulated bits of what can only be called occult lore, including some ideas about astrology and pyramidology from a California Klan leader named San Jacinto Capt. Even references to lost continents and the civilizations found their way into Swift's sermons.[13]

The connection between this theological amalgamation of ideas and conspiracy theory was clear early on. Depictions of Jews as leaders of a satanic conspiracy against America and all Christian civilization popped up as early as 1953.[14] By 1954, Swift peppered his religious sermons with references to "ADL goons" attacking Senator McCarthy for his exposure of our "hidden masters. . . . Is it Barney Baruch or Felix Frankfurter?"

Seedliner rhetoric turned some conspiratorial references into coded messages—clear to the initiated but unlikely to be noticed by anyone else. When Swift despairs that we have let the treasury "tax us with the burdens of Babylon," he refers to the Babylonian conspiracy, through which the Jews seized control of American finance with the income tax and the Federal Reserve System. Some "mystical anti-Semitism" has been attributed to Swift's seedliner definition of the Jews, in that it gives them a "special potency by a mystical dimension that identifies with a concept beyond themselves." Swift's sermons were also used to urge his followers to fight back: "It is time we decide who is going to run our nation. The Christian majority, or the Jews who have sought to take it over in the last thirty years."[15]

Until the arrival of the civil rights movement, seedliner sermons (and increasingly, printed manifestos) simply elaborated a version of the hidden hand conspiracy. A small group of "first generation" Identity theologians—primarily Swift, Conrad Gaard, William Potter Gale, and Bertrand Comparet—accounted for almost all the conspiratorial output. The ratio of current politics to biblical interpretation in Swift's own sermons began tilting toward the former early on. One 1955 sermon was dominated by the theme of "treason." President Eisenhower was dismissed as "a tool of Barney Baruch and his crowd." Rockefeller's United Nations ("the dreaded '5th column'") constituted the "greatest conspiracy against Christian civilization that has ever been erected in your time." (The actual construction of the UN headquarters in New York showed that Nostradamus's prediction about New York's fall was about to come true.) The Jews were creating an economy "which would build a World Order that would subordinate any Christian nation." To top off the sermon, Swift pointed to America's vast influx of Jews who had fled the Nazis: "Self evident that they didn't kill six and a half million because they're found on every Main Street of every town with the money they printed with the plates Mr. Morgenthau gave them. The secret is out."[16]

The seedliner conspiracy was laid out in full by Conrad Gaard in his 1955 book *Spotlight on the Great Conspiracy*. Some fifty pages of seedline biblical history concludes with the emergence of the Illuminati, which, having taken over both political parties, has not bothered to organize a "new 'liberal' Party" in the United States to promote its goal: the "One World Collectivist State." Behind Gaard's Illuminati stand the "Dragon Cult" plotters (the dragon relating back to the serpent and thus to Satan and Cain's evil Jewish seedline), who represent "Oriental Dictatorship," the absolute enemy of America's "Occidental Constitutionalism." The gulf between these two "Ways of Life" is so great that neither compromise nor coexistence is possible.[17] After drawing on seedliner theory that leads back to a Khazar-Zionist hidden hand conspiracy, Gaard returns to the Founders' "Occidental Constitutionalism," which allows Christian people to enjoy the freedom of limited government. This is what the forces of "Oriental Dictatorship" cannot abide: "The atheistic, anti-Christian Illuminati, and their deluded stooges, of course, could not recognize such a divine heritage, much less make it the basis for a social and governmental order, because the hidden Masters of the Illuminati were the same Satanically inspired plotters who had invented the Babylonian totalitarian 'kingdom of this world order' as a substitute for JeHoVaH's perfect program." Gaard concludes on a high note. White Christians, the "remnant of Israel," will rise up and defeat the conspiracy in an apocalyptic battle.[18]

By 1957, Swift was using his sermons to expose such elements of the conspiracy as the Asiatic flu and all the other viruses "released in your country . . . as an experiment, that is their Germ Warfare." The flu shots, like the flu itself, were part of this conspiracy. "You do not need a flu shot," Swift told his followers, "All you need, my friends, is to wake up." By 1962, Swift was simply recounting the Rothschilds' conspiracy to destroy American financial independence (although he did combine this with the Cecil Rhodes conspiracy to recapture the United States). In the wake of the Kennedy assassination, Swift warned that the "powers of Anti-Christ" were pushing "THE DISARMAMENT OF THE CITIZENS OF OUR NATION IN VIOLATION OF THE BILL OF RIGHTS." They were trying to take the guns needed "to cope with the vast number of conspiratorial forces that are at work in our society."[19] As the 1960s wore on, Swift's rhetoric became more and more militaristic, claiming that "a lot of preachers" were going to receive "quite a shock when they find out that the Lord is a man of war." In non-broadcast speeches before friendly audiences, Swift began advocating killing blacks. In 1970, Swift died in Tijuana, where he had gone in a desperate attempt to cure his diabetes—untreated because he "distrusted the 'Jewish' American medical establishment."[20]

Christian Identity Conspiracism

Wesley Swift was instrumental in establishing several organizations in California: the Anglo-Saxon Congregation of Los Angeles, the California League against Communism, and even the Pyramid Club. But it was Swift's Church of Jesus Christ–Christian, founded in Lancaster, California, in 1946, that first embodied seedline theology. Congregations of the church sprang up throughout the state, attracting like-minded preachers. One of these was Conrad Gaard. Another was Bertrand L. Comparet, deputy city attorney for San Diego, whose sermons could be innovative. He interpreted the book of Isaiah as a commentary on the United States, for it described a nation that was "tall and smooth shaven."[21] For over two decades, Comparet produced a stream of short books on the Jews—some of these biblical exegesis (e.g., *The Mark of the Beast*), others standard denunciations of the Jewish financial conspiracy (e.g., *Merchants of Babylon*). He preached Christian Identity until his death in 1983, infusing his sermons with the responsibility of "our race . . . to rule the world according to Yahweh's laws."[22]

Another early associate of Swift's was Oren F. Potito, who became the East Coast head of the Church of Jesus Christ–Christian after moving to Saint Petersburg, Florida. In the 1960s, Potito was also a high-ranking member of the National States' Rights Party, which began interacting with the Swift church to take the fight "against the enemies, the Jews and their stooges right into their own homes." At the open meeting held by the two groups in Los Angeles in 1963, threats to kills blacks and Jews abounded.[23] Like Comparet, Potito produced both Christian Identity religious tracts (*Jesus Christ Was Not a Jew*) and wholly secular diatribes (*The Federal Reserve Bank*). Potito's *The Conspiracy* applied Nesta Webster's Jewish-Masonic-Marxist Illuminati to World War II. In Potito's eyes, Hitler is the innocent victim of a war "brought on and concluded according to a deliberate plan developed and carried out by a conspiracy of a small, centrally directed group of Jews high in the governments of nearly every nation." In a Holocaust denial tract, Potito explained that Jewish control of the government led to the removal of any religious identification on census questionnaires "to keep us from finding out that there were five million more Jews in the United States than the birth rate could account for."[24]

Closely associated with both Potito and Swift was former Admiral John G. Crommelin, a violent racist and antisemite. Not a religious figure by any means, Crommelin's close association with the leaders of Christian Identity rested solely on his political views about the "worldwide Communist Jewish Conspiracy." Crommelin lost seven elections in his home state of Alabama because he refused "to make a deal with the Devil, (in other words, the Communist Jews) to get the necessary funds" for his campaign. It probably did not matter, however, since "they would steal the election from you, and they do it; because the voting machines are the greatest robbers ever invented. . . . I think voting machines are a Communist-Jewish invention. In fact I'm sure of it." Crommelin was confident of prevailing in the fight against the Jewish Communists because the menace of racial integration was uniting the white race:

> The real reason for the first Civil War was the attempt on the part of the Rothschilds in 1861, to stir up trouble between the North and the South, so they could get in here and take control over the country: I think the same thing is true now. . . . But there is . . . a tremendous factor in our favour.
>
> In 1861–1865 we had the White People completely divided between the North and the South with White Christians fighting the White Christians. Now . . . we have the White Man from the north fighting

along-side the White Man from the south. . . . I do believe that God has set this up for us to WIN.[25]

The most important of Swift's early colleagues was retired army colonel William Potter Gale, largely because of his additions to Christian Identity thinking. Not as prolific as some of the other preachers, Gale did lay out his ideas in his 1963 tract, *The Faith of Our Fathers*. (Its frontispiece suggests its content: a heroic depiction of Gale in clerical collar beneath an eagle clutching a cross, with a confederate battle flag backdrop.) Gale's interpretation of the Bible is avowedly racist but also intergalactic, for it begins: "This is a story about a race of people who exist on the planet Earth."[26] The story is quite peculiar, even by the standards of Christian Identity and British Israelism. It begins with the extraterrestrial, pre-Adamite "Enosh," who had inhabited the earth for "possibly millions of years" before "catastrophes beyond imagination or comprehension" destroyed their ancient civilizations. The story finally settles down into a more familiar Christian Identity struggle between "Ad-am's celestial family on Earth" and various satanic forces.[27]

Gale's epic culminates in America, to which our forefathers came "to advance the Faith of Jesus Christ and to form a GOVERNMENT under His Laws." Building on Bertrand Comparet's *America Is a Bible Land*, Gale continues: "They came to this land, the New Jerusalem that had been promised to God's Is-ra-el and which had been described perfectly in the Scriptures. . . . They formed thirteen colonies as they were from thirteen tribes." Although the "blindness" of history would have us believe Satan's story that Pilgrims and Puritans were fleeing religious persecution, Gale sets us straight: "These sovereign States of the great nation of His Kingdom were formed by men of the Adamic race and their women were mighty in their tasks. This nation and this government were founded by white men and white women who were Christians. They fought their way across the wilderness and built a great nation. In the name of the God of our Fathers, this nation will remain a white man's land and a white man's government. Until the Arch-angel calls the end of time."[28] At this point, biblical narrative gives way to the conspiracy against America. From the beginning, when George Washington "was given a vision of the dark clouds of Satan's children coming over the land," the conspiracy was directed by the "Yehudi" (i.e., international Jews): "As usual, they remained to themselves and continually plotted against Ad-am's children and their Yah-ve. They became storekeepers, lenders of money, pawn-brokers and termites in government just as they had always done.... Their leaders remained in Holland and Switzerland but planned and directed their activities on an international basis. They were never loyal to a nation that took them in. They sent their hirelings to the new nation and with their international money power they seduced many of Ad-am's children who were blind as to their origin." Beyond the standard usury of the "international money power," the Jews in Gale's account began and ran the slave trade, had Lincoln assassinated, and debased our legal system.[29]

The lasting significance of Gale's thought lies not in this rehash of the hidden hand conspiracy, but in his interpretation of American history. Of primary importance is the idea that the Articles of Confederation are "perpetual, never to be repealed or amended." Gale also attaches perpetual status to the "Ordnance [sic] of the Territories," which he says determines the addition of states to the Union. Government under the articles not only stressed state sovereignty but was also based in the Holy Bible and "organic law" and operated under a monetary system free from "usury." The Constitution, thus, is more or less an addendum to the articles that gives the federal government "absolutely NO 'rights.'" As Gale saw it, the Articles of Confederation are still in effect. Among other things, this means that American government is officially Christian, the Supreme Court has no basis for interpreting the Constitution, and all amendments to the Constitution after the Bill of Rights are illegal. These ideas constitute the basis of the Posse Comitatus movement (founded by Gale around 1969), as well as the entire legal doctrine used by the sovereign citizens, organized tax resisters, and numerous financial scams.[30]

The second distinctive element in Gale's work is his adamant position in favor of taking the fight to the Jews and their puppets, the blacks, as well as "Ad-am's blind children" (Gentiles who do the Jews' bidding). This last group resided largely in northern cities since "the brethren of the South were better prepared to resist Satan's children because of their way of life and their knowledge of the Word." From the beginning, Southern resistance brought intensified Jewish warfare against the South: "The Yehudi leaders knew that these Southern men would be a constant source of trouble to their plans. . . . The sons of Satan recognized the sons of God and feared them. . . . The sons of Satan knew that they must bring about a mongrelization with the Enosh [blacks] to effectively destroy the sons of God. Their land must be taken from them and their women folk subjected to the heathen." Thus, the Civil War, and the Reconstruction, was overseen by a "Yehudi Stooge." When Southern men formed the Ku Klux Klan "for the recovery and the protection of their people," the organization prospered, "as their mission was to bring righteous government to the people." Even an amazing "false flag" operation in which "Yehudi agents," dressed as masked Klansmen, terrorized blacks and Catholics to destroy the good name of the Klan, could not destroy the South.[31] But now, in the "Midnight Hour" as Gale called it, the Jews were mounting another campaign to destroy the South. The "Enosh were to be employed as front-line troops against Adam's children while the Yehudi sat back in the tall grass out of danger." Faced with this onslaught, the "sons and daughters of the Most High"

> would suddenly realize that they have been waiting for the Heavenly Father to do the things that He had sent them into the Earth to do in His name. . . . They were told to be his "battle-axe" and to fight Satan on Earth. They are to occupy the Earth and rule in righteousness with Him at the head of their government. Until this is done, no peace with Satan can be obtained. It has been fore-ordained that victory is to be theirs but they must be brave enough to "fight" and shed their blood in sacrifice if necessary. When they do that, victory is theirs![32]

This was a different type of Christian premillennialism. Rejecting the idea of "waiting for the Heavenly Father," the Christian Identity creed as sculpted by Gale and Swift maintained that the sons and daughters of God "would not be raptured into the Kingdom of God in the last days, but would have to fight to establish the Kingdom on Earth, in an all out war."[33]

Similar rhetoric emanated from the Church of Jesus Christ–Christian and the Christian Defense League, a more militaristic organization also founded by Wesley Swift. As early as 1959, a league flyer feared that an "ORGANIZED WAR" threatened the "preservation of our White Christian heritage." In the early 1960s, the league also forged an alliance with J. B. Stoner's equally racist and violent National States' Rights Party.[34] Wesley Swift's sermons reflected the more intense racism, describing the "fury of White Christian civilization when it realizes how betrayed and bilked it has been." Swift continued, "Now you find that as the sons and daughters of God wake up, they want to march. . . . It will be the fastest sweeping march to cleanse this nation ever seen in the history of God's Kingdom." If evil forces try to stop them, "then war is part of the picture."[35] Gale was even more strident, telling groups in the Los Angeles area that "pure whites" must fight "the non-pure . . . even if we have to take up arms and make their blood run in the streets." Gale advocated assassinating California's Governor Brown, Attorney General Mosk, and Senator "Kikel" (Senator Thomas Kuchel, a moderate Republican). In a broadcast sermon, Gale told the Jews that, if they tried "to harm us in any way, every Rabbi in L.A. will die within 24 hours." Shortly afterward, Gale gave a speech in which, referring to the arrest of General Walker during the integration of the University of Mississippi, he warned: "Anytime you try to kidnap me or any of my associates under any of these circumstances in the future, we will kill you."[36]

Organized Resistance to the Conspiracy

Gale's warning was not hollow talk. While other rhetorically violent groups—such as James Madole's neo-Nazi National Renaissance Party— had engaged in symbolic and theatrical activities, Gale and Swift meant business. No later than 1960, Gale founded the California Rangers, a paramilitary group that could "put 20,000 fully armed and trained men into the streets of Los Angeles within six hours after an emergency." Around the same time Swift was designing Operation AWAKE (Army of White American Kingdom Evangelists) as "the defense division of the Church of Jesus Christ, Christian." This group was clearly modeled on William Pelley's Silver Shirt organization of the 1930s, with an AWAKE militia in every state, a subsidiary AWAKE district posse in every congressional district and, for each posse, any number of chapels of thirteen Christian Soldiers each. The group's instructional manual required every chapel leader to join Pedro del Valle's Defenders of the American Constitution.[37] (Del Valle, a former Marine Corps Lieutenant General was a strong proponent of the Khazarian Jew version of the hidden hand conspiracy but wasn't involved in Christian Identity.) By the mid-1960s, Gale and Swift were behind three paramilitary organizations, the Christian Defense League, the California Rangers, and AWAKE, "designed to defend the country in case of takeover," as Oren Potito explained. California's attorney general saw them as "a secret underground guerrilla force, . . . linked with other non-military organizations by a common ideology and leadership."[38]

As the "movement" became more paramilitary, Swift had reason to fear that his Church of Jesus Christ-Christian might lose its religious— and tax exempt—status. Accordingly, Swift handed off to Richard Butler the leadership of the Christian Defense League, which was to "act as a liaison to 'patriotic groups' but never participate in any action."[39] Gale focused his attention on the California Rangers and the AWAKE militias, and both Gale and Butler stepped up their working relationships with other right-wing but non–Christian Identity organizations, such as the National States' Rights Party. Church of Jesus Christ-Christian preachers Oren Potito and Charles "Connie" Lynch were important figures in the National States' Rights Party, as was Admiral John Crommelin, who spoke at Swift's meetings in Los Angeles on topics such as how the Rothschilds incited the Civil War.[40] They also forged some links with the Minutemen, organized by Robert DePugh to "take any action—no matter how brutal—that may be required to renew the protection of the United States Constitution for future generations."[41] The resulting nexus of organizations was suspected by the FBI in an array of violent acts, including the bombing of the Sixteenth Street Baptist Church in Birmingham and the murder of Medgar Evers in Mississippi. They were also suspected of plotting to kill President Kennedy and Martin Luther King Jr. in 1963. And although Gale claimed the suspicion was based on "lies . . . planted by the Jews," it has not entirely dissipated.[42]

Two developments spread Christian Identity to a wider audience. On Swift's death in 1970, Richard Butler took over the ministry of the Church of Jesus Christ–Christian, moved its headquarters to Hayden Lake, Idaho, and renamed it Church of Jesus Christ Christian–Aryan Nations. By this time, the Satanic-Jewish conspiracy was taken completely for granted. Christian Identity had never articulated a distinctive conspiracy; its focus was biblical rather than topical. The particulars of the actual conspiracy perpetrated by the Jews, their dupes, and their puppets were not original ideas. Swift, Comparet, Gaard, Potito, and Gale all simply expropriated those elements of the hidden hand conspiracy that suited them.

Butler's Aryan Nations kept all the Christian Identity and British Israelism underpinnings and added a gloss of the "symbolic heraldry" of the "Aryans, a Race of Gods." Butler further provided official twelve-point Weltanschauung (e.g., "RACE is the Blood and Soul of the Nation"), twelve "Foundation Stones" of redemption, a "Theopolitical Platform," and a ten-article "Platform for the *Aryan National State*." These points were buttressed with excerpts from a 1919 "confession" by Jewish Nazi Arthur Trebitsch, in which he admitted that his own "venomous program" provided "further proof that organized Jewry follows those Machiavellian principles for the enslavement of the peoples of this planet and the destruction of all higher humanity, culture, and civilization which are outlined in the 'Protocols of the Learned Elders of Zion.'"[43]

In the Aryan nation Butler envisioned, white Christians would be freed from "the swinepen dominated by the alien which they now serve." Citizenship would be limited to whites; noncitizens could visit "the Republic, but only under the custodianship of a citizen." Jews would be "repatriated," their wealth "redistributed," and "Jew Talmudic anti-Christ Communism made a capital crime. "True Positive Christianity" and an "Aryan cultural viewpoint" would be mandatory in schools and all media of communications. This would put an end to "Usury," the "Jew-'Law Merchant' judicial system," and anything else that threatened "the purity of the race."[44]

Foremost among those things that threatened the purity of the race was the federal government, which had been forcing racial integration on white-owned businesses and white-controlled local governments for some time. William Potter Gale's response was to create an "unorganized militia"—based on his idea that all military draft-age men constituted a de facto unorganized militia—named after the Posse Comitatus Act of 1878. Important symbolically, that act had marked the end of post–Civil War Reconstruction by removing federal troops from the South. Since Posse Comitatus generally translates as "Power of (or to) the County," the group came to stand for the idea that no legal authority beyond county government was legitimate. Thus, the highest legal authority anywhere in the United States was the county sheriff. An early flyer for the posse in Michigan explained that the "Police Law Manual" gave sheriffs priority in making arrests and that "the sheriff may require suitable aid—(Posse)!!!"[45] Gale himself continued leading his Ministry of Christ Church and for some time wrote newsletters and pamphlets on "Identity" and "the anti-Christ Jews." This ministerial side of Gale's operation was distinct from the Posse Comitatus. Although the antisemitism of the posse derived directly from Christian Identity, no effort was made to articulate this theological basis. Thus, more than Butler's Aryan Nations, the Posse Comitatus was a secular organization.[46]

The establishment of Aryan Nations and the Posse Comitatus marked a turning point for Christian Identity in that the churches and the secular organizations became more distinct. Beginning in the 1970s, Christian Identity churches and "ministries" proliferated and, by most estimates, now number in the hundreds. Most are small, but some have achieved a regional or even national presence through newsletters and broadcasting. The theology they preach has been described as "the thread that binds otherwise isolated hate groups into a small national movement," as the churches draw people in.[47] The case of a Colorado parishioner of Pete Peters's LaPorte Church of Christ illustrates the process:

> "At first I tried to dispute it, tried to prove this theology was wrong," said Ted Weiland, a 32-year-old from Denver. . . .
>
> "I was like those people who have been brainwashed to think it's white supremacy, racism or discrimination," he said. "But there has been a historical case of mistaken identity. We are the real Jews, the chosen people of the Bible." . . .
>
> Weiland was convinced by Peters' arguments, especially his theory connecting the Jews to communism. . . . "The Bible says the antichrist deceives, and the false Jews fit the bill better than anyone else," he said. "We believe there will be an invasion of America. I look at my own weapons at home in terms of possible invasion, and we stockpile cans of food for that possibility."[48]

While this makes Reverend Peters seem theologically antisemitic, it does not quite do justice to a man who complained that it is hard to tell "the truth concerning the Jewish push for their socialistic, communistic, antichrist, One-World government" since these same Jews "control the media and use the hysterical smear label (and misnomer) of anti-Semitism whenever someone has the courage to shed light on their evil deeds."[49]

It is typical for Christian Identity leaders to maintain both a religious role while heading a separate, political organization, as Gale did. Robert Miles was the pastor of the Mountain Church of Jesus Christ the Savior and head of the United Klans of America in Michigan. Sheldon Emry ministered to the Lord's Covenant Church in Phoenix while working with the Citizens Emergency Defense System, a "private militia" funded by Missouri white supremacist John R. Harrell. James Warner, in addition to founding the New Christian Crusade Church in Metairie, Louisiana, revived Wesley Swift's Christian Defense League to help fight "outright dictatorship by organized Jewry."[50] But there are, of course, organizations with only tenuous links to actual churches or ministries. Many of these are quite extreme, frequently leading to violence bordering on insurrection.

The ideological origin of these groups in the ideas of Swift and Gale accounts for much of the extremism. The biblical basis for their antisemitism and racism, derived from Swift, gives members of these groups a sense of righteousness that is hard to imagine. Christian Identity has been characterized as a world-rejecting religious movement. Whereas most of the religious movements that have arisen in recent times are either positive world-affirming or at least grudgingly world-accommodating, world-rejecting movements are based on the Manichean dichotomy already associated with conspiracism. After separating the world into "good and evil, order and chaos, or the sacred and profane," a religion such as Christian Identity "identifies and rejects the modern world and the current social order as evil, corrupt, and illegitimate."[51] Thom Robb, long-time Klansman and director of the White People's Committee to Restore God's Laws (among other positions), is fairly representative as he claims the backing of the "laws of God as set forth in the Holy Bible" for his war on "the black plague and Jew parasites that are destroying our race and nation." The alternative American history articulated by William Potter Gale adds to the sense of righteousness. The Posse Comitatus ideology, as well as that of its offspring, the sovereign citizens, is based on the belief that "the true history of the United States—and thus the true laws, the true obligations of citizens, the true government—had been hidden from the American citizen by a massive, long-lasting conspiracy."

14

THE GOVERNMENT CONSPIRACY AGAINST "US"

> The passage of time will make it clear to even the more slow among us
> that the government is the foremost threat to life, and liberty of the folk.
>
> Louis Beam, "Leaderless Resistance"[1]

Christian Identity is one "core feature of right-wing extremism," embodied in such variants as militias, sovereign citizens, Freemen, and common law courts. But there are other sources of inspiration, and the differences between Christian Identity groups and other white supremacist and antisemitic groups can be minor. People concerned about the patriot movement frequently conflate Christian Identity with neo-Nazi, Aryan paganist, or Yockeyite groups. Researcher Tanya Sharpe, for instance, has collapsed everything into "the antigovernment, paramilitary survivalist/conspiracy mentality."[2] This is reasonable given the common belief of all these forces that America has been betrayed, that the Jews orchestrated the conspiracy behind this betrayal, and that the ultimate goal of the conspiracy is the destruction or subjugation of the white race.

The Patriot Movement

Conspiracy theories have been useful to patriot groups as a recruiting tool and to justify the claim that the federal government has lost its legitimacy, so that "when a government becomes a tyranny it is no longer legitimate, and therefore, citizens have a right to revolt and to free the sovereign people from the yoke of oppression."[3] Some patriot groups focus simply on fighting the "federal tyranny" that betrays constitutional values, while others have given up even on "CONstitutionalism" as "nothing more than a mindless worship of a façade of spurious legitimacy behind which a murderous, corrupt and idiotic regime cowers." Some wage a Racial Holy War (RaHoWa) that, once won, will "usher in a new golden-age for the Aryan race." Still others think of themselves as the resistance to the Zionist Occupational Government (ZOG). In practice, these differing rationales and their corresponding terminology do not matter much.[4] Aside from their religious zeal, the primary distinguishing feature of Christian Identity groups is geographical: they predominate in rural America, especially in a swath running roughly from Arkansas to the Pacific Northwest.

The shift to rural America began when Richard Butler moved the Church of Jesus Christ–Christian from southern California to northern Idaho and rechristened it Aryan Nations. Around the same time, James Ellison left San Antonio to "establish a refuge" as the Lord had instructed him. By the mid-seventies, Ellison's rural Arkansas compound, Zarephath-Horeb, was home to his survivalist group, The Covenant, the Sword, and the Arm of the Lord. The extremist community of Elohim City, Oklahoma, which became well known only after the Oklahoma City bombing in 1995, was also founded around this time. Much of this rural migration was associated with paramilitary survivalism. One feature of the Covenant, the Sword, and the Arm of the Lord was the Endtime Overcomer Survival Training School, and both Elohim City and the Aryan Nations compound were armed camps. John R. Harrell, who had been putting on rural gun-oriented "freedom festivals" in downstate Illinois for some time, established his own "private militia," the Citizens Emergency Defense System under the leadership of Jack Mohr, a "psychopolitics" mind-control conspiracist. Harrell identified a "Mid-America Survival Area"—defined by its corners: Lubbock, Texas; Scotts Bluff, Nebraska; Pittsburgh; and Atlanta—he believed to be "defendable" against invasion by an "alien force."[5]

Rural areas were vulnerable to the Christian Identity message, even in its virulent forms. The farm economy suffered badly in the 1970s, with increased energy costs and lower commodity prices. Farm foreclosures created an "existential insecurity" that Christian Identity preachers could easily whip up into hatred. James Wickstrom, head of "counterinsurgency" for the Posse Comitatus, portrayed the farmer as the "Twentieth Century Slave" who was at the mercy of Jewish "land-grabbing devils."[6] This fear of losing control of the land was exacerbated by a 1976 change in federal law that brought more land under the administration of the Bureau of Land Management, the U.S. Forest Service, and other agencies. A "sagebrush rebellion" of state and local officials in the West fought these changes in the courts but lost.

As rural America continued to suffer economically into the 1980s, conspiracism flourished. Various groups and their periodicals began to characterize the foreclosure problem as intentional. Ruth Nichols's quarterly newspaper *Farm Tempo* decried the "horrendous premeditated plot to rob farmers of their land." Behind this "so cunningly conceived and so cleverly executed" conspiracy stood the Federal Reserve System. While Nichols stopped there, other periodicals went further. The Patriots Information Network's newsletter routinely implied Jewish control of the conspiracy, and *The Upright Ostrich* cited Eustace Mullins's standard "Rothschilds rule the U.S." conspiracy.[7] In this situation, Christian Identity militants pressed their advantage. William Potter Gale continued to promote the goals of the Posse Comitatus in radio "sermons" featuring less and less religious content: "Yes, we're going to cleanse our land. We're going to do it with a sword. And we're going to do it with violence. 'Oh,' they say, 'Reverend Gale, you're teaching violence." You're damned right I'm teaching violence! God said You're going to do it that way, and it's about time somebody is telling you to get violent, whitey." Gale broadcast threats against Jews—as did Sheldon Emry, who attacked the Moral Majority for supporting "the antichrist Jews"; James Warner, who warned Jews to "keep their big noses out of our racial and religious affairs"; and many others.[8] By 1983, Christian Identity groups were organizing for war on what was seen as the Zionist Occupation Government. Ellison's Covenant, the Sword, and the Arm of the Lord launched a series of bombings, justified in the group's "ATTACK" manifesto on the grounds that "every action of the enemy shall be met with equal and opposite reaction."[9] Ultimately, an Aryan Nations Congress brought together Richard Butler, James Ellison, Robert Miles (at the time, head of the Michigan Klan), and others. Their plan to overthrow ZOG led to yet another new group, the Brüder Schweigen, or, as they were universally known, The Order (a name taken from William Pierce's racist revenge novel *The Turner Diaries*).

Robert Mathews, The Order's leader, issued his Declaration of War on November 25, 1984—a date now commemorated by right-wing extremists.[10] Although accompanied by a lengthy and accusatory letter to Congress, Mathews's actual declaration is fairly short:

It is now a dark and dismal time in the history of our race. All around us lie the green graves of our sires, yet, in a land once ours we have become a people dispossessed. Our heroes and culture have been insulted and degraded. The mongrel hordes clamor to sever us from our inheritance. Yet our people do not care.

Throughout this land our children are being coerced into accepting nonwhites for their idols, their companions, and worst of all for their mates. . . . Evidence abounds that a certain, vile, alien people have taken control of our country. How is it that a parasite has gained dominion over its host? Instead of being vigilant our fathers have slept.

What are we to do? How bleak these aliens have made our children's future. All about us the land is dying. Our cities swarm with dusky hordes. . . . Our farms are being seized by usurious leeches and our people are being forced off the land. The capitalists and communists pick gleefully at our bones while the vile, hook-nosed masters of usury orchestrate our destruction.

We hereby declare ourselves a free and sovereign people. We claim a territorial imperative that will consist of the entire North American continent north of Mexico. As soldiers of the Aryan Resistance Movement (ARM) we will conduct ourselves in accordance with the Geneva Convention.

We now close this Declaration with an open letter to congress and our signatures confirming our intent to do battle. Let friend and foe alike be made aware: This Is War! We . . . declare ourselves to be in a full and unrelenting state of war with those forces seeking and consciously promoting the destruction of our faith and race. Therefore, for Blood, Soil, and Honor, and for the future of our children, we commit ourselves to battle. Amen![11]

Members of The Order were already rampaging through the West, committing robberies and giving the proceeds to the Covenant, the Sword, and the Arm of the Lord. The Order had gained notoriety for murdering Denver radio personality Alan Berg and was being hunted by federal authorities. At this same time, the legend of North Dakota farmer Gordon Kahl was growing. In keeping with his Posse Comitatus beliefs, Kahl refused to pay taxes, calling them "tithes to the Synagogue of Satan, under the 2nd plank of the Communist Manifesto."[12] In 1983, Kahl killed two federal marshals trying to arrest him and fled to Arkansas where he was killed some months later in shootout at the home of a fellow Posse Comitatus member.

Crimes such as these brought a serious federal response; William Potter Gale himself was arrested and convicted of issuing death threats against a federal judge. Robert Mathews was killed in 1984 in an FBI siege of Whidbey Island, near Everett, Washington, and in 1985 twenty-three members of The Order were indicted on a variety of federal racketeering charges. For a time, it appeared that the violence that grew out of Swift and Gale's Christian Identity had run its course, but the respite turned out to be brief. In 1990 President George Herbert Walker

Bush used the unfortunate phrase "new world order" to mark the end of the Cold War, putting conspiracists across the board on high alert. The disastrous 1992 federal assault on Randy Weaver's home in what is commonly called Ruby Ridge and the next year's equally unpopular and lethal siege of David Koresh's Branch Davidian compound near Waco generated massive antigovernment backlash. In this context the Brady Handgun Violence Prevention Act (the "Brady Bill"), which mandated background checks, was seen in a very suspicious light. By 1994, violence in the West against federal agencies as benign as the Forest Service marked the return of Christian Identity–fueled militias.[13]

The militia "movement" is often dated from the establishment of the Montana Militia in 1994, although militias existed earlier. Some see two phases of militias: one more inspired by Christian Identity and the ideas of William L. Pierce (especially *The Turner Diaries*); the second dating from the mid-nineties and more inspired by new world order conspiracism.[14] Depending on the breadth of definition, the militia movement may or may not be considered the same as the Christian patriot movement. It certainly has some roots in the "township" movement that originated in Nehemiah Township, Idaho, in 1982 and was devoted to the "preservation, protection, and sustenance of our Aryan race." Similarly to the Posse Comitatus position, sovereign townships used "Anglo-Saxon" law and "Yahshua Christian" law, and considered any other governments' laws that conflicted with their own to be invalid.[15] Although the specific "legal" terms are not used uniformly across the patriot movement, Anglo-Saxon law seems to be much the same as organic law, the underlying documents of which are "the Magna Carta, the Declaration of Independence, the Articles of Confederation, and the Bill of Rights" but not necessarily the Constitution. This body of law is seemingly threatened by the "Talmudic Law" that serves as the basis of "the current welfare state: the mob rule of democracy."[16]

In 1996, the Southern Poverty Law Center distinguished between militias and patriot groups, identifying over four hundred of the former and three hundred of the latter. Others have lumped them together as white supremacist groups.[17] Essentially, the idea of forming "militias" derived from William Potter Gale's reading of the Constitution as promoting "unorganized militias" to guard against government tyranny. Because of the problems other antigovernment groups had encountered with infiltration by law enforcement, Louis Beam (of the Aryan Nations) added the idea of "leaderless resistance," which in practice meant no large-scale organization—hence the hundreds of small groups that the Southern Poverty Law Center identified.[18]

Martyrs

In the aftermath of the declaration of war and surging right-wing violence in the 1990s, martyrdom became something of an inspirational fixation in the militia and Christian patriot movements. While conspiracists had long recognized those who had suffered at the hands of the conspiracy, serious martyrdom began with the 1983 death of Gordon Kahl, the North Dakota rancher and Posse Comitatus member. The posse's James Wickstrom, who held the "land-grabbing Jews" responsible for Kahl's death, immediately proclaimed that "Gordon Kahl will prove to be a martyr for all the people who seek freedom in America." William Potter Gale claimed that Kahl was killed "because he was teaching this law of posse comitatus, and the banking system and the reason for the foreclosures in the farms, the result of the Federal Reserve System." Richard Wayne Snell, who became a martyr himself, generated stories of government torture and even of federal agents' killing a local sheriff to keep him from exposing their torture of Kahl.[19]

The next year, the siege that killed Robert Mathews, head of The Order, raised the standard of martyrdom among white supremacists in particular. Women for Aryan Unity offered their tribute to Mathews and his comrades for their work to establish a "Territorial Homeland for our people" and for sacrificing "what they could" to provide "a future for white children." The Brüder Schweigen "news page" paid tribute to all members of The Order victimized by the government. And David Lane (regarded as a prisoner of war and martyr himself) maintains a tribute page filled with posts from followers worldwide:

The system took you down, but your memory will live for a thousand years and inspire whites to stand up against those who want to destroy us! . . . (Ireland)

He fought for our race and he gave up everything a man can give for his ideals and ideas. We won't give up Robert! (Poland)

Robert was a hero of our race. He read the Turner Diaries and he lived the Turner Diaries! (USA)[20]

William Pierce's *The Turner Diaries* has provided inspiration for many would-be martyrs. The protagonist, Earl Turner, begins as a reluctant resister of Zionist control but becomes "a white Aryan hero and martyr who leads the 'Great Revolution' in which millions of American Jews, Blacks, Hispanics, and 'race-traitors' are exterminated on the climactic 'Day of the Rope.'"[21]

In the 1990s, government actions began to generate more martyrs with a much broader appeal. The siege of Randy Weaver's house in Idaho left many people uneasy. Weaver was not killed, but his wife and infant son were. Weaver himself accused the government of carrying out "a ZOG ambush" in which "Samuel Hansen Weaver and Vicki Weaver are Martyrs for Yah-Yahshua and the White Race." The siege was so important to the idea of oppressive government ruthlessly wiping out patriots that both the beginning and end of the siege are singled out as "deadly dates" on the "Calendar for Right-Wing Extremists."[22] Louis Beam of the Aryan Nations predicted:

The federals have made a terrible error in the Weaver case that they will long regret. . . . Long after Weaver is tried and has been freed by the courts as an innocent man wrongfully accused, there will be 10,000 White men in this country . . . with a burning desire to see the federals pay for their crime against nature. Tens of thousands will now see clearly the face of an enemy that before they could not visualize. . . .

Mark my word, this incident, like the murder of Gordon Kahl, will not go away. . . . Men across this nation will sit quietly in their homes planning, praying and waiting. Then someday, without a signal from anyone—yet as if a signal had came [*sic*] from everyone—they will walk quickly out their front doors with a look of grim determination on their faces. . . . Payback, some will call it. For others it will be an act of true patriotism in the spirit of Lexington and Concord.[23]

Even more widely known than Ruby Ridge is "Waco," the shorthand term for the government's next fiasco, the siege of David Koresh's Branch Davidian compound. Almost everyone agrees that government agencies handled both standoffs badly and tried to obscure their culpability. But among militias, Waco provided more evidence of the government's persecution of the innocent. The Branch Davidians became martyrs despite the fact that the sect's beliefs were not particularly compatible with Christian Identity, the extreme Right, or white supremacy. The thing that made them martyrs was simply the government's assault.[24]

At the same time, Timothy McVeigh is conspicuously absent from the roster of martyrs because of the widespread belief across the militia-white supremacist world that the bombing of the Alfred P. Murrah Federal Building was a false-flag operation. One theory links the bombing to an aborted military coup against President Clinton because of his "treason" and murder of Vince Foster, as part of an extreme extension of the Whitewater scandal. Some simply blame federal law enforcement, especially the FBI's campaign of provocations designed to incite militias to violence as an excuse to wipe them out.[25] A more convoluted conspiracy centers on the nearby Elohim City religious compound, which was said to be filled with rejected Aryan Nations applicants, recruited by Anti-Defamation League "agents" with the support of the Southern Poverty Law Center, twin nemeses of white supremacists. Anti-Defamation League agents, so conspiracists claim, carried out the actual bombing with the approval of a federal government desperate to discredit the militias. The proof lies in Elohim City's survival: "If Elohim City wasn't an SPLC [Southern Poverty Law Center] False Flag operation, the FBI would have called in the Air National Guard and carpet bomb[ed] Elohim City. The FBI leveled Waco, slaughtered Randy Weaver's family, but they left the Elohim City terror base untouched?"[26]

Martyrs continued to accumulate. Gordon Kahl's advocate, Richard Wayne Snell, achieved martyrdom for killing a pawnbroker he thought was Jewish. As the appeals of Snell's murder conviction were exhausted and his execution loomed, the Militia of Montana newsletter *Taking Aim* lamented "an American patriot to be executed by the Beast." Retroactive martyrs were created, too. Kathy Ainsworth, a fifth-grade teacher with a secret life, had been killed by police in 1968 as she attempted to bomb the home of a prominent Jewish resident of Meridian, Mississippi. Decades later, Women for Aryan Unity began celebrating the birthday of "Our Fallen Sister," signing off: "We will never forget!" Eventually martyrdom managed to reach down to the level of Marvin Heemeyer of Granby, Colorado, who tried to destroy that town with an armored bulldozer before shooting himself in despair. Heemeyer had just lost what was described as a "garden-variety zoning dispute."[27]

The creation of martyrs became particularly important in the world created by William Potter Gale, William L. Pierce, and Robert Mathews for several reasons First, while conspiracists had long complained of victimization, the suffering of specific individuals made it viscerally real. Louis Beam's account of Ruby Ridge featured a graphic description of Vicki Weaver's head exploding while her baby, "covered with the crimson blood of it's [*sic*] mother, fell to the floor in screams of ununderstanding terror." This sort of violation demanded retaliation. By the time of the Malheur, Oregon, standoff in 2016 between those occupying a wildlife refuge and law enforcement, "rank and file" patriots had become adamant to avenge those arrested or killed. Supporters' Facebook posts held that "America was fired upon by our government" and asked: "Will we allow this government to continue slaughtering, and to set an example that we must bow to them alone?"[28]

Second, dates commemorating martyrdoms take on real meaning and inspire others. National Martyrs Day (not an actual holiday) falls on December 8 to mark the death of Robert Mathews. The Northwest

Hammerskins host rock festivals to mark the day, featuring bands such as Beer Hall Putsch. The neo-Nazi organization Stormfront has used the occasion to tout Mathews as a "yeoman farmer . . . burned to death by a secret police task force." Richard Kemp, youngest surviving member of The Order, addressed the Confederate Hammerskins Martyrs Day gathering by telephone from prison. "Let each of us be so inspired by the devotion of our fallen comrades," Kemp told the crowd, "that we lift their standards as we march into the future."[29] Even more inspirational is April 19, the date in 1995 when Timothy McVeigh (or whoever) blew up the Murrah Building in Oklahoma City. Everyone noted that this was the second anniversary of the destruction of the Branch Davidian compound, but it also marked the tenth anniversary of the federal takeover of the Covenant, the Sword, and the Arm of the Lord compound in Arkansas. It was also the very day when Richard Wayne Snell was executed, and militia members are proud to note that the date commemorates the first shots of the American Revolution at Lexington and Concord.

Third, and ultimately most important, the existence of martyrs means that there must in fact be a conflict. Guerilla wars and resistance movements have always had their martyrs, whether Che Guevara or members of the French Resistance in World War II. A list of martyrs tells people that they are not conspiracists imagining a Zionist Occupation Government, but real fighters, prepared to give their all to protect beleaguered white Christian America against the real forces of the ZOG.

Fighting the Zionist Occupation Government

In the wake of the Oklahoma City bombing in 1995, the existence of militias became widely recognized, but their conspiratorial basis and the conspiracy theories promoted by their members remained obscure. In part, this was because the underpinning of Christian Identity conspiracism had become so ingrained that militia members simply accepted that "the Jewish conspiracy has assumed vast proportions" and that its primary aim "is to erode white rights."[30] Yet conspiratorial ideas pervaded the militias, as Kenneth Stern reported: "Go to a militia meeting and pick up the literature. There are charts of 'The Conspiracy to Rule the World,' showing the House of Representatives connected to the Illuminati, the Illuminati connected to London's Hellfire Club, the Hellfire Club connected to Oxford, Oxford to the Bilderbergers, the Bilderbergers to the Federal Reserve, the Federal Reserve to the United Nations."[31] The Covenant, the Sword, and the Arm of the Lord published various conspiratorial items, ranging from *Witchcraft and the Illuminati* to a pamphlet listing "100 facts" about the Jews (background for their Christian Army "training manual"). The Citizens for Liberty, a Christian patriot group in Washington, offered for sale John Robison's *Proofs of a Conspiracy*. The Phoenix-based Police against the New World Order decoded the colored dots placed on rural mailboxes to guide the new world order troops: blue told the troops to send you to a FEMA concentration camp; pink doomed you to slave labor; and red dot meant you would be killed on the spot. In 1995, militia leaders testifying before a Senate committee described FEMA concentration camps, told of UN troops secretly scattered around the country, explained how the federal government itself had blown up the Murrah Building in Oklahoma City, and told the senators that the government was using "weather-control techniques so the new world order could starve millions of Americans" (they estimated eighty-five tornadoes caused by the government across America's heartland).[32]

Across the patriot movement, the Jewish conspiracy had become the Zionist Occupation Government: ZOG.[33] Gordon (Jack) Mohr, head of the Christian Patriots Defense League's Emergency Defense System and a religious proselytizer, lectured on the need for armed citizens' groups to fight for "the defense of white Christian civilization" in the face of ZOG's effort to establish "One World Dictatorship!"[34] The use of the term "ZOG" does little to distinguish militia and patriot ideas from earlier antisemitic conspiracy theories. Their distinctive conspiracism arises from William Potter Gale's organic law ideology laid out in 1963, which was the basis for "the myth of the Organic Constitution," according to which: "The Constitution is a divinely inspired document in which human agency is secondary to God's will. Only the original Constitution and Bill of Rights as signed by the Founders is the supreme Law of the Land and this law should be interpreted in the light of Biblical understanding. All later amendments, laws and regulations are 'unconstitutional' in the sense that they 'create a federal constitution in opposition to the original."[35] Despite the obvious religious rationale for the organic Constitution, the main point behind it is racial. While all Constitutional amendments were considered suspect, the Fourteenth Amendment was singled out as a key part of the conspiracy against the white race, because it ensured citizenship to former slaves. A country "is like a home to a people," wrote Erst LaFlor. "White men struggled to build a beautiful house for their children and future generations. And then, just as they were nailing on the last board, negroes were made citizens and given full run of the house."[36] During the school desegregation campaign of the 1960s, Dan Smoot had issued a call for a "first-rate political figure" to spearhead a drive to have the Fourteenth Amendment "resubmitted" for ratification, since its original ratification had been coercive and fraudulent. Smoot was certain that, in the aftermath of *Brown v. Board of Education*, the amendment would fail.[37]

A defining document in the struggle against ZOG is *The Citizen's Rule Book*, from around 1990. The *Rule Book* accepts the first twelve amendments to the Constitution as legitimate but describes all subsequent ones as having taken effect despite "serious doubt" about their legality. The important amendment is the fourteenth, section one of which provides citizenship to "all persons born or naturalized in the United States." The *Rule Book* interpretation, universally adhered to by white supremacist groups, is that this section provides only "2nd, 3rd, or whatever status of citizenship one selects for oneself, as opposed to Freeholder with full sovereign rights." That is, blacks and immigrants can have (at best) second-class citizenship.[38] Needless to say, efforts by the government to apply a normal interpretation of the Constitution are seen as contributing to a conspiracy to undermine the 'real' Constitution as well as God's will. Similarly, in the *Rule Book* version of the Constitution, the Seventeenth Amendment, providing for the direct election of senators, is not as innocuous as commonly thought, since "this moved us from a complex Republic to a simple Republic much like the style of government in the Soviet Union. States' rights were lost and we were plunged headlong into a democracy of which our forefathers warned us was the vilest form of government because it always ends in oppression."[39]

Fighting the ZOG was not just a war of words, however. Gale's advocacy of violence found an appreciative audience among those with what Tanya Sharpe has called "the antigovernment, paramilitary survivalist/conspiracy mentality." The Phineas Priesthood—"the warrior priesthood of the Christian Identity movement" open to those of "pure Levite lineage (not a Khazarian imposter)"—have taken it on themselves to enforce the Christian Identity prohibition of race mixing. In 1996, Eric Rudolph (who planted a bomb at that year's Atlanta Olympics) expanded the range of targets by bombing a gay nightclub. Both race mixing and homosexuality are, of course, promoted by the Jewish conspiracy to destroy white America's morality and "spiritual life." Militia members also became involved in antiabortion violence, especially after 1994 legislation to ensure safe access to clinics demonstrated "anti-Christian tyranny and defiance of God's law."[40] Joe Holland, of the North America Free Militia, bridled at being called a "tax-resister," telling reporters that he would oppose the federal government "until such time as it stops carrying out abortions in its murder clinics and stops supporting the national advancement of homosexuals." Equally conspiratorial, one Paul deParrie, a pro-life activist, accused the government, "drunk on the blood of the innocent," of fomenting "a pogrom against all who subscribe to a Judeo-Christian belief system." Citing the government's assaults on Randy Weaver and David Koresh, deParrie claimed that the government considered "anyone who doesn't bow down to Pax Americana and the New World Order a subversive."[41]

Sovereign Citizens

Of all the "patriot" groups that emerged toward the end of the century, the sovereign citizens can lay the strongest claim to an original conspiracy theory, although its derivation is hard to determine. The term "sovereign citizen" has rightly been referred to as a "catchall phrase for people with a variety of similar but idiosyncratic beliefs." In court, they often speak a weird quasi-legal "gibberish," such as this defendant's refusal to accept counsel: "There will be no exceptions, no consent, unequivocal no. I will not accept a title law nobility in common law venue. I do not waive common law venue. No one is going to represent me as sworn in from the appellate branch of the Supreme Court which is voluntary jurisdiction. And you better start reading your law. Why do you think the code commissioner is now putting the codes back into special television programs that came out just recently because of the edict we put on the Joint Chiefs of Staff?"[42] Despite their variety, sovereign citizens agree that they are not subject to federal law, as the federal government is illegitimate and has no jurisdiction over them. They refuse to get driver's licenses, use odd punctuation in their names, and make use of cryptic legalisms. Oklahoma City bombing conspirator Terry Nichols, for instance, would write "TDI" next to the zip codes on his letters to indicate that he was submitting to the use of these federal codes only under "Threat, Duress, Intimidation."[43] Most accounts stress the influence of William Potter Gale's Posse Comitatus on the ideas of sovereign citizens, but the mix of ideas is more complex and appears to date back to the work of Robert DePugh, head of the Patriotic Party and the Minutemen

The party and the resistance group were closely bound together under DePugh's leadership—both strongly anti-Communist and opposed to the civil rights movement. But conspiratorial ideas lay behind the groups' pronouncements. DePugh's 1966 self-published book *Blueprint for Victory*, for example, laid out a total resistance plan to fight the "One-World conspirators," described in the coded antisemitism of the hidden hand conspiracy as "the parasitic 'sons of the devil.'" A "special appeal" for DePugh's legal defense (for conspiracy to rob a bank) featured cover art showing the traditional pyramid with an eye atop it and the legend "Illuminati Bureaucratic Traitors." DePugh's messages embodied several themes that would take root among the "amalgam of tax resisters and racist 'Christian Identity' believers who coalesced around Gale's ideas of 'citizen government'" and emerged as the sovereign citizens.[44]

First, DePugh's rhetoric foreshadowed the idea of an illegitimate government turning citizens into subjects or even slaves. Stopping the tyrannical "Police State" necessitated taking a stand for freedom over "servitude," refusing to "submit docilely" to government persecution. Second, a "sovereign" approach to resistance involved innovative interpretations of law, as when readers were instructed to refuse to file taxes and write "PROTEST" on their 1040 tax forms. If, as was likely, they got a "threatening" letter from the IRS, they could fight back using Michigan Statute 28-410 against "malicious threats to extort money."[45] This "sovereign" tax resistance was pioneered by DePugh and A. J. Porth, "a brilliant patriot tax consultant." A 1968 seminar by Porth was advertised with the claim that the Internal Revenue Service was "a communist front organization!" (under the control of its "Commissar" Sheldon Cohen) "operating as a collection agency for International Communist Financiers!!!"[46] A third theme that led into sovereign thinking came directly from Posse Comitatus: the vital importance of "Common Law, which is the foundation of all our laws. . . . Even federal authorities must yield to county law enforcement officials in the enforcement of the common law."[47] Faced with federal "Dictatorship," "*WE THE PEOPLE* must keep Law and Order. This can be done at a *county level* through your *Sheriff*! Request that your county sheriff form a posse to keep law and order. Such a posse has jurisdiction over vigilante groups and federal troops. Federal troops *cannot* make arrests. Vigilante groups *cannot* make arrests. A sheriff and his posse *CAN* make arrests!"[48] Sovereign citizen ideas were inherent in both DePugh's Minutemen and Patriotic Party and in Gale's Posse Comitatus. This is not surprising since the two men worked together; in fact Gale was one of the supporters of the legal defense fund aimed at keeping DePugh out of prison.

Common Law is a cornerstone of sovereign citizens' beliefs. The organic constitutional system was, they believe, based on common law but later "secretly replaced by a new government system based on Admiralty Law." Admiralty law was then overlaid with the Uniform

Commercial Code, which deprives people of their sovereign rights by usurping the jurisdiction of the common law. The sovereign citizen seeks to countermand this jurisdictional shift by writing "Without Prejudice (UCC 1-308.4)" above his signature on legal documents.[49] Common Law also provides the rationale for sovereign people's courts and the obscure Three Notary Panel, which (its advocates say) has subpoena power and can authorize liens, rule laws unconstitutional, and fight foreclosures. In keeping with these beliefs, Tea Party activist John Darash organized a "network" of trial and grand juries for Common Law courts "as is our unalienable right and duty secured under the Fifth Amendment to do."[50]

Undermining the Constitution's Common Law with Admiralty Law and the Uniform Commercial Code allowed the government to implement its plan to enslave its own citizenry. First, the Fourteenth Amendment "created an artificial person-corporate entity-franchise entitled 'Citizen of the United States.'" Then, the establishment of the Federal Reserve System and the planned bankruptcy of 1933 (in which "every 14th Amendment 'Citizen of the United States' was pledged as an asset to fiancé [sic] the Chapter 11 reorganization") created a debt-based worthless paper money economy that benefited only bankers.[51] Finally, the 1933 "abandonment" of the gold standard "substituted its citizens as collateral for the country's debts by pledging each citizen's future earnings to foreign investors." Thus, "a secret United States Treasury account is set up for each citizen at birth, some large sum of money is placed in it or pledged to it . . .—$630,000 is a common number—. . . . As a consequence, they say, two separate identities are created. The corporate shell account, the one pledged as security, is the 'strawman' to which sovereign citizens refer and, in their view, is separate and distinct from their true flesh and blood identity."[52] As puzzling as this is already, a racist addition to this conspiracy rests on the idea that the Fourteenth Amendment was never truly ratified. Racists and opponents of immigration claim that the amendment created two classes of citizens: natural born citizens and Fourteenth Amendment citizens, whose claim to full citizenship is somehow weaker.[53] For sovereign citizens, this same distinction separates de jure citizens (original, common law citizens) from Fourteenth Amendment de facto citizens of the "corporation" that the United States became in 1878. The latter are "federal citizens" or "vessels" who have "bargained away their freedoms by accepting benefits from the United States government."[54]

To summarize, we have: (1) the replacement of a common law constitutional nation by a maritime/martial law corporation "doing business as" the United States, (2) the creation of second-class citizens without sovereign standing, and then (3) the use of those citizens as collateral to finance a bankrupt "nation," all converging to enslave Americans under illegitimate rule. Declaring one's sovereignty in myriad ways is required to break free of this slavery. Doing this successfully also compels the Internal Revenue Service to give you back the strawman money in your secret Treasury account. Not surprisingly, this feature has led to the sovereign movement's being swamped with get-rich-quick schemes that instruct you on how to fill out the proper paperwork to get your money.

Although its roots are deeply imbedded in the mulch of racism, sovereign citizen ideas have attracted some blacks. A popular conspiratorial variation rests on the work of Noble Drew Ali, who based his Moorish Science Temple of America on the idea that black Americans were Moors who had lived in North America before the revolution. Black sovereigns add to this the idea that their immunity from American law was affirmed by treaty between the United States and Morocco in 1787. Thus, the Fourteenth Amendment does not affect their status as citizens. Less cohesively, sovereignty has popped up among indigenous peoples across the nation. An effort to reinstate the "Sovereign Kingdom of Hawai'i" as the de jure reign of King Akahi Nui (instead of the de facto regime of the state of Hawai'i) failed when the "puppet masters" managed to shut down communications because of a tsunami warning caused by an earthquake ("set off and controlled by HARP [sic] and DARPA?").[55]

The worldview of sovereign citizens is so intense and peculiar that members of this movement are a major concern for law enforcement and the courts. Aside from the many instances when sovereigns have been involved in shootouts with the police, they have caused considerable harm by filing injunctions and issuing liens against the property of public officials—what has come to be called "paper terrorism." They flood the courts with paperwork featuring "odd or seemingly inane use of secondary legal materials, statutes, and overruled, misunderstood, or outdated case law." They are, however, considered competent to stand trial. Even though their beliefs appear delusional, legally they are not. Regardless of its content, any belief held by a considerable number of people cannot constitute evidence of insanity.[56]

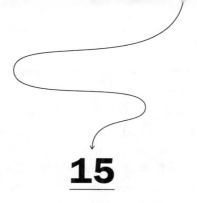

15

CONSPIRACISM REBOUNDS

TRUTHERS, BIRTHERS, AND THE NEW MILITIAS

These aren't conspiracy theories. These are facts.

Lance Garrison, Kansas State Militia[1]

Conspiracism is about a hundred years old. The *Protocols of the Learned Elders of Zion* began to be circulated outside Russia during the Bolshevik Revolution, and very shortly thereafter Nesta Webster published her first conspiratorial books. Over the decades, conspiracism evolved and branched out into different versions, from the secret government/hidden hand to mind-controlling psychopolitics to shape-shifting human-reptilian hybrids posing as our political leaders. During the last few years, conspiracism has become so imbedded in the popular mind that the once-menacing Illuminati has become a punchline. Websites filled with photographs of celebrities making triangular hand gestures or of crackpots with photoshopped tinfoil hats define the weird end of conspiracy theory for most people. The more serious side of conspiracism in the twenty-first century was first defined by the 9/11 attacks and the obsessive "truther" conspiracism that followed them. By the time that burst of conspiracism faded, the election of Barack Obama brought the racist right-wing conspiracism that lurked beneath the surface to prominence in American politics.

Despite the panoply of different conspiracy theories that arose between Nesta Webster and 9/11, none has wholly disappeared. In part, this is because the technologies of social media have made it easy to rekindle and spread any conspiracy theory. The dominant strand of conspiracism—the continuum from secret government to hidden hand to one-worlder to new world order—continues to be widely propagated, with perhaps an infinite number of subtle variations. Texe Marrs, for example, promotes a basic Zionist conspiracy with roots in the Kabbalah. Herbert G. Dorsey III recycled Webster's thesis with particular emphasis on the Knights Templar. Miguel Bruno Duarte's "shadow government" is primarily the work of the Illuminati, with Communist and Freemasonic support. Deanna Spingola focuses solely on the Rothschilds. David Allen Rivera provides an apocalyptic end-times interpretation. And Doc Marquis offers an occult version in which the *Protocols* were created by the Illuminati to discredit the Jews while the Illuminati establish Satan as "their Masonic Christ."[2] There are many more.

There is hardly a topic that contemporary conspiracists have allowed to disappear. Ellen McClay devoted her 2008 talk at the National Conference on Private Property Rights to the rise of UNESCO. Fundamentalist David Stewart, in his attack on evolution, brings back the specter of G. Brock Chisholm, Canadian psychiatrist and head of the World Health Organization until 1953. Conspiracy theorist Jennifer Lake was still fighting the polio vaccine conspiracy in 2008; Charlotte Iserbyt extolled the merits of the 1953 Reece Committee hearings on philanthropic foundations in a 2011 Alex Jones interview. Long-time John Birch Society member Alan Stang explained once again that Franklin Roosevelt "arranged" the attack on Pearl Harbor. And Glenn Beck generated some blowback by promoting Elizabeth Dilling's 1934 *Red Network* as well as the works of the intensely antisemitic Eustace Mullins.[3]

In keeping with the improvisational nature of modern conspiracy theorizing, other ideas have been merged with the standard new world order conspiracy. Jüri Lina interprets the Illuminati's overthrow of czarist

Russia within an astrological framework, while David Allen Rivera's two-and-a-half-hour PowerPoint presentation explains his apocalyptic conspiracy using the movie *The Matrix*, and P. D. Stuart explains how the American Revolution turned the United States into "a Jesuit enclave." Alex Christopher's "ultimate 'Unseen Hand'" behind the Illuminati turns out to be the railroad industry, a fact Christopher learned from a man who had actually "participated in the organizational plans for the 'New World Order.'" For Christopher Jon Bjerknes, the entire Zionist conspiracy centers on Albert Einstein.[4] Conspiracists from across the decades have been cited and their ideas recycled. Charlotte Iserbyt "suspects" that she owns the only surviving copy of the American Historical Association's 1934 Report of the Commission on Social Studies, which lays out the "plan for a Socialist America." (She does not.) Both Miguel Duarte and David Rivera bring back the same misinterpretation of Carroll Quigley's work that led Quigley to sue right-wing conspiracists in the 1960s. And Jüri Lina buys Major General Count Cherep-Spiridovich's claim that German chancellor Bismarck was aware of the Jewish hidden hand conspiracy to assassinate Lincoln and tried to thwart it.[5]

Other conspiracies have survived as well, although some now have seemingly few followers. Conspiracy theories having to do with health, medicine, and nutrition held their own or even gathered momentum in the early years of the century. Conspiratorial ideas about HIV/AIDS, for example, showed no sign of fading away, and every subsequent epidemic, right up to the Zika virus, has generated suspicions ranging from Big Pharma's profiting on death to new world order population control.[6] Similarly, the conspiracism that led to widespread suspicion of vaccines (primarily measles, mumps, and rubella vaccination, but with spillover effects) continues to have a great many casual adherents.[7] Other health threats have had their ups and downs. The conspiratorial end of the opposition to genetically modified foods seems to be holding its own. The view that chemtrails exist and are part of the plan to kill off or stupefy millions of people is riding high at present. But the cancer threat posed by electromagnetic fields near power lines and even fear of the mind-controlling High Frequency Active Auroral Research Program (HAARP) have faded considerably.[8]

9/11 and the Truth

All other conspiracy theories faded—at least for a while—in the wake of the 9/11 attacks, the only event since the Kennedy assassination powerful enough to generate extensive conspiracies of its own. Most of the avalanche of conspiratorial interpretation of 9/11 took place outside the long-established frameworks of conspiracism. The two basic "theories" around which suspicions gelled were LIHOP (let it happen on purpose) and MIHOP (made it happen on purpose). The LIHOP allegation was basically that the Bush administration knew (or suspected) that an attack was coming but did nothing to prevent it so it could pursue its war plans in the Middle East. The more severe MIHOP allegation was that the attacks were a false flag operation carried out by the Bush administration for the same reason. Both terms cover a variety of scenarios. The LIHOP scenarios are conceptually simple, and they barely rise to the level of conspiracy "theory." The MIHOP scenarios, in contrast, are genuinely theoretical, involving many more participants, long-term planning, and a leap of faith. In practice though, the line between LIHOP and MIHOP is often skirted, as illustrated by David Ray Griffin, a major voice of 9/11 conspiracism, in his book *The New Pearl Harbor*:

> I have often been asked whether there are any "smoking guns" pointing to complicity by the Bush administration. This is a question I did not explicitly address in the body of the book. Rather than focusing on those reported events that most strongly suggest such complicity, I instead presented a *cumulative* argument, suggesting that what is most persuasive, assuming the truth of at least a significant portion of the reported evidence, is that so many lines of evidence all seem to point in the same direction. . . . I said, in other words, that we have some *prima facie* smoking guns.[9]

The degree to which 9/11 conspiracism was genuinely spontaneous and self-contained is reflected in the obsessive attention paid to technical details, media inconsistencies, and timelines (e.g., "Despite this extensive body of credible evidence establishing Flight 93's impact time at 10.06am, NORAD and the 9/11 Commission asserted that the impact was at 10.03am."). This ad hoc, context-free conspiracism was often criticized, especially after "trutherism" began to decline. The *Guardian* excoriated the prominent MIHOP film *Loose Change* for depicting "a closed world: comprehensible, controllable, small," and thus easier to deal with than "the chaos which really governs our lives."[10] Nevertheless, around the edges of 9/11 conspiracism, many people did try to put the event in a larger context of familiar conspiratorial figures. One obvious choice was the Illuminati. Dominion theologian Gary North used the attack to repeat his Illuminati-oriented rehash of Carroll Quigley's ideas. Rick Martin used the attack to expose the Illuminati's long-range goal of "elimination of most of the world's human population." Although some members of Congress were aware of the Illuminati's plans, Martin claimed, they were frightened into silence when their fellow congressman Gary Condit "was made a patsy in the abduction and subsequent murder of Chandra Levy."[11]

Some of these efforts were extremely idiosyncratic, perhaps the work of just one person. One such theorist, under the moniker the Smoking Man, noted the "startling coincidences" linking 9/11 with the Oklahoma City bombing. Building his case on the fact that "20th hijacker" Zacarias Moussaoui had attended flight-training school at Max Westheimer Airport near Norman, Oklahoma, Smoking Man notes that "a squadron of the Civil Air Patrol (CAP) . . . still gathers at Westheimer every week. Coincidentally, several of the alleged 9/11 hijackers rented apartments in Delray Beach, Florida from a woman whose husband was a member of the CAP."[12] Equally bizarre but more thoroughgoing is an article posted by the Awaken Research Group ("Debunking 'Caveman' Conspiracy Theories since 2002"). A saga going back to the 1980s details a 9/11 conspiracy designed primarily to benefit the Teachers Insurance and Annuity Association—College Retirement Equities Fund for university professors. Among the conspirators were the Massachusetts Institute of Technology plasma and fusion lab, North Atlantic Treaty Organization, the Bonanno organized crime family, the Teamsters Union, JPMorgan Chase, the Boeing Corporation, and of course Hillary Clinton, who together managed to fight off New York Mayor Rudy Giuliani's efforts to expose the false flag attack they used to cover their theft of hundreds of billions of dollars.[13]

There have been efforts to link the 9/11 attacks to the Kennedy assassination, but these have been no more enduring than these idiosyncratic conspiracies. Radio host Philip Coppens maintained that "the 'lone assassin' template" used to deny Kennedy assassination conspiracy theories could be at work with 9/11, but this works only if one thinks of Osama Bin Laden as a lone assassin. Coppens went on to list parallels between the two events. Citing Operation Northwoods, a military proposal for secret action against Cuba that was rejected by Kennedy, Coppens ignores the nonexistence of the operation, saying: "Substitute Cuba with Afghanistan and Iraq and 9/11 is born." Gary Kohls, of Medical Professionals for 9/11 Truth, echoes the (anti-)lone assassin argument but focuses more on "the obvious false flag operation of 9/11," which he likens to several others—"the Berlin Reichstag Fire, Operation Northwoods, and the Gulf of Tonkin episodes (google them) readily come to mind." Kohls's writing displays the obsessive nature of much of the 9/11 conspiracism: "To continue to ignore the truths uncovered by the multitudes of thoughtful, highly intelligent and courageous prophetic voices world-wide and to continue to believe the absurd official theories when there is overwhelming evidence to the contrary is to go helplessly along with the evil agenda of shadowy, exploitative, psychopathic powers that are not your friends."[14] Most of those who find connections between 9/11 and the Kennedy assassination are in the "deep politics" camp pioneered by Peter Dale Scott. By linking "deep events" (those that reveal the workings of "the deep state, that part of the state that is not publicly accountable"), Scott and others try to piece together the clandestine power structure. In much of this analysis, similarity between the roads to American attacks on Cuba and in Iraq is key.[15]

The most widely believed of the larger 9/11 conspiracy theories blamed the attacks, not surprisingly, on the Jews. This was certainly the case across the Muslim world, where "conspiracy theories about the Mossad's culpability for the attacks mushroomed." (The Mossad is Israel's Intelligence Service.) Although Muslims in the Middle East had long been obsessed with conspiracy theories centered on Israel, "a new and more aggressive form of conspiracy theory and attendant demonization of the 'conspirators' took on worldwide proportions."[16] The Anti-Defamation League's investigation supported the importance of the Mossad to conspiracy theories centering on Israeli government or corporate spying in America. This tied in with the "WTC7" subtheory, in which the 7 World Trade Center building was destroyed on purpose to eliminate incriminating documents. The second major antisemitic conspiracy theory laid out a vague financial plot according to which the "Jewish owners" of the World Trade Center orchestrated the attack for the insurance money.[17]

The same array of charges that circulated in the Middle East dominated the conspiracy theories of the right-wing (and especially white supremacist) elements in the United States. Headlines in the intensely antisemitic newspaper *The Truth at Last* charged that Israeli firms had moved out of the World Trade Center before the attack and that the FBI was questioning Israelis about spying. Ohio congressional candidate Jim Condit took advantage of the fact that campaign ads cannot be censored to air TV spots featuring claims such as: "Many competent researchers believe that pro-Israeli, pro-New World Order traitors pulled off the 9-11 terror attacks" as part of their effort to establish "world tyranny headquartered in Jerusalem." The aged Eustace Mullins declared the attacks to be "essentially a Mossad campaign, spearheaded by the ADL." (In his paranoia, Mullins appeared to view 9/11 as a subsidiary operation of the campaign by the ADL and the Gannett Newspapers to discredit him personally.) Gordon "Jack" Mohr, who claimed to have predicted an attack "such as" 9/11 because of "the illegal and unscriptural acts of our government . . . as we have appeased the antichrists of Zionism," expressed surprise that this analysis led to his being "reviled as a '*hatemonger*.'" Mohr's September 2001 *Terrorist Intelligence Report* summarized the entire hidden hand conspiracy, beginning with the establishment of the Federal Reserve System and culminating in control over America by the "heathen 'blood suckers'" of the Zionist Occupation Government. America allowed this to happen, according to Mohr, and thus the 9/11 attacks are merely "the evil chickens of our DISOBEDIENCE to God . . . 'coming home to roost.'"[18]

The Zionist-Israeli conspiracy has shown considerable staying power even as general attachment to 9/11 conspiracy theories has declined. In 2009, the ADL noted with alarm the prevalence of antisemitic 9/11 conspiracy posts on the internet. Louisiana-based Nazi David Duke did not question Al-Qaeda's role in the attacks but excused them as resistance to Jewish domination. Duke argued that "the Jewish-Supremacist controlled media" would never question the official story since then "they will have to admit the power and control which Jewish Supremacists have over Western governments." Louis Farrakhan went further, flatly accusing "lying, murderous Zionist Jews" for the attacks.[19] Illuminati conspiracist Henry Makow, abridging an unspecified work by 9/11 conspiracist Christopher Bollyn, dug into the past of William Jeffrey, director of the National Institute of Standards and Technology when that organization issued a 2005 report on the destruction of the world Trade Center. Makow could discredit the report since Jeffrey was a "crypto Jew" whose father had changed the family's surname from Jaffe to Jeffrey in 1952. This connection between Zionism and 9/11 is used less to explain the attacks than as just another club with which to beat the Jews. As one example, Joy Karega, like other antisemites, not only supported Louis Farrakhan's views on 9/11 but also accused Israel of the Charlie Hebdo killings in Paris and of shooting down a Malaysian airliner over the Ukraine, bringing back the specter of Jacob Rothschild in the process. She was fired as an assistant professor at Oberlin College.

Obama's New World Order

As a boon to conspiracism, just as 9/11 was beginning to fade, Barack Obama was elected president. Even before his election, lawsuits challenged his citizenship, giving rise to the "birther" movement. Birtherism was not the first such attack on a president. Franklin Roosevelt's "Jewish ancestry" had been bandied about by conspiracists in the 1930s but never rose to the level of an issue. By 2008, however, media and politics had changed enough that the even more implausible charge that Obama was born in Kenya (or Indonesia) found a wide audience.[20] Such people as Donald Trump, TV money enthusiast Lou Dobbs, and "family values" presidential candidate Alan Keyes repeated and added to the conspiracy, and among Republican voters it was widely believed. On the reemerging neo-patriot right, birtherism provided a fresh opportunity to challenge the government. In "An Open Letter to Barack Obama," We the People Foundation chairman Robert Schulz stressed the "escalating constitutional crisis" that would follow from having "a *usurper*" in the White House, a crisis that could not be resolved legally: "Congress would be unable to remove you, a *usurper*, from the Office of the President on Impeachment, inviting certain political chaos including a potential for armed conflicts within the General Government or among the States and the People to effect the removal of such a *usurper*."[21]

This level of conspiracism did not emerge from nothing. Years of 9/11 trutherism had helped make conspiracism a familiar, even acceptable, approach to politics. Moreover, there were specific connections between trutherism and birtherism. Frank Gaffney, a disenchanted Reagan administration defense spokesman who accused Obama of hiding both his Kenyan birth and Muslim religion, had earlier invented a MIHOP 9/11 theory that placed conservative activist Grover Norquist at the center of the conspiracy. Philip Berg, who brought an early suit challenging Obama's eligibility, had in 2004 filed a LIHOP lawsuit against George W. Bush, alleging a FEMA plan to establish a secret government. Orly Taitz, a California lawyer who filed a similar suit on behalf of Alan Keyes's American Independent Party, abandoned the legal route after a judge fined her $20,000 for using the court for "a political agenda disconnected from any legitimate legal cause of action." Taitz promoted a conspiracy according to which Obama would fill FEMA concentration camps with his enemies. (The sudden attention to FEMA may well reflect the unpleasant publicity that agency received during and after Hurricane Katrina in 2005.)[22]

Antigovernment conspiracism became institutionalized during the 2008 election and throughout Obama's first term as president. For example, opposition to the North American Union and its supposed "NAFTA Super Highway" roared back to life. As shaped by conspiracy-minded Obama opponents such as Pat Buchanan, Lou Dobbs, and Jerome Corsi (all of whom promoted the birther charges), those issues were transformed into a direct assault on American sovereignty. Similarly, a July 2008 conference sponsored by Tom DeWeese's antienvironmental American Policy Center and Phyllis Schlafly's "pro-family" Eagle Forum introduced the United Nations 1992 sustainable development plan, Agenda 21, to the conspiracy world. This "anti-human document" represented the new world order's "new world theology" of replacing God with nature. The John Birch Society (for which the 2008 conference marked a return to prominence) also attacked "The New False Religion," claiming that "advocates of UN world government have drafted an Earth Charter, which they compare to the Ten Commandments and keep in an 'Ark of Hope.'"[23]

Militia groups, which had peaked in 1996 before beginning a ten-year decline, rebounded from perhaps fifty in number in 2007 to over two hundred by 2009. The Obama election also corresponded with a spike in sovereign citizen threats against judges and prosecutors and an increase in tax resisters sufficient to cause the Department of Justice to create a National Tax Defier Initiative.[24] New groups, many drawing on the 1990s patriot movement, proliferated. Just after the election of Obama, Robert Schulz (whose "usurper" ad was about to appear in the *Chicago Tribune*) gathered more than a hundred "delegates" from across the country to plan "Continental Congress 2009." Schulz had emerged out of the tax resister movement, while his co-organizer, Edwin Vieira, and many of the delegates had been active in the militias of the 1990s. Nativists and neo-confederates were represented, including one Robert Crooks, creator of a video demonstrating "how to keep a Home Depot parking lot empty" by shooting immigrants as they tried to cross the border. Continental Congress 2009 tried to draw in people affected by the economic collapse of 2008. A flyer advertising this "Historical People's Summit," which devoted much of its space to explaining that income tax is "a legal and constitutional *fraud*," began:

401(k) Losses? Unemployed? Foreclosed? There is a CAUSE . . . and a SOLUTION!

Our nation suffers because we have abandoned the Constitution

Economic catastrophe resulting directly from the *privately-owned* Federal Reserve bank cartel and fiat currency based on limitless debt

Unconstitutionally imposed, *unapportioned*, direct (*slave*) taxes on the labor of Americans

Unconstitutional bailouts of *private* banks and endless Middle-East military conflicts started unlawfully without a formal "Declaration of War"

And the most grievous injury: A servant government that refuses to be held accountable by responding to the People's repeated Petitions for Redress of Grievances

This is, of course, the same international banking conspiracy pioneered by secret government conspiracists decades earlier. And in case anyone might overlook the role of the Fed, the People's Summit was held on Jekyll Island, Georgia, where the Federal Reserve System was created. Participants were showered with information about Obama's agenda that would "collapse the Republic," the menace of sustainable development, the plan by the government to use "transportation choke points" to round up troublemakers and send them to FEMA camps, and many other conspiracist greatest hits.[25]

In March 2009, the Oath Keepers was created by Stewart Rhodes, a former Ron Paul libertarian. Rhodes had laid out his vision of the threat facing America a year earlier when Hillary Clinton was the frontrunner for the Democratic nomination:

Imagine that Herr Hitlery is sworn in as president in 2009. After a conveniently timed "domestic terrorism" event (just a coincidence, of course) . . . she promptly crams a United Nations mandated total ban on the private possession of firearms . . . proclaiming a national emergency and declaring the entire militia movement (and anyone else Morris Dees labels "extremists") to be "enemy combatants." . . . Hitlery declares that such citizens are subject to military tribunal handpicked by the dominatrix-in-chief herself. Hitlery then orders police, National Guard troops and active military to go house-to-house to disarm the American people and "black bag" those on a list of "known terrorists," with orders to shoot all resisters.[26]

The way to head off this standard militia conspiracy nightmare was to ensure that police and military would in fact keep their oaths to uphold the Constitution by refusing to obey the government's orders to round everyone up and put them in concentration camps. Rhodes's group was, to a remarkable degree, a retread of Jack McLamb's early 1990s group Police against the New World Order, whose 1992 "action plan" laid out the same threat and remedy. In order to "stop or 'kill off' the ongoing, elitist, covert operation which has been installed in the American system with great stealth and cunning," those who signed on to McLamb's Operation Vampire Killer 2000 resolved that "WE WILL, BY EVERY MEANS GIVEN UNTO US, UPHOLD OUR OATHS AND FULFILL OUR SWORN DUTY TO OUR COUNTRYMEN."[27]

Leaders of the neo-militia and patriot groups worked closely together. Rhodes and Richard Mack were heavily involved in Second Amendment marches and rallies. Mack and McLamb worked the "anti-government speaking circuit" together. Mack combined the Oath Keeper idea with William Gale's posse comitatus idea to create the Constitutional Sheriffs and Peace Officers Association. Reviving the idea that the county sheriff held ultimate legal authority, Mack declared them to be "constitutionally empowered to be able to keep federal agents out of the county."[28] Another old militia hand, Mike Vanderboegh, formed a more civilian-based group to defend the Constitution. Vanderboegh's III Percent

Patriots were named after the notion that only 3 percent of the colonists rose up against British oppression during the American Revolution. Although not legally bound by an oath, Three Percenters were no less resolved to fulfill their duty to their countrymen: "The Three Percent today are gun owners who will not disarm, will not compromise and will no longer back up at the passage of the next gun control act. . . . We will not obey any further circumscription of our traditional liberties and will defend ourselves if attacked. . . . We are committed to the restoration of the Founders' Republic, and are willing to fight, die, and, if forced by any would-be oppressor, kill in the defense of ourselves and the constitution that we all took an oath to uphold against enemies foreign and domestic."[29] Between the election of 2008 and the end of President Obama's first term, dozens, perhaps hundreds of such groups were established. The John Birch Society had been reborn to the point where it cosponsored the 2010 Conservative Political Action Conference meeting. Some no doubt faded away and some may have been web-only groups, but the upsurge was still impressive. A few at random: the Tenth Amendment Center (nullifiers), Freedom Advocates, the oxymoronically named Sovereignty International, the Christian Liberty Guard (to judge from their website photo, four men and two dogs), Restore the Republic, the neo-Klan organization League of the South, the Third Continental Congress, and Christian Exodus, a group determined to establish theocracy in South Carolina.[30]

Many of these minor groups faded away after Obama's reelection, but they did not all disappear. Some were reduced to their core membership "who feel as if they have lost their only home. . . . They get increasingly frustrated and sometimes go out in a blaze of glory." The result was an increase in "lone wolf" and small group attacks. At the same time, a troubling increase in reported connections between such groups and the military was beginning to emerge. These were not well received reports—a 2009 Department of Homeland Security report was downplayed largely because it reported that the "willingness of a small percentage of military personnel to join extremist groups during the 1990s because they were disgruntled, disillusioned, or suffering from the psychological effects of war is being replicated today."[31] While the military may be reluctant to admit it, it has been plagued by this problem, as neo-Nazis and RaHoWa fighters find military bases to be fertile ground.[32]

Obama's election marked the third burst of right-wing conspiracism since around 1970, when Christian Identity groups and the fading neo-Nazi groups built on white fears and rural resentment to create the conspiracist idea that the federal government would eliminate their racial privilege and run roughshod over their land. Early militias, the Aryan Nations, and the Posse Comitatus embodied this thinking. As these groups in turn began to wane in the 1990s, a series of deadly confrontations—Gordon Kahl, Randy Weaver, Waco—generated a surge of new, much more violent groups, a wave that expanded rapidly before fading after the 9/11 attacks. With Obama's election came a new type of group: militia-like, but more respectable—Mike Vanderboegh's Three Percenters, Stewart Rhodes's Oath Keepers, Richard Mack's Constitutional Sheriffs and Peace Officers Association. Although distinct, these groups overlapped and many of their leaders interacted regularly with the Tea Party and other conservative groups. Right-wing conspiracism was about to enter the political mainstream.

16

CONSPIRACISM ENTERS
THE MAINSTREAM

Area Man Passionate Defender of What He Imagines Constitution to Be

The Onion, November 14, 2009

Two features of the burst of right-wing conspiracism accompanying the 2008 election and Obama's presidency stand out. Most striking is the overwhelming emphasis on defending the American Revolution and the Constitution. Much of this was symbolism, but meaningful symbolism: the Gadsden Flag (with the coiled rattlesnake) and its Don't Tread on Me slogan, Robert Schulz's Continental Congress 2009, and, for that matter, his group We the People. The Oath Keepers' first "muster" was held on April 19, the anniversary of the battles at Lexington and Concord, in Lexington, Massachusetts. The sovereign citizens in Maine renamed themselves the Constitutional Coalition. Every issue was presented in its constitutional context as part of a conspiracy to destroy the nation—from Obama's foreign birth to the income tax. The Constitution was, however, the version grounded in William Potter Gale's ideas: an organic Constitution given to the founders directly by a Christian God. Thus, "patriots" could oppose the government while upholding their constitution: the one the federal government refused to recognize and constantly violated.

A second noteworthy feature, though it proved to be temporary, was the marked diminution in the level of antisemitism on the conspiratorial Right. The 1992 Police against the New World Order action plan against the new world order had included predictable diatribes against the Rothschild banking empire, but its Oath Keeper heirs never appear to mention the Jews. As late as 2002, Edgar Steele, a holdover Aryan Nations member, wrote an essay entitled "It's the Jews Stupid!!!"[1] But by 2008 views like this were hard to find emanating from patriot groups. This might be attributable to better public relations and coded messages, but even the Anti-Defamation League in 2009 found negligible antisemitism. While they identified many instances of racist imagery and rhetoric, the ADL also detected rhetoric attacking Obama as a Nazi and his proposals as Fascist. Placards carried at protests against Obama's proposed health care legislation featured messages such as "Oh S#!t / It's 1939 Germany all over again / Obama's HR3200 = Hitler's T4" to "When we smell the burning flesh from the ovens it will be to [sic] late for us all." And while the latter is crude and objectionable, it is hard to imagine that it was motivated by antisemitism. This is not to say that antisemitic conspiracism disappeared, but it appeared to have been separated from the increasingly constitutionalist patriot conspiracism.[2]

Tea Party Conspiracism

Right-wing patriot groups were able to broaden their base by going mainstream. Militias began collecting food for food banks, conducting blood drives, and "getting together an open-carry group who will openly carry our firearms and pick up trash." They considered their armed patrols on the lookout for illegal aliens to be a civic service. Eventually, they even portrayed the carrying of their automatic weapons to the local Jack in the Box as a public service and seemed upset when people were afraid.[3] The main break with their past practices, however, was becoming involved in electoral politics through the Tea Party movement. Although it began as an "astroturf" movement—that is, a seemingly grassroots-based citizen group backed by right-wing money—the Tea Party exploded spontaneously, splitting into at least half a dozen overlapping groups and becoming an important vehicle for Ron Paul's 2008 presidential bid. After the election, various Christian rightist, patriot, and neo-militia leaders made their way into these groups, considerably changing their character.[4]

From its beginning and as its name implies, the Tea Party movement had been inspired by the American Revolution and the Founders. Some enthusiasts attended rallies decked out in eighteenth-century costumes, notably featuring tricorne hats. The history they espoused, though, was a peculiar form of "historical fundamentalism"—not just "kooky history; it was *anti*history": "Marked by a belief that a particular and quite narrowly defined past—'the founding'—is ageless and sacred and to be worshipped; that certain historical texts—'the founding documents'— are to be read in the same spirit with which religious fundamentalists read, for instance, the Ten Commandments; that the Founding Fathers were divinely inspired; that the academic study of history . . . is a conspiracy and, furthermore, blasphemy; and that political arguments grounded in appeals to the founding documents, as sacred texts, and to the Founding Fathers, as prophets, are therefore incontrovertible."[5]

These conceptions were all in keeping with the organic Constitution idea of William Potter Gale but filtered through a different conspiracist, W. Cleon Skousen. An anti-one-worlder, anti-Communist conspiracist since the 1950s, Skousen had turned his attention to early American history in the 1980s, publishing *The 5,000 Year Leap* and *The Making of America: The Substance and Meaning of the Constitution* in quick succession.[6] Combining the organic Constitution with the Mormon version of British Israelism, Skousen portrayed a divinely inspired nation created by founders whose deep Christianity protected them from Enlightenment ideas. These books stirred some controversy, primarily over Skousen's view of slavery (especially his contention that "the slave owners were the worst victims of the system") and eventually faded into obscurity before Glenn Beck single-handedly brought them back to prominence, after Skousen's death in 2006 at the age of ninety-two.[7]

Skousen's argument, much like Gale's, is based on a religious take on natural law as the only basis for government. Legal scholar Jared Goldstein drew out the implications: "For Skousen, natural law means God's laws and encompasses the necessity for 'limited government,' the right to bear arms, protections for the family and the institution of marriage, the sanctity of private property, and the avoidance of debt. Such natural law principles, Skousen claims, are not subject to change by mortal legislators. Legislation contrary to God's laws is a 'scourge to humanity' and is therefore unconstitutional."[8] Like Gale, Skousen interpreted much of American history as a betrayal of natural law. Socialists, working secretly for wealthy bankers and the "dynastic rich" began America's fall, and government policies from the Progressive Era onward accelerated its decline to the point that "today, almost everything the government does is unconstitutional."[9] Skousen's main departure from Gale's version of constitutional purity stems from his Mormon theology. Despite their belief that America is "under attack by modern secret combinations seeking to eliminate liberty," Skousen and his followers do not blame the Jews. Latter Day Saint theology is philosemitic. One study of conspiratorial Mormon rhetoric concluded that "no mention of general Jewish influence can be found within these circles and even criticism of certain bankers or political leaders who happen to be Jewish, never makes mention of their heritage."[10]

As this conspiratorial constitutionalism made its way into politics by way of the Tea Party, the absence of the virulent antisemitism that had characterized Christian patriot groups made it more acceptable to mainstream conservatives. Parts of the conspiracy suffered a loss of coherence without the Jews—notably those parts having to do with the Federal Reserve System and its "fiat" currency, and the abandonment of the gold standard. Ever since Representative McFadden's diatribes eighty years earlier, the central tenet of the financial conspiracy had been that the Jews were stealing "our" money. But, by the time Ron Paul published his version of the conspiracy in 2009, the Jews were gone, leaving the rationale for and beneficiaries of the financial "cartel" a mystery. Even Skousen's son Joel, who analyzed the "strategic" aspects of the new world order as "a predator movement," was unable to solve the mystery. Posing the question, "why destroy the tremendous prosperity that even these conspirators for global power enjoy," the younger Skousen has no answer and can say only that "Most people do not sufficiently understand real evil."[11]

Glenn Beck declared that Skousen's *The 5,000 Year Leap* "changed my understanding of the United States government and our founders," and he touted the book on his show. *The 5,000 Year Leap* was reissued in 2009, and an updated edition of *The Making of America* also appeared. Skousen's National Center for Constitutional Studies organized seminars for Tea Party groups nationwide, teaching a mix of vaguely Anglo-Israelite biblical and "free market" constitutionalism. After learning that Karl Marx invented the income tax and that national parks subvert the Constitution, Tea Party students realized the importance of grasping "the founding principles to understand where the country has gone off track." Seminars devoted specifically to a close reading of *The Making of America* stressed the federal government's "usurpation of power" and consequent illegitimacy. Attending a seminar in Fairmont, West Virginia, Alexander Zaitchik summarized its program as having three major pillars: "Understanding the divine guidance that has allowed the United States to thrive; rejecting the tyrannical, implicitly sinful, nature of the modern federal government; and preparing for a divine reckoning that will bring down America's government and possibly tear society as we know it asunder, thus allowing those with sound principles—i.e., godly NCCS [National Center for Constitutional Studies] graduates—to rebuild the republic along 'sounder' more pious lines."[12] The seminars did their work. Referring to Skousen's history, a United American Tea Party video admonished the public that it was "time we learn and follow the FREEDOM principles of our Founding Fathers." Even more pointedly, the Abingdon/Bristol/SW Virginia Tea Party's website attracted members with this statement: "We are called racist. Hatemongers. Right wing nut-jobs. Domestic terrorists. All by our own Department of Homeland Security. We are none of those things. We don't want to 'fundamentally change' America. We want to fundamentally RESTORE our country to the divinely inspired vision that our Founders fought for, risking everything. We are the Tea Party Movement. WE HAVE A LOT TO DO!!! Join us." After interviewing attendees at the Tea Party National Convention in 2010, Jonathan Kay, whose earlier work had dealt with the 9/11 truth movement, wrote that "it has become clear to me that the movement is dominated by people whose vision of the government is conspiratorial and dangerously detached from reality."[13]

The electoral success of politicians supported by the Tea Party in 2010 brought conspiracy theories into politics as never before. This has been apparent at the congressional level, but state and local politics has probably been affected even more. Virtually every issue has now been couched in a conspiracist context to a greater or lesser degree. And some issues have existed solely as conspiracy theories. The concept of a conspiracy meme began to spread. The central logic of the conspiracy meme, according to Ted Goertzel, who pioneered the concept, "is to question, often on speculative grounds, everything the 'establishment' says or does and to demand immediate, comprehensive answers to all questions." Answers that conspiracists do not find convincing, Goertzel adds, "are taken as proof of conspiratorial deception."[14] The ubiquity of the conspiracy meme contributed to a problem that has only grown worse: the term "conspiracy theory" has begun to lose its meaning. This problem actually has two parts, which work together to create a knot of confusion. First, "conspiracy theory" has been increasingly applied to things that are neither conspiratorial nor theoretical. Second, actual conspiratorial ideas are often couched in circumspect language that is not explicitly conspiratorial, making it hard to tell whether calling some statement a conspiracy theory is correct.

Exactly when "conspiracy theory" began to be applied too widely is hard to say. During the debate over President Obama's health care package in 2009, Sarah Palin, the Republican nominee for vice president, introduced the term "death panels," which became a rallying cry against "Obamacare" on the far Right. Widely disparaged as fraudulent, death panels were never discussed at that time as a conspiracy theory.

An article at the fact-checking journalism website PolitiFact quoted dozens of people on both sides of the issue, and although many pejorative terms were used, conspiracy theory was not one of them. The closest hint of conspiracism was a statement by the spokesman for the American Association of Retired Persons: "If your start-out stance is being distrustful of government, then this fit right into your worldview."[15]

By 2014, however, this more accurate assessment was clearly giving way to conspiratorial rhetoric, especially on the Left. Allen Clifton, cofounder of the website Forward Progressives, noted "death panels" as one of "the asinine conspiracy theories conservatives have used against Obama." And journalist Ed Kilgore noted that, given Palin's "taste for conspiracy theories and her less than rigorous commitment to facts, it was easy for her to start raving about 'death panels.'"[16] Pigeonholing ideas or terms as conspiracist began moving into standard conservative rhetoric as well. As early as 2011, Hugh Hewitt, a conservative law professor and radio-show host, continually tried to define Kevin Williamson's analysis of growing Wall Street support for Obama as a "Bilderbergerish" conspiracy. When Williamson referred to brokers as "these guys," Hewitt responded: "When you say these guys, are they in a clubhouse somewhere? . . . How many of them are they? Are they getting together at the Harvard Club on the 3rd floor in the Library Wednesday night for drinks to decide the world?"[17]

The second part of the problem—the fact that mainstream rhetoric began to reflect conspiracy theories without explicitly articulating them—exacerbated the problem of distinguishing conspiracism from political hyperbole. Implicit conspiracy references require prior knowledge to decode—but prior knowledge of what? The Tea Party's conspiratorial underpinning was the ongoing betrayal of American tradition and values—"the cleverly hidden, devious and insidious town by town destruction of our Constitutional Republic . . . by our own government."[18] This notion derived from the patriot movement (militias, sovereign citizens, posse comitatus), its loosely affiliated Christian Identity church movement, and the constitutional history of William Potter Gale and Cleon Skousen.

Tea Party conspiracism inherited considerable racism and antisemitism from these sources but generally made some effort to downplay the antisemitism. The betrayal conspiracy also represented an extension of the one-worlder, anti-UN conspiracism of the 1950s. Neither the one-worlder conspiracist theorists nor the new world order Tea Party conspiracists looked behind the scenes to a larger Illuminati or Talmudic or Masonic source of evil. Instead, the betrayal conspiracy featured two interacting forces trying to destroy America: from the patriot movement, the federal government itself, and from the one-worlder conspiracists, the United Nations and any other internationalist organizations.

But, the racism and antisemitism were not gone. They began reshaping this betrayal conspiracy soon after the Tea Party's success. Implicit in much of the anti–civil rights rhetoric, this bigotry found its voice in the early 1970s. Books such as Wilmot Robertson's *The Dispossessed Majority* (followed in short order by *Ventilations*, a diatribe against those who found his first book to be racist) and Erst LaFlor's *The Betrayal of the White Race* stripped down the conspiracy to its basic element. The same spirit of intolerance infused Ben Klassen's Church of the Creator and many of the militias of the 1990s. These extreme racists, especially neo-Nazis and neo-confederates, were early users of the internet, which "dovetailed nicely with the notion of leaderless resistance." Electronic bulletin boards used for communication and recruitment by groups such as Aryan Nations, the White Aryan Resistance, and the Klan carried the message of racism under the radar of polite society.[19]

Eventually this underground network emerged as the "alt-right." This twenty-first-century manifestation of intolerance "intellectualized" the betrayal of whites in terms of a conspiracy against Western civilization, an idea that can be traced back to Francis Parker Yockey's *Imperium* and James H. Madole's version of an Aryan "renaissance." The loose-knit alt-right has only one common defining characteristic: adherence to the notion of white supremacy. And while some of its adherents flaunt their racism, others use the term "white identitarian" to try to avoid the stigma of racism, making interaction with less racist groups possible.[20]

Conspiracism Everywhere

The result of all these forces has been an unprecedented level of conspiracism. Examples are boundless, both of conspiratorial thinking and of calling things conspiracy theories that are not. For example, a 2015 article about presidential hopeful Ben Carson headlined his "Satanic Sabbath persecution conspiracy." Carson, a Seventh-Day Adventist, had told churchgoers in Australia that, in the United States, "there has to be a return first to a religious awakening, and, more than likely, any persecution, particularly of the Sabbath, will come from the right, not from the left." This statement reflects Adventist prophecy and is theological apocalypticism delivered to a religious audience, not a "conspiracy."[21] The other side of the problem—unrecognized conspiracism—was exemplified a few months earlier when former Florida congressman and Fox News regular Allen West made news with a blog post (since removed): "Sharia Law Comes to Walmart?" West recounted an experience he and his daughter Aubrey had shared:

> There was a young man doing the checkout and another Walmart employee came over and put up a sign, "No alcohol products in this lane." So being the inquisitive fella I am, I used my additional set of eyes—glasses—to see the young checkout man's name. Let me just say is was NOT "Steve."
>
> I pointed out the sign to Aubrey and her response was a simple question, how is it that this Muslim employee could refuse to service customers based on his religious beliefs, but Christians are being forced to participate in events contrary to their religious beliefs?
>
> Boy howdy, that is one astute young lady.

This vignette make sense only in the context of two conspiratorial ideas: first, that the government is engaged in a campaign to "crush" (as West put it) the rights of Christians and, second, that there is a conspiracy trying to establish Sharia law in the United States. Both of these are manifestations of a conspiracist belief in a larger effort to destroy America.

The issue died when Walmart explained that, under state law, minors such as the clerk in question were not allowed to sell tobacco or alcohol. West had reacted to a "conspiracy" that existed only in his mind. Unlike Carson's sermon, West's post was conspiratorial, but the press tended to treat it as a slip up rather than a conspiracy theory.[22]

The increasingly casual use of conspiracy to describe other things is blurring the lines in political analysis. A typical news report about the fact that two Federal Election Commission members were considering opening presidential debates to third party candidates focused on the Republican contention that this would favor the Democrats in 2016. Some Republicans even suggested that was the intent, but nothing in this tiny controversy merited the headline, "GOP Conspiracy Says Efforts to Open Debates a Ploy to Elect Democrats." Similarly, Rand Paul's charge that Vice President Cheney promoted the war in Iraq because his former employer Halliburton would get a "billion-dollar no-bid contract" was a serious accusation of conflict of interest, but it was not Paul's "own conspiracy theory about 9/11."[23]

Anything having to do with Muslims can generate a conspiracy theory in America, and sometimes these in turn can generate their own reality. Belief in President Obama's foreign birth and secret adherence to Islam make it small leap to the conspiratorial belief that he is "allied with our Islamist enemies in a 'Grand Jihad' against America" and perhaps guided by the principles of Kenyan anticolonialism.[24] This context made alarming the public an easy task for anti-Muslim activists "bent on spreading the illusory fear that Islamic laws and customs (also known as Shariah) are taking over American courts." National politicians joined in, expressing their fears of "this creeping attempt . . . to gradually ease Sharia law and the Muslim faith into our government." First in Oklahoma, then in states across the South, activist groups put anti-Sharia ballot measures before the public with the strong suggestion that a pro-Sharia conspiracy made the move necessary. Sometimes this conspiracy was linked to immigration reform (a "tool of Satan that will lead to the enactment of Sharia law and usher in the End Times"). The original ballot measure's author, Oklahoma representative Rex Duncan, suggested that time was running out and his measured needed to be passed "while Oklahoma is still able to defend itself against this sort of hideous invasion."[25]

Both anti-immigrant and anti-Muslim fears were inflamed by conspiracy theories built around the army's Special Operations Forces training event Jade Helm 15 held largely in Texas. Making the same kind of conspiracy-based leaps that led Allen West to think Walmart had succumbed to Sharia law, conspiracists took FEMA storm shelters to be "death domes," imagined a network of secret tunnels was somehow related to gun confiscation, and claimed that Blue Bell ice cream trucks were to be used as portable mortuaries. The Oath Keepers theorized a government conspiracy to identify "resistance leaders" to be sent to concentration camps; radio-show host Alex Jones posited a third-term coup by Barack Obama; action movie star Chuck Norris thought the point was to take over Texas; Texas representative Louie Gohmert hit all these conspiratorial notes, concluding: "People who have grown leery of federal government overreach become suspicious of whether their big brother government anticipates certain states may start another civil war or be overtaken by foreign radical Islamist elements, which have been reported to be just across our border."[26] Texas Governor Greg Abbott assured voters he would order the Texas State Guard to "monitor" the situation even though the exercises had been coordinated with state and local officials months earlier. Senator Ted Cruz agreed with Gohmert, calling the reaction a "natural consequence of our untrustworthy federal government." Online comments were markedly less politic.[27] As with so many conspiracist flashpoints, the furor over Jade Helm reflected an issue of the day, immigration. In the early 1960s, a similar reaction greeted the army's Operation Water Moccasin, which was said to enable the United Nations' plan to flood the South with troops from Africa. Then in the 1990s, militias took a Marine Corps training exercise to be a stealth effort to "weigh the armed forces willingness to shoot American citizens in a gun confiscation program." The main difference in Jade Helm was that a great many public officials joined in the conspiratorial frenzy.[28]

Government efforts to disarm Americans were also the driving belief behind the burgeoning "false flag" interpretation of highly publicized shootings and other deadly attacks. The exact interpretation varied: the attack might be the work of a government willing to kill innocent people in its push for gun control, or the entire event may have been staged by the government for the same purpose. The former variation had been around for some time; it was applied to the Oklahoma City bombing and featured in some of the more extreme 9/11 conspiracies. The idea of the government's staging a massacre is newer, emerging out of the Sandy Hook School shooting in December 2012 and heavily reinforced by the Boston Marathon bombing the following April. Distinctively, arguments for these conspiracies were carried on almost exclusively online and were heavily visual, with photographs and short videos dominating. Many of these featured "crisis actors," people supposedly paid by the government to portray victims in one massacre after another, which conspiracists thought proved that the events are "controlled by the evil ones." Side-by-side photographs of people who more or less resembled each other were spread around the internet with captions such as "Another 'CRISIS ACTOR'?? Boston Runner 'Rebecca Roche' is Sandy Hook Teacher 'Kaitlin Roig.'"[29]

These conspiratorial interpretations were not spontaneous rumors. An early study found the conspiratorial alternative narratives about mass shootings to have distinctive online "signatures" that suggested a purposive campaign. They also noted the co-occurrence of the hashtag #falseflag with #obama, #nra, and #teaparty.[30] It seems fairly likely that the campaign was motivated by the reelection of President Obama. Orly Taitz, whose birther lawsuits had been thrown out some years earlier, was among those playing up the Sandy Hook massacre as part of Obama's determination to seize patriots' guns, tweeting: "Obama and his regime are trying to disarm all of us, in order to gain an absolute power."[31]

As shootings and other violent events have continued, the conspiratorial narrative has moved beyond gun control as people tie it to their own conspiracies. Lyndon LaRouche placed the blame for the Orlando nightclub shootings in 2016 on the British, the Saudis, and the FBI—"the same people who brought you 9/11." Alex Jones, conversely, credited the false flag operation to President Obama's (and German chancellor Merkel's) effort to silence "dissenters" like himself. "Oh my gosh," Jones imagined Obama saying, "we've got to pass other hate laws to deal with right-wingers and stuff, and we need your guns of course, so you can't protect yourself."[32] Even the violent confrontations and vehicular murder during the 2017 Charlottesville neo-Nazi rally have been molded by Jones into a false flag narrative, complete with crisis actors and agents provocateur paid by George Soros, who is beginning to replace the Rockefellers in the conspiracist pantheon. Responses to Jones's video cast additional blame on everyone from the "Berkeley-educated" Charlottesville mayor (who held back the police) to the Jews (some of whom could be connected to the murderous driver).[33]

The debate over the "common core" standards promoted by the Department of Education have similarly become imbedded in conspiracism. Aside from the standard concern over "Communism," conspiracists have linked the standards to the federal government's larger goal of promoting homosexuality. "We don't want our children to be taught to be anti-Christian, anti-Catholic and anti-American," the Alabama Senate's education committee was told by Terry Bratton, an Alabama tea party leader. "We don't want our children to lose their innocence, beginning in pre-school or kindergarten, told that homosexuality is OK and should be experienced at an early age and that same-sex marriages are OK." In Florida, the awarding of a contract for developing new school accountability tests associated with common core galvanized religious conservatives. Representative Charles Van Zant addressed their concerns about American Institutes for Research, which had received the contract, telling a crowd to

> go on their website. Click the link to what they are doing with youth, and you will see what their agenda really is. They are promoting as hard as they can any youth that is interested in the LGBT agenda and even name it 2-S, which they define as having two spirits. The Bible says a lot about being double-minded. These people . . . will promote

double-mindedness in state education, and attract every one of your children to become as homosexual as they possibly can. I'm sorry to report that to you—I really hate to bring you that news, but you need to know.[34]

Even issues at the state and local level have received similar treatment, as conspiracy theories link them to larger issues and contrived controversies. Local zoning efforts have become inseparable from the conspiracy theories surrounding the UN's nonbinding sustainable growth recommendations known as Agenda 21. According to comedian Victoria Jackson, this 1992 resolution "uses environmentalism to promote the global redistribution of wealth, communism." Senator Ted Cruz filled in what this means in practice: the abolition of golf courses, pastureland, and even paved roads. State legislatures have considered—and Alabama has succeeded in—banning any local planning that embodies any of the Agenda 21 suggestions. Agenda 21 conspiracism has killed local initiatives ranging from bike paths to oyster bed restoration.[35]

There may not be an issue that has been overlooked by conspiracists. Anti-Indian activists in Montana have discovered that "Federal Indian policy is tying in and being coordinated with international and United Nations goals, and the long-term goal of the United Nations and Agenda 21 is that the states go away."[36] Senate Republicans in Georgia, to prepare for their fight against President Obama's Rural Council (which they equated with Stalin's five-year plans and China's Great Leap Forward), held a four-hour briefing that characterized the council as Obama's plan "to force everyone into the cities from whence our ancestors fled." According to conservative activist Field Searcy, host of the briefing, this goal could only be reached by widespread mind control: "They do that by a process known as the Delphi technique. The Delphi technique was developed by the Rand Corporation during the Cold War as a mind-control technique. It's also known as 'consensive process.' But basically the goal of the Delphi technique is to lead a targeted group of people to a pre-determined outcome while keeping the illusion of being open to public input."[37]

New Dynamics of Conspiracy Theorizing

During the 2016 presidential election, conspiracy theorizing reached a new level, becoming the pervasive characteristic of Donald Trump's campaign in particular. To some degree, this may have been an election-driven acceleration of the trend in conspiratorial thinking since the rise of the Tea Party. Clearly, the increase was also fueled by Trump himself, who had expressed 9/11 conspiracy ideas and had been a prominent "birther." Behind the scenes, however, changes in the nature of social media may well have contributed to both more conspiracism and a different dynamic of conspiracy theory development and distribution. The very algorithms designed to build on what users of social media have attended to in the past can create a "filter bubble" of reinforcing information—whether essentially accurate news or mean-spirited bigotry or deranged speculation. The information tends to be both repetitive and disaggregated, often passed along from one person to another after only cursory attention. Information becomes "stories" that "jump from platform to platform, reaching new audiences and 'going viral' in ways and at speeds that were previously impossible."[38]

This process reinforces the ad hoc nature of modern conspiracism, increasingly spread by networks of anonymous conspiracists who may well be fed information by politically interested parties. The stories that emerge out of this process are uncertain and unverifiable, and when they break into wider discourse, the rhetoric used is usually referential, implicit, or oblique. Donald Trump himself has been prolific enough to provide examples of all three styles. In one of his last forays into birtherism, Trump tweeted at the end of 2013: "How amazing, the State Health Director who verified the copies of Obama's 'birth certificate' died in a plane crash today. All others lived." The obvious reference to a fading, but still ongoing conspiracy theory makes this tweet perfectly comprehensible.[39] By the time he was running for president, Trump had moved on to less obvious remarks. Talking with right-wing radio-show host Michael Savage, Trump said about the death of Justice Antonin Scalia two days earlier: "Well, I just heard it today, just a little while ago actually, I just landed and I hear it's a big topic, the question, and it's a horrible topic, but they say they found the pillow on his face, which is a pretty unusual place to find a pillow." This statement clearly entertains the idea that Scalia was murdered, although Trump does not explicitly mention any type of foul play. It is an implicit nod to the conspiracy theories that were already swirling around the internet.[40] On the other side of the admittedly fine line between implicit and oblique lies Trump's remark in the wake of the Orlando nightclub shooting. Referencing Islamic terrorism, Trump said of President Obama on Fox News: "He doesn't get it, or he gets it better than anybody understands." Trump continued by saying that Obama "is not tough, not smart—or he's got something else in mind."[41] Somewhere behind these oblique comments lies the Obama-as-secret-Muslim conspiracy.

A peculiar event that occurred during the presidential transition period may illustrate how inferential and oblique rhetoric can build on social network conspiracism to create serious real-world problems. On December 4, 2016, a young man named Edgar Welch entered the Comet Ping Pong pizzeria in Washington, DC, wielding a rifle, to rescue the "child sex slaves" he believed were being held there. Finding no captive children, Welch surrendered to police. Initially the incident seemed inexplicable, even random, but was actually linked to a conspiracy spread by, among others, incoming National Security Adviser Michael Flynn, who in November had tweeted: "U decide—NYPD Blows Whistle on New Hillary Emails: Money Laundering, Sex Crimes w Children, etc. . . . MUST READ!" Flynn's tweet was too oblique to be held against him, but his son (and "chief of staff") Michael Jr. fared worse for his more direct tweet on the day of the incident: "Until #Pizzagate proven to be false, it'll remain a story. The left seems to forget #PodestaEmails and the many 'coincidences' tied to it." Flynn Junior lost his position on the transition team.[42]

What, exactly, either Flynn was talking about is not clear, and few could figure out the "coincidences" that linked a DC pizzeria, Clinton campaign manager John Podesta, and an imaginary pedophilia cult. News reports generally offered a brief explanation along the lines of

National Public Radio's: "Internet users have developed a wholly fictitious conspiracy theory that maintains Comet Ping Pong is the site of an international Satanic child abuse cabal hosted by powerful Democrats, including Hillary Clinton. Speculation and fabrications tied to the bizarre conspiracy theory have been relentlessly circulated by politically motivated fringe sites."[43] Which internet users fabricated this theory is rarely addressed. Flynn senior's original tweet did not mention the pizzeria but tagged alt-righter Mike Cernovich and his Danger and Play website, where connections were being bandied about: for example, an artist, Marina Abramović, emailed lobbyist Tony Podesta, inviting him to a dinner party and asking if his brother John might like to come. Abramović joked about her "spirit cooking," a reference to her 1996 portfolio of prints of that title, which was an occult reference going back at least to the Victorian era's Aleister Crowley. Cernovich elaborated on the hidden meaning of the invitation: "Occult symbolism, as I've reported on extensively, is done openly to taunt the public. It's a form of power and control. Secret societies do not want to remain secret."[44] Cernovich's efforts were part of the larger network focused on Satanic child abuse and bloody rituals. Some of the participants in that network interpreted other emails from John Podesta about pizza, or pasta, as coded messages. And, since Comet Ping Pong was Podesta's go-to pizza restaurant, others examined the images on that restaurant's menus and discovered coded pedophilia instructions—a long-standing and constant internet phobia. Soon, a 2010 internet frenzy that had tried to link both Bill and Hillary Clinton to child sex trafficking in Haiti was recycled to buttress the #PizzaGate story.[45]

Comet Ping Pong's owner, James Alefantis, and even his employees started receiving death threats via texts, tweets, and Facebook postings. These were presumably inspired by tweets such as one from Subhia (@ ExtinctMedia):

Hillary Clinton Friend's fake name:
"James Alefantis" =
J'Aime les enfants =

I love children
#PizzaGate #SpiritCooking #Twittergate

Right-wing websites featured headlines such as "Pizzagate: How 4Chan Uncovered the Sick World of Washington's Occult Elite." New hashtags such as #LittleLivesMatter and #LolitaExpress drew internet users into the conspiracy. When Reddit banned the r/pizzagate conspiracy board because of the threats, the reaction was predictable. On r/The_Donald, a pro-Trump subreddit (i.e., forum for a specific topic on the website Reddit), a former moderator declared, the "entire mod team and everyone else is tightening up our opsec [operations security] and putting on our battle-armor." Imagining the persecution they were about to face, others wrote, "We have all made life insurance videos. We have all vowed to continue the fight. You have only increased our number. This morning we were numerous, tonight we are legion."[46]

Reddit's action did not, of course, stop the growth of the conspiracy. Atlantabobby included a video with his post purporting to show "Hillary Clinton baby sacrifices" ("Hillary Clinton, and her close inner circle of 'Luciferian worship cult' associates, deserve to burn in Hell"). BulbechilLen was suspicious that, while "researching" #PizzaGate, "mysteriously my internet turned off." Writing under #Mommicide, AleahRN added the tags #PizzaGate Networks and #Pedophocracy to make it easy for anyone to follow up on her message: "I know thousands of moms that had their children JUDICIALLY KIDNAPPED." Conspiracists with other agendas worked the issue into their narratives. Writing about the presidential race from a white betrayal perspective, Mr. Rockwell opined that "if the Hag wins it will be apropos that the final possible nail in the White race will be brought on by a woman with links to Satanism and satanic rituals."[47] Reddit was widely accused of being part of the conspiracy for "censoring pedo activity. Isint [sic] that being an accomplice to crime?" That question was posed under the heading RIP Seth Rich, an allusion to another flash-in-the-pan conspiracy theory that Hillary Clinton had ordered Democratic National Committee staffer Rich killed either because he had leaked her emails or just "knew too much."[48] The anonymity provided by Twitter let people hide behind names such as TommySteamer (accompanying photo of an infant sitting on a chamber pot suggests that Steamer is not the person's actual last name), so that when they link popular TV chef Guy Fieri to the conspiracy for having touted the restaurant's clam pizza, they cannot be held accountable. As a natural extension of this anonymity, apparent posts from political figures (Rep. Steven Smith) and celebrities (Roseanne Barr [@therealroseanne]) may well be bogus. Eventually, all this activity boiled over as Edgar Welch took matters into his own hands.[49] The tools of social media seem to have turned the future of conspiracism into a frightening now.

17

THE ATTACK ON SCIENCE

HIV/AIDS is a man-made disease associated with a CIA-linked vaccination genocide

> Dr. Leonard Horowitz, "Medical Conspiracy Theories and Media Behaviors"

The concept of global warming was created by and for the Chinese in order to make U.S. manufacturing non-competitive.

> Donald J. Trump, tweet, November 6, 2012

As conspiracism has become more prominent in daily life, its impacts have multiplied. In recent years, conspiracism has spilled over from politics to science as never before. The baleful effect of conspiracy theories on science recently reached the point where scientists held an unprecedented nationwide series of protest marches on Earth Day 2017. Astrophysicist Adam Frank elaborated: "It's a measure of how bad things have gotten that there is talk of this March for Science at all. . . . Do we really want to spend a day walking around holding up a sign that says 'Science Is Our Children's Future'? Well, we certainly want people to understand how deeply that's true. But given a choice, we'd rather get the new satellite data loaded up on the computer so we can start doing some spectral analysis."[1] Science today faces challenges ranging from everyday people who fear having their children immunized to powerful politicians who maintain that climate change is a hoax. Overwhelmingly, the term used for such antiscience thinking is "denialism," which connotes a purposive rejection of science rather than mere thoughtless nonacceptance. Scientific breakthroughs and theories have long been resisted by people who felt their beliefs challenged, going back at least to Galileo. More recently, the Idaho legislature removed all references to climate change from the state's K–12 science curriculum.[2] Denialism, however, does not fully describe this thinking since more often than not conspiracism lies behind it.

The bulk of the news about science denialism in recent years has focused on two issues: climate change and vaccines. But conspiracy theories about science and the scientific establishment are long-standing and have touched on every scientific discipline. Even without going back to the Scopes "monkey trial" of evolution, or the fluoride scare of the 1950s, or the moon-landing hoax (not that any of these has disappeared), conspiracy-buttressed denials of accepted science are easy enough to find. Many of them are perpetuated by relatively small groups of people with some idiosyncratic belief. Some spring from larger conspiracy theories. Former Minnesota governor Jesse Ventura is among those who believe that the federal government's secret "germ-warfare" lab on Plum Island in Long Island Sound is the source of Lyme disease. Doing his best to elaborate a conspiracy theory, Ventura challenged his readers to "guess" who was responsible before revealing that it was "a former top Nazi scientist named Eric Traub, who'd been brought to the U.S. under top-secret Project PAPERCLIP. . . . This was at the start of the Cold War, and the idea was to grab these Dr. Strangelove types before the Soviet Union did. Traub had formerly worked under Heinrich Himmler, who ran Hitler's SS, and he'd been lab chief at a secret Nazi bio-warfare lab looking into animal diseases. That seems to have been the model for Plum Island."[3] Health entrepreneur Mike Adams used the news coverage of dangerous levels of lead in the drinking water of Flint, Michigan, to tout his own study free from "all corporate money, government influence and all the blind, obedient 'consensus' science narratives that only end in stupidity." Adams's "study" found that "Obama's EPA" had poisoned "an estimated 10 million Americans with brain-damaging contaminants." Not surprisingly, Adams is also a leading conspiracist in the anti-GMO movement, which was embraced by 2016 Green Party presidential candidate Jill Stein.[4]

Among those who believe that the CERN Large Hadron Collider near Geneva has opened a portal to a parallel universe, some suspect that this was the secret goal all along. But this interpretation pales in comparison to the conspiracists who claim CERN is a continuation of the Illuminati's Project Blue Beam, a cosmic light show so compelling that it will eliminate all resistance to the Antichrist's new world order.[5] There is much discussion online of the conspiracy to control the weather, including the government's creation of synthetic "snow" storms to distract people from "big government tyranny." Tesla's followers continue to reveal the widespread conspiracy to suppress his electro-gravitics technology. And Donald Zygutis's *The Sagan Conspiracy: NASA's Untold Plot to Suppress the People's Scientist's Theory of Ancient Aliens* speaks for itself.[6]

The conspiratorial idea that most often ties together smaller scientific conspiracies is population control. Stanley Montieth, a leader in this school of thought, explains that the conspiracy is detailed on the Georgia Guidestones. This anonymously constructed 1980 Stonehenge-like edifice in rural Georgia features humanistic homilies in several languages and has become a conspiratorial icon of evil—beginning around the time of Obama's election it has routinely been defaced with anti-NWO graffiti. Montieth, like many others, interprets the "Druid-like monument" as instructing those on "the dark side." Montieth details coded messages aimed at Margaret Sanger's Planned Parenthood followers, who "fully intend to 'exterminate' a significant portion of the world's population" in order to "cleanse" our society of its "human weeds." The Sanger acolytes are working on behalf of the radical environmentalists, who want "a wild and healthy planet" to enjoy for their own elite pleasure.[7]

Population control is also the most common conspiracy theory involving the medical establishment generally and 'big pharma' in particular. The ad copy for Kevin Galalae's *Killing Us Softly: The Global Depopulation Policy* categorizes "GMOs, vaccines, artificial diseases like AIDS, fluoride," and others as "weapons of mass sterility and selective morbidity that affect nearly every human being on the planet." Jennifer Lake claims that the polio vaccine is "the greatest bioweapon 'nerve agent' ever to be perpetrated upon humankind." Dr. Nancy Turner Banks, an HIV denier, paints AIDS as a man-made weapon of war that the elite use "against those populations they consider expendable and the rest whom they wish to control." Leonard Horowitz, a former dentist and proponent of pseudoscientific conspiracy theories, accuses mainstream medicine of genocide, adding: "I say genocide with a strict definition meaning: the mass killing of people for economic, political and/or ideological reasons."[8]

These are extreme examples, but there are literally thousands of them. Some seem relatively harmless, no worse than believing in the Loch Ness Monster or casting horoscopes. But in some areas of vital public concern, much of this conspiracism and the denialism it supports is harmful indeed.

The Development of Conspiracism: Health and Medicine

Public health issues have been affected by conspiracy theories for decades, whenever spurious cures have come under attack from medical authorities. Typically, the issue is first portrayed as a "controversy" with a medical "democracy" on one side fighting know-it-all elitists on the other.[9] The battle over the supposed cancer cure Laetrile lasted for decades and illustrates how conspiratorial thinking emerges from the so-called controversy. In the 1940s, Laetrile advocates initially limited themselves to making medical claims in public venues to try to pressure the medical establishment (including regulatory bodies) to approve their cure. Ultimately unsuccessful, they shifted to a "freedom of choice" approach, attacking the medical establishment and quoting Patrick Henry's "Give

Me Liberty or Give Me Death." This tactic attracted support from the John Birch Society, and by the 1970s, Laetrile advocates began casting the government not just as an obstacle to medical progress but a threat to people's liberty as well. "The point is freedom," complained right-wing newspaper columnist and Laetrile ally James J. Kilpatrick. "We lose it by chunks, by bits, by grains. Daily we yield more authoritarian control to the state and to the experts."[10]

Such a turn toward conspiracism is typical of people who believe that they have discovered something miraculous, whether a medical cure, a technological breakthrough, or lost arcane wisdom. When the experts reject or ignore their find, they reject the experts. In medical areas, where government approval is also involved, rejection routinely flowers into conspiracy. Thus, Dr. Stanislaw Burzynski has been "persecuted" by the FDA, which refuses to approve his cancer cure (antineoplastons) because his success "has angered the pharma-medical-industrial complex"—not because of its arrant quackery. His is just one of many medical "options," such as the Gerson Therapy, that have been "forbidden," as a Gerson-produced video makes clear: "*Cancer: The Forbidden Cures* is a fascinating documentary that exposes the corruption of the cancer industry and the extreme measures they will take to discredit, imprison, and professionally destroy any physician who treats cancer patients using natural or alternative methods. . . . They have and will go to extreme measures to prevent the truth about effective natural treatments from reaching the public and interfering with their revenue stream." Under this onslaught of extreme measures, it is remarkable that the Gerson Therapy has thrived for over ninety years.[11] The exact nature of the extreme measures is generally unspecified, but in 2015, internet chatter attributed the "mysterious" deaths of five holistic medical practitioners to a murderous conspiracy by Big Pharma and the FDA. This level of conspiracism is common among the "crusaders and defenders" who have exposed the "monolithic agent of evil" that is the medical establishment.[12] Extreme measures should not be surprising, as Dr. Brad Case, author of *Thugs, Drugs and the War on Bugs*, explained in an interview: "Well, if people finally knew that vaccines cause autism, like we now know that smoking causes cancer and emphysema, especially if we knew that THEY knew and have known for a long time and did nothing about it, then there would be such an uprising that they wouldn't just get sued, they'd probably get the guillotine."[13]

Old conspiracy theories have sometimes been recycled for attacks on the medical establishment. Nancy Turner Banks falls back on an antisemitic version of Emanuel Josephson's 1952 indictment of "the Rockefeller-Gates-Flexner-Simmons-A.M.A. gang" that seized control of American medicine after World War I. Banks also plagiarizes Eustace Mullins's 1988 depiction of the Rockefeller-Rothschild "medical conspiracy against America."[14]

The growth of a conspiratorial framework has made it more likely that any health controversy will be plunged into mistrust, paranoia, and conspiracism. When state health departments began to crack down on the raw milk fad in 2010, many people argued that raw milk was not dangerous, as the FDA and other public health agencies claimed. Conspiracists went further, generating internet stories such as "The witch-hunt that's taking it to one of America's healthiest food choices." David Icke began his assessment by stating "when a government declares something, we already know from their track record of being perpetual liars that the opposite of what they are saying is true," and Mike Adams took his stand on Alex Jones's Infowars website, declaring that "we will not be treated like food slaves by a corrupt criminally-run government that wishes to force everyone to drink DEAD MILK."[15] The raw milk issue came and went in a year, but a constant stream of such issues keeps conspiracism going. The conspiratorial backdrop of the anti-vaccination movement is nearly twenty years old and shows little sign of disappearing. Dr. Andrew Wakefield himself, the man whose fraudulent research began the vaccine controversy in 1998, continues to accuse the Centers for Disease Control of orchestrating a conspiracy to discredit his research. Anti-vaccination conspiracism has been well covered in academic and popular literature but continues to worry public health officials.[16]

Perhaps the most worrisome area of health-related conspiracism today is epidemiology. Both predictable epidemics, such as influenza, and unexpected pandemics, such as Ebola, are now routinely imbedded in conspiracy theories from the moment they are discovered, causing difficulties for health officials worldwide. Conspiracism first hit with the AIDS pandemic, leading to a cultlike denialism. Further, a variety of conspiracy theories declared AIDS to be a man-made viral agent designed to wipe out gay men, or African American men, or even Africans in their entirety.[17] In South Africa, where HIV denialism in government resulted in thousands of deaths, beliefs about AIDS in President Mbeki's cabinet were reputedly based in Milton William Cooper's bizarre conspiratorial opus *Behold a Pale Horse*.[18]

In recent years, conspiracy theories have been regularly applied to influenza outbreaks, some featuring accusations that Mexicans were being sent to the United States as "walking germ warfare weapons." Mike Adams's videos about the swine flu outbreak in 2009 featured Adams himself rapping:

> The big drug companies are makin' a killing
> Collectin' the billions and gettin' away like a James Bond villain
> Cause they're willin' to do almost anything
> Just to make money with the flu vaccine[19]

During the Ebola scare, right-wing conspiracy pioneer Phyllis Schlafly accused President Obama of allowing the disease into the United States as part of his conspiracy to destroy the country, while popular singer Chris Brown tweeted that Ebola was part of a population control conspiracy. And some conspiracy theories about the Zika virus became entwined with those about the measles, mumps, and rubella vaccines, although most simply stressed the profits certain to accrue to the Rockefellers from the sales of Zika vaccines.[20]

Undermining Science with Conspiracy Theory: Climate Change

The corporate campaign against climate change is quite different from the conspiracy theories about health issues. Its most peculiar feature is that, while the outlines of the campaign are well known, millions of people in the United States continue to believe its claims. Generally called climate change deniers, they often insist on the term "skeptic" to make their position appear more reflective and open to discussion (HIV denialists, conversely, prefer "dissident").[21] By either designation, they are steeped in conspiracy theories. Science writer David Suzuki described their view of climate change "as a massive plot or hoax perpetrated by the world's scientists and scientific institutions, governments, the UN, environmentalists and sinister forces to create a socialist world government or something."[22]

The uncertainty behind Suzuki's "or something" arises because there is no climatological equivalent of Big Pharma, which health conspiracists rely on as an anchor for their claims. Accordingly, the campaign against climate change has focused on the apolitical and nonideological Intergovernmental Panel on Climate Change (IPCC), which is disparaged as a "political" and "ideological" body determined to find evidence of climate change. Moreover, the suggestion is often made that IPCC scientists gain financially from their affiliation; they are even paid to travel to "exotic locations" for meetings. Despite its relatively humdrum origin (established in 1988 by the UN Environmental Panel and the World Meteorological Organisation), the IPCC has been described as a "hidden world . . . made up of very few players." This elite, according to conspiracists, naturally controls all climate data and keeps any dissident voice from being heard through its self-serving peer review requirement for publishing. Conspiracists claim that all this amounts to "a real conspiracy, . . . beyond argument."[23]

Behind such claims lies the energy industry and its manifold front groups, many with names intended to create confusion with actual scientific organizations. In the United States, most of these are funded through the industry's Heartland Institute.[24] Foremost among Heartland's creations is the Nongovernmental International Panel on Climate Change (NIPPC), which has distributed, among other activities, its packet of instructional materials titled *Climate Change Reconsidered* to schools and colleges nationwide. After reassuring teachers that NIPCC is "wholly independent of political pressures and influences," the cover letter accompanying the packet asked them: "Will you tell your students the 'science is settled' on global warming, as the United Nations' Intergovernmental Panel on Climate Change (IPCC) claims it is? Or will you explain to them that real science is never settled—that the essence of science is skepticism?"[25] Similar denialist organizations funded in part by the Heartland Institute include the Science and Public Policy Institute, Craig Idso's Center for the Study of Carbon Dioxide and Global Change, and the International Climate Science Coalition. For several years, Heartland and NIPCC organized annual meetings, called the International Conference on Climate Change, where participants exchanged conspiratorial views on climate change. Heartland president Joseph Bast referred to it as part of "Obama's anti-energy agenda," while Heartland policy adviser John Dunn called it "enviro-fascist madness," adding the comforting afterthought that "warm is good for people, . . . the people that warm spells kill are already moribund." Former president of the Czech Republic Václav Klaus, having already declared climate change to be a "communist conspiracy," declared: "It is identical to communism—identical not similar." The 2012 conference was marred by controversy over a Heartland billboard featuring a mug shot of Ted Kaczynski (the Unabomber) with the legend, "I still believe in Global Warming. Do You?" Since that time, the conferences have become more sporadic.[26]

The information that filters down from these pseudoscientific organizations reaches the public through "an ecosystem of hyperpartisan media outlets," from which it emerges in an even more conspiratorial context. One Brian Sussman releases most of his denialism through his Eco-Tyranny website, where the "socialist agenda" conspiracy prevails, but he sometimes softens his message for outlets such as *Forbes*, where the conspiracy is limited to the federal government's tireless efforts to control ever more of America's land.[27] The right-wing Media Research Center keeps the public apprised of the mainstream media's contribution to the climate change agenda with stories such as "Networks Hide the Decline in Credibility of Climate Change Science." Alex Jones has linked the climate change agenda to chemtrails (which have been accused of "geoengineering" the climate to make it conform to IPCC models). Jones has also claimed that chemtrails do not affect "globalists" because they receive a "special detox." And Breitbart's regular contributor on environmental issues, James Delingpole, subsumes climate change into the grand environmental conspiracy that, "after militant Islam, probably represents the biggest political and economic threat to the world today because its tentacles spread so far and because its influence is so insidious . . .—the 'climate change' scare especially—is the hard left's Trojan Horse; unlike the Soviets, unlike the Nazis, it intends to destroy Western liberal civilization not from without but from within."[28]

The overriding tactic of the campaign against climate change has been to attack scientists, depicting their work as political. This tactic had featured prominently in battles over repressed memory research in the 1990s and quickly spread to medical research. For example, Dr. Joseph Sonnabend, after objecting to being portrayed in an HIV-denialist film as supporting its claims, was accused of having "sold out to corporate pseudo-science." [29] Scientists in many disciplines have reported attacks ranging from cyberbullying and public abuse to "elaborately-formatted multi-page dossiers" alleging research misconduct. The most notorious single example was the campaign waged against "Recursive Fury," a paper by Stephan Lewandowsky and his colleagues that found science denialism more common among both conspiracy theorists and advocates of free market economics. Threats of libel actions led to the paper's being withdrawn, which in turn led to outrage among scientists. Lewandowski was also pilloried on line, and his integrity was routinely questioned.[30]

The campaign against climate science reached its conspiratorial apex when thousands of emails were hacked and released to climate deniers in 2009. The emails were the basis of an avalanche of accusations depicting the IPCC as the center of a worldwide conspiracy of corrupt scientists. Led by polemicists such as Brian Sussman and James Delingpole, the accusations were expanded into book-length papers and actual books through the efforts of denialist front organizations and their press allies. Denialist politicians seized the opportunity to undermine the upcoming Copenhagen round of climate talks by alluding to "the revelations of appalling practices by the so-called climate change experts."[31] As we have come to expect, exonerations of the scientists—investigations found no misleading of the public, no conspiratorial behavior, no climate change "hoax"—were simply used to expand the conspiracy to include the investigators. As the *Wall Street Journal* explained: "Global warming alarmists claim vindication after last year's data manipulation scandal. Don't believe the 'independent' reviews." Despite its hollowness, "Climategate" did undermine the public's acceptance of climate change, to the point where denialists tried to revive the charges in 2011 with "Climategate 2.0."[32]

As with conspiratorial broadsides on public health, the concerted attack on climate scientists had an impact beyond the issue itself. As one study noted, the campaign diminished public trust in scientists, "primarily among individuals with a strongly individualistic worldview or politically conservative ideology."[33] As scientific discourse was increasingly swamped by political debate, scientists could simply be portrayed as "hyping . . . flimsy studies—melting Himalayan glaciers; vanishing polar ice—to press the political point." Scientists were depicted as elitists who wanted the public to blindly believe in their message. The informational packet sent to schools by the NIPCC headlined its denialist message: "Don't just *believe* in global warming. *Understand* it." In this context the efforts of the IPCC to warn of the consequences of global warming could be written off as a propaganda campaign by "the Left," as the former chief economist at the Heritage Foundation, Stephen Moore, did, in terms reminiscent of hidden hand conspiracy rhetoric: "I mean, they've taken this dingbat idea of global climate change and they've put it in the schools, they've put it in the movies, they've put it in the media and the churches—you know, I'm Catholic, even the Pope talks about climate change. So it's very alarming how this propaganda campaign, that they made this stuff out of, almost completely out of thin air and they've convinced millions and millions of thought leaders that this stuff is real."[34]

Science denialism is notoriously hard to dislodge. Entire academic conferences have been held to help scientists cope with the problem.[35] Alfred Moore has broken down the problems conspiracism causes for public policy into several areas, the first of which is distraction. The National Aeronautics and Space Administration has wasted immeasurable time trying to counter moon-landing hoax conspiracists; public health agencies have had to come up with strategies to combat AIDS denialists and to convince parents in the grip of anti-vaccination conspiracies to have their children immunized; there are issues facing atmospheric scientists, but their need to focus on activists' chemtrails conspiracies "may be taking attention away from real underlying problems that need addressing."[36] The problems caused by distraction are hard to assess because they are typically actions that are not taken because they are crowded out by the need to counter conspiracist beliefs.

The diminution of popular trust in scientists has been exploited by politicians increasingly over the last decade. Senator Inhofe has famously labeled climate change a hoax, and the less well-known Representative Lamar Smith (chairman of the House Science, Space, and Technology Committee) routinely calls it a scam. No serious contender for the Republican nomination for president has been able to support the science of climate change for years, a situation conservative columnist David Brooks attributes to fear that the antiscience "thought police will knock on their door and drag them off to an AM radio interrogation."[37]

Many vested interests appear happy enough to use conspiracism to undermine science for their own benefit; best known among these are the tobacco and energy industries. But in addition, a surprising array of conspiratorial individuals seem perfectly willing to disparage or undermine science. There are HIV denialists motivated by a clear disgust for what they imagine to be the gay lifestyle among the "syphilitic bath house veterans" who refuse to take responsibility for their "self-destructive behavior." What are now called SLAP-activists (for the **S**ecret **L**arge-Scale **A**tmospheric Spraying **P**rogram using chemtrails) work to undermine science and even threaten scientists. Young-earth creationists fighting evolution have incorporated the "Climategate controversy" into their science bashing. Andrew Schlafly, founder of Conservapedia, attacks Albert Einstein and his theory of relativity as a liberal Zionist conspiracy. As the editors of *Scientific American* have reiterated, "The new science denialism is creating an existential crisis like few the country has faced before."[38]

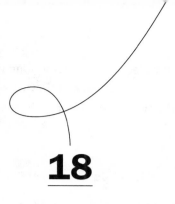

18

DEMOCRACY AND CIVIL SOCIETY

Three years ago, our lab decided these conspiracy theories were too marginal and salacious to be the focus of our research. Almost that it was beneath our dignity to pay attention to and promote this kind of content. What a terrible mistake that was. It seems to me we weren't the only ones who made it. . . . I hope it is not too late.

Kate Starbird, "Information Wars"[1]

As conspiracism has become more prominent in daily life, its impacts have multiplied. In American politics, conspiracy theories first became an integral part of political debates, taking many politicians by surprise during the town hall meetings held to discuss Obama's health care plan. Tea Party activists accused government officials of "trampling on our constitution" and demanded "their country back," and gun-wielding patriots offered veiled threats. In short order, conspiracism moved into electoral campaigns, hitting its stride in 2016. Today, conspiracism has made the transition from electioneering to government itself, and concern is growing over its effect on democracy.[2] In addition to these more existential concerns, there is the much more immediate phenomenon of conspiracy-related violence, including serious attacks and mass shootings. These are, of course, rare and often written off as the work of the mentally ill, but they are fostered by conspiracism more than is generally known.

The Sharp Edge of Conspiracism: Extreme Violence

The link between conspiratorial beliefs and violent behavior is not surprising, given the array of violence-prone groups that grew out of the "anti-government, paramilitary survivalist/conspiracy mentality" prevalent on the extreme Right in the 1980s and 1990s.[3] The Posse Comitatus, Aryan Nations, The Order, various state militias, the sovereign citizens, and the Phineas Priesthood all committed violent acts. In some cases, as with The Order, violent attacks, including assassinations, were planned in detail. In other cases, notably the sovereign citizens, almost all fatal incidents were spontaneous, often the result of unplanned interactions with law enforcement.[4] Many violent acts have been clearly tied to a group, but the connection can be obscure, in keeping with the Aryan Nation's principle of leaderless resistance. Small cells of terrorists give themselves names suggesting their inspiration: Sons of Gestapo, Team Viper, Army of God, League of the Silent Soldier, Sons of Liberty, or Third Continental Congress.[5] And there are lone wolves, not really part of any organized group but inspired by conspiracism.

Seemingly random shootings are the hallmark of the lone wolf, and despite a wealth of instances in which evidence suggests conspiratorial thinking, cause and effect remain difficult to sort out. This is partly because there are few shootings and bombings to analyze but also because lone-wolf conspiracists often have such muddled and paranoid ideas that the question of their sanity arises. Conspiratorial mind-control beliefs and similar paranoid fantasies are common, as are secret messages; one would-be bomber claimed to have "discovered a secret map detailing a planned UN takeover mistakenly printed on a box of Trix."[6] Joseph Parent and Joseph Uscinski have found some evidence that conspiracy-minded individuals are more accepting of—perhaps even prone to—violence than other people. While "the relationship between conspiracy theory and violent impulses is complicated," Parent and Uscinski admit, together they form a "toxic combination."[7]

The complexity is well illustrated by Jared Loughner, who singled out Representative Gabrielle Giffords for assassination—wounding her and thirteen others and killing nine people in Tucson in 2011. Loughner's online statements and videos have been described as a "bizarre and toxic stream-of-consciousness conspiracism" and seem to have been influenced by occultism.[8] Loughner apparently held a wide variety of conspiratorial ideas, from our enslavement by the Federal Reserve, to vague 9/11 beliefs, to the conviction that all of NASA's activities were hoaxes. Some reported on Loughner's intense concern with grammar, originally writing it off as a personality quirk. But it seems more likely that Loughner was influenced by sovereign citizen ":David-Wynn: Miller's" theory that the authorities use grammar as a tool in their conspiracy to control the public. ":Miller" illustrates the control by "explaining" his name in terms of his theory: "Because I use prepositional phrases, through punctuation, which is classified as hieroglyphics, which makes me a life, l-i-f-e.... David is an adjective, Miller is a pronoun, two adjectives are a condition of modification, opinion, presumption, which modifies the pronoun, pro means no on noun. So therefore, I'm not a fact. I'm a fiction."[9] In a video, Loughner claimed that "the government is implying mind control and brainwash on the people by controlling grammar." Loughner had a conspiratorial framework, however inchoate, which he targeted onto Giffords. People on the Left suggested that a map released by Sarah Palin showing twenty members of Congress (including Giffords) as they would appear in the crosshairs of a telescopic gunsight tilted Loughner's conspiracism toward violence, especially as Palin tweeted "Don't Retreat, Instead RELOAD" as a reinforcing comment.[10]

In a multination study of extremist violence, Jamie Bartlett and Carl Miller concluded that conspiracism tends to exaggerate extremist views and propel some individuals toward violent acts in three ways.[11] First, conspiracism exaggerates the "otherness" of one's opponents. This is fully in keeping with the Manicheanism of so much conspiracy thinking but can also show up in smaller ways. Chris Mercer, who killed nine people at Umpqua Community College in Oregon in 2015, distanced himself from the type of person who would become his victim in a blog post. "Most people," Mercer wrote, "will spend hours standing in front of stores just to buy a new phone. . . . I used to be like that."[12] The second way in which conspiracism leads to violence stems from its tendency to delegitimize moderate views, again feeding into a dichotomous world-view in which people are either with you or against you. Your opponent becomes your enemy as hostility erodes any finer distinctions. The Norwegian mass murderer Anders Behring Breivik exemplified this thinking when he lumped together four enemy groups of pro-Islamic traitors, from the cultural, political, and media elite constituting Category A down to the compliant drones of Category D.[13] The third spur to violence provided by conspiracism, especially the more apocalyptic variety, is the idea that violent acts may be necessary to "wake up" the public. Joseph Stark, a "tax resister" who flew an airplane into an Internal Revenue Service building in Austin, Texas, exemplified this in his suicide note/manifesto: "I can only hope that the numbers get too big to be white washed and ignored that the American zombies wake up and revolt; it will take nothing else. I would only hope that by striking a nerve that stimulates the inevitable double standard, knee-jerk government reaction that results in more stupid draconian restrictions people wake up and begin to see the pompous political thugs and their mindless minions for what they are."[14]

The conspiratorial backgrounds of lone wolves vary considerably. Sometimes their conspiracism is not overt or is overshadowed by even more peculiar ideas, and sometimes the conspiracism does not emerge quickly. In 2010, John Patrick Bedell, firmly in the grip of a libertarian version of a deep-state conspiracy theory (involving both a narco-conspiracy and mind-controlled sex slaves), drove from California to the Pentagon, where he wounded two guards before being killed. Paul Ciancia, who in 2013 killed a Transportation Security Administration officer and wounded four other people at Los Angeles International Airport, carried with him a "manifesto" outlining the Federal Reserve "fiat money" version of the new world order conspiracy. Dylann Roof's 2015 massacre of worshippers in a South Carolina AME church was inspired by the racial holy war rhetoric reflecting a conspiracy by Jews and blacks against the white race.[15] Sometimes the conspiracism behind attacks is abstract to the point of being generic. In 2014, Jerad and Amanda Miller of Las Vegas killed two police officers in a stand against "tyranny" as Jerad declared in a lengthy and redundant post clearly inspired by Robert Mathews's Declaration of War:

> May the best men of our beloved nation stand and fight tyranny, without fear and without regret. May we stand proud as free men instead of kneeling as slaves. May we offer our children a free and just world. . . . We cannot fail in this endeavor of Liberty, if we do we risk leaving our orphaned children to the will of tyrants . . . the longer we wait, our enemies become better equipped and recruit more mercenaries of death, willing to do a tyrants bidding without question. . . . We certainly stand before a great and powerful enemy. I, however, would rather die fighting for freedom, than live on my knees as a slave. Let it be known to our children's children that free men stood fast before a tyrants wrath. . . .[16]

Sometimes the conspiracism motivating an attack is long-standing. When James von Brunn attacked the Holocaust Memorial Museum in Washington, DC, in 2009, killing a security guard, he was portrayed as a racist, a white supremacist, and/or a Holocaust denier. All true, but these views were also strongly embedded in a conspiratorial framework von Brunn had maintained since reading John Beaty's "Khazarian Jew" conspiracy opus, *The Iron Curtain over America*, in 1964.[17] In 1981, in keeping with his understanding of the "International Banking Cabal," von Brunn decided to place the Federal Reserve Board of Governors under citizen's arrest. Following a script seemingly lifted from the movies, von Brunn explained that he

> intended to hold the Board prisoners in the Board Room, demand that their fellow conspirators at CBS provide national TV-hookup; then,

over TV to figuratively hand over the felons to the American people with an explanation of my charges against the FED. I then intended to hand over the prisoners, unharmed, to the President of the United States. I expected to stand trial in a U.S. Federal District Court, and prove the Fed's culpability to a jury of my peers. I expected the jury to find the FED guilty and my citizens' arrest of the felons upheld by statute.

This plan went wrong from the beginning, and, as he related in his "racialist guide for the preservation and nurture of the white gene pool," von Brunn was railroaded into prison by "a biased Negro jury . . . and Jew Judge."[18]

Wish Fulfillment Conspiracies

People such as von Brunn, or Jerad and Amanda Miller, or Jared Loughner are fortunately very uncommon. But there are others with an anti-government conspiracist framework who are attracted to violence but not driven to random killings. In 2014, Cliven Bundy orchestrated a standoff with officials of the Bureau of Land Management over grazing fees. Bundy, a follower of the sovereign citizens, owed over a million dollars in back fees accumulating since 1992, when Bundy had decided the federal government was illegitimate. In short order, hundreds of armed men, "truck drivers, pizza deliverymen, and ex-cops from as far away as New Hampshire and Georgia" made their way to Bunkerville, Nevada. One described how moved he was by "Americans, refusing to cow to the federal government, blindly, like cattle. They were taking a stand." As Weldon Travis, a participant, wrote in his paean to the Battle of Bunkerville: "Some had quit their jobs, not knowing when they might return to their families. Sounds like our forefathers, right?" Signs and banners attached to a chain-link fence carried messages such as "RIP Freedom Public Land First Amendment," "Big Government Takeover Here's Your Proof Who's Next?" and "How long are people of the Western states going to put up with Marshall [sic] Law imposed by the BLM?"

Bunkerville quickly became an armed paramilitary camp—Camp Tripwire—with a guarded perimeter and snipers posted on Interstate overpasses.[19] Two years later, Cliven's son Ammon led the occupation of the Malheur Wildlife Refuge in Oregon to protest the imprisonment of two men convicted of arson. Again, supporters came in droves in response to Bundy's Facebook post: "ALL PATRIOTS ITS [sic] TIME TO STAND UP NOT STAND DOWN!!!" The people drawn to such armed confrontations often seem to be living out a fantasy in which they forgo their normal lives for the excitement of standing up against the oppression "by a 'foreign' government." And when, as in Oregon, they are acquitted, the fantasy is reinforced.[20]

In the world of patriot conspiracism, this scenario has been a popular fantasy at least since William Pierce's 1978 white supremacist revenge novel *The Turner Diaries*. Timothy McVeigh was apparently captivated by this novel, and his bombing of the Murrah Building was based on a key scene from it.[21] During the militia heyday, novels like John Ross's *Unintended Consequences* (in which the leaderless resistance assassinates Bureau of Alcohol, Tobacco, and Firearms agents and politicians until the government rescinds all its unconstitutional laws) and James Wesley Rawles's *Patriots* (in which a band of survivors escapes to north Idaho where they fight off outsiders and restore the Constitution) provided inspiration. More recently, Mike Vanderboegh, the founder of the III Percent Patriots, created a novel on his blog entitled *Absolved*. It depicted the struggle of a group of Alabama patriots against thugs from the Bureau of Alcohol, Tobacco, and Firearms after a Waco-like incident kicks off government repression. Like *The Turner Diaries*, Vanderboegh's novel has the distinction of inspiring real events. A copycat plot by north Georgia militia members to spread the poison ricin in several cities and "take out" public officials "to make the country right again" was thwarted in 2011.[22] There are, of course, a great many more such excursions into armed fantasy, such as Matthew Bracken's popular Enemies Trilogy, and these can be worked into ongoing conspiracy theories.[23] The ironically named website the Daily Sheeple featured an article titled "15 Doomsday Fiction Books That May Soon Become

Reality." Such fantasies are reinforced on a great many survivalist and prepper websites that advertise "non-GMO survival seeds," "survival property" for "strategic relocation to Idaho & Montana," and of course military gear such as gas masks, high-capacity magazines, lightweight body armor, and night vision units.[24]

Probably even more important, since not all conspiracists care to read, music supports some of the most violent conspiracists. The subgenre of country hate music dates back to the civil rights movement when the United Klans of America sold dozens of records, most simply and offensively racist, but others—"Stand Up and Be Counted" or "The Money Belongs to Us"—echoing conspiracy themes. More recent music is similarly not overtly conspiratorial, its viciously racist lyrics instead focusing on white supremacism. Today the best-known area in this musical genre is the völkish white supremacist music of bands beginning with RaHoWa in the early 1990s. The neo-Nazi Hammerskins have used their music festivals as a recruiting tool for years now; their 2016 Hammerfest in Georgia featured bands such as Beer Hall Putsch, Ironwill, and Hate Your Neighbors. This music stresses the need for whites to fight against the conspiracy to destroy them.[25] The band RaHoWa's song "Ode to a Dying People" conveys the common message of the "betrayal" of the white race by the forces in charge of contemporary society. As with so much similar rhetoric, it mimics the self-pitying tone of Robert Mathews:

> It's all over except for the crying;
> With a whimper instead of the roar of a lion
> The greatest race ever to walk the earth, walk the earth;
> Dying a slow death with insane mirth
> The tomb has been prepared, our race betrayed, our race betrayed
> White man, fight the flight toward the grave.

The song was later covered by the Swedish singer Saga, an inspiration to Anders Behring Breivik, who describes Saga as "courageous" and "the most talented patriotic musician in the English speaking world."[26]

Some people are drawn into violent, confrontational situations by immersing themselves in conspiratorial fantasies about the collapse of society. People can become so obsessed with "the end of the world as we know it" (TEOTWAWKI) that it becomes "Doom Porn," which can be thought of as "applied conspiracism." Conspiracists convinced of an impending apocalyptic battle will begin "preparing for TEOTWAWKI, because they appear to have a deep-seated, almost nihilistic wish for everything just to end."[27] There are people who find these doomsday scenarios perversely appealing and unconnected to conspiracy theories. Many TEOTWAWKI adherents are more attuned to power grid failures, pandemics, or other catastrophes than to conspiracies. Their deepest concern is escaping the boredom of everyday life, as underscored on their websites—of the "105 ways TEOTWAWKI changes everything," the top three are the demise of lawn mowing, traffic jams, and video games.[28] Some people, however, combine TEOTWAWKI with the immediacy of SHTF—"shit hits the fan," the ideas of which were initially a response to the civil rights activities in the 1960s. Even before the Watts Riots in Los Angeles, a 1965 advertisement headlined "We Will Survive" offered the book *Form Your "Home Guard" Now* that "tells you what you need—what to expect—how to defend and protect— what enemy forces are planning." One could also purchase Wally Butterworth's phonograph record, "Arm your home with GUNS against drunken negro rioters" (flip side: "Democratic Traitors Disarm USA for One World Government").[29] Unlike the TEOTWAWKIists, the daydreams of SHTFers are not about the end of mowing the lawn, but like those of one "Dan C.," who imagines "handling an active shooter situation" in the big-box store where he works: "I have spent considerable time studying this issue and even more time thinking about what one should do." Although advised to avoid confrontation, Dan C. envisions himself darting to the firearms section of the store and loading up to handle the situation.[30]

The conspiracy theory shared among SHTFers is that the federal government is wholly illegitimate and a betrayal of the Constitution, kept in power only through intimidation and deceit. The federal government and its globalist allies conspire constantly to destroy America. Occasionally, someone will expound on details of the globalist agenda, but the topic usually is how, exactly, the government plans to enforce martial law.[31] All federal government policies are treated as aspects of the determination to squash Americans. These policies often do not exist; environmental "proposals," for instance, that will make Americans "pay for the privilege of breathing the air and living on this planet have also signaled an impoverished and tightly controlled future." The ultimate point is that the government must be fought. In the words of the editor of the online SHTF journal *SHTF Plan*:

> Our founders believed that the people have the RIGHT to resist tyranny and that if tyranny was entrenched that we had an OBLIGATION to fight and destroy it. . . . Freedom is predicated, necessitates, and requires a distrust of those who would rule us. We as a people have forgotten this to our detriment. . . . I see dark days ahead for us in which the country a [*sic*] separated not unlike it was during the Revolutionary war. On one side the tories and on the other the patriots. One side will stand for their government while the other will stand for the nation."[32]

This sort of belief cannot be the only cause of deadly attacks such as those of Jared Loughner or James von Brunn. But it is hard to ignore the conspiracism behind Jerad and Amanda Miller's trek to join the Battle of Bunkerville before returning to Las Vegas and shooting two police officers—their part in the fight against tyranny.

The Threat to Democracy

Both the conspiracy-driven violence and the emergence of science denialism have impacts on public policy. Law enforcement agencies and the court systems have found it necessary to devote considerable attention to handling mass shootings, organized resistance such as at Bunkerville and the low-level but constant threat posed by sovereign citizens. Many analysts have bemoaned how conspiracy theories and the misinformation they spawn "distort the debate that is crucial to democracy" and divert attention from real issues.[33] Imaginary conspiracies such as those over Sharia Law or the federal government's preparations for attacking Texas during Jade Helm 15 pop up from time to time. But more serious imaginary conspiracies such as the government's determination to impose draconian environmental restrictions on everyone in keeping with the UN's Agenda 21 proposals have hampered local planning efforts for years.[34]

All indications are that this situation is worsening. Republican representative Devin Nunes noted that, in 2003, about 10 percent of his communications from constituents was "conspiracy-theorist nonsense," a figure that he estimated in 2016 to have risen to 90 percent. Much of this nonsense is denialist conspiracism that underlies people's refusal to allow their children to be vaccinated. Such noncooperation also stems from the increasingly polarized politics fostered by the Manicheanism of conspiracist thinking. More troublingly, in government itself the "norms of partisan restraint have eroded in recent decades," rendering "our democratic institutions increasingly dysfunctional."[35] Distraction, distortion, and noncooperation are not, of course, separate in practice. The birther movement, for example, relied entirely on distorted information, was a political distraction, and served as a rationale for noncooperation. Still, they are useful distinctions.

The greater question, being raised in many quarters, is to what degree conspiracism constitutes a threat to democracy itself. There are two aspects to this concern. One is how much conspiracist depictions of reality can manipulate or badly distort public opinion. The other centers on authoritarianism, its capacity to destroy democracy, and its relationship to conspiracism. The idea that the "informed public" (theoretically the bedrock of democratic government) can be manipulated is not new; it goes back at least to Walter Lippmann's 1925 *The Phantom Public*. Not surprisingly, new information technologies and practices lie at the center of today's concern. There has been, it is argued, a "shift in paradigm" as the amount of easily available conspiracist information has increased. "News" stories "grounded on conspiracy theories tend to reduce the complexity and are able to contain the uncertainty they generate," creating a "climate of disengagement from mainstream society and officially recommended practices.[36] If conspiracy theories can, as psychologists suggest, reduce uncertainty with simplifying narratives, many people will turn to and accept them. This tendency is even more pronounced if the matter at hand involves any moral judgment and is accompanied by greater levels of interaction (e.g., comments) with conspiracist narratives.[37]

The attraction of conspiracist narratives and stories is increasingly reinforced by the very algorithms used to provide people with information. On Facebook, now many people's primary source of information, "once people join a single conspiracy-minded group, they are algorithmically routed to a plethora of others." At the same time, countervailing information is algorithmically rejected, so that a 'filter bubble" is created: "Join an anti-vaccine group, and your suggestions will include anti-GMO, chemtrail watch, flat Earther (yes, really), and 'curing cancer naturally' groups. Rather than pulling a user out of the rabbit hole, the recommendation engine pushes them further in. We are long past merely partisan filter bubbles and well into the realm of siloed communities that experience their own reality and operate with their own facts."[38] This is what philosophers call a crippled epistemology, in which the information any one person receives is constantly reinforced, contributing to individual intransigence and social polarization. Conspiracy theorizing is implicated in this process as a key source of simplifying, uncertainty-reducing, popular misinformation. Moreover, social-web activity features a notorious "asymmetry of passion," leading to conspiracists' being greatly overrepresented (hence the fact most online information about vaccines is anti-vaccination). Thus, early hopes that new technology's expansion of accessible information would lead to greater "collective intelligence" is being supplanted by fear of "a sort of 'collective credulity.'"[39]

This serendipitous fit between the characteristics of conspiracism and technological advancement is not quite the entire story. Online practices such as trolling and astroturfing compound the difficulty of achieving collective intelligence. Hoaxes, parodies, and satires, often posing as "alternative news sources," routinely fool conspiracists, who repost them or work them into the evidence for their conspiracy.[40] Astroturfing and false tweets, when used to spread conspiracies, raise the question of attribution. Anonymously generated information played a key role in the PizzaGate claims. It can be quite difficult to know who is behind a conspiracy theory and why it is being put forth.

The second point of the argument that conspiracism threatens democracy has two variants of its own: that conspiracism is cultlike to the point of being antidemocratic and that conspiracism is a bridge to authoritarianism. The first variant is less common and is often made implicitly, but the interaction between cultish and conspiracist thinking was noted in the wake of the failure of Y2K end-of-the-world predictions. Evangelical Y2K conspiracists maintained their beliefs with two "mutually supportive discourses"—both Manichean and apocalyptic: "A fundamentalist dispensationalism that interprets all world events as part of a grand narrative culminating in the Second Coming of Christ, and an entrenched conspiracism that regards the current political system as both hopelessly corrupt and a pawn in the hands of the powerbrokers of the New World Order. When Y2K failed to usher in the Antichrist, the discourse shifted from dispensationalism to conspiracism."[41] After the similar Mayan calendar doomsday narrative of 2012, the same connection was noted, this time between New Age apocalyptic and conspiratorial "milieus." And at least one assessment of the Tsarnaev brothers, who carried out the Boston Marathon bombing, implicitly painted them as cultists in their conspiracism.[42] Above all else, however, the election of Donald Trump has generated depictions of him as, in effect, the leader of a conspiracist cult of "white grievance."[43] The cultish interpretation of conspiracism intensifies the in-group versus out-group dynamics along with the bigotry and scapegoating that accompany them. In addition, political intransigence and a Manichean outlook are presumably intensified. But in the end, cults do not seem to add much to our understanding of apocalyptic conspiracy theories. We may be saying nothing more here than that cults are inherently conspiratorial.

Conspiracism as a bridge to authoritarianism, which is by definition a threat to democracy, is a more substantive point but often an ambivalent one. Authoritarians appear to use conspiracy theories for their propaganda value, even if they do not personally believe those theories. Vladimir Putin casts the West as the villain in the Russian version of the hidden hand conspiracy. Some analysts think he does so cynically, even if the Russian military and security services accept the idea.[44] In 2016, Sir Richard Evans summed up three-and-a-half-years' worth of interdisciplinary work at Cambridge's Conspiracy and Democracy Project in this curiously ambivalent fashion: "It's not a case of conspiracy theories threatening democracy, whatever else it might be. By themselves, such theories may reinforce political suspicion and prejudice but they're not the origin of it. So: they can in some circumstances be something of a threat to democracy, but on the whole, I think it's fair to conclude that the scale of the threat is fairly limited."[45] Some make a more forceful case that conspiracism is related to authoritarianism and thus to the threat authoritarianism poses to democracy. Again, the election of Donald Trump has brought the issue to the foreground, but analytically Trump constitutes a confounding variable. If Trump tapped into and activated an authoritarian impulse that he continues to act on, then he constitutes a threat to democracy and so does the underlying impulse. Trump is also a notorious conspiracist, as are many of his followers. But: did the conspiracism help generate or activate the authoritarianism? And, if it did, was conspiracism *necessary* for generating authoritarianism? In other words, would bigotry and xenophobia and misogyny have been sufficient to "activate the base" of Trump supporters without conspiracism? Those who see conspiracism as a bridge to authoritarianism answer the first questions positively. They see conspiracism as playing a vital role—intensifying and hardening the bigotry in a way that supports authoritarian politics.

The starting point for this argument is new research into an "authoritarian dynamic" of intolerance (INTOLERANCE = AUTHORITARIANISM × THREAT), by which "social conservatism" is actually authoritarianism—a "functional predisposition" that can be activated by a "normative threat."[46] Researchers found that actual threats to people's well-being such as terrorism have the capacity to evoke authoritarian behavior in people whether or not they had a functional predisposition to authoritarianism. But they also found that social changes perceived as threatening would activate authoritarianism in those with a predisposition to it but have no impact on others. And while social changes can seem threatening on their own, conspiracy theories have always been tailor-made to make them seem so. This leads to the conclusion that conspiracy theories, if not vital to the rise of overt authoritarianism, are certainly an ideal vehicle to that end.[47]

One can easily see the same dynamic, with conspiracism at its core, in the rise and radicalization of the Christian patriots in the late twentieth century. Equally obvious was the expansion of this dynamic into the political mainstream with the election of Barack Obama, a president who faced an unprecedented level of conspiracy theories. The rise of the Tea Party introduced Cleon Skousen's "fundamentalist vision of the Constitution," which served as a means of "channeling nationalistic and authoritarian impulses."[48] Adam Gopnik made the current argument during the 2016 presidential campaign, telling readers that the details of Trump's latest conspiracy theory did not really matter. "What should hold our attention," Gopnik said, is Trump's "mainstreaming of conspiracy theories, and the hate speech that usually accompanies them. All fascism takes on a peculiar national tone, and where the national tone of Germany lent itself to anti-Semitic theories, that of the United States involves paranoia about secret government actions, of the kind that the radio host and Trump partisan Alex Jones engages in so much."[49]

While all these links are hard to prove, a consensus appears to be developing around the danger of conspiracism to a democratic civic culture. The psychological literature, perhaps even more so than a few years ago, reflects the view of most researchers that conspiracist ideation is not "harmless fun" but carries serious social consequences. Researchers studying the effects of social media—the filter bubbles and siloed communities—are especially concerned. The scientific community has begun to band together as the various conspiratorial attacks on different areas of science threaten to cohere under Donald Trump into "an authoritarian tendency to base policy arguments on questionable assertions of fact and a cult of personality."[50] Those on the Left find "conspiracism—and the racism it builds on . . . the greatest long-term threat that we need to tackle," a right-wing populism that carries with it "the implied threat of an armed political culture."[51]

At present, conspiratorial thinking, its increasing de facto linkage to right-wing and authoritarian politics, and the conspiracy-friendly imperatives of web-based communications have all combined in American politics to create a situation many people find extremely ominous. At the same time, no one wants to circumscribe free speech or have an authority designate which ideas are reasonable and which are conspiracist nonsense. It may be comforting to think that the situation will resolve itself or that a shift in political beliefs will undo it. But the evidence suggests otherwise.

ACKNOWLEDGMENTS

I would like to thank the University of Chicago Press for being the type of institution that still accepts tangible mail and that is willing to take a chance on an essentially random retired professor with a plausible manuscript. I have worked with four people there, each helpful, friendly, and remarkably patient. In particular: executive editor Tim Mennel, editorial associate Rachel Kelly Unger, senior manuscript editor Yvonne Zipter, and promotions manager Tyler McGaughey. There must be others who deserve my thanks, but I do not know their names. It has been a pleasure. Thanks.

NOTES

Introduction

1   Such terms as "worldview" and "belief system" are used interchangeably. For example, Michael J. Wood and Karen M. Douglas use "worldview" in their title and then switch to "belief system" in "Online Communication as a Window to Conspiracist Worldviews," *Frontiers in Psychology*, vol. 6, article 836 (2015). See also Nigel James, "Militias, the Patriot Movement, and the Internet: The Ideology of Conspiracism," *Sociological Review* 48, no. 2 (2001): 64–92; Élise Hendrick, "Conspiracism: A (Further) Definition," *Meldungen aus dem Exil* (blog), July 21, 2015, https://meldungen-aus-dem-exil.noblogs.org/post/2015 /07/21/conspiracism-a-further-definition/; Roland Imhoff and Martin Bruder, "Speaking (Un-)Truth to Power: Conspiracy Mentality as a Generalised Political Attitude," *European Journal of Personality* 28, no. 1 (2014): 25–43.

2   Quotations: Victoria Jackson, "I Found Agenda 21 in Lynchburg, VA!," April 1, 2014, http://victoriajackson.com/10914/found-agenda-21-lynchburg-va (accessed April 8, 2014; no longer available at that site); and Southern Poverty Law Center, "The Players: Anti-Agenda 21 Activists," in *Agenda 21* (SPLC, 2014), 15.

3   Bar codes: Art Kohl, "The Beast (666) Is Coming," Faith Bible Baptist Church, accessed May 11, 2018, http://www.fbbc.com/messages/beast.htm. Chemtrails: Jonathan Vankin and John Whalen, *The World's Greatest Conspiracies* (Citadel Press, 2010), 14.

4   Richard Hofstadter, "The Paranoid Style in America Politics," in *The Paranoid Style in American Politics and Other Essays* (Alfred A. Knopf, 1965), 29.

5   For an overview of definitional efforts, see Brian L. Keeley, "Of Conspiracy Theories," *Journal of Philosophy* 96, no. 3 (1999): 109–26; Lee Basham, "Living with the Conspiracy," *Philosophical Forum* 32, no. 3 (2001): 265–80, and "Malevolent Global Conspiracy," *Journal of Social Philosophy* 34, no. 1 (2003): 91–103; Steve Clarke, "Conspiracy Theories and Conspiracy Theorizing," *Philosophy of the Social Sciences* 32, no. 2 (2002): 131–50; Brian Keeley, "*Nobody* Expects the Spanish Inquisition! More Thoughts on Conspiracy Theory," *Journal of Social Philosophy* 34, no. 1 (2003): 104–10; Charles R. Pigden, "Conspiracy Theories and the Conventional Wisdom," *Episteme* 4, no. 2 (2007): 219–32; Pete Mandik, "Shit Happens," *Episteme* 4, no. 2 (2007): 205–18; David Coady, "Introduction: Conspiracy Theories," *Episteme* 4, no. 2 (2007): 131–34.

6   Ted Goertzel, "Belief in Conspiracy Theories," *Political Psychology* 15 (1994): 733–44, and "The Conspiracy Meme," *Skeptical Inquirer*, vol. 35, no. 1 (January–February 2011). See also Juha Räikkä, "On Political Conspiracy Theories," *Journal of Political Philosophy* 17, no. 2 (2009): 185–201; and Robert A. Goldberg, "Enemies Within: The Conspiracy Culture of Modern America," John O'Sullivan Memorial Lecture, Department of History, Florida Atlantic University, 2010, http://www.fau.edu/artsandletters/osullivan/images/robert-a-goldberg -booklet.pdf.

7   Sharon Parsons et al., "A Test of the Grapevine: An Empirical Examination of Conspiracy Theories among African-Americans," *Sociological Spectrum* 19, no. 2 (1999): 201–22, quote on 201; Tom Jensen, "Democrats and Republicans Differ on Conspiracy Theory Beliefs," press release, Public Policy Polling, April 2, 2013, https://www.publicpolicypolling.com/polls/democrats-and-republicans -differ-on-conspiracy-theory-beliefs/.

8   For criticism, see Christopher Thresher-Andrews, "21% of US Voters Believe Obama Is the Anti-Christ: The Problem with Conspiracy Polling," Psychology of Conspiracy Theories, May 8, 2013, https://conspiracypsychology.com/2013 /05/08/21-of-us-voters-believe-obama-is-the-anti-christ-the-problem-with -conspiracy-polling/comment-page-1/; and Jesse Walker, "It's All a Conspiracy: The Limitations of Research into Paranoia and Conspiracy Theories," *Slate*, May 20, 2014, http://www.slate.com/articles/technology/future_tense /2014/05/conspiracy_theory_research_can_t_be_believed.html. For improvements, see Robert Brotherton, Christopher C. French, and Alan D. Pickering, "Measuring Belief in Conspiracy Theories: The Generic Conspiracist Beliefs Scale," *Frontiers in Psychology*, vol. 4, article 289 (2013); and Martin Bruder et al., "Measuring Individual Differences in Conspiracy Theories across Cultures: Conspiracy Mentality Questionnaire," *Frontiers in Psychology*, vol. 4, article 225 (2013).

9   Presidential Debate News, "GOP Conspiracy Says Efforts to Open Debates a Ploy to Elect Democrats," *IVN*, ,September 9, 2015, https://ivn.us/2015 /09/09/gop-conspiracy-says-efforts-open-debates-ploy-elect-democrats/; David Corn, "Ben Carson and the Satanic Sabbath Persecution Conspiracy," *Mother Jones*, October 2, 2015, https://www.motherjones.com/politics/2015 /10/ben-carson-sabbath-persecution-satan-conspiracy/; Brian Tashman, "58 Donald Trump Conspiracy Theories (and Counting!): The Definitive Trump

Conspiracy Guide," *AlterNet*, May 3, 2016, https://www.alternet.org/right
-wing/58-donald-trump-conspiracy-theories-and-counting-definitive-trump
-conspiracy-guide.

10   Jesse Walker, "What I Saw at the Conspiracy Theory Conference," *Hit & Run*
      (blog), *Reason*, [reason.com] March 15, 2013, http://reason.com/blog/2015/03
      /18/what-i-saw-at-the-conspiracy-theory-conf.

11   David Aaronovich, *Voodoo Histories: How Conspiracy Theory Has Shaped
      Modern History* (Riverhead Books, 2010), 5; Karen M. Douglas and Robbie M.
      Sutton, "Does It Take One to Know One? Endorsement of Conspiracy Theories
      Is Influenced by Personal Willingness to Conspire," *British Journal of Social
      Psychology* 50 (2011): 544–52, quote on 544.

12   False beliefs: David Barron et al., "Associations between Schizotypy and
      Conspiracist Ideation," *Personality and Individual Differences* 70 (2014):
      156–59. Pseudoscience: Maarten Boudry and Johan Braeckman, "Immunizing
      Strategies and Epistemic Defense Mechanisms," *Philosophia* 39, no. 1 (2011):
      145–61. See also Massimo Pigliucci, *Nonsense on Stilts* (University of Chicago
      Press, 2010); and Ben Goldacre, *Bad Science* (Fourth Estate, 2009). On crippled
      epistemology, see Robert Brotherton and Silan Eser, "Bored to Fears: Boredom
      Proneness, Paranoia, and Conspiracy Theories," *Personality and Individual Dif-
      ferences* 80 (2015): 1–5; Michiel Van Elk, "Perceptual Biases in Relation to Para-
      normal and Conspiracy Beliefs," *PLoS ONE*, vol. 10, no. 6 (2015); Cass Sunstein
      and Adrian Vermeule, "Conspiracy Theories: Causes and Cures," *Journal of
      Political Philosophy* 17, no. 2 (2009): 202–27. Nihilistic: Alex Seitz-Wald, "Why
      People Believe in Conspiracy Theories," *Salon*, April 26, 2013, https://www
      .salon.com/2013/04/24/why_people_believe_in_conspiracy_theories/. Magical
      thinking: Eric J. Oliver and Thomas J. Wood, "Conspiracy Theories, Magical
      Thinking, and the Paranoid Style(s) of Mass Communication" (Working Paper
      Series, University of Chicago Department of Political Science, June 2012).

13   Charles R. Pigden, "Popper Revisited, or What Is Wrong with Conspiracy The-
      ories?," *Philosophy of the Social Sciences* 25, no. 1 (1995): 3–34; Jaron Harambam
      and Stef Aupers, "Contesting Epistemic Authority: On the Boundaries of Sci-
      ence," *Public Understanding of Science* 24, no. 4 (2015): 466–80.

14   Karl Popper, *The Open Society and Its Enemies*, 5th ed. (Princeton University
      Press, 1966), 2:95. On the religious parallel, see Brian Bennett, "Hermetic
      Histories: Divine Providence and Conspiracy Theory," *Numen* 54, no. 2 (2007):
      174–209. There are many instances of the term's being used pejoratively much
      earlier than Popper. See P. W. Slosson, "The Conspiracy Superstition," *Unpopu-
      lar Review* (April 1917), 395–407.

15   Keeley, "Of Conspiracy Theories"; Clarke, "Conspiracy Theories"; Neil Dag-
      nall et al., "Conspiracy Theory and Cognitive Style: A Worldview," *Frontiers in
      Psychology*, vol. 6, article 206 (2015).

16   See Justin P. Friesen, Troy H. Campbell, and Aaron C. Kay, "The Psychological
      Advantage of Unfalsifiability and the Appeal of Untestable Religious and Political
      Ideologies," *Journal of Personality and Social Psychology* 108, no. 3 (2014): 515–29.

17   Hannah Darwin, Nick Neaves, and Joni Holmes, "Belief in Conspiracy Theo-
      ries: The Role of Paranormal Belief, Paranoid Ideation, and Schizotypy," *Per-*

sonality and Individual Differences 50 (2011): 1289–93; Jan van der Temple and James E. Alcock, "Relationships between Conspiracy Mentality, Hyperactive Agency Detection, and Schizotypy: Supernatural Forces at Work?" *Personality and Individual Differences* 82 (2015): 136–41; Scott Radnitz and Patrick Underwood, "Is Belief in Conspiracy Theories Pathological? A Survey Experiment on the Roots of Extreme Suspicion," *British Journal of Political Science* 47, no. 1 (2015): 113–29.

18   Quoted segments in order: Rick Pimentel, "Conspiracy Theory," *Philosophy News*, March 17, 2012, http://www.philosophynews.com/post/2012/03/17/Conspiracy-Theory.aspx; Floyd Rudmin, "Conspiracy Theory as Naive Deconstructive History," New Democracy World, April 2003, 3, http://www.newdemocracyworld.org/old/conspiracy.htm; Rebecca Moore, "Reconstructing Reality: Conspiracy Theories about Jonestown," *Journal of Popular Culture* 36, no. 2 (2002): 201; Harambam and Aupers, "Contesting Epistemic Authority," 3. According to one George Washington, the CIA created the term "conspiracy theorists" to discredit its critics ("In 1967, the CIA Created the Label 'Conspiracy Theorists' . . . to Attack Anyone Who Challenges the 'Official' Narrative," February 23, 2015, https://www.zerohedge.com/news/2015-02-23/1967-the-cia-created-phrase-conspiracy-theorists-and-ways-attack-anyone-who-challenge)—debunked in: Robert Blaskiewicz, "Nope, It Was Always Already Wrong," *Skeptical Inquirer* (August 8, 2013), https://www.csicop.org/specialarticles/show/nope_it_was_always_already_wrong.

19   Ginna Husting, "Once More with Feeling: Conspiracy Theories, Contempt, and Affective Governmentality," Metabunk.org, May 13, 2015, https://www.metabunk.org/attachments/once_more_with_feeling-_conspiracy_theories_contempt_and_affective_governmentality-pdf.4957/, 5; Jack Z. Bratich, *Conspiracy Panics: Political Rationality and Popular Culture* (SUNY Press, 2008).

20   Lance deHaven-Smith, *Conspiracy Theory in America* (University of Texas Press, 2013). See also Mathijs Pelkmans and Rhys Machold, "Conspiracy Theories and Their Truth Trajectories," *Focaal—Journal of Global and Historical Anthropology* 59 (2011): 66–80.

21   Lee Basham and Matthew R. X. Dentith, "Social Science's Conspiracy-Theory Panic: Now They Want to Cure Everyone," *Social Epistemology Review and Reply Collective* 5, no. 10 (2016): 12–19, quote on 13.

22   Jaron Harambam and Stef Aupers, "'I Am Not a Conspiracy Theorist': Relational Identifications in the Dutch Conspiracy Milieu," *Cultural Sociology* 11, no. 1 (2016): 113–29; Moore, "Reconstructing Reality"; Ted Goertzel, "Conspiracy Theories in Science," *EMBO Reports* 11, no. 7 (2010): 493–99; Antonis Sapountzis and Susan Condor, "Conspiracy Accounts as Intergroup Theories: Challenging Dominant Understandings of Social Power and Political Legitimacy," *Political Psychology* 34, no. 5 (2013): 731–52; Kevin Loria, "Conspiracy Theorists See Themselves as Critical Thinkers—Here's Why," *Business Insider*, October 11, 2016, http://www.businessinsider.com/conspiracy-theorists-critical-freethinkers-sheeple-2016-10. Citizen journalists in: Bratich, *Conspiracy Panics*, 208. See also "Deniers Are Not Skeptics," petition to news organi-

zations organized through *Skeptical Inquirer* (October 26, 2015), https://www
.csicop.org/news/show/deniers_are_not_skeptics.

23 Mark Lane-Galileo comparison in Rudmin, "Conspiracy Theory," 3. See also
    Robin Ramsay, "Of Conspiracies and Conspiracy Theories: The Truth Buried
    by the Fantasies," talk given at Unconvention '96, Institute of Education,
    London, now published as *Political Notes*, no. 128, April 20, 1996, http://www
    .serendipity.li/eden/laconspi.html.

24 See, as a random example, Jonathan Elinoff, "33 Conspiracy Theories That
    Turned Out to Be True, What Every Person Should Know . . . ," Infowars, Jan-
    uary 6, 2010, https://www.infowars.com/33-conspiracy-theories-that-turned
    -out-to-be-true-what-every-person-should-know/.

25 Witch panics: Wood and Douglas, "Online Communication." Holocaust:
    Räikkä, "On Political Conspiracy Theories." Quoted segments in order:
    Moore, "Reconstructing Reality"; Pigden, "Popper Revisited"; Keeley, "Of
    Conspiracy Theories." On "epistemically warranted" ideas, see Matthew R. X.
    Dentith, "When Inferring to a Conspiracy Might Be the Best Explanation,"
    Social Epistemology 30, nos. 5–6 (2016): 572–91. See also Dagnall et al., "Con-
    spiracy Theory and Cognitive Style"; and Joel Bunting and Jason Taylor, "Con-
    spiracy Theories and Fortuitous Data," *Philosophy of the Social Sciences* 40, no. 3
    (2010): 567–78.

26 Ordinary people: Radnitz and Underwood, "Is Belief in Conspiracy Theories
    Pathological?" See also Rob Brotherton, "We're All Conspiracy Theorists,"
    Utne Reader, June 2016, https://www.utne.com/science-and-technology/were
    -all-conspiracy-theorists-zeoz1606zfis. Quotation from Räikkä, "On Political
    Conspiracy Theories," 187.

27 See James A. Patterson, "Changing Images of the Beast: Apocalyptic Conspir-
    acy Theories in American History," *Journal of the Evangelical Theological Society*
    31, no. 4 (1988): 443–52; David Lobb, "Fascist Apocalypse: William Pelley
    and Millennial Extremism" (paper presented at the conference of the Center
    for Millennial Studies, November 1999), now published in *Journal of Millen-
    nial Studies*, vol. 2, no. 2 (Winter 2000), http://www.mille.org/publications
    /winter2000/lobb.PDF; Matthew A. Sutton, "Was FDR the Antichrist? The
    Birth of Fundamentalist Antiliberalism in a Global Age," *Journal of American
    History* 98, no. 4 (2012): 1052–74.

28 Noam Gidron and Bart Bonikowski, "Varieties of Populism: Literature Review
    and Research Agenda" (Weatherhead Working Paper Series no. 13-0004,
    Harvard University, 2013, https://scholar.harvard.edu/gidron/publications
    /varieties-populism-literature-review-and-research-agenda). Disloyal: Rafael
    Di Tella and Julio J. Rotemberg, "Populism and the Return of the 'Paranoid
    Style': Some Evidence and a Simple Model of Demand for Incompetence as
    Insurance against Elite Betrayal" (NBER Working Paper No. 22975, December
    2016, http://www.nber.org/papers/w22975). Steven Van Hauwaert, "Shared
    Dualisms: On Populism and Conspiracy Theory," Counterpoint, accessed
    May 15, 2018, http://counterpoint.uk.com/shared-dualisms-on-populism-and
    -conspiracy-theory/; Betty A. Dobratz and Lisa K. Waldner, "The White Power

Movement's Populist Connection to the Tea Party Movement in the United States," *Athens Journal of Social Sciences* 3, no. 3 (2016): 181–93.

29 Basham, "Malevolent Global Conspiracy." Christopher Thresher-Andrews, "An Introduction into the World of Conspiracy," in "The Psychology of Conspiracy Theories," special issue of *PsyPAG Quarterly*, no. 88 (September 2013), 5–8; Oliver and Wood, "Conspiracy Theories." Malevolent collusion: Dagnall et al., "Conspiracy Theory and Cognitive Style." Secret machinations: Sunstein and Vermeule, "Conspiracy Theories: Causes and Cures."

30 Viren Swami and Rebecca Coles, "The Truth Is Out There," *Psychologist* 23, no. 7 (2010): 560–63. "Preternaturally effective" comes from Richard Hofstadter's "The Paranoid Style in American Politics" to describe the populists' view of the bankers and politicians who conspired to maintain the gold standard, not as a general definition of conspiracism.

31 Three prominent conspiracists selected at random: William Guy Carr, *Pawns in the Game* (National Federation of Christian Laymen, 1954); William L. Pierce, "The Trouble with People," November 7, 1976, available at http://www.the-savoisien.com/blog/index.php?post/The-trouble-with-people-William-L.-Pierce; Gordon (Jack) Mohr, "America—Wake Up!!" archived at https://israelect.com/reference/JackMohr/jm070.htm (accessed May 15, 2018).

32 Richard Hofstadter, "The Pseudo-Conservative Revolt—1954," in *The Paranoid Style*, 44–45.

33 Thomas F. Pettigrew, "Social Psychological Perspectives on Trump Supporters," *Journal of Social and Political Psychology* 5, no. 1 (2017): 107–16.

34 Matt A. Barreto et al., "The Tea Party in the Age of Obama: Mainstream Conservatism or Outgroup Anxiety?" *Political Power and Social Theory* 22 (2011): 1–29. Marc Hetherington and Elizabeth Suhay, "Authoritarianism, Threat, and Americans' Support for the War on Terror," *American Journal of Political Science* 55, no. 3 (2011): 546–60. See also Radnitz and Underwood, "Is Belief in Conspiracy Theories Pathological?"; Evan Osnos, "The Fearful and the Frustrated," *New Yorker*, August 31, 2015, 50–59; Amanda Taub, "The Rise of American Authoritarianism," Vox, March 1, 2016, https://www.vox.com/2016/3/1/11127424/trump-authoritarianism. Hofstadter credits the term "pseudo-conservative" to Theodore Adorno's *The Authoritarian Personality*.

35 Brian Bennett, "Hermetic Histories," 174; Daniel Jolley and Karen M. Douglas, "The Social Consequences of Conspiracism: Exposure to Conspiracy Theories Decreases Intention to Engage in Politics and to Reduce One's Carbon Footprint," *British Journal of Psychology* 105 (2014), 25.

36 Counter-discourse: Sapountzis and Condor, "Conspiracy Accounts," 732. Epistemic authorities: Brotherton and Eser, "Bored to Fears," 1. Conspiracy meme: Goertzel, "The Conspiracy Meme," 1. See also Philippe Huneman, "The True Cost of Conspiracy Theories," openDemocracy, December 17, 2015, https://www.opendemocracy.net/conspiracy/suspect-science/philippe-huneman/true-cost-of-conspiracy-theories; Alessandro Bessi et al., "Trend of Narratives in an Age of Misinformation," *PLoS ONE*, vol. 10, no. 8 (2015); Włodislaw Duch, "Memetics and Neural Models of Conspiracy Theories," arXiv.org, August 19, 2015, https://arxiv.org/abs/1508.04561.

37   See, e.g., the film *Loose Change*, written and directed by Dylan Avery, originally produced in 2005. See also "Debunking 9/11 Conspiracy Theories,"
PopularTechnology.net, September 11, 2011, http://www.populartechnology
.net/2009/06/debunking-911-conspiracy-theories.html. Zionist new world
order versions: Gordon (Jack) Mohr, "Israel Is at War and Losing!" *Winter
Intelligence Report*, 2001; Eustace Mullins, "The Secret of 9/11: The Drumbeat
for War," *Spectrum* 4, no. 5 (2002): 68; Zander C. Fuerza, *Masters of Deception—
Zionism, 9/11 and the War on Terror Hoax* (self-pub., 2013), available at Zionist
Report, January 30, 2016, https://zionistreport.com/2016/01/ebook-masters-of
-deception-zionism-911-and-the-war-on-terror-hoax/.

Chapter One

1   Nesta H. Webster, *Secret Societies and Subversive Movements* (Boswell Publishing, 1924), 1.
2   Gordon S. Wood, "Conspiracy and the Paranoid Style: Causality and Deceit in
the Eighteenth Century," *William and Mary Quarterly* 39, no. 3 (1982): 401–41,
quote on 410.
3   Ibid., 407.
4   Keith Thomas, "Just Say Yes," review of *Inventing the People: The Rise of Popular
Sovereignty in England and America* by Edmund S. Morgan, *New York Review of
Books*, November 24, 1988.
5   Wood, "Conspiracy and the Paranoid Style," 410.
6   Ira D. Gruber, "The American Revolution as Conspiracy: The British View,"
William and Mary Quarterly 26 (1969): 360–72, quote on 368. Secret emissaries: J. L. Bell, "Conspiracy Theories of the Revolution," *Boston 1775* (blog),
July 16, 2006, http://boston1775.blogspot.com/2006/07/conspiracy-theories-of
-revolution.html.
7   Selfish factions: David Brion Davis, introduction to "Ideological Responses
to the French Revolution (1795–1802)," pt. 3 of *The Fear of Conspiracy: Images
of Un-American Subversion from the Revolution to the Present*, ed. David Brion
Davis (Cornell University Press, 1971), 35. Coterie: Gruber, "American Revolution," 360. See also Ed White, "The Value of Conspiracy Theory," *American
Literary History* 14, no. 1 (2002): 1–31; and Gordon S. Wood, "Rhetoric and
Reality in the American Revolution," *William and Mary Quarterly* 23, no. 1
(1966): 3–32.
8   See Bernard Bailyn, "A Note on Conspiracy," in *The Ideological Origins of the
American Revolution* (Belknap Press of Harvard University Press, 1967),
148–58.
9   Wood, "Conspiracy and the Paranoid Style," 431–32.
10   "The French Revolution and the Bavarian Illuminati," Grand Lodge of British
Columbia and Yukon, 2002, http://freemasonry.bcy.ca/texts/robison-barruel
.html#2.
11   Mike Jay, "Darkness over All: John Robison and the Birth of the Illuminati Conspiracy Theory," MikeJay.net, 2015, https://mikejay.net/darkness-over-all/, 6–7.

12   Seth Payson, *Proofs of the Real Existence, and Dangerous Tendency, of Illuminism* (Samuel Etheridge, 1802), 6. Payson's defense of Robison's mental condition is repeated in Webster, *Secret Societies*, 3–8.

13   Vernon Stauffer, "New England and the Bavarian Illuminati," Ph.D. diss., Columbia University, 1919, 202.

14   Jay, "Darkness over All," 10. Barruel's criticism can be found in "The French Revolution and the Bavarian Illuminati."

15   See "Roots of Twentieth Century Conspiracy Theory," Grand Lodge of British Columbia and Yukon, 2009, http://freemasonry.bcy.ca/anti-masonry /mythology_secret.html. See also "The French Revolution and the Bavarian Illuminati"; John M. Roberts, *The Mythology of Secret Societies* (Charles Scribner's Sons, 1973); and Adam Zamoyski, *Phantom Terror* (Basic Books, 2015), chap. 2. Barruel's book is titled *Memoirs Illustrating the History of Jacobinism* (London: Printed for the translator by T. Burton, No. 11 Gate Street, Lincoln's-Inn Fields, 1798).

16   Walter Edwin Peck, "Shelley and the Abbé Barruel," *PMLA* 36, no. 3 (1921): 347–53, quote on 348.

17   Jay, "Darkness over All," 7.

18   Paul Simpson, *That's What They Want You to Think: Conspiracies, Real, Possible, and Paranoid* (Zenith Press, 1973), 210; S. R. Shearer, "The Origins of the Illuminist Myth: The Fabrication of the Protocols of the Learned Elders of Zion," AntipasMinistries, accessed May 15, 2018, http://www.antipasministries.com /html/file0000130.htm.

19   Serge Moscovici, "The Conspiracy Mentality" (theatrical performance), and Dieter Groh, "The Temptation of Conspiracy Theory (Part 1)" (oversimplifying construct)—both in *Changing Conceptions of Conspiracism*, ed. Carl F. Graumann and Serge Moscovici (Springer-Verlag, 1987), 154 and 11, respectively.

20   Michael Shermer and Pat Linse, "Conspiracy Theories," *Skeptic*, 2015, https:// www.skeptic.com/downloads/conspiracy-theories-who-why-and-how.pdf. See also Karen M. Douglas et al., "Someone Is Pulling the Strings: Hypersensitive Agency Detection and Belief in Conspiracy Theories," *Thinking and Reasoning* 22, no. 1 (2016): 57–77.

21   Katy Waldman, "It's All Connected," *Slate*, September 16, 2014, http://www .slate.com/articles/health_and_science/science/2014/09/apophenia_makes _unrelated_things_seem_connected_metaphors_paranormal_beliefs.html.

22   James Perloff, "About James Perloff," JamesPerloff.com, accessed May 15, 2018, https://jamesperloff.com/about-james-perloff/; Gary L. Wean, "The Anatomy of a Conspiracy of Race Riots and Revolution," *Contact*, August 19, 1994, 1.

23   Gerald Burton Winrod, *The Hidden Hand—the Protocols and the Coming Superman* (Defender Publications, 1933), 11.

24   Arie W. Kruglanski, "Blame-Placing Schemata and Attributional Research," in *Changing Conceptions of Conspiracism*, ed. Graumann and Moscovici, 219–30.

25   Jennifer A. Whitson and Adam D. Galinsky, "Lacking Control Increases Illusory Pattern Perception," *Science* 322 (2008): 115–17; Michiel Van Elk, "Perceptual Biases in Relation to Paranormal and Conspiracy Beliefs," *PLoS ONE*, vol. 10, no. 6 (2015); Richard Landes, "The Jews as Contested Ground in Post-

modern Conspiracy Theory," *Jewish Political Studies Review* 19, nos. 3–4 (Fall 2007): 2.

26   Robert Brotherton and Christopher C. French, "Belief in Conspiracy Theory and Susceptibility to the Conjunction Fallacy," *Applied Cognitive Psychology* 28 (2014): 238–48; Jennifer Whitson, Adam Galinsky, and Aaron Kay, "The Emotional Roots of Conspiratorial Perceptions, System Justification, and Belief in the Paranormal," *Journal of Experimental Social Psychology* 56 (2015): 89–95; Raluca Petrican and Christopher T. Burris, "Am I the Stone? Overattribution of Agency and Religious Orientation," *Psychology of Religion and Spirituality* 4, no. 4 (2012): 312–23; Jan van der Temple and James E. Alcock, "Relationships between Conspiracy Mentality, Hyperactive Agency Detection, and Schizotypy: Supernatural Forces at Work?" *Journal of Personality and Individual Differences* 82 (2015): 136–41; Annika Svedholm, Marjaana Lindeman, and Jari Lipsanen, "Believing in the Purpose of Events—Why Does It Occur, and Is It Supernatural?" *Applied Cognitive Psychology* 24 (2010): 252–65.

27   David Casacuberta, Carolina Figueras, and Roser Martínez, "The R Files: Applying Relevance Model to Conspiracy Theory Fallacies," *Journal of English Studies* 1 (1999): 45–55.

28   Nesta Webster, *World Revolution: The Plot against Civilization* (Small, Maynard & Co., 1921) and *Secret Societies*. See also "Nesta H. Webster's *Secret Societies*," Grand Lodge of British Columbia and Yukon, 2001, http://freemasonry.bcy.ca /anti-masonry/webster_n.html.

29   Ezra Pound, *America, Roosevelt and the Causes of the Present War* (Peter Russell, 1951); published in Italian in Venice, 1944; Wesley Swift, "Crushing the Serpent" (sermon), Dr. Wesley Swift Library at christogenea.org, August 1957, https://swift.christogenea.org/articles/crushing-serpent-8-0-57.

30   Richard Hofstadter, "The Paranoid Style in American Politics," in *The Paranoid Style in American Politics and Other Essays* (Alfred A. Knopf, 1965), 37–38.

31   Martha F. Lee, "Nesta Webster: The Voice of Conspiracy," *Journal of Women's History* 17, no. 3 (2007): 81–104.

32   Jeffrey M. Bale, "Political Paranoia v. Political Realism: On Distinguishing between Bogus Conspiracy Theories and Genuine Conspiratorial Politics," *Patterns of Prejudice* 4, no. 1 (2007): 45–60, quote at 47n4.

33   Groh, "The Temptation of Conspiracy Theory (Part 1)," 11; G. William Domhoff, "C. Wright Mills, Floyd Hunter, and Fifty Years of Power Structure Research," *Michigan Sociological Review* 21 (2007): 1–54. See also G. William Domhoff, "There Are No Conspiracies," Who Rules America? (website), March 2005, https://whorulesamerica.ucsc.edu/theory/conspiracy.html.

34   Volker Heins, "Critical Thinking and the Traps of Conspiracy Thinking," *Philosophy and Social Criticism* 33, no. 7 (2007): 787–801, quote on 791–92.

35   Bale, "Political Paranoia," 51–52; Hofstadter, "The Paranoid Style," 31–32.

36   Oren Potito, "Our Rulers. Who Are They?" *National Christian News* 3, no. 5 (1965): 1.

37   Ernie Lazar, "Nature and Purpose of Political Conspiracy Theories," Ernie Lazar Google Page, August 6, 2011 (rev. December 12, 2017), https://sites .google.com/site/ernie124102/ct-1.

38   Steven R. Goldzwig, "Conspiracy Rhetoric at the Dawn of the New Millennium: A Response," *Western Journal of Communication* 66, no. 4 (2002): 492–506, quote on 493–94.

39   Frank Capell, "The Scope of Soviet Activity in the U.S.," *Herald of Freedom*, January 17, 1964; Ameen Rihani, *The Descent of Bolshevism* (Stratford Co., 1920), 54; Jim Keith, *Saucers of the Illuminati* (IllumiNet Press, 1999), 81.

40   Michael Howard, *The Occult Conspiracy* (Destiny Books, 1989); William Schnoebelen, *The Light behind Masonry* (2006), DVD, and *Masonry: Beyond the Light* (Chick Publications, 1991); Jan Van Helsing, *Secret Societies and Their Power in the 20th Century* (Ewertverlag, 1995).

41   John McManus, "Know Thine Enemy," speech given at the Saint Joseph Forum, South Bend, IN, March 24, 2000, archived at archive.org/details/JohnMcManusKnowThineEnemy032400; Jim Marrs, *The Illuminati: The Secret Society That Hijacked the World* (Visible Ink Press, 2017); Des Griffin, "The Rothschild Dynasty," Bible Believers (website), accessed May 15, 2018, https://www.biblebelievers.org.au/slavery.htm; Terry Melanson, "The All-Seeing Eye, the President, the Secretary and the Guru," Illuminati Conspiracy Archive, July 2001, http://www.conspiracyarchive.com/NWO/All_Seeing_Eye.htm. Melanson claims to be quoting Weishaupt on the new world order.

42   "Freemasonry," n.d., http://www.overlordsofchaos.com/html/freemasonry_.html (this page no longer exists at this site).

43   Eric John Phelps, "Mystery Babylon Religion Based in Rome: Heart and Soul of Jesuit-Authored Illuminized Freemasonry Now Ruling the Nations for the Benefit of the Pope in Rome," Vatican Assassins, July 15, 2010, http://vaticanassassins.org/2010/07/15/mystery-babylon-religion-based-in-rome-heart-and-soul-of-jesuit-authored-illuminized-freemasonry-now-ruling-the-nations-for-the-benefit-of-the-pope-of-rome/; John Buckley, *Prophesy Unveiled* (Xulon Press, 2007).

44   Dieter Groh, "The Temptation of Conspiracy Theory (Part 2)," in *Changing Conceptions of Conspiracism*, ed. Graumann and Moscovici 26–28.

45   Roberts, *Mythology of Secret Societies*, 208.

46   Zamoyski, *Phantom Terror*, 350.

47   P. W. Slosson, "The 'Conspiracy' Superstition," *Unpopular Review* 7, no. 4 (1917): 395–407, quote on 397. See also "Roots of Twentieth Century Conspiracy Theory," Grand Lodge of British Columbia and Yukon, 2009, http://freemasonry.bcy.ca/anti-masonry/mythology_secret.html.

48   Wilson Carey McWilliams, review of *The Mythology of Secret Societies* by J. M. Roberts, *Journal of the American Academy of Religion* 43, no. 2, book review supplement (June 1975): 406–8, quote on 407. See also Slosson, "Conspiracy Superstition"; Roberts, *Mythology of Secret Societies*; "Roots of Twentieth Century Conspiracy Theory."

49   Shearer, "Origins of the Illuminist Myth," 4, 5. See also Norman Cohn, *Warrant for Genocide* (Harper & Row, 1966).

50   Roberts, *Mythology of Secret Societies*. See also Thomas Frost, *The Secret Societies of the European Revolution 1776–1876* (Tinsley Brothers, 1876), 2 vols.

51 A Disraeli example selected at random: Richard Stone, "Who Are the Illuminati?" The Truth Seeker, April 24, 2004, http://www.thetruthseeker.co.uk/?p=
101. The quotation is spoken by a character in Disraeli's 1844 novel *Coningsby;
or, The New Generation*. Henry Makow, "How the Illuminati Rig the Game:
The Dreyfus Affair," Aladdin's Miracle Lamp, March 16, 2016 (reprinted from
September 16, 2009), https://aladinsmiraclelamp.wordpress.com/2016/03/16
/how-the-illuminati-rig-the-game-the-dreyfus-affair/.

52 Tony Bonn, "Did London Banksters Really Threaten America in 1865?," *The
American Chronicle* (blog), September 23, 2012, theamericanchronicle.blogspot
.com/2012/09/did-london-banksters-really-threaten.html; "Federal Reserve
Bank [Inc.] a Murderous History: Banksters, the World's Worst Gangsters," South-
East Asian Water and Power Alliance, March 21, 2014, www.seawapa.co/2014/03
/federal-reserve-bank-inc-murderous.html; Mark Owen, "What You Didn't Know
about John Wilkes Booth and Jesse W. James," Illuminati Conspiracy Archive,
January 19, 2011, http://www.conspiracyarchive.com/Articles/Booth-Jesse-James
.htm. Both men had supposedly faked their own deaths with help from their fellow Knights of the Golden Circle Masons. See also Gyeorgos Ceres Hatonn, *The
Best of Times, the Worst of Times* (Phoenix Source Publishers, 1993), 109–11.

53 Sheikh Nazim, "Illuminati Origins of Wahabism," *My Beliefs* (blog), May 18,
2012, https://mybeliefs.co.uk/2012/05/18/illuminati-origins-of-wahabism/;
David Livingstone, "Ibn Taymiyya, and the Occult Origins of the Salafi Movement," *Conspiracy School* (blog), August 1, 2013, http://www.conspiracyschool
.com/blog/ibn-taymiyya-and-occult-origins-salafi-movement no date.

54 Frost, *Secret Societies*; the Illuminati is covered in chap. 1 of vol. 1.

55 George F. Dillon, *The War of the Antichrist with the Church and Christian Civilization* (M. H. Gill & Sons, 1885), 52–53.

56 John Daniel, *Scarlet and the Beast* (Day Publishing, 2007), 391. See also "A
Peek at 'Satan's Game Plan,' Written by Masons in 1871," Bible Probe message
archives, July 1, 2005, http://bibleprobe.com/archive/messages/46.html.

57 Pike's letter has been featured on websites ranging from Alex Jones's Infowars
to jesus-is-savior.com to the Daily Mail online. For some people, the distinction
between Satan and Lucifer is vitally important.

58 W. R. Jones, "Palladism and the Papacy: An Episode of French Anticlericalism
in the Nineteenth Century," *Journal of Church and State* 12, no. 3 (1970): 453–73.
See also Edmund Frank, "A Hoax," trans. Suzanne D'Aoust, Grand Lodge of
British Columbia and Yukon, 1997, freemasonry.bcy.ca/texts/taxil_confession
.html, reprinted from *l'Illustration*, no. 2827 (May 1, 1897); William Guy Carr,
The Conspiracy to Destroy All Existing Governments and Religions (originally a
pamphlet), 1958 (CPA Publishing, 2000). Carr first laid out the three world
wars conspiracy in *Pawns in the Game* (Federation of Christian Laymen, 1954).

59 Ellic Howe and Helmut Möller, "Theodor Reuss: Irregular Freemasonry in
Germany, 1900–1923," *Ars Quatuor Coronatorum* 91 (1978): 28–46.

60 Thomas Anderson, *Revolution: The Rise against the New World Order* bk. 5 (self-
pub., 2010).

61 Peck, "Shelley and the Abbé Barruel," 348.

Chapter Two

1   Alexander McKenzie-McHarg, "The Transfer of Anti-Illuminati Conspiracy Theories to the United States in the Late Eighteenth Century," Academia.edu, June 26, 2016, https://www.academia.edu/26501331/The_Transfer_of_Anti -Illuminati_Conspiracy_Theories_to_the_United_States_in_the_Late_Eighteenth _Century.

2   Cited in Vernon Stauffer, "New England and the Bavarian Illuminati," Ph.D. diss., Faculty of Political Science, Columbia University, 1918, 227.

3   Gordon S. Wood, "Conspiracy and the Paranoid Style: Causality and Deceit in the Eighteenth Century," *William and Mary Quarterly* 39, no. 3 (1982): 401–41, quote on 443.

4   David Brion Davis, "Some Themes of Countersubversion: An Analysis of Anti-Masonic, Anti-Catholic, and Anti-Mormon Literature," *Mississippi Valley Historical Review* 47, no. 2 (1960): 205–24. See also Michael Butter, *Plots, Designs, and Schemes: American Conspiracy Theories from the Puritans to the Present* (Walter de Gruyter, 2014), 27; Robert A. Goldberg, *Enemies Within* (Yale University Press, 2001), 1, 2.

5   David Osgood, "A Discourse" delivered on Thanksgiving Day, February 19, 1795, excerpted in David Brion Davis, ed., *The Fear of Conspiracy: Images of Un-American Subversion from the Revolution to the Present* (Cornell University Press, 1971), 44.

6   Fisher Ames, "Laocoön" (1799), reprinted in Davis, ed., *The Fear of Conspiracy*, 53. See also Richard Hofstadter, "The Paranoid Style in American Politics," in *The Paranoid Style in American Politics and Other Essays* (Alfred A. Knopf, 1965), 13–14.

7   Jedidiah Morse, "A Sermon, Exhibiting the Present Dangers, and Consequent Duties of the Citizens of the United States of America," delivered on the Day of National Fast, April 25, 1799, excerpted in Davis, ed., *The Fear of Conspiracy*, 47. See also Charles J. G. Griffin, "Jedediah Morse and the Bavarian Illuminati: An Essay in the Rhetoric of Conspiracy," *Central States Speech Journal* 39, nos. 3–4 (1988): 293–303; and Rachel Snell, "Jedidiah Morse and the Crusade for the New Jerusalem," BA thesis, University of Maine, 2006.

8   "From Thomas Jefferson to Bishop James Madison, 31 January 1800," Founders Online, accessed May 16, 2018, https://founders.archives.gov/documents /Jefferson/01-31-02-0297. A Bedlamite refers to an inmate of Bedlam, an English insane asylum.

9   Stauffer, "New England and the Bavarian Illuminati," 11–12n11.

10 Seth Payson, *Proofs of the Real Existence, and Dangerous Tendency, of Illuminism* (printed for the author by Samuel Etheridge, 1802), iii; John Wood, *A Full Exposition of the Clinton Faction and the Society of the Columbian Illuminati* (printed for the author, 1802). Ward's tract (which, even by the standards of its day, has an unconscionably long title) was apparently self-published in New York in 1828.

11 Kate Carté Engel, "Triangulating Religion and the American Revolution through Jedidiah Morse," *Common-Place*, vol. 15, no. 3 (2015), http://www .common-place-archives.org/vol-15/no-03/engel/#.WvxYdqQvzX4.

12   Timothy Dwight's "century sermon" quoted in Stauffer, "New England and the Bavarian Illuminati," 25; Goldberg, *Enemies Within*, 1, 2; Tappan ("A Discourse Delivered in the Chapel of Harvard College," June 19, 1798) quoted in Davis, *The Fear of Conspiracies*, 49.

13   Daniel Sullivan, Mark J. Landau, and Zachary Rothschild, "An Existential Function of Enemyship: Evidence That People Attribute Influence to Personal and Political Enemies to Compensate for Threats of Control," *Journal of Personality and Social Psychology* 98, no. 3 (2010): 434–49; Zachary Rothschild et al., "A Dual-Motive Model of Scapegoating: Displacing Blame to Reduce Guilt or Increase Control," *Journal of Personality and Social Psychology* 102, no. 6 (2012): 1148–63, quote on 1148.

14   Aaron C. Kay et al., "Compensatory Control—Achieving Order through the Mind, Our Institutions, and the Heavens," *Current Directions in Psychological Science* 18, no. 5 (2009): 264–68; Mark J. Landau, Aaron C. Kay, and Jennifer Whitson, "Compensatory Control and the Appeal of a Structured World," *Psychological Bulletin* 141, no. 3 (2015): 694–722; Piercarlo Valdesolo and Jesse Graham, "Awe, Uncertainty, and Agency Detection," *Psychological Science* 25 (2014): 170–78.

15   Paul Goodman, *Towards a Christian Republic* (Oxford University Press, 1988), 5.

16   Butter, *Plots, Designs, and Schemes*; Goodman, *Towards a Christian Republic*, chap. 4; Jeffrey L. Pasley, "Conspiracy Theory and American Exceptionalism from the Revolution to Roswell" (paper presented at a symposium in honor of Bernard Bailyn, Harvard University, May 13, 2000); Hofstadter, "The Paranoid Style," 23.

17   See, throughout, Goldberg, *Enemies Within*; Davis, ed., *The Fear of Conspiracy*; Richard Hofstadter, *Anti-Intellectualism in American Life* (Alfred A. Knopf, 1970).

18   David Brion Davis, "Some Themes of Countersubversion," in *The Fear of Conspiracy*, ed. Davis, 18; John Robison quoted in Hofstadter, "The Paranoid Style," 11. Paranoia and pornography quotation: Arthur Goldwag, *The New Hate* (Pantheon, 2009), 220. See also Goodman, *Towards a Christian Republic*, chap. 5; and Jesse Walker, *The United States of Paranoia* (HarperCollins, 2013).

19   Larry Haapanen, "Anti-Masonic Party," in *Conspiracy Theories in American History: An Encyclopedia*, ed. Peter Knight (ABC-CLIO, 2003), 76.

20   Thurlow Weed, "On the Abduction of Captain Wm. Morgan," notarized affidavit, September 9, 1882, JR's Rare Books and Commentary, accessed May 16, 2018, http://www.jrbooksonline.com/HTML-docs/thurlow_weed.htm (caveat: jrbooks is not wholly reliable). See also Hofstadter, "The Paranoid Style," 14–18.

21   Goodman, *Towards a Christian Republic*, 8.

22   Apocalyptic framework: Hofstadter, "The Paranoid Style," 17. One of the greatest evils: Goodman, *Towards a Christian Republic*, 20. Engine of Satan: David Bernard's *Light on Masonry*, 1829, cited in Hofstadter, "The Paranoid Style," 17. "Address to the People of the United States," *The Proceedings of the United States Anti-Masonic Convention, Held at Philadelphia, September 11, 1830*, Internet Archive, accessed May 16, 2018, archive.org/details /proceedingsunit01hollgoog, 152 (enemies of the human race), 159 (abuses).

23   Surveillance in Goodman, *Towards a Christian Republic*, 8; licentiousness throughout chaps. 4 and 5. Rites and oaths discussed in "Address to the People" and in Hofstadter, "The Paranoid Style," 18.

24 "Jedediah Morse and the Illuminati," Grand Lodge of British Columbia and Yukon, accessed July 10, 2018, freemasonry.bcy.ca/anti-masonry/morse.html.

25 Goldwag, *The New Hate*, chap. 5. See also Walker, *The United States of Paranoia*; and Hofstadter, "The Paranoid Style," 19–23.

26 Samuel Morse, *Foreign Conspiracy against the Liberties of the United States* (Leavitt, Lord & Co., 1835), 62. Morse's chapters had earlier been published as a series of essays by the *New York Observer*.

27 Ibid., 72, 74.

28 Lyman Beecher, *A Plea for the West*, 2d ed. (Truman & Smith, 1835), 131, 54. Levin quoted in John A. Forman, "Lewis Charles Levin: Portrait of an American Demagogue," *American Jewish Archives Journal*, 12, no. 2 (October 1960): 176, http://americanjewisharchives.org/publications/journal/PDF/1960_12_02_00_forman.pdf.

29 Levin quote in Forman, "Lewis Charles Levin," 178. Silent, systematized: Beecher, *A Plea for the West*, 148. Prowling: *New York Protestant Vindicator*, December 24, 1834, quoted in Goldwag, *The New Hate*, 206. Oath: Robert Blaskiewicz, "For Fear of a Jesuit Planet," *Skeptical Inquirer* (April 1, 2013), https://www.csicop.org/specialarticles/show/this_week_in_conspiracy_for_fear_of_a_jesuit_planet.

30 Bo Ekehammar et al., "What Matters Most to Prejudice: Big Five Personality, Social Dominance Orientation, or Right-Wing Authoritarianism?" *European Journal of Personality* 18 (2004): 463–82; Jarret T. Crawford and Jane M. Pilanski, "The Differential Effects of Right-Wing Authoritarianism and Social Dominance Orientation on Political Intolerance," *Political Psychology* 35, no. 4 (2014): 557–76; Marc Hetherington and Elizabeth Suhay, "Authoritarianism, Threat, and Americans' Support for the War on Terror," *American Journal of Political Science* 55, no. 3 (2011): 546–60.

31 Roland Imhoff and Martin Bruder, "Speaking (Un-)Truth to Power: Conspiracy Mentality as a Generalised Political Attitude," *European Journal of Personality* 28, no. 1 (2014): 25–43. See also Amanda Taub, "The Rise of American Authoritarianism," Vox, March 1, 2016, https://www.vox.com/2016/3/1/11127424/trump-authoritarianism; and Monika Grzesiak-Feldman and Monika Irzycka, "Right-Wing Authoritarianism and Conspiracy Thinking in a Polish Sample," *Psychological Reports* 105 (2009): 389–93.

32 On Puritan antipapism, see James Allen Patterson, "Changing Images of the Beast: Apocalyptic Conspiracy Theories in American History," *Journal of the Evangelical Theological Society* 31, no. 4 (1988): 443–52; Samuel F. B. Morse, "A Foreign Conspiracy against the Liberties of the United States," excerpted in Davis, ed., *The Fear of Conspiracy*, 95 and 97; Beecher, *A Plea for the West*, 53.

33 Justin D. Fulton, *Washington in the Lap of Rome* (W. Kellaway, 1888), vii–ix.

34 Ibid., vii. The most prominent organization involved in the spread of this false information was the American Protective Association. See Hofstadter, "The Paranoid Style," 22–23. See also Goldwag, *The New Hate*, 228.

35 David S. Reynolds, "The Slave Owners' Foreign Policy," review of *This Vast Southern Empire: Slaveholders at the Helm of American Foreign Policy* by Matthew Karp, *New York Review of Books*, June 22, 2017, 51; Goldberg, *Enemies Within*, 11.

36 David Brion Davis, *The Slave Power Conspiracy and the Paranoid Style* (Louisiana State University Press), 1969, 85. Aristocracy: Henry O'Reilly, *Origin and Objects of the Slaveholders' Conspiracy* (Baker and Godwin, 1862).

37 George W. Julien, "The Strength and Weakness of the Slave Power," 1852 speech in Cincinnati, excerpted in Davis, ed., *The Fear of Conspiracy*, 122–23; Beverly Tucker, *The Partisan Leader* (Rudd & Carleton, 1861). According to the title page, Tucker's book was written and "secretly printed" in 1836 but then suppressed. Leonard L. Richards, *The Slave Power: The Free North and Southern Domination* (Louisiana State University Press, 2000). See also Goldberg, *Enemies Within*, 9, and Butter, *Plots, Designs, and Schemes*, 29–30.

38 William Goodell, *Slavery and Anti-Slavery*, 1852, excerpted in Davis, ed., *The Fear of Conspiracy*, 111–19; Goldberg, *Enemies Within*, 102–48. See also Goldwag, *The New Hate*, chap. 4; and Walker, *The United States of Paranoia*.

39 John Smith Dye, *History of the Plots and Crimes of the Great Conspiracy to Overthrow Liberty*, quoted in Davis, ed., *The Fear of Conspiracy*, 135. There was no evidence that Presidents William Henry Harrison and Zachary Taylor (the other two presidents) had even been assassinated, nor, for that matter, that they were particularly illustrious. See Joseph Yannielli, "The Assassination of Zachary Taylor," Digital Histories at Yale, November 22, 2013, http://digitalhistories.yctl .org/2013/11/22/the-assassination-of-zachary-taylor/.

40 Goldwag, *The New Hate*, 180; "Debates at the Anti-Masonic Convention (1830)," excerpted in Davis, ed., *The Fear of Conspiracy*, 180–81.

41 Cabal: Kay, *Among the Truthers*, 33. Greatest crime: William H. Harvey, *A Tale of Two Nations* (1894), quoted in Richard Hofstadter, "Free Silver and the Mind of 'Coin' Harvey," in *The Paranoid Style*, 295.

42 Martin Walbert, *The Coming Battle* (W. B. Conkey, 1899).

43 E. J. Farmer, *The Conspiracy against Silver in the United States*, 1886, excepted in Davis, ed., *The Fear of Conspiracy*, 188–89. Bondholders' conspiracy: Hofstadter, "Free Silver," 257.

44 A. J. Warner, speech at the Second National Silver Convention, 1892, excerpted in "The British Plot to Enslave the World," in *The Fear of Conspiracy*, ed. Davis, 193.

45 Manifesto: Hofstadter, "The Paranoid Style," 8. H. C. Baldwin, speech at the Second National Silver Convention, 1892, excerpted in "The British Plot to Enslave the World," in *The Fear of Conspiracy*, ed. Davis, 194.

46 Money power: Gordon Clark, "Shylock as Banker and Conspirator," excerpted in Davis, ed., *The Fear of Conspiracy*, 195; John Reeves, *The Rothschilds: The Financial Rulers of Nations* (A. C. McClurg & Co., 1887). Rhetorical symbol: Virgil W. Dean, "Another Wichita Seditionist?," *Kansas History* 17, no. 1 (1994): 50–64, quote on 53.

47 Hofstadter, "Free Silver," 267.

48 Ibid., 293–300.

49 Ignatius Donnelly, *Caesar's Column* (F. J. Shulte, 1890), *Atlantis: The Antediluvian World* (Harper & Brothers, 1882), and *The Great Cryptogram: Francis Bacon's Cipher in the So-Called Shakespeare Plays* (R. S. Peale, 1888).

50 Ignatius Donnelly, "Preamble," in "The Populist Party Platform," People's Party convention, 1892, accessed May 16, 2018, http://www.wwnorton.com

/college/history/america7_brief/content/multimedia/ch22/documents_04
.htm.

51 L. J. Rather, "Disraeli, Freud and Jewish Conspiracy Theories," *Journal of the History of Ideas* 47, no. 1 (1986): 111–31, quote on 123. See also Alex J. Beringer, "'Some Unsuspected Author': Ignatius Donnelly and the Conspiracy Novel," *Arizona Quarterly* 68, no. 4 (2012): 35–60.

52 Grant E. Hamilton, "Their New Jerusalem," cartoon in *Judge* magazine, January 23, 1892; Watson Heston, "History Repeats Itself," cartoon in *Sound Money*, April 15, 1896.

53 See Goodman, *Towards a Christian Republic*, chap. 3.

54 Beecher, *A Plea for the West*, 11.

55 Davis, "Introduction," in *The Fear of Conspiracy*, ed. Davis, xxii–xxiii. This connection has never entirely disappeared, as evidenced by the rise of the Tea Party movement. See Jill Lepore, *The Whites of Their Eyes* (Princeton University Press, 2009).

56 On Protestantism, see Goodman, *Towards a Christian Republic*, chap. 4; see also Butter, *Plots, Designs, and Schemes*; and Goldberg, *Enemies Within*. On anti-intellectualism, see Hofstadter, *Anti-Intellectualism in American Life*.

57 Haapanen, "Anti-Masonic Party," 76.

58 Wood, "Conspiracy and the Paranoid Style," 441.

Chapter Three

1 Stephen Eric Bronner, *A Rumor about the Jews: Antisemitism, Conspiracy, and the Protocols of Zion* (Oxford University Press, 2003), chap. 3.

2 Eugen Weber, *Apocalypses* (Pimlico, 2000), esp. "The Jews: An Interlude," 129–37.

3 Monika Richarz, "The History of the Jews during the Nineteenth and Early Twentieth Centuries," *Discussion Papers Journal*, vol. 1, no. 8, p. 8, accessed May 16, 2018, http://www.un.org/en/holocaustremembrance/docs/pdf /Volume%20I/The_History_of_the_Jews_in_Europe.pdf.

4 Norman Cohn, *Warrant for Genocide* (Harper & Row, 1966), 170. On the distinction between Judeophobia and antisemitism, see Bronner, *A Rumor about the Jews*, chap. 3.

5 "Satan's" pamphlet: Brian Cathcart, "The Rothschild Libel: Why Has It Taken 200 Years for an Anti-Semitic Slur That Emerged from the Battle of Waterloo to Be Dismissed?," *Independent*, May 3, 2015, https://www.independent.co .uk/news/uk/home-news/the-rothschild-libel-why-has-it-taken-200-years -for-an-anti-semitic-slur-that-emerged-from-the-10216101.html. Disraeli: L. J. Rather, "Disraeli, Freud, and Jewish Conspiracy Theories," *Journal of the History of Ideas* 47, no. 1 (1986): 111–31. Eckert and Goedsche: S. R. Shearer, "The Origins of the Illuminist Myth: The Fabrication of the Protocols of the Learned Elders of Zion," Antipas Ministries, accessed May 16, 2018, http:// www.antipasministries.com/html/file0000130.htm.

6 S. M. Dubnow, *History of the Jews in Russia and Poland* (Jewish Publication Society of America, 1918), 188.

7   Cohn, *Warrant for Genocide*, 60. Osman-Bey's book was translated into English in 1878.

8   Shearer, "Origins," 6.

9   On the creation of the Protocols, see Cohn, *Warrant for Genocide*, or more briefly, Shearer, "Origins."

10   This is called the Nilus edition after Sergei Nilus. The Marsden translation is the one most often encountered in the United States.

11   Bronner, *A Rumor about the Jews*, 59–60.

12   The series "The International Jew: The World's Foremost Problem" ran from May 22 to October 2, 1920, in the *Dearborn Independent*.

13   Cohn, *Warrant for Genocide*, 253. See also "Is There a World-Wide Jewish Peril?" *Current Opinion* 69 (December 1920): 840–43, quotation from *America* on 842. "Forgeries" is typically used to describe the *Protocols*, although they are not strictly speaking forgeries of anything; they are simply bogus.

14   Cohn, *Warrant for Genocide*, 24–25.

15   See, for an example of the *Protocols* explained, the pamphlet *Read about the Protocols* (Patriotic Publishing Company, [1934]).

16   Elizabeth Dilling, *The Red Network* (1934), *The Roosevelt Red Record and Its Background* (1936), *The Octopus* (as Reverend Frank Woodruff Johnson; 1940)—all self-published. The quote is from Glen Jeansonne, *Women of the Far Right: The Mothers' Movement and World War II* (University of Chicago Press, 1996), 167.

17   Jeansonne, *Women of the Far Right*, 172 (Van Hyning), 177 (Washburn).

18   Gerald B. Winrod, *The Hidden Hand—the Protocols and the Coming Superman* (Defender Publications, 1934), *The Truth about the Protocols* (Defender Publications, 1935), *Adam Weishaupt: A Human Devil* (Defender Publications, 1935). See also ADL, *The Winrod Legacy of Hate*, 2012, https://www.adl.org/sites /default/files/documents/assets/pdf/combating-hate/The-Winrod-Legacy-of -Hate.pdf. Smith quotation in: Glen Jeansonne, "Preacher, Populist, and Propagandist: The Early Career of Gerald L. K. Smith," *Biography* 2, no. 4 (1979): 322; John O. Beaty, *Iron Curtain over America* (Wilkinson Publishing Co., 1951); Jack B. Tenney, *Zion's Trojan Horse: A Tenney Report on World Zionism* (Standard Publications, 1953).

19   Robert S. Robins and Jerrold M. Post, *Political Paranoia: The Psychopolitics of Hatred* (Yale University Press, 1997), 182–87, quotation on 183. See also Donna Kossy, "The Anglo-Israelites," originally appeared at http://home.pacifier.com /~dkossy/anglo.html (accessed September 10, 2106), a now-defunct website, but is reprinted in her *Kooks: A Guide to the Outer Limits of Human Belief* (Feral House, 1994).

20   On Sawyer, see Robins and Post, *Political Paranoia*, 185. See also "Prof. Charles A. L. Totten: an introduction," History and Time of the Kingdom, accessed May 16, 2018, http://www.fwselijah.com/totten.htm; and Michael Marinacci, "Wesley Swift and the Church of Jesus Christ–Christian," *Califia's Children* (blog), January 26, 2015, http://califias.blogspot.com/2015/01/wesley -swift-and-church-of-jesus-christ.html. Rand's linguistic analysis cited in Kossy, "The Anglo-Israelites," 4.

21   Marvin L. Lubenow, "Pre-Adamites, Sin, Death and the Human Fossils," *Journal of Creation* 12, no. 2 (August 1998): 222–32, https://creation.com/journal -of-creation-122. See also Marinacci, "Wesley Swift and the Church of Jesus Christ–Christian"; Viola Larson, "Christian Identity: A 'Christian' Religion for White Racists," *Christian Research Journal*, Fall 1992; and Louis S. Lapides, "The 'Christian Identity' Movement in America" (paper prepared for the North American Lausanne Consultation on Jewish Evangelism, April 4–5, 1989).

22   Steven Plaut, "The Khazar Myth and the New Anti-Semitism," JewishPress .com, May 9, 2007, http://www.jewishpress.com/indepth/front-page/the -khazar-myth-and-the-new-anti-semitism/2007/05/09/.

23   James Allan Patterson, "Changing Images of the Beast: Apocalyptic Conspiracy Theories in American History," *Journal of the Evangelical Theological Society* 31, no. 4 (1988): 443–52, quote on 443.

24   Paul Goodman, *Toward a Christian Republic* (Oxford University Press, 1988), chap. 4. See also Arthur Goldwag, *The New Hate* (Pantheon, 2012); Robert A. Goldberg, *Enemies Within* (Yale University Press, 2001); Michael Butter, *Plots, Designs, and Schemes: American Conspiracy Theories from the Puritans to the Present* (Walter de Gruyter, 2014).

25   Chip Berlet, "Dances with Devils: How Apocalyptic and Millennialist Themes Influence Right Wing Scapegoating and Conspiracism," *Public Eye* 12, nos. 2–3 (Fall 1998): 1–22 (April 16, 1999, rev. version available online at https://www .politicalresearch.org/wp-content/uploads/downloads/2013/02/Dances_with _Devils.pdf); Kenneth L. Gentry Jr., "Antisemitism and Dispensationalism," *Against Dispensationalism* (blog), July 20, 2011, http://againstdispensationalism .blogspot.com; Patterson, "Changing Images of the Beast"; Matthew A. Sutton, "Was FDR the Antichrist? The Birth of Fundamentalist Antiliberalism in a Global Age," *Journal of American History* 98, no. 4 (2012): 252–65.

26   Cohn, *Warrant for Genocide*; Weber, *Apocalypses*.

27   Weber, *Apocalypses*, 182. See also Ernest Reisinger, "The History of Dispensationalism in America," accessed July 10, 2018, http://www.reformedreader.org /hda.htm.

28   Nancy Koester, "The Future in our Past: Post-millennialism in American Protestantism," *Word and World* 15, no. 2 (1995): 137–44, quote at 137n1. On the social impact of early American evangelical Protestantism, see Richard Hofstadter, *Anti-Intellectualism in American Life* (Alfred A. Knopf, 1970), chap. 4.

29   Hofstadter, *Anti-Intellectualism in American Life*, 121.

30   Paul W. Rood II, "The Untold Story of the Fundamentals," *Biola Magazine*, Summer 2014, http://magazine.biola.edu/article/14-summer/the-untold-story -of-the-fundamentals/. See also Matthew A. Sutton, *American Apocalypse: A History of Modern Evangelism* (Harvard University Press, 2014), chap. 3.

31   William Bell Riley, *Protocols and Communism* (L. W. Camp, 1934). See also Clement Pulaski, "William Bell Riley and Fundamentalist Anti-Semitism," True Sons of Abraham, February 6, 2016, http://truesonsofabraham.com /riley.htm. Other quotations: Timothy P. Weber, "How Evangelicals Became Israel's Best Friend," *Christianity Today*, October 5, 1998, https://www .christianitytoday.com/ct/1998/october5/8tb038.html.

32 Richard Hofstadter, "The Paranoid Style in American Politics," in *The Paranoid Style in American Politics and other Essays* (Alfred A. Knopf, 1965), 38, 29–30. See also Michael Barkun, *A Culture of Conspiracy* (University of California Press, 2003).

33 Michael Barkun, *Religion and the Racist Right: The Origins of the Christian Identity Movement* (University of North Carolina Press, 1997), chap. 9.

34 William Potter Gale, *The Faith of Our Fathers* (Ministry of Christ Church, 1963), 33, 29. See also Wesley Swift, "Crushing the Serpent" (sermon), Dr. Wesley Swift Library at christogenea.org, August 1957, https://swift.christogenea.org/articles/crushing-serpent-8-0-57, and "The Power behind the Red Revolution," Dr. Wesley Swift Library at christogenea.org, June 18, 1962, https://swift.christogenea.org/articles/power-behind-red-revolution-6-18-62.

35 Winrod, *Adam Weishaupt*, 10; Gerald L. K. Smith, "If the Crusader Quits, What Happens?" (Christian Nationalist Crusade, ca. 1980); Tal Brooke, *One World* (End Run Publishing, 2000), 208.

36 Barkun, *A Culture of Conspiracy*, chap. 2, quotation on 23.

37 J. Gordon Melton, *Encyclopedic Handbook of Cults in America* (Garland, 1986), 68–75; John L. Reynolds, *Secret Societies* (Arcade, 2006), 148–55. On the suspicion of Freemasonry, see George F. Dillon, *The War of Antichrist with the Church and Christian Civilization* (M. H. Gill & Son, 1885). See also James Webb, *The Occult Underground* (Open Court, 1974).

38 Webb, *Occult Underground*, chap. 3. See also Melton, *Encyclopedic Handbook of Cults in America*, 87–92.

39 Melton, *Encyclopedic Handbook of Cults in America*, 73–75; Terry Melanson, "The Vril Society, the Luminous Lodge and the Realization of the Great Work," Illuminati Conspiracy Archive 2001, http://www.conspiracyarchive.com/NWO/Vril_Society.htm.

40 Peter Staudenmaier, "Anthroposophy and Ecofascism," Institute for Social Ecology, 2009, p. 6, http://social-ecology.org/wp/2009/01/anthroposophy-and-ecofascism-2/.

41 Nicholas Goodrick-Clarke, *Occult Roots of Nazism: Secret Aryan Cults and Their Influence on Nazi Ideology* (Tauris Parke, 2004), 2.

42 Webb, *Occult Underground*, 11.

43 Respectively: Melton, *Encyclopedic Handbook of Cults in America*, 89; Melanson, "The Vril Society"; Fredrik Bendz, "Anthroposophy," The Page of Reason (website), January 28, 2001, http://www.update.uu.se/~fbendz/pseudo/anthropos.html; Goodrick-Clarke, *Occult Roots of Nazism*, 108.

44 Paul A. Erikson, "The Indo-European Hypothesis in Nineteenth Century Physical Anthropology," Digital Assets Library, accessed May 17, 2018, http://digitalassets.lib.berkeley.edu/anthpubs/ucb/text/kas047_048-009.pdf, 166. Degeneration: Christopher B. Krebs, *A Most Dangerous Book* (W. W. Norton, 2011), 191–203.

45 Melanson, "The Vril Society," 2.

46 Nicholas Goodrick-Clarke, *Black Sun: Aryan Cults, Esoteric Nazism, and the Politics of Identity* (New York University Press, 2002), 80.

47 Goodrick-Clarke, *Occult Roots of Nazism*, 108. On Steiner, see Staudenmaier, "Anthroposophy and Ecofascism," 5–7.

48 Blavatsky discussed in Goodrick-Clarke, *Black Sun*, 80; quotation is Goodrick-Clarke's. Steiner is quoted in Bendz, "Anthroposophy."

49 Krebs, *A Most Dangerous Book*, 200.

50 Oscar Handlin and Mary F. Handlin, *Danger in Discord: Origins of Anti-Semitism in the United States* (ADL of B'nai B'rith, 1948), 19.

51 Goodrick-Clarke, *Occult Roots of Nazism*; Cohn, *Warrant for Genocide*; James Webb, *The Occult Establishment* (Open Court, 1976), chap. 5.

52 UFOs discussed in Melanson, "The Vril Society." Landig discussed in Goodrick-Clarke, *Black Sun*, 3–4. See also Jan Van Helsing, *Secret Societies and Their Power in the 20th Century* (Ewertverlag, 1995).

53 "L.T. McFadden, U.S. Fascist Ally, Beaten at Polls" Jewish Telegraphic Agency, November 8, 1934, https://www.jta.org/1934/11/08/archive/l-t-mcfadden-u-s -fascist-ally-beaten-at-polls; Hudson in Goodrick-Clarke, *Black Sun*, 73; Count Cherep-Spiridovich, *The Secret World Government; or, "The Hidden Hand"* (Anti-Bolshevist Publishing Company, 1926); Eugene N. Sanctuary, *Are These Things So?* (World Alliance Against Jewish Aggressiveness, 1934).

54 Hofstadter, *Anti-Intellectualism in American Life*, 134. On the Klan, see John M. Werly, "Premillennialism and the Paranoid Style," *American Studies* 18, no. 1 (1977): 39–55. See also Leo P. Ribuffo, *The Old Christian Right: The Protestant Far Right from the Great Depression to the Cold War* (Temple University Press, 1983).

55 William Dudley Pelley, *We Offer You the Scourge of Cords*, Private Manual no. 1 of the Silver Shirts of America (self-pub., 1933), 3, 4. See also David Lobb, "Fascist Apocalypse: William Pelley and Millennial Extremism" (paper presented at the Fourth Annual Conference of the Center for Millennial Studies, November 1999), now published in *Journal of Millennial Studies*, vol. 2, no. 2 (Winter 2000), http://www.mille.org/publications/winter2000/lobb.PDF.

56 Elizabeth Dilling, *The Red Betrayal of the Churches*, Red Network Bulletin (self-pub., ca. 1938).

57 Arno C. Gaebelein, *The Conflict of the Ages* (Our Hope, 1933), 188. Both Winrod books published by his Defender Publishers, 1935.

58 "Edith Starr Miller," Grand Lodge of British Columbia and Yukon, 2006, http://freemasonry.bcy.ca/anti-masonry/miller_e/miller_e.html; Christina M. Stoddard (writing as "Inquire Within"), *Trail of the Serpent* (Boswell Publishing Co., 1936).

59 "William Dudley Pelley, International Fascism, and the Sirius Tradition," pts. 3 and 4, *Visup* (blog), February 9, 2014 (http://visupview.blogspot.com/2014 /02/william-dudley-pelley-international.html) and February 16, 2014, (http:// visupview.blogspot.com/2014/02/william-dudley-pelley-international_16.html), respectively; Sanctuary *Are These Things So?*, app. A, 392–96; William Kullgren, "Astrological Indications for 1942," *Beacon Light*, vol. 10, no. 2 (January 1942).

Chapter Four

1 Letter to Geraldine Parker of Women United, April 14, 1941 quoted in "The Case of George Deatherage and Women United," *The Hour*, January 12, 1943, 1.

2   Webster's trilogy: *The French Revolution: A Study in Democracy* (Constable and Company, 1919), *World Revolution: The Plot against Civilization* (Small, Maynard & Company, 1921), and *Secret Societies and Subversive Movements* (Boswell, 1924). Quotation in *Secret Societies*, 1. See also "Nesta H. Webster's *Secret Societies*," Grand Lodge of British Columbia and Yukon, 2001, http://freemasonry .bcy.ca/anti-masonry/webster_n.html.

3   Martha F. Lee, "Nesta Webster: The Voice of Conspiracy," *Journal of Women's History* 17, no. 3 (2005): 81–104, quote on 92.

4   Winston Churchill, "Zionism versus Bolshevism," *Illustrated Sunday Herald*, February 8, 1920, 5; Howell A. Gwynne, *The Cause of World Unrest* (Grant Richards Ltd., 1920), 9–10.

5   The series ran from May 22 to October 2, 1920; the book was printed and distributed in 1920. See Leo Ribuffo, "Henry Ford and the International Jew," *American Jewish History* 69, no. 4 (1980): 437–77.

6   William Hard, *The Great Jewish Conspiracy* (American Jewish Book Company, 1920), 16–17. In the United Kingdom, Israel Zangwill and in France, Salomon Reinarch made similar arguments.

7   Editorial, *Christian Science Monitor*, quoted in "Henry Ford's Jewmaniacy," *American Hebrew*, September 3, 1920. The *Christian Science Monitor* story was recycled by the White Citizens' Council of Louisiana in the periodical the *Councilor* as "Monitor Warned Americans about Illuminati Plans in 1920" (ca. 1960s). The *Councilor* also claimed that the *Monitor*'s exposure of the Jewish Illuminati led to the editor's being "eased out" of his job because of liberal pressure (4). Catholic weekly cited in: "Is There A World-Wide Jewish Peril?" *Current Opinion*, December 1920, 842.

8   Robert Edward Edmondson, *"Anti-Semitic" Causes of Today*, booklet (self-pub., 1937[?]), 3–4. Ernest Elmhurst, *The World Hoax* (Pelley Press, 1939), 13, puts the number from the Lower East Side at 276. Father Coughlin, in his November 20, 1938, radio address, listed fifty-six high-ranking Russian Jews and three non-Jews married to Jewesses based on information provided by "the Nazis," collected with other sermons in *"Am I an Anti-Semite?"* (Condon Printing Co., 1939), 38.

9   Charles Parkhurst, *The Leper in the House*, pamphlet (National Security League, 1920).

10   Easley in: R. K. Murray, *Red Scare* (University of Minnesota Press, 1955), 87–88. The DAR in: Kevin C. Murphy, *Uphill All the Way: The Fortunes of Progressivism, 1919–1929* (self-pub., 2013), http://www.kevincmurphy.com/uphilltoc .html. Evolution in: Susan Jacoby, *The Politics of Unreason* (Pantheon, 2008), 85 (Jacoby and Bryan quotations).

11   Oscar Handlin and Mary Handlin, *Danger in Discord: Origins of Anti-Semitism in the United States* (ADL of B'Nai B'rith, 1948), 22.

12   Robert Singerman, "Contemporary Racist and Judeophobic Ideology Discovers the Khazars, or, Who Really Are the Jews" (Rosaline and Myer Feinstein Lecture, Temple University, 2004), 5.

13   Ibid. Romanism: Paul M. Winter, *What Price Tolerance?*, excerpted in David Brion Davis, ed., *The Fear of Conspiracy* (Cornell University Press, 1971), 243;

Count Cherep-Spiridovich, *The Secret World Government; or, "The Hidden Hand"* (Anti-Bolshevist Publishing Association, 1926), 3.

14 Marcus Eli Ravage, "A Real Case against the Jews," *Century Magazine*, January 1928, 346–50, quotations on 348 and 350. Despite being an obvious satire, Ravage's article is periodically cited as evidence of the Jewish conspiracy by antisemitic conspiracists. During World War II, it was offered for sale by the Aryan Bookstore in Los Angeles as a pamphlet titled *Bombshell against Christianity* written by "Marcus Ravage, a Hebrew." See *Joe Kamp, Peddler of Propaganda* (Friends of Democracy, 1942[?]), 20. See also Edmondson, *"Anti-Semitic" Causes of Today*, 6; and Robert H. Williams, *The Ultimate World Order* (self-pub., 1950), 38–39.

15 Gerald B. Winrod, *The Truth about the Protocols* (Defender Publications, 1935), 28th unnumbered page.

16 "Jewish Activities in the United States," *Dearborn Independent*, reprinted in Davis, ed., *The Fear of Conspiracy*, 239.

17 Winrod, *Truth about the Protocols*, 21. Charles Coughlin's "Money Control," quoted in William Dudley Pelley, *Hidden Empire* (Pelley Publishers, 1938), 15. Coughlin's "Not Anti-Semitism but Anti-Communism," in his *"Am I an Anti-Semite?,"* 79. American Guards pamphlet *National Copperhead Bulletin* reproduced in Americanism Committee, *Subversive Activities in America First Committee in California*, Report no. 1, (American Legion, 1941), 7; Edmondson, *"Anti-Semitic" Causes of Today*, 10; Cherep-Spiridovich, *Secret World Government*, 19.

18 Denis Fahey, *The Mystical Body of Christ in the Modern World*, 2nd ed. (Brown and Nolan, 1938), 89. In his testimony before the Dies Committee in 1939, George Van Horn Moseley stated: "As illustrating the tremendous power of organized Jewry, it must be noted that the '*British White Paper*' referred to was followed by a revised '*White Paper*' omitting entirely the reference to the role of Jews in Bolshevism!" *Buried Manuscript Resurrected* (transcript of testimony, June 1,1939), pamphlet (Christian Nationalist Crusade, 1939).

19 Pelley, *Hidden Empire*, 6; Fahey, *Mystical Body of Christ*, 90. Fahey lists Lenin's nationality as Russian but adds: "Some authors are convinced that Lenin's mother was a Jewess."

20 Antony Sutton, *Wall Street and the Bolshevik Revolution* (Arlington House, 1974), app. 2, "The Jewish-Conspiracy Theory of the Bolshevik Revolution."

21 On McFadden's speeches, see Edward Flaherty, "Myth #10: The Legendary Tirade of Louis T. McFadden," Political Research Associates, September 6, 2010, http://www.publiceye.org/conspire/flaherty/flaherty10.html; "Antisemitism in House of Congress," Jewish Telegraphic Agency, May 1, 1934, https://www.jta.org/1934/05/01/archive/anti-semitism-in-house-of-congress; and: "L. T. McFadden, U.S. Fascist Ally, Beaten at Polls," Jewish Telegraphic Agency, November 8, 1934, https://www.jta.org/1934/11/08/archive/l-t-mcfadden-u-s-fascist-ally-beaten-at-polls.

22 Pedro del Valle, "May God Save Our Nation from Traitors Who Rule Her," *Common* Sense, August 1966, 1; Sheldon Emry, *Coming Soon: America without Debt, Crime, or War* (self-pub., 1970), sheldonemrylibrary.com/Books/Coming

%20Soon.pdf; Richard C. Cook, "Louis T. McFadden (1876–1936): An American Hero," *Dandelion Salad* (blog), July 21, 2008, https://dandelionsalad .wordpress.com/2008/07/21/louis-t-mcfadden-1876-1936-an-american-hero -by-richard-c-cook/. McFadden was not assassinated.

23 A. N. Field, *The Truth about the Slump: What the News Never Tells* (self-pub., 1932); Gerald B. Winrod, *The Hidden Hand—the Protocols and the Coming Superman* (Defender Publications, 1934), 21; Pelley, *Hidden Empire*, 6; George Edward Sullivan, *Wolves in Sheep's Clothing* (Sodality Union of Washington, DC, 1937[?]); George Armstrong, *Rothschild Money Trust* (self-pub., 1940), app. 2, "Rabbi Reichorn's Funeral Oration,1869"; Robert Edward Edmondson, "Jew-Ruled U.S. Enterprises" (leaflet), February 9, 1940, http://digital-library .csun.edu/cdm/singleitem/collection/InOurOwnBackyard/id/235.

24 Handlin and Handlin, *Danger in Discord*, 35; Carey McWilliams, *A Mask for Privilege: Anti-Semitism in America* (Little, Brown & Co., 1948), 192.

25 Elizabeth Dilling, *The Roosevelt Red Record and Its Background* (self-pub., 1936), 13.

26 Eugene Sanctuary and Harry A. Jung, *The Man behind the Men behind Roosevelt* (American Vigilant Intelligence Federation, Inc., 1936). This booklet in fact carries no authorship but is credited to Sanctuary and Jung (who ran the federation). "The Rape of Our Nation's Schools," *Fiery Cross*, November 1970, 11.

27 On the Blue Eagle, see Gerald B. Winrod, *The NRA in Prophecy and a Discussion of Beast Worship* (Defender Publishers, 1935[?]); and "Fascism in America," *Life*, March 6, 1939, 62. On the big three, see Edmondson, *"Anti-Semitic" Causes of Today*, 4–5; and William Dudley Pelley, *The Reds Are upon Us* (self-pub., 1938), 13–33;

28 Pelley, *Hidden Empire*, 2–3. The designation "Roosevelt's Right Arm" is used by Edmondson. It is hard to tell where these designations originate or how widely they were used. Pelley, in his list, refers to Herbert Feis as "the brains of the State Department." In his "invisible government" pictograph, Robert Edmondson declares Brandeis to be the "Braintrust 'Godfather,'" and elsewhere makes a distinction between a "Baruch Protege" and a "Baruch 'Contribution.'" Edmondson's pictograph reproduced in John L. Spivak, "Plotting the American Pogroms," *New Masses*, October 9, 1934, 11.

29 Carl H. Mote, *The New Deal Goose Step* (Daniel Ryerson, 1939), 95–96. The "Economists" quotation from the *Protocols* heads Pelley's list.

30 Perkins accusation reported in the *Life* article "Fascism in America," 63; Eugene Sanctuary, *Are These Things So?* (World Alliance against Jewish Aggressiveness, 1934), 398–99; Spivak, "Plotting the American Pogroms," 11.

31 Gerald B. Winrod, *The Jewish Assault on Christianity* (self-pub., 1935), quotation on last page (unnumbered).

32 Mote, *New Deal Goose Step*, 93 and 95–96; Sanctuary, *Are These Things So?* 399; Pelley, *Hidden Empire*, 15; Garner quoted in "Seditious Publications Still Flourish in the U.S.," *The Hour*, no. 150, February 22, 1943, 3, http://jfk.hood .edu/Collection/Weisberg%20Subject%20Index%20Files/H%20Disk/Hour %20The/Item%2005.pdf.

33 Gerald L. K. Smith, *Too Much and Too Many Roosevelts* (Christian Nationalist Crusade, 1950), 5; Pelley, *Hidden Empire*, 7; Dilling, *Roosevelt Red Record*, 5.

34   Smith, *Too Much and Too Many Roosevelts,* 59–61. Smith attributes his claim to a
      Washington, DC, newspaper, but he actually excerpts a Gerald Winrod article,
      "Roosevelt's Jewish Ancestry," *The Revelator,* October 15, 1936, published in
      Wichita. Pelley cited in "The Repercussions of Hitlerism in the United States,"
      typescript document credited to the American Jewish Committee, ca. 1936
      (https://archive.org/details/TheRepercussionsOfHitlerismInTheUnitedStates).
      According to this document, Pelley's assessment of Jewishness encompassed
      such unlikely candidates as newspaper magnate William Randolph Hearst
      (Herzog) and former vice president Charles Dawes.

35   "World Service Was Hitler's Propaganda Source for U.S. Subversive Publica-
      tions," in "Special Sedition Trial Edition!," *Anti-Nazi Bulletin* 9, no. 3 (July–
      August 1944): 10. As late as 1942, one A. M Windhorst announced at a World
      Events Forum, "Roosevelt is a Jew, and so is everyone who ever came from
      Holland!" Reported in "Voices of Defeat," *Life,* April 13, 1942, 86.

36   Smith, *Too Much and Too Many Roosevelts,* 59 and 64.

37   Pelley, *Hidden Empire,* 15; Pelley, *Reds Are upon Us,* 9; Sanctuary, *Are These Things
      So?* iii, iv. (The quote within Sanctuary's quote is from Encyclopaedia Britan-
      nica, 11th ed. [1910], s.v. "Beaconsfield, Benjamin Disraeli, Earl of," quoting
      Lord Beaconsfield.) Edmondson, *"Anti-Semitic" Causes of Today,* 8 and 11.

38   Pelley, *Hidden Empire,* 9.

39   Nomad, "The Roots of Right Wing Religious Extremism: The Winrod Legacy
      1/2," *Nomadic Politics* (blog), April 22, 2013, https://nomadicpolitics.blogspot
      .com/2013/04/the-roots-of-right-wing-religious.html. On fundamentalists,
      see Matthew A. Sutton, "Was FDR the Antichrist? The Birth of Fundamentalist
      Antiliberalism in a Global Age," *Journal of American History* (2012): 1052–74,
      quote on 1062; James B. True, in his newsletter *Industrial Control Report,* Feb-
      ruary 11, 1939; Dilling, *Roosevelt Red Record,* 3.

40   *Buried Manuscript Resurrected,* 9.

41   Americanism Committee, *Subversive Activities,* pt. 4. See also John Roy Carl-
      son, *Under Cover* (E. P. Dutton, 1943), 240–43; "Terror Specialists," *Anti-Nazi
      Bulletin* 6, no. 4 (March 1940): 10.

42   "Women United. . . . Against USA!" *News Letter* 5, no. 144 (May 7, 1941): 2–4,
      2 (reproduction of Hudson reporting). *News Letter* was published the News
      Research Service, founded by the Los Angeles Jewish Community Committee
      in 1939.

43   Glen Jeansonne, *Women of the Far Right: The Mothers' Movement and World
      War II* (University of Chicago Press, 1996), 45–56, 50 ("Damn Jews"), 51 (Molly
      Pitchers). See also Theodore Irwin, *Inside the Christian Front* (American Coun-
      cil on Public Affairs, March 1940).

44   According to Jeansonne (*Women of the Far Right,* 42), Lindbergh "tended to
      believe conspiracy theories." See also *Is Lindbergh a Nazi?,* booklet (Friends of
      Democracy, 1941[?]). Moran quoted in the *Life* article "Voices of Defeat," 100.
      Deatherage quoted in "Defendants Dossiers Reveal Vast Network of Racial,
      Religious, and Political Subversion," in "Special Sedition Trial Edition!," *Anti-
      Nazi Bulletin* 9, no. 3 (July–August1944): 12. Baldwin quoted in Jeansonne,
      Women of the Far Right, 132.

45 Headline in *Christian Free Press* of Glendale, Cal., May 1938. Dilling in *The Octo-pus* (self-pub., 1940), 3; George Deatherage in the *News Bulletin* of the American Nationalist Confederation, April 23, 1938; Moseley in "Buried Testimony," 7; Westphal quoted in photo caption, *News Letter* 5, no. 144 (May 7, 1941): 1.

46 *The Dearborn Independent*, quoted in "Jewish Activities in America," in *The Fear of Conspiracy*, ed. Davis, 239; Armstrong, *Rothschild Money Trust*, app. 1, "Protocol No. 7"; de Aryan quoted in "Voices of Defeat," 88 and 98.

47 "Here Are Some Samples of the Poison Spread by the Alleged Conspirators," in "Special Sedition Trial Edition!," *Anti-Nazi Bulletin* 9, no. 3 (July–August1944): 8–10, 9 (reproduction of cover of Sanctuary's pamphlet *War Guilt and Warmon-gers*), 10 (reproduction of cover of Deatherage's publication *World-Service*).

48 Howland Spencer, "The Trap-Door," editorial in the *Post* (Highland, NY), reprinted as a flyer by the Edmondson Economic Service, no date. Rexford Guy Tugwell was one of Roosevelt's economic advisers.

49 Ernst Goerner, *Gentile Freemasons*, pamphlet (n.p., 1939), 6–7; "Onward Jewish Soldiers," leaflet (Anti-Communist Federation of America, 1939); Farber cited in Jeansonne, *Women of the Far Right*, 110; Waters quoted in *Life* magazine's "Voices of Defeat," 90.

50 "News Behind the Jews," *Liberation*, January 7, 1938, 6.

51 Curtis quoted in: Amanda Bradley, "Women of the Far Right—Part 2: Cath-erine Curtis, Laura Ingalls, & Agnes Waters," Counter-Currents Publishing, April 7, 2011, https://www.counter-currents.com/2011/04/women-of-the-far-right-part-2-catherine-curtis-laura-ingalls-and-agnes-waters/; Goerner, *Gentile Freemasons*. Molly Pitchers in Jeansonne, *Women of the Far Right*, 51; Moseley in *Joe Kamp, Peddler of Propaganda*, 15; Baldwin in "Women United," 5; Thorkelson's "remarks" collected as *Steps toward British Union, a World State, and International Strife*, pamphlet (n.p., 1940[?]). Martin J. Higgins claim about Eden's wife reported in "Voices of Defeat," 91.

52 Armstrong, *Rothschild Money Trust*; William Kullgren, "Astrological Indica-tions for 1942," *Beacon Light* 10, no. 2 (January1942): 4 (canceled election), 60–61 (Thorkelson address). The text of Kullgren's predictions makes it clear that they were written before American entry into the war.

53 Don Bell, "Who Are Our Rulers?" *American Mercury*, September 1960, 135; *The Secret Government of the Soviet Union*, pamphlet (n.p., 1958).

54 Gary Wean, "The Anatomy of a Conspiracy of Race Riots & Revolution," *Con-tact*, August 19, 1994.

55 G. Edward Griffin, *The Creature from Jekyll Island* (American Media, 1998).

Chapter Five

1 Garet Garrett, "The Revolution Was" (1944), in his *The People's Pottage* (West-ern Islands, 1951), 9–10; riverbank cave anecdote in "About the Author," 140.

2 Biographical sketches of all defendants can be found in "Defendants Dossiers Reveal Vast Network of Racial, Religious, and Political Subversion," in "Spe-cial Sedition Trial Edition!," *Anti-Nazi Bulletin*, vol. 9, no. 3 (July–August 1944).

3   'J' Canaan Greene's Facebook page, The Truth Be Told, reveals dozens of pho-
     tographs and paintings in which men have their hand in their coat.
4   Howell Gwynne, *The Cause of World Unrest* (Grant Richards Ltd., 1920), 9–10.
5   Gerald Winrod, *The Truth about the Protocols* (Defender Publications, 1935), 10.
     Cartoon and quotation in William Dudley Pelley, *Talmud and the Protocols*, in
     an apparently self-published "replica edition" (1937[?]) of the periodical *New
     Liberation*.
6   Martha F. Lee, "Nesta Webster: The Voice of Conspiracy," *Journal of Women's
     History* 17, no. 3 (2005): 81–104.
7   *Thus Speaks the Talmud*, pamphlet (Twentieth Century Crusaders, 1936);
     Eugene Sanctuary, *The Talmud Unmasked* (self-pub., 1939).
8   Croaking frogs: Gerald Winrod, *The Jewish Assault on Christianity*, booklet
     (self-pub., 1935). Intellects: Winrod, in *Revelator*, October 18, 1936. Other char-
     acterizations of Gentiles in William Dudley Pelley, *The Hidden Empire* (Pelley
     Publishers, 1938), 7–9, and the introduction to Ernest Elmhurst's *World Hoax*
     (Pelley Publishers, 1939), 1–7. See also "Behind the Scenes," Gerald B. Win-
     rod's introduction to his *Adam Weishaupt: A Human Devil* (Defender Publica-
     tions, 1935), 7–9.
9   Richard Hofstadter, "The Paranoid Style in American Politics," in *The Paranoid
     Style in American Politics and Other Essays* (Alfred A. Knopf, 1965), 37–38.
10   In different language, this is much the same idea as conspiracism's creation of
     a hermetic history, as noted in the introduction.
11   Maarten Boudry and Johan Braeckman, "How Convenient! The Epistemic
     Rationale of Self-Validating Belief Systems," *Philosophical Psychology* 25, no. 3
     (2012): 341–64, quote on 354. See also Maarten Boudry and Johan Braeckman,
     "Immunizing Strategies and Epistemic Defense Mechanisms," *Philosophia* 39,
     no. 1 (2011): 145–61; Robert Brotherton, "Towards a Definition of 'Conspiracy
     Theory,'" in "The Psychology of Conspiracy Theories," special issue of *PsyPAG
     Quarterly*, no. 88 (September 2013), 9–14; Steve Clarke, "Conspiracy Theories and
     Conspiracy Theorizing," *Philosophy of the Social Sciences* 32, no. 2 (2002): 131–50.
12   Brian L. Keeley, "Of Conspiracy Theories," *Journal of Philosophy* 96, no. 3
     (1999): 109–26, quote on 120. See also Chris Volkay, "Is This Article on Con-
     spiracies Part of a Conspiracy?" *Skeptical Inquirer*, vol. 35, no. 2 (September–
     October 2007).
13   Epistemic defense mechanism: Boudry and Braeckman, "Immunizing Strat-
     egies and Epistemic Defense Mechanisms," 145; Cass Sunstein and Adrian
     Vermeule, "Conspiracy Theories: Causes and Cures," *Journal of Political Philos-
     ophy* 17, no. 2 (2009): 202–27; Ted Goertzel, "Conspiracy Theories in Science,"
     EMBO Reports 11, no. 7 (2010), 494. Viruses: Albert A. Harrison and James M.
     Thomas, "The Kennedy Assassination, Unidentified Flying Objects, and Other
     Conspiracies: Psychological and Organizational Factors in the Perception of
     'Cover-Up,'" *Systems Research and Behavioral Science* 14, no. 2 (1997): 125.
14   Quotation in: Goertzel, "Conspiracy Theories in Science," 494. Topics: Harri-
     son and Thomas, "The Kennedy Assassination," 125.
15   Winrod, *The Hidden Hand—the Protocols and the Coming Superman* (Defender
     Publications, 1933), 23. "Kept press" in: Elmhurst, *World Hoax*, 10; Ernst

Goerner, *Gentile Freemasons*, pamphlet (n.p., 1939), 8; "Luce Called High Priest of New Deal Smear Gang" and "Smear Brigade Setting Stage to Keep Roosevelt In" *America Speaks*, no. 17 (April 1944), 1; Kamp quotation in *The Fifth Column vs. the Dies Committee* (Constitutional Educational League, 1941), 25.

16   "The Great American Triumvirate," *Social Justice*, December 5, 1938, back cover. Advertising control in: Robert Edward Edmondson, *"Anti-Semitic" Causes of Today*, booklet (self-pub., 1937[?]), 8.

17   Coughlin letter reproduced in *Is Lindbergh a Nazi?*, booklet (Friends of Democracy, 1941[?]), 9; George Armstrong, *Rothschild Money Trust* (self-pub., 1940), 3; Eugene Sanctuary, *Are These Things So?* (World Alliance against Jewish Aggressiveness, 1934), vii.

18   William Dudley Pelley, "Poor Old George Arliss Becomes a Jewish Propagandist," *Liberation*, January 27, 1934, 1.

19   William Dudley Pelley, "Are You Revolutionary-Minded through Jewish Entertainment?" *New Liberator*, November 7, 1937, 2.

20   Robert Edward Edmondson, *"Anti-Semitic" Causes of Today*, 9, and *The Movies: A Jew Monopoly* (American Vigilante Bulletin, October 14, 1938), 1.

21   Lee, "Nesta Webster," 92; Winrod, *The Hidden Hand*, 20. Anti-Communist Federation handbill reprinted in "Fascism in America," *Life*, March 6, 1939, 59.

22   Sanctuary, *Are These Things So?*, dedication page.

23   American Women against Communism objective: "To the Women of America," flyer reproduced in *News Letter* 5, no. 144 (May 7, 1941): 6; Elizabeth Dilling, *The Red Betrayal of the Churches*, Red Network Bulletin (self-pub., ca. 1938), 11 ("Red" Service), 5 (Christian Dupes), and *The Octopus* (self-pub., 1940), 5 (Christian Gentiles). In *The Red Network* (self-pub., 1934), Dilling devotes pages 33–38 to the Methodists' turning "Socialistic."

24   Sanctuary, *Are These Things So?*, 399; Pelley, "Are You Revolutionary Minded?" 2; Jacob Thorkelson, *Steps toward British Union, a World State, and International Strife*, pamphlet (n.p., 1940[?]), 28.

25   Sanctuary, *Are These Things So?*, 9–10 (Protocol sixteen), iv (quotations about public schools).

26   Dilling, *The Red Network*, 10; Charles E. Coughlin, *I Take My Stand* (self-pub., 1940), 7; Edmondson, *"Anti-Semitic" Causes of Today*, 10. Colleges: George E. Sullivan, "America's Insidious Foes," *Social Justice*, December 5, 1938, 10.

27   John Kasper, "Abolish the Public Schools! Now!" *Thunderbolt*, no. 18 (May 1960), 3.

28   Nesta Webster, *Secret Societies and Subversive Movements* (Boswell Publishing Co., 1924), 344.

29   Winrod, *The Hidden Hand*, 19–20. Protocol one quoted in: Sanctuary, *Are These Things So?*, 9.

30   Dilling, *Red Network*, 26–28. Bebel quotation on 27; dots of elision are Dilling's. Gerald L. K. Smith, *Too Much and Too Many Roosevelts* (Christian Nationalist Crusade, 1950), 38–39.

31   Carl Stempel, Thomas Hargrove, and Guido H. Stempel III, "Media Use, Social Structure, and Belief in 9/11 Conspiracy Theories," *Journalism and Mass Communication Quarterly* 84, no. 2 (2007): 356. See also Ian Reyes and Stef Aupers,

"'Trust No One': Modernization, Paranoia and Conspiracy Culture," *European Journal of Communication* 27, no. 1 (2012): 22–34.

32   Sunstein and Vermeule, "Conspiracy Theories: Causes and Cures"; Gregory A. Poland and Robert M. Jacobson, "The Clinician's Guide to the Anti-Vaccinationists' Galaxy," *Immunology* 73 (2012): 860. See also Eric J. Oliver and Thomas J. Wood, "Conspiracy Theories, Magical Thinking, and the Paranoid Style(s) of Mass Opinion" (working paper series, University of Chicago Department of Political Science, June 2012); and Quassim Cassam, "Vice Epistemology," *Monist* 99, no. 2 (2016): 159–80.

33   Jamie Bartlett and Carl Miller, *The Power of Unreason: Conspiracy Theories, Extremism, and Counter-Terrorism* (Demos, 2010), https://www.demos.co.uk /files/Conspiracy_theories_paper.pdf?1282913891. See also Benjamin R. Warner and Ryan Neville-Shepard, "Echoes of a Conspiracy: Birthers, Truthers, and the Cultivation of Extremism," Communication Quarterly 62, no. 1 (2014): 1–17. On bigotry, see "Unraveling Anti-Semitic 9/11 Conspiracy Theories," ADL, May 25, 2003, https://www.adl.org/news/article/unraveling-anti-semitic-911 -conspiracy-theories; Tanya T. Sharpe, "The Identity Christian Movement: Ideology of Domestic Terrorism," *Journal of Black Studies* 30, no. 4 (2000): 604–23; and Jelle van Buuren, "Spur to Violence? Anders Behring Breivik and the Eurabian Conspiracy," *Nordic Journal of Migration Research* 3, no. 4 (2013): 205–15.

34   Letter to the editor, *Women's Voice*, March 28, 1946, 12.

35   Dan Anderberg, Arnauld Chevalier, and Jonathan Wadsworth, "Anatomy of a Health Scare: Education, Income and the MMR Controversy in the UK," *Journal of Health Economics* 30 (2011): 515–30.

36   Daniel Jolley, "Are Conspiracy Theories Just Harmless Fun?" *Psychologist* 26, no. 1 (2013), 61. On globalization, see Alasdair Spark, "Conjuring Order: The New World Order and Conspiracy Theories on Globalization," *Sociological Review* 48, no. 2 (2000): 48–62 (discussion of casual adherence on 58–59).

37   "Anti-Vaccination Websites Use 'Science' and Stories to Support Claims, Study Finds," Johns Hopkins University Bloomberg School of Public Health, press release, November 3, 2015; Orac, "Conspiracy Theories: The Dark Heart of Alternative Medicine," *Respectful Insolence* (blog), March 20, 2014, https:// respectfulinsolence.com/2014/03/20/conspiracy-theories-the-dark-heart-of -alternative-medicine/. See also Michael Specter, *Denialism* (Penguin, 2009), chap. 2: "Vaccines and the Great Denial."

38   Jamie Bartlett and Carl Miller, "A Bestiary of the 9/11 Truth Movement: Notes from the Front Line," *Skeptical Inquirer* 35, no. 4 (July–August 2011): 3; Ben Goldacre, *Bad Science* (Fourth Estate, 2009), xii.

39   Webster, *Secret Societies*, 43–48.

40   John Stokes, review of *Secret Societies and Subversive Movements* by Nesta H. Webster, *Ars Quatuor Coronatorum* 36 (1924): 113.

41   Winrod, *Adam Weishaupt*, 10 and 43.

42   David Lobb, "Fascist Apocalypse: William Pelley and Millennial Extremism" (paper presented at the 4th annual conference of the Center for Millennial Studies, November 1999), 1, now published in *Journal of Millennial Studies*, vol. 2, no. 2 (Winter 2000), http://www.mille.org/publications/winter2000/lobb

.PDF. The quotation from *Reality* is featured on the cover of every issue. *Reality* can be found on the website of the International Association for the Preservation of Spiritualist and Occult Periodicals (http://www.iapsop.com/archive /materials/reality_pelley/).

43 Suzanne G. Ledeboer, "The Man Who Would Be Hitler," *California History* 65, no. 2 (June 1986): 126–36. See also "The Repercussions of Hitlerism in the United States" (1935?) and "William Dudley Pelley" (April 14, 1939), both typescript documents by the American Jewish Committee, http://ajcarchives.org /ajcarchive/DigitalArchive.aspx. Rabbis: *The Reds Are upon Us* (First Council, 1938), 7.

44 Gullible, unenlightened: *The Reds Are upon Us* 11 and 4; Dumb workingmen: Pelley, *Hidden Empire*, 5; Asleep: Pelley, introduction to Elmhurst's *World Hoax*, 3.

45 William Dudley Pelley, *We Offer You the Scourge of Cords*, Private Manual no. 1 of the Silver Shirts of America, (self-pub., 1933), 22–23.

46 Lee, "Nesta Webster," 91. See also the final section ("The End") in Winrod, *Hidden Hand*, 30–32.

47 Webster's preface to *Secret Societies* is an extended attack on bad reviews of her earlier book, *The French Revolution*. Fry's comments to Nazi agent Ubald von Roll are reported in *News Letter*, no. 112, October 30, 1940.

48 Russia and America: Pelley, introduction to Elmhurst's *World Hoax*, 2 and 3. Psychic Radio: *New Liberator*, June 1931, quoted in "Repercussions of Hitlerism," 2.

49 Scenarios of death in Pelley, *We Offer You the Scourge of Cords*, 3. Mystical 17: American Jewish Committee, "William Dudley Pelley," 5.

50 Revelations in Lee, "Nesta Webster," 88, 100n38. Magicians in Webster, *Secret Societies*, 172.

51 William Dudley Pelley, "The Messy State of the Union," *Liberation*, January 7, 1938, 6.

52 Prophecies in Clifford R. Hope Jr., "Strident Voices in Kansas between the Wars," *Kansas History* 2, no. 1 (1979): 60. Quotation from Winrod, *The Hidden Hand*, 28.

53 Winrod, *Adam Weishaupt*, 13; Pelley (writing as H. Sing Woo), replica edition of *The New Liberation*, 7; Webster, Secret Societies, 324.

54 Webster, *Secret Societies*, 3; "Other Books by Gerald B. Winrod," advertisement attached to *The Hidden Hand*.

55 Pelley, *We Offer You the Scourge of Cords*, 7; *The Reds Are upon Us*, 3 and 10.

56 Kullgren quotes from "Impeach Roosevelt and Repeal the New Deal Laws," and "The Truth about Hitler and the Present World Crisis," *Beacon Light* 7, no. 8 (August 1939): 7, 11, respectively, http://www.iapsop.com/archive/materials /beacon_light/beacon_light_v7_n8_aug_1939.pdf; survivalism in Preparation, *Beacon Light* 8, no. 6 (June 1940): 29–35, http://www.iapsop.com/archive /materials/beacon_light/beacon_light_v8_n6_jun_1940.pdf. Full issues of the *Beacon Light* can be found on the website of the International Association for the Preservation of Spiritualist and Occult Periodicals: http://www.iapsop.com /archive/materials/beacon_light/.

57 Sanctuary, *Are These Things So?*, 397, 392.

Chapter Six

1 Yiddish accent: Glen Jeansonne, *Women of the Far Right: The Mothers' Movement and World War II* (University of Chicago Press, 1996), 16; Steve Rendall, "Glenn Beck's Jewish Problem," FAIR, November 15, 2010, https://fair.org/home/glenn-becks-jewish-problem/.

2 Eugene N. Sanctuary, *Are These Things So?* (World Alliance Against Jewish Aggressiveness, 1934), app. A: "Some Claims of the Occult Forces," 392–96.

3 Nesta Webster, *Secret Societies and Subversive Movements* (Boswell Publishing, 1924), 7–8; Robert Edward Edmondson, "Jew-Ruled U.S. Enterprises" (leaflet) February 9, 1940, http://digital-library.csun.edu/cdm/singleitem/collection/InOurOwnBackyard/id/235; George Armstrong, *Rothschild Money Trust* (self-pub., 1940), 4; Charles E. Coughlin, "Persecution—Jewish and Christian," in *"Am I an Anti-Semite?"* (self-pub., 1939), 39; Sanctuary, *Are These Things So?*, i.

4 McFadden interview in "Anti-Semitism in House of Congress," *Jewish Daily Bulletin*, May 1, 1934, 3, archived by the Jewish Telegraphic Agency: http://pdfs.jta.org/1934/1934-05-01_2833.pdf; Robert Edward Edmondson, *"Anti-Semitic" Causes of Today*, booklet (self-pub., 1937[?]), 1; "Let Us Look at the Record," *Social Justice*, December 5, 1938, 8.

5 George Van Horn Moseley, testimony before the House Committee on Un-American Activities, June 1, 1939, published as *Buried Manuscript Resurrected*, pamphlet (Christian Nationalist Crusade, 1939), 9; Dilling, *The Octopus*, 3.

6 Armstrong, *Rothschild Money Trust*, 4; Ernest Elmhurst, *World Hoax* (Pelley Press, 1939), 3; Dilling quoted in "Voices of Defeat," *Life*, April 13, 1942, 91; Richard Crawford, "Anti-semitic Publisher Made a Name in San Diego: C. Leon de Aryan's 'The Broom' Lashed out at Jews, FDR, Unions and Communists," *San Diego Union Tribune*, June 2, 2011, reprinted under the title "The San Diego Crackpot," in Crawford's *San Diego Yesterday* (History Press, 2013); Gerald L. K. Smith, *Too Much and Too Many Roosevelts* (Christian Nationalist Crusade, 1950), 31.

7 On the connection between paranoia and narcissism, see Erich Wulff, "Paranoiac Conspiratory Delusion," in *Changing Conceptions of Conspiracy*, ed. Carl F. Graumann and Serge Moscovici (Springer-Verlag, 1987), 171–90; Dilling in: Jeansonne, *Women of the Far Right*, 84.

8 Howland Spencer, "The Trap-Door," editorial in the *Post* (Highland, NY), distributed as a leaflet by Edmondson Economic Service, no date. Simonds died of pneumonia.

9 Pelley's "despatch" in: "The Silver Shirts: Their History, Founder and Activities," *AJC Bulletin*, no. 3 (August 24, 1933), http://ajcarchives.org/AJC_DATA/files/THR-34.PDF.

10 *Buried Manuscript Resurrected*, 8 (Meranus Plan), 2 (Hudson anecdote).

11 Waters quoted in Jeansonne, *Women of the Far Right*, 146. Edmondson to Chief Justice Charles Evans Hughes, January 18, 1935, Securities and Exchange Commission Historical Society, http://sechistorical.org/museum/search/?q-first=Edmondson&record-type=type%3APapers.

12 Elizabeth Dilling, *The Red Network* (self-pub., 1934), 5.

13 Gerald B. Winrod, *Adam Weishaupt: A Human Devil* (Defender Publishers, 1935), 7; Carl H. Mote, *The New Deal Goose Step* (Daniel Ryerson, 1939), vi.

14 William Dudley Pelley, *Hidden Empire* (Pelley Press, 1938), 5–6; Elmhurst, *World Hoax*, 10; "We Are Herded as Sheep," *X-Ray*, March 7, 1942, 1; Smith, *Too Much and Too Many Roosevelts*, 3.

15 *Joe Kamp, Peddler of Propaganda* (Friends of Democracy, 1942[?]), 8, 12–13; Albert E. Kahn, "Dangerous Americans," *Reader's Scope*, January 1945, 72–74.

16 See ADL, *The Winrod Legacy of Hate*, 2012, https://www.adl.org/sites/default /files/documents/assets/pdf/combating-hate/The-Winrod-Legacy-of-Hate .pdf; Jeansonne, *Women of the Far Right*, chap. 12; "William Dudley Pelley, International Fascism, and the Sirius Tradition," pts. 3 and 4, *Visup* (blog), February 9, 2014 (http://visupview.blogspot.com/2014/02/william-dudley-pelley -international.html) and February 16, 2014, (http://visupview.blogspot.com /2014/02/william-dudley-pelley-international_16.html), respectively.

17 Dilling in: Christine K. Erickson, "'I Have Not Had One Fact Disproven': Elizabeth Dilling's Crusade against Communism in the 1930s," *Journal of American Studies* 36 (2002): 473–89, quote on 483. Gill in: *Joe Kamp, Peddler of Propaganda*, 12. Garner in: Virgil W. Dean, "Another Wichita Seditionist?" *Kansas History* 17 (1994): 50–64, quote on 55.

18 Sustained attacks on intellectuals can be found in Mote, *New Deal Goose Step*, iii–xii; Carter O'Connor, *What's Cookin'?*, booklet (Constitutional Educational League, 1942); Elizabeth Dilling, *The Red Betrayal of the Churches*, Red Network Bulletin (self-pub., ca. 1938). Einstein in: Sanctuary, *Are These Things So?*, 10–15, quotes on 11 and 14; and in Dilling, *Red Network*, 48.

19 Erickson, "I Have Not Had One Fact Disproven," 482; first quote, Dilling's; second quote, Erickson's.

20 Marek Martin, "Ham and Eggs, Not Half So Mad as California's Vast Orange Dump," *Social Justice*, December 5, 1938, 16.

21 Theodore W. Adorno et al., *The Authoritarian Personality*, quoted in Richard Hofstadter, "The Pseudo-Conservative Revolt—1954," in *The Paranoid Style in American Politics* (Alfred A. Knopf, 1965), 44.

22 Gerald L. K. Smith's Christian Nationalist Crusade distributed Moseley's speech as a pamphlet titled *Army General Exposes Jews*, and William Dudley Pelley's Pelley Press published it as *The Speech of Major General Moseley*. See also "Jews Seek War, Finance Communism, Gen. Moseley Tells Philadelphia Rally," *News from All over the World*, March 30, 1939, 4, archived by the Jewish Telegraphic Agency: http://pdfs.jta.org/1939/1939-03-30_098.pdf. Pelley quoted in: Geoffrey R. Stone, "Free Speech in World War II: 'When Are You Going to Indict the Seditionists?,'" *International Journal of Constitutional Law* 2, no. 2 (2004): 347.

23 George Deatherage, "Has Martin Dies Sold Out to the Jewish Bankers?" *Beacon Light* 7, no. 8 (August 1939): 38–45; *Is Lindbergh a Nazi?*, booklet (Friends of Democracy, 1941[?]).

24 Joseph Kamp, *The Fifth Column in Washington*, pamphlet (Constitutional Educational League, June 1940). See also O'Connor, *What's Cookin'?*, 26.

25   De Aryan quoted in Crawford, "The San Diego Crackpot," 2; "Suicide of the Hollywood Motion Picture Industry" (flyer), Committee on Unemployment, Hollywood Actors and Technicians, no date. The same claim was made in Dan Gilbert's *Hell over Hollywood: The Truth about the Movies!*, Christian Newspapermen's Committee to Investigate the Motion Picture Industry, 1942. Pelley quoted in American Jewish Committee, "William Dudley Pelley," 7. McWilliams quoted in the "Special Sedition Trial Edition!," *Anti-Nazi Bulletin* 9, no. 3 (July–August 1944): 4. The Molly Pitchers pamphlet in Glen Jeansonne, *Women of the Far Right*, 51.

26   The *Tribune* story is reproduced in "When Do We Eat?," *Anti-Nazi Bulletin* 8, no. 4 (August 1943): 3. Herbert Lehman was director general of the United Nations Relief and Rehabilitation Administration and had been one of the founders of the Lehman Brothers Investment Bank; Edward Stettinius was head of the Lend-Lease Administration. Alice Waters quoted in "Voices of Defeat," *Life*, April 13, 1942, 90.

27   O'Connor, *What's Cookin'?*, 18 and 19.

28   "Make America Hungry," *Gaelic American*, June 19, 1943, 1. A. H. Lane, *The Hidden Hand*, pamphlet (MCP Publications, [1938]), distributed by Eugene Sanctuary, 1942 (http://www.thechristianidentityforum.net/downloads/The -Hidden.pdf); "Churchill's Jewish OGPU Terrorizes and Jails Patriots of Great Britain," flyer, August 13, 1940. The OGPU had been the Soviet secret police agency until 1934, when its name changed and its acronym became the NKVD.

29   "Will It Take a Civil War to End Jew Control?," *Liberation*, January 14, 1939. Pelley quoted in David Lobb, "Fascist Apocalypse: William Pelley and Millennial Extremism" (paper presented at the fourth annual conference of the Center for Millennial Studies, November 1999), 5, now published in *Journal of Millennial Studies*, vol. 2, no. 2 (Winter 2000), http://www.mille.org/publications /winter2000/lobb.PDF. Moseley quoted in "Fascism in America," *Life*, March 6, 1939, 61. Waters quoted in Jeansonne, *Women of the Far Right*, 143. McWilliams quoted in the "Special Sedition Trial Edition!," *Anti-Nazi Bulletin* 9, no. 3 (July–August 1944): 5.

30   "UnAmerican Persecution of Christian Patriots Must Stop" (fundraising letter), Protestant War Veterans of the United States, Inc., n.d.; "A Special Appeal," Patriotic Research Bureau, January 14, 1944.

31   Henry H. Klein, *Republic on Trial*, pamphlet (self-pub., 1944); Waters quoted in "Fifth Column snake," *The Jewish Veteran*, June 1963, 6.

32   "Don't Stab Our Boys in the Back!! Wake Up, Americans!!" reproduced in *Anti-Nazi Bulletin* 9, no. 1 (February–March 1944): 4; Edward James Smythe, "INDICTMENT," Protestant War Veterans of the United States, Inc., 1945; Homer Maertz, *UNCIO Unmasked*, pamphlet (Pioneer News Service, 1945).

33   Letter sent by Agnes Waters on behalf of the National Blue Star Mothers, a group given that name apparently in hopes that people would think it was the patriotic organization Blue Star Mothers. The Jewish press covered this story heavily, especially as Waters mailed the letters using the congressional franking privilege: "Congressional Frank Used as Group Tell Mothers of Dead Jews to Blame," *Jewish Post* (Indianapolis) May 4, 1945, 5.

34 "Drive the Money Changers out of the Temple," *Women's Voice*, March 28, 1946, 3; *Freemasonry Is Jewry!*, pamphlet (Women's Voice, n.d.); *Don't Frighten Me*, pamphlet (Women's Voice, April 24, 1947), 7; *At the Root of It All—Anti-Gentilism* pamphlet (Women's Voice, 1946?).

35 Gerald B. Winrod, *Communism in Prophecy, History, America* (Defender Publications, 1946), and "Americanism and Illuminism," *Defender*, October 1949, 5. Also see ADL, *The Winrod Legacy of Hate*. Gerald L. K. Smith (writing as Mr. X), *The Roosevelt Death—a Super Mystery*, pamphlet (Christian Nationalist Crusade, 1947), 14. For an overview of the groups and literature of the time, see George Kellman, "Anti-Jewish Agitation," *American Jewish Year Book* 51 (1950): 110–16.

36 "Special Notice to All Jews" (leaflet) and "Vote Jewish" (flyer), both unattributable to any organization; "Anonymous Hate Campaign," *The Facts* (ADL), December 1946.

37 De Aryan, quoted in the Los Angeles ADL's "'V' Committee Report," November 27, 1951; Robert Edward Edmondson, *I Testify Against the Jews* (1954; rpt., Sons of Liberty, 1985). Petition and quotation on page "H."

38 Robert H. Williams, *The Untold Story of State Medicine* (Fireside Publishing Co., 1948), 15; George Van Horn Moseley, "What Jews Can We Trust?" (open letter/flyer) n.d.; Robert H. Williams, *The Anti-Defamation League and Its Use in the World Communist Offensive*, pamphlet (Closer-Ups, 1947); "Facts Regarding the Community Chest You Should Know" (flyer), National Blue Star Mothers, 1949.

39 The Boss and photographs: Robert H. Williams, *Know Your Enemy*, booklet (Williams Publications, 1956), 36 and front cover. Machiavellian: Henry H. Klein, "Frankfurter over the White House," *Women's Voice*, February 2, 1951, 8. Iron hand: Revilo P. Oliver, "Diabolical Minds Direct the Communist Conspiracy," *Common Sense*, July 1–15, 1959, 1. Asiatic Jews: "The Coming Red Dictatorship" (leaflet) *Common Sense*, 1959. Kennedy: "Kennedy Betrays Voters," *Thunderbolt*, January 1961, 1.

40 Benjamin H. Freedman, "The Truth Will Stand on Its Own Merit—a Jewish Defector Warns America" (speech given at the Willard Hotel, Washington, DC, 1961). Audios of the still popular speech can be found on YouTube; the forty-six-minute version is an abridgment. The Khazar theory had been Freedman's staple argument for some time. See his "Brainwashed USA Christians Duped by Unholiest Hoax in All History," *Fact for Fact* (newsletter), April 1959.

41 Revilo P. Oliver, "Marxmanship in Dallas," pts. 1 and 2, *American Opinion*, February 1964, 13–28, and March 1964, 65–78, respectively.

42 See Ernie Lazar, "Eustace Mullins and the Conspiratorial Extreme Right," Ernie Lazar Google Page, rev. May 21, 2017, https://sites.google.com/site /ernie124102/mullins.

43 A. Ralph Epperson, *The Unseen Hand* (Publius Press, 1985); William T. Still, *New World Order: The Ancient Plan of Secret Societies* (Huntington House, 1990); Robert Henry Goldsborough, *Lines of Credit, Ropes of Bondage* (Washington Dateline Publishers, 1989); Alex Christopher, *Pandora's Box* (self-pub., 2007).

Chapter Seven

1   "Yiddish Marxists Plot USA Defeat by USSR," *Common Sense*, October 15, 1950; Ralph E. Ellsworth and Sarah M. Harris, *The American Right Wing*, Occasional Paper No. 59, University of Illinois Library School (University of Illinois Graduate School of Library Science, 1960), 3.

2   Ellsworth and Harris, *American Right Wing*, 20, 23.

3   Irwin Suall, *The American Ultras* (New America, 1962), 4. See also Walter Wilcox, "The Press of the Radical Right: An Exploratory Analysis" (paper presented to the Association for Education in Journalism, University of Michigan, Ann Arbor, August 28, 1961), reprinted in *Journalism and Mass Communication Quarterly* 39, no. 2 (1962): 152–60; Richard Hofstadter, "The Pseudo-Conservative Revolt—1954," in *The Paranoid Style in American Politics and Other Essays* (Alfred A. Knopf, 1965).

4   Francis Cardinal Spellman, *Communism Is Un-American*, pamphlet (Constitutional Educational League, ca. 1946); Robert Welch, *The Blue Book of the John Birch Society* (Western Islands, 1959), xiv–xv.

5   Norman Dodd, *The Dodd Report to the American People* (Long House Publishers, 1954), 1. New York media: "Communism Can Be Destroyed Overnight!!!" *Dayton Independent*, June 7, 1951, 1. On the other hotbeds, see Joseph P. Kamp, *Meet the Man Who Plans to Rule America*, pamphlet (Constitutional Educational League, 1958); Edward J. Mowery, *HUAC and FBI—Targets for Abolition* (Bookmailer, 1961). Myron Fagan, *"Red Stars"—the Reds Are Back in Hollywood* (Cinema Education Guild, 1961).

6   Harvey Springer, "The Rape of Fundamentalism by the Federal Council of (Anti) Christ in America," *Western Voice*, September 20, 1945; *Is There a Pink Fringe in the Methodist Church?*, pamphlet (Committee for the Preservation of Methodism, 1951). Spiritual Bolshevism in: H. L. Birum Sr., "God's Segregation of Family, Church, Believer, Nation, Language & Races," *National Renaissance Bulletin*, July 1955. See also Dan Smoot, "The National Council of Churches," *Dan Smoot Report*, February 29, 1960. The Federal Council of Churches more or less became the National Council of Churches in 1950.

7   Jo Hindman, "Terrible 1313," *American Mercury*, January 1959, 5–15. On the Consumers Union: untitled news brief in the American Legion's *The Firing Line*, August 15, 1952, 1. On the YWCA: Joseph Kamp, *Behind the Lace Curtains*, pamphlet (Constitutional Educational League, 1948). On the Community Chest: "Facts Regarding the Community Chest You Should Know" (flyer), National Blue Star Mothers of America, 1949.

8   Emanuel M. Josephson, *Roosevelt's Communist Manifesto* (Chedney Press, 1955), quotation on book jacket.

9   See, for examples: Kent Courtney and Phoebe Courtney, *America's Unelected Rulers* (Conservative Society of America, 1962); Emanuel M. Josephson, *Rockefeller "Internationalist": The Man Who Misrules the World* (Chedney Press, 1952); Joseph P. Kamp, *We Must Abolish the United States* (Hallmark Publishers, 1950); Dan Smoot, *The Invisible Government* (Dan Smoot Report, Inc., 1962).

10   "The White Man's Party" (flyer), American Guard, 1937. Charles B. Hudson, in his newsletter *America in Danger!*, January 19, 1942.

11   Morgenthauists: Austin J. App, quoted in "Writer Calls Present Peace 'History's Most Terrifying,'" *Think Weekly*, January 26, 1947, 3. Kangaroo Court: "Roosevelt Betrayed Poland," *Think Weekly*, January 26, 1947, 2.

12   Austin J. App, "Slave-Laboring German Prisoners-of-War," and "Ravishing the Conquered Women of Europe"—both cited in "Think Weekly," *The Facts* (ADL), December 1946, 3; Einar Åberg's *The War Criminals* cited in *The Facts* (ADL), December 1946, 17; Ludwig A. Fritsch, *The Crime of Our Age* (self-pub., 1947), quotation from author's foreword.

13   Francis Parker Yockey, *Imperium* (Westropa Press, 1948), 234.

14   Johan Schoeman, "A Reverie on Nuremberg," *Women's Voice,* February 2, 1951, 13; Kenneth Goff, *Hitler and the Twentieth Century Hoax* (self-pub., 1954), 8. Payback: "Glances at the News," *Women's Voice*, April 24, 1947, 2. It should be noted, regarding the quote in text that (1) FDR rejected the plan, (2) Morgenthau is spelled wrong, and (3) Frankfurter had nothing to do with it. "Germany under the Equalitarian Jackboot," *Northlander*, October 1960, 1. The *Northlander* was published in Scotland but distributed in the United States.

15   James H. Madole, "The Program for the National Renaissance Party," and "Adolph Hitler, the George Washington of Europe," *National Renaissance Bulletin*, October 1953 and May 1953. Weishaupt was not Jewish, but Madole's spelling his name as "Weisshaupt" might be intended to make it appear so.

16   U.S. House of Representatives, Committee on Un-American Activities, *Preliminary Report on Neo-Fascist and Hate Groups* (Washington: U.S. Government Printing Office, 1954), 14–15; the front-page plea mentioned in text is included in Exhibit No. 6, 29.

17   "Brotherhood?" (flyer), National Renaissance Party, 1953.

18   Louis Marschalko, *The World Conquerors* (Joseph Sueli Publications, 1958), 7, 10.

19   James H. Madole, "The Program for the National Renaissance Party," and "Jewish Labor Czars Call for Military Invasion of Mississippi," *National Renaissance Bulletin*, January 1956, 3.

20   Nicholas Goodrick-Clarke, *Black Sun* (New York University Press, 2002), 3. Eustace Mullins, "Adolph Hitler: An Appreciation," *National Renaissance Bulletin*, October 1952, 4.

21   Goodrick-Clarke, *Black Sun*, 76. See also Revilo P. Oliver, "The Shadow of Empire: Francis Parker Yockey after Twenty Years," *American Mercury*, June 1966 (online at http://www.revilo-oliver.com/news/1966/06/the-shadow-of-empire-francis-parker-yockey-after-twenty-years/).

22   Yockey, *Imperium*. Quoted words and phrases on 176, 199, 202, 218, 234, and 219, respectively. Yockey has been accused of plagiarizing Catholic ideologue and Nazi Party functionary Carl Schmitt. See Sebastian Linderhof, "Concealed Influence: Francis Parker Yockey's Plagiarism of Carl Schmitt," *Occidental Quarterly* 10, no. 4 (Winter 2010–11): 19–62.

23   Madole's title: Goodrick-Clarke, *Black Sun*, 73. See also James H. Madole, "'The New Atlantis': A Blueprint for an Aryan 'Garden of Eden' in America,"

pt. 10, *National Renaissance Bulletin*, January–February 1976, 1; and Nicholas Goodrick-Clarke, "James Madole and the National Renaissance Party," *National-Satanist Worldview* (blog), August 27, 2016, https://nationalsatanist .wordpress.com/2016/08/27/james-madole-the-national-renaissance-party/.

24 See the introduction to Francis Parker Yockey's *Imperium*, i–xvii. Signed by Willis Carto, the introduction is also credited to Revilo P. Oliver, either on the grounds that he wrote it or that Carto plagiarized it. See also Jeffrey Kaplan, "The Postwar Paths of Occult National Socialism: From Rockwell and Madole to Manson," in *Cult, Anti-Cult and the Cultic Milieu: A Re-examination*, ed. Jeffrey Kaplan and Heléne Lööw (published in manuscript form at researchgate.net).

25 A long list of books advertised in *Attack!*, a Yockeyite newspaper, features dozens of books on Nordic history and the mythology of ancient Europe, but nothing Christian at all: "BOOKS Yule Special BOOKS," *Attack!*, December 1971, 7.

26 "America, Which Way?," *National Renaissance Bulletin*, January–February 1963, 1.

27 Quoted in David Livingstone, "Eustace Mullins: Occultist and Disinfo Agent of the Far-Right," *David Livingstone's Blog*, Conspiracy School, January 19, 2016, http://www.conspiracyschool.com/blog/eustace-mullins-occultist-and -disinfo-agent-far-right. See also "Are You Rugged Enough?" (flyer), Christian Youth Corps, 1965.

28 Oliver, "Shadow of Empire," 2; Fred Farrel, "Let's Put a Real Show on the Road—or Get Off the Road," *Common Sense*, September 1, 1970, 1–2.

29 Michael Barkun, *A Culture of Conspiracy* (University of California Press, 2003), 18–33, quote on 18. Spengler: Goodrick-Clarke, *Black Sun*, 75.

30 Advertisement and quotations from "Editorial," *Attack!*, Fall 1969, 3.

31 Curtis B. Dall, representing the Liberty Lobby, testimony before the Senate Finance Committee in 1962, quoted in Scott McLemee, "Spotlight on the Liberty Lobby," *CovertAction Quarterly*, no. 50 (Fall 1994), 50. On Carto's alliances and fallings out, see also Paul W. Valentine, "Power Base for Hard Right," *Washington Post*, May 16, 1971, A1, A8; and Margot Metroland, "Remembering Willis Carto: July 17, 1926–October 26, 2015," Counter-Currents Publishing, October 29, 2015, https://www.counter-currents.com/2015/10/remembering -willis-carto-july-17-1926-october-26-2015/.

32 "Help Us Build a Better America—Join NYA!," *Attack!*, August 1973, 5.

33 Quotations from Federal Bureau of Investigation, Freedom of Information/ Privacy Acts Release, "Subject: William Luther Pierce," https://archive.org /details/foia_Pierce_William_L.-HQ-1, 84.

34 On Pierce's plan, see *Attack!*, February 1974. On the American Nationalists, see *IX Flashback (Troop 9 News)*, pamphlet (American Nationalist, 1974), 5–6.

35 There is another Church of the Creator having nothing to do with Klassen or white supremacy. A legal dispute over use of the name was settled when Klassen's organization was recreated as the Creativity Movement. Ben Klassen, *The White Man's Bible* (Church of the Creator, 1981), 410–11.

36 "Dubious Counsel from Yeats," *Instauration* 1, no. 1 (December 1975): 6. See also Hubert Collins, "In Memoriam: Wilmot Robertson," Social Matter, July 8, 2014, https://www.socialmatter.net/2014/07/08/memoriam-wilmot

-robertson/. RaHoWa: Eric Hawthorne, "Enter the Racial Holy War," *Racial Loyalty*, January 1992, 1. Plan: Macaba, *The Road Back* (Noontide Press, 1973), 2.

37 On Cosmotheism, see William L. Pierce, "Creating a New Society," *Action*, August 1976. William Gayley Simpson, *Which Way Western Man?* (self-pub., 1978); Revilo P. Oliver, "Protecting Our Freedoms," Liberty Bell, September 1987, available online at http://www.revilo-oliver.com/rpo/Protecting_Our _Freedoms.html; Michael O'Meara, "The Jitterbugs and the Vabanquespieler: On Yockey's America," *Occidental Quarterly*, vol. 10, no. 4 (Winter 2010–11), https://www.toqonline.com/archives/v10n4/TOQv10n4OMeara.pdf.

38 Ben Klassen, "This Planet Is All Ours," *Racial Loyalty*, August 1998, 4, 5.

39 On the Creativity Movement's disdain for Christianity, see Alejandro Beutel, "Key Concepts to Understanding Violent White Supremacy," Research Brief, National Consortium for the Study of Terrorism and Responses to Terrorism, April 2017. Conspiratorial quotations from issue 16 of *Imperium*: "White Racial Loyalists Exposed!" by Brother Smith, xviii, and "Shootings, Rebels and Gays, Oh My!" by Rev Logsdon, xii and xiii, *Imperium*, August 42 A.C. This date probably corresponds to 2015; Hale's calendar begins with the founding of the Church of the Creator in 1973.

40 "Kevin MacDonald," Southern Poverty Law Center, accessed May 23, 2018, https://www.splcenter.org/fighting-hate/extremist-files/individual/kevin -macdonald. On Boas: Kevin MacDonald, "Robert Trivers Continues the Tradition of Moral Critique," *Occidental Observer*, January 2, 2012, https://www .theoccidentalobserver.net/2012/01/02/robert-trivers-continues-the-tradition -of-moral-critique-4/. See also Lee D. Baker, "The Cult of Franz Boas and His 'Conspiracy' to Destroy the White Race," *Proceedings of the American Philosophical Society* 154, no. 1 (2010): 8–18.

41 Jacob Siegel, "The Alt-Rights Jewish Godfather," *Tablet*, November 29, 2016 http://www.tabletmag.com/jewish-news-and-politics/218712/spencer -gottfried-alt-right, and, "European Roots of Trump's 'America First,'" *Politico*, January 23, 2017, https://www.politico.eu/article/the-european-roots-of/. See also Oliver, "Protecting Our Freedoms."

42 See Jeff Nesbit, "What Is the Alt-Right?" *US News & World Report*, September 12, 2016, https://www.usnews.com/news/articles/2016-09-12/what-is -the-alt-right; and JimBowie1958, "Paleoconservatives, White Nationalists, 1488ers and the New Alt-Right Defined," Clean Debate Zone, August 30, 2016, http://www.usmessageboard.com/threads/paleoconservatives-white -nationalists-1488ers-and-the-new-alt-right-defined.523807/.

43 On intellectual antisemitism, see George Michael, "Professor Kevin MacDonald's Critique of Judaism: Legitimate Scholarship or the Intellectualization of Anti-Semitism?" *Journal of Church and State* 48 (2006): 779–806; Jared Taylor, "Jews and American Renaissance," American Renaissance, April 14, 2006, https://www.amren.com/news/2006/04/jews_and_americ/. Spencer quoted in: Charles Tanner, "Richard Spencer: Alt-Right, White Nationalist, Anti-Semite," Institute for Research and Education on Human Rights, January 5, 2017, https://www.irehr.org/2017/01/05/richard-spencer-alt-right-white -nationalist-anti-semite/.

44 Heidi Beirich and Mark Potok, "Schism over Anti-Semitism Divides Key White Nationalist Group, American Renaissance," *Intelligence Report*, August 11, 2006, https://www.splcenter.org/fighting-hate/intelligence-report/2006 /schism-over-anti-semitism-divides-key-white-nationalist-group-american -renaissance. Friendly venue in: Tanner, "Richard Spencer."

45 On Regnery's career, see Lance Williams, "Meet the Ex-GOP Insider Who Cre-ated White Nationalist Richard Spencer," Center for Investigative Reporting, July 21, 2017, https://www.revealnews.org/article/meet-the-gop-insider-who -created-white-nationalist-richard-spencer/. On Francis's career, see "Sam Francis," Southern Poverty Law Center, accessed May 23, 2018, https://www .splcenter.org/fighting-hate/extremist-files/individual/sam-francis. Statement of principles in: Chris Haire, "The Problem with Sam Francis," *Haire of the Dog* (blog), *Charleston City Paper*, April 14, 2010, https://www.charlestoncitypaper .com/HaireoftheDog/archives/2010/04/14/the-problem-with-sam-francis.

46 Breitbart quoted in: Chip Berlet, "Collectivists, Communists, Labor Bosses, and Treason: The Tea Parties as Right-Wing Populist Counter-Subversion Panic," *Critical Sociology* 38, no. 4 (2012), 569.

47 Eyes on the Right, "Alt-Right Crowd Spreads Conspiracy Theories about Secret Pedo Ring at D.C. Pizza Parlor," Angry White Men (website), Novem-ber 23, 2016, https://angrywhitemen.org/2016/11/22/alt-right-crowd-spreads -conspiracy-theories-about-secret-pedo-ring-at-d-c-pizza-parlor/. See also Alice Marwick and Rebecca Lewis, *Media Manipulation and Disinformation Online* (Data and Society Research Institute, 2017), https://datasociety.net /pubs/oh/DataAndSociety_MediaManipulationAndDisinformationOnline.pdf.

48 "Race War Richard Spencer," n.d., francisparkeryockey.com.

Chapter Eight

1 "Awake America! To the Dangers of World Government" (flyer), Defenders of George Washington's Principles, 1945(?).

2 Catherine P. Baldwin, corrected testimony before the Senate Committee on Foreign Relations, placed in the *Congressional Record* by Senator William Langer, July 28, 1945.

3 George W. Armstrong, *Third Zionist War* (self-pub., 1951[?]), 5 (petition).

4 Jew-infested vehicle: "United Nations," *American Nationalist*, January 25, 1953, 2. Suppression: L. Fry, "Communism Triumphant," *Women's Voice*, July–August 1955, 7. Fully informed: "Christians Awake" (leaflet), Christian Patriots Cru-sade, 1956(?); Robert Edward Edmondson, *I Testify against the Jews* (self-pub., 1953), 289–90. Vermont riflemen: "Oath of Defiance to the United Nations Flag," *Common Sense*, August 15, 1954, 2.

5 Jack B. Tenney, "The Fight to Save America," acceptance speech as vice pres-idential nominee of the Christian Nationalist Party, September 14, 1952; also published as *"The Anti-Defamation League" & "The Fight to Save America"* (Sacred Truth Publishing, 2010). Tenney's obsession with Zionism is evident in his books and pamphlets, such as *Zion's Trojan Horse* (Standard Publications,

1954) and *Zionist Network* (Standard Publications, 1953). "U.N. Conspiracy to Rule World," *American Nationalist*, December 1954, 1. Billy James Hargis and Julian E. Williams, "United Nations—a Confidential Report," *Christian Crusade*, 1957(?), 4.

6   Phyllis Schlafly, "New World Order, Clinton-Style," *Phyllis Schlafly Report*, June 1994, 2.

7   World Court: Helen Allen, "Warning: Our Country in Jeopardy," *Common Sense*, January 1, 1960, 2. World Bank: "Shall the Money Lords Destroy Us?" (leaflet), Constitutional Money Alliance, 1951. Subversive organizations: Mary M. Davison, *The Profound Revolution* (Greater Nebraskan, 1966), 21. The "uniformity" charge was the refrain in Lillian Roberts's leaflet, "UNESCO: The Greatest Threat to America's Youth," Freedom Club of the First Congregationalist Church of Los Angeles, May 1952.

8   American Flag Committee, "A Report to the American People on UNESCO," inserted in the *Congressional Record* by Rep. John T. Wood as "The Greatest Subversive Plot in History," October 18, 1951. Later distributed as a flyer by local groups such as American Challenge of Athens, Alabama, 1962.

9   "UNESCO: Communism's Trap for Our Youth," by Paul Harvey, news analyst, inserted in the *Congressional Record* by Rep. James B. Utt under "Extension of Remarks," September 4, 1962. Later distributed as a flyer by To Restore American Independence Now (T.R.A.I.N.), an ad hoc committee of the John Birch Society, 1976(?).

10 Statue: Robert H. Williams, *The Ultimate World Order* (self-pub., 1950[?]), 15 (photograph and quotation). Mural: Dan Smoot, "UNESCO," *Dan Smoot Report*, April 4, 1960, 1. See also "Hate Art" (pamphlet), Keep America Committee, 1955(?).

11 Billy James Hargis, *Threats to Christian Education*, pamphlet (Christian Crusade, n.d.), and *The Truth about UNESCO*, pamphlet (Christian Crusade, n.d.).

12 Emanuel M. Josephson, *Rockefeller "Internationalist": The Man Who Misrules the World* (Chedney Press, 1952), 4.

13 Ibid., 121 (milk) and 37 (regimentation).

14 Catherine P. Baldwin, *And Men Wept* (Our Publications, 1954), iii–iv (McFadden). Baldwin's early career is sketched out in Glen Jeansonne, *Women of the Far Right: The Mothers' Movement and World War II* (University of Chicago Press, 1996), 131–35.

15 Catherine Baldwin, *Undermining America through the Foundations of Cecil Rhodes, Andrew Carnegie, Lord Northcliffe, Rockefeller, and the 20th Century Fund, Inc.*, pamphlet (Defenders of the Constitution of the United States of America, 1940[?]).

16 "Women for the United States of America," *The Facts* (ADL), January 1947, 7–12. Wesley Swift, "The Power behind the Red Revolution," Dr. Wesley Swift Library at christogenea.org, June 18, 1962, https://swift.christogenea.org /articles/power-behind-red-revolution-6-18-62.

17 Baldwin, *Undermining America*, 3 and 7.

18 B. Carroll Reece, remarks in the House of Representatives, August 20 1954, circulated as a pamphlet, 1.

19 Augustus G. Rudd, "Education for the New Social Order," *Vital Speeches of the Day* 14, no. 22 (September 15, 1948): 6.

20 American Flag Committee, "A Report to the American People on 'UNESCO,'" 1.

21 William Fulton's articles in the *Chicago Tribune* series "Rhodes' Goal: Return U.S. to British Empire" (July 15-31, 1951) are reprinted by phreedomphan in blog posts titled, "Scholars Exposed," pts. 1 and 2, *America's Enemies* (blog), April 13, 2012. Quotation from the July 17, 1951, article titled "Scholars Help British Cash in on U. S. Billions: Rhodes Men Hold Key Dole Jobs," pt. 1 of the blog post (https://americasenemies.wordpress.com/2012/04/13/scholars-exposed-part-1/). See also Swift, "Power behind the Red Revolution."

22 Norman Dodd, *The Dodd Report to the Reece Committee on Foundations"* (Long House, 1954), 8, 1 (Reece pamphlet).

23 Baldwin, *And Men Wept*, 2.

24 The quote is from ibid., 157.

25 Ibid., 29.

26 Rose L. Martin, *Fabian Freeway* (Western Islands, 1966), ix. See also Paul W. Shafer and John Howland Snow, *The Turning of the Tides* (Long House, 1962), part 1. Gary North, *Conspiracy—a Biblical View* (Dominion Press, 1986), 13. North misspells the title of the novel as *Philip Drew, Administrator*. North was not the first to notice House's novel. A headline in Harvey Springer's weekly newspaper *Western Voice*—"Shocking Discovery: New Deal Was Outlined in Book Written in 1912"—may have been the earliest (August 29, 1946).

27 American Legion cited in Ed Dieckmann, "Network for World Control," flyer distributed by the Network of Patriotic Letter Writers, n.d.; Kenneth Goff, "1776–1955," fundraising letter, 1955; William Guy Carr, "The Conspiracy to Destroy All Existing Governments and Religions," *News behind the News*, April 1958, 9.

28 Rothschilds: Don Bell, "Who Are Our Rulers?," *American Mercury*, September 1960, 136–37. Myron Fagan, *UN Is Spawn of the Illuminati*, pamphlet (Cinema Educational Guild, 1966), 5–6.

29 Shafer and Snow, *Turning of the Tides*, 164. See also Jennings C. Wise, *Woodrow Wilson, Disciple of Revolution* (Paisley Press, 1938).

30 Flyer for a rally sponsored by the Loyal American Group, December 1948.

31 Robert Welch, *The Blue Book of the John Birch Society* (Western Islands, 1959), 44; Dan Smoot, "Invisible Government—Part I," *Dan Smoot Report*, June 12, 1961, 188, 192; Alton Thatcher, "The Invisible Government," *Common Sense*, January 1, 1968, 4. Illuminati in: Myron Fagan, "Our Invisible Government Made Visible, Part 1," *News-Bulletin*, January 1962.

32 Dan Smoot, *The Invisible Government* (Dan Smoot Report, Inc., 1962); David Wise and Thomas B. Ross, *The Invisible Government* (Random House, 1964). The quotation in the text is taken from a 1964 CIA review of *The Invisible Government* (https://www.cia.gov/library/readingroom/docs/CIA-RDP80B01676R001300140001-4.pdf).

33 H. G. Wells, *The New World Order* (Sacker & Warburg, 1940). For a conspiratorial interpretation of Wells's book, see Michael Steinberg, "H. G. Wells Plots

the World Empire," *Executive Intelligence Review* 33, no. 12 (March 24, 2006): 11–13. Possible first use as a pejorative term: Charles W. Phillips, "Lease Lending for the New World Order in China," *Individualist*, no. 133, July 22, 1941, 1. Cartoon accompanying "The Hidden Enemy of Christianity," *Common Sense*, August 1963, 1.

34 Jon A. Yoder, "The United World Federalists: Liberals for Law and Order," *American Studies* 12, no. 1 (1972): 109–30.

35 Kent Courtney and Phoebe Courtney, *America's Unelected Rulers* (Conservative Society of America, 1962); on brainwashing, see chap. 4. Oren Potito, "Our Rulers—Who Are They?," *National Christian News*, May(?) 1965, 1. Don Bell, "Proofs of a Conspiracy to Build a Total, Managed Global Society," pt. 2, *Don Bell Reports*, September 15, 1972, 2.

36 Carroll Quigley, *Tragedy and Hope* (Macmillan, 1966).For a nonconspiratorial assessment of Quigley's ideas, see Daniel Brandt, "Clinton, Quigley and Conspiracy: What's Going on Here?," originally published at *NameBase NewsLine*, no. 1, April–June 1993, which is no longer available; reprinted by the website BeyondWeird.com: https://www.beyondweird.com/conspiracies/cncia006 .html. For a conspiratorial assessment, see Gerry Docherty and Jim MacGregor, "New World Order: The Founding Fathers," Global Research, April 26, 2015, https://www.globalresearch.ca/new-world-order-the-founding-fathers /5445255.

37 W. Cleon Skousen, *The Naked Capitalist* (self-pub., 1970). Lawsuit threat: Brandt, "Clinton, Quigley and Conspiracy," 3.

38 Gary Allen, *None Dare Call It Conspiracy* (Concord Press, 1971). That it was planned to be given away is clear from the message on the title page: "You may have received this book through the mail. It is a gift from a concerned American who has read the book. The donor believes that the survival of our country hinges on the public becoming aware of the material contained herein. All he asks is that you read the book. Thank You." Allen recycled his charges in *Richard Nixon: The Man behind the Mask* (Western Islands, 1971). Allen's trilateralism: John Rees, "An Interview with Gary Allen," *Review of the News*, February 27, 1980, reprinted at http://www.whale.to/b/allen1.html.

39 Seth Payne, "Satan's Plan: The Book of Mormon, Glenn Beck and Modern Conspiracy" (paper presented at a regional meeting of the American Academy on Religion, Calgary, May 10, 2014), 6. See also The Red Phone Is Ringing, "He Blinded Me with Skousen," Daily Kos, May 19, 2010, https://www.dailykos .com/stories/2010/5/19/867891/-.

40 G. Edward Griffin, "The Future Is Calling: Secret Organizations and Hidden Agendas," pt. 2, Freedom Force International, 2013, https://s3-us-west -2.amazonaws.com/freedomforce/pdf/futurecalling2.pdf. Welch, *The Blue Book*, sec. 2, 33–46. Quigley quoted in: Eric Samuelson, "An Introduction to the 'Little Sister' of the Royal Institute of International Affairs: The U.S. Council on Foreign Relations," Bible Believers, accessed May 23, 2018, https://www .biblebelievers.org.au/nowcfr.htm. Garbage: Rudy Maxa, "The Professor Who Knew Too Much," *Washington Post Sunday Magazine*, March 23, 1975. G. Edward Griffin, "The Quigley Formula," a lecture that is widely avail-

able, including from Ron Paul Forums (http://www.ronpaulforums.com
/showthread.php?258041-Video-G-Edward-Griffin-The-Quigley-Formula;
video).

41   Davison, *Profound Revolution*, 81. "Repeal the U. N. Charter *Now!*" *Patriot*,
     June–July 1968, 2.

42   Edward J. Hatfield Jr., "An Open Letter on the Death of J. Edgar Hoover,"
     May 5, 1972, ia801708.us.archive.org/19/items/foia_Pierce_William_L.-HQ-2
     /Pierce_William_L.-HQ-2.pdf, 11–12.

43   Robert Welch, *More Stately Mansions* (Western Islands, 1966); "The Com-
     munist Manifesto," *Family Heritage Series*, vol. 2, lesson no. 72, 1974, https://
     robertwelchuniversity.org/Family%20Heritage%20Series/Lesson%2072.pdf;
     the *Family Heritage Series* is part of Robert Welch University's "Home School
     Support" program. See also Donald Kimelman, "Illuminati Tentacles Grasp
     Bircher World," *Baltimore Sun*, April 20, 1975, A-19–20.

44   "Kissinger's Goal Is World Government," *Thunderbolt*, August 1972, 2; Gary H.
     Kah, *En Route to Global Occupation* (Huntington House, 1992); Dennis L.
     Cuddy, *Chronological History: The New World Order*, pamphlet (self-pub.,
     1996[?]); Samuelson, "An Introduction to the 'Little Sister,'" 2; John Cole-
     man, *The Tavistock Institute of Human Relations: Shaping the Moral, Spiritual,
     Cultural, Political and Economic Decline of the United States of America* (Global
     Review Publications, 2006).

45   Robert Welch, *The Neutralizers* (John Birch Society, 1963). Myron Fagan rou-
     tinely used "masterminds" in his reports to his followers. Medford Evans, *The
     Usurpers* (Western Islands, 1968). Arch Roberts called liberals "mattoids" (a
     combination of genius and fool) apparently just for fun. Wire-pullers: Pedro del
     Valle, "An American Patriot Speaks Out," *American Mercury*, November 1960,
     107. Edward Hatfield relied on the phrase "eastern establishment" in flyers put
     out by his Citizens for American Survival.

46   Brian Desborough, "Stop Misleading the Children, Mr. Jennings" (apparently
     reprinted from the *California Sun*, 1999), http://www.whale.to/b/desborough
     .html.

Chapter Nine

1   Upton Close [Josef Washington Hall] and John Howland Snow, *The Plan to
    Enslave Congress and You (Revealed and Documented)*, American Papers no. 4
    (Washington, DC: Broadcasts, Inc., 1950).

2   Carl Mote, *The New Deal Goose Step* (Daniel Ryerson, 1939), v.

3   Richard Hofstadter, *Anti-Intellectualism in American Life* (Alfred A. Knopf,
    1970), 3.

4   Clarence Manion, "Our America," in *The Key to Peace: A Formula for the
    Perpetuation of Real Americanism* (Heritage Foundation, 1951); Dan Smoot,
    "Impeaching Earl Warren," pt. 1, *Dan Smoot Report*, January 30, 1961, 35;
    Robert Welch, *A Letter to the South on Segregation*, pamphlet (John Birch Soci-
    ety, 1956).

5 Joseph Kamp, *We Must Abolish the United States* (Constitutional Educational League, 1950), 47. Red-ucators: Verne Kaub, "A Layman's Guide to the National Council of Churches Constitutional Convention," *Challenge*, February 1951, 4. Pseudo-intellectuals: Olivia O'Grady, *Beasts of the Apocalypse* (O'Grady Publications, 1959), 11. So-called scholars: Edgar Bundy, "Communism's Latest Ally—the New Per-version of the Bible," message delivered at the Lockland Baptist Church, n.d. Negro intellectuals: Manning Johnson, *Color, Communism and Common Sense*, pamphlet (The Alliance, 1958).

6 "Who Played the Fool, the Legion or Those Blatherskite 'Intellectuals'?" *The Firing Line*, December 1, 1952, 1–2.

7 Gerald B. Winrod, "Persecuted Radio Preachers," *Defender*, October 1949, 13–15. Jesus ban: W. D. Herrstrom's *Bible News Flashes*, cited in "The Combination of Religion and Hatred," *The Facts* (ADL), August 1946, 7.

8 Macy's: *Think Weekly*, July 14, 1946, 2. ADL: Upton Close, editor's note to Robert H. Williams's, *The Anti-Defamation League and Its Use in the World Communist Offensive*, pamphlet, Closer-Ups Supplement no. 1 (Closer-Ups, 1947).

9 Marilyn Allen, "F.B.I. Persecutes Utah Patriot," letter dated April 16, 1959, *Thunderbolt*, no. 12 (September 1959), 5. See also Eustace Mullins, "The Atlanta Report," leaflet (M&N Associates, 1959[?]); and "The Untold Facts behind the Synagogue Bombing," *National Renaissance Bulletin*, September–October 1958, 1–5.

10 Myron Fagan, "What Is This Thing Called 'Anti-Semitism'?," *News-Bulletin* (of the Cinema Educational League), November–December 1951, 10–11. This article includes copies of detailed correspondence between Fagan and California Bar Association officials. Robert H. Williams, *The Ultimate World Order* (self-pub., 1950), 72–74.

11 Joseph Kamp, *With Lotions of Love . . . to Walter Winchell*, pamphlet (Constitutional Educational League, 1944), fourth page; Eustace Mullins, "Writer Charges Oil Company with Breach of Contract," press release, February 20, 1956. Jewish Officials: Eustace Mullins, "Attention Readers!" (flyer?), n.d., and "Police State Terror on Lincoln Avenue" (press release) December 16, 1959.

12 Myron Fagan, "Year-End Report for Our Members" (attached to fundraising letter), January 1962; 5; Fred Schwarz, instructions accompanying form letter, 1961; Karl Prussion, "'Legal Czar' Mosk, A.C.L.U. and California Board of Education Attack 'Heads Up' Editor," *Heads Up*, June–July 1963, 3; Robert Welch, *Blue Book*, 4th ed. (Western Islands, 1961), ix; and "The ADL-IADI Axis," *News & Views*, November 1958, 15.

13 Joseph Kamp, *Senator McCarthy's Methods*, pamphlet (Constitutional Educational League, n.d.). Kamp wrote a series of pamphlets accusing the *New York Times*, the Scripps-Howard newspaper chain, the *Atlantic Monthly*, and the Ford Foundation of attacking McCarthy. See *Headlines*, November 1, 1953, an issue of Kamp's newsletter devoted entirely to the "CONSPIRACY against MCCARTHY."

14 Attack the lies: informational pamphlet on Citizens for American Survival (n.d.), "action program" no. 9, 4; Gerald L. K. Smith, fundraising letter for the Christian Nationalist Crusade, 1970. John Doe: "The Plan" (flyer), American Family Forum, 1968(?).

15   Eustace Mullins, *The Gentle Art of Thought Control*, pamphlet "extracted" from
     World Economic Review, July 1986; Michael Collins Piper, "Zionist Influence on
     the American Media," special report from American Free Press Newspaper,
     2003; Donald J. Trump, "We should have a contest as to which of the Net-
     works, plus CNN and not including Fox, is the most dishonest, corrupt and/or
     distorted in its political coverage . . . ," tweet, November 27, 2017, 6:04 a.m.

16   *The Brainwashing Manual* is generally credited to Goff. It has also been claimed
     by (or at least on behalf of) L. Ron Hubbard, inventor of Dianetics and founder
     of Scientology, and by one Charles Stickley, who may or may not have existed.
     See Massimo Introvigne, "L. Ron Hubbard, Kenneth Goff, and the 'Brain-
     Washing Manual' of 1955," Centro Studi sulle Nuovo Religioni, January 25,
     2014, http://www.cesnur.org/2005/brainwash_13.htm.

17   See Morris Kominsky, "The Great Crusade: The Psychopolitics Hoax," chap. 12
     of *The Hoaxers* (Branden Press).

18   Kenneth Goff, *Are the People of America Being Brain-Washed into Slavery?* (self-
     pub., 1955[?]), first page; this is the same book as The Brainwashing Manual.
     Fred Schwarz, Communism Diagnosis and Treatment (World Vision, Inc.,
     1963[?]), 37; Herb Blackschleger, *Hide! A Challenge to the Devotees of Freud,
     Pasteur, Darwin and Marx* (Meador Publishing Co., 1959), 103 ("brainwashed"
     quotation).

19   Editorial, *Santa Ana Register*, quoted in Kominsky, *The Hoaxers*, 114. See also
     Margaret L. Hartley, "Whose Mental Health? The Psychology of Suspicion,"
     Southwest Review 46, no. 4 (1961): 269–79; and "Siberian Concentration Camp
     Now Ready For You—and I Do Mean YOU!" *Women's Voice*, March 1956, 16.

20   Sinister bill: Wickliffe B. Venard Sr., *50 Years of Treason in 100 Acts* (self-pub.,
     1964), 31. Railroaded: Usher Burdick, "Remarks," *Congressional Record*,
     June 4, 1957.

21   Contemporary accounts, such as a chronology of the "steps toward mind
     control" often ignore the Soviets entirely, stressing instead Progressive Era
     organizations and their Rockefeller funding. "Steps toward Global Mind
     Control under the Banner of Mental Health and Education," Jesus-Is-Savior
     .com, accessed May 24, 2018, https://www.jesus-is-savior.com/Family/Parents
     %20Corner/mind_control.htm. This undated chronology ends in 2003; it could
     well be the work of Dennis L. Cuddy.

22   "One Worlders," *News behind the News*, January 1957, 1.

23   Revilo P. Oliver, "Introduction to *The Anti-Humans* by D. Bacu," published as a
     free-standing essay by Soldiers of the Cross in 1971 (Kenneth Goff's organiza-
     tion), online at http://www.revilo-oliver.com/rpo/Anti_Humans.html.

24   Eugene Pomeroy, "Fight the Two Worst Threats," *American Mercury*, Decem-
     ber 1958, 141; O'Grady, *Beasts of the Apocalypse*, 20. On Walker, see Revilo P.
     Oliver, "Commentary," appended to Frederick Seelig's *Destroy the Accuser*
     (Freedom Press, 1976), 141–42.

25   Aluminum: Leo Spira, *The Drama of Fluorine—Arch Enemy of Mankind* (Lee
     Foundation for Nutritional Research, 1953). Zionists: "Fluoridation Poison in
     Drinking Water," *Common Sense*, October 15, 1954, 1–2, 4. Charles B. Hudson,
     "Poison," *Women's Voice* February 22, 1951, 5.

26 "Rev. Kenneth Goff's Testimony," *News behind the News*, March 1958, 6. Secret Police: "The Romance of Fluorides (No.1)," *American Capsule News*, February 4, 1956.

27 "At the Sign of the Unholy Three" (flyer), Keep America Committee, May 16, 1955.

28 "Say 'NO' to Poison-Fluorine in Your Drinking Water" (flyer), Citizens Committee against Fluoridation, La Crosse, WI, distributed by Constitutional Educational League, n.d. Survey: Donald R. McNeil, "America's Longest War: The Fight over Fluoridation, 1950—," *Wilson Quarterly* 9, no. 3 (Summer 1985): 150; the quote within the quote is from the survey). See also Ralph E. Ellsworth and Sarah M. Harris, *The American Right Wing*, Occasional Paper No. 59, University of Illinois Library School (University of Illinois Graduate School of Library Science, 1960), 12–13.

29 Jo Hindman, "Secret *Cum* Files—a Leftist Wedge," *American Mercury*, October 1958, 48. "Cum" is Hindman's shorthand for "cumulative." Revilo P. Oliver, "Americans Speak Out," *American Mercury*, January 1960, 125.

30 Ad copy for Skousen's recording, "Building Balanced Children," in the Key Records catalog, n.d.

31 "An Evil and Subversive Thing: The Anti-Mental Health Movement," Hogg Foundation for Mental Health, accessed May 24, 2018, http://www.hogghistory .org/an-evil-and-subversive-thing/. Newsletter quoted on fourth page of print version.

32 Gene Birkeland, "Deliver Us from Evil," *American Mercury* 88 (March 1959), reprinted at American Education Watch, *Exposing the Global Road to Ruin through Education*, http://www.americaseducationwatch.org/uploads/7/9/1/7 /7917170/exposing_the_global_road_to_ruin_full.pdf, 3.

33 See, for instance, Jared Atwell, "The Work of a Super-Patriot: Allen Zoll and the National Council for American Education," history thesis, University of North Carolina at Asheville, 2003. DAR quotation in: Harry Bach, "Censorship of Library Books and Textbooks in American schools, 1953-1963," *Journal of Secondary Education* 40, no. 1 (1965): 8.

34 E. Merrill Root, *Brainwashing in the High Schools* (Devin-Adair, 1958). See also "What Is Happening to America's Youth?" *News and Views*, May 1965, 14–15; Matt Cvetic, "The Thought Control Brigade," and "The Mental Health Goldbrick," *American Mercury*, October 1958, 137–38 and March 1959, 123–26, respectively; "Does UNESCO Oligarchy Rule PTA?" *Guardians of Our American Heritage*, December 1955, 3; Dan Smoot, "UNESCO," *Dan Smoot Report*, April 4, 1960, 110. Smoot is quoting the booklets.

35 Martha Andrews, "Education or Indoctrination?" *Common Sense*, January 15, 1967, 3.

36 John Kasper, "Abolish the Public Schools! Now!" *Thunderbolt* (exact date unknown) 1960, 3.

37 Birkeland, "Deliver Us from Evil," 1. Smoot, "UNESCO," 110.

38 John Steinbacher, "The Child Seducers Revisited," *American Mercury*, Fall 1970, 6, 7.

39 Ezra Taft Benson, "Godless Forces Threaten Us," *Conference Report*, October 1969, 60–64, quote on 61; Gary Allen, "Hate Therapy," *American Opinion*, Jan-

uary 1968; Don Bell, *Don Bell Reports*, May 3, 1968; "Sensitivity Training is . . . Mental Suicide!" *Fiery Cross*, April 1971, 7.

40   Ed Dieckmann Jr., "Network for World Control," *American Mercury*, Winter 1969. Distributed as a flyer by the Network of Patriotic Letter Writers; quotation on second page of flyer.

41   Menticide: "Sensitivity Training," *News and Views*, October 1968, 6–8. Robots: "The Plan" (flyer), American Family Forum, 1968(?). Editorial: "Freedom from What? Now They Would Subvert Parental Authority," *Nashville Banner*, January 14, 1964, excerpted in "What Is Happening to America's Youth?" *News and Views*, May 1965, 16.

42   David Noebel, *Communism, Hypnotism and the Beatles* (Christian Crusade Publications, 1965), 1. See also Carl F. Lyons, "Soviet Blueprint for Total Immorality Unleashed Fifty Years Ago Hurled the United States into Abyss of Moral Degradation," *Common Sense*, January 15, 1967, 1.

43   Drugs: Birkeland, "Deliver Us from Evil," 4. Movies and folk songs: "What Is Happening to America's Youth?" 17 and 18. Representative Utt quoted in "Rock Plot?" *Billboard* 81, no. 18 (May 3, 1969): 48. Lab tested: Noebel, *Communism, Hypnotism and the Beatles*, 10.

44   Jo-Ann Abrigg, "In the Name of Education," *Phyllis Schlafly Report*, December 1976, 3; Constance E. Cumbey, *The Hidden Dangers of the Rainbow* (Huntington House, 1985), 212; Charlotte T. Iserbyt, *The Deliberate Dumbing Down of America* (Conscience Press, 1999), xv.

45   Michael A. Aquino, introduction (November 2003) to Colonel Paul E. Valley with Major Michael A. Aquino's *From PSYOP to Mind War: the Psychology of Victory* (Psychological Operations Group, U.S. Army Reserve, 1980), 2, https://flowofwisdom.files.wordpress.com/2013/07/mindwar-mindwar_co_authored_by_michael-aquino.pdf.

46   Richard Condon, foreword to Walter Bowart's *Operation Mind Control* (Dell, 1978), 14–15.

47   William R. Pabst, "Concentration Camp Plans for U.S. Citizens" (transcript of a taped report) 1979, no page numbers, posted on https://www.scribd.com/document/87119956/Concentration-Camp-Plans-for-u-s-Citizens (accessed July 13, 2018). Pabst's aerosols may be the earliest conspiratorial reference to chemtrails.

48   Gordon (Jack) Mohr, "The Psychopolitical Indoctrination of America," pt. 1, Israel Elect of Zion, accessed May 24, 2018, https://israelect.com/reference/JackMohr/jm020a.htm.

49   Eustace Mullins, "Sigmund Freud: Antichrist Devil," Whale, May 10, 1997, ttp://www.whale.to/b/mullins49.html. Lewin and Tavistock: Ron Patton, "Project Monarch: Nazi Mind Control," *PARANOIA: The Conspiracy Reader*, reprinted at Whale, accessed May 24, 2018, http://www.whale.to/b/patton.html. Martin Cannon, "The Controllers: A New Hypothesis of Alien Abduction," pts. 1–4, Biblioteca Pleyades, ca. 1990, https://www.bibliotecapleyades.net/sociopolitica/esp_sociopol_mindcon04.htm; apparently an excerpt from Cannon's book *The Controllers: Mind Control and Its Role in the "Alien" Abduction Phenomenon* (Feral House, 1996).

50   Cannon, "The Controllers," pt. 1, third page. Assassins and agents: Cathy O'Brien and Mark Phillips, *TRANCE Formation of America* (Reality Marketing, 2005); Rebecca Moore, "Reconstructing Reality: Conspiracy Theories about Jonestown," *Journal of Popular Culture* 36, no. 2 (2002): 200–220; Patton, "Project Monarch"; Brice Taylor, *Thanks for the Memories* (Brice Taylor Trust, 1991). Research: O'Brien and Phillips, *TRANCE Formation of America*, third page of chap. 1. WARNING: Cisco Wheeler and Fritz Springmeier, "The Illuminati Formula to Create an Undetectable Total Mind Control Slave," Biblioteca Pleyades, accessed July 13, 2018, https://www.bibliotecapleyades.net/sociopolitica /mindcontrol/mindcontrol_index.htm.

51   Elaine Showalter, *Hystories: Hysterical Epidemics and Modern Media* (Columbia University Press, 1997); Elizabeth Loftus, "On Science under Legal Assault," *Daedalus* 132, no. 4 (Fall 2003): 84–86; Evan Harrington, "Conspiracy Theories and Paranoia: Notes from a Mind-Control Conference," *Skeptical Inquirer*, vol. 20, no. 5 (September–October 1996), https://www.csicop.org/si/show /conspiracy_theories_and_paranoia_notes_from_a_mind-control_conference.

52   Harrington, "Conspiracy Theories and Paranoia," 2; the "*sic*" and ellipses are Harrington's.

53   Cannon, "The Controllers," 24–25; Taylor, *Thanks for the Memories*, 1; Patton, "Project Monarch," 11–12.

54   Mohr, "Psychopolitical Indoctrination of America," 8; the internal quote and irregular ellipses are Mohr's, although there is no indication whom he is quoting.

Chapter Ten

1   Ezra Taft Benson, "Godless Forces Threaten Us," *Conference Report*, October 1969, 63. Fourteenth Amendment: "Impeaching Earl Warren," pt. 1, *Dan Smoot Report*, January 30, 1961, 37–38. Fourteenth and Fifteenth Amendments: Erst LaFlor, *The Betrayal of the White Race* (self-pub., 1970). Sixteenth Amendment: "Bulletin No. 6," Congress of Freedom, October 31, 1953, 5. Seventeenth Amendment: Myron Fagan, "The Illuminati and the Council on Foreign Relations," Bible Believers, accessed May 24, 2018, http://www.biblebelievers.org .au/illuminati.htm. Headquarters: Revilo P. Oliver, "All America Must Know the Terror That Is upon Us," *Conservative* Viewpoint, June 1966, 10. Federal Reserve: Wickliffe B. Venard, *50 Years of Treason in 100 Acts* (self-pub., 1964), 1–6. Marilyn Monroe: Frank Capell, *The Strange Death of Marilyn Monroe* (Herald of Freedom, 1964), 6.

2   *Catalogue of Publications and Training Aids of the Church League of America*, November 1967; Key Records, catalog, n.d.

3   *Open Forum Speakers' Bureau Presents Exciting Speakers, Leadership You Can Be Proud Of*, brochure (Amarillo, TX, n.d.).

4   Schwarz's events for which programs can be found online include: Greater Miami School of AntiCommunism, 1961; Washington [DC] School of Anti-Communism, 1964; Tidewater Schwarz-Philbrick Anti-Communist Rally, 1966; Anti-Subversive Seminars (New York and Washington, DC), 1969.

Dallas Freedom Forum, program, 1960. On the 1962 Dallas Freedom Forum and the Reagan speech, see Edward H. Miller, *Nut Country* (University of Chicago Press, 2015), 30–32. On the National Indignation Convention: see "Finding Aid—FBI and Other Files (Ernie Lazar Collection)," August 2016 at https://crws.berkeley.edu/sites/default/files/shared/images/pubs/FINDING%20AID%2008-23-16.pdf, p. 37. "Project Alert!" (flyer), 1961.

5   Hargis: "First Annual National Anti-Communist Leadership School," Tulsa, Oklahoma, January 29 to February 2, 1962 (program). See also John M. Werly, "Premillennialism and the Paranoid Style," *American Studies* 18, no. 1 (1977): 48–50.

6   "Ninth Annual National Session, the Congress of Freedom, Inc.," Columbus, Ohio, April 6–10, 1960. A different Congress of Freedom, affiliated with the Citizens Council of Louisiana, also featured conspiracists.

7   "Soldiers of the Cross Christian Patriotic Training Institute" (brochure), four sessions, July 15 to August 17, 1969. Dallas Rocquemore, *Get Ye Up into the High Mountains* (Pilgrim Torch, 1968) ("Why not make it a Christmas present to those of your loved ones?"—ad copy).

8   Nero-like powers: Elizabeth Dilling, "Pharisee Police State Has Barred Common Sense," *Common Sense*, October 15, 1958, 4. Even jokingly: Myron Fagan, *United Nations Is United States Cancer*, pamphlet (Cinema Educational Guild, n.d.), 6.

9   "Our Goal—50 Million White Members in America" (leaflet), White Circle League (Chicago), 1954.

10 Clarence Manion, *The Key to Peace: A Formula for the Perpetuation of Real Americanism* (Heritage Foundation, 1950), published in abridged form as *Our America*, pamphlet (Heritage Foundation, 1951), 16, 17–18.

11 Ben Moreell, "To Communism . . . via Majority Vote," speech to the marketing division of the American Petroleum Institute, Chicago, November 10, 1952, https://archive.org/stream/ToCommunism . . . viaMajorityVote/ToCommunismViaMajorityVote_djvu.txt, and "Engineers—Scientific and Social," speech to the Society of Automotive Engineers, Detroit, January 14, 1953, http://www.pirate4x4.com/forum/general-chit-chat/849421-social-engineering-speech-1953-admiral-ben-moreell-seabees-founder.html.

12 Norman Dodd, *The Dodd Report to the Reece Committee on Foundations* (Long House, 1954), 10, 12. Karl Kurtz, "1313: A Famous (or Infamous) Landmark of Public Administration," National Council of State Legislatures, March 18, 2010, http://ncsl.typepad.com/the_thicket/2010/03/1313-landmark-of-public-administration.html.

13 John F. Brennan, "The Radical Right, the National Municipal League Smear File, and the Controversy over Metropolitan Government in the United States during the Postwar Years," *Public Voices* 13, no. 1 (2013): 28 and 30.

14 William Guy Carr, "The Conspiracy to Destroy All Existing Governments and Religions," *News behind the News*, April 1958, 10; Jo Hindman, organizational chart titled "The Metropolitan Government Network (in Part)," 1961, reproduced in her *Blame Metro . . . When Urban Renewal Strikes!* (Caxton Printers, 1966); Kent Courtney and Phoebe Courtney, *America's Unelected Rulers* (Conservative Society of America, 1962).

15   Four steps: Jo Hindman, "The 'Metro' Monster," *American Mercury*, July 1959,
      50. Metrocrats: "Metro Tyranny," memo (?), Citizens for Constitutional Gov-
      ernment, February 11, 1972. Brainwashing: Courtney and Courtney, *America's
      Unelected Rulers*, 38.
16   "Why Not Go First Class?," John Birch Society leaflet, n.d.; Merwin K. Hart,
      Economic Council Letter, no. 525, 1962.
17   Pedro del Valle, "Defeat the Civil Rights Bill of 1963 S-1731," *Common Sense*,
      September 1, 1963, 4; "One Worlders to Surrender U.S.—Egghead Wreckers at
      Work," *Common Sense*, January 1, 1963, 1.
18   "The N.A.A.C.P. Is Not Controlled by Negroes" (leaflet), American National-
      ists, 1957.
19   Allen's diatribe cited in *The Facts* (ADL), December 1946, 19. Marilyn Allen,
      Alien Minorities and Mongrelization (Meador Publishing, 1949). Stoner cited in
      "Mass Murder Urged by Tennessee Hitler," *Bulletin and Washington Newsletter*
      (ADL), September 1946, 2.
20   Eustace Mullins, "Communism Hits South with Non-segregation," *Common
      Sense*, July 1, 1954, 1; James H. Madole, "Professional Tolerance Merchants
      Foment Civil War in Dixie," *National Renaissance Bulletin*, September 1955;
      "DEATH! to the Traitors" (flyer), Christian Patriots Crusade, 1958.
21   National Citizens Protective Association (of Saint Louis) handbill, n.d. (1955?);
      Bryant Bowles, "Left-Wing Papers Lie to Northerners," *National Forum*, mid-
      August 1954, 1; James H. Madole, "The Catholic Church and Racial Matters,"
      National Renaissance Bulletin, October–November 1957, 3; "Emmett Till Is
      Alive" (flyer), American Anti-Communist Militia, 1955.
22   "Jews Organize Negro Sit-Ins," *Thunderbolt*, 1960; Oren Potito, "Segregate or
      Integrate: Which Way for Christians?" *Thunderbolt*, September 1962, 12.
23   Joseph Beauharnais, "Bye Bye Blackbird," *White Circle League of America*,
      April 4, 1968, 3.
24   Wilmot Robertson, *The Dispossessed Majority* (Howard Allen, 1972), and *Venti-
      lations* (Howard Allen, 1972); quotation from *Ventilations*, 55.
25   Robert Williams, *Know Your Enemy* (Williams Publications, 1956), 17.
26   "Remember the Nightmare of Trumbull Park Homes and the Police State?"
      (flyer), White Circle League (Chicago), 1954; "Race-Mixing Scorecard," *Revere*,
      September 1956, 4; "Why Does the Application Specify 'White Race'?" (flyer),
      Christian Defense League, 1964(?). Dickinson quoted in "Selma—Saga of
      Debauchery and Immorality," Cinema Education Guild, 1965. This was prob-
      ably written by Myron Fagan, head of the guild, who is not wholly reliable.
27   Archibald B. Roosevelt, preface to *Red Intrigue and Race Turmoil* (Alliance, Inc.,
      1958), 4, 5.
28   "Leninists Plan Provocations for Violence—Prepare for Strategic Moment,"
      Heads Up, April–May 1963, 1.
29   The photograph of Martin Luther King Jr. was distributed in 1957 by the Geor-
      gia Commission on Education, a group fighting school desegregation. By the
      early 1960s, the White Citizens Council of Louisiana undertook a campaign
      to blanket the South with billboards featuring the photo because "leftwing
      newspapers may refuse to tell the whole truth, but we can tell the story on

billboards" (from a fundraising letter signed by the council's president Courtney Smith, May1965). See also "Civil Rights Red Fronters," *Common Sense*,
August 1963, 4; and Julia Brown, "Please *Don't* Help Glorify Martin Luther
King" (pamphlet) John Birch Society, Truth about Civil Turmoil (TACT) Committee, n.d.

30   "The Gesell Report—Military Dictatorship," *Common Sense*, 1 September
1963, 3.

31   Selma: American Flag Committee, *Newsletter* no.68, Spring 1965, 1. President
Johnson: Herbert Butterworth, *Role of Race Riots in Plan for World Government
by LBJ*, phonograph record, 1965. Watts: Karl Prussion, "Watts Insurrection—
Result of Communist Civil Rights Movement," *Heads Up*, August 1965, 1.
Detroit: George Kindred, Patriotic Party spokesman, quoted in the *Patriot*,
June–July 1968, 4. Chicago: flyer distributed by the Chicago Committee to Sup-
port Your Local Police, Inc., 1968.

32   "Evidence Links SCEF to Havana Terrorist and NAACP Chief," *Councilor*,
April 2, 1966, 2; Alan Stang, "Lest We Forget," *Review of the News*, April 24,
1968, 4.

33   Sabotaging: Revilo P. Oliver, "After Fifty Years," *Attack!*, Fall 1969, 4. See also
John Steinbacher, "The Child Seducers Revisited," *American Mercury*, Fall
1970, 5–8. Gandhi: "The Baptist World Alliance—Alliance with What?" *News &
Views*, June 1965, 12–13. Swarming peaceniks: "Pacifists Demonstrate in Pentagon," *On Target*, October 1, 1965, 1.

34   Robert Shelton, editorial, *Fiery Cross*, August 1970, 2. See also "Guerrilla Warfare," pt. 7, *AVG Report*, September 1971, 2.

35   Don Bell, "Executive Orders: The Broad Highway to Dictatorship," *Don Bell
Reports*, February 4, 1972. See also W. Frank Horne, "Presidential Powers over-
rule Congress," *Common Sense*, September 1, 1963, 1.

36   John R. Rarick, "Regional Government—the New Federal Soviets by Executive
Order," *Congressional Record*, February 16, 1972. Closer working relationships:
Executive Order 11647, February 10, 1972, appended to Rarick's remarks.

37   "Information on Citizens for American Survival," flyer, n.d.

38   McDonald revelation and accompanying scenario in William R. Pabst, *Concentration Camp Plans for U.S. Citizens* (self-pub. 1979), which Pabst describes as
an "updated report."

39   Untitled document from the lobbying campaign against the Montana
Constitutional Convention by the Committee for Constitutional Government, 1972, University of Montana Law Library, http://www.umt
.edu/media/law/library%5CMontanaConstitution%5CCampbell
/CitizensForConstitutionalGovernment-Excerpts.pdf, 30.

40   Phoebe Courtney, *Beware Metro and Regional Government* (Independent American, 1973), esp. chap. 7: "'1313'—Regional Government's Trojan Horse"; Don
Bell, "The Contrived Evolution of Regional Government," *Don Bell Reports*,
most of 1974; maps in pt. 17 (August 23, 1974) and pt. 15 (August 9, 1974). A
compact version of Bell's argument (also with map) can be found in "The 'New
Socialism' in the United States: The Planners to Replace the Politicians," *Don
Bell Reports*, September 21, 1973.

41   "The Silent Revolution" (pamphlet), Association for Land Use Planning by Land Owners, Inc., 1976, 3–6.

42   Nate Brown, "Say Goodbye to the 50 States, Get Ready for FEMA Regions for the North American Union," *Christian Journal*, June 3, 2016, https://christianjournal.net/nwo/50-states-fema-regions-north-american-union/; "The United States Was Officially Abolished in 1972!" Spingola Speaks, accessed April 24, 2018, http://www.spingola.com/regionalism_maps.htm.

43   Plans: Upton Close, "Give Me Your Guns," *Closer Up*, September 27, 1963; Wesley Swift, "Jacob's Time of Trouble" (sermon), 1963, https://israelect.com/ChurchOfTrueIsrael/swift/swjacob-trouble.html.

44   Soviet Jews: "You're at a Party" (flyer), Right Brigade, 1965. Don't let them: untitled flyer, Right Brigade, n.d. Last bastion and final analysis: reader appeal, *Patriot*, June–July 1968, 10.

45   Coins: "Silver Coins Soon Unavailable," *On Target*, October 1, 1965, 3. Sports: Lawrence Dunegan, taped "reminiscences" of a speech given in 1969 by an unnamed member of the "Order" (tape no. 2: "NWO Plans Exposed by Insider in 1969," Rense Alt News, August 26, 2011, http://rense.com/general94/nwoplans.htm. Homosexuals: Revilo P. Oliver, "Commentary," appended to Frederick Seelig's *Destroy the Accuser* (Freedom Press, 1967), 156, 163–64.

46   Gerald L. K. Smith, *Too Much and Too Many Roosevelts* (Christian Nationalist Crusade, 1950); Joseph Kamp, "Meet the Man Who Plans to Rule America," *Headlines*, 1958; Myron Fagan, *The Strange Cases of Chet Huntley and Ed Murrow*, booklet (Cinema Educational Guild, 1961).

47   See, for instance, Ronald Reagan, "What Price Freedom?," an address to the Dallas Freedom Forum, February 27, 1962 (broadcast on local television on March 22).

48   Carr, "The Conspiracy to Destroy All Existing Governments and Religions," 2; Jo-Ann Abrigg, "In the Name of Education," *Phyllis Schlafly Report*, December 1976, 1 (experts), 2 (Third Force); Ed Dieckmann, "Network for World Control," news clipping distributed by the Network of Patriotic Letter Writers, ca.1969, 2. Do-gooders and 1313: Don Bell, "Who Are Our Rulers?," *American Mercury*, September 1960, 135. Posers: Curtis B. Dall, first page of foreword to June Grem's *The Money Manipulators* (Enterprise Publications), 1971.

49   Benjamin Freedman, speech to "a military organization in Washington, D.C., 1974," HugeQuestions.com, accessed July 13, 2018, http://hugequestions.com/Eric/TFC/Freedman1974speech.html.

50   Grem, *Money Manipulators*, second page of author's preface; Mary M. Davison, *Profound Revolution* (Greater Nebraskan, 1966), 75; Dall, foreword to Grem, *Money Manipulators*.

Chapter Eleven

1   U.S. House of Representatives, *Americans Missing in Southeast Asia: Final Report, Together with Additional and Separate Views of the Select Committee on Missing Persons in Southeast Asia* (Washington: U.S. Government Printing Office), vii.

2   See Gordon B. Arnold, *Conspiracy Theory in Film, Television, and Politics* (Prae-
     ger, 2008); and David Harper, "The Politics of Paranoia: Paranoid Positioning
     and Conspiratorial Narratives in the Surveillance Society," *Surveillance and
     Society* 5, no. 1 (2008): 1–32.

3   Bill Kaysing and Randy Reid, *We Never Went to the Moon: America's Thirty Bil-
     lion Dollar Swindle* (Health Research, 1976), 5.

4   Ibid., 7, 8 (questions), 19, 20, 23 (captions), 26 (desert), 45 (buffet).

5   William Brian II, *Moongate* (Future Science Research Publishing Co., 1982),
     145; Ralph René, *NASA Mooned America!* (self-pub., 1992).

6   Roger D. Launius, "Denying the Apollo Moon Landings: Conspiracy and Ques-
     tioning in Modern American History" (paper delivered at the forty-eighth
     American Institute of Aeronautics and Astronautics Aerospace Sciences meet-
     ing, January 6, 2010), 8–9.

7   See, for instance, Whitley Streiber, *Communion* (Beech Tree Books, 1987);
     John A. Keel, *Operation Trojan Horse* (IllumiNet Press, 1996); Jason Colavito,
     "Should Public Libraries Promote Stan Gordon's Bigfoot-UFO Conspiracy
     Theories?" *Jason Colavito* (blog), April 21, 2014, http://www.jasoncolavito.com
     /blog/should-public-libraries-promote-stan-gordons-bigfoot-ufo-conspiracy
     -theories. For an overview, see Phil Patton, *Dreamland* (Villard, 1998).

8   See Michael Specter, *Denialism* (Penguin, 2009); Orac, "Conspiracy Theories:
     The Dark Heart of Alternative Medicine," *Respectful Insolence* (blog), March 20,
     2014, https://respectfulinsolence.com/2014/03/20/conspiracy-theories-the
     -dark-heart-of-alternative-medicine/; Ben Goldacre, *Bad Science* (Fourth
     Estate, 2009); Jeanne Bergman, "The Cult of HIV Denialism," The Body (web-
     site), Spring 2010, http://www.thebody.com/content/art57918.html; Helen
     Epstein, "Ebola in Liberia: An Epidemic of Rumors," *New York Review of Books*,
     December 18, 2014, 91–95.

9   Walter H. Bowart's *Operation Mind Control* (Dell, 1978), for example, is
     difficult to categorize ideologically. Right wing 9/11: Eustace Mullins, "The
     Secret of 9/11: The Drumbeat for War," Spectrum 4, no. 5 (November 2002):
     68–73, https://dokumen.tips/documents/spectrum-v45002.html; Zander
     Fuerza, *Masters of Deception: Zionism, 9/11 and the War on Terror Hoax* (self-
     pub., 2013). Difficulty of categorizing 9/11: David Hawkins, "'Manufactured
     Shock'—How Teachers, NATO and the Mob Staged an Al-Qaeda 9/11," *Awaken
     Research Group*, vol. 1, no. 4 (2006), https://issuu.com/infowarbooks/docs
     /-manufactured-shock----how-teachers--nato-and-the-. H. Bruce Franklin,
     M.I.A. or Mythmaking in America (Lawrence Hill Books), 1992.

10   Viren Swami, Tomas Chamorro-Premuzic, and Adrian Furnham, "Unan-
     swered Questions: A Preliminary Investigation of Personality and Individual
     Difference Predictors of 9/11 Conspiracist Beliefs," *Applied Cognitive Psychol-
     ogy* 24 (2010): 759. See also Viren Swami and Adrian Furnham, "Examining
     Conspiracy Beliefs about the Disappearance of Amelia Earhart," *Journal of
     General Psychology* 139, no. 4 (2012): 244–59; Michael Wood, Karen Douglas,
     and Robbie Sutton, "Dead and Alive: Beliefs in Contradictory Conspiracy
     Theories," *Social Psychology and Personality Science* 3, no. 6 (2012): 767–73;
     Harvey J. Irwin, Neil Dagnall, and Kenneth Drinkwater, "Belief Inconsistency

in Conspiracy Theorists," *Comprehensive Psychology*, vol. 4 (2015), https://doi
.org/10.2466/17.CP.4.19. For a contextual treatment, see ADL, *Rage Grows in
America: Anti-Government Conspiracies*, November 2012, https://www.adl.org
/sites/default/files/documents/assets/pdf/combating-hate/Rage-Grows-In
-America.pdf.

11   Joel Achenbach, "The Age of Disbelief," *National Geographic*, March 2015,
     30–47; Pope Brock, *Charlatan: America's Most Dangerous Huckster, the Man Who
     Pursued Him, and the Age of Flimflam* (Crown, 2008); Art Swift, "Majority in
     U.S. Still Believe JFK Killed in Conspiracy," Gallup, November 15, 2013, http://
     news.gallup.com/poll/165893/majority-believe-jfk-killed-conspiracy.aspx;
     Intelligence Report Staff, "Paper Terrorism," *Intelligence Report*, Fall 2017, 39
     (reprinted at https://www.splcenter.org/fighting-hate/intelligence-report/2017
     /paper-terrorism).

12   Robert N. Proctor, "Agnotology: A Missing Term to Describe the Cultural Pro-
     duction of Ignorance (and Its Study)," in *Agnotology: The Making and Unmaking
     of Ignorance*, ed. Robert N. Proctor and Londa Schiebinger (Stanford University
     Press), 2008. See also David Kaiser and Lee Wasserman, "The Rockefeller
     Family Fund vs. Exxon," *New York Review of Books*, December 8, 2016, 31–35.

13   The term "gadflies" is attributed, in this context, to geneticist Sean B. Car-
     roll in Steven Novella, "Features of Denialism," *Neurologicablog*, Septem-
     ber 12, 2014, https://theness.com/neurologicablog/index.php/features-of
     -denialism/. Ben Goldacre is more severe, seeing such people as being "guilty
     of an unforgivable crime," in *Bad Science*, 335. Vaccine study: "Anti-Vaccination
     Websites Use 'Science' and Stories to Support Claims, Study Finds," press
     release, Johns Hopkins University Bloomberg School of Public Health, Novem-
     ber 3, 2015. Irwin quoted in Bergman, "The Cult of HIV Denialism."

14   HIV: Charles Dervarics, "Conspiracy Beliefs May Be Hin-
     dering HIV Prevention among African Americans," Popula-
     tion Reference Bureau, February 1, 2005, https://www.prb.org
     /conspiracybeliefsmaybehinderinghivpreventionamongafricanamericans/.
     Nancy Turner Banks, "The Brothers Flexner," Slide Share, 2010, https://
     www.slideshare.net/drimhotep/the-brothers-flexner-by-nancy-turner-banks
     -mdmba. Polio: Morris A. Bealle, "$15,000 Reward If You Can Prove Salk
     Vaccine Isn't a Fake," *American Capsule News*, June 17, 1961; Jenny Lake, "Polio
     Then, Now, and Forever," 2008, accessed November 5, 2015, iamthewitness
     .com/news/2008.11.06-Polio.Then.Now.and.Forever.html (website no longer
     available). Holocaust: David Hoggan, *The Myth of the Six Million* (Noontide
     Press, 1969); Michael A. Hoffman II and A. Wyatt Mann, *Tales of the Holohoax:
     A Journal of Satire*, vol. 1, no. 1 (1989).

15   Orac, "Conspiracy Theories: The Dark Heart," 4. See also Maria Konnikova, "I
     Don't Want to Be Right," *New Yorker*, May 16, 2014; G. William Engdahl, *Seeds
     of Destruction* (Global Research, 2007); Kaiser and Wasserman, "Rockefel-
     ler Family Fund." See also Naomi Orestes and Erik M. Conway, *Merchants of
     Doubt* (Bloomsbury Press, 2010).

16   Stephan Lewandowsky, Michael E. Mann, Linda Bauld, Gerard Hastings,
     and Elizabeth F. Loftus, "The Subterranean War on Science," *Observer*, no.

9 (November 2013), https://www.psychologicalscience.org/observer/the
-subterranean-war-on-science.

17 Russell L. Blaylock, "When Rejecting Orthodoxy Becomes a Mental Illness,"
Hacienda Publishing, August 15, 2013, http://www.haciendapub.com/articles
/when-rejecting-orthodoxy-becomes-mental-illness-russell-l-blaylock-md.

18 Anonymous nurse quoted in: Epstein, "Ebola in Liberia," 92. Toxic drugs:
Bergman, "The Cult of HIV Denialism."

19 See Jeremy Stahl, "The Theory vs. the Facts: 9/11 Conspiracy Theorists
Responded to Refutations by Alleging More Cover-Ups," Slate.com, September 7, 2011, http://www.slate.com/articles/news_and_politics/trutherism
/2011/09/the_theory_vs_the_facts.html; Quassim Cassam, "Bad Thinkers,"
Aeon, March 13, 2015, https://aeon.co/essays/the-intellectual-character-of
-conspiracy-theorists; Željko Pavić, "Science and Pseudoscience in Postmodern Societies," *Informatologia* 46, no. 2 (2013): 145–53. Sagan quoted in Susan
Jacoby, *The Age of American Unreason* (Pantheon, 2008), 210.

20 Creation scientist: David J. Stewart, "Evolution, Communism and the NWO . . .
Devilution!" Jesus-Is-Savior.com, accessed May 29, 2018, https://www.jesus
-is-savior.com/Evolution%20Hoax/devilution.htm. Lucifer Project: Conrado
Salas Cano's reply to Brian Dunning's article in: Brian Dunning, "Lucifer Is Not
Quite Dead Yet . . . ," *SkepticBlog*, November 4, 2010, http://www.skepticblog
.org/2010/11/04/lucifer/. Similarly, Jim Keith's *Casebook on Alternative 3*
(IllumiNet Press, 1994), is based entirely on a British television program about
the elite fleeing earth for Mars, aired as a hoax. Keith treats the program as a
double-bluff revelation of a true conspiracy.

21 Sincere environmentalists: Miguel A. Faria Jr., "Liberal Orthodoxy and
the Squelching of Political or Scientific Dissent," Hacienda Publishing,
August 19, 2013, http://www.haciendapub.com/articles/liberal-orthodoxy-and
-squelching-political-or-scientific-dissent-miguel-faria-jr-md?report=reader.
Green agenda: Victoria Jackson, "I Found 'Agenda 21' in Lynchburg, Va.!,"
April 1, 2014, http://victoriajackson.com/10914/found-agenda-21-lynchburg
-va (accessed April 8, 2014; no longer available at that site). Inhofe quoted in:
Farron Cousins, "Climate Denier Jim Inhofe Goes Full Conspiracy Theorist
in Unhinged Rant about Global Warming," *Desmog* (blog), August 2, 2016,
https://www.desmogblog.com/2016/08/02/climate-denier-jim-inhofe-goes
-full-conspiracy-theorist-unhinged-rant-about-global-warming.

22 Neil Dagnall et al., "Reality Testing, Belief in the Paranormal, and Urban
Legends," *European Journal of Parapsychology* 25 (2010): 25–48; Ken Drinkwa-
ter, Neil Dagnall, and Andrew Parker, "Reality Testing, Conspiracy Theories,
and Paranormal Beliefs," *Journal of Parapsychology* 76, no. 1 (2012): 57–75;
Neil Dagnall et al., "Conspiracy Theory and Cognitive Style: A Worldview,"
Frontiers in Psychology, vol. 6, no. 206 (2015). See also Michiel Van Elk, "Perceptual Biases in Relation to Paranormal and Conspiracy Beliefs," *PLoS ONE*,
vol. 10, no. 6 (2015); Jennifer A. Whitson, Adam D. Galinsky, and Aaron Kay,
"The Emotional Roots of Conspiratorial Perceptions, System Justification, and
Belief in the Paranormal," *Journal of Experimental Social Psychology* 56 (2015):
89–95; Emilio Lobato et al., "Examining the Relationship between Conspir-

acy Theories, Paranormal Beliefs, and Pseudoscience among a University Population," *Applied Cognitive Psychology* 28, no. 5 (2014): 617–25; Jane L. Risen, "Believing What We Do Not Believe: Acquiescence to Superstitious Beliefs and Other Powerful Intuitions," *Psychological Review* 123, no. 2 (2016): 182–207; Karl Popper, *The Open Society and Its Enemies*, 5th ed. (Princeton University Press, 1966), 2:95.

23   Albert A. Harrison and James M. Thomas, "The Kennedy Assassination, Unidentified Flying Objects, and Other Conspiracies: Psychological and Organizational Factors in the Perception of 'Cover-Up,'" *Systems Research and Behavioral Science* 14, no. 2 (1997): 113–28.

24   Hynek quoted in Brad Steiger, *Project Blue Book* (Ballantine Books, 1976), 3.

25   On experimental aircraft, see Patton, *Dreamland*. On the CIA's activities, see; Philip J. Klass, *UFOs—the Public Deceived* (Prometheus Books, 1983), 13–21.

26   Steiger, *Project Blue Book*, back cover.

27   Keel, *Operation Trojan Horse*, 7. Keel's book had been published in 1970 under the title *UFOs*. It was not successful, a fact Keel blamed on a conspiracy to release his book "to coincide with the great stock market crash of 1970" (*Operation Trojan Horse*, 7). Lord Peter Hill-Norton, introduction to Timothy Good, *Above Top Secret* (William Morrow, 1988), 8–9; John G. Fuller, *The Interrupted Journey: Two Hours Aboard a Flying Saucer* (Dial Press, 1966). For a skeptical account, see Brian Dunning, "Betty and Barney Hill: The Original UFO Abduction," *Skeptoid*, podcast no. 124 October 21, 2008, https://skeptoid.com/episodes/4124. For a "textbook" image of a Zeta Reticulan, see the 2011 movie *Paul*, directed by Greg Mottola (NBC Universal), DVD.

28   Harrison and Thomas, "The Kennedy Assassination," 114.

29   In order: Whitley Streiber, blurb for Good's *Above Top Secret*, inside front cover; Milton William Cooper, *Behold a Pale Horse* (Light Technology Publishing, 1991), 230; Jim Keith, *Saucers of the Illuminati* (IllumiNet Press), 1999.

30   Steiger, *Project Blue Book*. First book on Roswell: Charles Berlitz and William L. Moore, *The Roswell Incident* (Grosset & Dunlap, 1980). Stanton T. Friedman and Don Berliner, *Crash at Corona* (Marlowe & Co., 1992), chap. 6; Milton William Cooper, "MAJESTYTWELVE," Hour of the Time (website), 1997, http://www.hourofthetime.com/majestyt.htm.

31   Supersecret group: Friedman and Berliner, *Crash at Corona*, 55. World government: Cooper, "MAJESTYTWELVE."

32   Keith, *Saucers of the Illuminati*; Martin Cannon, "The Controllers: A New Hypothesis of Alien Abductions," pts. 1–4, Biblioteca Pleyades, ca. 1990, https://www.bibliotecapleyades.net/sociopolitica/esp_sociopol_mindcon04.htm.

33   Illuminati-led conspiracy: Milton William Cooper, "Secret Societies/New World Order," Plausible Futures Newsletter, April 8, 2007, http://plausiblefutures.com/secret-societies-and-the-new-world-order/. Apology in: Cooper, "MAJESTYTWELVE."

34   Oscar Magocsi, "Alien Influences on Earth" (excerpts from "The Buzz Andrews Story"), OscarMagocsi.com, 1984, http://www.oscarmagocsi.com/index.php/alien-influence-on-earth. See also Luca Scantamburlo's interview with William

Rutledge ("Alien Spaceship Wreck on the Moon," *Magocsi Blog,* June 30, 2007, http://www.oscarmagocsi.com/index.php/blog/33-alien-spaceship-wreck-on -the-moon); and Mary-Ann Russon, "World UFO Day: Alien Girl and the Secret Apollo 20 Mission," *International Business Times,* updated July 1, 2014, https:// www.ibtimes.co.uk/world-ufo-day-alien-girl-secret-apollo-20-mission-1454928.

35 See, for example, Norma Cox, "Illuminism in the Ozarks," JR's Rare Books and Commentary (website), June 1989, http://www.jrbooksonline.com/HTML -docs/Cox_Illuminism.htm.

36 Philip J. Corso, *The Day after Roswell* (Pocket Books, 1998); Tim Swartz, "Technology of the Gods," StealthSkater Archives, 1997, http://www.stealthskater .com/Documents/Swartz_1.pdf. Although Swartz's article is dated 1997, he refers explicitly to Corso's 1998 book.

37 Martin Davis, "Saucers, Secrets and Shickshinny Knights," St. John of Jerusalem Research Web Site, accessed May 30, 2018. http://www.orderstjohn.org /lumpen/saucers.htm.

38 Conspiracy explanation: Romeo Vitelli, "The Tesla Conspiracy," *Providentia* (blog), August 2, 2009, http://drvitelli.typepad.com/providentia/2009/08 /the-tesla-conspiracy.html%20; Alex Knapp, "Nikola Tesla Wasn't God and Thomas Edison Wasn't the Devil," *Forbes,* May 18, 2012, https://www.forbes .com/sites/alexknapp/2012/05/18/nikola-tesla-wasnt-god-and-thomas-edison -wasnt-the-devil/#263d764a1a21. Supernatural: Pam Kohler, "Was Tesla the Conduit between Fallen Angels and Our Technology?," Salvation and Survival (website), December 4, 2014, https://www.salvationandsurvival.com/2014/12 /was-tesla-conduit-between-fallen-angels.html; Christian Soderberg, "Illuminati's Biggest Crime? Suppressing Tesla Technology," HenryMakow.com, June 6, 2010, https://www.henrymakow.com/nikola_tesla.html. WTC Towers: Judy D. Wood, *Where Did the Towers Go? Evidence of Directed Free-Energy Technology on 9/11* (New Investigation, 2010).

39 William Lyne, *Pentagon Aliens* (Creatopia Productions, 1999), vi, 220. Tesla conspiracies are popular on the libertarian Right. See, for example, David Jerale, "Myths and Rumors Persist in the Tale of Legendary Inventor Nikola Tesla," *Libertarian Republic,* September 12, 2013, https://thelibertarianrepublic .com/evil-capitalists-prevent-nikola-tesla-creating-free-energy/.

40 Cox, "Illuminism in the Ozarks"; Stan Deyo, *Cosmic Conspiracy* (West Australian Texas Trading, 1978); Brian Desborough, "The Illuminati—Past and Present," *Spectrum,* November 2002, 36.

41 See Terry Melanson, "The Vril Society, the Luminous Lodge and the Realization of the Great Work," Illuminati Conspiracy Archive, 2001, http://www .conspiracyarchive.com/NWO/Vril_Society.htm; Vojislav Milosevic, "Nikola Tesla Was Murdered by Otto Skorzeny?" *Sign of the Times,* February 13, 2012, https://www.sott.net/article/241580-Nikola-Tesla-Was-Murdered-by-Otto -Skorzeny; Kevin McClure, *The Nazi UFO Mythos* (Skandinavisk UFO Information, 2004), http://www.sufoi.dk/e-boger/boger/The%20Nazi%20UFO %20Mythos.pdf; Erich J. Choron, "Operation 'Highjump' and . . . the UFO Connection," Biblioteca Pleyades, accessed May 30, 2018, https://www .bibliotecapleyades.net/antarctica/antartica11.htm.

42   Daniel Loxton and Donald R. Prothero, *Abominable Science!* (Columbia University Press, 2013). Other popular, but relatively conspiracy-free areas include astrology, prophecy, and ghosts.

43   Klass, *UFOs—the Public Deceived*; Donald R. McNeil, "America's Longest War: The Fight over Fluoridation, 1950—," *Wilson Quarterly* 9, no. 3 (Summer 1985): 149.

44   Peter Dale Scott, *Deep Politics and the Death of JFK* (University of California Press, 1993); Franklin, *M.I.A. or Mythmaking in America*; Evan Harrington, "Conspiracy Theories and Paranoia: Notes from a Mind-Control Conference," *Skeptical Inquirer*, vol. 20, no. 5 (September–October 2016), https://www.csicop .org/si/show/conspiracy_theories_and_paranoia_notes_from_a_mind-control _conference; Launius, "Denying the Apollo Moon Landings."

45   Colavito, "Should Public Libraries?"

46   Ian Reyes and Jason K. Smith, "What They Don't Want You to Know about Planet X: *Surviving 2012* and the Aesthetics of Conspiracy Rhetoric," *Communication Quarterly* 64, no. 2 (2014): 1–31, quotes on 12 ("avoided acknowledging" [Reyes and Smith]), 13 (from Master's website).

Chapter Twelve

1   John K. Weiskittel, "Freemasons and the Conciliar Church," *Athanasian*, vol. 14, no. 4 (1993). Steve Lightfoot's website lennonmurdertruth.com has been hacked and abandoned.

2   Marilyn Ferguson, *The Aquarian Conspiracy: Personal and Social Transformation in the 1980s* (J. P. Tarcher, 1980).

3   Ibid., 18 (pragmatic and transcendental), 19 (conspiracy of love). On mysticism, see Sunita Samal, "Culture of Conspiracy: An Explanation of Politics," *Research on Humanities and Social Sciences* 2, no. 5 (2012): 97–106. On the influx of Eastern religions, see J. Gordon Melton, "What Is a cult?," pt. 1 of *Encyclopedic Handbook of Cults in America* (Garland Publishing, 1986).

4   Michael Barkun, *A Culture of Conspiracy* (University of California Press, 2003), 19.

5   Kevin A. Whitesides, "2012 Millennialism Becomes Conspiracy Teleology," *Nova Religio: The Journal of Alternative and Emergent Religions* 19, no. 2 (2015): 30. UFO link and global extinction: Oscar Magocsi, "Alien Influences on Earth" (excerpts from "The Buzz Andrews Story"), OscarMagocsi.com, 1984, http://www.oscarmagocsi.com/index.php/alien-influence-on-earth.

6   Constance Cumbey, *The Hidden Dangers of the Rainbow* (Huntington House, 1983), eighth page.

7   Ibid., 153. The manifesto ("Humanist Manifesto II") is available at the American Humanist Association website (https://americanhumanist.org/what-is -humanism/manifesto2/).

8   Edward B. Jenkinson, "The New Age Rage and Schoolbook Protest," *Library Trends* 39, nos. 1–2 (1990): 38.

9   Gary North, *Unholy Spirits: Occultism and New Age Humanism* (Institute for Christian Economics, 1988), 13–14; Texe Marrs, *Dark Secrets of the New Age*

(Crossway Books, 1987) and *Mystery Mark of the New Age* (Crossway Books, 1988), vi.

10 Lyndon LaRouche, "The Aquarian Conspiracy," from chap. 2 of Executive Intelligence Review, *Dope, Inc.*, 3rd ed. (Executive Intelligence Review, 1992), reprinted at https://www.biblebelievers.org.au/aquarian.htm. As early as June 1980, Citizens for LaRouche had produced a pamphlet titled *Stamp Out the Aquarian Conspiracy* (http://wlym.com/archive/oakland/brutish/Aquarian.pdf).

11 Serge Monast, "The Greatest Hoax—NASA's Project Blue Beam," apparently originally broadcast by the International Free Press Network of Québec in 1994, transcribed by SweetLiberty.org on a page titled "The Greatest Hoax" (http://www.sweetliberty.org/issues/hoax/bluebeam.htm).

12 Stanley K. Montieth, *The Population Control Agenda* (self-pub., 1996[?]), and *Brotherhood of Darkness* (Hearthstone Publishing, 2000). "Destructive one-fourth" attributed to Barbara Marx Hubbard, "one of the leaders of the New Age movement" (*Brotherhood of Darkness*, 133–34). Suicide song: Jenkinson, "The New Age Rage and Schoolbook Protest," 38.

13 Dennis L. Cuddy, *National Mental Health Program: Creating Standards for the New World Order* (Bible Belt Publishing, 2004), 27–28.

14 Tal Brooke, *One World* (End Run Publishing, 2000), 73.

15 Texe Marrs, "Occult Magic of the Jewish Cabala," Power of Prophecy, accessed July 13, 2018, http://www.texemarrs.com/012006/occult_magic_of_jewish _cabala.htm.

16 David Icke, *The Biggest Secret* (David Icke Books, 1999); excerpted at https:// www.bibliotecapleyades.net/biggestsecret/esp_biggest_secret_4.htm. See also Jeffrey Roberts, "The Biggest Secret: Do Reptilian-Human Hybrids Run Our World?" *Collective Evolution*, October 17, 2013, http://www.collective -evolution.com/2013/10/17/david-ickes-theory-of-the-reptilian-human-hybrid -apocalypse/.

17 Brian Desborough, interviewed by Rick Martin: "A Follow-Up Interview with Brian Desborough," *Spectrum*, November 2002, 56. The foremost blood-lines conspiracist is probably Fritz Springmeier, author of *Bloodlines of the Illuminati*, 1995, https://www.cia.gov/library/abbottabad-compound/FC /FC2F5371043C48FDD95AEDE7B8A49624_Springmeier.-.Bloodlines.of.the .Illuminati.R.pdf.

18 David Icke, *Children of the Matrix* (Bridge of Love, 2001). On accusations of antisemitism, see Jon Ronson, "Beset by Lizards," *Guardian*, March 17, 2001, https://www.theguardian.com/books/2001/mar/17/features.weekend; David Icke, *Alice in Wonderland and the World Trade Center Disaster* (Bridge of Love, 2002). Online, Icke did develop a fourth dimensional version of his 9/11 response.

19 See, for example, Nicholas Haggar, *The Secret Founding of America* (Watkins Publishing, 2007); and Robert Hieronimus, *Founding Fathers, Secret Societies* (Destiny Books, 2006).

20 Ad copy for *Secret Mysteries of America's Beginnings*, vol. 1, *The New Atlantis* (DVD), Cutting Edge Bookstore, accessed May 30, 2018, http://www .cuttingedge.org/detail.cfm?ID=1134.

21 "Freemasonry and Washington, D. C.'s Street Layout," Freemasonry Watch, accessed April 30, 2018, http://freemasonrywatch.org/washington.html.
22 Ibid.
23 Arno Gaebelein, *The Conflict of the Ages* (Our Hope, 1933). That the illustration was not in the original book can be inferred from its explanation, which refers to the 1950s writings of William Guy Carr. The illustration was probably inserted into the online edition of Gaebelein's book by the antisemitic, anti–new world order conspiracist Stan Rittenhouse.
24 Pfefferkorn, *At the Root of It All . . . Anti-Gentilism*, pamphlet (Women's Voice, 1946), 12.
25 Doc Marquis, *America's Occult Holidays* (Cutting Edge Ministries, 2010), DVD, advertisement for the series (https://www.yumpu.com/en/document/view /11915675/former-illuminist-satanist-doc-marquis-despatch-magazine-home-). Railroad symbolism: James Shelby Downard and Michael A. Hoffman II, *King Kill 33* (Independent History and Research, 1998), 19. Numerology of Dealey Plaza: Kent D. Bentkowski, "Dealey Plaza: Freemasonic Symbolism in the Death of JFK," *The Kentroversy Papers* (blog), June 22, 2007, http://kentroversypapers .blogspot.com/2007/06/dealey-plaza-esoteric-freemasonic.html.
26 Robert Howard, "Destruction of the Trade Centres: Occult Symbolism Indicates Enemies within Our Own Government," Saxon Messenger (website), 2002(?), https://saxonmessenger.christogenea.org/pdf/destruction-trade -centres-occult-symbolism-indicates-enemies-within-our-own-government. Howard's interpretation was based on what he calls "Albert Pike's Masonic Master Plan" but also included the Illuminati and Satanic forces.
27 "Top Ten Illuminati Symbols Hidden in Plain Sight," Illuminati Agenda (website), April 4, 2014, http://www.illuminatiagenda.com/top-ten-illuminati -symbols-hidden-in-plain-sight/.
28 Frame of reference: Fritz Springmeier, *Be Wise as Serpents*, "special pre-publication edition" (self-pub., 1991), http://www.nommeraadio.ee/meedia /pdf/RRS/Be%20Wise%20as%20Serpents.pdf, 4. "Why Does the Illuminati Insert Symbols in Movies, TV and Other Media?" IlluminatiRex (website), accessed May 30, 2018, https://www.illuminatirex.com/illuminati-symbols-tv -movies-media/.
29 David Icke, "Reptilian Programs," in "The Real Matrix," Biblioteca Pleyades, accessed April 30, 2018, https://www.bibliotecapleyades.net/biggestsecret/esp _icke05.htm.
30 Quotations in: Bradley Loves, "What Is the True Agenda of the Archon?" 2012: What's the Real Truth?, November 30, 2014, https://jhaines6.wordpress.com /2014/11/30/what-is-the-true-agenda-of-the-archon-anunnaki-draco-cabal -what-are-they-really-trying-to-achieve-here-on-the-earth-and-why-do-you -need-to-know-by-bradley-loves/. Cube symbolism: "The Saturn Matrix: Saturn Cube Illuminati Symbolism in Media and Corporate Logos," Inspire to Change World, June 12, 2017, http://www.inspiretochangeworld.com/2017/06 /saturn-matrix-saturn-cube-illuminati-symbolism-media-corporate-logos/.
31 Chip Berlet, "LaRouche, Antisemitism, and German Memory," *Research for Progress* (blog), 2008, http://www.researchforprogress.us/dox/larouche

/antisemitism.html. LaRouche himself has maintained that both international Jewish and international communist conspiracies are "false-trail pursuits." Klan connection: Editors of Executive Intelligence Report, *The Ugly Truth about the ADL* (Executive Pub, 1992).

32   Lyndon LaRouche, "The Secrets Known Only to the Inner Elite," *Campaigner*, vol. 11, nos. 3–4 (May–June 1978), http://laroucheplanet.info/pmwiki/pmwiki .php?n=Library.INNERELITES.

33   The royal drug trade is outlined in Executive Intelligence Review, *Dope, Inc.*, which, if not written by LaRouche, is written under his aegis. For recent attacks, see "British, Saudi and FBI Complicity Exposed in Orlando Mass Killings: The Same People Who Brought You 9/11" (leaflet), LaRouche Pac, June 16, 2016, https://larouchepac.com/20160616/british-saudi-and-fbi -complicity-exposed-orlando-mass-killings-same-people-who-brought-you, and "Anglo-Saudi War and Terror Machine Stands Exposed in Florida—Go for Targets & Bring It Down" (leaflets), LaRouchePAC, June 14, 2016, https:// larouchepac.com/20160614/anglo-saudi-war-and-terror-machine-stands -exposed-florida-go-targets-bring-it-down.

34   All advertised on the Tarpley website: tarpley.net.

35   Anton Chaitkin, "The Lincoln Revolution," Schiller Institute, https://www .schillerinstitute.org/fid_97-01/fid_981_lincoln.html, reprinted from their magazine *Fidelio*, vol. 7, no. 1 (Spring, 1998); Donald Phau, "The Treachery of Thomas Jefferson," *Campaigner* 13, no. 2 (March 1980): 5–32. Miguel Bruno Duarte, "Illuminati," Inter-American Institute, December 11, 2012, http:// archive.is/20130415221337/theinteramerican.org/commentary/414-illuminati .html.

36   John A. Williams, *The Man Who Cried I Am* (Little, Brown, 1967).

37   Jones's 1972 sermon is transcribed in "The King Alfred Plan & Concentration Camps," Q1059-2 Transcript, Alternative Considerations of Jonestown and Peoples Temple (website sponsored by the Special Collections of Library and Information Access at San Diego State University), last modified on February 18, 2016, https://jonestown.sdsu.edu/?page_id=27332. Energy crisis argument in: Sagittarius [Carl L. Shears], *The Countdown to Black Genocide* (Nuclassics and Science Pub., 1973). Both the latter and the *King Alfred Research Newsletter* are advertised by researcher Mae Brussell in advertising flyer no. 338, July 21, 1978 (http://www.maebrussell.com/Bibliography%20Sheets/338 -339s1.pdf).

38   Music and radio: Steven Best and Douglas Kellner, "Rap, Black Rage, and Racial Difference," *Enculturation* 2, no. 2 (1999), https://pages.gseis.ucla.edu /faculty/kellner/essays/rapblackrageracialdifference.pdf, 9. Rex 84: "Chicago Gangs and the 'King Alfred Plan,'" *Northwest Research and Covert Book Report*, May 31, 2013.

39   "King Alfred Plan, Rex 84, NDAA, Op Garden Plot and the Plan for Dealing with a Disgruntled Disarmed Black America," July 8, 2016, aggregatepress .org (website no longer exists). White scientists: Best and Kellner, "Rap, Black Rage, and Racial Difference," 9. Laura M. Bogart and Sheryl Thorburn, "Are HIV/AIDS Conspiracy Beliefs a Barrier to HIV Prevention among African

Americans?" *Journal of Acquired Immune Deficiency Syndromes* 38, no. 2 (2005): 213–18; Sheryl Thorburn and Laura M. Bogart, "Conspiracy Beliefs about Birth Control: Barriers to Pregnancy Prevention among African Americans of Reproductive Age," *Health Education and Behavior* 32, no. 4 (2015): 474–87.

40   Cheryl King, "The King Alfred Plan," July 24, 2015, linkedin.com. Diamonds: Nancy Turner Banks, *AIDS, Opium, Diamonds, and Empire* (iUniverse, 2010).

41   Tiffanie Drayton, "Black Susceptibility to Conspiracy and Propaganda," 2016, clutchmagonline.com/2016/08/black-susceptibility-to-conspiracy -propaganda/.

42   Alasdair Spark, "Conjuring Order: The New World Order and Conspiracy Theories of Globalization," *Sociological Review* 48, no. S2 (2000): S46–S62, quotes on 47 (equal opportunity), 48 (Police against the New World Order,), 51 (Chomsky).

43   Jonathan Kay, *Among the Truthers* (HarperCollins, 2011), 31.

44   Daniel Pipes, *Conspiracy: How the Paranoid Style Flourishes and Where It Comes From* (Free Press, 1999). Criticism: Nigel James, "Militias, the Patriot Movement, and the Internet: The Ideology of Conspiracism," *Sociological Review* 48, no. 2 (2001): 78. Conspiracy fantasy: Michael Parenti quoted in Spark, "Conjuring Order," 54.

45   G. William Domhoff, "There Are No Conspiracies," Who Rules America?, posted March 2005, https://whorulesamerica.ucsc.edu/theory/conspiracy.html.

46   Peter Dale Scott, *Deep Politics and the Death of JFK* (University of California Press, 1993), xi.

47   Jim Garrison, *On the Trail of the Assassins* (Sheridan Square Press, 1988). See also Max Holland, "The Demon in Jim Garrison," *Wilson Quarterly* 25, no. 2 (2001): 10–17; Hamilton Nolan, "The Astounding Conspiracy Theories of Wall Street Genius Mark Gorton," *Gawker* (blog), April 10, 2014, http://gawker.com /the-astounding-conspiracy-theories-of-wall-street-geniu-1561427624; Mark Gorton, *50 Years of the Deep State,* WikiSpooks, November 22, 2013, https:// wikispooks.com/wiki/Document:Fifty_Years_of_the_Deep_State. Brussell's article "The Nazi Connection to the JFK Assassination" probably puts her over the line as well (reprinted from *Rebel*, January 1984, at http://www.maebrussell .com/Mae%20Brussell%20Articles/Nazi%20Connection%20oto%20JFK %20Assass.html).

48   See Jacques Laroche and Alexander Moore, "Conspiracism and 'Lone Nuts': Inevitable Adjuncts to Bloodshed in American Politics?" *Revue français d'études américaines* 69 (1996): 109–16.

49   Don DeLillo, *Libra* (Viking Press, 1988); James Ellroy, *American Tabloid* (Alfred A. Knopf, 1995). On Lombardi's work, see Patricia Goldstone, *Interlock* (Counterpoint, 2015).

50   Michael Kelly, "The Road to Paranoia," *New Yorker*, June 19, 1995, https://www .newyorker.com/magazine/1995/06/19/the-road-to-paranoia; Kenn Thomas, "Michael Kelly and Conspiracy Fusion," reprinted in his *Parapolitics: Conspiracy in Contemporary America* (Adventures Unlimited Press, 2006), 221–23. On the possibility of hoaxes, see Adam Gorightly, "Manson, Discordianism, and Fusion Paranoia," *Secret Transmissions* (blog), September 2016, http://www

.secrettransmissions.com/2016/09/manson-discordianism-fusion-paranoia
.html.

51   Sam Smith, "America's Extremist Center," *Progressive Review*, July 1995, http://
prorev.com/center.htm; Daniel Brandt, "The 1960s and COINTELPRO: In
Defense of Paranoia," Third World Traveler, July–September1995, http://www
.thirdworldtraveler.com/FBI/COINTELPRO_Paranoia.html.

52   Daniel Pipes, "Fusion Paranoia: A New Twist in Conspiracy Theories," *Jerusalem Post*, January 14, 2004, http://www.freerepublic.com/focus/f-news
/1057643/posts; Michael Weiss, "Socialism of Fools," *Dispatch* (blog), *New Cri-
terion*, vol. 36, no. 9 (October 8, 2009), https://www.newcriterion.com/blogs
/dispatch/socialism-of-fools.

53   "Fluoridation," *Revelations Awareness*, 1981, no. 11, https://issuu.com
/cosmicchannelings/docs/cosmic-awareness-1981-11. The entire issue was an
attack on fluoridation.

54   Niccoli Nattrass, *The AIDS Conspiracy; Science Fights Back* (Columbia University Press, 2012), 26; Alan Cantwell, "Paranoid/Paranoia—Media Buzzwords
to Silence the Politically Incorrect," Rense Alt News, January 10, 2005, http://
www.rense.com/general61/hhwe.htm.

55   Chip Berlet, "Crackpots, the Left, and 'Jewish Banker Cabals,'" *Z Magazine*,
November 1, 2007, https://zcomm.org/zmagazine/crackpots-the-left-and
-jewish-banker-cabals-by-chip-berlet/.

56   The October surprise conspiracy has the 1980 Reagan campaign cutting a
secret deal with Iran to keep President Carter from securing the release of the
American hostages there. See Robert Parry, *The October Surprise X-Files* (Media
Consortium, 1996) for a deep politics explanation. For a truly conspiratorial
deep politics assessment of the Wellstone "assassination" of October 2002,
see "Senator Paul Wellstone Assassinated by Covert US Terror Group Linked
to Bush," Vox News, October 25, 2002, http://www.voxfux.com/archives
/00000039.htm.

57   Tom Jensen, "Democrats and Republicans Differ on Conspiracy Theory
Beliefs," Public Policy Polling, April 2, 2013, https://www.publicpolicypolling
.com/polls/democrats-and-republicans-differ-on-conspiracy-theory-beliefs/;
"The Conspiratorial Mindset in an Age of Transition" (executive summary),
Political Capital Policy Research and Consulting Institute, December 20, 2013,
http://www.politicalcapital.hu/news.php?article_read=1&article_id=1467. See
also Steven Rosenfeld, "Study: How Breitbart Media's Disinformation Created the Paranoid Fact-Averse Nation That Elected Trump," *AlterNet*, July 20,
2017, https://www.alternet.org/investigations/breitbarts-disinformation
-dominated-right-wing-media-2016-creating-dark-paranoid-fact.

Chapter Thirteen

1   Paul deArmond, "Christian Patriots at War with the State," *Public Good
Archives* (blog), 1996, https://publicgoodarchivesblog.wordpress.com/archives
/christian-patriots-at-war-with-the-state/. See also "The Rise and Develop-

ment of the 'Christian' Identity Movement," chronological flow chart facing page 1 of Louis S. Lapides, "The 'Christian Identity' Movement in America" (paper prepared for the North American Lausanne Consultation on Jewish Evangelism," April 4–5, 1989), http://www.lcje.net/papers/1989/Lapides.pdf.

2   Dennis Tourish and Tim Wohlforth, "Prophets of the Apocalypse: White Supremacy and the Theology of Christian Identity," *Cultic Studies Journal* 17 (2000): 15–41, http://www.icsahome.com/articles/prophets-of-the-apocalypse -csj-17; "Christian Identity Movement," Religious Tolerance (website), May 30, 2006, http://www.religioustolerance.org/cr_ident.htm.

3   W. H. Poole, *Anglo-Israel or the Saxon Race Proved to Be the Lost Tribes of the Bible* (Bengough Bros., 1889); E. P. Ingersol, *Lost Israel Found in the Anglo-Saxon Race* (Kansas Publishing House, 1886).

4   Robert S. Robins and Jerrold M. Post, *Political Paranoia—the Psychopolitics of Hatred* (Yale University Press, 1997), 184. See also Donna Kossy, "The Anglo-Israelites," originally appeared at http://home.pacifier.com/~dkossy/anglo .html (accessed September 10, 2106), a now-defunct website, but is reprinted in her *Kooks: A Guide to the Outer Limits of Human Belief* (Feral House, 1994) . . .

5   Michael Marinacci, "Wesley Swift and the Church of Jesus Christ—Christian," *Califia's Children* (blog), January 26, 2015, http://califias.blogspot.com/2015/01 /wesley-swift-and-church-of-jesus-christ.html. See also Michael Barkun, *Religion and the Racist Right: The Origins of the Christian Identity Movement* (University of North Carolina Press, 1997), chap. 9; and Jon F. Schamber and Scott R. Stroud, "Mystical Anti-Semitism and the Christian Identity Movement: A Narrative Criticism of Dan Gayman's 'The Two Seeds of Genesis 3, no. 15'" (paper presented at the meeting of the National Communication Association, Seattle, November 9–12, 2000), 1–2.

6   Robert Singerman, "Contemporary Racist and Judeophobic Ideology Discovers the Khazars, or, Who Really Are the Jews" (Rosaline and Meyer Feinstein lecture, Feinstein Center for American Jewish History, Temple University, 2004), 8.

7   "Anglo-Saxon Federation of America," *The Facts* (ADL) January 1947, 5, 3.

8   Schamber and Stroud, "Mystical Anti-Semitism and the Christian Identity Movement," 11. See also "Revival of the Klan," *The Facts* (ADL), May 1946, 11.

9   Wesley Swift, "Crushing the Serpent" (sermon), Dr. Wesley Swift Library at christogenea.org, August 1957, https://swift.christogenea.org/articles/crushing -serpent-8-0-57.

10   Wesley Swift, "Children of the Stranger" (sermon), Dr. Wesley Swift Library at christogenea.org, November 27, 1960, https://swift.christogenea.org/articles /ws1960. On the pre-Adamites, see also Viola Larson, "Christian Identity: A 'Christian' Religion for White Racists," *Christian Research Journal*, Fall 1992, 2–4; and Tanya Telfair Sharpe, "The Identity Christian Movement: Ideology of Domestic Terrorism," *Journal of Black Studies* 30, no. 4 (2000): 604–23.

11   Tourish and Wohlforth, "Prophets of the Apocalypse."

12   Ibid. See also "Project Megiddo," pt. 3, "Christian Identity," FBI report, reproduced on the Center for Study of New Religions website, November 1999, http://www.cesnur.org/testi/FBI_006.htm.

13   Schamber and Stroud, "Mystical Anti-Semitism and the Christian Identity Movement." See also Larson, "Identity," 4; and Marinacci, "Wesley Swift and the Church of Jesus Christ—Christian."

14   Sermons by Swift and other seedliner preachers go back to the 1940s. Various sympathetic websites have posted sermons from as long ago as 1953. They have been transcribed from tapes made of sermons apparently aired on radio. (A sermon may end abruptly with the notation "tape ran out.") Sometimes the sermons are precisely dated, but sometimes only the year is available. The transcriptions also have questionable punctuation and frequently spell people's name phonetically (e.g., Brandise for Brandeis). Since these errors are not attributable to the speakers, they have been corrected here.

15   Wesley Swift, "Hour of Decision" (sermon), Dr. Wesley Swift Library at christogenea.org, 1954, https://swift.christogenea.org/articles/hour-decision -1954, and "The Nations That Will Survive" (sermon), Dr. Wesley Swift Library at christogenea.org, June 10, 1954, https://swift.christogenea.org/articles /nations-will-survive-1954. The Babylonian conspiracy: Bertrand Compa-ret, "Babylon's Money" (audio recording), Christogenea, 1970s (?), https:// comparet.christogenea.org/audio/babylons-money-side. Special potency: Schamber and Stroud, "Mystical Anti-Semitism and the Christian Identity Movement," 9.

16   Wesley Swift, "False Economy" (sermon), Dr. Wesley Swift Library at christogenea.org, 1955, https://swift.christogenea.org/articles/false-economy -1955.

17   Conrad Gaard, *Spotlight on the Great Conspiracy* (Destiny of America Corp., 1955), available at http://www.colchestercollection.com/titles/S/spotlight-on -the-great-conspiracy.html. The only version of Gaard's book on line is a 1993 reprint that has attached to it, without attribution, post-1955 material. More-over, the pagination in the reprint is uncertain because of reformatting. All the quotations appear to be in the page 50–55 range.

18   Ibid., 124 (?) and 175 (?).

19   Wesley Swift, "Crushing the Serpent," "The Power behind the Red Revolu-tion" (sermon), Dr. Wesley Swift Library at christogenea.org, June 18, 1962, https://swift.christogenea.org/articles/power-behind-red-revolution-6-18-62, "Time of Jacob's Trouble," (sermon), Dr. Wesley Swift Library at christogenea .org, November 16, 1963, https://swift.christogenea.org/articles/time-jacobs -trouble-11-16-63.

20   Wesley Swift, "Why You Cannot Turn Back" (sermon), Dr. Wesley Swift Library at christogenea.org, August 15, 1965, https://swift.christogenea.org /search/node/Why%20You%20Cannot%20Turn%20Back. An FBI report (July 24, 1963) quoted Swift as advocating killing "Negroes" in a speech to the Hollywood Women's Club on June 14, 1963, in "Gale, William Potter HQ1" at ia801209.us.archive.org/2/items/GaleWilliamP.HQ1/Gale%2C%20William %20P.-HQ-1.pdf, 108–10. Swift's death: Marinacci, "Wesley Swift and the Church of Jesus Christ—Christian."

21   Bertrand L. Comparet, "The Cain/Satanic Seed Line," Christogenea, accessed May 31, 2018, https://comparet.christogenea.org/sermons/cainsatanic-seed

-line and "America Is a Bible Land" (sermon), Christogenea, n.d., https://comparet.christogenea.org/sermons/america-bible-land.

22   Bertrand L. Comparet, *The Mark of the Beast* (New Christian Crusade Church, 1975), and *Merchants of Babylon* (New Christian Crusade Church, 1966). Yahwey's laws: Bertrand L. Comparet, "The Destiny of Our Race," Emporium of Truth, accessed May 31, 2018, https://emporiumoftruth.files.wordpress.com /2011/03/the-destiny-of-our-race.pdf, 3.

23   *Twelfth Report of the Senate Factfinding Subcommittee on Un-American Activities* (California State Senate, 1963), 198.

24   Oren F. Potito, "The Conspiracy," Resist.com, accessed May 31, 2018, https://www.resist.com/14Words/bio/TheConspiracy.pdf, and "The Fairy Tale," Resist.com, accessed May 31, 2018, https://www.resist.com/14Words/bio /TheFairytale.pdf.

25   "Admiral John G. Crommelin Addresses Swift Meeting in Los Angeles in 1963," Saxon Messenger, accessed May 31, 2018, https://saxonmessenger .christogenea.org/pdf/admiral-john-g-crommelin-addresses-swift-meeting -los-angeles-1963, 6 (voting machines), 8–9 (prediction).

26   Richard Potter Gale, *The Faith of Our Fathers* (Ministry of Christ Church, 1963), available at hotk.files.wordpress.com/2012/10/faith-of-our-fathers.pdf.

27   Ibid., 9–15.

28   Ibid., 27–28.

29   Ibid., 37–38.

30   Ibid., 29–33. See also J. M. Berger, "Without Prejudice: What Sovereign Citizens Believe" (paper written for the Program on Extremism at George Washington University, June 2016), https://extremism.gwu.edu/sites/g/files /zaxdzs2191/f/downloads/JMB%20Sovereign%20Citizens.pdf; John Færseth, "Militias and Conspiracy Culture," Hate Speech International, December 23, 2013, https://www.hate-speech.org/sovereign-citizens-militias-and -conspiracy-culture/; deArmond, "Christian Patriots at War with the State."

31   Gale, *Faith of Our Fathers*, chap. 8, 37–43, quote on 41. Gale did not use term "false flag," but claimed that Jews, while committing atrocities, would purposefully kill some Jews as well since "they think nothing of eliminating some lesser Yehudi to provide the confusion as to the guilty party" (49).

32   Ibid., 44–54, quote on 54.

33   Marinacci, "Wesley Swift and the Church of Jesus Christ—Christian," 7. See also "Project Megiddo," 2.

34   The liaison between the two groups was primarily the reverend Charles "Connie" Lynch. See "Background Information on the National States' Rights Party," Florida Legislative Investigation Committee, July 31, 1964, especially 11–14.

35   "Read This Message and Join In" (flyer), Christian Defense League, ca. 1959; Wesley Swift, "Wrath Shall Rise Up in Their Countenance" (sermon), Dr. Wesley Swift Library at christogenea.org, July 8, 1962, https://swift.christogenea .org/articles/wrath-shall-rise-their-countenance-7-8-62, and "Why You Cannot Turn Back," (sermon), Dr. Wesley Swift Library at christogenea.org, August 15, 1965, https://swift.christogenea.org/articles/why-you-cannot-turn -back-8-15-65.

36   FBI report of Harry Griffith, July 24, 1963; and FBI memo—both in "Gale, William Potter HQ1." Threat against rabbis quoted in Lapides, "The 'Christian Identity' Movement," 25.

37   Twenty thousand men: FBI report of Harry Griffith, July 24, 1963; and Operation Awake, FBI report, January 22, 1964—both in "Gale, William Potter HQ1."

38   *Para-military Organizations in California—California Rangers*, report by the Attorney General of California to the Legislature (Bureau of Criminal Identification and Investigation, April 12, 1965), 2 (Potito quotation), 9 (secret force).

39   FBI memo, March 12, 1964 in "Gale, William Potter HQ1."

40   "National States' Rights Party—Racial Matters," FBI report on the party's National Convention in Montgomery, AL, September 1–2, 1962. On Crommelin's speech, see "Admiral John G. Crommelin Addresses Swift Meeting."

41   William W. Turner, "The Minutemen," *Ramparts*, January 1967, 70 (quote), 72 (links to Swift and Gale). See also *Para-military Organizations in California*.

42   FBI report, October 6, 1964, and FBI memo on Gale speech of June 21, 1963—both in "Gale, William Potter HQ1." See also William Turner, "DePugh and the Minutemen: Wonderland of the Mind," *Ramparts*, June 1970, 11–12; and David Boylan, "A League of Their Own: A Look Inside the Christian Defense League," Cuban Information Archives, Document 0046, updated 2004, http://cuban-exile.com/doc_026-050/doc0046.html.

43   Richard G. Butler, *To Our Kinsmen* (pamphlet), describing Aryan Nations and membership application, https://www.scribd.com/document/288137950/AN-text-pdf, 7 (Trebitsch quote).

44   Ibid., 1 (swinepen quote), 6 (other quotations from the platform for the Aryan National State).

45   Untitled flyer signed by George L. Kindred, 1968.

46   See "The 'Identity Churches': A Theology of Hate," *ADL Facts*, Spring 1983, 14–15, https://archive.org/details/TheidentityChurchesATheologyOfHate; and Daniel Levitas, "The Terrorist Next Door," *New York Times*, November 17, 2002, https://www.nytimes.com/2002/11/17/books/chapters/the-terrorist-next-door.html, excerpt from *The Terrorist Next Door: The Militia Movement and the Radical Right*, by Levitas.

47   Michael D'Antonio, "The Identity Movement and Its 'Real Jew' Claim," Alicia Patterson Foundation, 1988, last updated April 11, 2011, http://aliciapatterson.org/stories/identity-movement-and-its-real-jew-claim. See also, Leah Nelson, "Church at Kaweah Spreads Hateful, Militant Christian Views" *Intelligence Report*, Spring 2012, 64–67.

48   D'Antonio, "The Identity Movement."

49   "Peter J. 'Pete' Peters," ADL, accessed July 13, 2018, http://archive.is/937q.

50   On Miles, see Robert E. Miles, "To Parade or Not to Parade," Stormfront.org, posted July 10, 2004, https://www.stormfront.org/forum/t141974/; "The Identity Churches: A Theology of Hate," *Facts* (ADL), Spring 1983, 10. See also Schamber and Stroud, "Mystical Anti-Semitism and the Christian Identity Movement," 6–7; and Lapides, "The 'Christian Identity' Movement," 37–42.

51   Matthew A. Lauder, *Religion and Resistance: Examining the Role of Religion in Irregular Warfare*, Technical Note 2009-049 (Defence R&D Canada—Toronto,

March 2009), 13. See also "The Combination of Religion and Hatred," *The Facts* (ADL), August 1946, 1–9.

Chapter Fourteen

1   Louis Beam, "Leaderless Resistance," originally written as a manifesto in 1983, published in the *Seditionist*, no. 12 (February 1992), and *Modern Militiaman*, no. 3 (October 1996), http://whitenationalist.org/lindstedt/mmmisu3.html #noleaders. Beam left the Aryan Nations in 1988.

2   Core feature: Timothy Baysinger, "Right-Wing Group Characteristics and Ideology," *Homeland Security Affairs*, vol. 2, article 3 (July 2006), https://www.hsaj.org/articles/166. Tanya Telfair Sharpe, "The Identity Christian Movement: Ideology of Domestic Terrorism," *Journal of Black* Studies 30, no. 4 (2000): 604–23, quote on 608. See also Sandi DuBowski, "Storming Wombs and Waco: How the Anti-Abortion and Militia Movements Converge," *Front Lines Research* 2, no. 2 (October1996):1-10.

3   Thompson Smith, "The Patriot Movement: Refreshing the Tree of Liberty with Fertilizer Bombs and the Blood of Martyrs," *Valparaiso University Law Review* 32, no. 1 (1997): 276–77.

4   CONstitutionalism: Martin Lindstedt, "Dress Rehearsal for Götterdämmerung," *Modern Militiaman* #8 April 19, 1998, http://whitenationalist.org/lindstedt/mm8wever.html. Golden-age: Matthew A. Lauder, *Religion and Resistance: Examining the Role of Religion in Irregular Warfare*, Technical Note 2009-049 (Defence R&D Canada—Toronto, March 2009), 14. On terminology, see Alejandro Beutel, "Key Concepts to Understand Violent White Supremacy," Research Brief, National Consortium for the Study of Terrorism And Responses to Terrorism (START), April 2017. See also *Investigating Terrorism and Criminal Extremism: Terms and Concepts*, version 1.0 (Bureau of Justice Assistance, U.S. Department of Justice, 2005-9).

5   Jessica Eve Stern, "The Covenant, the Sword, and the Arm of the Lord," in *Toxic Terror*, ed. Jonathan Tucker (MIT Press, 2000). On Elohim City, see Gustav Niebuhr, "A Vision of an Apocalypse: The Religion of the Far Right," *New York Times*, May 22, 1995, https://www.nytimes.com/1995/05/22/us/a-vision-of-an-apocalypse-the-religion-of-the-far-right.html. On Harrell, see Jon F. Schamber and Scott R. Stroud, "Mystical Anti-Semitism and the Christian Identity Movement: A Narrative Criticism of Dan Gayman's 'The Two Seeds of Genesis 3, no. 15'" (paper presented at the meeting of the National Communication Association, Seattle, 2000), 7. Robert M. Press, "They Play War Games in U.S. Countryside," *Christian Science Monitor*, March 23, 1981, http://www.csmonitor.com/1981/1323/132340.html. On the rural nature of Christian Identity groups in general, see Kenneth A. Stern, *A Force upon the Plain* (University of Oklahoma Press, 1997).

6   R. Georges Delamontagne, "Relationships between Varieties of Religious Experience and Manifest Hatred: A Sociological Analysis," *Journal of Religion and Society* 14 (2012): 18. Wickstrom: Mark Potok, "Timeline: Land Use and the

'Patriots,'" *Intelligence Report*, Fall 2014, 28 (reprinted at https://www.splcenter .org/fighting-hate/intelligence-report/2014/land-use-patriots). See also Viola Larson, "Christian Identity: A 'Christian' Religion for White Racists," *Christian Research Journal*, Fall 1992, 5.

7   Leonard Zeskind, "Far-Right Racist and Anti-Semitic Organizations Active in the Middle West and Iowa," Center for Democratic Renewal, 1985, 3 and 5 (reprinted at http://www.ajcarchives.org/AJC_DATA/Files/839.pdf).

8   "The Identity Churches: A Theology of Hate," *Facts* (ADL), Spring 1983, 7 (Gale), 8 (Emry), 10 (Warner). See also Daniel Levitas, "The Terrorist Next Door," *New York Times*, November 17, 2002, https://www.nytimes.com/2002 /11/17/books/chapters/the-terrorist-next-door.html, excerpt from *The Terrorist Next Door: The Militia Movement and the Radical Right*, by Levitas.

9   ATTACK is an acronym for Aryan Tactical Treaty for the Advancement of Christ's Kingdom. See Stern, "The Covenant, the Sword, and the Arm of the Lord," 148.

10   "Deadly Dates: Calendar for Right-Wing Extremists," an actual calendar created by the Institute of Finance and Management to identify "high alert" days when extra security precautions might be taken against right-wing extremists, who "have proven to be very concerned with the calendar" (http://sdrmonthly .com/content/resources/Deadly_Dates-_Calendar_for_Right-Wing_Extremists .pdf, 2011).

11   Robert J. Mathews, "Declaration of War," *Mourning the Ancient*, accessed May 2, 2018, http://www.mourningtheancient.com/mathews2.htm.

12   Statement of Gordon Kahl about the events surrounding his attempted arrest, February 13, 1983 (Outpost of Freedom [website], accessed June 1, 2018, http:// www.outpost-of-freedom.com/kahl01.htm). This statement is often referred to as a manifesto, but it is not. The *American Free Press*, June 16, 2003, pages B2 and B4, printed the "Text of the Final Affidavit of Gordon Kahl," a longer version of events dated February 25, 1983. This affidavit is more manifesto-like, assuming it is genuine. (Reprinted at https://www.amfirstbooks.com /IntroPages/Subscription_Periodicals/American_Free_Press/download_files /2003/AFP_20030616_Issue_23_Insert;_Final_Affidavit_of_Gordon_Kahl.pdf.)

13   *The Anti-Government Movement Guidebook* (National Center for State Courts, 1999), 4, 14–19. See also Ryan Lenz, "War in the West," *Intelligence Report*, Fall 2014, 20–26.

14   Stan C. Weeber, "Origins, Orientation and Etiologies of the U.S. Citizen Militia Movement, 1982–1997," *Free Inquiry in Creative Sociology* 27, no. 1 (1999): 57–66. See also *Shooting for Respectability: Firearms, False Patriots, and Politics in Montana*, report (Montana Human Rights Network, 2003), http://www .mhrn.org/publications/specialresearchreports/GunPaper.pdf.

15   See Paul deArmond, "Christian Patriots at War with the State," *Public Good Archives* (blog), 1996, https://publicgoodarchivesblog.wordpress.com/archives /christian-patriots-at-war-with-the-state/; "The NTC" (The Nehemiah Township Charter and Common Law Contract, 1982), December 2, 2014, https:// www.stormfront.org/forum/t169015. See also Michael Barkun, *Religion and the Racist Right* (University of North Carolina Press, 1997), 219.

16 Rudy Stanko, "Organic Law vs Talmudic Law," *Racial Loyalty* (newspaper), January 1992, 11.

17 Schamber and Stroud, "Mystical Anti-Semitism and the Christian Identity Movement," 5. See also Jay Taber, "A Mandate from God: Christian White Supremacy in the U.S.," *Intercontinental Cry* (magazine), April 4, 2014, https://intercontinentalcry.org/mandate-god-christian-white-supremacy-us/.

18 Paul deArmond, "Racist Origins of Border Militias," Public Good Project Report, October 2005, https://publicgoodarchivesblog.wordpress.com/whats-new/ (no longer available). See also Scott Stewart, "Grassroots Cells: Even More Dangerous than Lone Wolves," *Worldview*, August 20, 2015, https://worldview.stratfor.com/article/grassroots-cells-even-more-dangerous-lone-wolves; Beam, "Leaderless Resistance."

19 Wickstrom's prediction cited in Andy Mel, *Death of a Patriot* (Revival Press, 1986). Kahl's personal history: John A. Schumacher, *Gordon Kahl's Cult of Racial Purity* (self-pub., 2013). Gale and Snell quotations in: Levitas, "The Terrorist Next Door."

20 "Robert J Mathews 30 Years in Valhalla," WAU (Women for Aryan Unity), November 25, 2014, https://www.wau14.com/robert-j-mathews-30-years-in-valhalla/. Der Brüder Schweigen archives and posts, as well as the David Lane global posts, are available at http://www.davidlane1488.com/main.html. See also George Michael, "David Lane and the 14 Words," *Totalitarian Political and Religious Movements* 10, no. 1 (2009): 43–61.

21 Louis S. Lapides, "The 'Christian Identity' Movement in America" (paper prepared for the North American Lausanne Consultation on Jewish Evangelism, April 4–5, 1989), 45, http://www.lcje.net/papers/1989/Lapides.pdf; William L. Pierce, *The Turner Diaries* (National Vanguard Books, 1978).

22 Quotation: Conrad Goeringer, "The Randy Weaver Story: A New Aryan Saga (part 2 of 2)," Skeptic Tank, accessed June 1, 2018, http://www.skepticfiles.org/moretext/weaver.htm; Institute of Finance and Management, "Deadly Dates," 2.

23 Louis Beam, "1/4 Inch: The Randy Weaver Story," last updated December 29, 1996, http://www.louisbeam.com/14inch.htm. (Weaver's shotgun was sawed off to a quarter inch under the legal minimum for shotgun barrels.) The illustration attached to Beam's prediction depicts heavily armed United Nations troops prominent in the siege.

24 Garry Wills, "The New Revolutionaries," *New York Review of Books*, August 10, 1995, 54; Michael Barkun, "Appropriated Martyrs: The Branch Davidians and the Radical Right," *Terrorism and Political Violence* 19, no. 1 (2007): 117–24. On the government's efforts to learn from these fiascos, see Michael Barkun, "The Branch Davidian Standoff Twenty Years Later," *Reason Papers* 36, no. 1 (2014): 65–71.

25 Coup: Sherman Skolnick, "The Oklahoma Bombing and the Story of a Magazine," BeyondWeird.com, 1996, http://www.beyondweird.com/conspiracy/cn07-37.html. FBI: William L. Grigg, "They'll Be Back: PATCON, Oklahoma City, and Jesse Trentadue's Lonely Crusade for Justice," *Pro Libertate* (blog),

November 13, 2014, http://freedominourtime.blogspot.com/2014/11/theyll-be
-back-patcon-oklahoma-city-and.html.

26 "The Truth on the Oklahoma City Bombing," *Judicial-Inc Archive* (blog),
April 28, 2010, http://judicial-inc-archive.blogspot.com/2010/04/who-really
-orchestrated-okc-bombing.html.

27 On Snell, see Levitas, "The Terrorist Next Door," 7–8. It is possible that Snell
thought all pawnbrokers were Jewish. On Ainsworth, see "Happy Birthday
Kathy Ainsworth," WAU (Women for Aryan Unity), July 31, 2015, https://www
.wau14.com/happy-birthday-kathy-ainsworth/; and Chris Goodrich, "Book
Review: Klan and FBI Wounded in Hail of Bullets: *Terror in the Night: The Klan's
Campaign against the Jews* by Jack Nelson," *Los Angeles Times*, February 23,
1993, http://articles.latimes.com/1993-02-23/news/vw-330_1_jack-nelson.
On Heemeyer, see Martin J. Smith, "Martyr without a Cause," *Los Angeles
Times*, July 25, 2004, http://articles.latimes.com/2004/jul/25/magazine/tm
-bulldozer30.

28 Beam, "1/4 Inch." See also Lauder, *Religion and Resistance*, 15. Posts in: David
Neiwert, "Antigovernment Movement's Rank and File Want Retaliation for
Arrests, Death in Oregon, but Their Leaders Are Reluctant," *Hatewatch* (blog),
Southern Poverty Law Center, January 28, 2016, https://www.splcenter.org
/hatewatch/2016/01/28/antigovernment-movements-rank-and-file-want
-retaliation-arrests-death-oregon-their-leaders.

29 "Alert: Northwestern Hammerskins Annual Martyr's Day Celebration 2015, Washington State Weekend of December 5th and 6th," Puget
Sound Anarchists, November 24, 2015, https://pugetsoundanarchists.org
/alert-northwestern-hammerskins-annual-martyrs-day-celebration-2015
-washington-state-weekend-of-december-5th-and-6th/; "Re: December 8th:
Martyr's Day," Stormfront.org, December 8, 2007, https://www.stormfront
.org/forum/t443129/; David Holthouse, "Calling from Prison, Member of The
Order Delivers 'Martyr's Day' Address," *Hatewatch* (blog), Southern Poverty
Law Center, December 22, 2008, https://www.splcenter.org/hatewatch/2008
/12/22/calling-prison-member-order-delivers-%E2%80%98martyr%E2%80
%99s-day%E2%80%99-address.

30 Dennis Tourish and Tim Wohlforth, "Prophets of the Apocalypse: White
Supremacy and the Theology of Christian Identity," *Cultic Studies Journal* 17
(2000): 15–41, http://www.icsahome.com/articles/prophets-of-the-apocalypse
-csj-17; Philip Lamy, *Millennium Rage* (Plenum Press, 1996), esp. chap. 5, "Antichrist: The Myth of the Jewish World Conspiracy"; Leah Nelson, "Church at
Kaweah Spreads Hateful, Militant Christian Views" *Intelligence Report*, Spring
2012, 64–67.

31 Stern, *A Force upon the* Plain, 45–46.

32 Covenant, the Sword, and the Arm of the Lord publications in: Stern, "The
Covenant, the Sword, and the Arm of the Lord," 1. Robison's *Proofs* in: deAr-
mond, "Christian Patriots at War with the State," 5. Mailbox dots in: "'Patriot'
Conspiracy Theorist Jack Mclamb Dies," *Hatewatch* (blog), Southern Poverty
Law Center, January 13, 2014, https://www.splcenter.org/hatewatch/2014/01
/13/patriot-conspiracy-theorist-jack-mclamb-dies. Senate testimony in: Tour-

ish and Wohlforth, "Prophets of the Apocalypse," 3. Weather control also in Robert S .Robins and Jerrold M. Post, *Political Paranoia and the Psychopolitics of Hatred* (Yale University Press, 1997), 211–12.

33   The ZOG is considered "nonconcordant" (i.e., not universally accepted by white supremacist groups) by those who specialize in the study of such concepts. See Beutel, "Key Concepts to Understand Violent White Supremacy," 2. Similarly, see the discussion of the schism in the alt-right movement in: Chuck Tanner, "Richard Spencer: Alt-Right, White Nationalist, Anti-Semite," Institute for Research and Education on Human Rights, January 5, 2017, https://www.irehr.org/2017/01/05/richard-spencer-alt-right-white-nationalist-anti-semite/.

34   Gordon (Jack) Mohr, "Conspiracy to Deceive the Elect!!" Israel Elect of Zion, 1996(?), https://israelect.com/reference/JackMohr/jm007.htm.

35   DeArmond, "Christian Patriots at War with the State," 7. DeArmond appears to be quoting from *The Citizen's Rule Book*, 4th rev. (Christian Patriots, n.d.), https://famguardian.org/Publications/CitRulebook/citizen-rule-book.pdf. Gale's "constitutional" legacy is confusing. This "organic constitution" idea has been widely adopted by antigovernment "constitutionalists," including some in the Tea Party. Gale's other (and conflicting) idea was that the Articles of Confederation take precedence and that any part of the Constitution not in keeping with the articles is null and void. This more radical reinvention of America's founding documents underlies the localist views of the Posse Comitatus and the Township movement.

36   Erst LaFlor, *The Betrayal of the White Race* (self-pub., 1970), 3.

37   Dan Smoot, "Impeaching Earl Warren," pt. 1, *Dan Smoot Report*, January 30, 1961, 38.

38   *The Citizen's Rule Book*, 24.

39   Ibid., 25. See also J. M. Berger, "Without Prejudice: What Sovereign Citizens Believe" (paper written for the Program on Extremism at George Washington University, June 2016), 3–4, https://extremism.gwu.edu/sites/g/files/zaxdzs2191/f/downloads/JMB%20Sovereign%20Citizens.pdf.

40   Sharpe, "The Identity Christian Movement," 608, 618. Anonymous warrior priesthood quotation: "The Manchurian Oswald's Right Buttock," pt. 2, "Winding Up Little Timmy Tuttle," [whitenationalist.org, accessed June 1, 2018, http://whitenationalist.org/lindstedt/mnchosw2.html. Jewish conspiracy in Mohr, "Conspiracy to Deceive," 14. Anti-Christian tyranny in DuBowski, "Storming Wombs and Waco," 2. See also "ADL Investigation Reveals Strain of Anti-Semitism in Extreme Factions of the Anti-Abortion Movement," ADL Press Release, October 30, 1998, http://archive.is/zMSv.

41   Holland and deParrie quoted in DuBowski, "Storming Wombs and Waco," 2, 3.

42   *Anti-Government Movement Guidebook*, 13.

43   Joshua P. Weir, "Sovereign Citizens: A Reasoned Response to the Madness," *Lewis & Clark Law Review* 19, no. 3 (2015): 840.

44   Blueprint: *The Patriot*, June–July 1968, 1. Cover art: "Special Message" (leaflet), perhaps by Ken Duggan, n.d. (1968?). Amalgam: Weir, "Sovereign Citizens," 835.

45   "Stamp out the I.R.S. and the Federal Reserve Banking System," Patriotic
      Party Alert: "Stop the Police State," n.d., 5.
46   Advertisement/flyer, 1968.
47   "Stop the Police State," 1.
48   "Alarm," Patriotic Party, 1968.
49   Secret replacement: "Sovereign Citizens Movement," Southern Poverty
      Law Center, accessed June 1, 2018, https://www.splcenter.org/fighting-hate
      /extremist-files/ideology/sovereign-citizens-movement. Without prejudice:
      J. M. Sovereign: Godsent, *Title Four Flag Says You're Schwag!* (Sovereignty
      Press, 2009), 27.
50   Weir, "Sovereign Citizens," 8; Joshua Rhett Miller, "Tea Party Leader Says
      Group Seeks to Marginalize Him as 'Sovereign Citizen Guru,'" Fox News, Feb-
      ruary24, 2014, http://www.foxnews.com/politics/2014/02/24/tea-party-leader
      -says-group-seeks-to-marginalize-him-with-sovereign-citizen.html.
51   Vanessa Fimbres and Robert Kelly, "Free Your Mind—a Peek into the Matrix,"
      accessed May 3, 2018, http://www.americanssovereignbulletin.com/wp
      -content/uploads/2012/06/Free-Your-Mind-a-Peek-into-the-Matrix.pdf. See
      also Sovereign: Godsent, "Gold Dollars or Funny Money?," chap. 9 of *Title
      Four Flag Says You're Schwag!*
52   "A Quick Guide to Sovereign Citizens," University of North Carolina School of
      Government, November 2013, 2.
53   Some birthers used this reasoning to explain how someone "not having one
      drop of American blood in their veins" could become president, "destroying
      this country." See "The Fourteenth Amendment and a 'Natural Born Citizen,'"
      Birthers, accessed June 1, 2018, http://birthers.org/USC/14.html.
54   "Quick Guide to Sovereign Citizens," 2.
55   Leah Nelson, "'Sovereigns' in Black," *Intelligence Report*, August 24, 2011,
      https://www.splcenter.org/fighting-hate/intelligence-report/2011/%E2%80
      %98sovereigns%E2%80%99-black; "Quick Guide to Sovereign Citizens," 4;
      Teresa M. Blankenship, "Hawai'i Kingdom—Update 2—Exclusive," *American's
      Sovereign Bulletin*, July–August 2012, 11.
56   Intelligence Report Staff, "Paper Terrorism," *Intelligence Report*, Fall 2017,
      38–40 (reprinted at https://www.splcenter.org/fighting-hate/intelligence
      -report/2017/paper-terrorism). See also "Quick Guide to Sovereign Citizens,"
      1. Quotation and competence: Melissa L. Shearer and Christina M. Koenig,
      "Representing the Sovereign Citizen," *Voice for the Defense*, March 12, 2014,
      http://www.voiceforthedefenseonline.com/story/representing-sovereign
      -citizen.

Chapter Fifteen

1   Quoted in: Judy L. Thomas, "New Breed of Militias Puts on a Friendlier Face,
      But Critics Say It's Camouflage," *Kansas City Star*, September 11, 2010.
2   Texe Marrs, *Conspiracy of the Six-Pointed Star* (RiverCrest Publishing, 2011);
      Herbert G. Dorsey III, "The Historical Influence of International Bank-

ing," U.S.A. the Republic (website), 2004, http://www.usa-the-republic
.com/illuminati/cfr_3.html; Miguel Bruno Duarte, "Illuminati," Inter-
American Institute, December 11, 2012, http://archive.is/20130415221337
/theinteramerican.org/commentary/414-illuminati.html; Deanna Spingola,
"Before Rockefeller, There Was Rothschild," Springola Speaks, March 27,
2008, http://www.spingola.com/before_rockefeller.htm; David Allen Rivera,
Final Warning: A History of the New World Order (InteliBooks, 2004); Doc Marquis, *The Illuminati Protocols of Zion: The Plot against Israel*," Secrets of the Illuminati Series, DVD, accessed June 1, 2018, http://www.cuttingedge.org/detail
.cfm?ID=2227.

3   Ellen McClay, "A Word About UNESCO" (paper presented at the eleventh
annual National Conference on Private Property Rights, Albany, NY, October 13, 2007), https://prfamerica.org/speeches/11th/A-WordAbout-UNESCO
.html; David J. Stewart, "Evolution, Communism and the NWO . . . *Devilution!*" Jesus-Is-Savior.com, accessed May 29, 2018, https://www.jesus-is-savior
.com/Evolution%20Hoax/devilution.htm; Jennifer Lake, "Polio Then, Now,
and Forever"; Charlotte Iserbyt, "America's Road to Ruin," interview by Alex
Jones, May 2011, transcript of video, http://static.infowars.com/2012/01/i
/article-images/Iserbyt-AR2R-May2011.pdf; Alan Stang, "Zionism and the
Jewish Conspiracy," pt. 1, News with Views, February 17, 2009, http://www
.newswithviews.com/Stang/alan187.htm; Steve Rendall, "Glenn Beck's Jewish Problem," Fair: Fairness and Accuracy in Reporting, November 15, 2010,
https://fair.org/home/glenn-becks-jewish-problem/.

4   Jüri Lina, *Under the Sign of the Scorpion* (Referent Publishing, 2002); Rivera,
Final Warning, advertisement for 2004 video; P. D. Stuart, "The Revolutionary
War: How America Became a Jesuit Enclave," chap. 31 of *Codeword Barbêlôn:
Danger in the Vatican* (Lux-Verbi, 2006); Alex Christopher, *Pandora's Box—the
Ultimate "Unseen Hand" behind the New World Order* (Pandora's Box Publica-
tions,2007), second page of the introduction; Christopher Jon Bjerknes, *The
Manufacture and Sale of Saint Einstein* (self-pub., 2006), https://archive.org
/stream/ChristopherJonBjerknesTheManufactureAndSaleOfSaintEinstein
/SaintEinstein#page/n0/mode/2up.

5   The Red Phone Is Ringing, "He Blinded Me with Skousen," Daily Kos, May 19,
2010, https://www.dailykos.com/stories/2010/5/19/867891/-; Iserbyt, "America's Road to Ruin," 11; Duarte, "Illuminati," 17n5; Jüri Lina, "The Rothschilds'
Plan to Conquer America for the Bankers," *Barnes Review*, September–October
2004, 15.

6   See Jeanne Bergman, "The Cult of HIV Denialism," The Body (website),
Spring 2010, http://www.thebody.com/content/art57918.html; and Seth C.
Kalichman, "The Psychology of AIDS Denialism: Pseudocience, Conspiracy Thinking, and Medical Mistrust," *European Psychologist* 19 (2014): 13–22;
Leonard Horowitz, "Emerging Viruses—AIDS—Ebola," All-Natural, accessed
June 4, 2018, http://all-natural.com/horo-3/; Elsevier, "Zika Conspiracy Theories on Social Media Putting Vulnerable People at Risk," press release, May 24,
2016, https://www.elsevier.com/about/press-releases/research-and-journals
/zika-conspiracy-theories-on-social-media-putting-vulnerable-people-at-risk.

7   Anna Kata, "Anti-Vaccine Activists, Web 2.0, and the Postmodern Para-
     digm—an Overview of the Tactics and Tropes Used Online by the Anti-
     Vaccination Movement," *Vaccine* 30 (2011): 3778–89; Ben Goldacre, "The
     Media's MMR Hoax," chap. 16 of *Bad Science* (Fourth Estate, 2009); Saad B.
     Omer, "How Donald Trump's Conspiracy Theories about Vaccines Could
     Harm Public Health," *Washington Post*, January 11, 2017, https://www
     .washingtonpost.com/posteverything/wp/2017/01/11/how-donald-trumps
     -conspiracy-theories-about-vaccines-could-harm-public-health/?utm_term=
     .1ae686c705d3.

8   Jon Entine, "Most 'Dangerous' Anti-Science GMO Critic? Meet Mike Adams—
     Conspiracy Junkie Runs Alternative 'Health' Empire," Genetic Literacy Project,
     April 1, 2014, https://geneticliteracyproject.org/2014/04/01/most-dangerous
     -anti-science-gmo-critic-meet-mike-adams-conspiracy-junkie-runs-alternative
     -health-empire-more-influential-than-us-government-websites/; Christine
     Shearer et al., "Quantifying Expert Consensus against the Existence of a
     Secret, Large-Scale Atmospheric Spraying Program," *Environmental Research
     Letters* 11 (2016); Danny Lewis, "Calling All Conspiracy Theorists: Alaska's
     'Mind-Control Lab' Is Hosting an Open House," *Smithsonian*, August 25, 2016,
     https://www.smithsonianmag.com/smart-news/scientists-alaska-research-lab
     -are-holding-open-house-dispel-conspiracy-theories-180960255/.

9   David Ray Griffin, *The New Pearl Harbor* (Olive Branch Press, 2004), 196–97.

10   Philip Coppens, "9/11 + 11/22 = Conspiracy Plus: The Conspiracy Nation by
     Philip Coppens," Eye of the Psychic, accessed June 4, 2018, https://www
     .eyeofthepsychic.com/nine-eleven/; George Monbiot, "Short Changed," *The
     Guardian*, February 6, 2007. The popularity of 9/11 conspiracy theories appears
     to have peaked in 2005.

11   Gary North, "World Trade Center Building 7 and Conspiracy Theories,"
     LewRockwell.com, November 8, 2004, https://www.lewrockwell.com/2004
     /11/gary-north/the-redblue-map-vs-conspiracy-theories/; Rick Martin,
     "Secret Rulers of Planet Earth: The Illuminati," *Spectrum*, 4, no. 5 (November
     2002): 52, http://www.fourwinds10.com/siterun_data/spectrum/volume4
     /S0405.pdf.

12   The Smoking Man, "Rise of the Fourth Reich: the OKC Bombing, KuwAm,
     Mohammed Atta and 9/11," *Rielpolitik* (blog), September11, 2015, https://
     rielpolitik.com/2015/09/11/rise-of-the-fourth-reich-the-okc-bombing-kuwam
     -mohamed-atta-and-911/.

13   David Hawkins, "'Manufactured Shock'—How Teachers, NATO and the Mob
     Staged an Al-Qaeda 9/11," *Awaken Research Group*, vol. 1, no. 4 (2006), https://
     issuu.com/infowarbooks/docs/-manufactured-shock----how-teachers--nato
     -and-the-

14   Coppens, "9/11+11/22"; Gary G. Kohls, "Duty to Warn: 9/11 and Cognitive Dis-
     sonance," Global Research, September 3, 2013, https://www.globalresearch.ca
     /duty-to-warn-911-and-cognitive-dissonance/5347923.

15   Peter Dale Scott, "JFK, 9/11 and War," 911Truth.org, August 18, 2007,
     http://911truth.org/jfk-assassination-911-war/, and "The Hidden Govern-

ment Group Linking JFK, Watergate, Iran-Contra and 9/11," Who.What. Why (website), October 5, 2014, https://whowhatwhy.org/2014/10/05/the -hidden-government-group-linking-jfk-watergate-iran-contra-and-911/. See also Robert Bonomo, "JFK and 9/11: The Common Threads," *Unz Review*, November 29, 2013, http://www.unz.com/rbonomo/jfk-and-911-the-common -threads/; and Laurent Guyénot, *JFK–9/11 50 Years of Deep State* (Progressive Press, 2014).

16   Richard Landes, "The Jews as Contested Ground in Postmodern Conspiracy Theory," *Jewish Political Studies Review*, vol. 19, nos. 3–4 (Fall 2007). On Muslim conspiracism generally, see Marvin Zonis and Craig M. Joseph, "Conspiracy Thinking in the Middle East," *Political Psychology* 15, no. 3 (1994): 443–59. For an example of Arab conspiracism after 9/11, see Michael Collins Piper, "Zionist Influence on the American Media" (speech, Zayed International Centre for Coordination and Follow-Up [an Arab League think tank], March 10, 2003), http://americanfreepress.net/Supplements/Zayed%20Report.pdf.

17   "Unraveling Anti-Semitic 9/11 Conspiracy Theories," ADL, May 25, 2003, https://www.adl.org/news/article/unraveling-anti-semitic-911-conspiracy -theories.

18   "Terrorism Strikes America: What They're Saying," ADL, November 28, 2001. See also "Unraveling Anti-Semitic 9/11 Conspiracy Theories," 13–14; Eustace Mullins, "The Secret of 9/11: The Drumbeat for War," *Spectrum* 4, no. 5 (November 2002): 68–73, http://www.fourwinds10.com/siterun_data /spectrum/volume4/S0405.pdf; Gordon "Jack" Mohr, "Addendum," *From the Watchman's Corner Winter Intelligence Report*, December 2001, https://israelect .com/reference/JackMohr/int_report_12_2001.pdf, 17 (prediction); *From the Watchman's Corner Terrorist Intelligence Report*, September 2001, https:// israelect.com/reference/JackMohr/terr_int_report_9_2001.pdf, 2 (ZOG) and 5 (chickens).

19   ADL, "Anti-Semitic 9/11 Conspiracy Theories Abound on Social Networking Sites," 2009; David Duke, "9-11: Israel, the True Cause of Terrorism against America," DavidDuke.com, September 11, 2012, https://davidduke.com/9-11 -israel-the-true-cause-of-terrorism-against-america/; Tamar Pileggi, "Farrakhan: 'Lying, Murderous Zionist Jews' Behind 9/11," *Times of Israel*, March 6, 2015, https://www.timesofisrael.com/jewish-graves-desecrated-on-mount-of -olives/.

20   See Doctor Conspiracy, "The Debunker's Guide to Obama Conspiracy Theories," Obama Conspiracy Theories, 2017, http://www.obamaconspiracy.org /bookmarks/fact-checking-and-debunking/the-debunkers-guide-to-obama -conspiracy-theories/.

21   "An Open Letter to Barack Obama," advertisement placed in the *Chicago Tribune*, December 1, 2008, by We the People Foundation for Constitutional Education, Inc. On the origin of the birther charges, see Loren Collins, "The Secret Origins of the Birthers," Birth of a Notion, June 22, 2011 (updated September 18, 2016), http://birthofanotion.com/home/the-secret-origin-of-the -birthers.

22   On Gaffney, see David Keene, "When Conspiracy Nuts Do Real Damage,"
      Washington Times, April 17, 2016, https://www.washingtontimes.com/news
      /2016/apr/17/david-keene-when-conspiracy-nuts-do-real-damage/. On Berg
      and Taitz, see ADL, *Rage Grows in America: Anti-Government Conspiracies*,
      November 2012, https://www.adl.org/sites/default/files/documents/assets
      /pdf/combating-hate/Rage-Grows-In-America.pdf, 14–17. On Taitz's lawsuits,
      see Jennifer McGee, "Conspiracy Theory in the Age of the Internet: The Case
      of the 'Birthers,'" Akima Shukutoku University Knowledge Archive March 15,
      2011, 57–62 (downloadable as a PDF at scholar.google.com). On the return
      of FEMA as a threat, see Larry Keller, "Fear of FEMA," *Intelligence Report*,
      Spring 2010, 12–17 (available online at https://www.splcenter.org/fighting-hate
      /intelligence-report/2010/fear-fema).

23   On the North American Union conspiracy theories, see Chip Berlet, "The
      North American Union: Right-Wing Populist Conspiracism Rebounds," *Public
      Eye* 23, no. 1 (Spring 2008): 1, 11–19. Kyle Mantyla, "The Far Right's Latest
      Boogeyman: Environmentalism," Right Wing Watch, December 15, 2008,
      http://www.rightwingwatch.org/post/the-far-rights-newest-boogeyman
      -environmentalism/. See also Benjamin Warner and Ryan Neville-Shepard,
      "Echoes of A Conspiracy: Birthers, Truthers and the Cultivation of Extrem-
      ism," *Communication Quarterly* 62, no. 1 (2014): 1–17.

24   Militias: ADL, *Rage Grows in America*, 28–29. Threats and resistance: Mark
      Potok, "Timeline: Land Use and the 'Patriots,'" *Intelligence Report*, Fall 2014,
      29 (reprinted at https://www.splcenter.org/fighting-hate/intelligence-report
      /2014/land-use-patriots).

25   Heidi Beirich, "Midwifing the Militias," *Intelligence Report*, March 2, 2010,
      https://www.splcenter.org/fighting-hate/intelligence-report/2010/midwifing
      -militias; "Continental Congress 2009" (flyer), We the People Founda-
      tion for Constitutional Education, Inc., accessed May 7, 2018, https://
      wethepeoplefoundation.org/UPDATE/misc2009/OST-WTP-FLYER-3.pdf.

26   Stewart Rhodes, "Enemy at the Gate: Just Following Orders," *S.W.A.T. Maga-
      zine*, April 2008, https://www.swatmag.com/article/enemy-gate-just-following
      -orders/, quoted in "Elmer Stewart Rhodes," accessed July 16, 2018, https://
      www.splcenter.org/fighting-hate/extremist-files/individual/elmer-stewart
      -rhodes-0. Morris Dees founded the Southern Poverty Law Center.

27   *Operation Vampire Killer 2000: American Police Action Plan for Stopping World
      Government Rule*, Police against the New World Order, 1992, reprinted at
      http://musicians4freedom.com/wp-content/uploads/2012/05/Jack-McLamb
      -Operation-Vampire-Killer-2000-Police-and-Military-Against-the-NWO.pdf;
      quotations on third page.

28   "Hamilton Group Promoting Extremism, Not 'Celebrating Conservatism': Sec-
      ond Militia Speaker Coming to Town in Two Months" (press release), Montana
      Human Rights Network, August 14, 2009, http://www.mhrn.org/publications
      /specialresearchreports/McLambBriefingPaper.pdf. See also Potok, "Time-
      line: Land Use," 30.

29   Three Percenter quoted in ADL, *Rage Grows in America*, 28. See also Spencer
      Sunshine with Rural Organizing Project and Political Research Associates, *Up

in *Arms: A Guide to Oregon's Patriot Movement* (Political Research Associates, 2016), http://www.rop.org/wp-content/uploads/Up-in-Arms_Report_PDF-1 .pdf; and Potok, "Timeline: Land Use," 29–30.

30   The "web only" qualification is used in ADL, *Rage Grows in America*, 29. Jo Freeman, "Libertarians Invade the 2010 Conservative Political Action Conference," JoFreeman.com, February 2010, https://www.jofreeman.com /rightreport/cpac.html. The list of groups is taken from ADL, *Rage Grows in America*; and Beirich, "Midwifing the Militias." See also Justine Sharrock, "Oath Keepers and the Age of Treason," *Mother Jones*, March–April, 2010, https://www.motherjones.com/politics/2010/02/oath-keepers/.

31   *Rightwing Extremism: Current Economic and Political Climate Fueling Resurgence in Radicalization and Recruitment*, Assessment, Office of Intelligence and Analysis, U.S. Department of Homeland Security, April 7, 2009, https:// fas.org/irp/eprint/rightwing.pdf. See also Charles P. Blair, "Looking Clearly at Right-Wing Terrorism," *Bulletin of the Atomic Scientists*, June 9, 2014, https:// thebulletin.org/looking-clearly-right-wing-terrorism7232; and Mark Pitcavage, "Cerberus Unleashed: The Three Faces of the Lone Wolf Terrorist," *American Behavioral Scientist* 59, no. 13 (2015): 1655–80.

32   John Hudson, "Neo-Nazis Are Using the Army as a Training Camp," *Atlantic*, August 21, 2012, https://www.theatlantic.com/national/archive/2012 /08/neo-nazis-are-using-army-training-camp/324485/; Daniel Trotta, "U.S. Army Battling Racists within Its Own Ranks," Reuters, August 21, 2012, https://www.reuters.com/article/us-usa-wisconsin-shooting-army -idUSBRE87K04Y20120821; Nadya Labi, "Rogue Element," *New Yorker*, May 26, 2014, 50–61 (available online at https://www.newyorker.com /magazine/2014/05/26/rogue-element).

Chapter Sixteen

1   *Operation Vampire Killer 2000: American Police Action Plan for Stopping World Government Rule*, Police against the New World Order, 1992, reprinted at http://musicians4freedom.com/wp-content/uploads/2012/05/Jack-McLamb -Operation-Vampire-Killer-2000-Police-and-Military-Against-the-NWO .pdf. Steele essay in: Heidi Beirich, "Midwifing the Militias," *Intelligence Report*, March 2, 2010, 5 (reprinted at https://www.splcenter.org/fighting -hate/intelligence-report/2010/midwifing-militias). An archive of sorts of antisemitic militia writing from the turn of the century can be found in Martin Lindstadt's "Stuff I Should Have Wrote, but Didn't," WhiteNationalist.org, rev. November 5, 2009, http://www.whitenationalist.org/lindstedt/goodstuf .html.

2   ADL, *Rage Grows in America: Anti-Government Conspiracies*, November 2012, https://www.adl.org/sites/default/files/documents/assets/pdf/combating-hate /Rage-Grows-In-America.pdf 10. The phrase "Hitler's T4" refers to the belief among Tea Partiers that Hitler's "health care system," was known as the "T4 Program" and included "death panels." See Doc Marquis, "The Illuminati's

7-Part Plan Towards the Creation of a New World Order," News with Views, December 15, 2014, http://www.newswithviews.com/Marquis/doc100.htm.

3   Judy L. Thomas, "New Breed of Militias Puts on a Friendlier Face, but Critics Say It's Camouflage," *Kansas City Star*, September 11, 2010, 2–3. Jack in the Box: Lauren McGaughy and David Rauf, "NRA Blasts Open Carry Supporters," *San Antonio Express-News*, June 2, 2014.

4   Chip Berlet, "Collectivists, Communists, Labor Bosses, and Treason: The Tea Parties as Right-Wing Counter-Subversionist Panic," *Critical Sociology* 38, no. 4 (2012): 565–67.

5   Jill Lepore, *The Whites of Their Eyes* (Princeton University Press, 2010), 16.

6   W. Cleon Skousen, *The 5,000 Year Leap* (National Center for Constitutional Studies, 1981), and *The Making of America: The Substance and Meaning of the Constitution* (National Center for Constitutional Studies, 1985).

7   Jared A. Goldstein, "The Tea Party's Constitution," *Denver University Law Review* 88, no. 3 (2011): 559–76, quote on 566. See also Rob Boston, "Troubling Textbooks," *Church and State*, September 2014, https://www.au.org/church-state/september-2014-church-state/featured/troubling-textbooks.

8   Goldstein, "Tea Party's Constitution," 567.

9   Ibid., 569. See also Alexander Zaitchik, "Fringe Mormon Group Makes Myths with Glenn Beck's Help," *Intelligence Report*, Spring 2011, https://www.splcenter.org/fighting-hate/intelligence-report/2011/fringe-mormon-group-makes-myths-glenn-beck%E2%80%99s-help.

10   Seth Payne, "Satan's Plan: The Book of Mormon, Glenn Beck and Modern Conspiracy" (paper presented at the meeting of the American Academy of Religion, Calgary, May 10, 2014), 8.

11   Ron Paul, *End the Fed* (Grand Central Publishing, 2009). By 2016, Paul was referring to the Fed itself as a "secret society." Joel M. Skousen, "Analysis of Strategic Threats in the Current Decade (2000–2010)," JoelSkousen.com, updated May 2010, http://www.joelskousen.com/threats.html.

12   Beck quotation: Boston, "Troubling Textbooks," 3. First seminar: "Profile: W. Cleon Skousen, History Commons, accessed June 4, 2018, http://www.historycommons.org/entity.jsp?entity=w_cleon_skousen_1. Second seminar: Zaitchik, "Fringe Mormon Group," 5.

13   Video: Sean Wilentz, "Confounding Fathers: The Tea Party's Cold War Roots," *New Yorker*, October 18, 2010, https://www.newyorker.com/magazine/2010/10/18/confounding-fathers. Website quoted in Berlet, "Collectivists, Communists, Labor Bosses, and Treason," 578. Jonathan Kay, "Tea Party Movement Is Full of Conspiracy Theories," *Newsweek*, February 8, 2010, http://www.newsweek.com/tea-party-movement-full-conspiracy-theories-75153.

14   Ted Goertzel, "The Conspiracy Meme," *Skeptical Inquirer*, vol. 35, no. (January–February 2011), https://www.csicop.org/si/show/the_conspiracy_meme.

15   Brendan Nyhan, "Why the 'Death Panel' Myth Wouldn't Die: Misinformation in the Health Care Debate," *Forum*, vol. 8, no. 1 (2010); Angie Drobnic Holan, "PolitiFact's Lie of the Year: 'Death Panels,'" PolitiFact, December 18, 2009, http://www.politifact.com/truth-o-meter/article/2009/dec/18/politifact-lie-year-death-panels/.

16　Allen Clifton, "A Breakdown of Some of the Asinine Conspiracy Theories Conservatives Have Used against Obama," Forward Progressives, May 5, 2014, https://
forwardprogressives.com/breakdown-asinine-conspiracy-theories-conservatives
-used-obama/; Ed Kilgore, "Who Will Lead the Fight against 'Death Panels' This
Time?," Washington Monthly, July 9, 2015, https://washingtonmonthly.com/2015
/07/09/who-will-lead-the-fight-against-death-panels-this-time/.

17　Conor Friedersdorf, "Ron Paul, Conspiracy Theories, and the Right," Atlantic,
December 29, 2011, https://www.theatlantic.com/politics/archive/2011/12/ron
-paul-conspiracy-theories-and-the-right/250638/.

18　Daneen Peterson, "How to Reverse the Communist UN Takeover . . .
One Country at a Time," Secure the Republic, October 17, 2012, https://
securetherepublic.com/blog/2012/10/17/reverse-communist-takeover/.

19　George Michael, "The New Media and the Rise of Exhortatory Terrorism,"
Strategic Studies Quarterly 7, no. 1 (Spring 2013): 42–43.

20　George Michael, "The Rise of the Alt-Right and the Politics of Polarization in
America," Skeptic, vol. 22, no. 2 (2017), https://www.skeptic.com/reading_room
/rise-of-alt-right-politics-of-polarization-in-america/.

21　David Corn, "Ben Carson and the Satanic Sabbath Persecution Conspiracy,"
Mother Jones, October 2, 2015, https://www.motherjones.com/politics/2015/10
/ben-carson-sabbath-persecution-satan-conspiracy/.

22　Erik Wemple, "Allen West Corrects Walmart-Sharia Story," Washington Post,
May 12, 2015, https://www.washingtonpost.com/blogs/erik-wemple/wp/2015
/05/12/allen-west-corrects-walmart-sharia-story/?utm_term=.ad3138a125a0.
Wemple's story does not use the word "conspiracy."

23　Presidential Debate News, "GOP Conspiracy Says Efforts to Open Debates
a Ploy to Elect Democrats," Independent Voter Network, September 9, 2015,
https://ivn.us/2015/09/09/gop-conspiracy-says-efforts-open-debates-ploy
-elect-democrats/; Rand Paul story: David Corn, "Rand Paul: The Most Inter-
esting Conspiracy Theorist in Washington," Mother Jones, October 20, 2014,
https://www.motherjones.com/politics/2014/10/rand-paul-truther-conspiracy
-theories/.

24　Friedersdorf, "Ron Paul, Conspiracy Theories, and the Right," 3, with reference to the National Review and to Newt Gingrich.

25　Illusory fear: Faiza Patel and Amos Toh, "The Clear Anti-Muslim Bias
behind Anti-Sharia Laws," Washington Post, February 21, 2014, https://
www.washingtonpost.com/national/religion/commentary-the-clear-anti
-muslim-bias-behind-anti-shariah-laws/2014/02/21/381d7a7a-9b30-11e3
-8112-52fdf646027b_story.html?utm_term=.2550e6fc02b5; Cathie Adams,
former chairwoman of the Texas Republican Party and current leader of the
Texas chapter of Phyllis Schlafly's Eagle Forum, quoted in Mark Potok and
Don Terry, "Margins to the Mainstream," Intelligence Report, October 27, 2015,
31–32 (creeping attempt and tool of Satan), online at https://www.splcenter
.org/fighting-hate/intelligence-report/2015/margins-mainstream. Duncan quoted in: "Oklahoma International and Sharia Law, State question 755
(2010)," Ballotpedia, accessed May 8, 2018, https://ballotpedia.org/Oklahoma
_International_and_Sharia_Law,_State_Question_755_ (2010).

26   Gohmert quoted in: Dahlia Lithwick, "Threats to Liberty," *Slate*, May 7, 2015, http://www.slate.com/articles/news_and_politics/jurisprudence/2015/05/jade _helm_15_fear_of_military_and_police_conspiracy_theorists_ignore_true.html. Random "leaps" recounted in: Potok and Terry, "Margins to the Mainstream," 11–16. John MacMurray, "Birchers, and Birthers, and Lies! Oh My!" *Dick and Sharon's LA Progressive*, May 9, 2015, https://www.laprogressive.com/jade -helm-15/.

27   MacMurray, "Birchers, and Birthers, and Lies!"

28   Thomas H. Kuchel, "The Fright Peddlers," *Cleveland-Marshall Law Review*, 13, no. 4 (1964): 4–6; Mike Blair, "Marines 'Attack' New Orleans and Mobile," *Spotlight*, September 9, 1996.

29   Robert Brotherton, "Conspiracy Theorising in the Wake of the Newtown Shooting," The Psychology of Conspiracy Theories (website), December 15, 2012, https://conspiracypsychology.com/2012/12/15/conspiracy-theorising -in-the-wake-of-newtown-shooting/; Alex Seitz-Wald, "Sandy Hook Truther Won't Quit," *Salon*, January 18, 2013, https://www.salon.com/2013/01/18 /james_tracy_wont_back_down/. Quotations and photographs formerly at http://thetruthfulone.com/false-flag-crisis-actors/; an image from that page can be found at https://www.pinterest.com/pin/400961173058166320/?lp =true. See also "Boston Marathon Crisis Actors! "Before It's News, April 22, 2013, http://beforeitsnews.com/conspiracy-theories/2013/04/boston -marathon-crisis-actors-2450330.html.

30   Kate Starbird, "Information Wars: A Window into the Alternative Media Ecosystem," *Medium*, March 14, 2017, https://medium.com/hci-design-at -uw/information-wars-a-window-into-the-alternative-media-ecosystem -a1347f32fd8f.

31   John Celock, "Orly Taitz Blames Sandy Hook Massacre on Obama," *HuffPost*, December 18, 2012, https://www.huffingtonpost.com/2012/12/18/orly-taitz -sandy-hook-obama_n_2325671.html.

32   "British, Saudi and FBI Complicity Exposed in Orlando Mass Killings" (leaf- let), LaRouche Pac, June 16, 2016, https://larouchepac.com/20160616/british -saudi-and-fbi-complicity-exposed-orlando-mass-killings-same-people-who -brought-you; Sam Reisman, "Alex Jones Already Calling Orlando a 'False Flag,'" Mediaite, June 13, 2016, https://www.mediaite.com/online/alex-jones -already-calling-orlando-a-false-flag/.

33   Aaron Sankin, "Charlottesville Conspiracy Theories Spread, Echoing 'False Flag' Claims," Reveal (from the Center for Investigative Reporting), August 13, 2017, https://www.revealnews.org/blog/charlottesville-conspiracy-theories -spread-echoing-other-false-flag-claims/.

34   "Far Right Sees Communism, Plot behind Schools' Common Core," *Intel- ligence Report*, Fall 2014, 5–6. Alabama Senate testimony in: Kurt Eichen- wald, "The Plots to Destroy America," *Newsweek*, May 15, 2014, http://www .newsweek.com/2014/05/23/plots-destroy-america-251123.html. Terry Bratton quoted in: *Public Schools in the Crosshairs: Far-Right Propaganda and the Common Core State Standards*, special report (Southern Poverty Law Center), May 2014. Van Zant quoted in Amy Sherman, "Lawmaker: Common

Core Testing Company Forces Children to Become 'as Homosexual as They Possibly Can,'" PolitiFact Florida, May 20, 2014, http://www.politifact.com /florida/statements/2014/may/20/charles-van-zant/common-core-testing -homosexual-possibly-can/.

35 Victoria Jackson, "I Found 'Agenda 21' in Lynchburg, Va!," April 1, 2014, http:// victoriajackson.com/10914/found-agenda-21-lynchburg-va (accessed April 8, 2014; no longer available at that site). Cruz quoted in Heidi Beirich et al., *Agenda 21: The UN, Sustainability and Right-Wing Conspiracy Theory*, special report (Southern Poverty Law Center), April 2014, 5, https://www.splcenter.org /sites/default/files/d6_legacy_files/downloads/publication/agenda_21_final _web.pdf. List of projects killed in: Eichenwald, "Plots to Destroy America." See also Karen T. Frick, David Weinzimmer, and Paul Waddell, "The Politics of Sustainable Development Opposition: State Legislative Efforts to Stop the United Nations' Agenda 21 in the United States," *Urban Studies* 52, no. 2 (2014): 209–32.

36 Ryan Lenz, "Seeing Red," *Intelligence Report*, Spring 2016, 26.

37 Tim Murphy, "Top Georgia GOP Lawmakers Host Briefing on Secret Obama Mind-Control Plot," *Mother Jones*, November 14, 2012, https://www .motherjones.com/politics/2012/11/georgia-senate-gets-52-minute-briefing -united-nations-takeover/.

38 Renee Diresta, "Social Network Algorithms Are Distorting Reality by Boosting Conspiracy Theories," *Fast Company*, May 11, 2016, https://www.fastcompany .com/3059742/social-network-algorithms-are-distorting-reality-by-boosting -conspiracy-theories. See also Alessandro Bessi et al., "Science vs Conspiracy: Collective Narratives in the Age of Misinformation," *PLoS ONE*, vol. 10, no. 2 (2015).

39 Brian Tashman, "58 Donald Trump Conspiracy Theories (and Counting!): The Definitive Trump Conspiracy Guide," *AlterNet*, May 3, 2016, https://www .alternet.org/right-wing/58-donald-trump-conspiracy-theories-and-counting -definitive-trump-conspiracy-guide, conspiracy theory 3.

40 Amy Davidson Sorkin, "Donald Trump's Scalia-Conspiracy Theory Pillow Fight," *New Yorker*, February 17, 2016, https://www.newyorker.com/news /amy-davidson/donald-trumps-scalia-conspiracy-pillow-fight. See also Caitlyn Yilek, "Trump Flirts with Suggestion That Scalia Was Murdered," *Ballot Box* (blog), *Hill*, February 16, 2016, http://thehill.com/blogs/ballot-box /presidential-races/donald-trump-justice-antonin-scalia-murdered-pillow -conspiracy-theory.

41 Jesse Walker, "Trump's Orlando Conspiracy," *Commercial Appeal*, June 16, 2016, http://archive.commercialappeal.com/opinion/national/jesse-walker -trumps-orlando-conspiracy-355701ce-8f6a-6cf0-e053-0100007f90ac -383216801.html/.

42 Aaron Blake, "Michael Flynn's Tweet Wasn't Actually about #Pizzagate, but Now His Son Is Defending the Baseless Conspiracy Theory," *The Fix* (blog), *Washington Post*, December 5, 2016, https://www.washingtonpost.com/news /the-fix/wp/2016/12/05/did-michael-flynn-really-tweet-something-about -pizzagate-not-exactly/?utm_term=.fcc4cc2d261f; Andrew Kaczynski, "On

Twitter, Michael Flynn Interacted with Alt-Right, Made Controversial Comments on Muslims, Shared Fake News," CNN, November 18, 2016, https://www.cnn.com/2016/11/18/politics/kfile-flynn-tweets/index.html; "Incoming National Security Advisor's Son Spreads Fake News about D.C. Pizza Shop," *Politico*, December 4, 2016, https://www.politico.com/story/2016/12/incoming-national-security-advisers-son-spreads-fake-news-about-dc-pizza-shop-232181.

43 Camila Domonoske, "Man Fires Rifle inside D.C. Pizzeria, Cites Fictitious Conspiracy Theories," *The Two Way* (blog), National Public Radio, December 5, 2016, https://www.npr.org/sections/thetwo-way/2016/12/05/504404675/man-fires-rifle-inside-d-c-pizzeria-cites-fictitious-conspiracy-theories.

44 Mike Cernovich, "Podesta Spirit Cooking Emails Reveal Clinton Inner Circle as Sex Cult with Connections to Human Trafficking," *Danger and Play* (blog), November 3, 2016, https://archive.is/52eqw. See also Carmen Celestini, "Wikileaks' October Surprise: With 'Spirit Dinners,' Conspiracy Goes Mainstream," *Religion Dispatches*, November 4, 2016, http://religiondispatches.org/wikileaks-october-surprise-with-spirit-dinners-conspiracy-goes-mainstream/.

45 Eyes on the Right, "Alt-Right Crowd Spreads Conspiracy Theories about Secret Pedo Ring at D.C. Pizza Parlor," Angry White Men (website), November 22, 2016, https://angrywhitemen.org/2016/11/22/alt-right-crowd-spreads-conspiracy-theories-about-secret-pedo-ring-at-d-c-pizza-parlor/. On the Haitian story, see Shani M. King, "Owning Laura Silsby's Shame: How the Haitian Child Trafficking Scheme Embodies the Western Disregard for the Integrity of Poor Families," *Harvard Human Rights Journal* 25, no. 1 (2012), esp. 7–11. See also "Fugitive Who Posed as Lawyer Following Haitian Earthquake Sentenced to 3 Years in Federal Prison for Alien Smuggling," U.S. Immigration and Customs Enforcement news release, June 16, 2011, https://www.ice.gov/news/releases/fugitive-who-posed-lawyer-following-haitian-earthquake-sentenced-3-years-federal.

46 Right-wing websites in Eyes on the Right, "Alt-Right Crowd Spreads Conspiracy Theories." Reddit reaction: Abby Ohlheiser, "Fearing Yet Another Witch Hunt, Reddit Bans 'Pizzagate,'" *Washington Post*, November 24, 2016, https://www.washingtonpost.com/news/the-intersect/wp/2016/11/23/fearing-yet-another-witch-hunt-reddit-bans-pizzagate/?utm_term=.14151400d5d3. The term "4Chan" refers to a message board for anonymous posts.

47 Mr. Rockwell, "Clinton Cabal to Be Brought Down by Jew Flashing His 'Weiner' . . . ?," November 6, 2016, http://everyoneisaracist.blogspot.com/2016/11/clinton-cabal-to-be-brought-down-by-jew.html.

48 Tweets in Eyes on the Right, "Alt-Right Crowd Spreads Conspiracy Theories," 4–7. Seth Rich conspiracy: Manuel Roig-Franzia, "Seth Rich Wasn't Just Another D.C. Murder Victim: He Was a Meme in the Weirdest Presidential Election of Our Times," *Washington Post*, January 18, 2017, https://www.washingtonpost.com/lifestyle/style/seth-rich-wasnt-just-another-dc-murder-victim-he-was-a-meme-in-the-weirdest-presidential-election-of-our-times

/2017/01/18/ee8e27f8-dcc0-11e6-918c-99ede3c8cafa_story.html?utm_term=
.6a9339bc4ad1.

49   Eyes on the Right, "Alt-Right Crowd Spreads Conspiracy Theories," 9–10.

Chapter Seventeen

1   Adam Frank, "Why I'd Rather Not March," "Cosmos & Culture: Commentary
on Science and Society," National Public Radio, February 12, 2017, https://
www.npr.org/sections/13.7/2017/02/12/513873493/why-id-rather-not-march.

2   Natasha Geiling, "Idaho Lawmakers Vote to Remove Climate Information from Science Curriculum," ThinkProgress, February 14, 2017, https://
thinkprogress.org/idaho-climate-science-school-curriculum-fc81d0b6d432/.

3   Jesse Ventura, *American Conspiracies* (Skyhorse Publishing, 2011), chap. 15.
See also Smaranda Dumitru, "Lyme Disease on Plum Island: Fringe Conspiracy Theory or Government Cover-Up?" Tick Talk: An Investigative Project on
Lyme Disease (State University of New York at New Paltz), accessed July 16,
2018, https://sites.newpaltz.edu/ticktalk/social-attitudes/story-by-smaranda
-dumitru/.

4   Mike Adams, "Obama's EPA Caught Covering up High Heavy Metals Pollution
across U.S. Cities as Federal Government Wages Multifaceted WAR against
Its Own Citizens," *Natural News*, June 21, 2016, https://www.naturalnews
.com/054428_heavy_metals_municipal_water_supply_EPA_cover-up.html;
Craig D. Pearcey, "Deconstructing the Conspiracy of Deliberate Poisoning of US Municipal Water," Science-Based Medicine, July 31, 2016, https://
sciencebasedmedicine.org/deconstructing-the-conspiracy-of-deliberate
-poisoning-of-us-municipal-water/. See also Jon Entine, "Most 'Dangerous' Anti-Science GMO Critic? Meet Mike Adams—Conspiracy Junkie Runs
Alternative 'Health' Empire," Genetic Literacy Project, April 1, 2014, https://
geneticliteracyproject.org/2014/04/01/most-dangerous-anti-science-gmo
-critic-meet-mike-adams-conspiracy-junkie-runs-alternative-health-empire
-more-influential-than-us-government-websites/; Jordan Weissman, "Jill
Stein's Ideas Are Terrible: She Is Not the Savior the Left Is Looking For," *Mon-
eybox* (blog), *Slate*, July 27, 2016, http://www.slate.com/blogs/moneybox/2016
/07/27/jill_stein_is_not_the_savior_the_left_is_looking_for.html.

5   Royce Christyn, "Some Believe Mysterious 'Floating Cities' Caused by CERN
Wormhole," YourNewsWire.com, February 17, 2017, https://yournewswire.com
/some-believe-mysterious-floating-cities-caused-by-cern-wormhole/. Project
Blue Beam was the invention of Québécois writer Serge Monast—see "The
Greatest Hoax—NASA's Project Blue Beam," transcribed from a radio broad-
cast by Monast (ca. 1994) by SweetLiberty.org on a page titled "The Greatest
Hoax" (http://www.sweetliberty.org/issues/hoax/bluebeam.htm).

6   Zach Toombs, "Conspiracy Theorists Think Government Planted 'Fake
Snow,'" Newsy, February 1, 2014, https://www.newsy.com/stories/conspiracy
-theorists-think-gov-t-planted-fake-snow/; Taimoor ul Islam, "Climate Control

Conspiracy Theories: Is HAARP Changing Our Weather?," *Science Times*, March 15, 2015, http://www.sciencetimes.com/articles/4252/20150315/climate-control-conspiracy-theories-is-haarp-changing-our-weather.htm. Tesla: Justin Deschamps, "Science Conspiracy: Suppressed Free Energy Science," Stillness in the Storm, November 13, 2013, https://stillnessinthestorm.com/2013/11/science-conspiracy-suppressed-free/. Donald L. Zygutis, *The Sagan Conspiracy* (New Page Books, 2016).

7 Stanley K. Montieth, *The Population Control Agenda* (self pub., 1995?), http://www.radioliberty.com/ThePopulationControlAgenda.pdf, 2, 4, and 5.

8 Ad copy for Kevin Galalae's *Killing Us Softly: The Global Depopulation Policy*, American Free Press Bookstore, accessed June 5, 2018, http://shop.americanfreepress.net/store/p/662-KILLING-US-SOFTLY-The-Global-Depopulation-Policy.html; Jenny Lake, "Polio Then, Now, and Forever," 2008, accessed November 5, 2015, iamthewitness.com/news/2008.11.06-Polio.Then.Now.and.Forever.html (website no longer available); Nancy Turner Banks, "The Brothers Flexner," Slide Share, 2010, https://www.slideshare.net/drimhotep/the-brothers-flexner-by-nancy-turner-banks-mdmba, 35; Len Horowitz, "DNA: Pirates of the Sacred Spiral" (lecture presented at the fourteenth annual UFO Congress Convention and Film Festival, Laughlin, NV, March 6-12, 2005), on video at https://www.youtube.com/watch?v=FStLvEy64vw.

9 An early example: Brock Pope, *Charlatan: America's Most Dangerous Huckster, the Man Who Pursued Him, and the Age of Flimflam* (Crown Publishers, 2008). For a contemporary example, see Vivian Goldschmidt, "Latest Osteoporosis News: Americans 'Too Dumb' to Recognize Medical Conspiracies," Save Our Bones, 2014, https://saveourbones.com/medical-conspiracies-big-pharma-finds-sneaky-way-to-expand-osteoporosis-diagnosis-new-study-on-bone-flexibility-and-more/.

10 James C. Petersen and Gerald E. Markle, "Politics and Science in the Laetrile Controversy," *Social Studies of Science* 9 (1979): 139–66, quote on 150.

11 Eric Merola, director, *Burzynski, the Movie* (Merola Films, 2010), video distributed by Gerson Health Media. "Angered the pharma-medical-industrial complex": ad copy for *Burzynski, the Movie*, accessed June 5, 2018, http://gersonmedia.com/product/burzynski-movie/. See also Orac, "Conspiracy Theories; The Dark Heart of Alternative Medicine," *Respectful Insolence* (blog), March 20, 2014, https://respectfulinsolence.com/2014/03/20/conspiracy-theories-the-dark-heart-of-alternative-medicine/; Massimo Mazzucco, director, *Cancer: The Forbidden Cures* (Luogocomune, 2010), video distributed by Gerson Health Media. "Fascinating documentary": ad copy for *Cancer: The Forbidden Cures*, accessed June 5, 2018, http://gersonmedia.com/product/cancer-forbidden-cures/. On Gerson's ninety years of being suppressed, see "Gerson Therapy: 90 Year-Old Powerful Natural Cancer Treatment You've Probably Never Heard Of," Mercola, August 14, 2011, https://articles.mercola.com/sites/articles/archive/2011/08/14/beautiful-truth-about-outlawed-cancer-treatment.aspx. Max Gerson's therapy consists essentially of a diet and detoxification regimen. It appears to have been first touted as a cancer cure in the 1940s.

12 Leslie Waghorn and Julia Bennett, "There Is No Holistic Murder Conspiracy Afoot. Seriously," The Scientific Parent, August 3, 2015, https:// thescientificparent.org/there-is-no-holistic-murder-conspiracy-afoot -seriously/#; Robert Blaskiewicz, "The Big Pharma Conspiracy Theory," *Medical Writing* 22, no. 4 (2013): 259.

13 Mary Arsenault, "An Interview with Dr. Brad Case," *Wisdom*, May 2011, http:// wisdom-magazine.com/Article.aspx/2166/; *Thugs, Drugs and the War on Bugs* was also available as a video from Gerson Health Media (gersonmedia.com no longer functioning).

14 Banks, "The Brothers Flexner," 35; Emanuel M. Josephson, *Rockefeller "Internationalist": The Man Who Misrules the World* (Chedney Press, 1952), 106; Eustace Mullins, *Murder by Injection* (National Council for Medical Research, 1988).

15 Dr. Joseph Mercola, "The Witch-Hunt That's Taking It to One of America's Healthiest Food Choices," Mercola, December 31, 2010, https://articles .mercola.com/sites/articles/archive/2010/12/31/us-government-sneakily -subsidizes-milk-industry.aspx; "The Raw Milk Conspiracy—Short Facts!," DavidIcke.com, September 16, 2011, https://forum.davidicke.com/showthread .php?t=183733; Mike Adams, "update" to "Raw Food Raid: Armed Agents Bust Raw Milk & Cheese Sellers," Infowars, August 3, 2011, https://www.infowars .com/raw-food-raid-armed-agents-bust-raw-milk-cheese-sellers/. The raid of a health food store by California law enforcement authorities was, by any reasonable standard, excessive.

16 Anna Almendrala, "Andrew Wakefield, Disgraced Anti-Vax Doctor, Returns with a Documentary at Tribeca Film Fest," *HuffPost*, July 26, 2016, https:// www.huffingtonpost.com/entry/andrew-wakefield-anti-vax-documentary -tribeca_us_56f4a125e4b0143a9b47dd7b; Anna Kata, "Anti-Vaccine Activists, Web 2.0, and the Postmodern Paradigm—an Overview of Tactics and Tropes Used by the Anti-Vaccination Movement," *Vaccine* 30 (2012): 3778–89; Daniel Jolley and Karen M. Douglas, "The Effect of Anti-Vaccine Conspiracy Theories on Vaccination Intentions," *PLoS ONE* 9, vol. no. 2 (2014); J. Eric Oliver and Thomas Wood, "Medical Conspiracy Theories and Health Behaviors in the United States," *JAMA Internal Medicine* 174, no. 5 (2014): 817–18; Saad B. Omer, "How Donald Trump's Conspiracy Theories about Vaccines Could Harm Public Health," *Washington Post*, January 11, 2017, https://www.washingtonpost .com/posteverything/wp/2017/01/11/how-donald-trumps-conspiracy-theories -about-vaccines-could-harm-public-health/?utm_term=.1ae686c705d3.

17 Nicoli Nattrass, "Understanding the Origin and Prevalence of AIDS Conspiracy Beliefs in the United States and South Africa," *Sociology of Health and Illness* 35, no. 1 (2013): 113–29.

18 Jeanne Bergman, "The Cult of HIV Denialism," The Body (website), Spring 2010, http://www.thebody.com/content/art57918.html; Charles Dervarics, "Conspiracy Beliefs May Be Hindering HIV Prevention among African Americans," Population Reference Bureau, February 1, 2005, https://www.prb.org /conspiracybeliefsmaybehinderinghivpreventionamongafricanamericans/; *Origin of the AIDS Virus: Briefing for the Office of the Honorable James A. Traficant, Jr., House of Representatives* (General Accounting Office, June 17, 2002),

https://www.gao.gov/new.items/d02809r.pdf; Didier Fassin, "The Politics of Conspiracy Theories: On AIDS in South Africa and a Few Other Global Plots," *Brown Journal of World Affairs* 27, no. 2 (2011): 39–50.

19   Quoted in Blaskiewicz, "Big Pharma Conspiracy Theory," 260.

20   Shawn Smallman, "Whom Do You Trust? Doubt and Conspiracy Theories in the 2009 Influenza Pandemic," *Journal of International and Global Studies* 6, no. 2 (2015): 1–24, quote on 5. Schlafly and Brown cited in: Ludovica Iaccino, "Ebola 'Caused by Red Cross' and Other Conspiracy Theories," *International Business Times*, October 16, 2014, https://www.ibtimes.co.uk/ebola-caused -by-red-cross-other-conspiracy-theories-1469896. Mark Drezde, David A. Broniatowski, and Karen M. Hilyard, "Zika Vaccine Misconceptions: A Social Media Analysis," *Vaccine* 34, no. 30 (2016): 3441–42. Rockefeller: Maddie Stone, "Conspiracy Theorists Think Zika Is a Biological Weapon [Updated: Or a Monsanto Front]," Gizmodo, February 16, 2016, https://gizmodo.com/these -zika-truther-theories-are-fantastically-insane-1756893104.

21   Naomi Oreskes and Erik M. Conway, *Merchants of Doubt* (Bloomsbury Press, 2010). See also David Kaiser and Lee Wasserman, "The Rockefeller Family Fund vs. Exxon," *New York Review of Books*, December 8, 2016, 31–35. On the terminology, see "Deniers Are Not Skeptics," a petition to news organizations organized through the *Skeptical Inquiry*, October 26, 2015, https://www.csicop .org/news/show/deniers_are_not_skeptics. The preference for "dissident" noted in Bergman, "The Cult of HIV Denialism," 2.

22   David Suzuki, "Conspiracies Fuel Climate Change Denial and Belief in Chem-trails," *Desmog* (blog), September 5, 2013, https://www.desmogblog.com/2013 /09/03/conspiracies-fuel-climate-change-denial-and-belief-chemtrails.

23   Exotic locations: S. Fred Singer, ed., *Nature, Not Human Activity, Rules the Climate* (Heartland Institute, 2008), https://www.heartland.org/_template-assets /documents/publications/22835.pdf, v. Hidden world: Hugh Morgan, introduction to John Costella, ed., *The Climategate Emails* (Lavoisier Group, March 2010), https://www.lavoisier.com.au/articles/greenhouse-science/climate-change /climategate-emails.pdf, iii, reprinted part of the SPPI Reprint Series by the Science and Public Policy Institute, June 8, 2010, iv, http://scienceandpublicpolicy .org/wp-content/uploads/2010/01/climategate_analysis.pdf.

24   Riley E. Dunlap and Aaron M. McCright, "Organized Climate Change Denial," in *The Oxford Handbook of Climate Change and Society*, ed. John Dryzek, Richard Norgaard, and David Schlossberg (Oxford University Press, 2011), 144–60. See also Graham Readfearn, "Trump Billionaires Have Poured Millions into Climate Science Denial," Truthout (website), January 17, 2017, https://truthout .org/articles/trump-billionaires-have-poured-millions-into-climate-science -denial/.

25   Steve Newton, "The Alternative Reality of the Heartland Institute's 'NIPCC' Report," *National Center for Science Education Blog* October 28, 2013, https:// ncse.com/blog/2013/10/alternative-reality-heartland-institute-s-nipcc-report -0015140.

26   Suzanne Goldenberg, "Heartland Reflects on Its Beating," *Guardian*, May 22, 2012, https://www.theguardian.com/environment/2012/may/22/heartland

-beating-climate-conference. Václav Klaus, National Press Club of Australia Address, July 26, 2011, https://www.youtube.com/watch?v=idKceFvO7AM.

27 Brian Sussman, "Earth Day's Red Underbelly," *Eco-Tyranny Book* (blog), Eco-Tyranny, April 21, 2015, http://www.eco-tyranny.com/eco-tyranny-book/earth-days-red-underbelly/, and "Drill It, Dam It, Log It: How to Fight Eco-Tyranny in America," *Energy Source* (blog), *Forbes*, May 7, 2012, https://www.forbes.com/sites/energysource/2012/05/07/drill-it-dam-it-log-it-how-to-fight-eco-tyranny-in-america/#7ed78ff8786b.

28 Julia A. Seymour, "Networks Hide the Decline in Credibility of Climate Change Science," Media Research Center NewsBusters, April 21, 2010, https://www.newsbusters.org/special-reports/networks-hide-decline-credibility-climate-change-science. Moore quoted in Ed Brayton, "Moore Combines Science Denialism with a Martyr Complex," Patheos.com, June 9, 2016, http://www.patheos.com/blogs/dispatches/2016/06/09/moore-combines-science-denialism-with-a-martyr-complex/. Alex Jones in: Graham Readfearn, "More Terrifying Than Trump? The Booming Conspiracy Culture of Climate Science Denial," *Guardian*, December 6, 2016, https://www.theguardian.com/environment/planet-oz/2016/dec/06/more-terrifying-than-trump-the-booming-conspiracy-culture-of-climate-science-denial. James Delingpole, "Why Conservatives Will Always Lose the War on Climate Change," Breitbart, April 9, 2016 http://www.breitbart.com/big-government/2016/04/09/conservatives-will-always-lose-climate-change/. The geoengineering argument frequently shows up in reader responses on climate science denial websites. A response agreeing with Brian Sussman said "any global warming that is occurring is due to geoengineering—intentional manipulation of the climate" (Randy Sandberg, response to Brian Sussman, "A Reply to the Eco-Activist-in-Chief," *Eco-Tyranny Book* (blog), *Eco-Tyranny*, October 27, 2015, http://www.eco-tyranny.com/eco-tyranny-book/a-reply-to-the-eco-activist-in-chief/).

29 Elizabeth Loftus, "On Science under Legal Assault," *Daedalus* 132, no. 4 (Fall 2003): 84–86. See also Evan Harrington, "Conspiracy Theories and Paranoia: Notes from a Mind-Control Conference," *Skeptical Inquirer*, vol. 20, no. 5 (October 1996), https://www.csicop.org/si/show/conspiracy_theories_and_paranoia_notes_from_a_mind-control_conference. Sonnabend in: Bergman, "The Cult of HIV Denialism," 4.

30 Stephan Lewandowsky et al., "The Subterranean War on Science," *Observer* 26, no. 9 (2013), 2; Stephan Lewandowsky et al., "Recursive Fury: Conspiracist Ideation in the Blogosphere in Response to Research on Conspiracist Ideation," *Frontiers in Psychology* 4 (2014): 73. See also Elaine McKewon, "The Conversation: Climate Deniers Intimidate Journal into Retracting Paper That Finds They Believe Conspiracy Theories," *Scientific American*, April 3, 2014, https://www.scientificamerican.com/article/climate-deniers-intimidate-journal-into-retracting-paper-that-finds-they-believe-conspiracy-theories/.

31 Examples of the accusations being expanded into book-length papers and actual books include the Science and Public Policy Institute reprint of John Costella's *The Climategate Emails*, and WorldNetDaily, a right-wing media

company, publishing Brian Sussman's *Climategate* through its WND Books subsidiary in 2010, as well as Senator James Inhofe's *The Greatest Hoax* in 2012. "Practices by the so-called climate change experts": Sarah Palin, "Sarah Palin on the Politicization of the Copenhagen Climate Conference," op-ed, *Washington Post*, December 9, 2009, http://www.washingtonpost.com/wp-dyn /content/article/2009/12/08/AR2009120803402.html.

32 See David Biello, "Scientists Respond to 'Climategate' E-Mail Controversy," *Scientific American*, December 4, 2009, https://www.scientificamerican .com/article/scientists-respond-to-climategate-controversy/; "Debunking Misinformation about Stolen Climate Emails in the 'Climategate' Manufactured Controversy," Union of Concerned Scientists, accessed June 6, 2018, https://www.ucsusa.org/global-warming/solutions/fight -misinformation/debunking-misinformation-stolen-emails-climategate .html#.WxgAh-4vzX4; Patrick J. Michaels, "The Climategate Whitewash Continues," *Wall Street Journal*, July 12, 2010, https://www.wsj.com/articles /SB10001424052748704075604575356611173414140. On the impact on public opinion, see Anthony A. Leiserowitz et al., "Climategate, Public Opinion, and the Loss of Trust," *American Behavioral Science* 57, no. (2013): 818–37. On the effort at revival, see James Delingpole, "Climategate 2.0," *Wall Street Journal*, November 28, 2011, https://www.wsj.com/articles /SB10001424052970204452104577059830626002226.

33 Leiserowitz et al., "Climategate, Public Opinion, and the Loss of Trust," 818. See also Karen M. Douglas and Robbie M. Sutton, "Climate Change: Why the Conspiracy Theories Are Dangerous," *Bulletin of the Atomic Scientists* 71, no. 2 (2015): 98–106, https://thebulletin.org/2015/march/climate-change-why -conspiracy-theories-are-dangerous8074; and Sander van der Linden, "The Conspiracy-Effect: Exposure to Conspiracy Theories (about Global Warming) Decreases Pro-Social Behavior and Science Acceptance," *Personality and Individual Differences* 87 (2015): 171–73.

34 Hyping: Bret Stephens, "Liberalism's Imaginary Enemies," *Wall Street Journal*, November 30, 2015, https://www.wsj.com/articles/liberalisms-imaginary -enemies-1448929043, quoted in Jonathan Chait, "How Republican 'Thought Police' Enforce Climate-Science Denial," *New York*, December 1, 2015, http:// nymag.com/daily/intelligencer/2015/12/how-gop-thought-police-enforce -science-denial.html. NIPCC packet shown in: Newton, "Alternative Reality of the Heartland Institute's 'NIPCC' Report." Moore quoted in Brayton, "Moore Combines Science Denialism with a Martyr Complex," 1.

35 Brendan Nyhan and Jason Reifler, "When Corrections Fail: The Persistence of Political Misperceptions," *Political Behavior* 32 (2010): 303–30. See videos from the conference Science Writing in the Age of Denial, University of Wisconsin–Madison, April 23–24, 2012 (sciencedenial.wisc.edu/videos).

36 Alfred Moore, "What Is The Problem With Conspiracy Theories?" *Conspiracy Theories* (blog), Conspiracy and Democracy: History, Political Theory and Internet Research, August 30, 2013, http://www.conspiracyanddemocracy.org /blog/what-is-the-problem-with-conspiracy-theories-2/. Chemtrail quotation: Christine Shearer et al., "Quantifying Expert Consensus against the Exis-

tence of a Secret, Large-Scale Atmospheric Spraying Program," *Environmental Research Letters*, 11 (2016), 9; Nicoli Nattrass, "Still Crazy after All These Years: The Challenge of AIDS Denialism for Science," *AIDS Behavior* 14 (2010): 248–51; Rose Cairns, "Climates of Suspicion: 'Chemtrail' Conspiracy Narratives and the International Politics of Geoengineering," *Geographical Journal*, vol. 182, no. 1·(December 2014).

37   Brooks quoted in Chait, "How Republican 'Thought Police.'" See also Readfearn, "Trump Billionaires Have Poured Millions."

38   HIV: Bergman, "The Cult of HIV Denialism," 3. SLAP-activists: Christine Shearer et al., "Quantifying Expert Consensus." Creationism: Larry Vardiman, "Climategate: Begging the Question," *Acts & Facts* 39, no. 5 (2010): 12–13, http://www.icr.org/article/climategate-begging-question/. Einstein: Joel L. Shurkin, "It's All Relative: You Say Einstein Is 'Jewish Science,' I Say 'Liberal Conspiracy,'" Jewish Telegraphic Agency, August 17, 2010, https://www.jta.org/2010/08/17/life-religion/its-all-relative-you-say-einstein-is-jewish-science-i-say-liberal-conspiracy. *Scientific American* editors, "Donald Trump's Lack of Respect for Science Is Alarming," *Scientific American*, September 1, 2016, https://www.scientificamerican.com/article/donald-trump-s-lack-of-respect-for-science-is-alarming/.

Chapter Eighteen

1   Kate Starbird, "Information Wars: A Window into the Alternative Media Ecosystem," *Medium*, March 14, 2017, https://medium.com/hci-design-at-uw/information-wars-a-window-into-the-alternative-media-ecosystem-a1347f32fd8f, concluding observation. Professor Starbird directs the Emerging Capacities of Mass Participation Laboratory at the University of Washington.

2   ADL, *Rage Grows in America: Anti-Government Conspiracies*, November 2012, https://www.adl.org/sites/default/files/documents/assets/pdf/combating-hate/Rage-Grows-In-America.pdf, 6–7. Brian Wheeler, "Are Conspiracy Theories Destroying Democracy?" BBC News, October 27, 2013, https://www.bbc.com/news/uk-politics-24650841.

3   Tanya Telfair Sharpe, "The Identity Christian Movement: Ideology of Domestic Terrorism," *Journal of Black Studies* 30, no. 4 (2000): 604–23, quote on 608.

4   Recently, sovereign citizens have been actively targeting law enforcement officers with greater regularity. See "Sovereign Citizen Extremist Ideology Will Drive Violence at Home, during Travel, and at Government Facilities," Intelligence Assessment, Office of Intelligence and Analysis, U.S. Department of Homeland Security, February 5, 2015, https://fas.org/irp/eprint/sovereign.pdf.

5   See *Terror from the Right*, a special report from the Southern Poverty Law Center's Intelligence Project (Southern Poverty Law Center, 2012).

6   High-profile examples of mind-control fantasists include Boston Marathon bomber Tamerlan Tsarnaev and Washington Navy Yard shooter Aaron Alexis. Donald Beauregard's Trix box hallucination in: *Terror from the Right*, 15.

7 Joseph Parent and Joseph Uscinski, "People Who Believe in Conspiracy Theories Are More Likely to Endorse Violence," *Chicago Tribune*, February 6, 2016, http://www.chicagotribune.com/news/opinion/commentary/ct-conspiracy-theories-and-violence-20160206-story.html. See also Mark Pitcavage, "Cerberus Unleashed: The Three Faces of the Lone Wolf Terrorist," *American Behavioral Scientist* 59, no. 13 (2015): 1655–80.

8 Tim Wise, "Paranoia as Prelude: Conspiracism and the Cost of Political Rage," Wise (website), January 10, 2011, http://www.timwise.org/2011/01/paranoia-as-prelude-conspiracism-and-the-cost-of-political-rage/; "Satanism 101—Jared Loughner's Satanic Video," *Stop Obama Now!!* (blog), accessed June 6, 2018, https://stop-obama-now.net/laughners-satanic-video/.

9 Max Read, "Why Is Jared Loughner Obsessed with Grammar?" *Gawker* (blog), January 10, 2010, http://gawker.com/5729241/why-was-jared-loughner-obsessed-with-grammar.

10 Jillian Rayfield, "'Sovereign Citizen' Sues Prosecutors for Grammar-Based Conspiracy," *Muckraker* (blog), Talking Points Memo, February 15, 2012, https://talkingpointsmemo.com/muckraker/sovereign-citizen-sues-prosecutors-for-grammar-based-conspiracy. See also Benjamin Radford, "Why Conspiracy Theories Provoke Violence," Seeker (website), January 30, 2014, https://www.seeker.com/why-conspiracy-theories-provoke-violence-1768258449.html; Max Fisher, "Did Sarah Palin's Target Map Play a Role in Giffords Shooting?" *Atlantic*, January 10, 2011, https://www.theatlantic.com/politics/archive/2011/01/did-sarah-palin-s-target-map-play-role-in-giffords-shooting/342714/. See also Wise, "Paranoia as Prelude"; and David Neiwert, "Sorry, Right-Wing Talkers: Loughner's Rampage Was a Clear Act of Political Terrorism Directed at a Liberal 'Government' Target," *Orcinus* (blog), January 17, 2011, https://dneiwert.blogspot.com/2011/01/by-dave-media-id19387-embedtrue.html.

11 Jamie Bartlett and Carl Miller, *The Power of Unreason: Conspiracy Theories, Extremism, and Counter-Terrorism* (Demos, 2010), https://www.demos.co.uk/files/Conspiracy_theories_paper.pdf?1282913891.

12 "Details Emerge about Oregon Killer: Conservative Who Loved Guns and Conspiracy Theories," *AlterNet*, October 2, 2015, https://www.alternet.org/civil-liberties/details-emerge-about-oregon-killer-conservative-who-loved-guns-and-conspiracy.

13 Kjetil B. Simonsen, "Conspiracism and Violence," *New Compass*, December 10, 2011, http://new-compass.net/articles/conspiracism-and-violence. See also Dean G. Pruitt, "Conspiracy Theories in Conflict Escalation," in *Changing Conceptions of Conspiracism*, ed. Kurt Graumann and Serge Moscovici (Springer-Verlag, 1987), chap. 11.

14 Joe Weisenthal, "The Insane Manifesto of Austin Texas Crash Pilot Joseph Andrew Stack," Business Insider, February 18, 2010, http://www.businessinsider.com/joseph-andrew-stacks-insane-manifesto-2010-2.

15 "John Patrick Bedell and the Lethal Lure of Conspiracy Theories," ADL, March 5, 2010, https://www.adl.org/news/article/john-patrick-bedell-and-the-lethal-lure-of-conspiracy-theories. Ciancia: "Alleged LAX Shooter Carried

Note with 'Patriot' References," *Intelligence Report*, Spring 2014, 5. Laura Miller, "Behind Dylann Roof's Race War: The Highly Motivated Secret White Supremacy Movement Working toward 'The Battle of Armageddon,'" *Salon*, June 24, 2015, https://www.salon.com/2015/06/24/behind_dylann_roofs_race _war_the_highly_motivated_secret_white_supremacy_movement_working _toward_the_battle_of_armageddon/. Roof's jailhouse statement shows the influence of Christian Identity conspiracy theories. See Edward Ball, "United States v. Dylann Roof," *New York Review of Books*, March 9, 2017, 4–8.

16 Chez Pazienza, "We're The Killers: Meet the Anti-Government Conspiracy Theorists behind the Vegas Shooting," Daily Banter, June 9, 2014, https:// thedailybanter.com/issues/2014/06/09/killers-meet-anti-government -conspiracy-theorists-behind-vegas-shooting/; quotation from Jerad Miller's Facebook page, dated June 2, 2014 (https://www.facebook.com/jerad.miller.1 /posts/717954731576700).

17 Adam Holland, "Holocaust Museum Shooter's Letters to Marine Corps General Show Longstanding Ties to Racist Right," *Adam Holland* (blog), June 16, 2009, http://adamholland.blogspot.com/2009/06/holocaust-museum -shooters-letters-to.html. Von Brunn had been given Beaty's book by Marine Corps Lieutenant General Pedro del Valle, a fixture of right-wing conspiracism from the 1950s to the 1970s.

18 James von Brunn, "*Kill the Best Gentiles!*" (Holy Western Empire, 1999), 382–87.

19 John M. Glionna and Richard Simon, "At Scene of Nevada Ranch Standoff, 'Citizen Soldiers' Are On Guard," *Los Angeles Times*, April 24, 2014, http://www .latimes.com/nation/la-na-nevada-range-war-20140425-story.html; Weldon Travis, "The Battle of Bunkerville: Victory over Oppression," Liberty Nation, April 16, 2017, https://www.libertynation.com/bundy-ranch-an-eyewitness -account/; Ryan Lenz, "War in the West," *Intelligence Report*, Fall 2014, 23 (photograph of signs and banners).

20 Matt Taibbi, "The Dumb and the Restless," *Rolling Stone*, January 7, 2016, https://www.rollingstone.com/politics/news/the-dumb-and-the-restless -20160107; Leah Sottile, "Why Was a 26-Year-Old Computer Whiz from Ohio the Last Man Standing at Malheur?" *Outside*, October 6, 2016, https://www .outsideonline.com/2122591/david-fry-malheur-holdout. Bundy post on Facebook, December 31, 2015, https://www.facebook.com/bundyranch/videos /937487166328092/. Foreign government: Aaron Bady, "Libertarian Fairy Tales: The Bundy Militia's Revisionist History in Oregon," *Pacific Standard*, January 7, 2016, https://psmag.com/news/libertarian-fairy-tales-of-the-bundy-family. On acquittal, see Andrew Gumbel, "How the Oregon Militia Acquittals Reflect the Influence of White Nationalist Agitators," Reader Supported News, October 29, 2016, https://readersupportednews.org/news-section2/318-66/39964-how-the -oregon-militia-acquittals-reflect-the-influence-of-white-nationalist-agitators.

21 "The Turner Diaries" (ADL, accessed June 6, 2018, https://www.adl.org /education/resources/backgrounders/turner-diaries) features a brief synopsis of the plot William L. Pierce's *The Turner Diaries* (National Vanguard Books, 1978). See also Jim Fulcher, "The American Militia Conspiracy Novel," *Studies in Popular Culture* 24, no. 1 (2001): 59–70.

22 Ross's novel (*Unintended Consequences* [Accurate Press, 1996]) features cover art showing a helmeted agent of the Bureau of Alcohol, Tobacco, and Firearms ravishing a supine and still blindfolded Lady Justice. Rawles's *Patriots* was first published in the early 1990s using shareware. On his book covers, blog, and so forth, Rawles uses a comma after his middle name in the fashion of sovereign citizens to distinguish himself from the government-created entity James Wesley Rawles. Carolyn Kellogg, "'Online Novel' Allegedly Inspired Georgia Terrorism Suspects," *Jacket Copy* (blog), *Los Angeles Times*, November3, 2011, http://latimesblogs.latimes.com/jacketcopy/2011/11/online-novel-inspired -georgia-terrorism-suspects.html. See also *Terror from the Right*, 45.

23 Matthew Bracken's *Enemies Trilogy: Enemies Foreign and Domestic* (2003), *Domestic Enemies: The Reconquista* (2006), and *Foreign Enemies and Traitors* (2009), all from Steelcutter Publishing.

24 "15 Doomsday Fiction Books That May Soon Become Reality," Daily Sheeple, November 12, 2014, http://www.thedailysheeple.com/15-doomsday-fiction -books-that-may-soon-become-reality_112014. The ads for survival gear and related products and services appear along the right-hand side of *SurvivalBlog* (https://survivalblog.com/). "Preppers" are one step removed from survival- ists. They lead normal lives, as opposed to living in a remote compound, but devote themselves to preparing for the day when the "shit hits the fan."

25 Beth Messner et al., "The Hardest Hate: A Sociological Analysis of Country Hate Music," *Popular Music and Society* 30, no. 4 (2007): 513–31. Klan records: "Snap- out Catalogue," advertisement in *Fiery Cross*, August 1970, 20. "RAHOWA! Music Band Gets Record Contract," *Racial Loyalty*, no. 77 (January 1992), 7 (text available online at https://archive.org/stream/RacialLoyalty77Jan1992 /eBook-BenKlassen-RacialLoyalty-Issue77_djvu.txt); Atlanta Anarchist Black Cross, "Neo-Nazi 'Hammerfest' Gathering Planned for Georgia, October 1st," It's Going Down (website), August 24, 2016, https://itsgoingdown.org/neo-nazi -hammerfest-gathering-planned-georgia-october-1st/. See also John M. Cotter, "Sounds of Hate: White Power Rock and Roll and the Neo-Nazi Skinhead Sub- culture," *Terrorism and Political Violence* 11, no. 2 (1999): 111–40.

26 Joe Stroud, "The Importance of Music to Anders Behring Breivik," *Journal of Terrorism Research* 4, no. 1 (2013) 5–18, reprinted at https://cvir.st-andrews .ac.uk/articles/10.15664/jtr.620/. Quotation about Saga: Breivik's mani- festo, under the pseudonym Andrew Berwick, *2083: A European Declaration of Independence* (2011), https://fas.org/programs/tap/_docs/2083_-_A_European _Declaration_of_Independence.pdf, 847.

27 Kyle Reardon, "Modeling Threats & Analyzing Risk: A Rebuttal against 'Doom Porn,'" *The Last Bastille* (blog), September 1, 2015, https://thelastbastille .wordpress.com/2015/09/01/modeling-threats-and-analyzing-risk-a-rebuttal -against-doom-porn/. (Warning: the term "doom porn" also refers to a subge- nre of actual pornography.) Both "TEOTWAWKI" and "SHTF" are commonly used internet terms. The end of the world as we know it (TEOTWAWKI) websites focus on the postapocalyptic situation everyone will soon face and are devoted to long-term strategies for survival. Shit hits the fan (SHTF) websites focus on the specific events likely to bring about TEOTWAWKI.

28   Just in Case Jack, "105 Ways Your Life Will Change after TEOTWAWKI," Skilled Survival, accessed June 6, 2018, https://www.skilledsurvival.com/life -after-teotwawki-part-1/. On boredom, see Steven R. Goldzwig, "Conspiracy Rhetoric at the Dawn of the New Millennium: A Response," *Western Journal of Communication* 66, no. 4 (2002): 492–506; and Robert Brotherton and Silan Eser, "Bored to Fears: Boredom Proneness, Paranoia, and Conspiracy Theories," *Personality and Individual Differences* 80 (2015): 1–5.

29   Book by Art Westerman and Kay Westerman, *Form Your "Home Guard" Now*, advertised in *Councilor*, February 2, 1965, 4. "Wally Butterworth Recordings Every American Should Own" (flyer with order blank), 1965.

30   Dan C., "Handling an Active Shooter Situation," *SHTF Blog*, accessed June 6, 2018, https://www.shtfblog.com/handling-an-active-shooter-situation/.

31   Compare, for example, Ivana Martyn, "The New America: Agenda 21 and the UN One World Government Plan," SHTFAmerica, July 9, 2016, http:// shtfamerica.com/2016/07/09/new-america-agenda-21-u-n-one-world -government-plan/; and "Martial Law: Can the Government Control over 300 Million People?" Preparing for SHTF, accessed June 6, 2018, https:// prepforshtf.com/martial-law-can-the-government-control-over-300-million -people/.

32   Pay for breathing: Mac Slavo, "Obama Killed Our Economic Freedom: Stagnation, Unemployment and Deteriorating Social Conditions," *SHTF Plan*, February 15, 2017, http://www.shtfplan.com/headline-news/obama-killed -our-economic-freedom-stagnation-unemployment-and-deteriorating-social -conditions_02152017. Our founders: "Love of Country vs Love of Government," August 22, 2014, shftjournal.com (website no longer active).

33   Brendan Nyhan, quoted in Kurt Eichenwald, "The Plots to Destroy America," *Newsweek*, May 15, 2014, 4, online at http://www.newsweek.com/2014/05/23 /plots-destroy-america-251123.html. See also Dahlia Lithwick, "Threats to Liberty," *Slate*, May 7, 2015, http://www.slate.com/articles/news_and_politics /jurisprudence/2015/05/jade_helm_15_fear_of_military_and_police_conspiracy _theorists_ignore_true.html.

34   Karen T. Frick, David Weinzimmer, and Paul Waddell, "The Politics of Sustainable Development Opposition: State Legislative Efforts To Stop the UN Agenda 21 in the United States," *Urban Studies* 52, no. 2 (2014): 209–32.

35   Nunes: Renee Diresta, "Social Network Algorithms Are Distorting Reality by Boosting Conspiracy Theories," *Fast Company*, May 11, 2016, https://www .fastcompany.com/3059742/social-network-algorithms-are-distorting-reality -by-boosting-conspiracy-theories; Steven Levitsky and Daniel Ziblatt, "Is Donald Trump a Threat to Democracy?" *New York Times*, December 16, 2016, https://www.nytimes.com/2016/12/16/opinion/sunday/is-donald-trump-a -threat-to-democracy.html.

36   Paradigm shift: Alessandro Bessi et al., "Science vs Conspiracy: Collective Narratives in the Age of Misinformation," *PLoS ONE* 10, no. 2 (2015): 2.

37   Ezra M. Markowitz and Azim F. Shariff, "Climate Change and Moral Judgement," *Nature Climate Change* 2 (2012): 243–47. Interaction: Bessi et al., "Science vs Conspiracy," 9.

38   Quotation in: Diresta, "Social Network Algorithms," 5–6.

39   Ibid., 9 and 10 (asymmetry). Collective credulity: Delia Mocanu et al., "Collective Attention in the Age of (Mis)Information," *Computers in Human Behavior* 51 (2014): 1198–1204. See also Dave Emory, "In Your Facebook: Virtual Panopticon," pt. 2, For the Record, no. 946, February 9, 2017, http://spitfirelist.com /for-the-record/ftr-946-in-your-facebook-a-virtual-panopticon-part-2/.

40   Mocanu et al., "Collective Attention in the Age of (Mis)Information," 2. Bessi et al., "Science vs. Conspiracy," 8–10. Iran's government news agency apparently fell for a satire from the *Onion* claiming Mahmoud Ahmadinejad was more popular than Barack Obama among rural white Americans: "Digital Wildfires in a Hyperconnected World," in *Global Risks 2013*, 8th ed. (World Economic Forum, 2016), 4.

41   Douglas E. Cowan, "Confronting the Failed Failure, Y2K and Evangelical Eschatology in Light of the Passed Millennium," *Nova Religio: The Journal of Alternative and Emergent Religions* 7, no. 2 (2003): 82.

42   Kevin A. Whitesides, "2012 Millennialism Becomes Conspiracist Teleology," *Nova Religio: The Journal of Alternative and Emergent Religions* 19, no. 2 (2015): 30–48. Tsarnaevs: Izzat Jarudi, "The Tipping Point: When Conspiracy Theories Become Dangerous," *Cognoscenti*, June 7, 2013, http://www.wbur.org /cognoscenti/2013/06/07/conspiracy-theories-tsarnaev-brothers-izzat-jarudi.

43   Paul Rosenberg, "Conspiracy Theory's Big Comeback: Deep Paranoia Runs Free in the Age of Donald Trump," *Salon*, January 1, 2017, https://www.salon .com/2017/01/01/conspiracy-theorys-big-comeback-deep-paranoia-runs-free -in-the-age-of-donald-trump/. See also Amanda Taub, "The Rise of American Authoritarianism," Vox, March 1, 2016, https://www.vox.com/2016/3/1 /11127424/trump-authoritarianism; and Evan Osnos, "The Fearful and the Frustrated," *New Yorker*, August 31, 2015, 50–59.

44   Serghei Golunov, "The 'Hidden Hand' of External Enemies," Policy Memo No. 192, PONARS Eurasia, June 2012, http://www.ponarseurasia.org/sites/default /files/policy-memos-pdf/pepm192.pdf, 2.

45   Sir Richard Evans, "Conspiracy Theories: A Threat to Democracy?" (lecture at the Museum of London, June 16, 2016), https://www.gresham.ac.uk/lecture /transcript/print/conspiracy-theories-a-threat-to-democracy/.

46   Karen Stenner, "Three Kinds of 'Conservatism,'" *Psychological Inquiry* 20 (2009): 142–59.

47   Marc Hetherington and Elizabeth Suhay, "Authoritarianism, Threat, and Americans' Support for the War on Terror," *American Journal of Political Science* 55, no. 3 (2011): 546–60. See also Taub, "Rise of American Authoritarianism."

48   Jared A. Goldstein, "The Tea Party's Constitution," *Denver University Law Review* 88, no. 3 (2011): 576.

49   Adam Gopnik, "Trump and the Truth: Conspiracy Theories," *New Yorker*, September 13, 2016, https://www.newyorker.com/news/news-desk/trump-and -the-truth-conspiracy-theories. Also see Ari Berman, "Donald Trump Is the Greatest Threat to American Democracy in Our Lifetime," *Nation*, November 28, 2016, https://www.thenation.com/article/donald-trump-is-the-greatest -threat-to-american-democracy-in-our-lifetime/.

50 *Scientific American* editors, "Donald Trump's Lack of Respect for Science Is Alarming," *Scientific American*, September 1, 2016, https://www.scientificamerican.com/article/donald-trump-s-lack-of-respect-for-science-is-alarming/.

51 Abby Scher, "Militias and the 'New Normal,'" *Democratic Left*, Winter 2016, reprinted at Democratic Socialists of America, January 11, 2017, https://www.dsausa.org/militias_and_the_new_normal.

INDEX

Note: As this is a book about conspiracism, many of the entries in the index refer to things that do not in fact exist and occurrences that did not happen.

Bush, George W., 277
Butler, Richard G., 139, 188, 245–47, 251, 253
Butterworth, Wally, 323

Caesar's Column (Donnelly), 42
Calderone, Mary, 173, 194
Cameron, W. J., 53–54, 233
Campaigner, 225
Cancer: The Forbidden Cures (film), 306
Canham, Erwin, 164
Cannon, Martin, 177, 209
Cantwell, Alan, 230
Capell, Frank, 21
Capt, San Jacinto, 235
Carnegie, Andrew, 149, 152
Carr, William Guy, 26, 153, 184, 194, 230
Carson, Ben, 291
Carto, Willis, 136–37, 139
Case, Brad, 306
Catholics: conspiracy of, 2, 28, 35–38, 40, 44,
    47, 233–34; in league with Jews, 71, 187;
    victims of conspiracy, 22, 214, 242
Center for the Study of Carbon Dioxide and
    Global Change, 310
Central Intelligence Agency, 154, 176–78, 198–
    99, 207–9, 212
Cernovich, Mike, 299
chemtrails, 3, 177, 196, 271, 310–11, 313
Cherep-Spiridovich, Arthur, 64, 71, 73, 90, 271
Chicago Tribune, 121, 151, 278
Chisholm, G. Brock, 167, 171, 174, 270
Chomsky, Noam, 228, 230
Christian Anti-Communist Crusade, 167, 181
Christian Crusade, 147, 182
Christian Defense League, 188, 244–45, 248
Christian Front, 83
Christian Identity, 234–35, 239–49, 254–55, 263
Christian Journal, 192
Christian Liberty Guard, 281
Christian Mobilizers, 83
Christian Patriots Crusade, 186
Christian Patriots Defense League, 261
Christian Science Monitor, 69, 164
Christopher, Alex, 126, 271
Churchill, Winston, 68, 84, 122, 125
Church League of America, 181
Church of Jesus Christ-Christian, 239, 244–46,
    251
Church of the Creator (Creativity Movement),
    138–39, 290

Ciancia, Paul, 318
Citizens Emergency Defense System, 248,
    252, 261
Citizens for American Survival, 191
Citizen's Rule Book, The, 262
civil rights movement, 2, 66, 75, 162, 182,
    185–90, 198, 237, 262, 264, 290, 322–23;
    controlled by Jews, 126, 187–88; controlled
    by the Kremlin, 188–90; miscegenation in,
    45, 187–88
Clark, Gordon, 43
Clifton, Allen, 289
climate change conspiracy, 308–14
Clinton, Bill, 258, 299
Clinton, Hillary, 1, 274, 279–80, 299–300
Close, Upton (Josef W. Hall), 163
Cohn, Norman, 59
Coin's Financial School (Harvey), 42
Coleman, John, 158
Coming Race, The (Bulwer-Lytton), 60
Common Sense (newspaper), 132, 186, 189
Communism, Hypnotism and the Beatles
    (Noebel), 181
Communist Manifesto, The (Marx and Engels),
    98, 130
Comparet, Bertrand L., 237, 239, 241
concentration camps, 52, 114, 167–68, 176–77,
    191–92, 261, 277
Condit, Gary, 273
Condit, Jim, 275
Condon, Richard, 176
Conflict of the Ages, The (Gaebelein), 65, 222
congressional investigations: Church Com-
    mittee (FBI and CIA activities), 198;
    Dies Committee (House Committee on
    Un-American Activities), 81, 83, 94, 115,
    120; House Select Committee on Assas-
    sinations, 199; House Select Committee
    on Missing Persons in Southeast Asia,
    199; Iran-Contra Hearings, 226; Kennedy
    Hearings (on Tuskegee experiments), 199;
    Overman Committee (on Bolshevism),
    69–70; Pike Committee (on intelligence),
    199; Reece Committee (on philanthropic
    foundations), 129, 150–51, 184, 270;
    Rockefeller Commission on CIA Activities
    in the United States (not strictly speaking
    congressional), 198–99; Watergate Hear-
    ings, 198
Congressional Record, 146

Howard, Michael, 22
Hudson, Charles B., 64, 82, 115, 130, 132, 169
humanism: LaRouche's favorable view of, 224–25; as a threat, 175, 195, 216–17, 304
Huntley, Chet, 164–65, 194
Husting, Ginna, 7
Hynek, J. Allen, 206

Icke, David, 219–20, 223, 307
Illuminati: Bavarian, 23–27, 29–32, 131; creation of myth, 23–32; essentially random use of by conspiracists, 1, 4, 10, 22, 52, 68, 102–4, 109, 143, 153–54, 157, 174, 184, 208–9, 211, 220–23, 238, 264, 270, 273; illuminized Freemasonry, 15–17
Imperium (periodical), 139
Imperium (Yockey), 133–36, 290
Independent Farmers, 182
Inhofe, James, 206, 313
Instauration, 138
intellectuals, 130, 135, 148, 152–54, 161–63, 188; academics and their organizations, 77, 151–56, 160–62, 165, 172–73, 175, 190, 205, 217, 271, 309–11; anti-intellectualism, 33, 44, 170; Einstein, 107, 118, 125, 194, 271, 314; experts/social engineers/planners, 153, 155, 160, 170–71, 183–84, 194, 227, 285; Rhodes Scholars, 149–53, 189; right-wing, 133, 138, 140–41
International Climate Science Coalition, 310
International Jew, The (Ford), 69
Invisible Government, The (Smoot), 154
Iron Curtain over America, The (Beaty), 319
Irwin, Matt, 203
Iserbyt, Charlotte, 175, 270–71

Jackson, Victoria, 296
Jade Helm 15, 293, 325
Jefferson, Thomas, 30–31
Jesus Christ Was Not a Jew (Potito), 240
Jewish Peril, The (pamphlet), 51, 68
Jewish Question, The (Sawyer), 234
Jews: behind Bolshevism, 57, 68–70, 73–74; behind the New Deal, 66, 76–80, 85–86, 94, 100, 105–6, 123, 134, 158, 161, 188; international, 2, 50–52, 68–72, 80, 90, 123–25; as Khazars, 54–55, 62, 70–71, 126, 211, 233–34, 238, 263; lists of in govern-

ment, 77–78, 85–86, 125–26; in the nineteenth century, 17, 19, 40, 42–43, 48–51; seedliner theory of, 54, 63, 233, 235–38; as Talmudists/Cabbalists, 48, 50, 78, 91–92, 95, 108, 111, 132, 232
John Birch Society: 1950s heyday, 64, 128, 136, 154, 156, 165, 181, 270, 306; 1960s transition to Illuminati conspiracy, 21, 157; 2008 return to prominence, 278, 281
Johnson, Lyndon B., 75, 189
Joly, Maurice, 51
Jones, Alex, 2, 270, 293, 295, 307, 310, 329
Jones, Jim, 226
Josephson, Emanuel M., 148–49, 307

Kaczynski, Ted (the Unabomber), 310
Kah, Gary, 158
Kahl, Gordon, 254, 256, 258
Kamp, Joseph, 94, 117–18, 120–21, 155, 162, 164, 194
Karega, Joy, 276
Kasper, John, 97
Kay, Jonathan, 228, 288
Kaysing, Bill, 200–201, 203
Keel, John, 207
Keeley, Brian, 1
Kelley, Michael, 230
Kemp, Richard, 260
Kennedy, John, 2–3, 8, 21, 126, 160, 198–99, 202, 212, 223, 229, 238, 274
Kennedy, Robert, 21
Keyes, Alan, 277
Kilgore, Ed, 289
Killing Us Softly (Galalae), 305
Kilpatrick, James J., 306
King, Martin Luther, Jr., 2, 187, 189, 190, 194, 199
King, Stephen, 215
King Alfred Plan, 225–27
Kissinger, Henry, 158, 178
Klan: groups, 54, 64, 72, 77, 82, 134, 173, 190, 224, 234, 243, 248, 281, 290, 322; individual leaders, 53, 71, 186, 195, 234, 236, 249, 253
Klassen, Ben, 127, 138–39, 290
Klaus, Václav, 310
Klein, Henry H., 123
Know Your Enemies (Mohr), 232
Know Your Enemy (Williams), 125
Kohls, Gary, 274

Koresh, David, 255, 258
Kullgren, William, 66, 86, 108, 111

Lady Queenborough. *See* Miller, Edith Starr
LaFlor, Erst, 262, 290
Lake, Jennifer, 270, 305
Landes, Richard, 18
Landig, Wilhelm, 63
Lane, David, 140, 256
Lane, Mark, 8
Lanz von Liebenfels, Jörg, 60–62
LaRouche, Lyndon, 214, 217, 224–25, 294
Lazar, Ernie, 21
League of the South, 281
Leese, Arnold, 122
Leggett, George, 136
Lehman, Herbert, 125
L'Enfant, Pierre, 221
Lerner, Max, 161
Levin, Lewis, 36
Lewandowsky, Stephan, 204, 311
Lewin, Kurt, 177
Liberation, 122
Liberty Lobby, 136
Libra (DeLillo), 229
Lightfoot, Steve, 215
Lina, Jüri, 270–71
Lincoln, Abraham, 40, 242
Lindbergh, Charles, Jr., 82, 94, 120
Loeb, Harold, 121
Lombardi, Mark, 229
Loughner, Jared, 317
Loves, Bradley, 214
Lovett, Robert Morss, 120
Lowman, Myers, 182
Ludovici, Anthony, 139–40
Lynch, Charles "Connie," 245
Lynch, W. W., 181
Lyne, William, 211

MacDonald, Kevin, 140
Mack, Richard, 280
Madole, James H., 132–36, 164, 186, 244, 290
Maertz, Homer, 123
Magocsi, Oscar, 209
Mailer, Norman, 229
Making of America, The (Skousen), 285, 287
Makow, Henry, 276
Manchurian Candidate, The (Condon), 176

Manion, Clarence, 162, 183
Manual for Survival (Baarslag), 181
Mark of the Beast, The (Comparet), 239
Marquis, Doc, 222, 270
Marrs, Jim, 22
Marrs, Texe, 214, 217, 219, 270
Marsden, Victor, 51, 70
Marshall, Thurgood, 189
Martin, Rick, 273
Martin, Rose, 153, 181
martyrs: Ainsworth, 259; Branch Davidians,
    258; Dilling, 114, 119; Heemeyer, 259; Kahl,
    256; David Lane, 256; Mathews, 256, 259;
    McFadden, 75; Snell, 259; Turner (fic-
    tional), 257; Walker, 169; Randy, Samuel,
    and Vicki Weaver, 257, 259
Marx, Karl, 69, 108, 129, 132, 167, 287
Marx Brothers, 85
Marxism, Marxists, 125, 127, 142, 157, 175, 186,
    219, 228, 240
Masters, Marshall, 212–13
Mathews, Robert, 253–54, 256, 259, 319, 322
McCarthy, Joseph, 162
McClay, Ellen, 270
McDonald, Larry, 191
McFadden, Louis, 63, 74–75, 112, 149, 286
McGinley, Conde, 86, 131–32, 185–86
McLamb, Jack, 280
McManus, John, 22
McVeigh, Timothy, 258, 260, 321
McWilliams, Carey, 76
McWilliams, Joseph, 121–22
Media Research Center, 310
medical/health conspiracies, 239, 304–8; elec-
    tromagnetic fields, 271; epidemics, 204–5,
    271, 308; fluoridation of water, 52, 169–70,
    212, 230, 305; genetically modified organ-
    isms, 204, 271, 304–5; HIV/AIDS, 203–5,
    226, 230, 271, 305, 308; influenza, 19, 58,
    238, 308; Lyme disease, 303; polio, 169–70,
    203, 270, 305; syphilis, 106; vaccines, 203–
    4, 271, 305–7, 326
Melanson, Terry, 23
Memoirs Illustrating the History of Jacobinism
    (Barruel), 16–17, 22, 29–30
Mercer, Chris, 318
Merchants of Babylon (Comparet), 239
Mid-America Survival Area, 252
Miles, Robert, 248, 253

new world order, 12, 21–23, 86, 121, 126, 130, 137, 143, 153–58, 161, 167, 176, 180, 227–28, 255, 261, 263, 270–71, 276, 278, 287, 290, 304, 318–19, 327; Black genocide version, 226; Jewish/Zionist conspiracy, 11, 124, 237–38, 275, 284; New Age conspiracy, 218–19; Satanic conspiracy, 58

New World Order (Still), 126

Nicholas I (czar), 23

Nichols, Terry, 264

9/11 conspiracies, 272–76; connection to Kennedy assassination, 274; LIHOP (let it happen on purpose), 272, 277; MIHOP (made it happen on purpose), 272–73, 277; "truthers," 101, 274; Zionist conspiracy, 275–76

Nixon, Richard, 157, 190–91

Noebel, David, 181, 195

None Dare Call It Conspiracy (Allen), 18, 181

None Dare Call It Witchcraft (North), 217

Nongovernmental International Panel on Climate Change, 309, 312

Noontide Press, 260

Norquist, Grover, 277

Norris, Chuck, 293

Norris, Kathleen, 82

North, Gary, 153, 217, 273

Northwest Hammerskins, 260

Nunes, Devin, 325

Oath Keepers, 279–80, 282–84

Obama, Barack, 5, 27, 140, 269, 276–84, 288–89, 293–98, 304, 308, 310, 315, 329

O'Brien, Cathy, 178

occult, 16, 21–22, 26–27, 34, 47, 59–63, 65–67, 75, 86, 89–90, 102–3, 105–9, 118, 178, 206, 208, 236, 270, 300, 317; new age occultism, 214–19; occult fascism, 134–37; occult revival, 59–63; occult symbolism, 221–24, 299

Occult Roots of Nazism, The (Goodrick-Clarke), 47

Occult Significance of Blood (Steiner), 62

Occult Theocrasy (Lady Queenborough), 27, 65

O'Connor, Carter, 121

Octopus, The (Dilling), 52, 110, 113

Oklahoma City bombing, 251, 258, 260–61, 264, 273, 293

Oliver, Revilo, 87, 126, 134–35, 139, 161, 168, 170, 182

O'Meara, Michael, 139

one-world government conspiracy, 58, 137, 144, 146, 167–68, 174, 215, 217, 219, 248, 261, 285, 323; a.k.a. globalists, 151, 158, 194, 311, 324; one-worlders, 21–22, 48, 126, 153–55, 164, 174, 188, 190, 194, 217, 264, 270, 290

Onion, 283

Open Conspiracy, The (Wells), 215

Open Forum Speakers' Bureau, 181

Operation Vampire Killer 2000, 280

Order, The (Brüder Schweigen), 125–54, 256, 260, 316

Osgood, David, 30

Oswald, Lee Harvey, 202

Our Israelitish Origin (Wilson), 53

Overlords of Chaos, 23

Pabst, William, 176, 191

Palin, Sarah, 288–89, 317

Pandora's Box (Christopher), 126

Parent, Joseph, 316–17

Patriotic Party, 157, 264

Patriots (Rawles), 321

Paul, Rand, 292

Paul, Ron, 137, 285–86

Payson, Seth, 31

Pegler, Westbrook, 162

Pelley, William Dudley, 64–65, 75, 77–80, 91, 95–96, 103–6, 108, 114–15, 117–22, 245

Pentagon Aliens (Lyne), 211

Perkins, Frances, 78

Perloff, James, 18

Peters, Pete, 248

Philip Dru, Administrator (House), 153, 159

Phineas Priesthood, 263, 316

Phoenix, River, 160

Picasso, Pablo, 147

Pierce, William Luther, 87, 134, 137, 139, 253, 255, 257, 321

Pike, Albert, 26

Piper, Michael Collins, 166

Pipes, Daniel, 228, 230

Pittman, R. Carter, 182

Pizzagate, 298–301

Podesta, John, 298–99

Police against the New World Order, 261, 280, 284

Pomeroy, Eugene, 168

Popper, Karl, 6, 206

population reduction conspiracy, 10, 23, 223, 273, 305; in league with environmentalists, 218–19, 304–5